FRENCH COLONIALISM IN TROPICAL AFRICA

1900–1945

FRENCH COLONIALISM
IN TROPICAL AFRICA
1900–1945

by
JEAN SURET-CANALE

TRANSLATED FROM THE FRENCH
BY TILL GOTTHEINER

PICA PRESS

NEW YORK

Published in the United States of America in 1971 by
PICA PRESS
Distributed by Universe Books
381 Park Avenue South, New York, N.Y. 10016

First published in 1964 by Éditions Sociales, Paris,
as *Afrique Noire*, Vol. II: *L'Ère coloniale 1900–1945*
This translation © C. Hurst & Co. (Publishers) Ltd., 1971

Library of Congress Catalog Card Number: 75–95756
ISBN 0–87663–702–0

Printed in Great Britain

CONTENTS

	Page
PREFACE	ix

PART ONE: THE DEVELOPMENT OF THE COLONIAL SYSTEM, 1900–1919

Chapter

I. The Trade-based Economy — 3
  1. *Traditional Colonial Trade* — 4
    (*a*) CHARACTER AND METHODS — 4
    (*b*) THE MONOPOLIST TRADING COMPANIES — 7
    (*c*) TRADE OPERATIONS — 11

  2. *The System of Large Concessions in Equatorial Africa* — 17
    (*a*) FIRST ATTEMPTS — 17
    (*b*) THE 'LARGE CONCESSIONS' — 20
    (*c*) TWO SYSTEMS OF EXPLOITATION — 24
    (*d*) FROM EXPLOITATION TO EXTERMINATION: THE MARTYRDOM OF THE CONGO — 26
    (*e*) THE GAUD-TOQUÉ AFFAIR — 34
    (*f*) THE DEPOPULATION OF EQUATORIAL AFRICA — 36

  3. *Economic Consequences* — 37
    (*a*) FRENCH EQUATORIAL AFRICA — 37
    (*b*) THE CAMEROONS — 41
    (*c*) FRENCH WEST AFRICA — 42
    (*d*) MINING — 49

II. Social Consequences — 59
  1. *The Advance of the Money Economy* — 59
  2. *The Decline of Slavery* — 60
  3. *The Disintegration of the Traditional Social Structures* — 67

III. The Administrative System — 71
  1. *Despotism and Direct Administration* — 71
  2. *Administrative Chiefdoms* — 79
  3. *'Assimilation' and 'Association'* — 83
  4. *Centralisation: the Government-General* — 86

IV. Pacification   93
  1. *The 'Pacification' of the Ivory Coast*   95
  2. *The 'Pacification' of other hard-cores of Resistance in
     French West Africa*   103
  3. *Operations in Equatorial Africa*   107
  4. *The Resistance in Togo and the Cameroons*   112

V. Imperialist Rivalries: the First World War   118
  1. *The N'Goko-Sangha Company, Agadir and the 1911
     Compromise*   118
  2. *Anti-Colonialism in France before 1914 and African
     Problems*   123
  3. *Conditions in French Black Africa around 1914*   129
  4. *The 1914–1918 War and the Black Troops*   134
     (*a*) THE BLACK ARMY   134
     (*b*) RECRUITMENT   135
     (*c*) RESISTANCE DURING THE WAR   139
  5. *Conquest and Annexation of Togo and Kamerun,
     1914–1919*   144
  6. *The Russian October Revolution and Africa*   146

PART TWO: THE ZENITH OF COLONIALISM, 1919–1945

INTRODUCTION   155
  I. Economic Exploitation   159
  1. *The Trade Monopolies*   159
     (*a*) CAPITAL   160
     (*b*) PHYSIOGNOMY OF THE FINANCIAL OLIGARCHY   167
     (*c*) TRADE AND ECONOMIC STRUCTURE   183
     (*d*) TRANSPORT AND INDUSTRY   194
  2. *Production*   218
     (*a*) THE DEVELOPMENT OF EXPORT CROPS   219
     (*b*) COMPULSORY CROPS   228
     (*c*) THE INDIGENOUS PROVIDENT SOCIETIES   235
     (*d*) MIGRATION AND FORCED LABOUR   244
     (*e*) THE SPOLIATION OF THE LAND: AGRICULTURAL,
           FORESTRY AND URBAN CONCESSIONS   255
     (*f*) THE MINES   268
     (*g*) THE CRISIS AND DEVELOPMENT EFFORTS   272
  3. *The Economic Balance Sheet*   294
     (*a*) PAUPERISATION   294
     (*b*) AFRICA, A DYING LAND   300

II. Political and Administrative Oppression   307

  1. *Colonial Administration*   307
    (*a*) GOVERNORS AND ADMINISTRATORS   307
    (*b*) THE SYSTEM OF CHIEFS   322
    (*c*) REPRESENTATIVE INSTITUTIONS   327
    (*d*) THE *Indigénat*—THE JUDICIARY SYSTEM 331
    (*e*) RECRUITMENT   336
    (*f*) THE FISCAL SYSTEM   341
    (*g*) DIRECT AND INDIRECT RULE   348
  2. *The Missions*   355
  3. *Culture and Education*   369
    (*a*) CULTURAL OPPRESSION   369
    (*b*) HISTORY OF AFRICAN COLONIAL EDUCATION 371
    (*c*) THE SPIRIT AND METHODS OF EDUCATION   379
    (*d*) THE TEACHING STAFF   386
    (*e*) CONCLUSION   391
  4. *Medical and Health Services*   395
    (*a*) HEALTH   395
    (*b*) MEDICAL ACTION   403

III. Social and Political Evolution   417

  1. *Social Evolution*   417
    (*a*) THE TOWNS   417
    (*b*) THE COUNTRY REGIONS   419
    (*c*) THE MARRIAGE PROBLEM: MARRIAGE SETTLE-
    MENT AND POLYGAMY   423
  2. *Political Life*   426
    (*a*) THE LAST ARMED UPRISINGS   426
    (*b*) RELIGIOUS MOVEMENTS   431
    (*c*) THE FIRST SIGNS OF MODERN POLITICAL LIFE 439
  3. *The Second World War, 1939–1945*   462
    (*a*) AFRICA IN THE WAR   462
    (*b*) THE WAR EFFORT   477
    (*c*) THE CONFERENCE OF FRENCH AFRICA AT
    BRAZZAVILLE   484

BIBLIOGRAPHY   491

INDEX   509

MAPS

French Equatorial Africa, 1939   xiii
French West Africa, 1939   xiv
Concessions in the Congo, 1900   xvi
  A*

II. Political and Administrative Oppression

  1. General Aspects 307
    (a) GOVERNORS AND ADMINISTRATORS 307
    (b) THE SYSTEM OF JUSTICE 307
    (c) REPRESENTATIVE INSTITUTIONS .....
    (d) The Judiciary ... indigenous 383
    (e) RECRUITMENT 326
    (f) THE LEGAL SYSTEM 383
    (g) DIRECT AND INDIRECT RULE 366
    2. The Missions 392

  B. Culture and Education 400
    (a) CULTURAL OPPRESSION .....
    (b) HISTORY OF AFRICAN COLONIAL EDUCATION 373
    (c) THE SYSTEM AND AIMS OF COLONIAL EDUCATION .....
    (d) THE TEACHING STAFF 380
    (e) IN SCHOOLS 400
    ... Social Mental Health .....
    (a) HEALTH 805
    (b) SOCIAL ACTION 405

III. Social and Political Evolution

  1. Social Evolution 377
    (a) TOWNS 377
    (b) THE COUNTRYSIDE .....
    (c) THE TRADE UNION MOVEMENT 370
    RENT AND POPULATION .....
    2. Political Life .....
    (a) THE LEGISLATIVE ASSEMBLIES 420
    (b) ELECTIONS MOVEMENTS .....
    (c) THE RISE OF MODERN POLITICAL LIFE 170
    (d) THE WORLD WAR, 1939–1945 .....
    (e) AFRICA IN THE WAR .....
    (f) THE WAR IN .....
    (g) THE CONFERENCE OF FRENCH AFRICA AT BRAZZAVILLE .....

BIBLIOGRAPHY .....
INDEX 505

MAPS

  French Equatorial Africa, 1939 .....
  French West Africa, 1939 .....
  Communications in the Colony, 1900 .....

PREFACE

When the idea of this work was conceived, an essential part of it was to be devoted to an analysis of the colonial system as it existed in tropical Africa under French domination. The need for elucidating, or, at least, seriously dealing with a number of problems relevant to the past and to pre-colonial structures led the author to write another book, which is intended as an introduction.* But since 1958 the movement of history has speeded up in that part of the world: the African colonial system, at that time in full crisis, has since, to a large extent, collapsed. Called by circumstances to return to Africa, first as director of the Guinea Institute of Research and headmaster of the Conakry Lycée, then as director of the Teachers' Training College at Kindia, the author was impelled to carry out urgent tasks, which delayed the completion of this study.

By 1962 the central theme, still a topic of current interest six years before, had become largely a matter of history. It seemed necessary, therefore, to devote a separate volume to this, and to reserve a third part for a study of the last fifteen or twenty years – the period of the crisis and collapse of the French colonial system in tropical Africa. Entitled *The Colonial Era* this book, therefore, centres around the economic, social and political system which came into being and reached its height between the years 1900 and 1945. Essentially historical in its approach, it none the less retains present-day interest; for the economic structures on which the system was based have remained more or less intact, and the social and political heritage weighs heavily upon the present independent African republics.

No ambitions beyond clearing some ground and opening up some horizons were intended in writing this book. It did not prove possible, for example, to throw light on the life and history of the African peoples during the period under review as would have been fitting. Such a study would involve an enormous amount of investigation on the spot, a task that can hardly be undertaken at the present time, and one which Africans alone can complete satisfactorily.

* *Afrique Noire occidentale et centrale: géographie, civilisation, histoire.* Paris, Editions Sociales, 1st ed., 1958; 2nd ed., 1961.

In contrast to the preceding volume, a work of synthesis of which the starting point was a study that had already been concluded, this volume, with a few exceptions, is based on direct contemporary material. Under these conditions it was not possible to undertake a systematic analysis of archives; and indeed these are accessible only for the period previous to 1913. Forgoing any claim to being exhaustive, the author had to content himself with printed sources, supplementing these, where it became indispensable, by some research into materials from accessible local archives. In other words, this is but a first approach opening the way to more detailed studies which, sometime in the future, will permit a more solid synthesis.

The approach being a critical one, some people may see in it a certain bias. That is a risk that has to be faced in dealing with a subject which, for so long, has been (and still remains) taboo. Officially condemned, colonialism still survives in the men, the spirit, and the institutions that do not tolerate anyone lifting the veil from their secrets. The risk is one that every investigation into the truth faces when it involves powerful interests. If anyone should doubt this, let him turn to the sources (nearly all of them 'colonial'), let him compare the facts that have been extracted with the versions of the numerous panegyrists of colonisation . . . and then let him form his own judgment.

Kindia
30 November, 1962   J. S.–C.

The present edition contains the author's revisions to 31 December, 1966.

MAPS

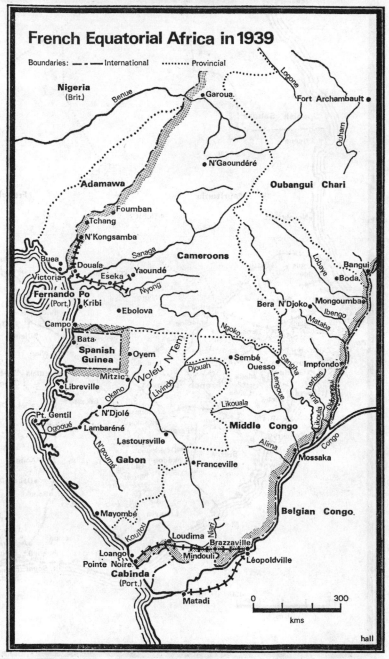

French Equatorial Africa in 1939

Boundaries: — · — International ········· Provincial

Nigeria (Brit.)

Benue

Garoua

Logone

Fort Archambault

Ouham

N'Gaoundéré

Adamawa

Oubangui Chari

Foumban

Tchang

N'Kongsamba

Sanaga

Cameroons

Buea

Douala

Yaoundé

Lobaye

Bangui

Victoria

Eseka

Boda

Fernando Po (Port.)

Kribi

Nyong

Bera N'Djoko

Mongoumba

Ibengo

Campo

Ebolova

Ngoko

Mataba

Bata

Spanish Guinea

Oyem

Woleu N'Tem

Djouah

Sembé

Ouesso

Impfondo

Mitzic

Okano

Livindo

Djouah

Likouala

Sangha

Lengoué

Likouala aux herbes

Libreville

Pt. Gentil

N'Djolé

Ogooué

Lambaréné

Likouala

Middle Congo

Oubangui

N'gounié

Lastoursville

Alima

Congo

Gabon

Franceville

Mossaka

Mayombé

Belgian Congo

Kouilou

Loudima

Niari

Brazzaville

Loango

Mindouli

Léopoldville

Pointe Noire

Cabinda (Port.)

Matadi

0   300

kms

hall

xiii

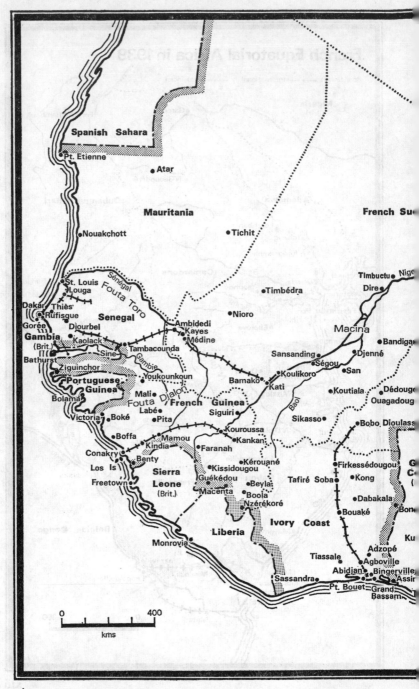

Spanish Sahara

Pt. Etienne

Atar

Mauritania

French Su

Nouakchott

Tichit

St. Louis
Louga

Sénégal

Fouta Toro

Timbédra

Timbuctu Nige

Diré

Dakar Thiès
Rufisgue

Senegal

Nioro

Macina

Gorée
Gambia
(Brit.)
Bathurst

Djourbel

Kaolack

Ambidedi
Kayes
Médine

Sansanding

Bandiga

Sine

Tambacounda

Gambie

Djenné

Ségou

San

Ziguinchor

Bamako

Koulikoro

Kati

Koutiala

Dédougo

Portuguese
Guinea

Youkounkoun

Fouta Dialon

French Guinea

Siguiri

Ouagadoug

Bolama

Mali

Baol

Bobo Dioulass

Victoria

Boké

Labé

Pita

Kouroussa

Sikasso

Boffa

Mamou

Kankan

Firkessédougou

G
C
(

Conakry
Los Is
Freetown

Kindia
Benty

Faranah

Kérouané

Kong

Sierra
Leone
(Brit.)

Kissidougou
Guékédou
Macenta

Beyla

Tafiré Soba

Dabakala

Bouaké

Bon

Boola
Nzérékoré

Ivory Coast

Ku

Liberia

Monrovia

Tiassale

Adzopé
Agboville
Abidjan Bingerville
Assir

Sassandra

Pt. Bouet Grand
Bassam

0   400

kms

xiv

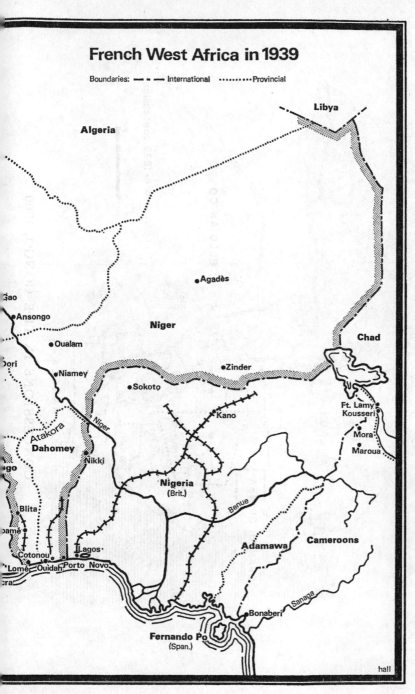

French West Africa in 1939

Boundaries: — ·· — International ·········· Provincial

Algeria

Libya

●Agadès

Niger

Chad

ʒao

●Ansongo

●Oualam

●Zinder

Dori

●Niamey

Niger

●Sokoto

Ft. Lamy
Kousseri

Kano

Atakora

Dahomey

Mora

Maroua

go

●Nikki

Nigeria
(Brit.)

Benue

Blita

bamé ●

Adamawa

Cameroons

Cotonou

●Lagos

Lomé Ouidah Porto Novo

cra

Bonaberi

Sanaga

Fernando Po
(Span.)

hall

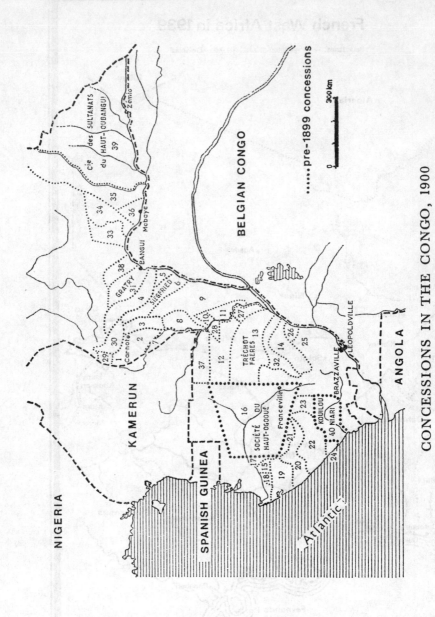

CONCESSIONS IN THE CONGO, 1900

.... pre-1899 concessions

300 km

Key to map: Concessions in the Congo, 1900

Name of Concessionaire	Company	Capital (francs)	Headquarters
1. Nouzaret	Cⁱᵉ. Com. et Coloniale de la Kadéi-Sangha	600,000	Paris
2. Durand	Cⁱᵉ. de la Haute-Sangha	1,200,000	Paris
3. Guynet	Société de l'Ekela Kadéi-Sangha	700,000	Paris
4. Cauvez	Cⁱᵉ. des Caoutchoucs et Produits de la Lobaye	2,000,000	Roubaix
5. David	Société du Baniembé	700,000	Paris
6. Siegfried	Société de l'Ibenga	1,500,000	Paris
7. Gazengel	Société de l'Ogooué N'Gounié	500,000	Paris
8. Mestayer	Cⁱᵉ. des Produits de la Sangha	1,500,000	Paris
9. Faure, Boutelleau, Desbrières	Cⁱᵉ. Française du Congo	3,000,000	Lille
10. Gimming et Campagne	Cⁱᵉ. de la Sangha	800,000	Paris
11. Ritaine, Descamps } see 37			
12. Nicol, Bernain			
13. Tréchot frères	Cⁱᵉ. Française du Haut-Congo	2,000,000	Paris
14. Jacta, Decourcelle	Société Agricole et Com. de l'Alima	800,000	Paris
15. Gazengel (cf. 7)			
16. Société du Haut-Ogooué			
17. Monthaye	Société des Factoreries de N'Djolé	600,000	Le Havre
18. Société du Bas-Ogooué			
19. Izambert	Cⁱᵉ. Générale du Fernan-Vaz	1,500,000	Paris
20. Devès	Société de la Setté-Cama	1,200,000	Paris
21. Leplus	Cⁱᵉ. de la Haute-N'Gounié	900,000	Paris
22. Vergnes, Lindeboom et Cie., Delignau	Cⁱᵉ. Française du Congo Occidental	1,800,000	Paris
23. Jobet	Société de l'Ongomo	800,000	Paris
24. Bazenet	Cⁱᵉ. du littoral Bavili	400,000	Paris
25. Bouvier	Cⁱᵉ. Agricole, Com. et Ind. de la Léfini	800,000	Lille
26. Romaire	Société de la N'Kéni et Kémé	700,000	Lille
27. Collas	Société de la Sangha équatoriale	800,000	Paris
28. Delineau, see 22			
29. Normandin	Cⁱᵉ. Com. et Coloniale de la Mambéré-Sangha	900,000	Paris
30. Compagnie Française du Congo	Cⁱᵉ. Com. de Colonisation du Congo Français	1,000,000	Paris
31. Gratry	Société des Etablissements Gratry-M'Poko	1,200,000	Lille
32. Cousin	L'Alimaïenne	800,000	Paris
33. De Brancion, Séguin }	Cⁱᵉ. du Kouango Français	2,250,000	Paris
34. De la Revelière			
35. Rémy Martin, Boulet, Mahieu, etc.	Cⁱᵉ. de la Kotto	2,500,000	Paris
36. Emile Martin	Cⁱᵉ. de la Mobaye	1,000,000	Paris
37. Mimerel, Paquier, Kunkler	Cⁱᵉ. de N'Goko-Sangha	1,280,000	Paris
38. Laroche, de Kergariou, Robin	Société Bretonne du Congo	300,000	Lille
39. Couvreux, Douchart, etc.	Cⁱᵉ. des Sultanats du Haut-Oubangui	9,000,000	Paris
40. Cⁱᵉ. propriétaire du Kouilou-Niari			

PART ONE
The Development of the Colonial System
(1900–1919)

CHAPTER I

THE TRADE-BASED ECONOMY

The military conquest of West and Central Africa was covered in an earlier volume but, apart from a few comments necessary for a proper understanding of the situation, the economic, political and social aspects of the colonising process were left aside.

Chronologically it is impossible to separate this aspect from military history. The establishment of the colonial system began with Faidherbe, but the conquest was not completed until the period 1934–6 (the occupation of Tindouf on the Mauretanian–Moroccan border in 1934, and the establishment of a regular link between Morocco and Senegal in 1936). In general terms, though, the conquest ended in 1900 with the Battle of Kousseri. There were still small local pockets of resistance to overcome, but it was now possible for colonisation proper to develop.

The economic and social system characteristic of the colonial empire was not properly established until the period 1900–14, and could not take root in the territories without this preceding epoch of conquest and annexation. Throughout this time, commercial activities surviving from the first colonial period (export of agricultural produce and raw materials, import of manufactured goods) continued to occupy a very important place in the economy, but with a new and decisive element: the export of capital to the colonies. In this way the great monopolies based on financial capital took control of the economy and indeed of the administration of the colonial territories, a control which enhanced and confirmed their position in the home country. This point will not be discussed further in this chapter,[1] which will be mainly a description of the basic features of colonial imperialism in the French territories of Black Africa.[2]

There was far less of a gap here than existed anywhere else between the traditional trade-based colonisation, which changed to Free Trade in the middle of the nineteenth century, and contemporary colonial imperialism. It was through the medium of trade that colonial development took place. Most capital was lodged in the commercial sector; investments in land or industry (which will be described in more detail below) were never to hold more than a secondary position.

This continuity in tradition did not exclude certain important changes in the form, structure and methods of commerce, especially that very fundamental change which involves the transition from 'free competition' to legal or *de facto* monopoly which operated to the profit of imperialist financial capital.

1. Traditional Colonial Trade

(a) CHARACTER AND METHODS

At this point it would be appropriate to describe the characteristic features of the old-fashioned trading firm on the African coast, either French (from Bordeaux or Marseilles), British (with a head office in Manchester or Liverpool) or German (from Bremen or Hamburg). From its European headquarters this head office was concerned with the purchase of goods in exchange for explosives and weapons of very poor quality,[3] commercial spirits, Manchester cotton, hardware and various poorly manufactured oddments. In the nineteenth century the first two commodities held pride of place, together with cotton materials. Between 1900 and 1914 their relative importance dwindled away to the point where the trade in weapons practically disappeared. There were various reasons. First was the prohibition or strict control of arms imports, the high import duties on weapons, and the need for import permits (which were often very expensive and difficult to obtain from the administrative authorities, for they were generally granted only to pro-French chiefs and dignitaries). Then the advance of Islam and the application of the Brussels Conventions affected the import of spirits.[4] Finally, and most particularly, the large reductions in the real income of the local population obliged them to spend the money they had at their disposal on the purchase of prime necessities, such as cotton fabrics, which remained high on the list of imports; manufactured goods, which increased greatly in proportion (these two categories tended to replace traditional products of African manufacture); and imported foodstuffs which were introduced for the first time – sugar and rice. Thus in imports to Guinea, spirits, which in 1897 had accounted for 7 per cent of the total value of imported goods, fell to roughly 3 per cent in 1900 (500,000 out of a total of 14,200,000 francs). Cotton fabrics formed more than one-third of the imports (5,300,000). On the other hand, in Dahomey, which was not influenced by Islam, spirits continued to make up almost one-third of the imports (4,300,000 out of 15,200,000), cotton fabrics taking only second place (2,900,000): these figures are also those given for 1900.[5]

This merchandise was purchased in Europe by the head offices. Average-sized firms made cash purchases, but larger firms, especially the British ones, bought on credit; this more progressive method of organisation gave them an opportunity to do a far greater volume of business. But they risked losses in case of forced sales to meet their liabilities.

The trade – like all trade in agricultural produce – had a seasonal character. The 'season of trade' took up a brief period of a few weeks or months, soon after the harvest; its occurrence varied according to the product and the region. During the rest of the year activity was limited, reduced largely to the sale of merchandise on credit. It was on a credit basis that the African middlemen were supplied. These were trading people along the coast to begin with and, later, trade agents charged with prospecting the bush.[6]

The very nature of these operations tied up capital (in the form of merchandise) over a longer period, and the trading firms could not seriously extend their operations except by using the banks. This circumstance aided the transformation of colonial commercial capital, the interpenetration of large business firms and banks holding the same interests – the Compagnie française de l'Afrique occidentale and the Marseillaise de Crédit (Marseilles Credit Bank), for example.[7] The Banque de l'Afrique occidentale took over from the Banque du Sénégal in 1901. Emile Maurel of Bordeaux presided over its board of directors.

The European firms generally had a central agency with shops in each colony run by a general agent interested in profit-sharing. Often, at least in the early stages, this general agent was a partner in the firm or a member of the owner's family. The trading stations in the bush were branches run by subordinates, which served both as purchasing centres and as shops; they both collected and weighed local products brought in by the peasants, and sold merchandise. What the African acquired he spent quickly. Most often this transaction was effected without the use of money. A similar role was played by a few secondary European firms 'of independent status', reduced to the sole act of selling, since they did not possess the means to make direct purchases in Europe, but had to turn for that purpose to the more important business houses with which they traded on a semi-wholesale basis. These 'independent' business firms were always few in number and most were far from stable; under favourable circumstances the small independent trader enjoyed advantages through his relation with the head of the trading post, but in times of crisis he was doomed to bankruptcy, and the big firms did nothing to set him afloat again – in fact, quite the contrary. Before 1900 the distinction between these two types of firm was not so clear. There were firms like that belonging to Verdier, who personally and on the spot ran his branch-office at Assinie and Grand-Bassam, with coffee plantations that still exist at Elima on the side. The same applied to the firm of Pastré of Marseilles, with Aimé Olivier[8] (Pastré's son-in-law) as general agent at Boloma in Portuguese Guinea, before they expanded their depots and trading posts into the Rivières du Sud and Fouta-Djalon. At this intermediary level, running several trading posts, partly importing direct and organising trade caravans, were the traders at Saint-Louis, African and half-caste, who extended their activity towards the Sudan as the conquest proceeded. By about the year 1900, mainly due to the crisis of the years 1900–1, these medium-sized businesses were largely eliminated or reduced to the role of subsidiaries.

With the completion of the conquest of West Africa between 1895 and 1901, foreign trade doubled, rising from 78,700,000 to 157,000,000 francs. It dropped again to 133,500,000 in 1902. Expansion followed by depression favoured economic concentration.

> The years that preceded 1900 saw the establishment of the big colonial companies which reduced the number and activity of the traders [at Saint-Louis and Gorée] and made serious inroads into their financial resources. Their descendants had to turn to administration and the liberal professions, or leave the country. Thus their influence on the population declined.[9]

In the centres one could find, alongside the trading stations, which they patronised, retailers with their own shops: Wolofs following the French troops, Sierra Leoneans in Guinea, who were to be outnumbered and replaced by Lebanese and Syrians, as we shall see later.

In the first period of colonisation, the trading stations and shops tended, for reasons of security, to be confined to the vicinity of administrative and military posts whose task, among others, was to 'protect commerce'. Since the custom at these posts was necessarily limited, those living in the bush could be reached in two different ways. Certain local chiefs (e.g. those of Fouta-Djalon) organised trade convoys with their vassals and captives, negotiating directly with the trading stations at the posts (in the case of Fouta with the trading stations along the coast). But in general this trade remained in the hands of African middlemen who, in Guinea and on the Ivory Coast, were called by the generic term of *dioula*.[10]

For a long time the coastal populations had formed a screen

between the European counting-house and the *dioula* or their local equivalents: the Apollonians of Assinie, the Douala of the Cameroons or the Bateke of the Congo. Some of them even conducted their own import or export: e.g. the 'jack-jack' of the coastal regions of the Ivory Coast, organised in independent villages, who carried on a direct trade in European cargoes. They were the first to be eliminated by the European occupation.

The *dioula* retained their important and indispensable role for a longer time. They collected produce in the interior for export, and exchanged it in the trading stations for trade commodities, which they then redistributed in the bush. The profession was not without risk. Generally the *dioula* handed over his goods on credit against the promise of delivery of raw materials when he next came that way; it was not always easy for him to collect his debts, and he had to make up for losses by calculating a profit margin of 300 to 400 per cent. Finally, he was always at the mercy of highwaymen or the cupidity of local chiefs, who did not stop short of assassination in order to lay hands on the coveted merchandise. The *dioula* often gathered in armed caravans and some of them, important figures, used dozens of carriers. Their market was far more widespread before the building of railways and the increase of outposts, since important trading stations were then only to be found in ports supplied by maritime or river navigation. In answer to reproaches made to the commercial companies that they had not penetrated into the interior, the head of the French West Africa Company objected that this was not the fault of the traders: the trading branches established at Kurussa, Siguiri, offered mediocre returns because of bad communications and danger from attack. Transports into the interior were carried more quickly and cheaply by indigenous caravanners.[11] Only the railways, he concluded, would change this state of affairs. In 1903 an official report estimated the number of *dioula* and carriers in their service at more than 100,000 for Guinea alone, with its population of two million. It should be noted, however, that they were concerned not only with trading as middlemen, but also with the large-scale trade of the interior: cattle from Sahel and dried fish from the Niger, exchanged principally for cola from the forest region.[12] In the Sudan, Niger and Chad, the trans-Saharan caravan trade, in the hands of the Moors and Arabs, retained its importance until 1914. For 'Upper Senegal and Niger' it still accounted for a quarter of the value of trade with Senegal in 1906.[13]

(b) THE MONOPOLIST TRADING COMPANIES

At the end of the nineteenth century and the beginning of the twentieth, the *de facto* monopoly of a small number of European firms grew stronger. Though this consolidation was accompanied by relentless internal strife, especially between French and foreign companies, it effectively prevented all possibility of new foreign intrusion into this field. At the same time came a progressive development of trading methods linked with a steady growth of means of communication and the consequent extension of the market towards the interior, due for the most part to 'pacification' and political annexation.

In Guinea, for instance, at the beginning of the twentieth century there were about twenty 'big' companies, each with more than two trade depots, and with a head office and general agent at Conakry. Of these companies, scarcely one-third were French, the French West Africa Company of Marseilles being by far the most important. Then came a large number of British firms which, for a long time, had had their main depots in Freetown, but which were forced to open up in Conakry by the 1897 customs regulations. Such were Paterson-Zochonis, and Broadhurst and Sons, both of Manchester; there were other foreign firms (Colin of Hamburg; Pelizaeus of Bremen; two Belgian companies; Ryff, Roth et Cie. of Switzerland), small then but destined to form the nucleus of the powerful Société commerciale de l'Ouest Africain (S.C.O.A.); also the Aaron Cohen Company of Tangier, conveniently cloaked in Spanish nationality.

In general terms a geographical division can be established as follows. In Senegal and the Sudan a group of Bordeaux business houses ruled more or less supreme. They were: Devès et Chaumet, Chavanel, Maurel et Prom, Delmas et Clastre, Rabaud et Cie., Buhan et Teyssère, Assémat, Vézia.

In 1896 one writer commented:

> . . . Trade in this country [Senegal] is in the hands of three or four big business houses which have formed a syndicate, a kind of Triple Alliance, which assures them a monopoly of all products, in all eventualities.[14]

The medium-sized businesses, notes the same writer, were allowed their share of merchandise on condition that they respected the purchase prices fixed by the 'big boys'.

In 1897 another author wrote:

> At the present time, five or six syndicated business houses from Bordeaux, headed by Maurel et Prom, Devès et Chaumet, Buhan et Teyssère, consider Senegal their private domain.[15]

On the Guinea coast and in the Congo there were Marseilles business houses, or firms with Paris-based capital: the Compagnie française de l'Afrique occidentale,[16] Mante et Borelli (Regis' successors), the Société coloniale de la côte de Guinée, the Compagnie française du Commerce Africain, the Comptoir commercial français, etc. At first they controlled only a small part of the trade, which was mainly in the hands of British houses from Liverpool and Manchester (especially in the Congo, but also in Guinea and Dahomey), and German houses from Bremen and Hamburg (especially in Dahomey, the Congo and, to a lesser degree, in Guinea).[17] From the beginning of the century until 1914, trade crises saw the disappearance of several of these minor firms and even some of the bigger ones (the crisis of 1900-1 had already played its part): Belgian companies, for example, and some Paris-based firms, which were| too deeply concerned with stock market speculations and lacked both the experience and the trade contacts of the Marseilles, Bordeaux or British firms. Concentration grew slowly, and at the same time, a whole series of carefully planned measures worked against British trade, which had originally been predominant on the coast of Guinea.

The Customs Act of 11 January, 1892, which put an end to the liberal regime inherited from the Second Empire (once it had eliminated the 'exclusive system'),[18] had the basic purpose of providing more favourable conditions for the export of French goods to the colonies. None the less, numerous international agreements limited the actual extension of a protectionist system. The Congo Basin was not involved: the Act of Berlin (26 February, 1885) stipulated equality of commercial opportunity for all the nations and even customs exemptions for a period of twenty years; the Act of Brussels (2 July, 1890) went back on this latter point by authorising dues not exceeding 10 per cent *ad valorem*, discrimination as such still being forbidden. This was the basis on which the Lisbon Protocol of 8 April, 1892, established a customs union between the French Congo, the independent state of the Congo and Angola, with a single tariff that remained valid until 2 July, 1911, on which date it was terminated by France. Similarly, the Anglo-French convention of 14 June, 1898, abolished all discriminatory dues between the Ivory Coast and Dahomey for a period of thirty years, as the result of which French trade improved as the system operated to its advantage in the Gold Coast and Nigeria.[19]

There remained Gabon as a field for a possible protectionist system in Equatorial Africa, and in French West Africa there was also the so-called 'free zone' which was not subject to restrictions of an international order; it consisted of Senegal, the Sudan and Guinea. Gabon simply applied the French tariff to all imports, which was not calculated to please the local traders. In Senegal and its Sudanese hinterland, customs and excise dues were levied, with the addition, after 1872, of a 5 per cent surtax on imported foreign goods. In Guinea, merchandise was affected only by consumer taxes, as in the Ivory Coast and Dahomey. In 1897 Governor Ballay had introduced a surtax on indirect imports, which affected all French and British goods that did not come directly from their country of origin; its purpose was to deprive Freetown of its role as clearing house for the Guinea trade, to the benefit of Conakry.

The Decree of 14 April, 1905, extended the Senegal system of a 5 per cent surtax to the entire 'free zone', and helped to strengthen the position of French trade.

This decree, apart from being extremely clear and precise, was inspired by certain fundamental ideas which should be examined more closely:

1. Products intended for trade, i.e. for purchase by the native population, were taxed.
2. Products intended for purchase by Europeans were exempt from customs dues.
3. Products coming from abroad or manufactured in an African region not under French control were subject to a surtax.

It is easy to see the protectionist, one might almost say the imperialist, trends which this decree was intended to satisfy. It seems to have been made in the interest of France rather than for the development of the colony.[20]

The effects of the surtax were revealed strikingly in the evolution of trade in Guinea: the share of French imports rose from 32 per cent in 1904 to 60 per cent in 1908.[21] In Dahomey, where this system did not exist, France's share in imports remained weak and even declined (24 per cent in 1908). In the years 1910–13 France supplied French West Africa with 44–48 per cent of its imports. In 1909, 59·2 per cent of exports from French West Africa went to France, this high percentage representing mainly groundnuts from Senegal, 73·4 per cent of whose exports went to France. In the other colonies, by contrast, countries other than France often held a major share. Germany took the main portion of palms and palm oil from Dahomey; in 1913, out of timber exported by French Equatorial Africa totalling 8,300,000 francs in value, Germany received 3,500,000, Great Britain 2,000,000, the Netherlands 1,200,000 and France 1,500,000.[22] Colonial trade complained of not finding in France sufficiently privileged outlets. Apart from a few cases under exemption, a minimum tariff had to be paid on colonial products on entry into France and only a few enjoyed tax remission. After 1900 Le Myre de Vilers, chairman of the budget for the colonies, demanded free entry for these. Little by little, under the pressure of interest groups, tax remissions or even exemptions increased (for rubber this came in 1906). Finally, a law passed in 1913, and intended to come into force in 1914, granted free entry for 'secondary colonial products' such as cocoa or coffee, where production was to be encouraged.[23]

German business interests were eliminated completely by the 1914–18 war. On the eve of the war certain features began to develop which took definite form in the period between the two world wars. One was the preponderance of several major firms: the Compagnie française de l'Afrique occidentale of Marseilles; the Bordeaux firms (Maurel Frères, Maurel et Prom, Peyrissac, Devès et Chaumet, Chavanel) firmly established in Senegal and the Sudan, less strongly along the Guinea coast, but forced back gradually into purely local or second-rate status; the British from Manchester; finally, beginning to make its impact, Ryff, Roth et Cie., which, in 1907, became the Société commerciale de l'Ouest Africain. In any case, from the beginning of the century, despite internal dissension, the large firms were few enough in number to reach an understanding among themselves to bar entry to the African market to any potential newcomer. Similarly there were successive transformations in the establishment and methods of work of the trading posts.

(c) TRADE OPERATIONS

At the end of the nineteenth century, individuals and, in particular, trade caravans would travel to the trading posts for direct exchange in kind: raw materials against commodities. In every case, the 'customers' only bought their products in order to procure certain coveted articles in exchange; the medium of money was not only useless, but it ran into obvious difficulties caused by the absence of coins and the generally non-monetised state of the country.

Here, as an example, is a description of the trading procedure used in Guinea:

When the porters of products, regardless of number, arrived at a trading post, they were housed in huts *ad hoc* and were given an arrival present. This first gift was called *sankiriba* – meaning, literally, the placing of sandals. It was made up most often of rice, biscuits, sugar, salt and meat, a little tobacco and some pieces of cloth. Its importance was based on the traders' approximated evaluation of the products brought. This was entirely a question of flair and chance. This done, the *dantégué* [arrival speech] was delivered. In this speech the *salétigui* [leader of the caravan] extolled the value of what he was bringing. . . .[24]

At the conclusion of his speech the goods were unwrapped and placed on the scales. Then came fresh discussions about prices. Once these were agreed upon, they were expressed in *gourdes* (silver five-franc pieces), the local currency; the amount was written up on a voucher, exchangeable for goods. Then new deliberations took place, brought to an end when special prices and supplementary gifts were offered to the leader of the caravan, who took over the task of convincing anyone who was still hesitant. Finally, a departure present was offered, and this played an essential role. If it was found pleasing, the members of the caravan – even if they had been swindled over everything else – would speak highly of the generosity of the trader and would attract new customers to him. If not, they would destroy the trader's name and put off potential customers.

With the imposition of taxes, the need for the population to conserve in money form a portion of the produce sold led to a growth in the import of metal coins (mainly in silver five-franc pieces).[25] However, direct exchange continued to predominate for a long time.

These commercial methods were upset towards the end of the nineteenth century with the arrival of the Syrians. The term was applied to all Levantines, citizens of the Ottoman Empire (predominantly Lebanese and mainly Christians), who came to settle in increasing numbers as small shopkeepers, particularly in French West Africa (in French Equatorial Africa, the Greeks and Portuguese were to play an analogous role on a smaller scale). Coming first alone, and as simple leaseholders of Africans, they gradually brought their wives over to join them and acquired land; the French mandate over Syria and Lebanon after the first world war placed them in an advantageous position since they were now French nationals. While keeping up their ties with their own country and sending their money there, many of them established themselves in Africa and made roots there.

The story of their settlement in Guinea, where the exporting of rubber was the predominant activity, might serve us as example. With variations due to the specific local trading conditions, it applies equally to other territories. The first Syrians arrived at Conakry in 1897, when customs regulations, aimed at freeing the young colony of Guinea from the commercial domination of Freetown, gave warm encouragement to business. The price of rubber was rising steadily, and expansion was in full swing. At first they were content to have stalls on the market selling odd goods, accepting balls of rubber by way of payment; but soon they turned to the purchase of rubber, undertaking to pay money for it, and their stalls continued to exist only as a matter of form. As a closely knit group, they charged one of their better-educated or more able members to gather up the produce each evening and to make the round of all the business firms the next morning, selling the entire collection to the one that made the best offer, even if the difference was only a matter of a few centimes.

Among the twenty-odd rival export houses, there was always one urgently needing to make purchases, even if very close to the current rate. Thus the Syrians could obtain the maximum price and at the same time cut out the trading stations from making direct purchases. The trading stations still pretended to continue their exchange in kind to give an outlet to trading merchandise, while the Syrians paid in money; moreover, the stations were in the habit of offering hospitality to the trade caravans and giving them presents. The Syrians saved on such outlays, thus rendering competition impossible. Within six months in 1898, the Syrians had acquired a monopoly over rubber.

In vain did the European firms, with the help of the colonial administration, try to eliminate this intrusion, which seriously curtailed their profits and forbade them access to the market. But the Syrians opened up shops, were better able to acquire goods, and took from the European business houses the sale of cloth which they hitherto controlled. In short, the Syrians managed, in the space of a few years, to take over a large part of the retail trade of the big European firms. It was the houses of second rank that suffered. Their retail sales were reduced until they became incapable of competing with the more important firms in wholesale or semi-wholesale trade. The two or three largest wholesale firms found it advantageous to put up with this state of affairs, gaining decidedly more by using the Syrians, who were content with little, as intermediaries rather than paying large salaries to the Europeans who were managers of trading stations, or availing themselves of retail traders as middlemen, who would demand greater margins.

There were only eighteen Syrians in Guinea in 1897, and from 1900 onwards they began to appear in Senegal. By 1913 their number had risen to 681, nearly all in Guinea and Senegal. After the First World War they established themselves on the Ivory Coast, where there had been only two in 1913. Over the entire area of French West Africa there were to be 4,500 in 1939 and 8,500 in 1953.

The Lebanese and Syrians contributed effectively towards the gradual replacement of the traditional system of exchange by barter at the trading stations, by payment in money. For the established businesses the old system had brought the advantage of avoiding the importation – and immobilisation – of cash, and of suppressing the real freedom of the customer to buy as he pleased. Nevertheless,

B

in the interior, direct exchange in kind continued to be the rule for a long time, and as late as 1939, in certain scattered areas, most transactions were still being carried on in this manner. A report, issued in 1903, on the situation in Guinea estimated that the Syrians had been really useful 'in maintaining competition among traders, and in keeping the prices of products at a rate that encouraged the local population to gather the harvest.'[26]

The groundnuts trade in Senegal was of a more advanced character: the product was cultivated and not simply gathered. After the end of the nineteenth century the methods for which it set the example spread, with certain local variations, to the majority of regions affected by the trade. In the tropical climate with very short rainy seasons, more than elsewhere, trade closely followed the rhythm of the seasons, opening up especially after the harvest, between the end of November and mid-December. First, the grower had to take his harvest to the 'port of call' (this term, employed originally in the proper sense to mean navigational ports on the River Senegal, was later applied to all trade centres, including railway stations). At Cayor and Baol, the grower used 'donkey-drivers', breeders and owners of pack-animals – the Laobé of Djoalu, Toucouleurs, Mauretanians; the last-named were generally associated with a trader, who gave them, by way of an advance, food and accommodation during their stay at the port, and paid a premium according to what they had brought. Thus they did not let the cultivator choose freely the shop to which he would bring his harvest. On the Sine-Saloum islands, transport was by boats; in the south of the same region, where sleeping-sickness precluded the use of draught animals, people carried the sacks on their heads.

If the choice of shop was not imposed on the cultivator in advance by his transporters, and if he was not tied to one trader through advances which the latter had granted him – 'credits for the rainy season', loans of supplies solicited at a moment of hardship, involving usurous interest rates – he would be besieged on arrival at the trading point by traders' touts, 'masters of the spoken word', who outrivalled one another in promises and vaunted the imported goods their patron had for sale in order to entice the customer. The peasant realised that, in the end, he would always be cheated to some extent, but he tried to defend himself and did not always allow himself to be fleeced. Aided by a liking for talk, he would bargain at length with the trader, and sometimes he would not even hesitate to consult other traders at the port before handing over his harvest to the one who made the best offer.

In a typical port of call, there would be a single road, of considerable width (there was sufficient space; unevenness of the ground was rare, and the people liked having an open outlook). If there were several streets, this denoted a large centre; the main streets generally contained permanent hard tracks down which carts could be wheeled to the station or the port. The rainy season (a dead season anyway) turned these streets into mud, while the dry season created a labyrinth of furrows of dried mud and sand into which the foot would sink. The traders' shops lined the street. Branch offices, trading stations belonging to large firms, or the establishments of independent European traders would consist of solid buildings. At best these were metal-framed with the first storey providing living quarters for the trader, the trading station agent or owner, with a verandah and a canvas roof. A more modest enterprise or a 'sub-trading station', run by a Lebanese merchant or a Wolof tradesman, would often consist of no more than a shanty made of boards. The layout was always the same: living quarters were either upstairs or at the back of the store, overlooking the yard. The Lebanese, to begin with, lived and slept in their shops, even on the floor amongst bales of merchandise.

The shop counter was placed parallel to the street, on to which the premises opened by wide wooden double-doors that were barricaded overnight with iron bars, chains and padlocks. The doorways were sufficient to light the interior. Windows would only complicate the construction and be appreciated by thieves. In important establishments there would be one or two night-watchmen, who would either sleep inside or lay out their mattresses on the verandah by the door. Where there was no watchman and the trader slept at the back, he would balance on top of the door some metal bowls which would fall and rouse him if anyone tried to open it.

In one corner, close to the entrance, stood the scales where the sacks of groundnuts were weighed. Checks by inspectors of weights and measures were very infrequent, and the good merchant was well acquainted with the art of coaxing his agents: there were few scales that had not been set false, to the trader's advantage, and the use of false weights was commonplace. A more subtle procedure consisted in offering a present, such as a pocket-knife or a hard pencil, to the customer, which was skilfully placed on the scale at the moment when the goods were weighed. At the back of the shop a corridor led to the *secco* or drying yard, a space with a hard-trodden floor enclosed by a corrugated iron fence fixed to posts: here seeds were emptied out and had to be kept under supervision to prevent fermentation, or damage by rodents or weevils.

The back half of the shop was divided off by a wooden counter, partly bare, partly covered with racks on which were set out tempting goods – cloth, hats, sugar, cola, etc. Against the wall, on shelves, stood the reserve stocks, including many bales of cloth; in a cupboard with glass or wire-mesh on the front were the 'luxury' articles, bottles of perfume, combs, alarm-clocks or shoes. On the floor were sacks of rice and millet. In the corner, well labelled, were objects left by the growers as tokens of advances received: jewellery, loin-cloths, etc. Between the two doors were heavy or cumbersome objects which were unlikely to be stolen, like large bowls. As elsewhere, the merchants did their best to pay with goods; but competition, particularly from the Lebanese, and the fact that the peasant had to possess coins to pay taxes and other charges, forced them to pay for an increasing portion of the harvest in money (the silver five-franc *gourde*). In the early days of trading, the company agents brought sealed sacks on the waggon-trains from Dakar to Saint-Louis, which they would throw to the agents at the trading stations on the quayside. For 'transactions' in more remote parts, the sacks of money would be carried farther by donkey or camel.

The expense of transporting money in this way was small compared with that of handling groundnuts, which were first placed in sacks as they left the drying yard; transported thus to the port, they were emptied out again in an open space, put in sacks to be transported on board ship on the heads of labourers, and finally emptied into the hold of the ship where they were freighted in bulk. The sacks generally belonged to the big trading firms who had to provide and renew them.

On the coast and in Senegal there was the appearance of free trade, but this was not true of the interior, where export produce, bought by the trading companies at very low prices on account of transport costs, and exchanged for imported goods that were highly priced for the same reason, was supplied by the peasants only under administrative pressure. The 'market' was controlled by the area commander and his guards, and had the appearance of a gathering of forced labourers come to bring their tribute in kind. The local business houses shared the quota by friendly agreement, or the commander held an auction, usually a faked one.

Having at their disposal a virtual monopoly masquerading as a free market, the Marseilles or Bordeaux firms in French West Africa vigorously opposed the system of large concessions, which won the day in the Belgian Congo, the French Congo and the Cameroons.

2. The System of Large Concessions in Equatorial Africa

(a) FIRST ATTEMPTS

French trade did not acquire important positions in the Congo, but a leading role was played by two English trading companies, Hatton and Cookson, and John Holt – 'established on the coast of the Congo for a long time and monopolising nearly all the trade'[27] – and by the German company, Woermann. The interior remained almost untouched.[28] It was difficult to strengthen the 'national' commercial position through customs arrangements, as Governor Ballay did in Guinea in 1897 to eliminate the competition of Freetown. The larger part of French Equatorial Africa, in effect, formed part of the 'Conventional Congo Basin',[29] throughout which, under the terms of the general Act of Berlin of 21 February, 1885, trade was free, with non-discriminatory tariffs ad valorem of 3, 5, 6 or 10 per cent (according to the nature of the merchandise) alone being tolerated under the Brussels Act of 1890. This was certainly not the determining cause of the special system which grew up in French Equatorial Africa (it did not exist in the Cameroons and, within French Equatorial Africa itself, it did not apply in Gabon); but it did contribute towards its success. The French trading companies were little interested in Gabon and the Congo, the Bordeaux companies never venturing there and the Marseilles firms only making a few tentative steps. The French companies were responsible for little more than a quarter of the trade in the Congo in 1892.

Faced with the shortage of French 'free' enterprise and the weakness of public assets, Brazza, the prime minister, contemplated appealing to the chartered companies to move into Ogooué and Kouila-Niari. A first agreement was signed between Brazza and Christophle, the governor of the Crédit Foncier and representative of a group of firms; this agreement, which envisaged the construction of a railway to Kouila-Niari and the concession of 20,000 square kilometres, was not followed up. This failure may have been due to the action of Belgian interests that were not anxious to see a railway line competing with their route to Leopoldville.[30] But, though reticent at first, investors in Paris and other European centres, who had been attracted by the prodigious profits reaped in the Congo Free State, began to take an interest in such undertakings.

Lacking an economic base in the area, the French companies expected the intervention of the political and administrative personnel of the colonies in their favour, and they were not disappointed. From 1891 on, Étienne, then under-secretary of state for the colonies,[31] drew up a plan creating big chartered companies which would hold virtually sovereign rights over vast territories for a period of ninety-nine years.

The fruits of the earth, of the hunt, and of fishing would be theirs free of charge. They would have police and judiciary rights on their lands, would be able to raise taxes, and would be free to sign treaties with neighbouring estates.[32]

Paul Leroy-Beaulieu presented his theoretical justification for this scheme in a report submitted to the Committee of French Africa at its session on 18 February, 1892, dealing with 'colonial companies and the rights which they should expect'. Étienne looked forward to the creation of these companies by decree, as authorised by traditional colonial legislation. But foreseeing the storms this project might raise, Freycinet, president of the council, preferred to submit it to parliament, where it was held up in committee. While the matter dragged on, Delcassé, under-secretary of state in 1893, 'quietly reached a decision on the question of the big colonial companies'. By a decree, the Société des études et d'exploitation du Congo français (Le Chatelier) was granted a series of minor concessions to be held in full tenure, and a large concession of 20,000 square km. in the basin of the Fernan Vaz, a general concession (including mining rights) with full tenure of the land developed at the end of thirty years. This was given by way of remuneration for 'studies' on the establishment of a railway line – rather, a joint rail and river route – from Brazzaville to the Atlantic. Another decree conceded to Daumas (a former agent of Régis et Cie. of Marseilles) 107,000 square km. on the Upper Ogooué for a period of thirty years, with free use of all the surface and subterranean wealth of the earth, the *monopoly of trade* (the concession being situated outside the Conventional Congo Basin) and the ownership of the land developed by the end of the concession. No budget dues were imposed upon him, but the concession-holder was to see to the provision of ports and the maintenance of the necessary police forces on his concession.

These two Congolese concessions did not encroach only on foreign commercial companies. At N'djolé, on the Ogooué, where Daumas established his head office, there were French trading stations belonging to settlers, several of whom were to gain concessions in 1899: Boggoi et Cie., Gazengel and Monthaye. William Guynet, soon to be found among the big business men of the Congo, appealed for the annulment of the concessions. Harry Alis, journalist and secretary-general of the committee of French Africa, attacked Le Chatelier in the journal *Débats*: this led to a duel in which Alis was killed.[33] In fact (as will be seen below) this protest of Daumas and

Le Chatelier's rivals (almost all of whom were later to be found among concession-holders) was not so much concerned with the principle of the system of concessions as with the fact that they had not received their share of the spoils. In any case, the share of French trade in the Congo rose from 26·04 per cent in 1892 to 41·8 per cent in 1893 and 47·1 per cent in 1894.

A third decree granted to the business house of Verdier – who for a long time had represented French interests on the Ivory Coast – a concession of 5,500,000 hectares in that colony, with a thirty-year monopoly of forest exploitation and full tenure of all lands developed. The levies demanded in return were insignificant: an annual tax of 5,000 francs to be paid into the local budget and a charge of 3 francs per log of timber exported.

On the Ivory Coast, protests were raised: the local administration (headed by Governor Binger), which had not been consulted, and rival commercial companies, objected vigorously.[34] Parliament, whose advice had not been asked, did the same. Radical and socialist deputies, moreover, attacked the whole principle of the system of concessions outright.

The concessions to Verdier and Daumas were annulled in 1896: Verdier, represented by the 'Compagnie française de Kong', finally obtained 300,000 hectares in full tenure by way of settlement, plus a fixed indemnity of 250,000 francs and fourteen annual payments of 125,000 francs each! As to the Daumas concession, it was annulled under the pretext that 'the company had not been constituted in the period foreseen'. Though his claim for sovereign and police rights was dismissed by the council of state, Daumas, represented by the Société commerciale et industrielle du Haut-Ogooué, received 'by way of compensation' the same territory, with the exception of customs rights, for a period of fifteen years! He was, moreover, to be responsible for food supplies for the administrative posts established on his concession, and to carry out various works (codicil of 1897). As to Chatelier's concession, it was revoked in 1897 – and replaced by another agreement benefiting the Société commerciale et industrielle du Congo français, which was renamed the Société d'études et d'exploitation du Congo français; in exchange for the 20,000 square km. on the Fernan Vaz, it was granted 30,000 square km. on both banks of the Kouilou and the Niari – with the exception, this time, of mining rights. On going bankrupt, it was bought up, in 1899, under the name of Compagnie propriétaire du Kouilou-Niari by a group of Belgian interests, who abandoned the project of establishing a railway line which, with the completion of the railway from Léopoldville in 1898, had lost its basic economic attraction.

(b) THE 'LARGE CONCESSIONS'

While the first concession-holders obtained advantageous 'com-promises', the colonial party opened a big propaganda campaign in favour of the colonial companies, presented as a panacea and a system of 'economic' colonisation (in fact, as will be seen, this system proved an expensive one). Étienne published a series of articles on this theme in Le Temps[35] and the theoretician Leroy-Beaulieu was called in. Finally, the minister Guillain set up a commission to draft the articles and conditions of forty limited companies to which, between March and July 1899, thirty-year concessions were accorded, covering almost 70 per cent of the territory of the Congo (the future French Equatorial Africa), that is to say, 650,000 square km.[36]

The biggest company (Société des Sultanats du Haut-Oubangui) received 140,000 square km., the smallest (Société de la N'Kémé-N'Keni) 120,000 hectares. The articles and conditions provided for full ownership of the conceded land if it was 'developed' – a condition considered to be fulfilled if there was a harvest of rubber on twenty feet per hectare in five years, or if it provided one domestic elephant per 100 hectares, or cultivation or constructions covering one-tenth of the area.

The companies were to pay into the colonial budget an annual rent, plus 15 per cent of their profits, give a surety bond and main-tain navigational services on the rivers for their territories. In principle, they enjoyed no delegation of sovereignty, and their agents were to 'avoid administrative or political interference' (Article 13 of the ministerial instructions of 24 May, 1899). Yet customs, administrative or military posts could be established, on request, in the territories under concession. In practice, however, the police forces (militia) were placed at the disposal of the company agents, and in the absence of the regular administrators, they assumed real political powers. The concessions entirely ignored the indigenous political organisation of the native population, who were thus placed at the mercy of the companies. 'Native reserves' were envisaged, but were never marked out.[37] As time passed, mergers reduced the number of chartered companies, the last of which was constituted as the 'N'Goko-Sangha' company (decree of 27 March, 1905), immediately appearing in the news.

It should be realised that the territories given to the companies were still largely unexplored.

When the Congo was parcelled off into vast concessions, just enough was known to assign to various companies the area of such and such a river, from which they often derived their names:

Eleka-Sanga, Lobai, Alima and so on; more precise delimitation did not exist except as a bait, since the majority of the rivers named were not even exactly plotted on the maps. Nevertheless, the directors would arrive at Brazzaville to collect information; but the administrators (among whom were men of ability and experience) often could not answer their questions: they had no maps, the sketches having been drawn up in Paris; some names were unknown to them, while others did double duty: claims, protests, quarrels . . . this was the beginning of the hoped for harmony.[38]

It was about the same period that two big chartered companies came into existence in the Protectorate of the Cameroon: the Süd-Kamerun company with a capital of 2,000,000 marks[39] (8 December, 1898), which was granted 72,000 square km., and the Nord-West Kamerun company (31 July, 1899), which received a grant of 80,000 square km. The Süd-Kamerun company's concession was granted in perpetuity for rubber exploitation, without any reciprocal obligation. The Nord-West Kamerun company, on the other hand, was pledged to allocate 100,000 marks to the exploration of Chad, to construct roads, canals, railways, and establish branch offices and plantations.[40] The 'model' from which they professed to derive their inspiration was, as we have already said, that of King Leopold II's ventures in the Congo Free State, the dividends of which evoked admiration in stockbroking circles. Admittedly it was known by then what methods had been employed to obtain these dividends. Even before Edmund D. Morel published his *Red Rubber*,[41] denouncing the atrocities perpetrated by King Leopold's agents, highly convincing revelations were published in 1900 by the *Neeuwe Gazet* of Antwerp and the *Kölnische Zeitung*; Pierre Mille referred to this in his book *Au Congo belge*.[42] Even the bulletin of the committee of French Africa had to take cognisance of the fact.[43] But the politicians prevailed, with the support of their Belgian *confrères* and models (nominees of King Leopold).

Apart from Parisian business circles there were Belgian and Dutch interests in the Congolese companies. Most prominent until the eve of the Second World War was Du Vivier de Streel, who had been departmental head to the minister for the colonies, Lebon, and who was managing director of several of these companies for more than thirty years. At the outset, many of the shares were purchased by the Belgians with an eye to speculation, and resold after the 'inflation'. Even before exploitation had begun, this led to big fluctuations on the stock exchange. The Belgians kept control of only a few companies where they expected success: several others were con-

B*

trolled by the 'Comptoir français colonial' of Paris. Half its directors were Belgians, one of them, moreover, being a director of the 'A.B.I.R.' in the Free State.[44] In 1907 the capital of the thirty-seven chartered companies in the French Congo was divided as follows: France, 43,600,000 francs; Belgium, 15,600,000 francs; the Netherlands, 1,100,000 francs.[45] In contrast, Bordeaux or Marseilles capital was almost absent. 'The Congolese companies roused little interest in Marseilles and the colony [the Congo] was one of those which came least within the range of the Marseilles field of action.'[46]

The Belgians owned shares in the Cameroon companies. The Nord-West Kamerun company included several German companies, including Woermann, which had only kept its establishments at Victoria, but took in fresh Belgian capital. The Süd-Kamerun company was largely Belgian: Colonel Thys, Leopold II's representative in these matters, held the vice-presidency; the headquarters was set up in Brussels, but after two years was transferred to Hamburg.[47]

When the system of large companies became predominant in Central Africa, the established trade put up opposition in French occidentale. A report by the Compagnie française de l'Afrique Africaine, published in 1900, condemned the system of concessions in operation there.[48] In 1901, private enterprise, entrusted with the construction of the railway line from Conakry to Niger, was forced to withdraw owing to bad management. A Franco-Belgian group, urged on by Colonel Thys, offered to continue the work, on condition that it received a concession of 120,000 hectares, but, in spite of the former Governor Ballay's support for the Franco-Belgian group, local traders (instigated by Governor Cousturier) caused obstructions; Cousturier gave preference to the construction being done under state supervision, financed by loans and resources from the colony's reserve of budget surplus.

Also in 1901, in return, Georges Borelli (of the Mante et Borelli Company, successors to Régis) obtained a railway concession in Dahomey on advantageous conditions (infra-structure to be paid for by the colony, a subsidy of 200 francs per kilometre built; taxes to be paid to the colony only in the event of the revenue exceeding 6,000 francs per kilometre. To this was added a concession of 300,000 hectares in three parts in the vicinity of the railway line, and the monopoly use of ports and docks within a radius of 200 km. around Cotonou. But faced with the protests of business competitors, and with difficulties involved in the exploitation of such a territory in a populated country like Dahomey, the Railway Company of Dahomey was forced to abandon its land concessions. By way of compensation it received the comforting indemnity of 4,000,000 francs in 1904.[49]

That the alarm raised by the traders was not without foundation could be seen from the fate suffered in Central Africa by the established businesses which, being mostly English, did not enjoy administrative protection. Arguing on the basis of their concessions, which gave them the right to all products of the soil, the companies aimed at a monopoly of purchase from the population and, similarly, a monopoly of sale of imported goods, since the use of money was still less widespread in the Congo than it was in French West Africa. British trading stations had been established on the Ogooué since 1884; now they found themselves persecuted, and fines were imposed upon them as a consequence of complaints of 'illegal activity' by the chartered company of the Ogooué-Ngunié. The same firms, established in 1857 and 1869 in the 'Conventional Congo Basin' zone, had their rubber seized by agents of the Compagnie du Congo occidental. A circular declared this seizure illegal; but the court of appeal at Libreville, in a judgement on 27 November, 1901, declared in favour of the chartered companies. It denied that trade carried on with the local population over a period of twenty years established an 'acquired right', and stated that the exclusive right of exploitation conceded to the Compagnie du Congo occidental did not constitute a commercial monopoly, as was forbidden under Article 5 of the Act of Berlin. The companies to fall victim to these measures were the two Liverpool firms, John Holt and Hatton and Cookson. The Liverpool–Manchester merchants took action, and it was not mere chance that their spokesman, E. D. Morel, member of the African section of the Liverpool chamber of commerce (which had little praise for French colonisation in West Africa), denounced the horrors of colonisation in the French Congo and the 'Free State' with great vigour.[50]

In September 1901 the Liverpool chamber of commerce lodged a solemn protest; and on 15 May, 1902, a meeting for the defence of British rights took place at the Mansion House. It was attended in person by John Holt, who was vice-president of the African section of the Liverpool chamber of commerce, and whose business was one of those most badly affected. The protests demanded that a new international conference on Africa be summoned to state precisely the terms of the Act of Berlin in respect to the Congo. (The Free State was likewise referred to.) A motion to that effect was passed by the House of Commons. The rebirth of the Entente Cordiale in 1904 put an end to this offensive; but the Foreign Office demanded compensation (the abandonment of the proposed trial of British merchants, and indemnities of 2,500,000 francs). The colony of the Congo had to pay heavy indemnities out of its budget to the British merchants. An agreement of 14 May, 1906, stipulated the annulment of judicial proceedings already begun and the grant of an indemnity of 1,500,000 francs, divided in equal parts between John Holt and Hatton and Cookson, of which 500,000 francs were payable immediately and the rest in ten annual instalments with a 4 per cent interest. Moreover, John Holt received 30,000 hectares of land of his own choice. But the rights of the chartered companies were upheld.[51] The weakness of 'free' trade, and the fact that it was represented mainly by foreign firms, prevented it from becoming an obstacle to the system of concessions.

(c) TWO SYSTEMS OF EXPLOITATION

Two systems of exploitation were thus established in French Black Africa. They had certain basic features in common, but clear differences in their manner of application.

The common features were rudimentary trade procedures; investment reduced to a minimum, and confined mainly to commerce and the transport of merchandise, almost insignificant in the productive sector. But in French West Africa trade was carried on under the auspices of 'freedom of trade' – while, in fact, the commercial companies had a monopoly; the 'independent' African peasant, who supplied the essentials of production, was exploited through the market. In the forest or semi-forest regions (Ivory Coast, Lower Guinea) there were a few European plantations (coffee, bananas) of which the vital development, incidentally, took place after the First World War. Some forest concessions were, likewise, accorded on the Ivory Coast. The development of this agricultural and forestry work under European direction was slight and remained limited geographically to humid regions and perennial plantations. In the entire savannah zone, the independent peasant produced his annual crops less expensively with traditional tools than using wage labour, badly paid though it was. In short, investment in agriculture, forestry and even mining was insignificant.

In 1905 the total capital invested in plantations and agriculture throughout French West Africa was valued at 2,368,000 francs (of which 1,000,000 was foreign), mainly in Guinea, the Ivory Coast and Senegal (25,000 francs only in Upper Senegal and Niger). In mining enterprises, reduced by degrees to the work of prospecting and stock exchange speculation, the capital invested in French West Africa rose to 2,685,000 francs.[52] A few figures will convey the extent of the concession. In 1898 they covered an area of 2,450 hectares on the Ivory Coast[53] (the Elima coffee plantation 200 hectares; coffee and cocoa plantations of Impérié at Bunua 150 hectares;

plantation of the Société coloniale de la côte de Guinée at Dabou 600 hectares – the latter two only partially developed).[54] By the beginning of 1912, concessions on the Ivory Coast had risen to 3,290 hectares (plus 40,000 hectares of forestry concession). In other colonies of the group it comprised: Senegal 6,300 hectares; Upper Senegal and Niger 2,829 hectares; Guinea 5,917 hectares; Dahomey 1,502 hectares.[55]

The extreme destitution of the peasant brought about by this situation was not the result of the 'free' play of supply and demand, but was brought about by the administration, which was at the beck and call of commerce. For one thing, the latter attended to the provision of export products for the European trade by means of compulsory cultivation, or forced deliveries at the lowest rate of taxed prices; it also transferred the general costs of running the colony to the African population through taxation and the requisitioning of labour (unpaid).

In French Equatorial Africa trade passed through the hands of the great colonial companies holding monopoly rights who, after 1900, established a syndicate, l'Union Congolaise. Nine of them grouped themselves together to organise joint navigation services as set out in their articles of association, and established the Messageries fluviale du Congo (1900). Three others (Compagnies des Sultanats, de la Kotto and de la Mobayé) created the Compagnie de navigation et de transports du Congo-Oubangui for the same purpose. Outwardly, their investments in agriculture, forestry and mining were more important, judging by the names of the companies and the activities laid down in their articles,[56] but in fact import and export constituted their real activity. However, the semblance of free trade often gave way to brutal plunder; for the companies considered the men and the product of their labour their own property.

The organisation of the chartered companies did not differ from that of the ordinary trade companies. The following description of the company of Ouahm et Nana (Ubangi) in 1905 was given by Commandant Saintoyant:

The Company, with French and Dutch capital, had at its disposal 20,000 square km., bordered on the east by the Ubangi–Chad porterage route. It owned a main trading station at Krebedjé (with one European director and three employees), a transit trading station at Fort-de-Possel and four trading stations, each staffed by two whites (an agent and his deputy) and a certain number of black agents recruited in Senegal, Sierra Leone and the Kasai. Their work was exclusively commercial with the somewhat absurd exception of poultry breeding at the main station.[57]

But transactions were carried on rather differently. By virtue of the deed of concession, the companies considered themselves owners of the products.

Consequently, when a native brought some produce of the soil to a trading station, valuing it at three francs, for example, he found himself being paid one franc, or he was told: 'I cannot pay for what is mine, but only for your labour of harvesting.' This franc was paid to him in the form of merchandise, and what merchandise! – often such extraordinary things as old uniforms, helmets and walking-sticks.[58]

(d) FROM EXPLOITATION TO EXTERMINATION: THE MARTYRDOM OF THE CONGO

The concession-holders showed no gratitude to the colonial administration for the efforts made in their favour. They made every demand upon it – primarily to back up the sanction of force to coerce the people to work, and to strip them of their property – and, on their side, they refused to submit to any control or even to fulfill obligations laid down in their statutes. From May 1899, the instructions of the commissioner-general of the Congo, de Lamothe, enjoined the local administration to render 'facilities and aid' to the company agents. No sooner had they been installed than the companies complained of not receiving all the aid required. What 'aid' meant can be seen from their accusations against the 'native populations irremediably lazy because they have never worked, since the administration has never demanded continuous work'.[59]

What was this 'laziness'? It is true that the population of the Congo, who had known neither the forcibly constructed village communities nor the relatively stable estates of West Africa, did not have the same working habits or even the habit of submission to alien discipline. But the real point was that right from the time of the conquest, before the establishment of the big chartered companies, the constant impressment for porterage between the coast and Brazzaville, and between Ubangi and Shari in Mandjal territory, had decimated the populations and provoked numerous revolts. To ensure the supply of provisions, arms and ammunition for Marchand's troops and to supply the Chad troops that were campaigning against Rabah, it was necessary to requisition numerous porters from among the scattered population over hundreds of kilometres, without any means of feeding or paying them. General Mangin cited, as an example, the troubles that occurred in Bassoundi territory in 1896 when Marchand's troops were passing through it. During a discussion between Dolisie (at the time lieutenant-governor of the Congo, under Brazza) and a local chief, Dolisie had one of the chief's followers disarmed for taking, in his opinion, a 'threatening attitude'. The chief demanded the restitution of the rifle and an indemnity, to which Dolisie replied by having the village burnt down and the palm trees felled. When the troops' porters were attacked, all the villages of the region were systematically burnt down.[60] Mangin observed philosophically:

> Setting fire to a village simply corresponds to a penance of several days' labour.[61] Since this work brings profit to nobody, I have never used this kind of punishment when I had to act severely: I always preferred to inflict a fine which would be of profit to the public exchequer, or forced labour in the general interest. But there were cases when an immediate chastisement became necessary, when it had to be proved on the spot who is master: I believe that burning should be used in such cases.[62]

To maintain contact with Chad, administrative porterage was established on a permanent basis.

The sub-divisions through which the route passed were charged with providing porters. Labour conditions were hard: the burden was 30 kg., the distance 25 km., the pay 1 franc.[63] The transports increased in number, and soon even the most willing lost heart. No food was provided, and the majority of the porters, people with no foresight [sic], had to cover their 80 to 100 km. suffering the pangs of hunger. Later on even this meagre salary was withheld, as a tax imposed on the village.[64]

Administrator Georges Toqué stated:

> We must transport more than 3,000 loads per month on men's heads. That is an absolute necessity. If these loads are not moved, the troops occupying Chad will be short of munitions when facing the enemy, and die of hunger. Since the military administration has left empty stores for the civil administration, it is absolutely impossible to give any pay to the porters.[65]

To find porters, the use of force became indispensable. A circular issued by Captain Thomasset on 16 October, 1901 (confirmed by instructions of Lieutenant-Colonel Destenaves dated 17 July, 1902), authorised heads of stations to inflict summarily up to fifty strokes of the cane, prison sentences and fines, or ultimately court proceedings. Circle commanders were authorised to pronounce sentences of deportation or death. Faced with the flight of the population who went to seek refuge in the Belgian Congo, they began to take women and children as hostages to force the men to submit to porterage, and even used women as porters. On 23 December, 1901, Toqué discovered in a camp of hostages in the bush the corpses of twenty women, and 150 women and children at the point of death through undernourishment.[66]

In 1903 the Mandja settled around Fort-Crampel, of whom there were between 16,000 and 18,000, had officially performed 12,370 days of porterage.[67] For the total of the populations subject to porterage, estimated at about 120,000, the number of days worked (excluding return trips) rose to 112,000 in 1902 and 101,066 in 1903, according to official figures. Since women, children, old people, chiefs and persons of standing were exempt from forced labour, the *Bulletin du Comité de l'Afrique française* estimated that the number of actual porters was as high as 12,000. Thus each one had to do ten days of porterage per year. But, taking into account the journey from the village to the station for the load and the time of the return trip, the *Bulletin* estimated that at least eighty days of porterage a year per subject were involved. 'And, we repeat', the *Bulletin* notes, 'all these figures give rather a low average.'[68] These figures did not include the days of forced labour on the construction or maintenance of roads,[69] culverts or administrative posts, carried out under exactly the same terms.

Cuvillier-Fleury noted elsewhere:

Badly nourished, overworked, often maltreated by foremen of little scruple, these unhappy people reached the end of their journey exhausted and ill. After a few days' rest, if they wished to return to their country, they had to bring themselves to beg to do the same trip in the opposite direction, and so to undergo the same sufferings. When they finally got back to their villages, they found their crops lying waste, their property pillaged.[70]

At the time when the chartered companies were being introduced, the poll tax (*impôt personnel*) made its appearance. It was aimed less at procuring resources for the administration than at easing the operation of the chartered companies. The minister of the colonies wrote in 1906:

You know that it was at the invitation of the chartered companies that one of my predecessors introduced a poll tax, nor are you unaware of the fact that in the Free State the tax at present levied constitutes one of the main means whereby the chartered companies obtain the required rubber.[71]

First it was levied in kind: in Upper Sangha, for example, for 1,000 persons counted, 1,000 kilos of rubber and 20 tusks of ivory were exacted. Fixed at 3 francs per head in 1902, the tax was raised to 5 francs in 1907, payable in rubber, handed over to the chartered companies and paid by the latter to the state. The decree of 11 February, 1902, establishing this poll-tax envisaged the progressive introduction of the payment of tax in kind and by instalments, beginning in 1904 and completed by 1908. But even at Brazzaville, the people were forced to pay one part of the tax in rubber, which they had to purchase at a higher price than that paid to them, so as to supply raw materials to the factory of M. William Guynet, Congo representative of the higher council for the colonies. As to tax collection, the administration of the colonies invited the general commissioner to employ Senegalese troops on service in the colony for this purpose, beginning in May 1902. A few months later, in August 1902, the new minister, Doumergue, added to the list of persons to be employed for tax collection the agents of the concessionaire companies.[72]

Through the ingenuity of the administration numerous supplementary taxes were added to the poll-tax: thus at Libreville a tax of 5 gold francs on tom-toms; one of 200 (later reduced to 100) francs was imposed on 'salt-houses' on the Congolese coast to prevent the exploitation of the local brine-pits, and so to force the population to buy the salt imported by the chartered companies. While the income from taxes doubled in French West Africa between 1902 and 1904, it more than quintupled in the Congo, rising from 90,970 to 507,793 francs. A circular sent out by Commissioner Gentil on 19 March, 1903, gave notice to officials that they would thenceforward be in line for promotion according to taxes collected.[73] This gave carte blanche for all manner of abuses. In the absence of regular checks, taxes were frequently raised two or three times. The system of 'hostages' was employed for the payment of taxes as for the provision of porters; above all, payment in kind through the chartered companies[74] made possible the most shameless pillage. Rubber was given a value far below the price operative in Guinea; for a piston gun, valued at 8–10 francs in Europe, the price of which could have increased by, at most, two or three times in transit, the companies exacted 200 kilos of ivory. Salt and cotton fabrics were sold at five times their price on arrival at the port. In Upper Ubangi, the establishment of free trade houses instead of the chartered companies resulted in the following changes: rubber paid for at 5 francs a kilo, opposed to 0·25 francs in the previous year; a chicken cost 2 instead of 0·60 francs; one load of porterage was paid for at 1·20 francs instead of – two spoonfuls of salt.[75]

Faced by flight and physical decline among the Mandja, a decree by Commissioner Gentil dated 2 December, 1904, suppressed forced porterage between Fort-Sibut and Fort-Crampel and replaced it by 'professional porterage'; but, due to the lack of 'professionals' to recruit, this remained a paper reform.

In fulfilment of this decree, some five hundred porters were recruited; rather they were pressed into service in the Lower Congo, in January 1905, and transported to the porterage route. The removal from home surroundings, the difficulties of finding food in this depopulated region, but most of all the inveterate horror of the blacks for any kind of regular and continuous work brought this experiment to nothing. The men deserted, and as we passed through [the Brazza mission in the summer of 1905] their group had been reduced to a very small number. We ourselves owed our porters to the old system of roll-call in the villages.[76]

At the same time, the chartered companies, anxious to supply their shareholders with hoped-for dividends, intensified every means of exploitation in the country; and the exploitation was devastating, since it exclusively affected the products of crop-harvesting and hunting, i.e. rubber and ivory. Their white staff were generally recruited from among the lowest strata of society, ne'er-do-weels or criminals trying their luck in the tropics.

They were recruited, Commandant Saintoyant wrote,

. . . from among people, who, having fallen on evil days in their own countries, had come to accept a post anywhere, in the roughest country. Badly paid, often obliged to sue their employers in court to get their pay, they seek to recoup themselves by doubtful means.[77]

Mangin, who can hardly be accused of tenderness, noted:

. . . seven concession agents, who, apart from two tolerable ones, are truly fiendish. Some of this may be the drunken bragging of ruffians, but it is disturbing to think that, without any supervision, these men are in direct contact with peoples who do not yet know us at all.

As examples of our race, they are a very bad choice, and we are storing up every kind of abuse, vengeance and repression, which are and will continue to be the history of this unhappy colony as long as there is no change in the system.[78]

The administration had not the power to exercise any control over the company agents and their activities. In 1905 there were a hundred officials in the Middle Congo – fifty-four in Brazzaville, twelve at Loango and only thirty-four over the rest of the territory, on account of shortage of staff, the 'reserved zones' (the 30 per cent of the territory without concessions) were not administered.[79] When a decree of 14 January, 1906, prohibited the delimitation of the 'Native reserves' intended in the concessions, there were violent protests from the companies. A decree of 9 October, 1903, planning for the establishment of reserves on one-tenth of the perimeter of the company land, remained a dead letter. However, on the whole, the officials tended to bow to the pressure, exerted through the demands and the insolence of company staff; advancement in their careers depended on the reports, favourable or otherwise, made about them by company representatives in higher places.

For the effects of the system we have only to read the testimony of Father Daigre, an old missionary, though hardly anti-colonialist as shown by certain passages of his text.

The majority of the villages responded with a refusal to harvest rubber, and in support of the administration flying columns of police were sent into the country. The natives did not try to resist, but several thousand of them, near the river, fled to the Belgian Congo. The rest hid in the bush, or in caves from which they were driven out with grenades.

The rebels did not give in for several weeks. Each village or group of villages was then occupied by one or several policemen assisted by a certain number of auxiliaries, and the rubber harvest began.

The crop involved was *landolphia humilis,* known by the colonials as grass rubber in contrast to forest rubber. It is a small shrub found very widely in the savannahs, whose deep roots secrete a second-grade latex.

A programme was worked out and the guards were charged with executing it. The work was done in common. After the morning roll-call, men and women alike were transformed into harvesters, and scattered to pull up the root-stock. On their return to the village each bundle was rigorously checked. They then beat the roots to separate the gum from the bark. The operation, a very long one, was done in running water in order to cleanse the rubber of all impurities.

At the end of the month, the harvest was taken to the market centre where the sale took place at the rate of fifteen sous per kilo.[80] The administration officials proceeded to the weighing, and the buyer taking delivery of the goods paid cash, not to the harvester but to the official, who rated the sum as part of the village tax. *Most of the people thus worked for nine consecutive months without receiving the slightest remuneration.* [Italics not in original.]

This forced labour continued for most of the first two years, because there was an abundance of the product, and food was still provided by the former cassava plantations. But the time came when the *landolphia* became scarce near the settlements, and the harvesters were removed to new settlements, often far away from the villages, where only the sick and young children were permitted to remain. In these deserted places the men worked under the supervision of the guards and their gang, living in infested shelters and dreadful promiscuity, completely exposed to the weather and often having no food besides roots and wild fruit. Towards the end of the month they were given two or three days to go and fetch food from the village, but most often they would return empty-handed since the crops had not been replanted.

Three months had been alloted for planting. But exhausted, discouraged, convinced that they would not be given time to care for their own fields, and that the harvest would be plundered or destroyed by wild animals, the natives hardly ever did any planting. It was then, by way of excuse, that the slogan was coined: 'These people are so slothful that they don't even plant their fields. It's hardly surprising that they are dying of hunger.' Slothful, it is true, but should we not see insecurity, confusion and bewilderment rather than slothfulness as the true cause for this distaste for planting?

Soon premiums in the form of various goods, spirits, meat, and even horses brought by the Bornu people from Chad, were widely distributed by the purchasing agents (the companies) to the village headmen and the police, inciting the latter to intensify the crop collection; this led to night work and to violence and extortion.

Auxiliaries posed as police and chased numerous harvesters who tried to elude forced labour, and one would meet long files of prisoners, roped by the neck, naked and pitiable. How many of these unhappy people, besotted by bad treatment, have I seen filing past along unfrequented roads. Starving and sick, they would drop like flies.

The sick and little children who had been abandoned in the villages died of hunger there. Several times I visited a region where those who were least ill did their best to feed them; and there I saw open graves from which the corpses had been removed to serve as food. Skeleton-like children rummaged among the piles of refuse to find ants and other insects to eat raw. Skulls and shin-bones were scattered along the approaches to the villages.

The situation worsened with the appearance of an epidemic.

This evil, unknown to medicine and called *ogourou* by the Banda, took the form of a total depigmentation of the body accompanied by œdema.[81] It passed in several big waves over a large part of the country and claimed thousands of victims, mainly in the rubber-growing areas.[82]

Comment would be superfluous. Father Daigre concludes:

As a consequence of this lamentable state of affairs, numerous villages survived simply as ruins; plantations ceased to exist, and the population was reduced to the direst misery and despair. Never had the people lived through such horrors, even during the worst periods of the Arab invasion. . . . Health services, it can truly be said, were non-existent in the colony, for there were only two or three doctors in residence at Bangui, the most distant point of the territory. . . . To distract attention, all the misery caused by the inhuman exploitation of rubber was put down to the sleeping sickness, which has certainly also been causing grave ravages for over ten years.[83]

In 1909 French West Africa had a total of twenty doctors. A study mission on sleeping sickness, set up under Dr. Martin in 1906 and in 1911 attached permanently to the Pasteure Institut at Brazzaville, could do no more than identify the disease. It stated that 'the date of appearance of the disease coincided in many points with our arrival in the country'.[84] And Dr. Curea, the lieutenant-governor of the Middle Congo, declared in *Le Temps*: 'I believe that scientific proof shows that it was overworking [the native] which provoked the extraordinary spread of sleeping sickness.'[85]

On the rivers of the Congo and the Ubangi the population had to endure a lesser degree of forced porterage; but they were exposed to the hardships of river navigation (forced labour for cutting timber, requisitioning of paddlers, provisions and fowls rounded up for passenger consumption, etc.). Professor Auguste Chevalier noted during his mission the devastation of the river banks. At Isasa, he found the village three-quarters burnt down. The few remaining inhabitants fled at the approach of the steamer *Dolisie*; and what remained of the village was immediately burnt down by the troops.

We watched a heart-breaking scene caused not by the natives but by the European army personnel travelling with us. From the indifference displayed by the officers who let it happen, I came to believe that such things must occur frequently, and now I turned my attention to the nature and origin of the troubles which occurred last February at Sangha, and last July here. . . .[86]

The concession-holders (still according to Chevalier) considered the natives as freely available for forced labour and proceeded to seize all their property, including cattle, under the pretext that the produce of the soil was included in the concession. The few plantations still kept by the village people were 'requisitioned' by the Europeans, the Senegalese, or their servants. Professor Chevalier quoted the opinion of heads of trading stations and of army officers: 'There is nothing to be got from these blacks here: the best thing to do is to exterminate them and so make the other regions more docile.'

(e) THE GAUD-TOQUÉ AFFAIR

It is clear that resistance was widespread and fierce, and its suppression grew in savagery. What could these unhappy people, who often had nothing beside assegais, do to defend themselves? Extermination continued systematically over the years. With the establishment of military posts moving towards the interior, it even increased. However, the moment came when the scandal broke publicly. The occasion was the Gaud-Toqué trial in 1905. The incriminating actions took place at Fort-Crampel in 1903.

Toqué was a well-known administrator, who received a citation from Lieutenant Mangin for his 'excellent conduct' with Marchand's force. He was the author of ethnographic and linguistic works, especially on the Banda. He enjoyed the confidence of his superiors, and Félicien Challaye noted: 'M. Bruel, who is in command of the region and lives at Fort-Archambault, is a personal friend of Toqué.'[87] Toqué's colleague, Gaud, on the other hand, had the reputation of being a ruffian; but he too was the author of ethnographic works on the Mandja. Another person implicated was a clerk of native affairs in the service of the militia named Proche, but he was finally exonerated.

Toqué had on various occasions, albeit discreetly, denounced the abuses of the system. But it seems that he had also participated in it. On leave in Paris, he refused to submit to the summons of a judge of Brazzaville, was arrested and, like Gaud, sent to the assizes. Proche, who had voluntarily returned to the colony, and appeared as a free defendant, was charged with having had two blacks shot without trial after they had fled at the arrival of the guards coming to requisition porters. Toqué was accused of causing the drowning of a black charged with the theft of a few cartridges. Gaud was accused of numerous assassinations and executions, of having let prisoners die of hunger, and of having baked a woman alive in an oven. Finally Gaud, together with Toqué, was accused of having made a servant drink a soup made from a human head, and above all, of blowing up a prisoner with a stick of dynamite tied to his body. This happened on 17 July, 1903, 'after a scene of lewdness'.[88]

This last affair caused a sensation. The victim, named Pakpa, was accused by Toqué of betraying him while acting as a guide and of leading him into an ambush. Toqué had written to Gaud, in May 1903, ordering him to arrest the man and have him shot. Gaud made the arrest on 12 July. The next day, Toqué returned to Fort-Crampel stricken with fever and went to bed. Gaud reported to him that there were three prisoners, among them Pakpa. Toqué ordered him to set the other two free, but of Pakpa he said: 'Treat him as you like.' On 14 July, Gaud blew him up with the dynamite tied to him and reported this to Toqué who observed: 'That mustn't get around.' Gaud replied: 'It looks absurd, but it will petrify the natives. After this they'll not raise a murmur.'[89]

Brazza, replaced a few years earlier, was sent to inspect, and in his party he had Félicien Challaye, a young philosophy graduate who, in his articles in *Le Temps* and the book he published in 1909, related the circumstances of the trial and placed it in a general perspective. Toqué defended himself by claiming that he had been included in the indictment for the very reason that he had denounced the crimes commited in Upper Shari, in which he said he had taken no part except under constraint and coercion. Challaye assumed that he tried to suppress the scandal caused by Gaud's crimes by covering them up; these were his superior's orders, and all the Europeans were behind him in doing so, 'for fear that Gaud might reveal all the scandals known to him, for example, that of the Nana massacre'.[90] Toqué summed up the situation prior to 1903:

It was a general massacre, perpetrated in order to make the service work. . . . Toqué, under examination, described the procedure employed to obtain porters before setting off for the outpost. Raids were made on the villages. The women and children were carried off; they were hidden in small huts so that passers-by should not see them. These women and children often died of hunger or smallpox; the women were raped by the local police. These hostages were not set free until the porters arrived. The same method was employed for tax collections.[91]

According to Félicien Challaye, Toqué did not use every means open to him for his defence. Pressure had been put upon him – even the promise of acquittal – not to expose the administration of Upper Shari and of the colony (to be exact, Bruel and Gentil), as he confirmed after being set free. On 26 August, 1905, Toqué and Gaud were finally sentenced to five years' solitary confinement with hard labour – which caused indignation among the Europeans in the Congo. But the court itself petitioned for the reduction of the sentence, and the two prisoners were soon released.[92]

In spite of all precautions, the scandal affected the upper echelons of the administration. Brazza, embittered by his previous disgrace and anxious to avenge his mission, clashed with Gentil, who was also involved in the investigation, and the whole European colony, including Mgr. Augouard who, in spite of his confused dealings with the administration, stood by Gentil.[93] In *L'Humanité* Gustave Rouanet directly attacked Gentil, who was accused of a series of crimes (maltreatment, summary executions, causing the death of militiamen by beating).[94] *Le Temps* made a clumsy reply claiming that these were 'deeds of war'[95] and that one of the summary executions under attack had been that of a 'British agent'. *L'Humanité* exposed a recent result of the 'hostage system': forty-five women and three children (out of fifty-eight women and ten children detained) had died of hunger at Mongumba, near Bangui, having been sent there by a touring commissioner in charge of native affairs. They had come from a region five days' march away and were huddled together in a hut 6 by 4·25 metres. The women, who nearly all died of hunger, had sacrificed themselves to save their children. A doctor, Major Fulconis, who had discovered this crime and saved the survivors, was reprimanded.

The scandal was finally hushed up. Brazza died at Dakar while returning from his mission; in February 1906 a big debate took place in the Chamber of Deputies in Paris, in the course of which Gustave Rouanet, Jaurès, Caillaux and Hubert placed the system of concessions on trial. But in the end the majority of the Chamber approved the refusal of the minister for the colonies to publish the report compiled from the work of the Brazza mission. The debate led merely to a juridical reform of the system, with no change in the methods used. Moreover, while the system continued, the administration took vigilant measure to avoid leakage.[96] In 1926 André Gide was to see scenes analogous to those described by Father Daigre between 1900 and 1914.

(*f*) THE DEPOPULATION OF EQUATORIAL AFRICA

The demographic consequences of what we have described can be imagined. At the beginning of the century the population of French Equatorial Africa was estimated at 15,000,000. In 1913, the yearbook of the Bureau of Longitudes estimated it at 10,000,000, the General Statistics of France at 9,00,0000. Bruel in his *French Equatorial Africa*, published in 1914, suggested a figure of 4,950,000 inhabitants. The 1921 census gave a figure of 2,860,868.

A pamphlet published by a settler who can hardly be reproached for liberal views, but who was undoubtedly anxious to attack the colonial administration, stated:

> The population of the three colonies of the Congo [Ubangi-Shari, the Middle Congo and Gabon] was 4,280,000 on 31 December, 1911, according to M. Bruel and official documents. During the official census of 1921 it was no more than 1,577,565. In other words, it has decreased by 63 per cent in ten years.[97]

In the editions of his book published after the First World War, Bruel blamed the approximate nature of census tallies and their exaggerated figures in order to explain this reduction. And in fact daring 'adjustments' were made several times while in many cases the administrators received orders to push up the population count so as not to discourage potential subscribers to shares in the chartered companies. But in the same work Bruel cited the example of a district where the population had diminished by 40 per cent between 1908 and 1916, and by another 40 per cent between 1916 and 1924. According to a military personage who was administrator of Upper Ubangi, the population of that region diminished by a quarter between 1903 and 1911.[98] Apart from famine and disease (sleeping sickness, in particular), the prolonged separation, due to requisitioning, of the men and women, often for nine out of every twelve months, and the physical exhaustion of the men, made them incapable of procreation. However, famine was the chief cause of the depopulation as shown by an official report:

> The native dies, primarily, because he lacks food. Famine is the principal cause of the depopulation of the Congo. It is that and that alone, long before the terrible sleeping sickness and epidemics and far more than these, which depopulates and destroys the colony.[99]

The demographic decline in a whole series of regions of French Equatorial Africa had no other cause, and it is fruitless to seek any mysterious 'psychological' reasons.

3. Economic Consequences

The balancing of the economy can be explained in terms of the prevailing system of colonisation.

(a) FRENCH EQUATORIAL AFRICA

In the Congo, the results achieved by the big chartered companies were uneven and bore no relation to the size of the territory under monopoly. Between 1900 and 1903 nearly all the companies recorded losses:

	Number of companies making a profit	Total profits (in francs)	Number of companies making a loss	Total losses (in francs)
1900	3	219,000	21	2,874,000
1901	2	114,854	28	4,369,000
1902	3	196,000	27	3,842,000
1903	8	1,017,000	23	2,275,000

On 31 December, 1903, the overall loss amounted to 11,700,000 francs, almost a quarter of the capital invested. But since this was a period when the companies were being established and making their first ventures, the figures were not abnormal. This result can in fact be ascribed largely to the speculative character of many of the companies, whose object was to make a 'fast buck' while the going was good rather than get down to serious activity. The allowances and various emoluments of the administrators often ate up much of the capital invested.[100]

The situation improved from 1904 onwards – by what methods and at what price we have already seen. By that date, six of the original forty companies had disappeared, three had merged with others, and one had a zero balance. Here are the results for 1904–6:

	Number of companies making a profit	Total profits (in francs)	Number of companies making a loss	Total losses (in francs)
1904	12	2,800,000	18	900,000
1905	17	4,900,000	14	990,000
1906	16	4,600,000	15	750,000

At the end of seven years of the concessions system, ten companies recorded approximately 10,000,000 francs profit since their foundation and twenty-one had their capital eaten away by a total loss of more than 9,000,000.[101] The rubber crisis, which partly explains the initial difficulties around 1901, recurred in 1907; the scandals already mentioned led to a partial reform of the concession system.

Between 1894 and 1898 the total turnover of commercial transactions in the Congo oscillated around the figure of 10,000,000 francs per year. In 1900 it rose sharply to about 18,000,000, but chiefly through imports made by the companies when they started their businesses. From 1902 onwards the trading figure fell to 13,800,000, i.e. back roughly to the figure of 1899. From then on there was a steady upward trend.

Foreign Trade of the French Congo
(in millions of francs)

Years	Total transactions	Imports	Exports
1896	9·5	4·7	4·7
1897	8·8	3·5	5·2
1898	10·5	4·8	5·6
1899	13·3	6·68	6·61
1900	17·9	10·4	7·5
1901	15·1	7·8	7·3
1902	13·8	5·5	8·3
1903	16·9	6·9	9·9
1904	21·1	9·0	12·1
1905	24·3	10·0	13·9
1906	29·5	13·0	16·4

Progress followed the same pattern in the following years, commercial transactions rising again after the 1907–8 crisis – caused by a drop in the price of rubber – to reach 41,500,000 francs in 1911 and 43,400,000 in 1912.

Setting aside the years 1900–1 when the chartered companies were being established, the value of exports exceeded that of imports. As a general rule, the colonial economy was tied to the principle of an excess in the value of imports; merchandise to be disposed of was sold at exceptionally high prices, and the values given to products purchased were abnormally low. One part of the import excess took the form of investments and of goods destined for consumption by Europeans in the colony, so that the profits exported from the colony to the metropolis were invisible. In the reverse situation, the weakness of capital contribution was made clear, and the cropping of local products was exceptionally intensive, without corresponding imports.

The chartered companies had the major share of commerce: 16,000,000 out of 24,300,000 in 1905 and 22,700,000 out of 29,500,000 in 1906. It is interesting to examine this in detail.

Year	General trade (in millions of francs)		Chartered company trade (in millions of francs)	
	Import	Export	Import	Export
1905	10·3	13·9	4·5	11·4
1906	13·0	16·4	6·7	15·7

A comparison of general statistics on possessions in the Congo and the trade of the chartered companies shows the high rate of imports by the small colonial enterprises and the almost total control of exports by the companies owing to the privilege they had been granted. A comparison of the companies' imports and exports throws light on the considerable difference between the value of imported goods in relation to that of exported products.[102]

The criticism caused by the administration of the companies and the bankruptcy of many of them led to a partial reform of the system in 1910. From the promulgation of a constitution for French Equatorial Africa in 1908, the principle had been adopted that the companies should be freed of the burden of administration, which should be left to the government. In practice, there was not much change, as the colonial administration did not possess the necessary manpower to take over from the companies. The latter, moreover, had all the means to force the administrators to grant them 'aid and support', and the 'control' that was technically in the administrators' power remained unenforced. The 'reform' of the system of concessions simply helped the companies that were in jeopardy; in exchange for renouncing their rights, which they were incapable of exercising, the losing companies gained substantial advantages and the annulment of part of their debts.[103]

Thus, a contract signed on 13 June, 1910, with eleven out of the thirteen chartered companies of the Sangha region, replaced the thirty-year concession by a sort of farming lease for a period of ten years, open to renewal, and limited to rubber production instead of every agricultural product. The area made over was considerably reduced, but this reduction was fictitious, since the area previously conceded had scarcely been penetrated. Moreover, the companies could arrange 'contracts' for the purchase of rubber with native communities in regions not under concession to them. At the same time, the merger of eleven companies into one body, named the Compagnie forestière de Sangha-Ubangi, gave them a more solid financial backing.

At the same time, a similar contract saved six companies in Gabon, out of eight in that region; these were also running at a loss. In return for their renunciation of 5,910,000 hectares theoretically conceded, they were granted full ownership of twelve 'plots' of 10,000 hectares plus one forestry concession.[104] Some of them, moreover, received the right for ten years, to exploit the forests situated along the water courses and lagoons in their former concessions to a depth of 5 km., in return for a tax of 0·50 to 1 franc per log exported. On the eve of the war the situation of the companies forming the Du Vivier de Streel Group was extremely prosperous. The 'reformed' companies had lost nothing except the commercial monopoly which they had shown themselves incapable of exercising. The *Bulletin du Comité de l'Afrique française* observed of them:

It can be said that the whole of their social capital had almost disappeared, and this loss left a mark on their activity. Nevertheless, without any direct profit to themselves, these companies immobilised considerable areas, interfering with competition, preventing the natives from purchasing merchandise which they required and depriving the colony of customs resources.[105]

In 1912 the following balance sheet could be drawn up: four companies had given up, twenty had been 'reformed' (eight had re-cast their concessions, while twelve had been limited to rubber) and nine retained their former status (among them the Société du Haut-Ogooué and the Compagnie propriétaire du Kouilou-Niari).

Distribution of Exports from the Congo in Value and Kind
(*in millions of francs*)

Year	Total	Rubber	Ivory	Timber
1896	4·7	2·6	1·4	0·7
1898	5·6	2·7	1·5	0·5
1905	13·9	7·4	4·0	2·1
1906	16·4	8·6	3·5	3·9

In the years up to the war, the export of timber from Gabon rose phenomenally (5,500,000 francs in 1912, 8,300,000 in 1913). The principal buyer was Germany, which used the wood for the manufacture of cigar boxes. The export of ivory, after reaching a peak of 210 tons in 1905 steadily declined; the important stocks accumulated in the villages had been pilfered and the systematic massacre of elephants led to a depletion of supplies.

As to the rubber, the record of 1906 (1,950 tons exported) was never reached again. The destruction of the settlements and the exhaustion of the population forced to collect it made 1,500 to 1,700 tons the highest possible figure. The drop in prices after 1911 put an end to the 'rubber era'; and from Gabon to Chad, the rubber crisis, added to the effects of 'pacification' and the repeated tax increases, caused the spread of famine in 1913–14.

(*b*) THE CAMEROONS

The evolution of the Cameroons was almost parallel to that of

French Equatorial Africa, but the great European plantations covered an even larger area. During the Puttkammer administration (until 1906) their development was a primary task. Von Puttkammer had been impressed by results obtained at Fernando Pò and at São Tomé. The methods employed were the same (the purchase of slaves in Dahomey and later in Liberia, under the pretext of 'recruitment').[106]

Plantations existed only in the neighbourhood of the coast, on the slopes of Mount Cameroon (British zone after 1918). In 1912–13 there were fifty-eight plantations in the Cameroons employing 17,800 of the native population, and covering in theory, 115,147 hectares, of which 22,225 were under cultivation and 11,393 under trees.[107] In practice, the more important investments included railways: the completion of the Bonabéri N'Kongsamba line in 1912 and the beginning of the Douala-Edea line, completed in 1914 over a stretch of 174 km., as far as Eseka. But the dominant investment was the rubber harvest, with the company agents requisitioning porters, food supplies and export products without paying the people. The more disciplined German administration put up some resistance to this: at Kribi, in 1907, it even went so far as to arm the population to resist the company agents![108]

A keen rivalry existed between the Süd-Kamerun company and the free merchants of Batanga and Kribi. The latter reproached the chartered companies for their extortionate practices, and the Süd-Kamerun company accused its rivals of selling arms and gunpowder to the people. After 1906 the company had to accept a reduction of a half of its territory conceded in 1899, which was now limited to 1,000,000 hectares in the still unexplored interior regions between Djouah and Sangha.

In spite of the considerable advantages bestowed on them, the big chartered companies ran into difficulties when the rubber crisis of 1907–8 worsened. To survive in French Equatorial Africa after 1909 they had to accept a reform of the privileges which they had been granted; this consisted of the renunciation of their prerogative rights in exchange for reduced land concessions with full tenure.

(c) FRENCH WEST AFRICA

In French West Africa large areas were under cultivation; yet crop gathering and stock grazing furnished the major value of exports right up to the eve of the war. In 1912, out of a total volume of over 104,000,000 francs, exports accounted for 52,500,000 (made up of rubber 24,000,000; oil-yielding plants 16,000,000;[109] timber 4,000,000; gum 2,800,000; cattle 2,000,000). Cultivated products made up 51,700,000 of the grand total, nearly the whole of which was furnished by oleagenous plants (groundnuts 40,000,000; palm oil and palm kernels 11,000,000). Other products represented only an insignificant amount: maize 300,000; cotton 150,000; copra 100,000; sesame 86,000; coffee 45,000; cocoa 25,000.[110]

Rubber held top place in French Equatorial Africa and in the Cameroons. It was a 'herbal' or liana rubber, with a limited yield and of mediocre quality. The principal producer was Guinea. Export began after 1870 in the Rivières du Sud – Rio Nunez, in particular. The region of Boké, which had produced and exported groundnuts and sesame, very quickly abandoned these crops to devote itself entirely to rubber gathering. When the liana crops in the Rivières du Sud were exhausted, the inhabitants abandoned cultivation and gathering and became *dioulas*; they exchanged the rubber gathered in the interior (Fouta-Djalon and the Manding Plateau) against barter goods. From 1890 onwards, Guinea exported 830 tons of rubber annually. In 1896–7 customs measures centering trade at Conakry, and the occupation of Fouta-Djalon, gave a new impetus to rubber gathering, and in 1898 this product made up 80 per cent of the value of exports from Guinea. A technical school was set up at Kouroussa, to train teachers to instruct the people in the art of making incisions and preparing the latex. Between 1900 and 1906, exports were approximately 1,500 tons per year, with a drop in 1901–2, due to the world crisis in rubber prices (the price dropped from 8·50 francs per kilo in 1899 to 4·40 francs at the beginning of 1901 to rise again to 8·50 francs in 1903, and above 9 francs in 1904). The enormous profits in the years 1899–1900 encouraged fraud: the lumps of rubber included up to 25 per cent impurity. During the crisis, Guinea rubber was more highly valued than rubber from the Congo.

Control measures were applied after 1901. The caravans were checked on arrival at Conakry and at the ports; the lumps were cut open and the stones and earth thrown out. A second check took place at the customs, where latex with too high a proportion of resin was rejected and the tested sacks and barrels were sealed. Finally, efforts were made to get rubber in strip-form to obviate fraudulent sale in lumps – which was how the 'Red Nigger' of Guinea was able to conquer the market. But it was difficult to apply controls over the whole of French West Africa. A decree of 1 February, 1905, sought to achieve radical results by forbidding the circulation of adulterated rubber. But it remained a dead letter since the agents at the trading posts opposed testing 'even under threat of arms'.[112]

In 1906 for the first time exports exceeded 1,500 tons, which was considered the maximum figure compatible with the preservation of the liana plantations. The price rose from 11 to 12 francs. A new crisis in 1907–8 was followed by a boom, and the climax came in 1909–10: production exceeded 2,000 tons; the price paid at Conakry rose to 15 and 20 francs (12 francs in the interior), while a kilo of rice cost 1 to 1.50 francs. The 'rubber fever' kept pace with the growth of the railway line from Conakry,[113] which reached Kindia in 1905 and Kouroussa in 1910.

On the Ivory Coast, rubber harvesting spread after 1899 with the establishment of the markets at Tiassalé and Aboisso. In 1906 rubber exports reached 6,400,000 francs; almost half of those in Guinea. Senegalese or Sudanese sub-traders organised the collection. Exploitation as a whole was less widespread than in Guinea, being still limited to the forest zone. Rubber accounted for a smaller portion of exports generally than in Guinea, and a larger part was taken up by palm kernels, palm oil, timber (mahogany) and cola. The Sudan and Senegal also produced significant quantities of rubber. In the Sudan, after 1896, rubber was accepted in payment for imports and brought by administrative convoys returning empty to Kayes.

At its height, in 1910, rubber production in French West Africa was estimated at more than 4,000 tons, representing a value of 32,000,000 francs and contributing 2,500,000 in taxes to the public revenue.

Rubber Exports from French West Africa

(*in tons*)

Year	Senegal and Sudan	Guinea	Ivory Coast	Total
1892	32	770	50	852
1900	440	1,464	1,052	2,956
1905	1,067	1,415	1,180	3,662
1909	1,265	1,810	1,242	4,317 (maximum)
1910	—	—	—	4,077
1911	—	—	—	3,537
1912	—	—	—	3,783
1913	149	1,455	962	2,566

The crisis reached its final stages after 1911. The hevea plantations, established in Asia in the preceding years, were beginning production. These plantations, producing higher grade rubber at less cost, furnished 12 per cent of world production in 1910; by 1913 this had reached 50 per cent. Meanwhile Africa's share of world production dropped to 25 per cent in 1912, 18 per cent in 1913 and 3–4 per cent in 1920.

The drop in prices and restriction of the market reduced rubber production in French West Africa to 1,500 tons between 1910 and 1913. Commercial transactions were cut down by 60 per cent and numerous outlying trading posts, whose entire activity had been centred on rubber transport, were forced to close. Like French Equatorial Africa and the Cameroons, Guinea suffered from the turning of the tide. By 1906 the disturbing results of rubber speculation had already made themselves felt. Not only export crops, such as oil-bearing plants in Lower Guinea, but even food crops were neglected to the point of causing a noticeable increase in the price of rice. From this time on, a shortage occurred in Fouta-Djalon and the Dinguiraye region at the beginning of each rainy season.[113]

In 1911 a European traveller noted the impossibility of procuring rice in Fouta-Djalon; his boy found it only at a Syrian shop, selling at a prohibitive price. Rubber must be held responsible for this state of affairs.

The European rush for this product has introduced into the rural customs of this country, which is endowed with this ill-omened wealth, two causes for deep disquiet: one is the abandonment of the less rewarding fields, and the other is the growth of porterage, a crushing labour which, as is widely known, often has little voluntary about it apart from the name.[114]

The collapse during the last few years before the war made matters much worse. During 1913–14 famine raged with greater severity in all of French West Africa, intensified by the growing financial burden of colonisation (steadily rising taxes, requisitioning, etc.); it was on the increase in French Equatorial Africa, and reached as far as Chad. It was less apparent on the Ivory Coast, where rubber was not the only cultivated commodity, and where the 'pacification' begun 1909–11 had stopped all progress in the rubber trade.

The First World War, with its growing demands on the populations (supplies of foodstuffs and raw materials to France – recruitment of men for military service) aggravated the misery and neglect, causing a number of uprisings. As part of the 'war effort' the export of rubber from French West Africa rose to 1,714 tons in 1915, even though the average purchase price did not exceed 2·50 francs per kilo in the interior and 'in spite of the troubled state of the Sudan'.[115]

Tropical Africa had not recovered from the rubber crisis on the eve of the war, when one author wrote:

In many territories and for a long time, the exploitation of rubber has been the native's only means of procuring the money he needs.[116]

C

The only production that showed real progress was that of groundnuts which was limited mainly to Senegal and, to a less extent, to the Sudan (Upper-Senegal-and-Niger). The total production reached some 300,000 tons. This progress was made possible, in the main, by increased cultivation, at the cost of food products and of fallow land which was essential for the good of the soil. Groundnuts accompanied the construction of the railway lines. At the end of the nineteenth century, the first attempt to grow groundnuts coincided with the building of the Dakar–Saint-Louis railway;[117] Cayor became the main supplier of groundnuts. A new link was established with the partial construction of the railway line from Thiès to Kayes, which was to provide a direct route between Dakar and the Sudan. The Thiès–Diourbel section, opened in 1909, made cultivation possible at Baol and Sine-Saloum. In 1910 the line was extended as far as Guinguinéo, and soon the Guinguinéo-Kaolack branch-line facilitated direct delivery to this port. (The chamber of commerce of Kaolack was set up in 1910 despite protests from the chamber at Rufisque.)

Groundnuts: Production Exported

Year	Senegal and Sudan	Guinea	Dahomey	Total
1892	46,790	103	—	46,893
1895	51,600	460	—	52,060
1900	140,911	900	50	141,861
1905	93,174	49	21	93,244
1910	233,600	560	17	234,177
1913	238,539	3,577	—	242,116

Groundnuts were planted even in Upper Senegal and along the Kayes–Koulikoro railway;[118] the extension of that line for another 42 km. along the Senegal River from Kayes to Ambidédi (departure point for the future line towards Thiès), avoided the river's dangerous rapids; from Ambidédi, groundnuts were sent by river-boat to Saint-Louis. (The Senegal River was navigable for only two to two-and-a-half months in the year.) However, this progress lacked a healthy basis. The yield was and remained mediocre at one ton per hectare, as against an average of two to three tons in other producer countries. It was noticed that the yield diminished in relation to the length of time the cultivation had been taking place. This was due to the shortening of the period during which the land lay fallow, and to the practice of leaving the fallow land bare and selling the straw; the soil thus became impoverished and was eroded by rain and wind. Formerly cultivated regions were partly abandoned in favour of new ones, and the most northerly regions of the cultivated zone (N'Kiambour and Cayor) were vacated. 'The Louga region has seen its population emigrate by thousands after the construction of the Thiès–Kayes line, and production dropped from 12,000 to 3,000 tons.'[119]

Finally, quality declined; the commercial oil content per grain diminished. This followed from the exhaustion of the soil, the spread of parasites, and the selection of wrong varieties. For this the traders were responsible, as they sold 'store reserves' rejected by exporters as seeds to the peasants. Poverty increased. The former traditional reserve granaries disappeared, and efforts by the administration to provide new ones (the establishment of 'indigenous provident societies') often led to additional exploitation of the peasants.

The third place in exports from French West Africa was held by the products of the oil palm together with rubber and groundnuts (87 per cent in value in 1909). Progress of exports was less important in this field. Between 1892 and 1909 the rubber exported multiplied five times, and the same was true of groundnuts between 1892 and 1913. In that same period, palm oil exports rose by only 40 per cent; palm kernels barely doubled.

Production Exported

(in tons)

PALM KERNELS

Year	Ivory Coast	Guinea	Senegal	Dahomey	Total
1892	1,130	2,300	1,244	14,400	19,074
1895	1,500	2,630	488	21,175	25,793
1900	3,107	3,180	430	21,986	28,703
1905	3,169	2,810	903	17,480	24,362
1910	5,423	4,580	1,449	34,784	46,236
1912	6,800	5,134	1,760	37,295	50,989
1913	6,949	5,172	2,021	26,371	40,513

Production in Togo in 1907: 4,346 tons

PALM OIL

Year	Ivory Coast	Guinea	Senegal	Dahomey	Total
1892	5,500	176	—	4,752	10,428
1900	4,340	62	—	8,920	13,322
1910	5,955	156	—	14,623	20,734
1913	6,014	284	—	7,971	14,269

Production in Togo in 1907: 998 tons

The extent of palm groves and the number of plants were estimated in 1920 as follows:

	Square km.	Millions of plants
Ivory Coast	7,000	42
Dahomey	6,000	36
Guinea (Rivières du Sud)	2,500	15
Togo	2,000	12

But due to lack of manpower and water the palms were only exploited to a limited extent (50 per cent in Dahomey, 33 per cent in the Ivory Coast, 25 per cent in Guinea). In theory the yield in Dahomey should have been 162,000 tons of oil (by ordinary pressure; by the use of industrial techniques the yield could have reached 200,000 tons) and 155,000 tons of palm-kernels. The proportion exported did not reach one-fifth in the case of palm-kernels and was little more than one-tenth in the case of oil, which was consumed locally on a large scale. This reflects the lack of any attempt at selection, the absence of mechanisation, all production being manual, and the poor conditions of preparation (the oil contained 20–50 per cent of fatty acids).

Other production accounted for only a small proportion of the total. The export of mahogany made fluctuating progress on the Ivory Coast, as we see below:

Export of Timber from the Ivory Coast
(*in tons*)

1892	7,000	1910	13,785
1900	13,000	1911	23,800
1905	9,600	1912	30,500
1907	20,000	1913	42,652

And after many poor results, cotton failed. In 1913 French West Africa supplied only an insignificant amount, half of what was produced in German East Africa and one-eleventh of production in British East Africa – countries that ranked only as medium producers. The rubber from Senegal (an average of 3,000 tons per year between 1910–13) represented a sizeable return. French West Africa exported only 350 tons of copra and a few hundred tons of cocoa. The Gold Coast was the main world producer with almost 100,000 tons. In 1892 the Ivory Coast supplied 35 tons of coffee for export, 75 tons in 1904, 23 tons in 1913. Tropical fruits did no better. The banana from China had been acclimatised in Guinea with some success: in 1903 the first export took place, of 7 tons; in 1914, 500 hectares were planted, but the absence of any system of organised transport led to failure.

In Senegal the development of groundnuts and the rubber rush led, as we mentioned above, to a reduction in food crops. There was an almost permanent shortage of cereals. Only maize was exported rather irregularly from Dahomey and Togo (Dahomey: 20,000 tons in 1908, 72 tons in 1911, 13,250 tons in 1913; Togo: 19,300 tons in 1907, 30,000 tons in 1908). The annual average import of rice from Indochina to French West Africa rose to 29,000 tons over the years 1906–15 and two-thirds of it went to Senegal. In 1914, the import of 63,000 tons of rice was unable to prevent famine.

(d) MINING

The exploitation of the mines was not important before 1914 except in French West Africa.[120] From the beginning of colonisation, and even before political annexation was achieved or consolidated, West Africa's traditional name for wealth in gold had attracted adventurers and speculators.[121] In the absence of all scientific prospecting their greed was naturally directed towards the regions where African gold-washers were already at work: Bambouk, Bouré and certain regions of the Ivory Coast.

This led to conflicts with the local population, whose rights from the very beginning were systematically ignored. Mining legislation established by the decree of 6 July, 1899, which was valid for all the colonies of continental Africa, reserved the 'surface deposits' for the traditional gold-washers within the limits of 'customary perimeters'. But great care was taken not to let the interested parties know of these clauses; and, moreover, how did one define 'surface deposits' in the case of quartz veins already exploited to a certain depth by the Africans? Adventurers and stock market speculators were preoccupied with rapid gains rather than investment; they did not understand anything of mining technology, and the few initiatives taken to introduce modern exploitation methods almost invariably ended in failure because of incompetence. Moreover, with only a few exceptions, the 'profitable' veins known to the traditional craftsmen did not produce the same yields under capitalist exploitation. The few methodical attempts made in Upper Guinea to start mining were cut short by the war.

Before 1900, treaties with local chiefs, and then the mining concessions granted by the colonial authorities, served as a pretext for the establishment of 'stock exchange' companies whose aim was to

extract gold from European speculators rather than from the Sudan. In 1896, as the result of a 'treaty' concluded by an adventurer with the chief of the village of Dioulafoundi (Bambouk), an Anglo-French group presided over by an English nobleman and a French general launched with great publicity a company bearing the promising title 'the Falémé Golden Valley'. A big banquet was held in London inaugurating its activity, but in practice it rapidly lost momentum and was abandoned. This state of affairs intensified after 1900 since methods remained unchanged. A plan was even mooted for the joint exploitation of gold and silk-cotton trees.

Treaties and permits were very rarely followed up by serious efforts. Captain Ballieu, who travelled in Bambouk in 1896, sought in vain 'for the sounds of miners' drills' and remarked upon 'the futility of their efforts and the frivolity of their search'. 'The prospectors visited the territories already being exploited by the natives, making demands of which the principal aim was simply the substitution of a European for a native.' Some of them did not even leave Paris, and limited themselves to demanding permits on the basis of indirect information, counting on the support of influential friends or those in high places. In Guinea in 1903 the majority of the permits were issued to 'aliases or speculators who had already sold their title-deeds'.[122] The ephemeral Compagnie minière du Soudan français held permits over an area of more than 150,000 hectares. The Compagnie minière de Falémé-Gambie had a monopoly of stakes in Bambouk and Bouré, forming a 'trust of mining rights over almost all the rivers of that region that could be dredged'. The mining 'movement' was stepped up in the Siguiri region of Guinea in 1907-8. To evade the clauses limiting concessions, the concession-holders formed themselves into groups. In 1908 there were eighty Europeans and a thousand workmen at the diggings in Siguiri.[123] The concession-holders often made efforts to evict the traditional gold-washers. In 1909 at Fatoya, they went so far as to dam a branch of the river in an attempt to prevent the washing of the alluvial deposits. This led, in 1914, to the eviction of the Compagnie des mines de Siguiri, since the administration became involved in political risks resulting from the companies' action. At the same time the companies led a violent campaign against the 1899 legislation. In 1910, the Compagnie minière du Soudan français, taking action against the gold-washers, proclaimed that

the French Government, whose banner everywhere carries the civilising [sic] ideal, will no longer tolerate the inhuman work of the natives in the Sudan because it is done without method . . . and leads to numerous accidents.

But this self-interested solicitude was not convincing. The techniques used by the companies were not superior to those of the traditional artisans; the company staffs, made up of adventurers, were generally incompetent, and the financial resources of the companies – eaten away by allowances for the administrators – were insufficient for the purchase and, above all, the transportation of the necessary equipment to the site. In 1910, the Société du Kémou transported expensive plant to Upper Falémé, but it could not be put into operation for lack of water. The Société commerciale et minière de Satadougou (Sudan) used up its resources in the transportation of its plant. Failure hit the Société de dragages aurifères [gold-dredging] du Tinkisso, which was established in 1906.

The commander of the circle of Satadougou wrote in 1908:

> Although almost the whole circle of Satadougou has been distributed out in concessions for prospecting and for the exploitation of mines, no actual plant has yet been installed.[124]

The administration took little notice of the friction caused by the methods of certain companies. The Kémou Company, for example, provoked a strike in 1910, doubtless one of the first in the Sudan.

On the Ivory Coast there was a similar series of financial speculations and technical failures. The Société française des gisements aurifères du Comoé et affluents (1907–14) exhausted its resources by having the parts of a dredger brought up the rapids of the Malamalasso. They were set up but never used, and the wreck still stands near the river's confluence with the Manzan. The results obtained on the Gold Coast led to the founding of numerous companies in the Bia and Sanwi regions: the Société minière de Kokumbo, whose administration noted from the start 'that there is priority of financial over industrial considerations' (1904). This view applied in most of the other mining companies on the Ivory Coast. The incidents in the Siguiri region led the administration to oppose European gold-mining activity in the Lobi country, then barely under control, where any intrusion might have led to difficulties (1913).

In conclusion, mining exploitation in French West Africa, when aimed largely at the extraction of gold, produced negligible results. In French Equatorial Africa, one of the first ores to attract attention was copper, found towards the end of the nineteenth century in the valley of the Niari, and the control of the copper deposits of that region was one of the causes of rivalry between Brazza and the representatives of Leopold II. The ore had already been mined by the Africans from whom, around 1900, the so-called Compagnie hollandaise took over.[125]

Mining, limited to the deposits at Mindouli, was done at first by having the ore carried across Loango on men's heads. The Compagnie minière du Congo français, set up in 1905 to reopen mining, included representatives of the main business groups in the Congo (Fondère, Guynet, Du Vivier de Streel), who constructed a narrow-gauge railway, completed in 1911, which facilitated the transport of the ore from Mindouli to Brazzaville, whence it was transported by Belgian railway (7,000 tons of ore between 1911 and 1914). Under these conditions, activity was aimed chiefly at creating an illusion in the eyes of shareholders rather than attaining valid economic results.[126]

REFERENCES

1. See J. Suret-Canale, *Afrique Noire occidentale et centrale: geographie, civilisation, histoire,* 2nd ed., pp. 183–5.

2. The following applies, except for a few details, also for Madagascar. Cf. P. Boiteau, *Contribution à l'histoire de la nation malgache.* Paris, Editions Sociales, 1958.

3. 'The rifles which were sold to the blacks were very dangerous arms for the marksman, but almost harmless against the enemy. They all have flintlocks and in the country where it rains seven months of the year (this refers to Guinea), they are of little use. The metal barrel was barely 2 mm. thick, and as the blacks have the annoying habit of loading their guns with enormous charges of gun-powder and over-heavy projectiles, accidents are frequent. These guns are sold at 10 to 20 francs on the spot, but their value in Liège or Manchester, the principal centres of manufacture, varies from 5 to 10 francs per piece.' (*Rapport d'ensemble sur la situation générale en Guinée française en 1903.* Conakry, Imprimerie Ternaux, 1904.) These figures and those which follow, it should be recalled, refer to gold francs (1 gold franc having the equivalent value of approximately 2·50 francs in 1963).

4. Import of spirits and alcoholic drinks into French West Africa (in value):
   1897: 6,200,000 francs
   1902: 5,500,000 francs
   1907: 6,800,000 francs

5.

	1887	1895	1900
	(in millions of francs)		
Import of alcoholic drinks	2·1	3·4	4·3
Import of cotton material	0·7	3·0	2·9
Total import	3·9	10·5	15·2

6. Credit granted to African intermediaries was, in spite of the risks incurred, a safe means of keeping control over them. The first German governor of Kamerun, von Soden, wrote a report on this subject to Bismarck: 'Fundamentally, it is a question . . . of a kind of slavery, worse than the old kind, and one whose only counterpart among us is found – with due respect – among professional usurers and brothel-owners. The whole affair is arranged from beginning to end in such a manner that the creditor, even in the most unfavourable case, will always gain something.' Report of 22 April, 1886 (Reichskolonialamt, No. 3827, Bl., 40 f.); cited in *Kamerun unter deutscher Kolonialherrschaft,* Berlin, Rütten und Loenig, 1960.

7. The same applies in Germany to Woermann and the Diskonto-Gesellschaft.

8. Made Count of Sanderval for services rendered to the Portuguese government.

9. Villard, 'Comment travailla Faidherbe', *Bulletin d'informations et de renseignements de l'Afrique occidentale française*, No. 204, 24 Oct., 1938.

10. The 'Hausa' of French Equatorial Africa and the Cameroon, etc.

11. F. Bohn, *Compagnie française de l'Afrique occidentale* (Rapport addressé à M. Cotelle, Conseiller d'Etat, Président de la Commission des concessions coloniales). Marseille, Imprimerie marseillaise, 1900.

12. Cf. R. Chudeau, 'Le grand commerce indigène de l'Afrique occidentale', *Bull. Sté. de Géographie commerciale de Paris*, 1920, pp. 398–412.

13. *Rapport d'ensemble sur la situation de la colonie du Haut-Sénégal-et-Niger en 1906.* Bordeaux, Gounouilhou, 1909.

14. Picrochole, *Le Sénégal drolatique*. Paris, Imprimerie Paul Dupont, 1896, pp. 8–9.

15. E. Lagrillière-Beauclerc, *Mission au Sénégal et au Soudan*. Paris, Tallandier, s.d. (1897).

16. Compagnie française de l'Afrique occidentale (French West Africa Company) founded in 1887, with a capital of 7,000,000 francs; it was, by the end of the century, the principal French firm in West Africa with counting-houses in Senegal, French and Portuguese Guinea, the Ivory Coast, Gambia, Sierra Leone, Nigeria. It succeeded the Compagnie du Sénégal et de la Côte occidentale d'Afrique, set up in 1881, which itself succeeded the firm of Verminck, founded in 1854.

17. The German firms purchased almost the whole of the maize and palms of Dahomey, two-fifths of the timber exported from French Equatorial Africa. (*Les colonies et la défense nationale*, Paris, Challamel, 1916.) They imported into Africa mainly spirits (29 per cent of spirit imports to French West Africa in 1907).

18. On this system see B. Schapper, 'La fin du régime de l'exclusif – Le Commerce étranger dans les possessions d'Afrique tropicale', *Annales africaines*, 1959, pp. 149–200.

19. This system was not denounced by France until October 1936.

20. G. Hervet, *Le Commerce extérieur de l'Afrique occidentale française*. Paris, Larose, 1911, p. 141.

21. *Bulletin du Comité de l'Afrique française*, No. 5, May 1909.

22. F. Rouget, *L'Afrique Equatoriale Française et le Commerce austro-allemand*. Melun, Imprimerie administrative, 1917. I: Les Bois.

23. Cf. Henri Brunschwig, *Mythes et réalités de l'impérialisme colonial français* (1871–1914). Paris, Armand Colin, 1960. (Chapter VI: La légende du protectionnisme.) Translated as *Myths and Realities of French Colonialism*. London, Pall Mall Press, 1965.

24. Yves Henry, *Le Caoutchouc dans l'Afrique occidentale française*. Paris, Challamel, 1907.

25. Gold circulated mainly near the British colonies. But it was hardly employed as money except by big business, and was, moreover, gradually replaced by banknotes; among the public it was increasingly hoarded as raw material for local jewellery-making.

The movement of administrative funds, in the interior, was done mainly in sealed boxes of 5,000 francs. In the Sudan (Upper-Senegal-and-Niger), banknotes were introduced at the beginning of 1904.

26. Op. cit., p. 75.

27. F. Rouget, *L'Expansion coloniale au Congo français*. Paris, Larose, 1906, p. 664.

28. 'While trade in the Congo was absolutely non-existent, that of the colonies we are speaking of (those of West Africa) rose, in 1898, to 62,000,000 francs in respect of Senegal, 17,000,000 in French Guinea, 11,500,000 in the Ivory Coast, 18,000,000 in Dahomey, making a total of 108,000,000 (not including the ex-colony of the Sudan, which, in the absence of precise documents, is not included

C*

in the figures given above).' (F. Bohn, *Compagnie française de l'Afrique occidentale* Marseille, Imprimerie marseillaise, 1900, p. 5.)

29. Conventional because it included, apart from the real hydrographic Congo basin, the Atlantic coast from latitude 2° 30′ south as far as the mouth of the Logé (Angola) and the coast of the Indian Ocean, from the Zambezi up to the Horn of Africa.

30. Cf. C. Coquery-Vidrovitch, 'Les idées économiques de Brazza et les premières tentatives de compagnies de colonisation au Congo français (1885–98)', *Cahiers d'études africaines*, 1965, V. 1, No. 17, pp. 57–82.

31. See vol. I, p. 207.

32. H. Brunschwig, *La Colonisation française*, Paris, Calmann-Lévy, 1949, p. 101.

33. Cf. R. Jeaugeon, 'Les sociétés d'exploitation au Congo et l'opinion française de 1890 à 1906', *Revue française d'histoire d'Outre-Mer*, 1962, pp. 353–437.

34. In his pamphlet *Trente-cinq années de lutte aux colonies* (Paris, L. Chailley, 1896) Verdier cast doubt on the sincerity of Binger in his hostility to concessions by affirming that, when asked by him in 1891 to become the head of a financial undertaking of the same kind, he accepted immediately.

35. Published later as a pamphlet Eugène Etienne, *Les Compagnies de colonisation*, Paris, Challamel, 1897.

36. Names of concessionaires (and those of the companies they made up) can be found in *La Quinzaine coloniale*, 1899, pp. 660–1.

37. Official text in *Annuaire du Gouvernement général de l'Afrique Equatoriale française*, 1912, Paris, Larose, 1912, vol. II.

38. Henri Lorin, 'La Crise du Congo français', *Questions diplomatiques et coloniales*, No. 91, December 1900, pp. 681–2.

39. A gold mark – 1·25 gold francs, which was a little more than 3 francs in 1963.

40. Cf. H. Brunschwig, *L'Expansion allemande outre-mer*, Paris, PUF, 1957, p. 158.

41. E. D. Morel, *Red Rubber*, London, Unwin, 1907.

42. Pierre Mille, *Au Congo belge*. Paris, A. Colin, 1899.

43. *Bulletin du Comité de l'Afrique française*, 1900, No. 5, pp. 187–8.

44. Cf. R. Jeaugeon, op. cit.

45. R. Cuvillier-Fleury, *La Main-d'oeuvre dans les colonies françaises de l'Afrique occidentale et du Congo*. Paris, Sirey, 1907.

46. Paul Masson, *Marseille et la colonisation française*. Marseille, Barlatier, 1906, p. 479.

47. *Bulletin du Comité de l'Afrique française*, 1900, No. 1, p. 39, and 1901, No. 1.

48. F. Bohn, *Compagnie française de l'Afrique occidentale* (Rapport adressé à M. Cotelle, Conseiller d'Etat, Président de la Commission des concessions coloniales). Marseille, Imprimerie marseillaise, 1900. See also *Bulletin du Comité de l'Afrique française*, Renseignements coloniaux, 1900, No. 4, p. 73.

49. Paul Masson, op. cit.

50. E. D. Morel, *Affairs of West Africa* (London, Heinemann, 1902), chapter XXVIII: 'The Concession regime in French Congo', and *The British Case in French Congo: the Story of a Great Injustice, its Cause and its Lessons*. London, Heinemann, 1903. See also Félicien Challaye, *Le Congo français*. Paris, Alcan, 1907.

On E. D. Morel, see a letter by Pierre Mille in *Le Courrier européen*, 1911, p. 467. In reply to Tardieu (who accused Morel of being a spokesman for the interests of British trade), Pierre Mille affirms that E. D. Morel was a completely disinterested man. The Congo Reform Association, which he brought into existence, was founded not by Liverpool merchants but by small people subscribing ten shillings. He belonged to the old Manchester School, for whom Free Trade was like a religious faith. He attacked the system of concessions in British Nigeria in *The Times*. He lost his job in leading the battle, which justified an open subscription held in his favour to which John Holt subscribed £100 (a fact that Tardieu did not fail to point out!). There can be no doubt that Morel was an honest man (compared with Tardieu whose corruptibility has been established); but it is also evident that his humanitarianism, like that of certain 'abolitionists' in the United States, coincided with the exact interests of the circles to whom he was personally linked.

51. The most complete account of this affair was given by J. Massiou, *Les Grandes concessions au Congo français*, Paris, Sagot, 1920 (very favourable to the chartered companies). See a recent study by S. J. S. Cookey, 'The Concession Policy in the French Congo and the British Reaction, 1898–1906', *Journal of African History*, 1966, VII, 2, pp. 263–78.

52. Cuvillier-Fleury, *La Main d'oeuvre dans les colonies françaises de l'Afrique occidentale et du Congo*, Paris, Sirey, 1907.

53. Not including the special case of the Verdier concessions (Elima belonged already to Verdier).

54. *Bulletin du Comité de l'Afrique française*, Renseignements coloniaux, 1900, No. 4. 'Rapport sur la situation générale de la Cote d'Ivoire en 1898.'

55. Ibid., No. 6, June 1912, p. 232.

56. In 1912–13 the plantations, fifty-eight in number, occupied 115,147 hectares in the Cameroon, of which 22,225 hectares were planted and 11,393 hectares in full production. (H. Labouret, *Le Cameroun*. Paris, Hartmann, 1937). We have found no figures for French Equatorial Africa.

57. J. Saintoyant, *L'Affaire du Congo*, 1905. Paris, Ed. de l'Epi, 1960, pp. 64 and 68.

58. Ibid., pp. 81–2.

59. *Bulletin du Comité de l'Afrique française*, 1900, No. 5, pp. 182–3.

60. Général Mangin, *Souvenirs d'Afrique* (Lettres et carnets de route). Paris, Denoël et Steele, 1936, book I.

61. One could not, in any case, call it the destruction of the palm-groves.

62. Général Mangin, op. cit.; E. D. Morel recalls 'the inevitable barbarity which characterised Marchand's hunt for carriers in the Upper Ubangi and Bahr El-Ghazal' (*Affairs of West Africa*, p. 251).

63. When they had the means to pay, and when they were willing to pay.

64. R. P. Daigre, *Oubanghi-Chari, témoignage sur son évolution (1900–40)*. Issoudun, Dillen et Cie., 1947, p. 111.

65. G. Toqué; cited by H. Brunschwig, *La Colonisation française*. Paris, Calmann-Lévy, 1949, p. 103.

66. F. Challaye, *Le Congo français*. Paris, Alcan, 1909.

67. *Bulletin du Comité de l'Afrique française*, 1904, No. 5. Alfred Fourneau, *Deux années dans la région de Tchad*, pp. 121–4.

68. Ibid., 1905, No. 1, p. 34.

69. Commandant Saintoyant gave the figure of 10,492 days of labour for clearing the undergrowth for the Possel-Crampel track, in the second half of 1903 alone. Payment: a spoonful of beads per day and two metres of fabric per month. (J. Saintoyant, *L'Affaire du Congo*, 1905. Paris, Editions de l'Epi, 1960, p. 75.)

70. R. Cuvillier-Fleury, op. cit., p. 60.

71. *Afrique française*. Renseignements coloniaux, 1906, No. 3, p. 85.

72. Cf. Jules Saintoyant, *L'Affaire du Congo*, pp. 44–5.

73. *L'Humanité* of 27 September, 1905, cites the text of the Gentil circular: 'My attention was, moreover, attracted by the small importance attached to the recovery of taxes. I have the honour of informing you that I consider it most important that you should make efforts to raise the figure in such a manner that it shall be as closely identical as possible to the provision laid down each year. I do not conceal from you that I shall judge you mainly on the results you attain in the

form of taxes on the Natives, which should be the object of your constant preoccupation.'

74. This came into general use after the Gentil circular of 27 April, 1905, entrusting the company agents with tax collection, which they were to pay to the colonies' exchequer.

75. *Revue indigène*, No. 67, November 1911, p. 647.

76. J. Saintoyant, op. cit., p. 77.

77. Ibid., p. 63.

78. Mangin, op. cit., vol. II: 'Tournée d'inspection au Congo (1908)', p. 207.

79. G. Bruel, *L'Afrique équatoriale française*, Paris, Larose, 1930.

80. The cost of rubber in Guinea at that same time was 4·50 francs per kilo at the beginning of 1901 (full crisis), 7·50 francs at the end of 1902, 9 to 9·50 francs per kilo at the beginning of 1904.

81. This 'illness' is not unknown: it can be seen in all big famines, and it raged in the German concentration camps.

82. R. P. Daigre, op. cit., pp. 113–16.

83. Ibid., p. 117.

84. Dr. Heckenroth, 'Rapport sur le fonctionnement du laboratoire de Brazzaville de l'Institut Pasteur depuis l'année 1906', *Revue Indigène*, No. 61, 30 May, 1911, p. 320.

85. Reproduced in *Revue Indigène*, No. 57, 30 January, 1911, pp. 58–9.

86. Auguste Chevalier, 'Mission Chari–Lac Tchad (1902–1904)', *L'Afrique centrale française*, Paris, Challamel, 1907, p. 23.

87. F. Challaye, op. cit.

88. *Le Temps*, 23 September, 1905. See also *Le Matin* of 15, 16, 17, 18, 20 and 22 February, 1905.

89. F. Challaye, *Souvenirs sur la colonisation*. Paris, Picard, 1935.

90. *Le Temps*, 24 September, 1905.

91. Ibid., 23 September, 1905.

92. After being set free Toqué published a book, *Les Massacres du Congo* (1907), in which he placed the system on trial and accused the administration directly. One of his superiors, M. de Roll, told him: 'Remember this: killing the blacks is not forbidden, only saying so, or being caught at it, or leaving traces; and it is better to kill twenty blacks than scratch one. The dead do not talk while a man who has been scratched will become a martyr in France' (op. cit., p. 105). The author has not been able to find this book in any library (some extracts appeared in a special number of Crapouillot dated January 1936: 'Expéditions coloniales – Leurs dessous, leurs atrocités'). Toqué was married in 1909 to an Alsatian woman (then of German nationality); invalided out of the army in 1914, he took up service under the Germans in the occupied zone, collaborated on *Bonnet rouge* and the *Gazette des Ardennes*. He was condemned to death by the 4th French Council of War on 25 July, 1919, and shot.

93. Cf. *Afrique noire*, vol. I, p. 187, note 1.

94. *L'Humanité*, of 26 and 27 September, 1905.

95. *Le Temps*, 28 September, 1905.

96. *Le Journal* of 19 July, 1912, indicates that the same methods were always used (forced porterage, raids by militiamen several days' journey from the posts, women taken as hostages, etc.).

97. R. S., colon du Congo: *Victor Augagneur et l'Afrique équatoriale française*, Bordeaux, Imprimerie coopérative, 1923, p. 7. This text is clearly inspired by an interest group linked to certain colonial companies.

98. Cf. P. Kalck, *Réalités oubanguiennes*, Paris, Berger-Levrault, 1959.

99. Report by Major Sargos to the governor-general of French Equatorial

Africa, 31 October, 1919, cited in *Victor Augagneur et l'Afrique équatoriale française*, p. 7.

100. Cf. Pierre Mille and Félicien Challaye, 'Les deux Congo . . .', *Cahiers de la Quinzaine*, 1906, 16th booklet, 7th series.

101. *Bulletin du Comité de l'Afrique française*, No. 5, May 1909: 'L'expérience congolaise', pp. 159–62.

102. *Possessions du Congo français et dépendances*. Rapport d'ensemble sur la situation générale en 1906. Paris, Larose, 1908, p. 110.

103. Texts in the *Annuaire du Gouvernement général de l'Afrique équatoriale française*, 1912. Paris, Larose, 1912, vol. II.

104. Speech by Governor Merlin to the October session of the government council of French Equatorial Africa, *Bulletin du Comité de l'Afrique française*, No. 11, November 1910, pp. 331 ff.

105. *Bulletin du Comité de l'Afrique française*, No. 3, March 1911: 'Le réveil de l'Afrique Equatoriale Française', p. 105.

106. That was the method that France largely used after 1848 – despite British protests – to continue the slave trade to the West Indies.

107. H. Labouret, *Le Cameroun*. Paris, Hartmann, 1937.

108. *Bulletin de l'Afrique française*, No. 4, April 1908, pp. 157–8.

109. The statistics included a part of palm-oil production and palm-kernels considered as gathering of the harvest, not plantations.

110. H. Cosnier, *L'Ouest-Africain français*, Paris, Larose, 1921.

111. H. Cosnier, op. cit., pp. 10–11.

112. Manual labour was furnished by requisition, often brought from far-distant regions including the Sudan. 'One has to work with rough and untrained people; these little-known blacks provided a veritable army of labourers and diggers; more than 10,000 to 12,000 men at a time in 1909' (*Revue Indigène*, No. 55, 30 November, 1910, p. 665).

113. *Rapport d'ensemble sur la situation générale de la Guinée française en 1906*. Conakry, Imprimerie Ternaux, 1907.

114. A. Guignard, 'Zig-zags en Afrique Occidentale française (II)', *Bulletin du Comité de l'Afrique française*, No. 10, October 1912, pp. 400–1.

115. H. Cosnier, op. cit., p. 8.

116. Ibid., p. 7.

117. We shall quote a significant text about the construction of the Dakar–St. Louis line, conceded to a private company: 'The idea was conceived of building a railway line in Senegal from Dakar to St. Louis. The large firms, with full employment in the metropolis, demanded 120,000 francs per kilometre. The Batignolle Company offered 80,000. In view of the special difficulties of a line through open desert, this was madness. Etienne, nevertheless, had the concession granted. But he took care to draw up the appropriate specifications. Ah! good tax-payers, it was a beautiful job. No ballast in laying the foundations of the route; sand was piled up and even shells; light rails were placed on top; a few occasional plank buildings served as stations; and off went the engine. A special clause in the contract stipulated that the line could be handed over by sections of twenty kilometres. When one section was thus finished [sic], a state engineer was invited out, who, with eyes shut, approved the work; the line was immediately declared open to traffic and the company gathered in the agreed sum, and construction continued. The line finished, a banquet was held. With the backing of official speeches the population of the metropolis was informed that a new route had just been opened to traffic and to the civilisation of France. Hardly had one year passed when the mounds of sand began to crumble everywhere, leaving the rails suspended in mid-air; the sandstorms overthrew the huts, the wooden beams were gnawed by insects, the engines were choked up with the dust; and there was no

more route, no station, no rolling stock. But as the State had taken over the work, all repairs were laid to its charge. Everything had to be done over again; the railway from St. Louis to Dakar cost 300,000 francs per kilometre! But the Batignolles Company had made a handsome sum.' (F. Delaisi, 'Comment on lance une conquête coloniale', *Le Crapouillot*, special number, January 1936, p. 47.)

As to exploitation, it was carried out as follows. The state guaranteed to the company an annual revenue of 1,154 francs per kilometre operated.... The regular expenses included costs of upkeep and operation (including the gross salaries of a considerable number of administrators provided as sinecures) and this compulsory revenue; takings were deducted from this . . . and the resulting deficit was made good by the state. (Ch. Rotté, *Les Chemins de fer et tramways des colonies*. Paris, Larose, 1910.) See also A. H. Canu, *La Pétaudière coloniale*. Paris, Chamuel, 1894.

118. The construction of the line from Kayes to the Niger provided hardly fewer scandals than that of the Dakar–St. Louis line. It had been started in 1881: 'Badly projected, established without method, too light to carry heavy traffic, it absorbed the fantastic sum of 24,000,000 francs [gold] in the construction of the first 54 kilometres. The despondent Parliament did not grant more than the bare credits for maintenance.' (Lucien Hubert, *L'veil du monde – L'Oeuvre de la France en Afrique occidentale*. Paris, Alcan, 1909, p. 125.)

Work was interrupted in 1885; when the material arrived on the spot Galliéni finished the line as far as Bafoulabé with the means available (that is to say, with unpaid forced labour), cf. *Afrique Noire*, vol. I, 2nd edition, p. 222.

'In 1888 the line was handed over to the military administration. But this railway line was useless; the gauge of the rails was, in places, 50 cm., elsewhere 60 cm., the infrastructure was deplorable, transfers from one train to another stops, prevented any organisation of heavy traffic.' (Lucien Hubert, op. cit., p. 125.) Everything had to be done over again.

119. H. Cosnier, op. cit., pp. 35–6.

120. In French West Africa the concessions granted to the big companies included the right to exploit below ground. Since no prospecting was carried out and there was no means of exploitation and transport, and above all because of the very spirit of the concession system, these rights were barely ever practised, unless stock exchange publicity was required. A large part of the information that follows is due to the kindness of M. J. Vogt, who put at our disposal his notes taken from the public archives of the former government-general of French West Africa and the Republic of Mali. The quotations without references are taken from the Archives of the federal ex-direction of Mines and Geology (Dakar).

121. On that period, in regard to Bambouk, see A. Ackermann, *Une Région aurifère de l'Afrique occidentale française: les territoires miniers de la Falémé*. Rixheim, F. Sutter, 1906, and Desplagnes, 'Les sources du Bakoy, régions aurifères soudanaises', *La Géographie*, XVI, 1907, pp. 225–35.

122. Federal Archives of French West Africa, 3 P 20/1903. Guinea.

123. Ibid., 3 P 6 bis/1909.

124. National Archives of Mali, Satadougou.

125. D. Levat, 'Notice géologique et minière sur la bassin cuprifère du Kouilou-Niari' (French Congo), *Annales des Mines*, 10th series, 1907, vol. XI: 'Mémoires', pp. 5–65.

126. Pobéguin, 'Mission d'étude au Moyen-Congo', *Afrique française*, 1920, No. 9–10, 11 and 12; and G. Bruel, 'Inventaire scientifique et économique du Moyen-Niari', *Afrique française*, *Revue Coloniale*, 1925, No. 4, pp. 101–19, and, above all, Nicolai, 'Recherche de minéralisations en cuivre, plomb, zinc, dans le bassin du Niari', *Revue de l'industrie minérale*, special number, January 1956.

CHAPTER II

SOCIAL CONSEQUENCES

1. The Advance of the Money Economy

The first economic aspect with considerable social consequences was the introduction and penetration of the market economy, to be referred to hereafter as the *money economy*.

We have seen that in the pre-colonial and early colonial period, Black Africa underwent some development of its market economy, with the appearance of commercial centres in the Sahel area, at the termini of the Trans-Sahara routes (Timbuktu, Djenné), and 'relay-markets' between the Sudan and the coastal regions (Kankan, Kong). Only the commercialisation of production was lacking. The use of money was practically unknown, cowrie shells and other equivalents taking its place. The countries of the Eastern Sahel, the Hausa cities in Ouadai, followed the Bornu in using the Maria Theresa dollar, introduced from Tripoli or the Nile basin.

European penetration, as we have said, came mainly through trade. The prime aim of colonisation was to achieve advantageous deals, unloading the products of European industry and obtaining in exchange raw materials or foodstuffs. The 'free' play of supply and demand helped to develop such exchanges, but the lure of European merchandise made a further contribution, because of either its novelty or its relative cheapness. This was the case with Lancashire cotton fabrics, which were far less solid and durable than those locally made, but far less expensive. However, this was not enough to reduce the importance of the closed circuit of home consumption which absorbed the largest part of African production, and which was the result of administrative coercion. The latter managed through taxation both to burden the masses with the expenses of administration and to produce the conditions necessary for business to run smoothly. At the same time, it forced the people to participate in the circulation of money; from then on, it became a pressing necessity for them to sell in order to raise tax money. Compulsory crops or deliveries to European traders at taxed prices had this effect.

We mentioned above the conditions under which the use of money began to spread, citing the example of Guinea. Its penetration into more remote regions (Niger, Chad and the interior of the Sudan, where the paleonigritic peoples had taken refuge) was extremely slow, and due more to fiscal constraint than to the demands of the market. In Chad, the administration had great difficulty in making French money accepted instead of the traditional three-franc thaler. The people ignored the new money and exchanged the thaler, at the same time, for five, six or seven francs. In North Cameroon the German administration took advantage of this by flooding the country with base coinage, taking the thaler at its exchange value; the use of the thaler was then forbidden and the old coins were withdrawn from circulation. The Bank of Senegal, which became the Banque de l'Afrique occidentale in 1905, issued banknotes, but they were used only in the transactions of commercial firms and did not come into widespread use until the First World War.

The development of the market economy is the first element we have to consider in order to understand the social evolution. The traditional social strata, the ancient hierarchies, were replaced by isolated individuals, legally 'equal' to other such individuals as sellers or purchasers of commodities. This corrosion of the ancient structures through the market economy was not in itself a new phenomenon, but its progress was amplified and accelerated. Parallel to this, administrative measures contributed to the social levelling and mixing of peoples. The displacement of populations accompanying the conquest had already, in a quite short space of time, surpassed in extent and intensity any such movements in earlier periods. The 'pacification' measures, of which more will be said below, had similar consequences. In the vicinity of the military posts and along the commercial routes, colonisation brought together a great diversity of people, more than in the villages, ranging from miserable social outcasts, former captives or fallen nobles, to self-made traders. Elsewhere, too, the spread and excessive severity of taxes, of forced labour and of other duties levelled all the 'natives', as French subjects, to a common norm.

2. The Decline of Slavery

It is in this context that one has to understand the hesitant and contradictory policy of the colonisers towards a problem which could not be ignored—slavery. Its abolition was the main 'humanitarian' pretext for colonisation, and it was under the banner of the fight against the barbarism of slavery that the Anti-Slavery Society of France[1] acted as patron of expeditions and made awards to explorers and conquerors. On the other hand, vigorous suppression of slavery was impossible for social reasons and dangerous politically. Hence the constant ambiguity of anti-slavery policy.

The anti-slavery of the colonisers was not simply a façade. As with certain abolitionists in the north of the United States at the time of the Civil War, there existed some very real economic interests behind the humanitarianism. Patriarchal or domestic slavery, as practised in Africa, presented a serious obstacle to colonial exploitation. Under this system the master, in principle, did not work at all or very little, and the surplus labour of the slave did not so much provide him with additional luxury as relieve him of the need to work. While the slave owed part of his labour to his master, at rates fixed by custom, the master in his turn was obliged to provide the slave with the means of subsistence, to feed him from his accumulated reserves from his profit over which he had not so much the right of disposal as of management. This closed system provided a tolerable life for the masters, and often a miserable one for the slaves, but one that never exposed them to isolation and destitution. The master, who by definition did not furnish any surplus labour himself, unproductively consumed the products of the slave's surplus labour, which never broke out of this circle. In the eyes of the colonisers it was a 'barbaric' system, because it presented an obstacle to the progress of their interests and the growth of their profits.

As practised in West Africa, it [domestic slavery] led to an easy and lazy life for men who, had they been adequately stimulated by self-interest [sic], could have become active workers anxious to enrich themselves by their labour.[2]

In brief, for important businessmen who were opposed to slavery it was not a question of abolishing it to ease the fate of the slave, but rather of making them do more work 'under the stimulus of self-interest', which, in fact, was confused with necessity – to the advantage of the colonisers. As for the former slave masters, they were to be turned away from the 'easy and lazy life', in other words put to work under the same terms as their former slaves, and for the profit of the same colonisers. Moreover, the suppression of slavery would weaken certain peoples or certain aristocracies which showed insufficient docility.

But, with the same political motive, the administration could not carry forward the suppression of slavery without grave inconveniences. 'Divide and rule' was the golden rule of the colonial administration as it had been that of the conquerors: to play on the tribal conflicts and social contradictions. And what better means was there of upholding this contradiction than the perpetuation of a social system in which there were masters and slaves, and what easier policy than to support the aristocratic minority against the masses that would bear the burden of colonisation? French colonial policy could never decide between these two contradictory lines of approach. It pursued each according to place and circumstances. In spite of official proclamations, slavery survived until our own times and disappeared in economically developed regions only with the advance of trading and capitalism, which supplanted it.

The Act of the Second Republic abolishing slavery in the colonies (27 April, 1848) was never really applied in Senegal. Faidherbe, in 1855, had the administrative council of the colony expressly proclaim that it would not be applied. During the conquest, slavery was not only allowed, but widely used. The conquered were distributed as captives to infantrymen and conscripted auxiliary troops, and they gave the French military a far from negligible revenue (the most honest sold their captives for the benefit of the exchequer). Elsewhere, the purchase of slaves was used as a means of recruitment for the army.[3] In the Sudan, the *oussourou* (right of the market)– legalised as a form of import tax on merchandise – was applied to the slave trade. An order, No. 111 of 14 March, 1893, signed by Archinard, fixed the details: a levy in kind – one slave out of ten – or a levy in money – either 200 francs or 10,000 cowries.

In 1887, Galliéni (later to become the laureate of the Anti-Slavery Society of France) established 'freedom villages' with a great deal of publicity. They were numerous in the Sudan and were also exceptionally set up in other regions, notably in the Congo. Officially this initiative was aimed at giving asylum and a means of subsistency to enemy slaves who sought refuge behind the French lines. This was the continuation of a tradition which, at the time of the struggle against the slave-traders, led to the creation of coastal centres for freed slaves (thus Libreville in Gabon). Their real object was to furnish manpower for the posts, near which they were established; the constant recruitment and requisitioning had driven this manpower far from the French routes and establishments. Refugees, deserters from the enemy and prisoners of war were thus thrown together, at the disposal of the army command.

It is quite certain that the main motive behind the spread of the freedom villages was that they presented an excellent solution to the problem of porterage and manpower – far better, in any case, than the system of going out, armed, to seek men every time the

need arose, and of seeing them escape at the first unguarded
moment – a slow, complicated and chancy system. In view of
policy demands and the scruples of public opinion, what in
Africa was a question of manpower was presented in Europe as a
humanitarian enterprise.[4]

In the Sudan the military authorities, followed by the civil
administration of Governor Albert Grodet in 1894, systematically
established 'freedom villages' near each post and along the supply
routes. Elsewhere a rather different policy was pursued. Senegal
kept up more liberal appearances. Although no document existed
prohibiting slavery or suppressing the slave trade, it had been
decided in 1881, with an eye to French public opinion, that any
slave who took refuge in a French post would be considered a free
man. The strict application of this statute would clearly risk worse
difficulties, involving 'friends' and allies of France. Thus official
instructions prescribed 'action with circumspection', and as a rule
no position was given to a 'freed' slave, who thus had no means of
subsistence and no choice but to find another master. As late as the
beginning of this century, slavery was still practised in all but name,
even by Europeans at Saint-Louis and Dakar, who bought slaves
for domestic help; they were taken to court and issued with a 'freedom patent', whereupon they were committed to their buyers, who
for this purpose acquired the office of 'tutor'.[5] This, it should be
made clear, was practised by people who were acquainted with
official instructions. The more or less hidden slave traffic continued
to be practised by the Moors, and kidnapping of children and adults
occurred even in Saint-Louis.[6]

The few attempts made to apply the laws of 1881, combined with
the Sudanese system of 'freedom villages', had unhappy results. At
Bakel, in 1896, the 'freedom village' had been crowded to excess,
and when 'trouble' developed, the slaves were simply sent back to
their former masters. On the other hand, Guinea, except for the
Sudanese part which was attached to it in 1899, remained a country
of classic slavery, which was denounced by the press. In August 1888
the administrator, Guilhon, declared in a report that he had proof
that 'all the [European] merchants of Nunez, with only two exceptions, are involved in the slave trade'.[7] The administrative report of
1890 indicated that the situation had not changed. Still at Nunez,
the administration took pride in an 'attempt' to suppress the slave
trade by an agreement counter-signed by seventeen chiefs, but
warned against 'over-precipitate' measures.

In practice, not only was slavery tolerated, but it was even
guaranteed by the exercise of the right of pursuit. Any fugitive

slave was returned to his master by the administration, even if he claimed maltreatment, unless he was redeemed for 150 francs. Even after the Ponty circular of 1901, which forbade it, pursuit continued to be practised for political reasons. (This fact was officially attested in 1906.)

In the Sudan, 'freedom villages' were systematically set up under the conditions described above. Those sent there included slaves who had escaped from enemy countries, slaves taken from their masters as a punishment or for political reasons, slaves paid for on the *oussourou* basis of 10 per cent of the transaction who had not been sold on behalf of the exchequer; finally there were rare cases of slaves coming from estates in liquidation – these the more liberal tradition set free. The population, without malicious intent, called these 'freedom villages' 'villages of the commander's slaves' – which was, in fact, what they were. The village chief, paid and appointed by the administration, 'held in relation to the circle commander . . . the functions usually given to the head slaves of a normal owner'.[8] The 'freedom villages' were exempt from taxes, as was the case with all slaves, the master paying for them, but, crushed by requisitioning and forced labour, they were a hell.

> The fugitive slaves preferred to choose a new master who would always give them what they needed, would not torment them with work that was beyond their strength, and left them in peace when they were tired or ill. This was not so in the freedom villages. What would one find there? Gangs of wretched men dying of hunger or on the brink of death, tired and yet, for example, forced to provide all the forced labour for the post and the circle porterage.[9]
>
> . . . The young people in the freedom villages did the same work at fourteen or fifteen years of age as route porters, far beyond their strength, and this affected their growth and their whole constitution.[10]

To this should be added the inadequacy of the land allocated (which was generally already appropriated) and its mediocre quality, the site of the villages having been chosen for practical reasons such as proximity to a post or to the route, and not for agricultural reasons. Where there were herds, they usually contained fewer animals than the average. The misery was such that free people were consigned to a freedom village as punishment.

> In one district that I passed through, an observer wrote, a custom had arisen that when a village could not or would not give the whole sum imposed [as taxes], a child would be taken and placed in a so-called freedom village until the tax was paid.[11]

The many fugitives from freedom villages were punished by prison sentences and the inhabitants could not move away without permits. Furthermore, these villages were widely used to supply labour (in effect, slave labour) for Europeans, for the missions, or to provide wives for soldiers. The missions thus acquired labour more economically than they could have done by the 'redemption' of slaves.

In the course of his brief governorship of the Sudan, Albert Grodet[12] took the first official measures against the slave trade. He did so both in response to public concern in France and also because the suppression of slavery corresponded to the wishes of the big economic interests, with which he had close links. Three decrees (30 December, 1894; 12 January and 11 May, 1895) prohibited the introduction of slaves into the Sudan for sale, and the movement of caravans. Slaves seized in contravention of these orders were to be installed in freedom villages! The effect of the decrees was virtually nil. The *dioulas* declared that their slaves were free and 'salaried porters'. From 1895 on, General de Trentinian, without abrogating the Grodet decrees, limited confiscation to cases where the slaves in the caravans were gagged or tied together!

The slaves themselves showed little enthusiasm for the measures taken 'for their sake'; when they took them seriously, they were ordered to be quiet. This was the case at Siguiri where, at the beginning of 1895, Grodet's measures provoked a riot among the captives. The circle commander, with Grodet's approval, inflicted sentences of several years imprisonment on six of the ring-leaders, and Grodet insisted that they should be detailed for the hardest labour at the post.

> After several demonstrations of this kind, the slaves should be convinced that they cannot misuse the advantages offered to them by our laws.[13]

Nevertheless, the continued protests of the French press forced the authorities to take certain measures: the Ponty circular of 1 February, 1901, suppressed the right of pursuit; finally the decree of 12 December, 1905, imposed a fine and from two to five years imprisonment on any person convicted of entering into 'a contract the purpose of which is the transfer of the liberty of a third person'. That was the first official act prohibiting the slave trade which applied generally in West Africa.[14] But it did not suppress slavery as such. 'The decree does not suppress vested interests. Natives owning domestic slaves are not affected.'[15] Another author observed: 'The four categories – free, freed, domestic captive and slave – continued to exist'[16].

A report issued in 1904 included under the term 'non-free' 2,000,000 out of the 8,250,000 inhabitants of French West Africa, the term 'non-free' being a euphemism which the administration imposed thenceforward to avoid protests which the proper term would arouse. In certain regions the rate was even higher, reaching 50 per cent. Slavery did not disappear, nor has it ever been formally prohibited; the trade was discreetly pursued right down to our own time, mainly in the more remote regions with strong traditions of slavery like Mauritania, Niger, Chad[18] and Fouta-Djalon. However, it gradually declined. The freedom villages also disappeared or were subject to communal law. Already in 1894 two district commanders in the Sudan asked for a reform of the system, not for humanitarian reasons, but to have more staff; they considered that the recruitment of manpower, which fell primarily on the freedom villages, should be extended to all. Tax exemption was suppressed in 1908–9. Between 1905 and 1910 the freedom villages were gradually abolished. In 1908 the indigenous agents of the administration were required to proclaim the 'liberation' of their slaves – an entirely theoretical proposition.

Wherever orders for the suppression of the slave trade were applied, and liberation took place on a large scale, it was done for political reasons. For instance, in 1909 Babichon, inspector of administrative affairs, had Alfa Alimou, the chief of the province of Labé (Guinea), arrested and sentenced to three years' imprisonment for 'slave trading'. He had been appointed to that post to replace Alfa Yaya, who was interned in Dahomey; it was, in reality, a pretext for applying the policy of suppressing the important chiefs and introducing direct rule.[19] In 1911 the same crime was ascribed to Alfa Yaya who, on his return to Conakry, was said to have tried to recover his slaves. (At that time the administration did not hesitate, illegal though it was, to exercise the right of pursuit in favour of its 'friends'.) In 1911, following the alleged revolt of the Fulani of Goumba in Guinea and the subsequent repression, 1,500 slaves were set free in order to destroy the political power of the Fulani in that region. This method was also employed elsewhere.

Nothing was changed for those who were loyal to the administration, except in a way that did not embarrass the masters. 'In Fouta-Djalon', an administrative report of 1911 noted, 'everything ended up with the paradoxical result of transforming the domestic slaves of the Foulas into free farmers paying rent four or five times as high as before, to the great joy of the "dispossessed" owners.'[20] Nor were these policies unaffected by economic considerations. In certain regions of the Sudan, the former slaves were encouraged to emigrate in order to force the owners to work: 'The owners who enjoyed the town life in the big towns of Niger, and were Islamic scholars, were quickly forced to return to their lands and work them, or they risked dying of hunger.'[21] Care was taken not to go to the same lengths with the slaves of the Fulani of Macina, since the latter were incapable of cultivating their own lands. As in Fouta-Djalon, common slavery was converted into *metayage*, or share-cropping, and the *diangal* which the slaves paid to their baptised masters was re-named 'leasehold rights'. Legal appearances were saved.

Though in certain regions there were a few cases where slavery survived to our own days, the institution as such was in decline after 1908–9. The steam-roller of colonisation oppressed one and all; it got rid of the chiefs, and eroded the traditional social distinctions without completely effacing them. On the other hand, since it used the local chiefdoms, traditional or imposed, which had an interest in maintaining servitude, the administration was hostile to any radical measures.

3. The Disintegration of the Traditional Social Structures

The development of the market economy and production contributed decisively in another way to the slow disintegration of the former social organisation. It speeded up the dissolution of the traditional community, which tended to disappear, leaving isolated individuals – buyers or sellers of goods. Where it did continue to exist, internal contradictions became sharper since elders or chiefs tended to use for their personal profit the common heritage, over which they possessed merely supervisory rights, and they neglected their duties towards the members of the community – sons, nephews, brothers, etc. The administration, impervious as it was to African realities, was ready to favour and sanction the usurpations in order to profit by having docile chiefs. Even in the towns the ancient collective ties had not disappeared, but they were being slowly destroyed, and the personal conflicts between chiefs and the mass of the people, between old and young, and men and women, revived. The dowry, formerly matrimonial 'compensation' and a sign of alliance between two families, turned increasingly into a form of bride purchase. The traditional society used the dowry to distinguish a married woman from a concubine slave. As slavery disappeared, the position of the married woman came closer to that of the concubine slave of former times.

The traditional hierarchy was also overthrown. Certain former slaves, having become (relatively) rich through trade or having become officials, acquired the status of 'dignitaries', and compared to them the fallen nobles cut sorry figures. But this could not be the starting-point of a new order. Colonial imperialism, by systematically extracting the fruits of surplus labour and even a large part of essential labour, prevented any form of local accumulation of capital among the Africans. The extreme misery of the standard of living formed an obstacle to any technical improvements. The 'banana machine', as the settlers on the Ivory Coast called the requisitioned Africans,[22] were paid little or nothing, and their labour thus cost far less than the machine or even the simplest tool. Any possibility of developing indigenous capitalism, or an indigenous bourgeoisie was thus extremely restricted.

The only sphere where the African could join in the network of colonial exploitation was trade, the major tool of that exploitation. But here, as we have seen, he was soon eliminated from any form of activity by better-armed competitors – company agents or the Lebanese and Syrians – and reduced to a secondary, mediocre role which often took the form of speculation or usury. The growth of usury, practised far more by the Lebanese and Syrians and the Europeans, including the administration (through the 'indigenous provident societies'), than by the Africans, worked its way right through the trade of colonial Africa. As a general rule the peasant was forced to seek advances from the trader on the promise of the coming harvest. Since his poverty made effective reimbursement risky, the trader would demand usurous rates, which his miserable condition forced the peasant to accept and which made it possible to deprive him of everything, or at least held him at the trader's mercy.

What Marx said in regard to the pre-capitalist period might well apply here:

> Usury centralises money wealth, wherever the means of production are disjointed. It does not alter the mode of production, but attaches itself to it as a parasite and makes it sick. It sucks its blood, takes away strength, and compels reproduction to proceed under even more disheartening conditions.[23]

But locally practised usury was only an accessory feature. Colonial exploitation by monopoly capital played the role on a far larger scale than usury had done in medieval Europe, the difference being that instead of permitting primitive accumulation on the spot,[24] as a basis for the subsequent development of industrial capitalism, it robbed the colonial country of this accumulation, which took place instead at home thanks to the profits and surplus profits exported. This accelerated the development that had characterised African society from the onset of trade – the slow disintegration of the traditional social strata, a sharpening of internal conflicts – resulting not from progress in conditions of production but from the continuous removal of the wealth produced and from misery growing ever more profound and widespread.

REFERENCES

1. Founded by Cardinal Lavigerie and approved by the papal brief of Leo XIII on 17 October, 1888.

2. R. Cuvillier-Fleury, op. cit., p. 31.

3. See vol. I, pp. 214–17.

4. Denise Bouche, 'Les villages de liberté en Afrique Occidentale Française', *Bulletin de l'Institut français d'Afrique noire*, 1949, No. 3–4, p. 529.

5. *Rapport confidentiel au Grand-Orient de France et au R. L. de la Fédération, Dakar.* Imprimerie de la Loge 'L'Etoile occidentale', 1904.

6. Same source. This remained so, in a Moorish setting, even at Dakar, until quite recently.

7. A. Demougeot, 'Histoire du Nunez', *Bulletin du Comité d'Etudes historiques et scientifiques de l'Afrique occidentale française*, vol. XXI, No. 2, 1938, pp. 274 ff.

8. Archives of the Government-General. Dakar. 248 Bamako. Cited by D. Bouche, op. cit., *Bulletin de l'Institute française de l'Afrique noire*, 1950, No. 1, p. 171.

9. Archives of the Government-General. Bamako. E 1/27/48 of 4 September, 1894.

10. Archives of the Government-General, Dakar. 248 Goudam.

11. G. Deherme, *L'Afrique occidentale française: action politique, économique et sociale.* Paris, Bloud et Cie., 1908, pp. 57–8.

12. On this person see vol. I, pp. 230–1, and M. Blanchard, 'Administrateurs d'Afrique Noir', *Revue d'Histoire des Colonies*, XL, 1953, pp. 377–430.

13. Denise Bouche, op. cit., p. 149.

14. The Act of 8 March, 1831, did not apply except to sea trade.

15. R. Cuvillier-Fleury, op. cit.

16. F. de Kersaint-Gilly, 'Essai sur l'évolution de l'esclavage en Afrique Occidentale Française', *Bulletin du Comité d'Etudes historiques et scientifiques de l'Afrique occidentale française*, 1924, No. 3, pp. 469–78.

17. Archives of the Government-General. 243.

18. In his instructions dated Fort-Archambault (28 February, 1911) Largeau, military commander of Chad, ruled: 'Shut your eyes. No stories of slaves, of liberation, etc.' The Anti-Slavery League bestowed its gold medal upon him in 1913 (General Hilaire, *Du Congo au Nil*, Marseilles, 1930, p. 81).

19. Cf. *Revue indigène*, No. 40, August 1909, p. 385, and Archives Nationales de la République de Guinée I.E.2 and I.E.7. Governor Liotard considered disastrous this initiative taken without his knowledge on the eve of the return of Alfa Yaya: Alfa Alimou, the personal enemy of Alfa Yaya, had been used by the administration and placed in this post to damage the supporters of the fallen chief. But once the arrest had been made, he gave instructions to the commander of the Labé circle to let the accusation stand and to make sure that there was no chance of an acquittal.

20. Denise Bouche, op. cit., 1949, p. 524. The substitution of the Métayage system for captives had been recommended by a circular of Governor Camille Guy. The annual report of the government-general of French West Africa for

1912 solemnly noted: 'In Fouta-Djalon . . . the practice of Métayage contracts is spreading more and more. It is worth noting that the former feudal chiefs have no scruples about recognising a capacity to sign a contract in their former agrarian serfs.' (Rapport Annuel 1912. Paris. Larose, 1915, p. 5.)

21. Paul Marty, *La Politique indigène du gouverneur-général Ponty*. Paris, E. Leroux, 1915, p. 14.

22. They were fed, on the Ivory Coast, on plantain bananas.

23. Karl Marx, *Capital*, vol. III, Chapter XXXVI, p. 700, edit. C. H. Kerr and Co., Chicago.

24. Primitive accumulation of the fifteenth to the eighteenth centuries took the form of concentration of capital by the expropriation of the peasants, the exploitation of the colonial peoples in America and Africa (Spanish and Portuguese colonisation, slave trade) and usury: that is to say, not on the basis of the capitalist mode of production but on that of the ancient forms of production, and, in the final analysis, on simple plunder.

CHAPTER III

THE ADMINISTRATIVE SYSTEM

1. Despotism and Direct Administration

The Second Empire, in the person of Faidherbe, gave French Black Africa the principles of its administration. The *senatus-consult* of 3 May, 1854, laid down the legislative system for the new colonies for nearly a century, up till the application of the 1946 constitution. The ancient colonies, the Antilles and Réunion, kept their special system. The 'other' colonies – and 'other' included all the conquests made right up to the end of the century – were left to the despotic powers of the head of state. Article 18 of the *senatus-consult* laid down: 'They shall be administered by decree of the Emperor until a statute be passed in respect of them by *a senatus-consult*.' This *senatus-consult* was never issued.

The Third Republic kept religiously to this decree, and the despotism of the authoritarian Empire continued in colonial affairs under the Republic. Unless expressly so decreed, acts passed by parliament did not apply to the colonies. The imperial senate, long before it actually disappeared, had forfeited its competence in colonial matters; but the *senatus-consult* of 21 May, 1870, which deprived it of that competence, did not abrogate any previous *senatus-consult*, which retained the validity of ordinary laws under the Third Republic.

It was the President of the Republic – in the place of the Emperor – and his government, or, to be exact, the minister of the navy and the minister for the colonies, who legislated by decree, extending to the colonies metropolitan legislation which they judged to be useful, or enacting special legislation for the purpose. Clearly, this legislative power had its limits: the colonial decrees of the President of the Republic could not modify existing laws, and they were open to annulment by the council of state. The parliament of the Third Republic had the right to pass laws for the colonies, but made little use of it. If it was considered necessary, the promulgation of laws which were to be applied in the colonies could be delayed indefinitely, or their effect could be limited by various expedients. Thus, the press law of 1881 (guaranteeing the liberty of the press) was applicable to the colonies by virtue of its Article 69, but when the point was raised, those colonies established after 1881 were ingeniously considered to be outside the law.[1]

Parallel to ministerial despotism ran the local despotism of the governors and administrators; the despotism of the lesser officials knew no limit other than that of their superiors. Faidherbe, formerly an army officer in Algeria, implanted the Algerian administrative system in Senegal, and it ultimately spread to all the French colonies. The division into 'circles' was imposed by Faidherbe. The officer – under the military system – and later the civil administrator ruled from the principal town over a certain number of posts, at first simple fortified strongholds, where a non-commissioned officer (later an administrator or an agent) represented him. This was in order to set up a network that would make possible the control of the country. The opposing strongholds (*tatas* or fortified villages) were destroyed, and the network was for ever being tightened to make resistance by the 'nomad' elements more and more difficult. ('Nomad' was the term applied to those who were seeking to preserve their independence by flight and constant changes of abode.)

In the Sudan it was the army that gave final form to the system; Galliéni provided a theoretical basis. He advocated the notorious 'oil stain' which, beginning from the strongholds, acquired dominion over the entire country. According to the promoters of the system, it was the infrastructure (of markets, schools, etc.) and its resulting benefits, which the army or circle police promised would help to win over the indigenous population and so extend the 'oil stain'. We shall soon see that matters were in reality somewhat different.

The European staff – colonial administrators and commissioners for native affairs – had inherited from the military period not only despotism but also total control. The circle commander or his deputy was in charge of administration, levied taxes, dispensed justice, carried out the function of police, ran the prisons and directed all public services. He was an autocrat and, except in centres where there was a substantial European population (which had to be dealt with tactfully), 'there was nothing to moderate the exaltation of authority and personal power'.[2] The administrative corps tried to the very end to preserve control, if not over all the branches of administration then at least over most of them; they were slow to tolerate the presence of trained personnel – doctors, teachers, purveyors of culture – however few in number; they long remained, and always did their best to show that they were, the masters.

All moral and effective authority, in all the branches of human activity, is centred in the hands of the administrator, who guards it jealously. That is the principal reason for the backward state in which they [the colonies] found themselves economically. Passive obedience has never been a factor in progress.[3]

The same observer estimated in 1921 that this was 'a prelude to normal administration, necessitated by circumstances which had lasted far longer than was reasonable'.[4] But the 'prelude' was to last right until the end of the system. The civil administration took over both its external forms and its vocabulary from the military. The civil commander, moreover, retained military or police powers; where he had no soldiers at his disposal, he had indigenous militia-men who became the 'circle police' of French West Africa.

There were clearly not enough European officials to ensure the total annexation of the country. It needed the collaboration of certain local people: direct auxiliaries (interpreters, commissioners, political agents, police) and indirect auxiliaries, the chiefs. To start with, as a necessity, recourse was had to the aid of the 'allied' or 'protected' local chiefs. But the notion of protectorate gradually brought about a change. The resident, at first a mere liaison officer, soon turned into an administrator supported by a garrison of soldiers. Posts multiplied in the interior of the 'protected' state, and the chief was reduced to an auxiliary role. It had been proposed that, following the British example, the most important chiefs of African states should be maintained, though reduced to a more or less ceremonial function. This had been the hope of Galliéni; but the system proved impractical. The majority of the great African states – the kingdoms of Ségou and Sikasso, and the state of Samory – refused to submit to French claims; so Archinard and his successors found it necessary to supress them. The maintained or installed 'allies' proved a disappointment. This was so with Aguibou at Bandiagara, Mademba Seye at Sansanding, Ago-li-agbo at Abomey and Alfa Yaya at Labé, who sought to continue exercising their traditional prerogatives while the French administration intended to issue all the orders. Nevertheless, certain kingships, based on particularly strong social structures, continued to exist, as for example that of Mossi; as did a number of chiefdoms, sultanates, or emirates of the desert or the border regions. A change of direction occurred in this policy at the beginning of the century. After 1900–1, conquest was virtually completed and the authorities turned to the 'steady suppression of the great chiefs and the destruction of their authority until the village becomes an administrative unit'.[5]

Between 1900 and 1910 the majority of the indigenous potentates, whether former enemies or friends, were eliminated – including those

who had been installed by the French conquerors. The treaties concluded with African potentates, without ever being formally abrogated, were considered as being relevant to metropolitan jurisdiction
alone; the kingdom of Abomey, for example, was suppressed by
simple decree of the governor; and in 1900 Ago-li-agbo, who had
been installed by France, was similarly overthrown, arrested and
interned in the Congo. In 1902, Aguibou, king of Macina, a faithful
ally of the French, was 'retired from office'. Even 'Fama' Mademba,
a French official who had been made 'king' of Sansanding, was
deposed in 1900 and lost his 'crown'; he was properly reinstated in
his role (with a decoration as consolation prize), but reinforced by a
commissioner for native affairs – himself under the commander of
Segou district. The kingdom of Mossi, though never suppressed,
was likewise reduced to a purely ceremonial role:

> In Mossi the system of direct administration inaugurated in 1905
> produced the expected results. [As a report on the situation in
> the colony of Upper-Senegal-and-Niger noted in 1906.] The
> people have accepted with confidence the substitution of our
> authority for that of Morho Naba. . . . Deprived of his political
> attributes, Moumeni has preserved his religious prestige in the
> eyes of the natives; he is the trustee of sacred fetishes, and he
> regularly holds ritual ceremonies.[6]

In the Congo the 'Makoko', paramount chief of the Bateke, who
had signed a treaty with Brazza, died in 1892. 'The official journal
of the colony did not shed one tear for this illustrious ally who had
been completely forgotten since the partition carried out at the
Berlin Conference', Mgr. Augouard noted ironically.[7] With the
establishment of the chartered companies, his successor, whom no
one had thought necessary to inform of the act of concession on his
lands, raised opposition to the companies' claims. A unit of Senegal
riflemen was dispatched, who killed a dozen Bateke in his entourage;
he himself was 'given rough treatment' and carried off to Brazzaville, where he died the following day.[8]

The Land Act of 23 October, 1904, put an end to the fiction of
'protectorates'. Until then a juridical distinction has been maintained between (1) territories of direct administration, subjected to
the same regulations as the national territory; (2) states reduced to
protectorates by right of conquest, and (3) states reduced to protectorates by treaty.[9]

In Senegal the first category applied to the principal towns, districts on which military, administrative or customs posts had been
built, territory within a radius of 1 km. from the 'ports of call' on
the coast and along the Senegal River, the coast between Dakar and

Saint-Louis to a depth of 2 km. and the land adjoining railway lines (1 km. on each side). In the third category, the African chiefs retained their rights over the land. In the 'conquered' protectorates the French state assumed their place and was considered proprietor of the 'empty ownerless lands'. In Senegal, the fiction of 'protectorates' was maintained until 1920 through the existence of two budgets, one for the 'countries of direct administration' and the other for 'protectorates'. This distinction had no other purpose than to bring the latter under the competence of the general council elected by the foundation members of the four communes of full mandate.[10] In fact, for a long time the administrative system was more or less the same everywhere.

By the unilateral Act of 23 October, 1904, the theoretical sovereignty of the African chiefs was wholly abolished.[11] All the territories of the colonies passed under the sovereignty of the French state, to which the 'empty' ownerless lands were already considered to belong.

As a result of this annexation, it was no longer the indigenous chiefs to whom the settlers and traders addressed themselves to obtain the lands they needed, but to the representatives of French authority who alone had the right to arrange the transfer of these lands, though the indigenous occupants had to be indemnified.[12]

The coming to power of the radicals, hostile to the clergy and the army, speeded up the trend towards 'direct administration'. Radicalism liked to present itself as an assimilator, but in fact for Black Africa there was no question of real assimilation, which was inconceivable within the framework of the colonial system. This trend led to the abolition or repudiation of traditional institutions, denounced as feudal or barbarian, and their replacement by the French colonial system of administration. The Alfa Yaya affair serves as an example. As chief of Labé, a province of Fouta-Djalon, he had taken the side of the French at the moment of conquest, and, thanks to the support of the administrator Noirot, the conqueror of Timbo, he had received his independence, being thereafter withdrawn from the authority of the Almamy.

In 1904 the governor of Guinea, Cousturier, former secretary-general and successor to Ballay, was superseded,[13] and replaced by Governor Frézouls, a radical who was determined to show up the disastrous character of the policy of his predecessors, who had depended on the big feudal chiefs. Alfa Yaya, the most prominent, became the scapegoat. By an 'easy manoeuvre', the governor lured Alfa Yaya to Conakry, where the chief appeared in great pomp with his retinue, expecting an official reception. He was quickly arrested, put aboard a ship, and then interned in Dahomey (1905). At this act the supporters of the former policy protested.

Among the acts that *roused universal censure and dishonoured those who committed them*, to borrow the very expressions of the minister for the colonies in his recent instructions to the commissioner-general of the Congo, should be included the breach of promise and the dishonour shown by certain representatives of the government towards the Natives administered by them. . . . Such is the view of the impartial public on the plot which put an end to the power of the former King of Labé, Alpha Yaya, who had most loyally helped the French government to take possession of Fouta-Djalon without a single shot being fired. It is known that, when summoned to Conakry for discussions a few months ago, Alpha Yaya, calm and confident as any man who has no cause to reproach himself, undertook this costly journey of several weeks with an escort of honour in answer to the appeal of the French representative; on leaving Government House he was arrested, put aboard a ship to Dakar and then deported to Dahomey.[15]

At the beginning of 1906, on the death of Almamy Baba-Alimou, the chiefs were asked not to designate a successor but to divide Fouta-Djalon into two chiefdoms where the two 'branches' of the Alfaya and Soriya were to rule.

Alfa Alimou, a personal enemy of Alfa Yaya and for that reason designated as chief of the province of Labé – with a territory far smaller in size than that under Alfa Yaya's authority – was condemned in 1909 to three years' imprisonment and demoted, the chiefdom of the province being suppressed. When Alfa Yaya returned from Dahomey at the end of his exile, the administration, which before his return had been seeking means of prolonging his absence, invoked an imaginary 'plot' to arrest him once again after a few weeks' stay at Conakry, in February 1911; he was interned, this time at Port-Etienne, and he died shortly afterwards. In April 1911, still in Guinea, steps were taken to crush the 'Ouali of Goumba', Tierno Aliou, an influential and respected *marabout;* he was condemned to death, extradited from Sierra Leone where he had sought refuge, and imprisoned at the convict prison at Fotoba in the Los islands, where he died in 1912.[16] In the course of his trial, counsel (appointed six days previously), having shown up the total lack of proof and the contradictory evidence, was answered by the public prosecutor that 'it is when witnesses contradict each other that they really speak the truth according to their conscience'.[17]

In the course of 1912, administrator Thoreau-Levaré proceeded to the complete dismemberment of the ancient provinces of Fouta-

Djalon so as to break up the ancient historic units. The Almamy Bokar Biro, of Timbo, was 'transferred' to the chiefdom of the canton of Daboula, outside his former territories. When in 1908 King Toffa of Porto-Novo (another faithful ally of France) died, his son was given the title of paramount chief (*chef supérieur*), and for an annuity of 25,000 francs had to promise to carry out the orders of the governor and the administrators.[18]

In short, after 1910 – to keep control over potentially powerful individuals and traditions that were still strong – a few 'provincial chiefs' or 'paramount chiefs' were still kept in existence, but their prerogatives were mainly honorary. As the role of the chiefs declined, the order of those directly subordinate to the administrators took on more importance: circle police, interpreters, agents and the like.

Little by little, the administration acquired the habit of passing over incompetent chiefs and of having their orders executed by assistants whose role was simply that of furnishing escorts and guards and doing police duty. . . .

Established as rulers in the villages, they brought heavy costs upon the inhabitants who had to provide food for their entourage: the favourite wife, the younger brother, the servant stable-boy who looked after the mount, all people with good appetites who demanded an exclusive cuisine and chicken at all meals.[19]

The guard on detachment was fully conscious of being indispensable; he did not hesitate to deputise for the chief, settling affairs, meting out justice according to his own standards and interests, and receiving presents. On return he would report that there was 'nothing new', or he would denounce some dark plot destined to compromise an arrogant chief who did not want to submit to his ways, or a jealous husband who had refused him an assignation with his third wife. The situation seems to be little different in most of Equatorial Africa,[20] where the same evil is rife, personified by the *tougourou* [militiamen] who are the terror of the villages. When the militiaman does not show up, his place is taken by the interpreter or the secretary, who is always correct, considerate, discreet and devoted, the obliging intermediary between the administrator, who does not speak the native language, and the natives who do not understand French. His tyranny is more enlightened, but no less heavy, and it is equally profitable. Circle police, interpreters or secretaries are nearly always the true chiefs of the country.[21]

For the administrator who drew this picture, all the evil obviously came from the native assistant, but in reality, the evil originated

D

from the despotism of the commander, in whose name his subordinates acted and from whom they sought personal gain. It has been claimed that this policy of direct administration was not intentional. Thus Georges Hardy wrote:

> Though not as a matter of deliberate intent, nearly all the principalities whose heads had concluded treaties with France have disappeared or are no more than empty forms. . . . The slowness and ineptitude of the local rulers in support of the work of colonisation, interpreted rightly or wrongly as a mark of ill-will, or as a sign of indisputable inferiority, have worn out the patience of the local authorities and have moved them to break up the traditional forms, which they found more cumbersome than useful, and to replace the representatives of ancient families as chiefs by small men without prestige, and too often without scruples. It thus happened that, around 1909, the term 'policy of association' was nothing but a cloak for direct administration of which the working could only be superficial.[22]

In reality, all the texts show that this policy of direct administration was perfectly deliberate and intentional. Its promoters, far from being bureaucrats, and ignorant of the facts, were perfectly well-informed, practical men; for instance, Thoreau-Levaré, responsible for the dismemberment of Fouta-Djalon, a former commissioner at Noirot, had held posts in Fouta or neighbouring regions from 1897 to 1914. He left a collection of 'Notes on the religious elders and influential personalities of Fouta' (at present in the archives of the administrative region of Mamou), which is an inexhaustible mine of information and was probably one of the sources used by Paul Marty for his studies on Islam in Guinea.

This policy was extolled by the officials. For instance Governor-General William Ponty declared before the Council of Government of French West Africa:

> We must destroy all hegemony of one race over another, or one ethnic group over another; fight the influence of the local aristocracies so as to make sure of the sympathies of the communities; *suppress all great principalities which nearly always act as a barrier between us and the mass of people under our administration.*[23] The application of these principles in Senegal and Guinea has begun to bear fruit.[24]

And the author cites as an example the removal of Alfa Alimou as chief of the Labé province. Specialist publications of the period express the same opinion. On the eve of the second deportation of Alfa Yaya, one author stated explicitly:

Here is no simple news-item; *this condemnation of Alfa Yaya and his supporters has profound political significance. We must unhesitatingly break up principalities which are immoral, if the designated chief does not live in the country itself, and dangerous if he has deep roots in the region of which he is in charge.*[25] On the contrary, how should we gain, if we divided the country into villages compact enough and inhabited enough to avoid crumbling, whose borders would conform to natural regions and whose inhabitants would have close ethnic ties? Such an organisation, rather like the Russian *mir*, would make it possible to have indigenous chiefs whose authority is real and directly effective, but who could be easily supervised. . . .

This system applied in Senegal, where the principalities (the more dangerous because they had historical origins) have nearly all been completely suppressed, yielded excellent results.[26]

The full application of this policy met with grave difficulties. It presumed the existence of a considerable European administrative personnel, with a perfect knowledge of the country and scattered over a large number of administrative posts. Before 1914 there had been a number of administrators, who had spent practically their entire careers in the same region after the conquest, knew the country and the people thoroughly, and spoke the local languages. After the war they became increasingly rare, and it became the habit to use administrators indiscriminately over every part of the empire, or at least over a group of territories. A large number of administrative outposts were abolished during the war, never to be re-established; administration became concentrated in a limited number of the main towns of the circle and in sub-divisions that covered several hundred villages. The intermediate link of the canton and the canton officer, each embracing up to about twenty villages, was enforced on a permanent basis.

2. *Administrative Chiefdoms*

The chiefs did not disappear. The French administration even created some where they had not existed before. But the institution, though it preserved the traditional appearances and utilised the same men and the same families, had a fundamentally new character. The traditional chiefdom gave way to administrative chiefdom.

The circle (or sub-division) was divided into cantons, the canton into villages. Under the authority of the circle commander indigenous canton village chiefs were named. At their level they were representatives of colonial despotism, workers for the administra-

tion in all capacities (policemen, judges, census-takers, tax-collec-
tors, crop agents, public works officials, etc.). These were men from
the traditional hierarchies, but they were quickly replaced when
they proved insufficiently docile, or otherwise according to the
whims of the administrators. These servants of France – interpreters,
agents, or even domestics – were often promoted by their masters;
the districts corresponding to the traditional chiefdoms were end-
lessly divided up or pieced together – for example in Fouta-Djalon.
In the purely tribal regions, where there were no political chiefs,
village and canton chiefs were imposed, and granted absolute
authority. The canton or village chief was no more than a cog in the
administrative machinery, often representing nothing 'traditional'
or 'customary'; the collegiate or democratic institutions, which
controlled and generally elected the chiefs, were reduced to a purely
formal role, and in some cases even ignored or suppressed.

It should again be emphasised that the despotism of the chiefs
was not a legacy of the African past, but a contribution of the
French system of colonial administration. There could hardly be a
poorer despot than such a chief, who was an official, and an unpaid
one at that. In the past he had received the 'customs' payments from
the European traders, various dues and taxes, and revenues of the
courts of justice. These traditional sources of revenue were taken
from him, at least officially, and he was left only with a rebate on
taxation. It was up to him to supplement his resources by 'fleecing'
the people under his administration; these extortions were tolerated
on condition that he did not let himself be caught at it. Essentially
it meant he had to make the men of his canton do unpaid work on
the fields he laid claim to, and construct or repair his huts without
pay. This procedure was considered 'normal' everywhere, and any
recalcitrant subject was punished for 'opposition to the exercise of
the functions vested in the canton chiefs'. But as there was no legal
basis for this forced labour on behalf of the chief, he could in fact be
sued, on the charge of having 'turned' to his profit requisitioned
labour which should not legally have been used except for the benefit
of the administration. When there was a scandal, whatever the
circumstances, it was always the chief who was held responsible,
never the administrator.

In view of the meagre advantages involved, the duties were many
and onerous: collection of taxes, requisitioning labour, compulsory
crop cultivation and provision of military recruits. He had to give
accommodation and food, on a royal scale and free of charge, to
emissaries or representatives of the administration on tour. He had
to entertain the agents or representatives of the chief town of the
circle who had been sent to deliver the orders of the commander;

to pay an educated secretary, and to maintain an armed body of law-enforcement agents, often complete blackguards.

When the chiefs were reproached for surrounding themselves with this doubtful crew, they would rightly reply: do you want us to collect taxes, and supply you with forced labour and conscripts, or not? We cannot do that by gentleness and persuasion. If the people are not afraid of being attacked and beaten, they will laugh at us.[28]

He enjoyed the support of the circle police, but that force could turn against him if he was not capable of executing the orders of his superiors with sufficient zeal and speed. The administrator had certain guarantees against the despotism of his superiors. If he received a bad report, this would at worst compromise his promotion. His career was rarely threatened. The chief had no such guarantees. From one day to the next an unforeseeable mistake, a difficulty in the execution of his orders, the ill-temper of the commander or the intrigues of some well-placed enemies could reduce him to nothing. He was lucky if his dismissal was not followed by imprisonment or deportation; for the excesses to which he was forced in the accomplishment of the tasks laid down by the administration, and which the latter pretended to ignore, were then invoked against him to justify the sanctions.

Very few administrators are aware of the smallness of the local chief's powers, in spite of their considerable influence. They act towards these collaborators as if they were true despots. When they receive from some office in the main town of the colony instructions demanding military recruitment, road repairs, the extension of the food crops, the introduction of the plough, of cotton, hemp or castor-oil plants in agriculture, they issue orders, and are surprised if, a few weeks later, these injunctions formulated with the customary precision and vigour have not been put into effect.
This command procedure might possibly succeed with autocrats, a few of whom have existed in Africa, but they are doomed to failure with individuals who are not and have never been tyrants.[29]

Whether they liked it or not, in other words, the chiefs had to become tyrants unless they wanted to compromise their position. For canton chiefs the advantages were still substantial in spite of the expense and risk, but the position of a village chief was very uneasy. The meagre rebates or dues which he could deduct did not make up for the responsibility which his superiors, from the canton chief to the circle commander, foisted upon him. The least delay with taxes or in the execution of orders was considered the responsibility of the village chief, who was arrested, imprisoned and flogged. In the tribal regions, where the people were accustomed to independence, there were great difficulties in filling such perilous posts in which the chief was caught between an inflexible administration, and the administered who did not recognise his authority. Elsewhere, the true traditional chief would hide himself behind a man of straw, either a man of low rank or a former slave, who bore the responsibilities in the eyes of the authorities and assumed the consequent risks. The so-called 'traditional' character of the chiefdom was always invoked as a pretext to justify arbitrary action and the cruelty of the colonial system of administration. All that bore a positive character in the traditional chiefdom – collective or democratic control, the powers and duties of a chief towards his subjects – was, in practice, pitilessly eliminated. Only the retrograde and negative features of the office of the chief, which were useful to colonialism, were maintained and encouraged.

Needless to say, the administration strove to use for its own ends the prestige and authority which the representatives of the traditional chiefly families still enjoyed. This was the purpose of an intervention by William Ponty in 1909, extolling the 'policy of races' that is, the choice of chiefs from the ethnic groups which they were to govern. But this policy, far from signifying a reaction against the system of direct administration, as the theoreticians of the Ecole[30] later pretended, continued in the same direction as before by 'decapitating' the aristocracies of other groups. The same was true of Van Vollenhoven's famous circular of 15 August, 1917, which marked an adaptation (to the necessities of the war) and not a radical change in orientation. No doubt he did denounce the abuses resulting from 'government by the circle police': but government by the canton chiefs, as we have seen, did nothing but replace the circle police by the followers of the canton chief, when he did not let them join in undertaking the same work. The reduction in European administrative personnel made direct administration impossible on the scale that it had hitherto been conceived. Van Vollenhoven insisted on the use of such indirect aids as the chiefs, and proposed measures deemed indispensable to consolidate their authority – respect for their customary titles, the bestowal of decorations, increased allowances, even consultation with the people. He condemned the abuse of administrative sanctions for unjustified ends, which had brought them into disrepute. But he made it clear that he was not calling for a return to the former state, and strongly reaffirmed the principle of direct administration.

They [the chiefs] have no power of their own, of any kind, for there cannot be two authorities in the circle, the French and the native; there can be only one. Only the circle commander gives orders; he alone is responsible. The indigenous chief is only an instrument, an auxiliary.

And he went on to state in precise terms:

These reasons [for making use of the chiefs] are not inspired by the chiefs' interests. They are not ancient sovereigns whose thrones *we want to preserve; the thrones either do not exist or have been overthrown by us, and will not be replaced.*[31] These reasons are inspired solely by the interest of the subject peoples under our authority. Between us and these people there must be a go-between, namely the chief.[32]

This stresses the fundamental change that colonisation brought about in the role and even the character of the chiefdom, of which 'traditional' forms, where they continued to exist, covered a new reality. This profound change should never be forgotten.

3. 'Assimilation' and 'Association'

The system of direct administration has often been held up as proof of a policy of 'assimilation' which had as its object the gallicising of the colonies to the point of turning them into simple transplanted copies of the French *départements*. But in reality, the system of colonial administration, despotic in principle, was absolutely opposed to the democratic institutions – democratic at least in form – which the Third Republic had established in France. The system of the right of citizenship made the indigenous populations of the colonies into French 'subjects' (not citizens), on whom the administrations could inflict prison, fines and corporal punishment by a simple ruling.

'Assimilation' had only a negative meaning: it suppressed or ignored the political structures that were truly African and the African culture, replacing them by colonial structures and colonial education – which were indeed 'French', but profoundly different from what existed at the same level in France itself. Nevertheless, the pretence that colonial policy led to the formation of a *'France d'Outre-mer'* was carefully cultivated. This was mainly for purposes of home policy. The French schoolchild or elector, profoundly ignorant of the colonial reality, was given to believe that the policy of direct administration was aimed at gradually raising the blacks of Africa to the condition of the French *à part entière*. Certain limited measures, pursued in contradiction to the general policy, kept up the illusion. For example, the communes of Gorée and Saint-Louis (1872), Rufisque (1880) and Dakar (1889) received French municipal status, as communes 'of full mandate'. In 1879 the 'originators' of the communes of full mandate in Senegal were granted the right (of which the Second Empire had deprived them) to elect a general council and to send a deputy to the French parliament.[33] They were thus like the inhabitants of the Antilles and Réunion, but in fact the completeness of this citizenship was contested for a long time.[34] For the people of the Antilles and Réunion, there was no ambiguity. But could the Senegalese of the privileged communes be considered citizens if they also retained a personal status claiming Islamic rights and polygamy, and consequently refused to enforce the civil code? On this score a long lawsuit had been fought between the inhabitants of the little island of Saint-Marie de Madagascar, an 'old colony' which had been incorporated into the colony of Madagascar, and the administration which attempted to reduce them to the status of subjects. The question was not settled definitely until the war: Deputy Blaise Diagne managed to persuade Clemenceau to introduce a law on 29 September, 1916, which proclaimed:

The Natives of the four Communes with full mandate in Senegal, and their descendants, are and shall remain French citizens and are subject to the military duties laid down under the Act of 19 October, 1915.

Surely the existence of these citizens was proof of the liberal intentions of France? There was another advantage: these 'citizens' could be used as auxiliary staff of the administration against the mass of their own people who remained 'subjects'. The same purpose was pursued with the granting of citizenship as a personal title to a few highly privileged persons;[35] a few officials or notables, as a special reward, were freed from native status – without, however, becoming full citizens.

After the First World War, to hamper the claims of the Africans who had taken the promises seriously, the alleged 'assimilation' was condemned as demagoguery and as incapable of being realised. It was replaced by a feigned policy of 'association', referring back to circulars of Ponty and Van Vollenhoven on the 'policy of races' and the use of indigenous chiefs. H. Labouret wrote:

The policy of association is based on respect for customs, manners and religions; everywhere it substitutes mutual aid for the exploitation of native energies and for the usurpation of their property and their lands. It stimulates their intellectual development. In other respects it is realistic and wise, preserving with resolute firmness all the rights and necessities of domination. It does not intend to create equality, which at present is too often impossible.[36]

In fact, this pretended 'association', linked to maintenance of the 'rights of domination', was nothing but the association of the horse and its rider; with the excuse of respect for customs (which, as the same author admitted, the administrators generally ignored since they had never seriously studied them), the colonial administration raised obstacles to all democratic claims. 'Manners' and 'customs' were identified with the chiefdom whose outward forms, as we have seen, were all that were kept.[37] Some more sincere – or more cynical – theoreticians of colonialism did not hesitate, before 1914, to jeer at the debates on association or assimilation, and the homilies on the blessings of colonisation. Charles Régismanset, a senior official in the ministry for the colonies and author of an *Essai sur la colonisation*, wrote under the ironic title 'La Colonisation européenne, un progrès?'

> Poor black humanity! Let us at least have the frankness to admit that if we take so much care of you, it is because you seem to us to constitute an inexhaustible reserve of labour. . . .
> We want to get as much as we can out of the African races; we want unlimited bales of rubber and ivory on the quays of Bordeaux and Le Harve, we want the groundnuts to grow, palm oil to fill the ships to the brim. That's all we want. There's no need here for science, justice, goodness and especially progress.
> I do not want black education to be pushed too far. . . . While they [the people] are weak, they will allow the right of the strongest. The day when the 'strongest' disarms, the day when they understand the admirable lie behind all these abstractions, they will hasten – the Annamites are giving us a foretaste of this – to denounce the alleged 'contract of association' and rise up against European tutelage and exploitation. . . .[38]

And he summed up:

> . . . unrealisable assimilation or hypocritical association, two systems in equally flagrant contradiction *of the facts*.[39]

Jules Harmand, in his work *Domination et Colonisation*[40] contrasts settlement with what he calls 'dominion'. Régismanset congratulated him on recognising that 'what lies at the base of all colonial policy is force.'[41] And Jules Harmand stressed:

D*

The conquerors should have no illusions on this score. However wise, experienced, clever and administratively able they may be, they will never inspire in those whom they claim to rule, after beating and subjecting them, those instinctive sentiments of affection and solidarity which make up a nation.[42]

4. Centralisation: the Government-General

The top administrative organisation within the framework of what we have just outlined is only of secondary interest. In West Africa as in the Congo, the stages of conquest led to successive adaptations. For a long time there was hesitation caused by the difficulty of reconciling centralisation under the authority of the governor of 'Senegal and dependencies' – Faidherbe's bequest – with the necessary autonomy of the newly established colonies. The same was true in the Congo, where the rivalry between Libreville in Gabon and Brazzaville in the Congo proper was expressed by vacillations between rigorous centralisation under the authority of the 'commissioner-general of the possessions of the French Congo and dependencies' and the relative autonomy of the colonies. In the years 1890–9 the effects of autonomy in the colonies often led to frontier conflicts and the resort on both sides to procedures reminiscent of those usual between countries at war with each other: for example, military expeditions and raids on the peoples subject to the authority of a 'rival' colony. This was true in particular of Senegal and Guinea, [43] the Sudan and Dahomey, etc.

The solution finally adopted was a constitution of groups or federations of colonies with a governor-general, distinct from and superior to the governors of the colonies; and ruling over the group, he formed a link between the governors and the minister, and surrounded himself with widely diversified central services which became more and more cumbersome. Governors and governors-general were assisted, the former by an administrative council and the latter by a legislative council, made up of leading officials and representatives of big business. From the first, centralisation won, with the governors-general becoming veritable proconsuls. They alone had the power to promulgate laws and decrees by virtue of a general order of the supreme court of appeal, and a consequent decree of 1902 making the governor-general the 'sole depository of the powers of the Republic'.[44] This trend increased until the very recent period of 'law cadres' (loi-cadres), and the legislation of 1946 raised the prerogatives of the governors-general (who became 'high commissioners') even further; it expressed itself in the growing demands on the general budget relative to the budgets of individual colonies.

The rule of financial autonomy resulting from Article 33 of the Financial Law of 13 April, 1900, was strictly applied in French West Africa from 1902. Except for military expenditure, all the costs of administration were henceforth charged to the colonies, including the salaries of officials on leave in France. Even before that date the majority of local budgets had been in deficit. But the governors were less concerned with using these liquid assets for development than with enlarging the 'reserve funds' that bore witness to the economy of their administration.[45]

Through a loan, French West Africa was able to build installations (65,000,000 francs in 1903, of which 45,000,000 was for ports and railways; 10,000,000 francs in 1907, of which 87,500,000 was for railways and 11,500,000 for ports). French Equatorial Africa, less favoured, had to resort to subsidies from France (about 700,000 francs annually) which proved wholly insufficient to provide for its development. Governor-General Merlin denounced the sorry state to which the colonial 'Cinderella' had been abandoned, and in 1909 he obtained a loan of 21,000,000;[46] in 1912–13 a loan of 172,000,000 was earmarked for railways, but the war nullified these projects. Of the German colonies, Togo managed to balance its budget in 1906; Kamerun absorbed important subsidies from the home country. Here the effort to provide installations had been far more intense than in the neighbouring French colonies.

Here we shall briefly summarise the administrative history of the territories under French occupation. In Senegal, the conflict between centralisation and decentralisation grew from the Second Empire onwards. Gorée, the port handling exports of groundnuts, with south-bound traffic, balked at its dependence on Saint-Louis. In 1854 it won the day, when two colonies were set up: Senegal (Saint-Louis and the river) and Gorée and Dependencies, under a special commander detached from the naval division stationed off the western coasts of Africa. Faidherbe's success on the river led to new changes in 1859, when Senegal annexed Gorée and the establishments along the Rivières du Sud as far as Sierra Leone. The commander of the naval division retained his authority over the establishments along the Guinea coast from Assinie to Gabon. In 1882 the colony of the Rivières du Sud was established; at one time it comprised the 'second arrondissement of Senegal' of Faidherbe's day, and all the trading establishments on the coast as far as Gabon (the former 'Etablissements français de la Côte de l'Or[47] et du Gabon'[47]), which until then had been administered by the 'supreme commander of Gabon'. It now came under the control of a lieutenant-governor, resident at Dakar, who was under the orders of the governor of Senegal. He took over the establishments at Benin (Porto-Novo), which had been under the commander of Gabon (1883).

In 1889–90, the colony of Rivières du Sud cut its ties with Senegal and Gabon, and in 1891 assumed the name of the 'Colony of French Guinea'. The 'independent' colonies of the Ivory Coast (1893) and Dahomey (1894) separated from it within a short time. In April 1896 a 'lieutenant-governor of Gabon', subordinate to Senegal, was named; from June the same year, an 'office of the commissioner-general of the government' took over the independent administration of Gabon and the Congo, which were reunited after 1891 under the name 'Possessions of the French Congo and Dependencies', with a lieutenant-governor for Gabon, subordinate to the comissioner-general. Similarly, the military command of the upper Senegal River (Haut-Fleuve), set up at Kayes, gave birth to the 'French Sudan', which, until its suppression in 1899, remained a military appendage (except for the brief spell of Grodet's civil government in 1893–5).

A decree of 16 June, 1895, established the 'government-general of French West Africa': at its head stood a civil governor-general, resident at Saint-Louis, whose function was that of governor of Senegal. That was in accordance with the trend of 'Senegalese' centralisation which soon provoked a contrary reaction. From the onset, Dahomey had remained outside the group, its governor having no other duties but to communicate to the governor-general duplicates of his reports to the minister. In 1896 the Ivory Coast and Guinea received partial autonomy. The conflicts resulting from this hybrid system provoked a return to centralisation: Dahomey was incorporated in the group in 1899; at the same time, the 'military' Sudan was dismembered; the Ivory Coast and Guinea were each allocated one part; Haut-Fleuve (Upper Senegal) and Bamako made up the territory of 'Senegambia and Niger', administered directly by a governor-general from 1902 to 1904. The rest was divided up into 'military territories'. In 1902 the government-general finally split off from Senegal, received its own budget and became centred on Dakar, while Saint-Louis was endowed with a separate 'lieutenant-governor of Senegal'.

The group that made up French West Africa took definite form in 1904 with the five colonies of Senegal, Guinea, the Ivory Coast, and Dahomey, and Upper-Senegal-and-Niger; the last-named colony was made up of the military territories and one part of Senegambia, the rest of it being incorporated into Senegal. To this were added the 'Territory of Mauritania', and in 1911 the 'military territory of Niger', detached from Upper-Senegal-and-Niger; the two became 'colonies' respectively in 1920 and 1921. An eighth colony, Upper Volta, was detached from Senegal and Niger in 1919, assuming in 1920 the name of French Sudan.

In the Congo the residence of the commissioner-general was established at Libreville. Under him he had lieutenant-governors for the Congo and Ubangi to whom were added a 'commissioner' for Shari and, in 1900, a commandant of the 'military territory' of Chad. In 1903 the commissioner-general moved his place of command again, this time to Brazzaville. In 1906 an administrative reform, inspired by that in French West Africa, established extreme centralisation with bad results. This was mitigated in 1908, at which time the commissioner-general took the title of governor-general. In 1910 the name 'French Congo' was replaced by 'French Equatorial Africa', with an organisation closely resembling that of French West Africa. The group comprised three colonies: Gabon, Middle Congo and Ubangi-Shari-Chad – the military territory of Chad was being set up as a fourth colony in 1920. The colonies of French Equatorial Africa were subdivided into 'regions' and 'districts', corresponding more or less to the 'circles' and sub-divisions' of French West Africa.

We can conclude with a note on the German administrative system in Kamerun and Togo. Bismarck, who had tolerated the colonial expansion rather than willed it, had hoped to delegate the care of administration to private colonial enterprises.

In the system which I call French, the national government claims the right each time to judge the merits of an enterprise, and gives it the financial go-ahead. In our system, we hand over the choice to commerce, to the individual, and if we see that the tree is taking root, is growing and prospering, and requires the protection of the empire, we grant it support.[48]

This system failed everywhere, and from the beginning proved impracticable in Togo and Kamerun, where the German merchants had neither the means nor the desire to administer the country. The 'syndicate' of interested traders, set up on 12 October, 1884, on Bismarck's order to take over colonial administration, ignored his advice and presented claims, while refusing categorically to underwrite expenses.[49] In 1884 it became necessary to send administrators and military personnel. At the head of the two colonies a governor, appointed by the Kaiser and responsible to him, assumed all civil and military powers and directed specialised services and subordinate officials. It was the 'French system' over again, not excluding its despotism, and it gave rise to the same abuses. Denounced in the Reichstag by the socialists (mainly by Bebel) and later by the Catholics of the centre, it brought a great deal of publicity and was condemned more severely than in France.

In Kamerun, the 'imperial chancellor of the protectorate, Leist, had the wives of Dahomey soldiers whipped in the presence of their husbands, which resulted in December 1893 in a revolt of the soldiers. He had female convicts brought to him from the prison at night for his sexual gratification. He was brought before a disciplinary council and condemned to be transferred to an equivalent post, with loss in seniority, for 'an error in the cause of duty'.

The scandal was such that the government had to quash the sentence, and a new judgement condemned him to dismissal from office.[50]

Assessor [Judge] Wehlan obtained admissions from accused persons by beating them with a cane; he condemned people falsely or without justification, on mere suspicion, and handed prisoners over to the soldiers, who executed them for their own amusement. He was condemned by the disciplinary council to a fine of 500 marks and removal to a post of equal standing. Captain Kannenberg had Kamerun chiefs beaten to death when they showed unwillingness to learn German. He was dismissed the service and condemned to three years in prison.[51]

REFERENCES

1. Cf. L. Rolland and P. Lampué, *Précis de législation coloniale*. Paris, Dalloz, 1940 (3rd edition).

2. H. Cosnier, op. cit., p. 141.

3. Ibid., introduction, p. xiv.

4. Ibid., p. 140.

5. *Rapport d'ensemble sur la situation générale de la Guinée française en 1906*. Conakry, Imprimerie Ternaux (1907).

6. *Rapport d'ensemble sur la situation dans la colonie de Haut-Sénégal-et-Niger en 1906*. Bordeaux, Gounouilhou, 1909, p. 18.

7. Mgr. Augouard, *Trente-six années au Congo*, vol. III, p. 16. Letter of 1 January, 1900.

8. Ibid., pp. 17–18.

9. Decree of 24 March, 1901.

10. It had the added advantage, in the eyes of the colonial administration, of leading to a permanent deficit in the first budget, which had to be made up from subsidies out of the second: in budgetary matters, this placed the general council of Senegal at the mercy of the governor! (cf. J. B. Corgeron, *Le Protectorat en Afrique occidentale française et les chefs indigènes*. Bordeaux, Y. Cadoret, 1920).

11. 'The empty ownerless lands in the colonies and the territories of French West Africa shall belong to the State' (decree of 23 October, 1904, Part II, Article 10).

12. *Rapport d'ensemble sur la situation générale de la Guinée française en 1906,* pp. 21-2.

13. He was appointed governor at St. Pierre and Miquelon.

14. *L'Afrique occidentale française* (Conakry), 11 February, 1911.

15. M. Crespin, 'Alpha Yaya et M. Frézouls', *Revue indigène*, 1906, No. 2, pp. 45-6.

16. National Archives of the Republic of Guinea, I.E.2, I.E.3 and I.E.7.

17. *L'Afrique occidentale française*, 22 September, 1911.

18. A. Akindele and C. Aguessy, *Contribution à l'étude de l'histoire de l'ancien royaume de Porto-Novo.* Dakar, Institut Français d'Afrique Noire, 1953.

19. They do no other than follow the example of their European superiors.

20. It is even worse, owing to the often artificial character of the chief system and the lack of authority of the chiefs.

21. H. Labouret, *A la recherche d'une politique indigène dans l'Ouest africain.* Paris, Editions du Comité de l'Afrique Française, 1931, p. 35.

22. G. Hardy, *Histoire Sociale de la colonisation française.* Paris, Larose, 1953, pp. 178-9.

23. Author's italics.

24. Report of the Governor-General W. Ponty to the Council of Government, 20 June, 1910. *Bulletin du Comité de l'Afrique française*, No. 7, July 1910.

25. Author's italics.

26. G. Teullière, 'Alpha Yaya et la politique indigène', *Revue indigène*, No. 67, November 1911, pp. 615-16.

27. The circle comprised generally two, three or four sub-divisions, one administered directly by the commander of the circle, the others by heads of sub-divisions (or administrators) surbordinate to the commander.

28. G. Vieillard, 'Notes sur le Peulhs du Fouta-Djalon', *Bulletin de 'Institut français d'Afrique Noire*, No. 1, 1940, p. 129.

29. H. Labouret, *A la recherche d'une politique indigène dans l'Ouest africain.* Paris, Editions du Comité de l'Afrique française, 1931, p. 94.

30. As in the case of Georges Hardy. The text quoted above by William Ponty suffices to contradict this interpretation.

31. Author's italics.

32. Circular of 15 August, 1917. *Bulletin du Comité de l'Afrique française.* No. 12, December 1917, p. 270.

33. When in 1840 Senegal received a regular system of administration it was limited to the island of Gorée, the port of St. Louis-du-Sénégal and some ports of call on the river. Dakar was not occupied until 1857. The royal ordinance of 7 September, 1840, laid down the powers of the governor, assisted by a council of administration (where local commerce was represented). A general council was established at St. Louis and an arrondissement council at Gorée. It was a more or less well-adapted copy of the institutions in France, analogous to the model used in the other 'old' colonies (Antilles, Réunion, the French West Indies).

34. For details of this question and the controversies to which it gave rise see Lamine Gueye, *De la situation politique des Sénégalais originaires des communes de plein exercise.* Paris, Ed. de la Vie Universitaire, 1922.

35. A decree of 25 May, 1912, laid down the following conditions for French subjects in French West Africa who wished to apply for citizenship:

1. to be born and domiciled in French West Africa;
2. to have attained the age of twenty-one years;
3. to know how to read and write or be holder of the Legion of Honour or the Médaille Militaire, or to have rendered exceptional services to France or the colony;
4. to give proof of the means of existence, a good life and behaviour;

5. to have rendered proof of devotion to French interests or of ten years of service in a public or private enterprise.

The colonial administration thus had all the means to raise obstacles to naturalisation; for it was violently hostile to the principle. The beneficiaries were insignificant in number.

36. H. Labouret, *A la recherche d'une politique indigène dans l'Ouest africain*. Paris, Editions du Comité de l'Afrique française, 1931, p. 13.

37. H. Labouret, op. cit., recognises this by observing: 'None of the remedies proposed for a situation judged defective since 1909 has succeeded. They were empirical, applying only to the chiefs, instead of considering the overall situation.'

38. Charles Régismanset, *Questions coloniales*. Paris, Larose, 1912, p. 94.

39. Ibid., p. 183.

40. Paris, Flammarion, 1910.

41. Ch. Régismanset, op. cit., p. 183.

42. Jules Harmand, op. cit., p. 153.

43. Examples quoted by C. W. Newbury, 'The Formation of the Government-General in French West Africa', *Journal of African History*, I, 1, 1960, pp. 111–28.

44. P. Lampué, 'La promulgation des lois et des décrets dans les Territoires d'Outre-mer', *Annales africaines*, 1956, No. 1, pp. 7–26.

45. In 1908 the 'reserve funds' of French West Africa ran to 9,800,000 as against 1,800,000 in 1895 (of this: general budget, 2,400,000; Guinea, 2,480,000; Dahomey, 1,500,000; Senegal, 1,100,000; Ivory Coast, 1,100,000; Upper-Senegal-and-Niger, 1,000,000). *Bulletin du Comité de l'Afrique française*, No. 4, April 1908, p. 129.

46. Entrusted to his 'friends' at the Lhoste Bank. Merlin, after leaving the administration, became director of a colonial bank. On his venality see General Hilaire, *Du Congo au Nil*. Marseille, 1930, p. 298.

47. Côte de l'Or, name of the future Ivory Coast.

48. Reichsanzeiger of 27 June, 1884 (cited by H. Brunschwig, *L'Expansion allemande outre-mer du XVe siècle à nos jours*, Paris, 1957, p. 131).

49. H. Stoecker, *Kamerun unter deutscher Kolonialherrschaft*. Berlin, Rütten and Loening, 1960, p. 84.

50. Ibid., p. 145.

51. H. Brunschwig, op. cit., p. 159.

CHAPTER IV

PACIFICATION

In the eyes of the great powers the victory at Kousseri sanctioned the domination of France over the territories which it had been allocated under treaties concluded with its imperialist rivals – in particular Great Britain and Germany. All that remained to be done was to make the populations acknowledge this authority. In certain regions, as along the coast, where the occupation was of long standing and settlements were relatively dense, the problem was virtually solved. The same applied where the existence of long-established states made it possible to use the ingrained habits of submission to authority, with recourse to local chiefs as mediators; this was the case in the Sudan.

This did not apply to the Saharan regions and the northern and eastern regions of Chad, where difficulty of access delayed effective possession.[1] Here establishments set up in the most important centres – which were separated by immense distances – had to be complemented by mobile police forces (*méharistes*).

In Mauritania, French penetration encountered the hostility of Ma El-Ainin, son of the religious reformer Mohamed Fadel. A native of Hodh, Ma El-Ainin took up residence in 1873 in Seguiet El-Hamra (still part of the Spanish Sahara). He claimed the authority of the Sultan of Morocco and with his brother's support kept the young Emir of Adrar, Ahmed Ould Aïda, under his protection. Coppolani, the first 'commissioner-general' of the Territory of Mauritania (1904), was killed in a surprise attack on Tidika. Adrar's resistance was finally broken by the Gouraud troops (1907–9), the capture of Tichit (1911) and the occupation of Oualata (27 January, 1912). Ma El-Ainin died in 1910 after being proclaimed sultan and having unsuccessfully sought to seize Fez. But Mauritania was exhausted.

The requisitioning of camels, oxen and sheep, which were indispensable for the transportation of food supplies for the troops, exhausted the country's main resource, livestock. It will take years to recoup the herds of camels, delicate animals, which literally wasted away on account of the inexperience of Gouraud and his followers.[2]

Of Taoudéni, the principal salt-mining centre, Captain Bonafous noted calmly that 'wars and the breaking-up of caravans' between 1905 and 1912 had caused the death by starvation of the entire population, which had to be totally replaced.[3]

El-Hiba, Ma El-Ainin's successor, proclaimed himself sultan and took Sous and Marrakesh (1912); beaten in Morocco, he fell back upon Adrar (January 1913). Lieutenant-Colonel Mouret, military commander of the territory, ignoring the possible diplomatic implications, replied with a raid on Smara, the capital created by Ma El-Ainin, in the middle of 'Spanish' territory; the stronghold was destroyed and Ould Aïda, who accompanied the Mouret, was reinvested in his functions as Emir of Adrar. In 1918 he was 'banished' to Saint-Louis, on the grounds that letters from the camp of El-Hiba had been found in his possession, then re-installed in 1920.

In Niger itself, Aïr was occupied in 1904, Kaouar and Bilma in 1905. But the position of these outposts remained precarious. In Chad, the occupation of Abéché, the capital of Wadai (1909), was followed by two reverberating disasters: the annihilation of the Fiegenschuh troops at Wadi Kadja in January 1910 and the defeat at Doroté on 9 November, 1910, when Colonel Moll, military commander of Chad, was killed. A general revolt of Wadai had to be suppressed in May–August 1911; the resistance of the Sultan of Dar Kouti, Mohamed-es-Senoussi (1911) and of his son Kamoun (1912) also had to be broken.[4]

The closeness of contested border areas and of those not under control prolonged the military operations for some time: in Borkou, the presence of a Turkish garrison until 1912 at Aïn Galakka[5] made resistance easier, Turkey not having recognised the Anglo-French treaty of delimitation of the borders of Chad, Libya and the Anglo-Egyptian Sudan. The Italian–Turkish war of 1912 and the loss of Libya by the Ottoman Empire made it possible for Colonel Largeau to take up residence in Aïn Galakka in 1913. General Hilaire described the capture of Aïn Galakka on 27 November, 1913, thus:

. . . wild confusion, each alley having to be taken, each house, one after the other, from the madmen determined to bury themselves to the last under the ruins of their sanctuaries, for their faith, their families and their ill-gotten property. The flames finally finished off the work of shrapnel, bullets and bayonets. . . . Street and house battles in the old way, without mercy being shown on either side, pillage and even . . . some rape.[6]

On the other hand, the absence of an effective Spanish occupation of Rio de Oro encouraged Moorish resistance to continue there until 1934–6; the occupation of Tindouf only took place in 1934.

In the forest regions, and in regions where the local tribes had never been subjected to organised states nor even recognised any superior political authority, the difficulties were greater; there was no native chiefdom there to rely on. In the absence of organised states, the actual penetration did not meet with serious obstacles, and the peoples tolerated the establishment of posts on condition that the French administrators and military staff did not interfere with their affairs. But any attempt to raise porters or to impose taxation caused hostilities to break out. Apart from the French posts and the occasional main lines of communication, the peoples remained effectively independent. The same applied to nearly all the territory of French Equatorial Africa (the interior of Gabon, the Middle Congo and Ubangi-Shari), the entire forest zone of the Ivory Coast, the forests of Guinea (where the Liberian frontier, theoretically, offered comfortable refuge), and the 'paleonigritic' tribes (the Coniagui and Bassari of the Senegal-Guinea region, the Dogon, and the mountain tribes of Atakora, Lobi and elsewhere).

To open up these territories for 'development', or in other words for colonial exploitation, the administrative system described above had to be imposed; not only a network of administrative and military posts, but the introduction of chiefdoms acting as intermediaries, permitting the raising of taxes, the supply of forced labour, and so on. This could not be imposed other than by force upon peoples accustomed to living in freedom.

On this process, by antithesis, colonial history has bestowed the name 'pacification'. It took the form of a long and cruel series of military operations, aimed at disarming the population and removing any possibility of resistance among them.

1. The 'Pacification' of the Ivory Coast

The 'pacification' of the Ivory Coast can serve as an example. It was the work of Governor Angoulvant, a 'theoretician' of the system, the apostle of 'strong-arm methods', who felt the need to explain and justify his actions at great length, although he left in the dark certain embarrassing aspects, on which some contemporary accounts can throw light.

The colony, established in 1893, and enlarged with part of the former military Sudan, seemed 'well in hand'. With the exception of the lands bordering Liberia, most of the territory had been thoroughly explored, and covered with a network of posts. And had not the last serious military operations (the fall of Samory, the Assikasso affair and the occupation of Baoulé in 1898–1900) sanctified the French annexation? A poll tax, already in force in the circles of the former Sudan, had been introduced all over the territory by 1901.

However, the establishment of a regular administration did not put an end to resistance in the forest region and around its edges, particularly in the Baoulé country. This latter region had been forcibly occupied since 1900, but guerrilla warfare continued incessantly.

The considerable porterage needed to supply thousands of men who occupied the country soon exasperated the Baoulé; their refusal gave place to numerous military operations which lasted throughout 1902 . . . and whose only result was to encourage further insurrection. The situation was complicated still further by the death of two very important individuals: Kouamé Guié, chief of the Warebros of Sakasso, heir to the conqueress of Baoulé, Aoura Pokou; and Acafou, the rich and influential chief of the southern N'gbans. The more so since the two chiefs fell to wrangling which, in the eyes of the natives, might, though wrongly [sic] assume a troublesome aspect.[7]

Between 1900 and 1906, revolt and military repression alternated without clear results; not only did the Baoulé remain partly unsubdued, and not only did the penetration of the upper region of the Cavally river and the Sassandra make no headway, but security was uncertain even in the lagoon region; attacks took place 8 km. from Bingerville, the seat of the colonial administration.[8] In 1908, when Governor Angoulvant took command, he summed up the situation thus:

The only areas occupied and effectively held were the north, the savannah (part of the former Sudan re-attached to the Ivory Coast), the coastal region in the south and a narrow strip of territory in the east, from Assinie to Indénié; Baouléland was half occupied. Eleswhere, there are only a few isolated posts under siege. *We receive no money* in the regions listed below as unknown, hostile or doubtful. *Trade does not exist and there is no security.*[9]

In his theoretical studies, Angoulvant rejected the 'absurdity' of 'peaceful penetration'. Colonisation could only be imposed by force.

Our enemy is our master, the story-tellers used to say. And if we do not hear this said in good French, it is thought and murmured in nearly all the dialects of Africa and elsewhere.[10]

The Africans were indifferent to the argument of the 'work of civilisation' (*l'oeuvre civilisatrice*), and

> continued to consider us as much as ever as intruders, reckoning that they were less wretched before our arrival. . . .[11] It cannot be supposed that the administrator's only mission is to please. The moment must come when he has to make demands. . . .[12] Let them try to find a country on this earth, however small, where the administration is loved, except by those who make a living from it . . . no such country exists. . . .[13] Certainly we have posts. But the officers in charge did not leave them. They would not have been able to do so except on the condition of never exercising any powers and of giving away a great deal. If our penetration is peaceful, it is due to the fact that our agents are content to remain inside their residences or to pay for the right of moving about unpretentiously at the price both of presents and their dignity.[14] Certainly explorers can move through new country a first time, and traders can traverse it. *They do not make any demands.* . . . But the head of a post is not placed in a region and paid simply to observe nature and pursue his ethnographical, botanical, geological or linguistic studies. He is there to administer. The meaning of this word administer is, after all, imposing rules, limiting individual liberties to ensure the freedom of all, gathering taxes, in subservience to the aims that are to be attained in the higher interests of civilisation.[15]

As to the 'higher interests of civilisation', Angoulvant gives a more explicit definition in one of his reports to the governor-general.

> In all that was done before, in the interests of the colony, military action was subordinated to political and administrative action, which in their turn must be determined by taking into consideration above all *the advantages which our settlers and our traders can expect and the economic interests at stake.*[16]

Angoulvant did not hesitate to impose his policy, in the name of the higher and well-understood interests of colonisation, in contrast to the short-sightedness of certain merchants who

> considered any region as pacified where they carried on their trade more or less freely; they did not worry whether the native paid taxes, did statute labour, or agreed to submit his disputes to justice.[17] What has to be established above all is the indisputable principle of our authority. . . . On the part of the natives, the acceptance of this principle must be expressed in a deferential welcome and absolute respect for our representatives whoever

they may be, in the full payment of taxes at a uniform rate of 2.50 francs, in serious co-operation in the construction of tracks and roads, in the acceptance of paid porterage, in the following of our advice [sic] in regard to labour, in recourse to our justice. . .[18] Signs of impatience or disrespect towards our authority, and the deliberate lack of goodwill are to be repressed without delay.[19]

From the outset of his administration Governor Angoulvant put his methods into operation. He started in November 1908 with operations in the Man region where the post, established in July that year, had been besieged by the Dan, 'indomitable savages . . . [who] wish to chase us out of the country'.[20]

Not being able to go far, owing to the weakness of our military forces, Captain Laurent [in charge of the post] limited himself to dealing rigorously with the village of Déagoui, quite close to the post. . . . He arrested the notables of the village of Gouapolé who, though compromised, had come to declare their loyalty.

The arrival of reinforcements finally made it possible to proceed to more serious matters.

On the next day, the repressive operations began against the villages close to the post. On the 8th, fires burnt on the four corners of the horizon: Ziélé, Kogoui, Gbouetongoui, Gouama and Man were destroyed; on the 9th and 10th it was the turn of the farming villages in the neighbourhood, whose stores of rice were taken to the post.[21]

In December 1909 the big village of Osrou in the lagoon region was visited with a similar punitive expedition. This was what Governor Angoulvant, who liked to be systematic, was to call the 'period of lack of means of action and setbacks'. It was to end at the beginning of 1910, with a large-scale 'setback', which nearly cost the governor-theoretician his post, but which finally permitted him to enter upon the 'period of brisk action and military expeditions'.

The construction of the railway line from the Ivory Coast had begun in 1904; from the coast the line crossed the forest zone towards Dimbokro. This first section was completed by the beginning of 1910. Then, on the morning of 6 January, all the Abbey forest people rose in rebellion. 'Between kilometres 40 and 120, the country rose as one in answer to a command.'[22] The railway and its installations were attacked, and between kilometres 24 and 42 alone the track was cut at twenty-five points. Neither the head of the post at Agboville, who knew the language of the country, nor the

Europeans, nor the Senegalese and Bambara living in the regions had in the least suspected that preparations for a revolt were afoot. On the eve of the rising, all the Abbey boys and women in their service disappeared.

Governor Angoulvant has nothing but contempt for these Abbeys:

Wild, savage, on the lowest rung of humanity, and, though near the railway, they refuse to come and see it; they lead a primitive life of nomads and hunters, and, so far, do not pay any taxes [but] are determined to oppose by force the penetration of their country.[23]

The governor, however, acknowledged that 'the Abbeys found the occasion propitious to take reprisals for the unfortunate conduct of certain wood-cutters, who have now disappeared[24] from the colony'.[25] The press of the period did not see the event as the 'savage' Abbeys' hostility to progress:

One must look for the real cause of the uprising in fear of being completely without weapons, of feeling themselves defenceless at the mercy of the administration. This fear will be understood when certain facts become known, like the following:

1. At Bingerville, in a single month, the people of the surrounding villages furnished 1,200 days of labour without seeing a centime's pay.

2. In the course of a peaceful talk, as the natives indicated they wished to get up to depart, they were shot at without any provocation.

3. Roads six metres in width were built all over the colony . . . the work was carried out without pay by the natives in regions where the population is scattered.[26]

The administration also undertook a general confiscation of firearms, without indemnity or reimbursement of the arms-tax levied that same year. It was a revolt of desperation.

The gravity of the situation was such that General Caudrelier, commander-in-chief of the troops in West Africa, and Governor-General William Ponty went to the scene. Angoulvant's policy was subjected to sharp criticism: he had wanted to move too fast.

The tax, which had ranged from 0·50 to 1 franc, or to 2 francs at the most, was suddenly raised to 4·50 francs. Its collection was put in the hands of police contingents exclusively.

Concrete results of these contingents: tax incompletely gathered at the cost of villages burnt down, chiefs and natives killed in large numbers, heads of chiefs put up on poles, the imposition of fines.[27]

The levying of taxes and fines everywhere met with one special difficulty – the shortage or non-existence of coin. Equivalents had to be accepted in their stead, valued at a rate of exchange that was greatly to the advantage of the colonial authorities: manillas (anklets)[28] at the rate of 30 francs for 15 bundles; oxen at 50 francs per head; gold dust at 100 francs for 50 grams.[29] A licence to carry firearms costing 5 francs had been imposed by Angoulvant (20 July, 1908) which hit 'all the natives of the colony, because all of them own a gun and some of them have two'.[30] Then, immediately after it had been levied, the disarming of the inhabitants was undertaken (21 August, 1909).

In all these extortions the 'colonial interest' was not forgotten. Here, for example, are the results of the Osrou operation, which was mentioned above:

> The village of Osrou had 14,600 francs levied in taxes. A contingent of 300 men was sent to collect this sum by force. Osrou was taken and condemned, after payment of the taxes, to a war fine of 100,000 francs, payable in silver within eight days!
>
> The village did not possess this exorbitant sum. There were those – and some allege that the idea was suggested by the local administration and certain officials agreed to it – there were those who *mortgaged the coming harvest*, this harvest being credited to the trading firms who paid the sum for the natives.[31]

But in the long run, the alarm caused by the revolt of the Abbeys turned out to be of service to Angoulvant. He was backed up by the governor-general; military reinforcements of nearly 1,400 men, all Senegalese, were sent to him. The enraged European settlers were in favour of 'strong measures'.

> Damage done to the track . . . the losses suffered by the traders along the route, by the mahogany growers whose timber-yards lined the road, were so serious that the most terrible repressions were authorised and justified. . . . The villages taken were burnt down. *No pity was shown to prisoners.* The severed heads were put up on poles by the railway stations or in front of the huts in the villages.[32]

Governor Angoulvant, with the necessary military strength at his disposal, did not limit himself to simple repressive operations; he wanted once and for all to break down all possibility of resistance. He himself enumerated and justified the means employed.

1. *Disarmament, the complete surrender of firearms.* The first and fundamental measure, 'the most effective sanction'. Angoulvant bluntly criticised Binger, who, in 1895, under the pretext that the

country was pacified and that local commerce would lose 300,000 francs per year, had annulled the decree forbidding the import of firearms into the colony. The guns provided by the trader may have been of limited range, but they constituted dangerous weapons in the forest, for ambushes. He was reproached for making them pay the tax and then confiscating the guns without indemnity. Those from whom they had been confiscated had, 'in general', not paid the tax; there could be no question of indemnity as it was a 'war-time measure'. It was also objected that the cessation of the arms trade had injured commerce and had left men and their crops without defence against wild beasts. A decree of 15 May, 1911, authorised the carrying of arms for 'a few safe privileged persons'.

In any event, the economic advantages of disarmament prevailed over the inconveniences.

With their firearms, which they loved to use more than anything else, the natives give themselves over far too much to the pleasures of the hunt, which thus becomes their exclusive source of food.[33]

Disarmed, the people of the forest were forced to abandon the hunt and take to agriculture, the only way to maintain commerce. By 30 September, 1914, 111,912 guns had been collected on the Ivory Coast.

2. *Arrest and internment outside the colony of chiefs and witch-doctors guilty of fomenting revolt.* Officially, there were 220 deported persons at Port-Etienne and in Dahomey. For the author this was 'insufficient' punishment. Capital punishment was needed (in fact, this was used without official sanction, as texts quoted above prove). He proposed the institution of criminal courts analogous to those existing in Indochina, and deplored this 'regrettable gap' in French institutions in West Africa. Governor Angoulvant was consoled, however, when he noted that exile to Port-Etienne nearly always led to the same result, namely death.

3. *Payment of retroactive taxes and war fine.* The people, subjected and disarmed as they were, had to pay taxes which could be back-dated to 1901. Moreover, reparations were imposed on them, the legality of which has been contested. The 1904 decree on the native population established their 'indisputable legality'. Moreover, their payment was no problem for the rich, thanks to their palm groves and gold-bearing deposits. Osrou, for example, was taxed 75,000 francs;[34] the district of Dabou 66,676 francs; the tribute to be paid by the Abbeys amounted to 79,700 francs; the Akoué paid 44,850 francs, the Attié 18,200 francs.

Their insolence came from their accumulated wealth; deprived of it, they were led to a more modest attitude and forced to work, which alone induces morality and educates races whose evolution has hardly begun.[35]

4. *Acceptance of annual taxes, of porterage and statute labour, opening up of roads and tracks.* Disarmed, deprived of their chiefs, plundered of their wealth, the people were forced into circumstances which gave them no choice as to whether or not to accept the demands of the administration, and furnish labour and products to the settlers and the traders.

5. *Destruction of camps and settlement in villages.* In view of the conditions of life offered by the forest and their level of social evolution, the forest people usually did not live in large settlements but in camps, limited to one big family, that were

> often remote one from the other, sometimes close together in fertile regions, but each with its own zone of cultivation and its own paths.[36]

This isolation favoured the 'taste for hunting', 'laziness', 'anarchy' and the 'absence of the chief's authority'. The camps were systematically destroyed, the inhabitants forced to establish themselves in villages founded near to posts or along the roads. This was to reinforce the authority of the chiefs and it offered more facilities for taking a census of the population. No one was to advance 'respect for traditions' as an objection to his policy; 'we are there to modify them'.[37]

The Akoué were resettled from 247 camps into seventeen villages; the N'gban from 312 camps into forty-seven villages.

The pursuit of this operation was to be permanent.

> . . . The regrouping done, it will still be necessary, in the years to come, to seek out and destroy camps which are being built anew, for various reasons; disputes with the chief, discord in the village, or simply persistence in the atavistic instincts of independence. . . . Granted, one must distinguish between established camps and temporary shelter necessitated by the distance of the fields, caused by crop rotation.[38]

Thus the 'period of brisk action' gave way to the 'period of slow action', to columns of troops and the policy of the 'oil stain', by which Governor Angoulvant 'pacified' the Ivory Coast between 1908 and 1916. As an author he acknowledged several times the 'energetic' and 'courageous' defence of the populations, only to qualify them later as 'savages . . . excited by spirits, fanaticised by witch-doctors'. After the 'Abbey expedition' (January–April 1910) he described the 'N'gban contingent' (30 May–31 July, 1910), 'independent, brave, tenacious people' who 'refused absolutely to give up their guns' and 'chased the head of post at Ouassou from their villages'.[39] Then followed the resistance of the Saléfoué, under the leadership of Boni N'Diolé (August–December 1910); then the 'Bandama' expedition (1 January–1 July, 1911) against the Nanafoué-Kpri, led by a woman, the chief of the village of Salekrou, who had already driven out the French in 1902. There were operations in the Zuénoula sector against the Nyas who had never 'been hostile . . . for a long time they had refused to pay their taxes, but decided to do so a short time ago'. They joined the revolt when they learnt that 'we want complete disarmament and the back payment of taxes'.[40] 'Captain Larroque went to punish the Yansuas, who had given an insolent reply to a request for porters . . . between the 20th and 25th, he burnt down all the villages of the Niono . . . from the 29th to the 31st, he razed to the ground five more large villages.'[41] In the sector of Sinfra 'the Fina, who refused to work on the roads, were attacked simultaneously by Captain Plomion and Captain Javouhey'.[42] In the West, the African population fled by the thousand to Liberia.

At the end of his administration Angoulvant knew how to 'refute the sophisms [notably that of 'peaceful conquest'] which have too often misled the thinking and compromised the interests of colonial France.'[43] He was promoted to the governor-generalship of French West Africa, followed by that of French Equatorial Africa. After leaving the service, he finished his career in politics and business. In 1924, Angoulvant had himself elected deputy for the French Indies 'under suspect conditions'.[45] Subsequently, if one is to believe General Hilaire, he became involved with liquor smuggling into the U.S.A. during Prohibition. Towards the 1930s he became one of the important agents of colonial finance capital, being member of the board of administration of, among others, the Compagnie générale des colonies, of the Banque commerciale africaine, the Compagnie d'exploitation forestières africaines, the Plantations réunies de l'Ouest africain, the Compagnie forestière sangha-Oubangi, and the Plantations et palmeraies de l'Ogôué.

2. The 'Pacification' of other Hard-cores of Resistance in French West Africa

With more or less method and at varying speeds, a policy inspired by the same principles was applied wherever resistance was found. In the forest regions of Guinea, the Guerzé, Manon, Toma and

Kissi had always resisted the Sudanese conquerors, for the last occasion at Samory. The frontier fixed by the agreement of 8 December, 1892, gave Liberia all the forest region, including Beyla. The operations against Samory soon led the French troops to cross this theoretical line. The vagueness in defining the frontier and the ineffectiveness of the Liberians' occupation of the area aided the resistance of the forest people. In 1894, at N'Zapa, Lieutenant Lecerf unexpectedly encountered a convoy of arms and munitions from Monrovia destined for Samory, and was killed.[46] The Toma massacred the Bailly and Pauly mission in 1898 without causing the least reaction.

In 1899 this sector was made part of Guinea, and organised into a 'military region' with Kissidougou, Sampouyara, Diorodougou and Beyla as advance posts.[47] The Conrart expedition, which set out to liberate the post of Diorodougou which was under constant attack from the Toma, finished by seizing the fortified village of Bafobakoro (28 February, 1900), but the French officer in charge of the operations was killed, while the enemy war chief Koko Tolno took refuge at N'Zapa on Liberian territory. A little later, operations were started against Chief Kissi Digo; and the centre of resistance, the village of Niadou, was burnt down by Lieutenant Crébessac.[48] The annual report for 1903 on the general situation in French Guinea noted:

> The spirit of independence of the natives is very great. They live in villages, each one independent of all the others. The authority of the village chiefs is very weak and that of the chiefs of the canton, whom we had hoped to set up in the military circles, is absolutely nil.[49]

In 1903, Franco-Liberian negotiations on frontier settlement failed, but were renewed in 1904–5; at the same time the Liberian commissioners Cummings and Loomax set about the occupation of the hinterland. A race broke out between the French and the Liberians to obtain the most favourable positions. In 1905, a party from the garrisons of Kissidougou, Sampouyara, Diorodougou and Beyla was reported to be in the south at Bamba, Bofosso, Kuonkan and Gouecké. Soon operations were undertaken to join the new posts with a road to run roughly parallel to the frontier. Numerous operations took place between 1905 and 1907: at Bamba, in the region of the great Millimou; at Bofosso, against Chief Kokogou; in the sector of Kuonkan the operations were intended to free the route Kuonka–Singuénou–Macenta–Bofosso, and were marked by the seizure of the Toma villages of M'Baléma and M'Balasso. In the

sector of Gouecké, Lieutenant Guignard destroyed the fortified
village of M'Palé.

But the most notorious episode of the Toma resistance took place
in the fortified village of Boussédou, to the east of Kuonkan. Colonel
Loomax, commander of the 'Frontier Force of Liberia', had sent
sharpshooters to various places and had the Liberian flag hoisted;
these operations had put the French on the defensive. At the beginning of 1907 the commander of the military region of Guinea arrived
at Kuonkan and authorised an attack on Boussédou. After a day of
battle (16 February, 1907) the French forces, who had taken the
first three palisaded entrenchments, arrived at a surrounding wall
and had to withdraw with heavy losses. Two months later the attack
was renewed, this time with artillery. After four hours of shooting
the assault failed, Lieutenant Guignard was killed and a retreat was
ordered. Two demoralised lieutenants abandoned their position and
returned to Kuonkan. The besieged, who knew that artillery would
finally destroy their palisades, profited from this break in the siege
to evacuate Boussédou during the night and make for Liberia. The
following morning (1 April, 1907) when the riflemen started the
assault after intense artillery shelling they found the village deserted.
A Swiss explorer, Dr. Volz, who had been rash enough to remain
alone in the village, was killed by gunshots. The French soldiers
declared they had noticed neither the Liberian flag flying above the
village nor the Swiss flag on the house of Dr. Volz.

Resistance continued in 1908: the frontier mission had to give up
work to the east of Guéckédou where it received a defeat at the
hands of Koko Tolno; the village of N'Zapa, former ally of Samory,
was burnt down in the course of 'reprisals' for the death of Lieutenant Lecerf in 1894; in the battle of Koyama, Dr. Mariotte, who
accompanied the mission, was mortally wounded. These important
operations came to an end in October 1911 with the capture of
Samoe and N'Zérékoré. The villages of Théassou, Bossou, and
Thuo were burnt down by the French troops, but Captain Héquet,
their commander, and Barthié, the agent at the trading post, who
had provoked the intervention of the troops at N'Zérékoré, were
killed.[50] In the Coniagi country no clashes occured as long as the
commander of the post of Boussourah did not try to levy taxes. In
April 1902 Lieutenant Moncorgé, heading a column of troops
formed of riflemen and Fulani auxiliaries furnished by Alfa Yaya (the
mortal enemy of the Coniagi) came to demand the levy. The war
chief of the Coniagi clan of Ityo, Yalou-Téné, had replied to a
previous request that he was ready to pay taxes in millet or groundnuts, but that he did not recognise money.[51] At a distance of 150
metres from the village, Moncorgé demanded that the chief should

appear before him. The chief refused three times. He had good reasons to be prudent because, a short time before, the same Moncorgé had lured the King of N'Dama, Thierno Ibrahima, into his hands, then surprised him in his sleep and sent him in chains to Conakry, whence he was deported to the Congo, to die six months later.[52] With the butt of his revolver Moncorgé knocked down one of the Malinké whom the chief had sent to him as a messenger. The Coniagi warriors immediately took up arms, and Moncorgé and his troops were annihilated during a two-hour battle, on 16 April, 1902. Two years later, in April 1904, a punitive expedition of 500 men with artillery arrived to 'avenge' Moncorgé. The villages were burnt down, the women and children who had taken refuge in the forest were massacred with cannon, and Yalou-Téné and his warriors committed suicide to the last man in the blockhouse of Ityo (13 April, 1904).[53]

In 1908, the Dogon[54] rebelled against the abuse of tax-levying. The village of Pesséma refused to let the deputy administrator enter on a census-taking tour, whereupon the village chief, his son and the dignitaries were arrested and interned at Nioro. In September–October 1908, a 'police tour' ravaged their crops in the plains to force them to pay taxes. In January 1909 the inhabitants of Ibissa again prevented the deputy Vieyres from entering their village. On 31 May, Administrator D'Arboussier was surprised and attacked in the Pelinga gorges, and in November Deputy Vieyres was killed in the village of Kinian. A reprisal contingent of 500 men with four artillery pieces was sent against them for the express purpose of driving them off their rocks and forcing them to rebuild their villages on the plain. The six rebel villages, grouped in four centres of resistance, were taken one after the other. The last point of resistance, Ibissa, was taken on 14 January, 1910. 'Pacification' had been achieved.

In Niger, the most important episode officially started with the action of Marabout Saidou in the Djerma country. The religious impulse given by this blind old man, denounced to the authorities by Djermakoye, the traditional chief of the Djerma, who was worried about his influence, contributed to crystallising the discontent; but matters came to a head over resistance to tax-levying. The village of Kabakitanda had refused to pay the taxes and had killed two policemen sent to supervise the tax-gathering. This may have been done only in self-defence. The military administration reacted by sending troops (17 December, 1905–4 January, 1906). 'Though holy war had not been declared, the impact of the pitiless reprisals was none the less clear.'[55] Denounced as being responsible for the rebellion, Marabout Saidou managed to flee to Nigeria. But the

extortions of the troops provoked general insurrection in the villages
on the river, from Goudel to Sansanné Hausa. When Lieutenant
Fabre met his death, a new repressive expedition had to be sent
(14–17 January, 1906). A few months later, the Sultan of Zinder
Ahmadu was accused of having instigated the uprising and having
sought the support of the Sultan of Kano; he was discharged from
office and deported (30 March, 1906). Mention could also be made
of the operations against the Lobi (1903) and against the chiefs of
Upper Gambia. The latter tried to use the British frontier to protect
themselves against submission (1901, Fodé Kaba; 1908, Bayaga).

3. Operations in Equatorial Africa

We have quoted only a few significant episodes from the 'pacification' of French West Africa. In Equatorial Africa the geographical
and social conditions mentioned as affecting the forest region of the
Ivory Coast were also present, but on a much vaster scale. Over a
limited territory and at the price of systematic action during a
period of eight years, Angoulvant managed to break the capacity of
the populations to resist. In consequence, it became possible for civil
administration to become established, with a network of posts spread
out over the territory. The indigenous chiefs henceforth served as
intermediaries for the administration which, from time to time,
without great effort, managed to repress the sporadic revolts; this
was not difficult, since the people had been virtually disarmed.

It was extremely difficult to apply the same method on a much
vaster territory, with scattered populations, or where the social
disintegration was even greater. The kingships of the great federations of tribes on the Ivory Coast, without altogether having the
qualities of a state, had offered more compact resistance, but also
allowed for submission *en bloc*. In Equatorial Africa the social
conditions recalled those of the forest regions of Guinea and the
paleonigritic people of West Africa. Moreover, the resources of men
and materials possessed by the 'pacifiers' were even more limited.
In 1908 there were 1,000 infantry in the Congo proper and 1,200
in Chad, as against 10,000 in the Cameroons.[56]

Furthermore, the special character of French colonisation in
Equatorial Africa, already mentioned, provoked prolonged and
desperate resistance. Occupation was therefore extremely slow, and
the period of setbacks and that of 'brisk action' – to use Angoulvant's
terminology – was protracted over decades, without ever completely
breaking down the resistance. From the turn of the century onwards,
first the Marchand mission, then the Chad expedition, and finally

the establishment and subsequent exactions of agents of the chartered
companies, led to an endless cycle of revolts and repressions. In 1900,
effective occupation was limited to a few posts and control of the
main lines of communication. By 1908, the progress achieved was
extremely modest. Between 1900 and 1908, revolts and reprisals
alternated continuously. There were operations in Sangha (1904)
and at Lobaye (1904–7). In Lobaye there was not a single administrative post. The agents of the chartered companies, Europeans and
Senegalese, made clear divisions of the country. A revolt broke out
in 1904. Chickens, palm wine and women were sent to the most
detested traders under pretext of a feast. When they were dead
drunk, the trading posts were invaded, the rifles seized and the
traders massacred.[57] A reprisal contingent scoured the region for
four years, but finally withdrew. In Upper Kotto (Ubangi) operations were conducted in 1906 against Chief Vridi Baram Bakié.
The chief was beaten on 7 April, 1907, but the region was soon
evacuated.[58]

With the establishment of a government-general, a series of big
operations were undertaken to 'pacify the country'. Mangin wrote
in 1908:

> The Congo, *a peaceful conquest*, has never been conquered or
> pacified. The metropolis today seems determined to give it the
> only instrument which may permit its development: military
> force.[59]

Reprisals were made easier by lack of unity among the population,
their resistance tactics being based on fixed defences – namely the
bandza, which was the forest equivalent of the *tata*, a blockhouse
several storeys high made of great tree trunks. But their complete
disarmament was far more difficult. The vast forest regions gave
them a chance to manoeuvre; rudimentary armament, limited of
necessity to projectile weapons, was enough to make ambush warfare
effective.

The 1908 operations, undertaken with insufficient troops, provoked uprisings on a wider scale. These were similar to those on the
Ivory Coast in 1908–9, the 'period of lack of means of action and of
setbacks' of Governor Angoulvant. In Gabon,

> apart from the sea, coast region, and the banks of the Ogooué,
> and possibly the immediate environs of Libreville, one could say
> that our authority is powerless, and nowhere can safety be
> assured.[61]

At the beginning of 1908, an agent of the charter company of
N'Goko-Sangha charged with opening up a trading post at the

frontier, was arrested by the people and handed over to the German troops in Kamerun. At the company's request it was decided to set up posts on the Ivindo. But the Woleu N'Tem area had to be evacuated, and the whole of Upper N'Gounié was in revolt under the leadership of the war chief Mavouroulou. Further to the east at Djouah Sembé, 'very tough battles' were fought by troops under the command of, first, Garnier and later Colonel Mangin. In May 1908 a shot which 'burst at an inopportune moment' on the delegates of the villages summoned for a discussion provoked a general revolt.[62] After the departure of the troops, the trading posts of N'Goko-Sangha were attacked and pillaged (August–October 1908).

In the south, 'police operations' took place in the Mayombe and in the environs of Loango in reprisal for attacks against the trading posts of the Compagnie du Congo occidental, but these led to no tangible results. Also in 1908, troops under Captain Prokos and Lieutenant Mourin operated on the Lobaye and the Upper Ubangi: the centre of resistance was the 'elephant hunter's village' Bera N'Djoko, situated in the mountain massif on the Upper Ibenga. At the end of 1908 it was stated that this 'den' had been occupied and that the rebels had surrendered;[63] however, operations against the same village carried on into 1909. In the valley of the M'Poko, 'where the behaviour of the agents of the chartered companies had compromised security',[64] operations were undertaken against Chief Kougouloutou in 1908–9. The results (the occupation of Ivindo, evacuation of Woleu N'Tem and 'pacification' of the N'Goko-Sangha region and the Middle Ubangi) were poor, if not actually negative.

Under these circumstances, new measures were taken in 1909. The circulars of Governor-General Merlin (April and September 1909) laid down a 'programme of penetration, and classification, in order of urgency, of the regions to be occupied'. This meant increasing the number of posts permanently established instead of scouring the country with troops whose action lost all meaning when they left the scene of their operations. From these 'solid bases' the troops were to radiate out to 'close in and surround' the insubordinate, and to cut off their possible route of escape.

An autonomous high command of troops was set up in 1909 in the Congo, which, up to that time, had been subordinate to the general French West African command. Operations continued throughout 1909–11, with more substantial results. During that period the region of Mayombe straddling the Loudima–Loango road was 'pacified'; in August–September 1909 the Sicre troops in the Mocabé country (Upper N'Gounié) subjugated the region and imposed a war tribute, but did not succeed in capturing Chief

E

Mavouroulou; military detachments were installed at Lastoursville and Franceville, on the Upper Ogouué, but remained isolated in the middle of unsubdued country.

The most important operations were undertaken along the frontier of Gabon and the Cameroons where, after the 1908 frontier agreement, it was a matter of asserting the rights of France. In 1909–10 Woleu N'Tem was reoccupied and the operations in the Okano basin were aimed at linking this region to the post of N'Djolé. French troops had to fight against 'armed bands' of *binzima* (described as 'brigands') who had gained the support of numerous villages and set up a regular military organisation with ranks and uniforms, including red berets. Reconnaissance in the territory of Ekoreti, ceded to France in 1908, had

> shown that this country, never occupied or reconnoitred, is practically in the hands of the Germans; the majority of the villages have trading posts in perfect condition, run by traders from the Cameroons.[65]

In Ivindo, and on the Middle Ogooué, the Debieuvre troops 'pacified' the Bakota country. In Djouah Sembé (N'Goko-Sangha region) the operation began in 1908 and continued without interruption (Garnier's troops, May–June 1909; operation under Captain Curault, August–September 1909; capture of the fortified villages of Goudou, June 1910; the Blaise contingent on the Upper Mossaka, July–August 1910; operations under Captain Geoffroy against the Sangha-Sangha in the region of the Djouah, who had attacked the trading posts of the Upper Ogooué Company, August–September 1911).

On the Middle Ubangi, Captain Prokos, with 250 riflemen and 750 guerrilla soldiers, conducted operations in the Lobaye, Ibenga and Motaba regions, which belonged to the Compagnie forestière Sangha-Oubangi (August–September 1909). Bera N'Djoko was taken a second time. Prokos was then replaced by Captain Calisti (July–August 1910) who took a company farther north against the M'Bi (November 1910–February 1911). The peoples of the M'Poko were subjugated in 1910–11. On the Upper Ubangi the operations were directed against the rebel Chief Baram-Bakié, whose fortress on the N'Dahaye river was seized on 10 May, 1909. Definite submission was not obtained until 1912. The conquest of Chad took place in a similar manner. The political crisis of 1911 and the abandonment to Germany of a large part of the territory, made the future uncertain; but the withdrawal of troops from the ceded regions made it possible to cover the rest of the territory with military units.

Drawing up a balance-sheet at the end of 1912, Governor-General Merlin noted that territory effectively occupied had risen from 26 to 60 per cent. Between 1908 and 1911 the military units had risen from 3,400 to 7,200 men, the number of administrative districts from seventeen to fifty, the number of posts from eighty-seven to 144. The number of administrative personnel had almost tripled.[67] But it was still insufficient to control the country.

There still remains 40 per cent of the territory where our administration does not, in fact, exercise more than a weak influence, and 20 per cent of that represents still unpenetrated land.[68]

In Gabon the occupation, limited in 1908 to the coastal regions and certain points along the course of the Ogooué, had spread to the Ogooué basin and the Cameroon frontier; but the country was not truly 'in hand'. The two townships of Lastoursville and France-ville were occupied by administrators with a force of 100 regional police, in the centre of a region of 80,000 square km. of unpenetrated country.

Scarcely anywhere can our agents accomplish the simplest acts of rudimentary administration except with the help of armed forces; gunfire resounds every day and at every turn.[69]

In the Middle Congo 'a good part of the Bateke country, the country of the Bamota, the upper basins of the Kouilou, the Mossaka and the Ofia, have never recognised any authority'.[70] In Ubangi one half of the territory under military administration was unoccupied and unexplored. Conquest was impossible, the occupation forces being 'obliged to undertake incessant operations in their zone of action'. Reprisals by police columns became a rule. Governor-General Augagneur noted:

I arrived at Brazzaville in August 1920. A few weeks before, a police round-up had exterminated 538 natives – men, women and children – according to the report on the round-up kept by officers in charge. (In French Equatorial Africa, police tours were the rule; they passed through various regions several times a year.) This slaughter moved no one, neither the governor of the colony, the interim governor-general, nor the general in supreme command of the troops. On the contrary, the military authorities demanded rewards from the minister of war for the officers who had commanded this killing.[71]

Just as I am finishing this preface, I learn that the Baya in the Boda region have revolted and fled into the bush; they were exasperated by the actions of the administration charged with the forced recruitment of workers and labourers; these were sent far from their homes, and up to half never returned. . . . This is what the strong arm leads to.[72] From the arrival of the Marchand mission and the Gentil troops to 1920, and intermittently until 1930, secret or narrowly localised risings followed in close succession. The main feature of French penetration in French Equatorial Africa was that it was peaceful [sic], but this did not exclude a long laborious period of conquest.[73]

4. The Resistance in Togo and the Cameroons

The Germans, in order to establish themselves in the north of Togo, had had to break down the insurrection in the Konkomba country, provoked by the brutalities of Dr. Grüner, who in the market at Binaparba had caused the death by shooting of seventy-nine men, women and children, and the wounding of twenty. A relief column under the command of Lieutenant von Massow had broken the revolt, though not without difficulties (May 1897–March 1898). At the same time, the multiple-barrelled guns (*mitrailleuses*) of the same von Massow overcame the resistance of the primitively armed Kabré clan (January 1898).[74] Between 1897 and 1900 numerous 'police troops' achieved 'pacification'.[75]

In Kamerun, in spite of the stipulations of the 1884 treaty, the German authorities had forbidden the Douala to trade on the Senegal (1895); that was the origin of the bitter grievance which reached a climax in 1914. In 1899 the Boulou, 'who, it appears, wished to keep the monopoly of trade between the coast and the interior of the country',[76] rose up and laid siege to Kribi. The war continued in the interior until 1901, and the centre was not finally subdued until 1911.

In the north, the Passarge expedition (1893–4) was no more than an armed exploratory mission. The fall of Tibati (1899) made it possible for the German forces to move northwards and permitted them to set up a series of key positions (capture of N'Gaoundéré, 1901; capture of Maroua, 1902; submission of the Mandara country and the establishment of the post at Mora, 1902). The chief figure in the conquest, Major Hans Dominik, left a trail of terror which recalls that of Combes in Upper Guinea.

It was a question of slow conquest rather than the repression of resistance to colonisation. The systematic elimination of the African traders in favour of German trade, as well as the numerous exactions and the brutality which was the rule in that period of colonial exploitation, led to a state of tension which explains the execution in 1914 of numerous chiefs and dignitaries who had up till then been faithful helpers of the German administration. The expropriation of the Joss plateau at Douala to set up a 'European town' brought the conflict to a climax among the people who, in 1884, had appealed for German protection. Rudolf Manga Bell, the heir of 'King Bell' enthroned in 1910, led the resistance to the planned expropriation and then to the decree confirming it, issued on 15 January, 1913. He was dismissed on 4 August, 1913.

The Douala hired lawyers in Germany, whither they illegally sent an emissary, Ngoso Din, secretary to Rudolf Manga Bell, as their spokesman. Their case seemed due for re-examination, when the colonial administration made it known that Rudolf Manga Bell had been arrested for 'high treason', having fomented a rising in collaboration with the chiefs of the interior, and for having made contact with foreign powers. The declaration of war brought this affair to a tragic end. The trial opened on 7 August, 1914, and finished the following day with the execution by hanging of Rudolf Manga Bell and Ngoso Din. At the same time a series of arrests and executions of dignitaries took place: Chief Martin Samba of Eboloa was shot on 8 August, to be followed by Chief Madola of Grand Batanga and, several days later, the chiefs of the Lamibé of Kalfu and Mindiff and five dignitaries from the court of Maroua.

It is doubtful whether there had indeed been a plot on the part of the dignitaries. Anxiety in the face of increasing tension might have provoked contacts between the chiefs of ethnic groups who had never been allies in the past. It seems that Rudolf Manga Bell had sent emissaries to the chiefs of the interior to try to obtain their support in his conflict with the German administration. Njoya, the one he had sent to the King of the Bomoum, was handed over to the Germans by the latter chief.[77]

It is far more probable that the plot was invented in its entirety by the German colonial authorities to put an end to the Douala affair and to terrorise the population, who had been driven to extremities just at the moment when the authorities had been placed in a dangerous position by the outbreak of war. Father Mveng evokes the atmosphere by speaking of 'a fire breaking out which had been smouldering for years'. One can understand such draconian measures. The 'Little Whites' had been expelled in the preceding year, and the use of pidgin English had been prohibited and declared a 'crime against the state'! The atmosphere in Kamerun on the eve of the war was highly explosive.[78]

REFERENCES

1. See vol. I, p. 247.

2. G. Désiré-Vuillemin, *Contribution à l'histoire de la Mauritanie de 1900 à 1934*. Dakar, Edition Clairafrique, 1962, p. 179.

3. Capitaine V. Bonafes, 'Taoudinii hier et aujourd'hui', *Revue militaire de l'Afrique ouest française*, No. 21, 15 April, 1934, pp. 1–24.

4. On this affair, see Afa Ti Goumbé, 'Notes sur Senoussi', *Le Courrier européen*, 1911, pp. 313–16. The author denies that Senoussi had Crampel assassinated; he is said to have been killed by the Banda tribe between N'Dele and Krebedje. He cites the testimony of administrator Mercuri and of Auguste Chevalier on this subject. He is characterised as 'a remarkable man, one of the few intelligent persons I have met in Africa . . . a well-informed, perspicacious chief, greatly loved by his people'. The Crampel affair was dug up to justify his liquidation.

5. Occupied by French troops in 1907, later evacuated.

6. General Hilaire, *Du Congo au Nil*. Marseille, 1930, p. 199.

7. F. J. Clozel, *Dix ans à la Côte d'Ivoire*. Paris, Challamel, 1906, p. 79.

8. A study undertaken in 1910 gave this partial list:

1896: Revolt of Zaranon. Assassination of administrator Poulle.

1898: Assikasso Affair. Osrou Revolt.

1899: Burning of the post at Toumodi.

1900–2: General revolt of the Baoulé.

1903: Mango Revolt.

1904: Bingerville attack.

1905: Agba contingent.

1906: Sassandra and Upper-Cavally operations.

1907: Contingent sent against the Gouro . . . etc.

('La situation politique en Côte d'Ivoire', *Bulletin du Comité de l'Afrique française*, No. 2, February 1910, pp. 60–2.) On the situation in the West of the Ivory Coast (Cavally and Sassandra basins) see: C. Wondji, 'La Cote d'Ivoire occidentale, periode de pénétration pacifique, 1890–1908', *Revue française d'histoire d'Outre-Mer*, L. 1963, pp. 180–1 and 346–81.

9. G. Angoulvant, *La Pacification de la Cote d'Ivoire*. Paris, Larose, 1916 (Author's italics – J.S.C.).

10. Ibid., p. 138.

11. Ibid., p. 32.

12. Ibid., p. 24.

13. Ibid., p. 22.

14. Ibid., p. 49.

15. Ibid., p. 22.

16. Ibid., p. 159. (Author's italics.)

17. Ibid., p. 191.

18. Ibid., p. 57 (Letter of the commander of the Lahou Circle, on the Dida country, of 29 July, 1908).

19. Ibid., p. 63 (Instructions of 26 November, 1908).

20. Ibid., p. 252.

21. Ibid., pp. 252 ff.

22. *Revue indigène*, No. 46, February 1910.

23. G. Angoulvant, op. cit., p. 281.

24. Obviously!

25. G. Angoulvant, op. cit., 281.

26. *Revue indigène*, No. 53, September 1910, pp. 518–19.

27. Jean La Bruère, 'Les événements de Côte d'Ivoire', *Revue indigène*, No. 46, February 1910, p. 104.

28. Manillas: copper anklets used as money on the Ivory Coast. (Their importation had been prohibited in 1895, but they continued to circulate.)

29. Marc Simon, *Souvenirs de Brousse*, 1961, pp. 83–4.

30. Ibid.

31. Ibid.

32. *La Dépêche de la Côte d'Ivoire*, 25 March, 1910.

33. G. Angoulvant, op. cit., p. 221. Exposé of the motives behind the 1910 budget, 24 June, 1909.

34. J. La Bruère, op. cit., has 100,000 francs: the figures given here are those approved by the Council of Government of French West Africa at its session on 21 June, 1910 (*L'Afrique ouest française*, 9 July, 1910); it is possible that the real levies may have been slightly higher than this.

35. G. Angoulvant, op. cit., p. 245. It should be noted that the confiscation of rifles, without indemnity or reimbursement of the firearms licence, was the equivalent of a heavy fine. The average price of a gun being 20 francs, the tax 5 francs, the *Revue indigène* (No. 55, 30 November, 1910) estimated the loss in 1910 at 600,000 francs. If one counts the total number of guns confiscated in 1914, one reaches a sum of around 2,800,000 francs (gold francs).

36. G. Angoulvant, op. cit., chapter I.

37. Ibid., II, chapter I.

38. Ibid., p. 216.

39. Ibid., p. 289.

40. Ibid., p. 335.

41. Ibid., p. 336.

42. Ibid., p. 338.

43. Ibid., preface.

44. On his morals see the views of General Hilaire who was Supreme Commander of Troops in French Equatorial Africa at the time of his administration: 'A fanatical politician, who used his knowledge to feather his own nest, and attended cynically to his own interests while haphazardly looking after those of the colonies' (General Hilaire, *Du Congo au Nil*, Marseille, 1930).

An example: in 1919 the Sangha-Ubangi company requested a modification of its concession, which he refused. The director-general of the company, Jean Weber, advised his agent in Africa to use 'peaceable diplomacy': on the occasion of an increase in capital, 8,000 shares (to a nominal value of 107 francs, rapidly quoted at the Stock Exchange at 150 francs) were offered to the governor-general who accepted . . . and sent the minister favourable recommendations on the requested modification. (F. Challaye, *Souvenirs sur la colonisation*. Paris, Picart, 1935.)

45. R. Runner, *Les Droits politiques des indigènes des colonies*. Paris, Larose, 1927.

46. The Toma Village of N'Zapa had concluded an alliance with Samory in 1891 and was to serve as a stage en route to Monrovia.

47. The posts of Sampuyara and Dirodougou were established in 1899.

48. *Histoire militaire de l'Afrique ouest française*. Paris, Imprimerie nationale, 1931.

49. *Rapport d'ensemble sur la situation générale de la Guinée française en 1903*. Conakry, Imprimerie Ternaux, p. 66.

50. See Baratier, *Epopées africaines*. Paris, Perrin, 1913 (pp. 15–34: La siège de Boussédou); A. Terrier, 'La frontière franco-libérienne', *Bulletin du Comité de l'Afrique française*, No. 4, August 1910, pp. 127–32; Lt. Bouet, 'Les Tomas', *Bulletin du Comité de l'Afrique française*, No. 8, August 1911, pp. 185–99, and No. 9 September 1911, pp. 220–46. The 1911 revolt in the Guerzé and Manon countries, was provoked by the levying of taxes. Contemporary administrative reports ascribe the cause to the activity of the Liberian commissioner Bernard, a naturalised Liberian from Martinique, who had urged the population to revolt.

Father Lelong notes on this: 'Reports compiled on the morrow of the 1911 uprising speak of Liberian agitators, as if the excessive charges which already hang over this people . . . was not enough to explain their reaction.' (M.H. Lelong, *Ces hommes qu'on appelle anthropophages*. Paris, Ed. Alsatia, 1946, p. 269).

51. National archives of the Republic of Guinea, I.D.18.

52. Crespin, 'La question du Coniagui', *Revue indigène*, No. 4, 1906, pp. 88–93.

53. National archives of the Republic of Guinea, I.D.18. A part of these documents has been reproduced by B. Maupoil, 'Notes concernant l'histoire des Coniagui – Bassari et en particulier l'occupation de leur pays par les Français', *Bulletin de l'Institut français d'Afrique noire*, XVI, 364, 1954, series B, pp. 378–89.

54. They were then called the Habé (a name used by the Fulani for the Dogon). Cf. 'La Pacification du pays Habé', *L'Afrique française, Renseignements coloniaux*, No. 3, March 1911.

55. 'Les révoltes de 1906 en Niger', *Revue militaire de l'Afrique Ouest française* No. 41, 15 April, 1939, p. 4.

56. Cdt. Vallier, *L'Organisation militaire du Congo français*. Paris, Charles-Lavauzelle, 1909, and *Une Etape de la conquête de l'Afrique equatoriale française (1908–12)*, edited by the technical section of colonial troops of the ministry of war. Paris, Fournier, 1921.

57. Cf. Challaye, *Souvenirs sur la colonisation*. Paris, Picart, 1935.

58. Cf. *Histoire militaire de l'Afrique équatoriale française*. Paris, Imprimerie nationale, 1931.

59. Ch. Mangin, *Souvenirs d'Afrique*. Vol. II: 'Tournée d'inspection au Congo (1908).' Paris, Denoël et Steele, 1936, p. 235.

60. A detailed description of the system of fortifications used in French Equatorial Africa will be found in Lt. Debrand, *La Conduite des petits détachements en Afrique equatoriale*. Paris, L. Fournier, 1911.

61. Governor-General Merlin, 'Discours d'ouverture à la session de 1909 du Conseil du gouvernement', quoted in *Une Etape de la conquête de l'Afrique équatoriale française*, op. cit.

62. *Une Etape de la conquête . . .* op. cit., p. 84.

63. *Revue indigène*, No. 32, 30 December, 1908, p. 550.

64. *Histoire militaire de l'Afrique équatoriale française*, p. 138. According to F. Challaye, *Souvenirs sur la colonisation*, 1,500 natives had been massacred by the company agents in that region in the course of one single year, 1906.

65. *Une Etape de la conquête*, op. cit., pp. 47–8.

66. They did not leave empty-handed. In Woleu N'Tem where, right from the beginning of the year 1912, the future cession of the territories was known, the order had been given to hasten the levying of taxes before the effective handing over of the posts to the German authorities. (*Une Etape de la conquête . . .* op. cit., p. 54.)

67. Opening speech of M. Merlin to the Council of Government of French Equatorial Africa, session of July 1912. In *Emprunt de l'Afrique équatoriale française*. Paris, Larose, 1913.

68. *Bulletin du Comité de l'Afrique française*, 1913, No. 1, p. 44.

69. Ibid., p. 45.

70. Ibid., p. 46.

71. Victor Augagneur, *Erreurs et brutalités coloniales*. Paris, Editions Montaigne, 1927, preface, p. x. He deals with an operation against the Karé, mountain people from Ouham-Pende. General Hilaire, the supreme commander, arraigned by Augagneur, claimed that the hundreds of dead were imaginary. It was, in his opinion, a 'tall story' of the commanding officers of the contingent, whose governor-general made it a pretext for undertaking an anti-militarist operation.

(*Du Congo au Nil,* op. cit., pp. 311–13.) Even if there was exaggeration, this 'tall story' must be symptomatic of the state of mind of the soldiers.

72. Ibid.

73. H. Zieglé, *Afrique equatoriale française.* Paris, Berger-Levrault, 1952, p. 100.

74. Cf. Cornevin, *Histoire du Togo.* Paris, Berger-Levrault, 1959, pp. 161–3.

75. Ibid., p. 164.

76. E. Mveng, *Histoire du Cameroun.* Paris, Présence africaine, 1963, p. 300.

77. Cf. Isaac Paré, *Les Allemands à Foumban, Abbia* (Yaoundé), March–June 1966, No. 12–13, pp. 211–31.

78. E. Mveng, op. cit., pp. 343–4.

CHAPTER V

IMPERIALIST RIVALRIES: THE FIRST WORLD WAR

The period of conquest was dominated by Franco-British rivalry. On the eve of final partition, the Fashoda affair brought about threats of war. Delcassé, who had given way to pressure and negotiated at the time of the affair, managed, despite the hostility of French public opinion, to push through the *Entente Cordiale* policy, which was sealed by the agreement of 8 April, 1904. The agreement dealt essentially with the partition of the zones of influence of the two powers and the settlement of disputes relating to their colonial possessions.

From that time on Franco-German rivalry came to the forefront. The acquisitiveness of German imperialism was centred on Morocco, one of the few still independent African territories, which the Anglo-French agreement of 1904 had left to France. Of this the spectacular 'visit' of Wilhelm II to Tangier in 1905 provided evidence. The international conference at Algeciras in 1906, however, shattered German ambitions.

The situation over Morocco became tense again during 1907-8. At the end of 1908 Kaiser Wilhelm, anxious to bring France to a more 'understanding' attitude towards his Balkan plans, proposed an agreement. This agreement was signed on 8 February, 1909. On Morocco, Germany resigned herself to recognising the political pre-eminence of France on condition that economic exploitation would be shared. In the event, French and German financiers joined in underwriting Moroccan railways and public works.

1. The N'Goko-Sangha Company, Agadir and the 1911 Compromise

When negotiations were held to settle the matter of economic collaboration in the Congo, the N'Goko-Sangha company came on the scene. It had been established in 1904 by the fusion of two chartered companies,[1] and its domain, within the framework of concessions granted in 1899, extended over 3,200,000 hectares. The directors of the company had never put to 'productive' use the 2,320,000 francs of subscribed capital, nor had there even been any effort to do serious business. The administrative reports reproached the company's agents for numerous extortions and even contraband arms trade.[2] Lacking other sources of revenue, the directors soon realised the profit they could derive from the frontier position of their concession in a region where no lines of demarcation had been drawn; the frontiers had been traced on a map geometrically.

After 1900, incidents occurred between the agents of the French companies and the German Süd-Kamerun company.[3] Soon the N'Goko-Sangha company complained to the council of state, claiming indemnities because the agents of 'the Süd-Kamerun' had gathered rubber on their territory. They withdrew their complaint when, at a cost of 325,000 francs, they were granted control of the 'Société d'exploration coloniale', another bankrupt chartered company in 1905. Their territory thus extended now over 7,000,000 hectares. Two months later, the company started a press campaign on a Franco-German incident (the Missoum-Missoum affair), which took place elsewhere in Kamerun,[4] and put in a new claim for 'indemnities', this time in the form of a grant of 3,000,000 hectares freehold. For the N'Goko-Sangha company from this time on, with the help of journalists and politicians in their pay, everything revolved around the quest for indemnities.[5] In 1907, having failed in a lawsuit brought in Hamburg against the Süd-Kamerun company, and after vainly demanding diplomatic intervention, the N'Goko-Sangha company claimed from the French government, by way of 'reparation', freehold tenure of 3,000,000 hectares and, moreover, the exclusive right to prospect for, and exploit, the mines over an area covering 7,000,000 hectares; the extension, prior to the due date, of the length of the concession, and the modification of Article 5 of its charter. This article referred to the proportion of non-French directors allowed on the board, whose numbers they wished to increase. Clearly this was a case of making money by selling shares to foreign financiers.

Germany was interested in the Congo. German imperialist circles worked out projects for a German *Mittel-Afrika*, which would link Kamerun and German East Africa (Tanganyika) by taking in the French Congo and the Free State of the Congo (the property of King Leopold II of the Belgians), both territories discredited in the eyes of the world by administrative scandals. In other words, the N'Goko-Sangha company demanded indemnities from the French government in the name of endangered 'national interests', and at the same time offered the advantages it had gained to German financiers! This campaign continued throughout 1908 and 1909, and the rectification of the frontiers laid down by the Convention of Berlin on 18 April, 1908, provided a new pretext.[6] These claims had no legal base whatever.

It [the N'Goko-Sangha company] cannot justify its claims, either in the name of honest dealing, or by clear-cut legal right. The reasons on which it bases its claims – difficulties in deriving benefit from its concessions owing to the presence of foreign merchants, and changes in its sphere of operations owing to frontier alterations – do not allow the company to claim any indemnity by virtue of the Charter.[7]

The managing director threatened the minister of the colonies, Milliès-Lacroix, and stated that he had behind him the entire press and 200 members of parliament.[8] An intensive press campaign continued to be waged in support of the 'injured' company, and among the leaders of this chorus was André Tardieu, the company lawyer who was also editor of the foreign policy column in Le Temps. According to Tardieu, three German firms had extracted ivory and rubber from more than 3,000,000 hectares of the N'Goko-Sangha company's possessions between 1899 and 1908; thirty-five German trading posts had been illegally set up, profiting from the scarcity of French administration in the territory conceded to the company.[9]

At that time a German suggestion was put forward aimed at 'prolonging' the agreement reached on Morocco by setting up a Franco-German consortium which would exploit the N'Goko-Sangha company's territory; the company would contribute its concession, and the Germans (specifically the Süd-Kamerun company) the capital. The Briand cabinet saw in this a means of putting an end to the endless claims of the N'Goko-Sangha company. With misgivings, the company accepted, on condition that the government first took a favourable decision on the question of indemnities! After numerous manoeuvres, an arbitrator, assisted by Governor-General Merlin, representing the government, and Tardieu, proposed an indemnity of 2,393,000 francs and 150,000 hectares with freehold tenure[10] (29 April, 1911). A meeting of shareholders soon decided to give 30,000 francs of this indemnity to their solicitors and 400,000 to their chairman to 'cover alleged outlays and as remuneration for their help'.[11] In May 1910, the N'Goko-Sangha company submitted a project for a consortium – and its managing director was most concerned about the 'commission' to be apportioned for this transaction. After some dilatoriness, on 22 November, 1910, the ministry of foreign affairs adopted the project for the consortium, and a convention was signed on 21 December between the ministry and the German ambassador.

In the end, however, the whole project miscarried. The 'Ligue française pour la défense des indigènes du Bassin conventionnel du Congo', with Félicien Challaye as its chairman (brought into being by, among others, Pierre Mille and Paix-Séailles, and the *Courrier européen*, which served as the Ligue's mouthpiece), led a campaign against indemnity. This campaign had the support of the socialist party, and Albert Thomas became its spokesman in the chamber. Parliament was hostile to the indemnity, and the government, on 25 January, 1911, annulled the decision of the arbitrators as legally unsound.[12] To make the consortium more acceptable, Pichon proposed the formation of a parallel Franco-German consortium which would function in the south of Kamerun. But 'the payment of indemnity having been dropped, the pledge given by the N'Goko-Sangha Company was also dismissed':[13] no indemnity, no consortium. With this blackmail, the company directors hoped to obtain satisfaction. They were deceived, for on 30 March, 1911, Messimy, the minister for the colonies, announced to the budget commission that, under these conditions, there would be no idemnity and no consortium.

To appease the anger of the Germans, who accused their French partners of bad faith, Caillaux, a cabinet minister who had urged agreement, asked one of the financiers interested in Congo affairs, Fondère, to negotiate with the Germans the construction of a railway line from the Congo to Kamerum as compensation for the failure of the consortium.

> An old companion of Brazza, and an ex-official of the Ministry for the Colonies, M. Fondère was and still remains the soul of big Congolese deals.[14]

Fondère was the founder of the Messageries fluviales which had a monopoly of navigation along the Congo and the Ubangi. He was, moreover, the spirit behind the 'Afrique et Congo' company, a trading and plantation-owning concern closely linked to the Messageries, and the managing director of two chartered companies in Gabon, Société des factoreries de N'Djolé and Société de l'Ogooué-N'Gounié. Finally he was managing director of the powerful Société forestière Sangha-Oubangui. This company proposed to buy up the N'Goko-Sangha company by paying the indemnity laid down by the arbitration proceedings. In Berlin he negotiated with Semler, the chairman of the Süd-Kamerun company and representative of a German colonial group, in the presence of the chairman of the N'Goko-Sangha Company. On his return to Paris, Fondère, with the assistance of three ministers, re-opened the project for the railway line, but it was turned down by the ministry for the colonies, which saw in this a covert seizure of the Congo by Germany.

At this point the 'Agadir Coup' broke out. The French had occupied the Moroccan town of Fez on 21 May, 1911, for which the Germans insisted on obtaining 'compensation'. As the negotiations dragged on and on, they felt they were being duped. On 1 July, 1911, the German warship *Panther* arrived outside Agadir and landed a small garrison. At the same time, a note declared the Moroccan question re-opened. Negotiations started up again in a state of extreme tension, and on two occasions the outbreak of war seemed imminent. Germany first demanded the entire Congo in exchange for Morocco. France refused, and in this had the support of Britain, which indicated to the Germans that their demands were excessive. Germany then demanded a piece of the French Congo to gain a foothold on the Congo and the Ubangi, cutting French Equatorial Africa in two; it demanded, moreover, that France should renounce its rights of pre-emption in the Belgian Congo in Germany's favour.[15] This was the preparation for German *Mittel-Afrika*.

A Franco-German agreement was finally signed on 4 November, 1911. Germany abandoned Morrocco to France (which established its 'protectorate' there in 1912), and received in exchange 259,000 square km. in French Equatorial Africa with access to the Atlantic south of Spanish Guinea and two points of contact on the right bank of the Congo and the Ubangi. France renounced its rights of pre-emption over Spanish Guinea, which henceforth became an enclave in the Cameroons. France received the small territory known as 'the Duck's Beak' between Logone and Shari, extending to 16,600 square km. It was due largely to British intervention that a compromise was reached. At the beginning of the crisis, Great Britain, with foresight, refused to give military aid, and recommended negotiations. When Germany laid claim to the entire Congo, the British government advised the German ambassador in London that his country's pretensions were excessive and let it be understood that war would be inevitable if they were upheld. Great Britain was not prepared to go to war simply to defend the interests of French imperialism. But it was not disposed either to let Germany profit from the situation to upset the African balance of power in its favour, and thus gain a serious advantage in their mutual commercial and maritime rivalry. Apart from these considerations, the German general staff was not ready for war and, in the French cabinet, Caillaux was firmly in favour of a Franco-German compromise. For these reasons war was avoided.

However, the compromise was badly received among imperialist circles with inclinations towards war, both in France and in Germany, and by 'public opinion' formed by the press in their pay. To be more exact, these circles tried to make the utmost capital out of the so-called 'humiliation' inflicted upon their respective countries, and so take the direction of affairs firmly in hand, isolating currents in favour of peace and intensifying preparation for war. In Germany, the disappointment of the colonial circles, who considered themselves 'sacrificed', resulted in the resignation of the secretary of state for the colonies, Dr. Lindequist, and was translated into a situation favourable to the increased influence of militarist circles and the vote for military measures in 1912.

In France, the minister Caillaux was accused of having 'sacrificed' the Congo: an appeal by Clemenceau to the senate foreign affairs commission, made with the secret knowledge of de Selves, the minister for foreign affairs, who was hostile to the agreement, revealed that the latter had not been kept informed of the negotiations undertaken by Caillaux concerning the Congo-Cameroons railway. Caillaux resigned and was replaced by a minister under the sway of Poincaré, the man of the Forges committee,[16] who was to have military service extended to three years and who was firmly resolved to prepare for conflict. Thus was accelerated the pressure for war, the plunge towards world conflict in which the rival imperialist powers were seeking to resolve both their internal contradictions and their external rivalries by imposing a new partition of the world, each with its own spheres of influence and its colonies.

2. Anti-Colonialism in France before 1914 and African Problems

We have so far mentioned anti-colonialism a number of times in this narrative. As the period of conquest progressed, it changed in character. Right-wing anti-colonialism disappeared; where it did exist, it was aimed less at the colonial activity itself than at the financial intrigues which it occasioned, and which gave them an opportunity to attack republican or radical politicians who were involved.

The natural solidarity felt by the French working class for the colonial peoples, fellow-victims of capitalist exploitation, was expressed increasingly through their political representatives and, in particular, through the spokesmen of the Parti socialiste unifié (United Socialist Party), which could legitimately claim to be the party of the French working class. This anti-colonialism, however, often expressed itself in a confused and hesitant manner, which revealed the strength of the opportunist current within the socialist party at the time that led to the party's collapse and self-betrayal in 1914.

Even before the unification of the socialists, the Parti ouvrier français (French Workers' Party) of Jules Guesde, representing the Marxist stream, had taken a stand against colonial policy. But even this position reflected the weaknesses, both sectarian and opportunist, of Guesdism. There was no fundamental analysis of the imperialist colonial phenomenon, nor was stress placed on solidarity with the peoples who had become victims of colonial aggression. The problem was posed essentially out of tactical considerations within the field of French politics, with one eye on the electors. Colonial policy was attacked in the name of 'the little soldier' sacrificed to the financiers' thirst for profits. It was undoubtedly an attack based on class considerations, which are indeed important, but the line of argument used did not in the end greatly differ from that of the anti-colonialists of the right, and in particular that of Paul Déroulède, who protested against the Dahomey expedition.[18]

Colonial policy is not and will not be [for the Parti ouvrier français] anything but speculation by the capitalist class, and a source of financial intrigues.[19]

When the Mayor of Marseilles, Flaissières, elected on the party ticket, warmly welcomed the 'hero of Dahomey' General Dodds (in May 1893), there was no reaction from the Guesdists – who were opposed to any official reception at the hôtel de ville and had made sure that half the 5,000 francs allocated for the occasion should be used for the injured and sick soldiers of Dahomey. The journal Le Socialiste (20 May, 1893) did not print the speech, and contented itself with congratulating the municipality of Marseilles for having 'refused to yield socialism . . . to General Dodds' sabres'.[20]

In 1895 the Romilly Congress of the Parti ouvrier français reiterated:

The XIIIth national congress of the P.O.F. raises its voice against colonial free-booting, for which no conscientious socialist will ever vote either a man or a penny.

This doctrinal position did not gain unanimous support. Bonnier, writing in Le Socialiste, stated that the socialists 'are not a priori enemies of all colonisation', and in the chamber Jourde voted in favour of military credits for the expedition to Madagascar as well as for the Act of Annexation (1896), while other Guesdist deputies voted against or abstained from the motion.[21]

In 1905, the very year when socialist unity was achieved, there appeared the first systematic analysis of the colonial phenomenon to be published in France from a socialist point of view. It was a pamphlet by Paul Louis entitled *Le Colonialisme*,[22] which seems to have introduced this term into the political vocabulary. It demonstrates the mechanism by which colonial expenditure paid by the mass of taxpayers – i.e. by the people – is converted into profits for capital. Paul Louis wrote:

We have seen that the subjugation of distant lands was to provide for the needs of capitalism and furnish it with new fields of activity and spoilation. It is the entire community which pays the costs of the expeditions, and which finances the cost of permanent bodies of occupation or civil administrations. It is the entire community which thus guarantees the arrears of colonial debts, when these debts, as happens in France, are contracted under the aegis of the metropolis.

The nation writes off the outlays involved in the development or the mere enlargement of the empire. That is the reason why parliaments of the nineteenth and twentieth centuries, which represent above all the greed of big business – the executive powers which attend to the interests of the bourgeoisie – do not hesitate to vote ever-increasing sums to colonialism and to squander the credits already approved. It is the bourgeoisie that always benefits: through the salaries of the officials, the provision of plant, and the awarding of contracts for public works.[23]

Paul Louis here replied to the Cartierists[24] and also, fifty-five years in advance, to M. Henri Brunschwig,[25] who has claimed that French colonialism was not based on financial interest since it cost far more than it brought in. But both forgot to mention who paid the costs and who reaped the profits. Nevertheless it might be said that Paul Louis did not succeed in demonstrating the new spirit of colonial imperialism of the end of the nineteenth and the beginning of the twentieth century. In this respect he fell short of the analyses not only of Lenin (1916) and Hilferding (1910), but even of Hobson (1902).[26] However, he pointed out with clarity the solidarity which united the working classes of the imperialist countries with the colonial peoples:

The working class will not let itself be taken in by the mirage of words, the seductions of humanitarian phraseology. It must recognise that there is no peaceful colonisation, that all colonisation is based on violence, war, the sacking of towns, sharing out of the loot, and slavery, however well or thinly disguised. Its autho-

rity is already sufficient to make its solidarity with the oppressed
native populations effectively felt, in re-claiming for the latter
their essential rights, safeguarding existence and subsistence; it
will profit from all debates held anywhere with the aim of frus-
trating overseas conquests, and pointing out the logical consequences of imperialist expansion.[27]

But even while correctly posing the question, the author explained
that it was impossible for the working class to raise obstacles to
colonisation. That, he said, would mean that the working class had
acquired mastery over the state, and had passed from the phase of
resistance to that of assault. It is true that the French working class
of the time had not the means to place obstacles in the way of
colonisation, but this reasoning, under the pretext of realism, led it
in effect to unite itself with the opportunist and bourgeois humani-
tarians, who bowed before colonialism as 'inevitable' and even
'necessary', and were content to demand its 'humanisation' – a
completely utopian aim. The duty of the working class was to
denounce colonial enterprise and to proclaim its solidarity with the
colonised peoples, even if, in the conditions of the time, no important
or immediate results could be hoped for, but it allowed that duty
to be blurred. Paul Louis, on the other hand, represented the
'revolutionary' trend. The opportunist position was represented by
the leadership of the socialist party, even including its 'specialists' on
colonial questions. Jaurès, who came from the ranks of bourgeois
republicans and was blinded by his admiration for Jules Ferry and
his scholarly work, showed himself hesitant and reticent to condemn
the principle of colonisation. It was only by degrees, in talks and
parliamentary speeches against the occupation of Morocco, that he
came out into the open. His condemnation referred to the motives
of the colonial movement, its methods, and its danger as a cause of
war, rather than to the principle of colonisation itself. But to Jaurès'
credit, one should remember the evolution of his ideas in a progressive direction which contrasted with those of Briand, Viviani or
Millerand, who moved from 'intransigent' socialism to reaction.[28]
But, as J. Bruhat observed, 'the theoretician is never on a par with
the man of action,[29] and Jaurès showed himself incapable of backing
up his denunciation of colonial enterprise with an analysis of the
phenomenon in depth.

Jaurès went against the current of the general evolution of the
Party. The national colonial policy had been rejected by the
Chalons congress of the party, and at Limoges and Nancy. At
Nancy, two reports were presented on the question but not discussed
at length, one by Paul Louis for the revolutionary trend, and the

other by Gustave Rouanet for the reformist trend. At the Toulouse congress (1908) the majority voted for the reformist motion, with a few reservations.[30] Gustave Rouanet, one of the socialists in the Chamber of Deputies specialising in colonial problems, went so far as to praise Brazza, 'the explorer who gave the Congo to France'.[31] In this speech Rouanet wanted to put on trial the crimes of colonisation committed in the Congo, which were on the agenda because of the Gaud-Toqué affair. He went on to support the authority of the Brazza mission, and his praises showed 'tactical' solicitude. What else could the average socialist voter think but that on one side there was 'good' colonisation, justified and glorious for France when men like Brazza were the promoters, and on the other abuses of the kind illustrated by the Gaud-Toqué affair? The same spirit is found in the report of an inquiry held for the socialist parliamentary group by Deputy Charles Dumas on the eve of the First World War, and published under the menancing title 'Set the Natives Free or Renounce the Colonies'.[32] In other words, colonisation can be allowed by the socialists on condition that the natives are given fundamental freedoms. Basically, the majority of socialists shared the views of the pacifist Félicien Challaye, who wrote:

> Colonisation is a necessary social fact. . . . But justice demands that the domination of the whites should not involve the worst consequences – slavery, robbery, torture, assassination – for the blacks. Justice demands that the natives should derive some advantages from our presence among them.[33]

Such an argument could not fundamentally embarrass the partisans of colonisation, since in its overall assumptions it took a position on their side. On the international level the situation was little different. At the congress of the International in 1900, the Dutchman Van Kol became the spokesman of 'colonial' socialism. At the Stuttgart congress of the International in 1907, Kautsky was grieved to have his report rejected.[34] The actions of the socialists or pacifists who stood up at the time against the malpractices of colonialism should not be overlooked or minimised, even if their positions were not always very consistent. The action of the socialist party was undoubtedly the most important because of the audience it commanded and because all the other political parties rallied to the colonial policy.[35] In tropical Africa, which concerns us, their interventions were limited, as they tended to turn more to North Africa, where the Moroccan question drew all attention, and eye-witness accounts were more numerous and more direct. We must refer again to the debate of 1906 on the situation in the Congo with the denunciation by Gustave Rouanet, who had already exposed the crimes of the Congo in a series of articles in *L'Humanité*. An important role was played, moreover, by *Le Courrier européen*, a bi-monthly founded in 1904 under the patronage of Edmund D. Morel. It served as a mouthpiece for the Ligue pour la défense des indigènes du Bassin conventionnel du Congo, whose main supporters were Paix-Séailles, Félicien Challaye and Pierre Mille. The League was not based on humanitarian considerations alone. While for some, like Challaye, this feeling was predominant, there can be no doubt that for others the main consideration was to have a means of attacking the chartered companies of the Congo and their monopoly. In that sense, the action of the League at the time of the N'Goko-Sangha affair belonged to the political sphere of home policy rather than that of anti-colonialist action.

We should mention finally the radical freelance writer Vigné d'Octon, who had already become well-known in 1900 for denouncing to the Chamber of Deputies, and in his book *La Gloire du sabre*, the crimes committed during the conquest of the Sudan. Vigné d'Octon, who was not returned to parliament in 1906, remained faithful to the anti-colonialism of the old-style radicals. Having little understanding of socialism, which was incompatible with his basic individualism, he turned towards anarchism. But in 1907 he concentrated his attention on North Africa and brought out a book *Les Crimes coloniaux de la IIIe République, Volume I – La Sueur du burnous*, published by Gustave Hervé in 1911.[37] Using this book as reference, the author launched a campaign of anti-colonialist conferences that were held all over France between 1911 and 1913. He ran a regular series of reports in *Guerre sociale*, Gustave Hervé's periodical, which published letters and contributions from Muslim correspondents in Algeria, but he was dropped by Hervé in June 1912, under the pretext of collaboration with the syndicalist campaign. This was the first step in the process whereby, in 1914, Hervé passed from frantic anti-militarism to exaggerated war propaganda.[38] It is significant that Vigné d'Octon, who had begun his career in West Africa and who had devoted to that region the most important of his interventions at the time of the conquest, did not return to the subject. The reason was that Sub-Saharan Africa was kept virtually sealed off to all those who did not have the right to go there in the course of their administrative and military duties, and the silence of those who had that right was assured by their professional oath.

Unwilling colonials, such as existed at the time of the conquest, capable of denouncing what they had witnessed, had died out; there remained only career colonials, who were morally and materially at one with the system. Vigné d'Octon never made a fundamental analysis of the colonial system. But, starting from a purely emotional reflex, he finally reached a more honourable position than the majority of socialists.

In his preface to *Crimes coloniaux*, he did not hesitate to write:

> I had this dream: at last there existed on this earth justice for all subject races and conquered peoples. Tired of being despoiled, pillaged, suppressed and massacred, the Arabs and the Berbers drove their oppressors from North Africa, the blacks did the same for the rest of the continent, and the yellow people for the soil of Asia.
>
> Having thus reconquered by violence and force their unconquerable and sacred rights, ravished from them by force and violence, each of these human families pursued the road of its destiny which for a time had been interrupted.
>
> And, forgetting that I was French – which is nothing – I remembered only one thing: that I was a Man – which is everything – and I felt an indescribable joy in the depth of my being.[39]

3. Conditions in French Black Africa around 1914

It was in the years when the First World War was imminent that the colonial system was finally established.

In the Sudan, the effects of the wars of conquest were beginning to die down. In the Congo, in Chad, and in the forest regions of French West Africa, on the other hand, 'pacification' operations were still in progress. In a country still suffering from exhaustion, the exactions of the colonisers became everywhere more and more crushing. The rate of the poll-tax kept rising rapidly; there was forced labour for road construction, the building of posts, the reconstruction of villages and compulsory crop cultivation, and labour was requisitioned for the construction of railway lines by private enterprise. The forest people of the Ivory Coast, paleonigritic tribes who had taken refuge in the hills, were deprived of their reserves. The social leveling – to the lowest level – was to force the peoples into work that was 'morally improving' – or otherwise beneficial to commerce. No progress was made in the techniques of production, nor in the development of an infrastructive. In 1917, Governor-General Van Vollenhoven underlined the poor state of such development. In 1914, the budget of French West Africa had devoted less than 2,500,000 francs to medical aid, and barely more than 2,000,000 to education; 1 per cent of the children of school age attended school. Agricultural services had to manage with allocations of 700,000 francs. Facilities such as posts and telegraph, public works, education and health, had to be satisfied with 'about half the sum which the city of Paris devoted to the upkeep of its streets and boulevards'.[40]

French Equatorial Africa had even worse provisions. The local budgets, their resources furnished almost exclusively by the poll-tax, were absorbed almost entirely by administrative and police personnel expenditures. Of Gabon's 972,000 francs revenue in 1911, the personnel in the districts accounted for 608,000 francs, and regional police and prison warders for 299,000 francs. Out of 25,000 francs allocated for education, only 5,406·84 francs were paid out. Four schools existed in 1910 – but three were closed on account of the shortage of teachers; at the school of Libreville, the only survivor, instruction was given by officials of the general administration who ran courses outside their office hours for a small additional remuneration. The Middle Congo spent less than 20,000 francs on education, and in Ubangi and Chad no money was allocated at all.[41]

The disappearance of funds and the deduction of even a part of the minimum necessary to assure the subsistence of the inhabitants by the widest variety of means, led annually to famine at times of shortage. The administration attributed this chronic situation to the peasant's 'lack of foresight', and from 1910 undertook to set up 'provident societies' which were meant at least to provide cultivators with the necessary seeds. The administrators quickly saw in this a means of filling their treasuries, by the use of funds coming in under compulsory quotas. The penury to which the populations were reduced put them at the mercy of the least crisis, whether of natural or social origin. These conditions combined to produce catastrophe in 1912 and 1914, when the crisis was of economic and social origin. The rubber crisis, with the collapse of market rates, had the worst effect on Guinea and the Congo. At the same time in 1912 and 1913, two years of drought and bad harvests followed upon each other in the Sudanic zone, from Senegal to Ouadai.[42] Archives are not accessible, and printed documents on this subject tend to be very laconic, so it is difficult to judge the extent and impact of the famine. But it caused the migration southwards of Saharan tribes, their settlement in new regions, and conflicts between them and the native people. In Macina, the first Touareg 'invasion' dates from the 1913–14 famine.[43] Numerous parents 'pawned', that is to say, temporarily ceded, their children as slaves as a means of procuring something to eat, often very little. Among the Dogon, there were cases of children being pawned for a handful of millet;[44] this was chiefly a way of shifting the responsibility for feeding hungry mouths on to others. The famine did not raise the number of slaves; on the contrary, tens of thousands of slaves were 'sent back' by their masters who renounced all obligation to feed them.[45] In the Sudan proper there were 250,000 to 300,000 victims. One may also note that the famine contributed to social levelling.

Here follows a description of the famine in the Bandiagara district, as given in the report of the commandant:

Two years of semi-drought (1911–12), followed by a year of complete drought, inevitably provoked a terrible famine. From the harvest of 1913 to that of 1914, grain and fodder crops were almost completely lacking. This led to heavy mortality among both people and animals.

As there had been no harvest in 1913, reserves were exhausted within a few weeks, so that the millet sold at 40 centimes a kilo in November had reached the price of 1 franc by February, and remained at that price until the harvest of 1914. Even at that excessive price it could not always be obtained. At that time a large part of the population was reduced to living off the fruits of trees, and later only their leaves.

In February, the villages began to thin out. Added to deaths came the exodus of a large part of the survivors to less stricken regions. To mention only the village of Bandiagara, a dozen people died there every day over a period of many weeks.

In short, the 1913–14 famine must have diminished the population of the district by about one-third. As to livestock, everything indicates that it was reduced by a half.[46]

Significant figures are given for Chad in texts quoted by Denise Moran and in material in local archives. Chad had just been conquered and was still under military administration. At first the French had been well received. It was hoped that they would put an end to the slave raids which the sultans had stepped up; but the people were soon disillusioned. First came the imposition of taxes. Colonel Moll declared:

Tax in kind is embarrassing and onerous. Let the native barter his grain and his materials before appearing at the cash-desk of the tax-gatherer.[48]

When nothing came, men were sent to collect the taxes. This led to

a general flight of the inhabitants towards the mountains. Taxes had to be levied by force, or seized by surprise . . . *manu militari*.[49]

Everything was sold *en masse* to sharp-shooters – a few Arabs who paid in thalers (Maria Theresa dollars). Prices fell 'below the market level', that is to say, below what the white man and his troops deigned to pay for their provisions – 'half or a third of the value of foodstuffs or articles'.[50] The people complained. 'Doudmourah [the dethroned former Sultan of Wadai] was satisfied with less; he took a few slaves and that was all.'[51] The military administration became even more insistent. The tax, 'half of which they had been happy to have levied by April, had now to be paid in full by March'; to the poll-tax was added a tax on livestock, consisting of one-thirtieth of the value of the herds. Counts were 'stepped up'. Revenue rose from 371,000 to 750,000 francs in 1911. At that date a report stated:

> It has become absolutely impossible to obtain anything whatso-ever from the people; they possess nothing except millet and *gabaks*,[52] which are respectively barely sufficient for their own nourishment and their dress.[53]

The general revolt of Wadai in May–August 1911 is easily explained by these conditions. The outbreak coincided with the arrival at Abéché on 21 March of a delegation that had come to protest against the payment of taxes in currency.[54] Colonel Largeau noted that scarcity in 1912 had been foreseen for 1912, and indi-cated also that the Kanem, 'requested' (sic) to pay the 1912 taxes in advance in September 1911, had fully settled everything by 31 December of that year.[55] To 'take the population in hand' the administration resorted to the same methods as in the Dogon country – systematic ravaging of crops on the plains and military operations in the mountains to dislodge the people from their hide-outs and force them to return to the plains.

In addition to the taxes, there was frequent requisitioning of road workers, porters and convoy foremen, all of whom the people, unaware of fine distinctions, classed generally as 'slaves' of the whites.[56] Conscript labour was paid for . . . when that proved pos-sible. A report stated:

> When the prices are known, the material furnished will be paid for. . . . This year, I have not been able to pay anyone except workers along the East–West route. Next year, it would be a good thing if I could start payment again on the two routes cleared through the undergrowth.[57]

The porters had to cross semi-desert zones without water-holes or villages, going without food for several days. For the repair of roads and posts, three months of forced labour without food was required. The head of a post noted:

> The natives have been taken on for statute labour and taxes for a period of eight months. They really have the right to a little rest.[58]

A military administrator decided to establish a market 'to force the Kirdi[59] to procure for themselves thalers for taxes'. In February, a thousand natives set off for the market 'encouraged by twenty Arab scouts'. The result was a fiasco, as no buyers turned up. And the administrator concluded indignantly: 'These people seem to have a horror of trade.'[60] To this were added extortions by non-commissioned officers, heads of posts, police, infantry and political agents. An inspection report noted that 'several army men send to France, by money order, up to ten times their pay'[61]. In a note to a sub-division, a circle commander observed:

Most often the villages furnish food free of charge. This procedure is lawful for our people, that is to say, for our agents whom we send on missions to the interior of one area. But it is intolerable that the scouts or riflemen of the neighbouring area should be fed without paying for it.

This was the setting for the 1913 famine. When the battalion commander (later General Hilaire) came to take over command, he found

all the fields abandoned, pillaged, burnt, bare; the majority of the villages deserted, in ruins, giving off the smell of human carnage to passers-by. On the no less deserted tracks, there were skeleton-like corpses which not even the jackals or hyenas would touch, and here and there emaciated persons in agony, with hollow eye sockets, bloated bellies, projecting ribs, limbs like knotted sticks, bones piercing the cracked skin, holding out a mummy's feeble hand towards food which one did not dare to offer them; hardly would they have swallowed it than they died.[62]

Nothing has been done to avert the famine.

In the almost deserted market of Abéché, across the wall from our post, human flesh was sold, cut into small pieces and arranged and presented as hyena meat.[63]

Major Hilaire laid the blame on the former head of the division, a Foreign Legion officer of Turkish origin, converted from Islam and a protégé of the Duchesse d'Uzès:

He sold to the people under his administration, at 100 per cent profit, all manner of trash brought from France in his luggage at the princess's expense. . . . Even during the famine he sold to the families of the infantry soldiers and the police millet at 2·50 francs per kilo which had been taken by the authorities as tax from the natives a few months before at 0·05 francs (their last supplies in the silos).[64]

During the epidemics that followed in 1916, 1917 and 1918 the losses reached 60 per cent and more:

> Everywhere up to 150 inhabitants at least out of a village of 200.[65]

A settler wrote:

> The horrors of the former régime have been exaggerated. . . . During the famine of 1898–9 the Sultan fed his subjects; in 1914, you let them die. The Arabs granted their captives villages of refuge, which you suppressed. There were no passes before; no hunting permits; no villages forced to live on the rocks, far from wells because the road passes that way. . . . The old subjection was easier than this. When we came, how many large villages were there, rich in cattle and in reserves of millet? They have dwindled and disappeared.[66]

To all these evils the war was to add others.

4. The 1914–1918 War and the Black Troops

(a) THE BLACK ARMY

From 1908 on, as part of the preparations for the imperialist war, the use of soldiers from the colonies, and from Black Africa particularly, was envisaged to provide 'cannon fodder'. Formations of black troops had been begun by Faidherbe in 1857 with the establishment of the 'Senegalese infantry'. They were used mainly in the conquest of Black Africa itself and to a small degree in other colonial operations, notably in Madagascar. They were used again during the military intervention in Morocco at the beginning of 1908. In European theatres of war they were used only on isolated occasions, generally in conjunction with Algerian troops; in the Crimean and Mexican wars, under the Second Empire, and in the 1870–1 war, a few Sengalese were in action at the battles of Wissemburg and Froeschwiller.

The master theoretician of a 'black army' was Colonel (later General) Mangin. In two articles in the *Revue de Paris*,[67] which aroused wide interest, he explained its value.

> The drop in the birthrate in France and the reduction of military training to two years have caused a considerable falling off in the total strength of the army, which is getting worse. The number of men called up in 1907 was 457,000; but since the introduction of the new Act, it is no more than 433,000. The statistics of male births foreshadow a drop in ten years to 399,000, and in twenty

years to 371,000. This is a loss of 62,000 men – the equivalent of four army corps.

By introducing conscription among the indigenous population of Algeria we could partly compensate for the weakening of our metropolitan forces; but the project under study is meeting with various objections from the European population in Algeria, who are afraid that in the case of insurrection, the Arabs, whom we would instruct and set free, would turn against us. But our Algerian settlers would be reassured if they felt themselves protected by regiments of Senegalese infantry, most of them fetishists.[68]

In 1910, a mission headed by Colonel Mangin, with Administrators Guignard and Le Hérissé, and Captains Cornet, Renard and Salaün as members, travelled through French West Africa to study the problem. They reached the conclusion that it was possible to raise 40,000 men in the region every year for a five-year period of service. This would provide a total strength five times higher than that required for the execution of the envisaged project. The governor-general of French West Africa, William Ponty, endorsed the conclusions drawn by the mission.

A dual proposition was formulated in 1911 on this basis by the minister for the colonies, Messimy, and Colonel Mangin: 1, the establishment of an Arab army (Algerian infantry) to reinforce the metropolitan army; 2, the formation of a black army for the defence of the colonial empire, especially in Africa 'and which might even, should the need arise, fight by the side of the other two'.[69] A decree of 1912 facilitated the creation of this 'black army'; natives of between twenty and twenty-eight years of age could be recruited by conscription for a period of four years, in case of a shortage of volunteers. Recruitment in the years preceding the war reached between 8,000 and 10,000 men per year.

(b) RECRUITMENT

At the time of the declaration of war there were 14,142 African infantrymen doing military service in French West Africa and 15,600 outside, mainly in Morocco. From September 1914 on, all the Senegalese battalions immediately available were shipped to France (two each from French West Africa, Morocco, and Algeria), and immediately sent to the front. At the same time expeditionary forces for action in Togo and Kamerun were set up in Africa.

The slaughter of the 1914 war rapidly led to a greater use of this source of manpower: in October 1915, 30,000 volunteers and conscripts were recruited to go to Europe. A decree of 9 October, 1915, ordered the mobilisation of natives over the age of eighteen in the

Senegalese infantry, to serve outside French West Africa for the duration of the war. The period of engagement was to be deducted from the time of compulsory service, and those taken on were to receive a call-up premium of 200 francs. By this means another 51,000 men were recruited in 1916, half of them from the traditional recruiting regions, Senegal and the Sudan. In 1917, seventeen Senegalese battalions were engaged in the battle of the Somme. The total number of infantrymen recruited had been 120,000. Much was said about the terror they would cause to the Germans – and their disregard for danger, which made it possible to use them largely as 'sacrificial' troops in places where the French were beginning to refuse to march.

It was readily believed at that time (taking into account the difficulties described below) that all that could be done had been done.

> The troops which could still be raised [in French West Africa] would not be worth the trouble needed to weld them into a unit, and to educate and equip them.[70]

In the middle of 1917 the necessity of using manpower from West Africa to 'revitalise France' was stressed. With this purpose in mind, Governor-General Joost Van Vollenhoven was sent to Dakar in June 1917 to replace Governor-General Clozel. In a speech on 7 June, 1917, he announced that the minister of supplies was the purchaser of the whole 1917 harvest in French West Africa of cereals both farinaceous and oil-yielding. Instead of employing requisitioning, he appealed to trading interests. An agreement was concluded between the business houses, grouped in a consortium of which Vézia was the representative, and the government, which undertook to buy at an agreed price all the products made available. But the products were made available, in fact, through compulsory crops and quotas which the population were forced to bring for sale, whether they liked it or not. This 'extravagant programme' took the form of 'raids' and enforced 'famine', 'with no result other than the export of a few thousand tons of sorghum which could not be preserved, and of paddy'.[71]

A few words must be said about Joost Van Vollenhoven. He has been depicted as a model administrator and patriotic hero, who resigned in protest against the excesses of military recruitment, and went to the front, where he was killed on 18 July, 1918: 'The equal of Bayard and La Tour d'Auvergne, and an example for future generations, having been one of the most brilliant among the most brave.'[72] The man's courage is beyond dispute, but his life work as a whole merits examination. Son of a Dutch settler in

Algeria, he had grown up in an environment which was later called 'ultra'. As a naturalised Frenchman, he attended the Ecole coloniale. After being an outstanding cadet, he soon became a member of the private office of Doumergue, the minister for the colonies in the Combes government. Two years after leaving the Ecole coloniale, he returned to it as an instructor; then he was secretary-general under various governments and goverments-general, *chef de cabinet* of the minister for the colonies, Lebrun–he negotiated the dismantling of the Congo in 1911 – then secretary-general of Indochina with Albert Sarraut (1912–14), and governor-general *ad interim* in his absence (1914–15).

Van Vollenhoven was intelligent, and a tireless worker, but endowed with steely ambition and an excessive taste for authority. Rather than serve his first campaign in the ranks, he chose to reach the summit as soon as he could by using the support of radical politicians. The latter, the 'loyal managers' of the capitalist society, were anxious to show that they could conduct the affairs of large-scale colonisation as well as and even better than the men traditionally associated with such affairs. His youth, his lightning career based on political 'influence', his lofty authoritarianism, and his foreign origin were enough to arouse the distaste of administrators and governors. 'He fought and suffered to establish himself.'[73] When, at the outbreak of the war, he held the rank of governor-general of Indochina, he revolted against the intrigues of his enemies who called him a '*boche*' and a shirker. In March 1915 he left for the front with the rank of sergeant. Despite his taste for authority, he also enjoyed taking risks. He volunteered for dangerous missions, was twice wounded, but could more often be found as a guest in officers' messes and with the staff than living in the trenches. He was twice earmarked for a staff appointment under the former Radical minister for the colonies, Messimy. He was commissioned lieutenant, and then, with sufficient military standing to face his detractors, he was named governor-general of French West Africa, where he carried out the mission described above. For six months he devoted himself to the task of proconsul, undertaking numerous tours, making speeches and issuing circulars: he carried out his role in a more absolutist fashion than any other governor-general, because he was also the representative of France at war. But he had to reckon with a higher authority than himself: at the end of 1917, Clemenceau decided that French West Africa should furnish not only foodstuffs but also men for the great slaughter.

The council of ministers decided on 8 January, 1918, to revive recruitment. A decree raised the upper age limit for recruitment to thirty-five years, and drew recruits from French Equatorial Africa.

To overcome the difficulties of this operation, which were already apparent, the authorities increased their promises. Additional orders established exemptions from taxation, family allowances, the granting of citizenship under certain conditions and reserved employment for ex-soldiers when they returned. Finally a 'psychological' measure was adopted. A mission was established on 11 January, 1918, and sent to French West Africa to intensify recruitment. It was under the direction of Blaise Diagne, the black deputy of the four communes in Senegal, who had been granted the title of 'commissioner of the Republic in West Africa', with the rank of governor-general.

Clemenceau, typically, had not consulted Van Vollenhoven, nor taken into consideration his advice on the advisability of recruitment. Van Vollenhoven might have accepted the task of carrying out this new policy; the one he had been entrusted with previously had, in most respects, paid even less attention to human realities. But what he could not accept was not to be anything other than top man. He wrote:

> The powers of the Republic cannot be split like a brioche. The governor-general is its sole depository; this is clear and definite, admitting of no doubt. [74]

There were also – an admission which he did not make, but which was to be made for him by other colonials – the humiliation, unacceptable to this son of an Algerian colon, who was a colonial ruler in his very soul, of having to share his powers with a black. He resigned and went back to the front.

With the help of the Diagne mission, 63,000 supplementary soldiers were recruited in 1918. [75] Of the 211,000 recruited in all, of whom 163,952 took part in battles in European theatres of war, an official announcement listed 24,762 who had 'died for France', not taking into account the innumerable 'missing', whose deaths could not be registered. The losses certainly exceeded one-tenth of the total number recruited, and probably reached about one-fifth. The quality of the troops did not always correspond to what had been hoped. Forced conscripts were not the same as the men recruited at the time of the conquest. Until 1914 the black army was a professional force, recruited mainly among the warrior peoples of Senegal and the Sudan. The infantrymen – mainly from military territories – had been privileged, their extortions tolerated; 'black funds' available to the officers had enabled them to 'encourage' the soldiers with 'bounty'. [76] An officer wrote:

> Let us not forget . . . that we have been able to raise recruits for

campaigns against the Ahmadu, the Samory and others, and we use their own soldiers after they have been defeated because we have wisely employed the only means which have ever made a good mercenary army: a share in the profits.[77]

That attraction had now disappeared, and, even worse, the families of the conscripted men were virtually abandoned. It was only in 1918 that the servicemen were given promises of a few limited advantages, with the after-thought of later making the 'ex-combatants' into a 'buffer group' (to use George Padmore's phrase)[78] as a support for the colonial administration. The ethnic composition of the troops changed. People of the forest regions, up to then an insignificant proportion, now accounted for half the total number of men. The chiefs who were given the task of furnishing recruits sent the poorest men, actual or former slaves, the outcasts of society, to make up the numbers: three-quarters of the contingents furnished by French West Africa between 1914 and 1918 were made up of such types.[79] This circumstance contributed to the destruction of former social relations. On their return, relatively privileged and independent, with pensions, marked out for reserved employment, and sometimes elected chiefs, these former captives rose to the level of their one-time masters, and even above them.

Sometimes, the chiefs used recruitment to get rid of those who could not be assimilated or were otherwise useless – the obstinate, the inveterately lazy, malingerers or the sick. It was kill or cure.

(c) RESISTANCE DURING THE WAR

This new exigency robbed the country of its youngest and most vigorous men. It came on top of the 'customary' exigencies, which were now further intensified by war taxation, forced labour, the supply of agricultural produce, etc. The country was already exhausted and frequently ravaged by famine. The difficulties did not appear all at once. After the famine of 1913–14, conscription into the army seemed to some an honourable way out. They expected from it either servitude, as in the past, or else honour and fortune. But this illusion was soon destroyed. This war had nothing in common with the African wars of former days, including those conducted by the colonisers. Those who left to fight in it rarely sent news. Their families were left with no help other than that of their closest relatives; a few repatriated soldiers and a few letters soon informed them of the horrors of the battles, the blood, the mud, the snow. Rumour propagated a fantastic picture, exaggerated perhaps, but was there any need to exaggerate? The return of the first wounded and mutilated soldiers spread terror.

The first uprising against recruitment began early in 1915. General Abadie attributed the revolts to

> poor propaganda, the composition and defective functioning of certain recruitment commissions, forced enrolment and arbitrary designation, delays in payment of premiums and indemnities to families, abuse in forced labour and subscription,[80] exaggerated accounts of the war brought by the first wounded men who were repatriated, and the actions of the fetishists.[81]

The first insurrection broke out in the Sudan, among the Bambara of Bélédougou. A column of troops led by Major Caillet 'brought them to reason'.[82] The leader of the insurgents, Diocé Traoré, blew himself up with his faithful companions in his *tata* at N'Koumé on 18 March, 1915.[83] 'A contingent formed in 1916 stormed the rebel villages and traversed the whole region under revolt.' But meanwhile, in March, the revolt spread to the circles of San, Koutiala, Bandiagara, Dori and Ouagadougou. From October 1915 to April 1916 alone, the repressions involved 2,500 infantrymen, 200 circle police, 2,000 supporters, with six cannons and four machine-guns.[86] The revolts continued in the Sudan until 1920 when, after a month of siege, the Dogon village of Tabi was captured (October–November 1920).

Hope of support from the Turks and the Germans provoked the Senussi to launch an offensive; they had remained independent in the Koufra oasis after the Italian victory. All over the Sahara and in the eastern Sudan, where advance posts, such as those of Dar Sila in Chad, had been evacuated in September 1914, revolts broke out. There was a general rising of the Touareg. The Targui chief Kaossen arrived at Ghat at the beginning of August 1916 with 200 regulars, a cannon and a machine-gun. He occupied Fort-Polignac and Djanet, which he held until 1918, and laid siege to Agadès. Combined Franco-British operations were needed to put an end to the resistance of the sultans in revolt at Dar Sila (Chad) and Darfur (Anglo-Egyptian Sudan) in 1916.[87]

The French who were in Africa for the Turco-Senussi offensive of 1916 will not forget the feeling of hope which passed through the whole of the Sudan in expectation of the raid of the Targui Kaossen, who were fortunately stopped before Agadès and thrown back to Aïr. Opposition to recruiting was intense, in spite of the recruiting campaign entrusted to Diagne – which mainly served publicly to humiliate the white members of the mission as they drove behind the triumphant chariot of the ebony-skinned high-commissioner – and this opposition caused a rising of fetishists and Muslims, and numerous revolts of a local character, which could have led to a holy war. . . .'[88]

This testimony by an officer of the colonial forces indicates the strength and extent of the movement which shook the whole of French West Africa. But in the end the revolts remained isolated local events, and were put down one after the other, like resistance during the conquest. The excesses of recruiting and of the 'war effort' in the frontier region caused migrations towards the neighbouring enclaves, mainly British, where there was no recruitment and where the fiscal situation was less onerous. In Dahomey the revolt began in January 1914, in the Holli country by the frontier with Nigeria, a marshy region covered with forests, which favoured guerrilla warfare. The first revolt failed, but a new rising took place (22 August, 1915 – 15 February, 1916), then a third (November 1916). The Holli chief was deported to Port-Etienne, where he died.

At the beginning of 1916 the Somba people of Atakora rose when an attempt at recruiting was made among them. Under the leadership of Gaba, from the village of Pelima, the young people took to the bush and the revolt spread to the regions of Tanguiéta and Kouandé. In September 1916 the Renard contingent ravaged the area, but without results. In January 1917 the movement spread to Middle Niger, and there were troubles at Kasadi and Gaya. In October 1916 a revolt broke out in the mountainous region of Borgou. Under the leadership of the king of the Nikki people, Chabi Prouka, and his war chief, Bio Guéra, the Bariba cut down bridges and telegraph lines, built road blocks and laid siege to the administrative post at Bimbéréké. In December 1916, repression was organised. Bio Guéra and his son were killed. The King of the Nikki escaped but was handed over to the French by Ago-li-agbo, and condemned to five years' internment; he died soon afterwards in the convict prison at Fotoba. Finally, from February 1917, an offensive was launched against the Atakora. Seven mountain refuges were taken by assault, and in the last (Dara Ouri) Gaba was killed with 300 or 400 men, women and children; the survivors, numbering about 300, were taken prisoner on 7 April, 1917. 'His [Gaba's] death in the last battle compelled the admiration of Major Renard, his adversary, and a similar view from the historian.'[89]

The last movement in the revolt against recruiting in Dahomey was that of the Sahoué (between Lake Ahémé and Lake Toho) in 1918. After the circle commander was killed, truly warlike operations were mounted, between 27 July, 1918, and 1 February, 1919.

. . . Military posts were established almost everywhere in the country of the Sahoué and notably in the neighbourhood of

F

watering points (Tokpa, for example, near Togo). *Any individuals who approached were killed:* there were many burnt-out huts and many dead – certainly more than a thousand.[90]

Reprisals continued for seven months and fifteen chiefs were deported to the Congo.

An example of the exodus movements was that of the Agni of Sanwi, whose country was on the frontier with the Gold Coast. Taxation of mahogany logs (free among the British), the suppression of the traditional kingship, and the forced cultivation of cocoa introduced by Governor Angoulvant had provoked numerous emigrations in 1913. The movement grew stronger with the war and recruiting, and involved the principal dignitaries. They demanded the restoration of a treaty concluded with France in 1843 and unilaterally suppressed by decree in 1900. During negotiations undertaken through the good services of the British district commissioner of Axim, they gave as conditions for their return the suppression of tax on timber logs, of forced and statute labour and of military recruiting. They finally returned after an agreement which promised them an amnesty was concluded in June 1918. But twelve of the chiefs who returned were immediately arrested and deported, finally being reprieved at the end of 1918.[91]

There were similar incidents on the other frontiers and in the whole of the Ivory Coast.

In 1915 numerous natives escaped to Liberia to avoid recruitment. From December 1917 to August 1918 a contingent operated in the Dida country whose inhabitants had revolted. Intensive recruitment had provoked numerous desertions [especially in the regions of Adzopé and Kong]; in Lobi there were several attempts to hold up the march of the detachments.[92]

In French Equatorial Africa revolts continued and were renewed against taxation, forced labour and requisitioning. Recruitment of porters and the requisitioning of foodstuffs for the detachments used against Kamerun increased the burden on the population.

In 1915 the resistance of entire tribes of the Bangana between Ouadda and Yalinga, who refused any tax assessment and all work for the benefit of the Compagnie des Sultanats, necessitated the sending of a military detachment.[93]

In the Years 1917–18

the collection of taxes or the establishment of certain posts became the occasion for hostile manifestations, for example among the Ivindo and the Woleu N'Tem.[94]

In the centre and east of Gabon, agitation reached such a degree that it led to full-scale military operations. In the Middle Congo, they were mounted in Lobaye (1917), Louessé (1916), Koudou (1917) and in N'Goko, which remained incompletely subjected. The troops met resistance from bands of 'army deserters coming from German units' in the New Cameroons. In Ubangi, the struggle took place in the Kotto basin, against Chief Gaiac, who was subjugated in May 1918; reprisal detachments systematically ravaged the country to induce famine. On the Upper M'Bomou, Sultan Mopoi, who had established himself on French territory in 1911 after being expelled from the Belgian Congo, was considered 'arrogant', and his arrest was decided upon in 1916. But the Sultan had 400 *bazinguers* (soldiers) who were well trained, and were equipped to one-third of their total number with quick-firing guns. After an attempt at a surprise attack by the head of the post on the person of the Sultan had failed, the French troops were beaten and the post evacuated. Belgian and British troops had to be called in for help in beating the Sultan in a battle on 17 March, 1916, and in his capture on 15 April. In 1919, resistance spread to the mountains of Ouham-Pendé and Ouham-Barga, where the caves served as refuge for the fighters from the Baya, Pana and Karé peoples. In Ouham-Pendé the Baya resisted in the Yadé caves; an assault on these was made between March and May 1919.

Chief Nome, the soul of the rebellion, surrounded in a cave with a few fanatics, refused to surrender and had himself killed after a heroic defence.[95]

Among the Pana, Chief Goibina, who had victoriously resisted the Germans for four months in 1914, was killed while making a raid on 23 April, 1919. Submission was completed by 1 May, 1919. The last uprising of the Karé, who still resisted in their caves, was on 14–17 June, 1920.[96] In Chad, the repression of movements linked to Senussi attacks[97] did not put an end to resistance and repression. In November 1917 the massacre of Abéché,

an atrocious tragedy, surpassing in cruelty and horror the worst abuses of even the most bloodthirsty of the old sultans, caused panic among the whole country and left an appalling memory for a long time.[98]

In 1918, recruiting for the army provoked new troubles and new repressions 'as at the first imposition of taxes'. Numerous villages, which had been constrained by the systematic ravaging of their crops to resettle in the plains, returned to their former settlements in the mountains.[99]

5. Conquest and Annexation of Togo and Kamerun, 1914–1919

The outbreak of war had been disastrous for the Allies in Europe, but by way of compensation, they had an easy success in Africa where German possessions, surrounded by French, British and Belgian territories, could not put up any serious opposition.

Togo, being impossible to defend geographically, was the first to give in. The governor, Major von Döring, on 5 August, 1914, proposed to his neighbours in the Gold Coast and Dahomey that the colony should remain neutral. However, Togo was invaded on the 6th simultaneously by the British and the French, who had greatly superior numbers. Von Döring had barely 1,500 men at his command, of whom 200 were Germans. He drew back to the radio station of Kamina where he capitulated on 26 August, after destroying the installations.

In Kamerun, however, the inaccessible forest and mountain zones made resistance easier. The German Colonel Zimmermann had some 3,500 men. The three-pronged attack against him was led from the sea coast by Colonel Meyer, from French Equatorial Africa by General Aymerich, and from Nigeria by Major-General Cunliffe. The immense extent of these fronts and the nature of the terrain made co-ordination as well as supplies for the troops difficult. In French Equatorial Africa requisitioning for military porterage for the Kamerun campaign caused 'the death of thousands of men, even the most robust'.[100]

This invasion received several setbacks, particularly in the north, but the Allies received reinforcements in 1915, in particular the Belgian contingents who came to reinforce the troops from French Equatorial Africa. They managed to mobilise 13,000 men, which enabled them to re-open the attack, but the operations dragged on for another year and became more costly. Garoua fell on 11 June, 1915, N'Gaoundéré on 19 June, after the rainy season the last centres of resistance were forced. On 22 December, 1915, Colonel Zimmermann, the governor, and the greater part of the German forces took refuge in Spanish Guinea, where they were disarmed and interned. Finally, on 18 February, 1916, the fort of Mora, which had been besieged since September 1914, capitulated. The troops of Equatorial Africa, who had furnished half the Allied armies engaged in Kamerun, suffered heavy losses – more than one-third of their total strength, not counting those who died after evacuation to the rear.[101]

Provisional agreements divided the administration of Togo and Kamerun between France and Great Britain (convention of 7 September, 1914, applying to Togo; agreement of 4 March, 1916, applying to Kamerun). While the Germans continued to expect victory in Europe, the realisation of a 'Mittel-Afrika' continued to figure among the German war aims. On the Allied side the French and the British had every intention of keeping the territories they had appropriated. A series of secret agreements, concluded between 1915 and 1917, had already laid down the division among the imperialists of the German and Turkish possessions. However, the Allies' propaganda – mainly after the entry of the United States into the war – was based on the principle of 'the right of peoples to self-determination'. Behind the 'idealism' of President Wilson was hidden America's desire to limit as much as possible the expansion of its European allies. In his message to the American Congress on 8 January, 1918, President Wilson laid down the principles of a 'just peace' in eighteen points. The fifth point touched on the colonial question, but already offered the means for the right of the peoples to self-determination to be isolated by reference to their 'interests' – a hint that the colonial peoples were incapable of exercising this right.[102]

Article 119 of the Treaty of Versailles deprived Germany completely of the right to possess colonies. Through propaganda, carried out from 1915 onwards, about the 'atrocities' of German colonisation, the European Allies had made the United States subscribe to this principle on the grounds that Germany had become morally unfit to colonise.[103] In an address to the American Senate in July 1919, Wilson declared:

> Germany must be deprived of her colonies because she would use them as objects of exploitation.[104]

There remained the question of reconciling the partition among the conquerors with Wilson's principles. Wilson had gone as far as envisaging that

> the German colonies should be declared the common property of the League of Nations and administered by the small nations.[105]

The idea of a mandate, defined in Article 22 of the Pact of the League of Nations, furnished a compromise solution. In practice, however, the French and British imperialists kept the German colonies which they had conquered. Legally, they were entrusted by the League of Nations with the 'tutelage' of the 'people still incapable of managing themselves in the particularly difficult conditions of the modern world', and had to submit to the League an annual report on their administration of the mandate territories. In concrete terms American imperialism imposed on the mandate-holders the principle of the 'open door' (freedom of exchange and commerce for all members of the League of Nations), freedom of conscience and religion (an open door to American missions) and the prohibition of military bases or of subjecting the people to military instruction (except police forces). Such were the principles of the 'B Mandate' to which Togo and Kamerun, among others, were subjected.

In spite of protests from the Weimar Republic, which claimed the mandate over the former colonies, an inter-Allied commission meeting in London on 19 May, 1919, ratified, except for a few details, the partition agreed to during the war by the French and the British. The Cameroons were divided into three parts. The former French territories annexed in 1911 were simply re-incorporated into French Equatorial Africa. The greater part of the rest (432,000 square km. with 2,800,000 inhabitants) was entrusted to France. Great Britain received two frontier strips adjoining Nigeria, with 550,000 inhabitants; the southern part comprised Mount Cameroon, with Victoria and Bouea (the former German capital), and the northern part, the emirate of Dikoa, was re-incorporated into the protected sultanate of Bornu. Togo was divided into two parts: the larger part consisting of roughly two-thirds of the territory with 747,000 inhabitants, with the coast and the capital Lomé, went to France, while a frontier strip adjacent to the Gold Coast with 185,000 inhabitants was entrusted to Great Britain. The Paris Convention of 8 September, 1919, finally settled the frontiers between Chad and the Anglo-Egyptian Sudan, and gave Dar Sila to France.

6. The Russian October Revolution and Africa

In appearance nothing had changed. Free of their German competitors, the victorious imperialists bore down even more heavily upon Africa. The golden age of colonisation was dawning, the time of great silence, when not a word reached the outside world about tropical Africa, not even a complaint. Judging by colonial publications of the time, one is led to believe that nothing was happening in Africa, where the peoples lived in peace and prosperity under the vigilant and enlightened tutelage of their administrators and governors. It was elsewhere, outside Africa, that the world imperialist system was first breached.

On 7 November, 1917, the Russian Revolution overthrew imperialism, proposed world peace, and proclaimed the right to freedom and independence of the peoples oppressed by Russian imperialism. Until then, the desire for liberty of the oppressed colonial peoples seemed to have no hope of success. They found themselves face to face with the monopolist front of an international class of exploiters, free to use all the resources and all the arms in the world.[106]

Resistance had not been lacking, but that seemed to have been the dying agony of a condemned world rather than the birth of a new. The socialists of Europe did not imagine, as we have seen, that an effective obstacle could be put in the way of colonial enterprise. In spite of the *cordon sanitaire* which was immediately established around Soviet Russia by international imperialism, the echo of the October Revolution reverberated throughout the world. The Russian revolution had proved that the system of oppression, crushing both the working classes of the home countries and the colonised peoples, was neither eternal nor invincible. It pointed to the solidarity that was necessary between the two categories of oppressed, between the socialist revolution in the industrial countries and the democratic anti-imperialist and agrarian revolution of the dependent peoples. The consequences were felt in first the neighbouring countries, those bordering on or close to the U.S.S.R. In semi-colonial China with its system of the 'open door' to the various imperialist powers, in the British Empire in India and in the Middle East, the crisis of the colonial system henceforth became more open.

There was a strong reaction even in North Africa. In 1920, the old radical Vigné d'Octon wrote:

. . . As I write these lines, there is not a single Arab, a single Bedouin from the extreme south of Tunisia to the western confines of Morocco, who does not know of the great Russian Revolution, and who, when facing the Orient, does not beg his God to make the reign of justice triumph, together with the Republic of the Soviets, over the land of Islam and the world.[107]

We possess no data which makes it possible to judge whether this phenomenon was also true of tropical Africa. It is certain, however, that a great awakening of consciences took place in this post-war period. The war had enabled African soldiers to see countries where the whites worked and were exploited. Some of them took part in mutinies at the end of the war, in Champagne, and with the Black Sea fleet. But the myth of the invincibility of the white man was not seriously shaken. What could be found to oppose the terrifying means of war which he possessed, and which were far superior to the Lebel guns and artillery which had been invincible in the wars of colonial conquest? The colonial system still felt confident. It needed the Second World War ultimately to break down its authority.

REFERENCES

1. The Compagnie des produits de la Sangha (Mestayer) and the Compagnie de la N'Goko-Ouesso (Mimerel, Paquier and Kunkler).

2. Cf. Maurice Viollette, *A la veille d'Agadir. La N'Goko-Sangha*, Paris, Larose, 1914. See also J. Caillaux, *Agadir: ma Politique extérieure*. Paris, Albin Michel, 1919.

3. Cf. *Bulletin du Comité de l'Afrique française*, 1900, No. 9, pp. 368–9.

4. *Bulletin du Comité de l'Afrique française*, 1905, No. 8, pp. 309–10.

5. Maurice Viollette, op. cit.

6. This Convention rectified the frontiers of the Cameroons and the French Congo by replacing the lines, which were largely theoretical, by water-courses, and by suppressing the 'Duck's Beak' formed to the north of the Tenth Parallel by the Shari and the Logone.

7. F. Challaye, *Un aspirant dictateur: André Tardieu*. Paris, Editions de la Révolution prolétarienne, 1930, p. 13. The articles in question are Nos. 3 and 29 of the specification.

8. The managing director was Mestayer, whom Caillaux described as follows: 'After rapidly dissipating a large family fortune, he had the lucky chance, thanks to connections in high places, of getting a concession in the Congo, whose degrees of longitude and latitude I would not swear that he knew. . . . His idle man-of-the-world mentality, his past as a Parisian prodigal, helped him to understand business as it is understood in the circles he frequented, where "to do business" meant to use social contacts and do no work, gaining large sums easily.' (J. Caillaux, *Agadir*, op. cit., pp. 57–8.)

9. André Tardieu, *Le Mystère d'Agadir*. Paris, Calmann-Lévy, 1912.

10. The company claimed 12,675,000 francs, the government proposed 903,000 francs; if one is to believe *Le Courrier européen* (1911, p. 141), there was collusion between Merlin (whose venality has been established) and Tardieu. This review cites, on this subject, a 'crushing report' from the Inspection of the Colonies.

11. J. Caillaux, op. cit., p. 64.

12. In *Le Courrier européen* (1911), p. 378, Félicien Challaye wrote, under the title 'First Victory': 'The indemnity of the N'Goko-Sangha will not be paid. . . . This is the effect of the campaign of the French League for the Defence of the Natives in the Conventional Basin of the Congo.'

13. J. Massiou, *Les Grandes concessions au Congo français*. Paris, Sagot, 1920.

14. J. Caillaux, op. cit., p. 79.

15. The 'independent state' was annexed by Belgium in 1908.

16. Grouping of big trusts of French steelworks directly interested in the military commands.

17. Cf. R. Thomas, 'La politique socialiste et le problème colonial de 1905 à 1920', *Revue française d'histoire d'Outre-mer*, 1960, pp. 213–45.

18. *Afrique Noire*, I, 2nd edition, p. 212.

19. A. Zévaès, *Histoire des partis socialistes en France*. Paris, Rivière, 1911; III: 'Les Guesdistes', pp. 100–2.

20. Cf. A. Olivesi, 'Les socialistes marseillais et le probleme colonial', *Mouvement Social*, No. 46, January–March 1964, pp. 27–66; Claude Williard, *Les Guesdistes*. Paris, Editions sociales, 1965, p. 63.

21. Claude Williard, op. cit., pp. 209–12.

22. Paul Louis, *Le Colonialisme*. Paris, Société Nouvelle de Librairie et d'Edition. 1905.

23. Paul Louis, op. cit., pp. 47–8.

24. 'Cartiéristes': supporters of ideas developed in 1958 by Raymond Cartier, pro-American journalist, violently hostile to 'aid' to the colonies or the former colonies of France.

25. Henri Brunschwig, *Mythes et réalités de l'impérialisme colonial français*. Paris, A. Colin, 1960. In English translation: *Myths and Realities of French Colonialism*. London, Pall Mall, 1965.

26. Lenin, *Imperialism, the Highest Stage of Capitalism*; Rudolf Hilferding, *Das Finanz Kapital*, Vienna, 1910; J. A. Hobson, *Imperialism*. London and New York, 1902.

27. Paul Louis, op. cit., p. 109.

28. Cf. Bruhat, 'Jaurès devant le problème colonial', *Cahiers Internationaux*, 94, March 1958, pp. 43–62.

29. Op. cit., p. 62.

30. R. Thomas, 'La politique socialiste et le problème colonial de 1905 à 1920', *Revue française d'histoire d'Outre-Mer*. 1960, 213–45.

31. Interpolation of 19 and 20 February, 1906.

32. Charles Dumas, *Libérez les indigènes ou renoncez aux colonies*. Paris, Eugène Figuière, 1914.

33. Félicien Challaye, *Le Congo français*. Paris, Alcan, 1909, p. 313. He recognised his mistake later, and the fact that the 'justice' he demanded was incompatible with the act of colonialism (see *Souvenirs sur la colonisation*. Paris, Picart, 1935): 'I too have tried to keep to the middle of the road, and have upheld the illusion that good might triumph. I thought: it all depends on a better administration. I had to convince myself that, fatally, and whatever the better persons do, the most covetous material interests are and always will be triumphant (and always at the expense of the natives).' (Félicien Challaye. Cited in Pierre Herbart, *Le Chancre du Niger*, preface by André Gide. Paris, Gallimard, 1939, p. 11.)

34. M. Rébérioux and G. Haupt, 'Le socialisme et la question coloniale avant 1914: l'attitude de l'Internationale', *Mouvement social*, No. 45, October–December 1963, pp. 7–38. That same year Kautsky published his work *Sozialismus und Kolonialpolitik*, which formed a pendant to the work by Paul Louis.

35. Assembly which expressed itself fully in support of the Radical Party, whose representatives, after Doumergue moved to the ministry for the colonies in the Combes cabinet, became the most zealous spokesmen of colonial policy.

36. Paul Vigné d'Octon, *La Gloire du sabre*. Paris, Flammarion, 1900.

37. Paul Vigné d'Octon, *Les Crimes coloniaux de la IIIe République*. Vol. I: 'La Sueur du burnous'. Paris, Editions de la Guerre sociale, 1911. The other volumes that were to follow, one on the battles in the Algerian–Morocco region from 1900–10, the other on the Foreign Legion and the military prison 'Biribi', never appeared and, it seems, were never written.

38. Cf. M. Rébérioux, 'La gauche socialiste française, la "Guerre sociale" et le "Mouvement socialiste" face au problème colonial', *Mouvement social*, No. 46, January–March 1964, pp. 91–104.

39. Op. cit., p. 8. On his character and work see J. Suret-Canale, 'L'Anti-colonialisme en France sous la IIIe République: Paul Vigné d'Octon', *Cahiers internatiounaux*, No. 107, September–October 1959, pp. 57–68.

40. Circular of 20 September, 1917. *Bulletin du Comité de l'Afrique française*, 1917, No. 9–10–11 (September–October–November), p. 353.

41. Government-General of French Equatorial Africa, *Comptes définitifs des recettes et des dépenses*. Financial year 1911. Paris, Larose, 1912.

42. 'The famine in 1914 in the Sudan was preceded in 1912 and in 1913 by drought, followed by a bad harvest throughout the immense territory from the Senegal to Chad, an area of 450 sq. km.' (Henri Labouret, *Famines et disettes aux colonies*. Paris, 1938.)

F*

43. Cf. Jean Gallais, 'La Vie saisonnière au sud du lac Debo', *C.O.M.*, 1958, II, pp. 117–41.

44. Henri Ortoli, 'Le Gage des personnes au Soudan français', *Bulletin de l'I.F.A.N.*, vol. I, 1939, pp. 313–24.

45. Félix de Kersaintgilly, 'Essai sur l'évolution de l'esclavage en A.O.F.', *B.C.E.H.S.*, 1924, No. 3, pp. 469–78.

46. Cited by E. L. Bélime, *Les Travaux du Niger*. Government-general of French West Africa, 1940, p. 17.

47. Denise Moran, *Tchad*. Paris, Gallimard, 1934. Quoting texts whose publication was prohibited, the author unfortunately often suppressed names of places and persons.

48. D. Moran, op. cit., p. 70. In the Congo, the chartered companies were interested in payment of tax in kind; in Chad, on the contrary, where merchandise could not be exported, it was more convenient to levy it in money.

49. D. Moran, op. cit.

50. Ibid.

51. Ibid.

52. Strips of woven cotton.

53. Ibid., p. 71.

54. Colonel Largeau, 'La Situation militaire du Tchad au début de 1912', *A.F.*, *R.C.*, 1913, No. 1, pp. 3–19.

55. Colonel Largeau, op. cit.

56. D. Moran, op. cit., p. 73.

57. Ibid.

58. D. Moran, op. cit., p. 81.

59. Mountain people not converted to Islam.

60. D. Moran, op. cit., p. 74.

61. Ibid., p. 86.

62. Hilaire, op. cit.

63. Ibid., p. 201.

64. Ibid., p. 202.

65. D. Moran, op. cit., p. 93. The pamphlet *Victor Augagneur et l'Afrique équatoriale française*, by R. S., colon du Congo (Bordeaux, Imprimerie coopérative, 1913), estimates that half the population was lost as the result of the 1913–14 famine at Ouadai. General Hilaire estimates that the population of Ouadai dropped from 700,000 in 1912 to 400,000 in 1914; Abéché, which had 28,000 inhabitants in 1912, had no more than 5,000 to 6,000 in July 1914. (Hilaire, op. cit., p. 91.)

66. D. Moran, op. cit., p. 230.

67. *Revue de Paris*, Numbers of 1 and 15 July, 1909.

68. *Bulletin du Comité de l'Afrique française*, No. 7, July 1909. For the general public Mangin developed his arguments in his book *La Force noire*, Paris, Hachette, 1910. On the controversies raised by the Mangin project, see Abdoulaye Ly, *Mercenaires noirs*. Paris, Présence africaine, 1957, notably pp. 33 ff.

69. *Revue indigène*, No. 61, 30 May, 1911, p. 279.

70. G. François, 'L'Aide de l'Afrique occidentale à la métropole', *Bulletin du Comité de l'Afrique française*, Nos. 5–6, May–June 1917, pp. 195–8.

71. H. Cosnier, op. cit., p. 148.

72. Quotation of Van Vollenhoven in a despatch of the Xth Army.

73. R. Delavignette, *Les Constructeurs de la France d'outre-mer*. Paris, Correa, 1946, p. 422.

74. R. Delavignette, op. cit., pp. 425–6.

75. The following is the official table of recruitment between 1914 and 1918 taken from A. Sarraut, *La Mise en valeur des colonies françaises*. Paris, Payot, 1923.

	1914	1915	1916	1917	1918	Total
French West Africa	29,742	34,655	51,913	13,831	63,208	193,349
French Equatorial Africa	—	3,766	—	—	14,164	17,910
	29,742	38,421	51,913	13,831	77,372	211,259

76. Abou Digu'en, *Notre Empire africain noir*. Paris, Charles-Lavauzelle, 1928.

77. Ibid., p. 63.

78. G. Padmore, *La Vie et les luttes des travailleurs nègres*. Petite Bibliothèque de l'Internationale Syndicale Rouge, XXXVII, Paris n.d.

79. Félix de Kersaintgilly, 'Essai sur l'évolution de l'esclavage en A.O.F.', *B.C.E.H.S.*, 1924, No. 3, pp. 469–78.

80. A study should be made of the 'subscriptions' (for national defence, war victims, etc.). The chiefs were evidently asked to participate, if they wished to give proof of 'loyalty' and their 'fidelity to France', which was evaluated according to the sum subscribed. It should be understood that these sums were obtained by supplementary contributions from their subjects. In the single year 1915 the Nomads of Mauritania, wretched as they were, 'subscribed' 60,000 gold francs for 'war-victims'. (G. Désiré-Vuillemin, op. cit., p. 210.)

81. General Abadie, *La Défense des colonies*. Paris, Charles-Lavauzelle, 1937.

82. *Histoire et épopée des troupes coloniales*. Paris, Les Presses modernes, 1956, p. 162.

83. *L'Artillerie aux colonies*. Paris, Imprimerie Villain et Bar, 1931, p. 148.

84. While awaiting a study on this question that is in preparation, let me mention, by way of example, that in the Bwa country (Bobo-Oulé) the revolt broke out in December 1915 over road works. A guard of the Commissioner for Native Affairs, Haillot, had forced a woman to work on the road with a one-day old baby. The baby died. The workers rose in revolt and killed the guard. The revolt seems to have been the result of accumulated atrocities performed by Haillot and certain officers (strangled prisoners, round-ups of young girls on the markets, rape accompanied by hanging, babies killed on their mothers' backs, etc.). The call-up of soldiers – at least in the memory of old men who lived at that time – does not seem to have played a determining role in this case. (M. Nazi Boni, *in litteris*. See, by that author, *Crépuscule des temps anciens*. Paris, Présence africaine, 1962, where this drama is described.)

85. *Histoire et épopée des troupes coloniales*. Paris, Les Presses modernes, 1956, p. 162.

86. General Abadie, op. cit.

87. *Les Troupes coloniales pendant la guerre 1914–1918:* 'Les senoussistes pendant la guerre 1914–1918.' Paris, Imprimerie nationale, 1931, pp. 483–98.

88. Abou Digu'en, op. cit., pp. 90–1.

89. R. Cornevin, *Histoire du Dahomey*. Paris, Berger-Levrault, 1962, p. 422.

90. M. Collery, 'Origine historique des cantons de la subdivision d'Athiémé', *Etudes dahoméennes*, 1952, VIII, p. 106.

91. H. Mouezy, *Assinie et le royaume de Krinjabo*. Paris, Larose, 1942, pp. 158–62.

92. *Histoire et épopée des troupes coloniales*. Paris, Les Presses modernes, 1956.

93. P. Kalck, *Réalités oubanguiennes*. Paris, Berger-Levrault, 1959, p. 48.

94. *Histoire militaire de l'Afrique équatoriale française*. Paris, Imprimerie nationale, 1931. It should be noted that the regions cited, like Upper-Sangha mentioned below, formed part of the New Cameroons (regions of French Equatorial Africa annexed by Germany by virtue of the 1911 agreements). The German ordinance of 4 December, 1912, fixing the rate of the poll tax in Kamerun, exempted the New Cameroons 'for political reasons'. Before evacuating it, the French administration had generally levied advance taxes for 1912. The reintroduction of the tax after two years of exemption was not well received.

95. *Histoire militaire de l'A.E.F.*, p. 327.

96. It was the repression of this uprising that Governor-General Augagneur denounced in the text cited above.

97. See above.

98. General Hilaire, op. cit., p. 328. The commander of Abéché (an alcoholic, already transferred for disciplinary reasons), on denunciation of an alleged 'plot', had two local chiefs murdered with the *'coupe-coupe'* by the Senegalese together with all their household and all the *faqihs* (Muslim clergy) of Abéché, more than a hundred persons in all.

99. D. Moran, op. cit.

100. *Victor Augagneur et l'A.E.F.*, by R. S., colon du Congo. Bordeaux, Imprimerie coopérative, 1923, p. 9.

101. A. Annet, *En colonne dans le Cameroun.* Paris, Debresse, 1949, pp. 118–19.

102. 'The free [sic], frank and absolutely impartial settlement of all colonial claims, founded upon the strict observance of the principle that in the determination of all these questions of sovereignty, the interest of the peoples under consideration must be borne in mind as much as the just claims of the governments whose rights are to be determined.' (Quoted by H. Brunschwig, *L'Expansion allemande outre-mer.* Paris, P.U.F., 1957, p. 182.)

103. Cf. *Les Crimes allemands en Afrique.* Paris, Comité de l'Afrique française, 1917.

104. Quoted by H. Brunschwig, op. cit., p. 181. In Germany people were indignant at the hypocrisy of this argument. It was pointed out that the French and English had committed the same atrocities and that they had been criticised, less often and that the French, English, and Belgians themselves used their colonies as 'objects of exploitation'. An official pamphlet put French colonisation on trial. (Reichskolonialministerium. Deutsche und französische Eingeborenenbehandlung: *Eine Erwiderung auf die im 'Journal officiel de la République française' vom 8 November, 1918, und 5 Januar, 1919, veröffentlichten Berichte.* Berlin, Dietrich Reimer, 1919.)

105. Ibid., p. 183.

106. W. Markov, *Sistemi coloniali e movimenti di liberazione.* Roma, Editori Riuniti, 1961, p. 42.

107. P. Vigné d'Octon, *La Nouvelle gloire du sabre.* Marseille, Petite Bibliothèque du Mutilé, n.d., p. 136.

PART TWO

The Zenith of Colonialism

1919–1945

INTRODUCTION

For the colonisers of tropical Africa, the years between the two wars constituted an era of security, yet with an undercurrent of anxiety. In spite of a few setbacks, serious only in Equatorial Africa, there was political stability. The administrative system, which a political observer in 1920 called a 'prelude to normal administration' – having 'lasted longer than is reasonable',[1] remained unchanged, and became consolidated in the same spirit of autocracy, bureaucratic routine and extemporisation.

The administrative ultra-conservatism was itself but the reflection of the opposition to economic progress. Between 1919 and 1939, and even up to 1945, the face of 'French' tropical Africa undoubtedly changed, but it was little in comparison with the profound transformations that occurred in the rest of the world. The introduction of the motor-car and, at the end of the period, the radio, represented the most important changes for Africa. 'Development' was not pushed further, and the existing system of trade persisted without many modifications.

There was a tendency to organise a more rational exploitation of the possessions that were kept in reserve. Immediately after the First World War and later during the world economic crisis, plans were drawn up. The only big enterprise initiated was that of the Niger Office, but compared with the size of the investment, the results were meagre. Even modest plans for improving the infrastructure, which had been conceived before 1914, remained unrealised. As regards railway lines, Roume, in 1904, had envisaged the construction of an East–West arterial route linking the various parts of French West Africa and providing access to the coast for various colonies: Guinea, the Ivory Coast and Dahomey. But with the coming of the motor-car, the main railway line, which was essentially of strategic importance, lost its attraction. As to 'lines of penetration', even those begun before 1914 were not completed. In Equatorial Africa one single project took twenty years to complete: the 512 km. Congo–Ocean line. We shall see under what conditions and at what a price it was achieved.

Thus the significant changes affected only the main towns and the big commercial ports. In the bush nothing changed. At Faranah, in Upper Guinea, the main commercial transactions were still conducted in 1939 by barter without the use of money. An administrator who crossed the canton of Soliman, a sub-division of Faranah, in October 1932, wrote: 'During this rapid tour I gained the impression that this region, which I visited in 1906, has not made any progress. On the contrary, as far as routes of communication go, there has been regress.'² In travelling across the Senegalese countryside, which he had visited for the first time at the end of the nineteenth century, Professor Auguste Chevalier received the same impression in 1947. The huts were still as miserable, the peasants still in rags; he asked: 'But what has happened to the millions of gold francs earned from the sale of peanuts?'³ And what of the regions where no roads existed? In 1947, as on the eve of the conquest, the officials moving about the forest region of Guinea used the 'hammock', a litter carried by four porters who were provided by the chief. To this should be added those requisitioned to carry the luggage, their number determined by the administrative grade of the traveller.⁴

This period of mediocrity and misery had its upheavals: one hardly dares to imagine the suffering caused by the arrival of a sadistic or unbalanced administrator or a famine due to natural catastrophe, the long period of hardship caused by the 'war efforts' of 1914–18 and 1939–45, or the depression from 1930 until 1936. Most often, when the drama was over, nothing changed.

In studying this period it becomes necessary to detach oneself from chronological continuity and to study each aspect of colonial exploitation separately, without hesitating, if need be, to go back before 1914, or to leave out the time of the Second World War, in order to find the elements needed to recognise a static reality. The unity of the period makes this possible.

It has already been said that this golden age of colonisation was also an age of great silence. Black Africa caused scarcely any worry. This was not true of Asia which was already in convulsions, or the Middle East and North Africa (the wars in Syria, Rif, and other places). Black Africa was not seriously 'contaminated' – this was stated quite openly in high places – and measures were taken to avoid any risk of contamination.

Before 1914 there was a naïve confidence in the millenial future of colonisation. This confidence took the form of a certain freedom in expressing points of view about colonisation and its methods (there were few who questioned the very principle). The year 1917 sowed doubt and mistrust. The eternal character of colonial enterprise was reaffirmed – it was something which provided a means of self-assurance – there was awareness of the perils that were threatening.

Thus, everything possible was done to prevent what was happening in Africa from filtering out, except through the colonial 'network'. No curious visitor was allowed to come and upset the calm of the authorities. Foreigners, in particular, were more or less excluded, and one could easily have counted the number of visas granted to those who had no business and were suspected of not supporting the colonial ethos – Americans, for example. Trips by journalists, when they took place at all, were usually initiated and subsidised to glorify the minister and the governor-general, and consequently the benefits of colonisation. At the same time they held up to public obliquy the badly informed and the embittered, who by their unseasonable criticism discouraged the courageous actors of the golden age of colonialism.

'The men in charge of our colonies are ready to show "their" land to a few citizens', wrote Albert Londres, 'but only by the light of a dim lantern.'[5] Those who dared to raise discordant voices were few indeed: Robert Poulaine of *Le Temps* (which was otherwise very moderate) Albert Londres, André Gide and Denise Moran, a teacher. These cast but a few beams of light upon a tragic reality. Commercial agents or colonial officers were silenced by their *esprit de corps* or simply by the desire not to spoil their careers. The Africans were gagged by the right of citizenship. Colonial publications like *Afrique française* and official reports published before 1914 did not say everything, but they said enough to enable the facts to be reconstructed without difficulty. The *Revue indigène* or the *Courrier européen* did not hesitate to keep the sore open.

Henceforth, hardly anything can be found apart from statistics or stereotyped accounts of development. For the rest, nothing was amiss – the political situation was excellent and the natives were kept well in hand. The true facts were kept 'confidential' and the reports were hidden in the archives where, to this very day, a researcher – or at least, one who is not right-thinking – has no access. For the first sign of political activity on the part of the Africans, we have no other source than allusions given in a circuitous way here and there, let fall by officials in moments of forgetfulness. Thus, it is still impossible to reconstruct the history of this period in all its detail and in its chronological continuity. Much will remain unknown for as long as the archives remain closed.[6]

REFERENCES

1. Henri Cosnier, *L'Ouest africain français*. Paris, Larose, 1921, p. 140.

2. Brière de l'Isle, 'Tournée dans le canton de Soliman du 25 au 29 octobre, 1932, inclus', *Archives de Faranah*, D.I.

3. A. Chevalier, 'Amélioration et extension de la culture des arachides au Sénégal', *Revue de botanique appliquée*, No. 295-6, May-June 1947, pp. 173-92.

4. In 1958, administrative forms used in Guinea to 'requisition' transport for officials still bore the words 'Number of Porters'.

5. Albert Londres, *Terre d'ébène*. Paris, Albin Michel, 1929, p. 260.

6. One could indeed make inquiries on the spot and gather information from witnesses surviving from that period, who are still numerous.

CHAPTER I

ECONOMIC EXPLOITATION

1. The Trade Monopolies

Seen within the general framework of contemporary colonial practice, the French colonisation in tropical Africa undoubtedly presents a number of special features. Of these the most obvious is the continuation of an economic system from another age. With this in mind an author wrote in 1957 that Black Africa remained

> a choice territory for the colonial commercial companies, with all the features they derive from the conditions in which they work – that is to say, a system of trade consisting of the collection and assembly at the ports of raw materials, which are exported in a crude state, and, in exchange, the distribution of imported manufactured goods.[1]

The export of raw materials and the import of manufactured goods remained characteristic of the economies of the colonised countries under the imperialist colonial system as it had been in the preceding period. But it was the export of capital to these countries that was to assume a decisive character. The monopolies which put their capital into agriculture and mining played the essential role; commerce was subordinate to production, and not the other way round as in the first colonial age.

West and Central Africa under French domination seem to have been an exception in this sense; here, as before, the economy was dominated by the commercial companies, and trade was fitted into the imperialist context. The legal monopoly of the older companies was replaced by a *de facto* monopoly of the financial oligarchy. Here, too, it was exported capital that controlled the economy, but its chosen domain was the import and export trade, and not production. As a consequence, the volume of invested capital remained very small.

The traditional trade was integrated by imperialism. Political and military control guaranteed and consolidated the monopoly of the commercial companies and the level of their profits. The weakness of production, and consequently of sales resulting from insignificant investment in production, was compensated for by the rise of profit margins. Commerce extracted more than surplus produce; it took part of the produce required for natural growth, and reduced the producer to penury. This presented an obstacle to all forms of accumulation, or any kind of technical progress. Monopoly, mercantilism, parasitism, stagnation: these, in short, were the main features of French colonisation in tropical Africa. They fit, moreover, into the general picture that can be drawn of French imperialism which, in spite of the size of its colonial possessions, preferred before 1914 to turn its activities in other directions: Russia, Turkey, Egypt, Latin America and elsewhere. Immediately before the First World War, France's trade with the colonies represented 12 per cent of her foreign trade – far from negligible, certainly, but still not decisive. Of foreign investment totalling 41,000,000,000 francs (gold), only 4,000,000,000 (of which 1,250,000 was a state loan) were committed to the colonies. This orientation of French overseas investment had a relation to the inflated rewards and commission that banks derived from certain foreign loans, and which were acquiesced in by countries with unstable economies like the Russian and Ottoman empires and Latin American republics. Further, in return for their loans, debtors in those countries were made to use a significant portion of the credits they received on purchases in France; manufacturing and armament trusts (mainly metallurgy), which were closely associated with the banks, gained profits this way. Thus capital gained both ways, and in addition fleeced the simple-minded French investor with a taste for safe bonds (and were there any safer than those guaranteed by the state?). How this type of operation worked is well known, in particular from the Russian loans. Thus, wrote Lenin, 'by contrast to British colonial imperialism, French imperialism can be qualified as usurous'.[2]

After 1919, according to estimates, French imperialism had lost two-thirds to three-quarters of its investments abroad, and was even less in a state to develop its colonial investments properly, although certain attempts were made. Essential investments continued to be made in the form of state loans, granted to Central and Eastern Europe, in particular. What was able to be spared for the colonies was mostly absorbed by North Africa – especially the newly-conquered Morocco – and Indochina.

(a) CAPITAL

In 1938 Frankel showed how slight was the investment made in the French territories of tropical Africa, particularly as compared with the British territories. The figures show a preponderance of public investment, which cannot really be considered imported capital, since it came mainly from local budgetary allocations, which included money provided from loans, repayable with interest by the colonial treasuries. According to Frankel, investment in the three groups of territories we are considering represents 5·94 per cent of investment in Africa as a whole, or 4·13 per cent if we only count private capital. The capital invested per head of population represents £2 sterling per person, as against £9·8 in the Portuguese colonies, which were far more backward, and £56 sterling in South Africa. Apart from the information given by Frankel, the only source available for an examination of these investments is an inquiry made by the ministry for the colonies in 1943,[3] which was based on a study of the annual reports published by the colonial companies and supplemented by questionnaires addressed to the latter. The object was to evelute the capital invested in Black Africa by France with a view, it seems, to possible bargaining with the Germans. In those circumstances it can be understood why the estimates should have been high, far surpassing those made by Frankel, at least in regard to private capital.[4]

Capital Invested from 1870 to 1936

(Estimated by Frankel in thousands of pounds sterling)[5]

Country	Investments			Capital not registered. % of registered capital (estimate)	Grand total
	Public	Private	Total		
French Equatorial Africa	15,248	5,000	20,248	5 (= 1,012)	21,260
French West Africa	16,477	12,500	28,977	5 (= 1,449)	30,426
Cameroons } Togo }	11,306	6,431	17,737[6]	5 (= 887)	18,624
TOTAL	43,031	23,931	66,962	3,348	70,310

The table on p. 162 was drawn up from balance sheets published by the companies. Foreign capital is excluded, at least that of companies which were foreign by their articles of association, a very artificial procedure since it excludes companies such as John Holt, Ollivant or King with their headquarters in Great Britain, but includes the French subsidiaries of the Anglo-Dutch Unilever trust – Nouvelle Société commerciale africaine, Compagnie du Niger français, Compagnie française de la Côte d'Ivoire. Likewise excluded in principle is capital deriving from company profits ploughed back

State of Investments from 1900 to 1940
(French West Africa, French Equatorial Africa, Cameroons, Togo)
(*in thousands of 1940 francs*)
Based on an enquiry by the Ministry for the Colonies

Sector of activity	Investments of Companies	Investments of Individuals	Total investments	% of Investments by sector (or group of sectors)	
Trade	8,761,962	1,752,392[2]	10,514,354	39	
Building societies	814,953	81,495[1]	896,448	3·5	48·5
Banks	1,556,732	—	1,556,732	6	
Industries	2,176,801	435,460[2]	2,612,161	9·6	17·1
Mines	1,860,304	186,030[1]	2,046,334	7·5	
Transport	879,150	87,915	967,065	3·6	3·6
Plantations	2,451,848	2,451,848[4]	4,903,696	18	
Stock-raising	71,450	14,290[2]	85,740	0·3	30·8
Forests	1,933,236	1,449,927[3]	3,383,163	12·5	
Total private investments	20,506,436	6,459,357	26,965,693	100	
Public investments (loans)	7,033,014	—	7,033,014		
GRAND TOTAL	27,539,450	6,459,357	33,998,707		

1. Contractual estimate: 10% of the company investmnets
2.   „   „   20   „   „   „
3.   „   „   75% „   „   „
4.   „   „   100% „   „   „

into the same business or reinvested in new companies, as well as what had been amassed by individuals.

The estimate of capital invested in each company comprises the following elements of their assets:

1, capital fully subscribed, excluding that deriving from the incorporation of marginal funds or reserves and without deduction of possible reductions in capital;

2, loans;

3, open or hidden reserves of marginal funds. Since the balance-sheet is almost always underestimated, for tax reasons, hidden investments are estimated at 5 per cent of declared investments, which is a modest approximation. However, the various reserves and marginal funds represent a large part of the reinvested or camouflaged profits, which are thus incorporated in the total investments;

4, amortisation;

5, credit accounts from the last balance-sheet.

The value of securities, representing capital invested in other companies, was excluded to avoid the same capital appearing several times, as was capital invested in other countries. Similarly, in cases of companies having interests elsewhere besides Black Africa, the part of their assets corresponding to the capital invested in other countries has been deducted. Clearly such calculations present great difficulties, and often only approximations are possible, notably in the case of building societies, banks and finance companies. Private investments, which cannot be valued exactly, have been estimated as a certain percentage of the total company investments, established contractually for each sector of the economy and varying from 10 per cent for building and transport investments to 100 per cent in the case of plantations. These figures seem to be arrived at judiciously, and take into account the state of affairs existing prior to 1940. Public investments are merely identified as colonial loans.

The sums have been recalculated for each period in terms of 1940 francs according to the following scale:

1 franc	1940 francs
gold	14.25
1928	2.8
1936	2.0
1937	1.8
1938	1.1

It should be noted that the coefficient of 14.25 f. (1940) for one gold franc notably exceeds the coefficient used elsewhere (about 12 according to various studies, cf. Marcel Piquemal, 'Exportation de capitaux aux colonies', *Economie et politique*, August–September 1957, pp. 69–70: index of reconversion of the account: 8.33; index of wholesale prices: 8.93).

The figures given do not represent the capital accumulated in tropical Africa under French domination, but capital exported from France to these countries. Part of the capital invested after 1900 was lost through bad management or through the effects of the various crises already referred to; not counting what was never effectively invested, but diverted or consumed in France by financial sharks, the 'animators' or certain companies created entirely with a view to speculation on the stock exchange. This, as we saw, was the case of certain chartered companies in the Congo. Conversely, capital derived from profits made on the spot and reinvested is excluded. This represents very little, as native capital was non-existent and the profits of the colonial companies were almost wholly exported. The only serious gap exists in the sphere of communications, where investment was made essentially by the state, out of local resources, as will be seen below.

Taking into consideration these factors and the margin of uncertainty which the estimates involve, the figures given convey some idea of the scale of investment, and certain conclusions can therefore be drawn:

1. Capital exported from France was extremely limited: 28,000,000,000 (1940) francs in forty years of private investment. Whatever the divergencies may be between the estimates of Frankel (who does not seem to have worked on such detailed figures) and the 1943 inquiry, both end up with very unimpressive figures, in comparison with what was invested in the other African territories, particularly the British.

2. Analysis of investment according to spheres of activity brings out the mercantile and parasitic character of capital in French tropical Africa: 39 per cent of investment, as in commerce, and nearly a half in the non-productive sectors, if banks and property investments are added to commerce. (Any classification by sector involves an arbitrary factor: most of the trading companies, whose assets are difficult to analyse, run commercial agencies, shipyards and maritime storage, lorry and cargo services, repair shops, agricultural and forestry concessions and other items.) The part attributed to commerce has thus been over-estimated, mainly at the expense of transport – most of the commercial companies provided their own road and even sea transport services – and to some extent at the expense of industry. But this error is at least partly compensated for by the classification as industry of port management enterprises (10 per cent of the industrial sector, with investments of 235,000,000 francs) and by the classification within the agricultural and forest sectors of the former chartered companies of French Equatorial Africa, whose work was, in fact, largely commercial.

The low private investment in the transport sector may seem surprising: but in 1940 – and these matters have not changed much in the years since then – the only visible installations colonisation had provided; these were few in number and mediocre in quality, and all near ports, railways and roads. The total investment remains insignificant, certainly less than 2,000,000,000 francs. Private investment, in fact, played but a minor role in these installations, and was used only by road haulage firms, coastal traffic and river navigation,[7] and by the railways from Dakar to Saint-Louis, which were constructed before 1900, and in Dahomey, prior to their repurchase by the government-general of French West Africa.[8] All the rest of the railway network, and the construction of a road system and ports, represents public investment. Expenditure was partly provided for by colonial loans;[9] but the local budgets or the reserve funds, made up of colonial taxes, constituted the main source of finance. Forced or 'statute' labour was largely used to lay the railways, and was used almost exclusively in the building of roads and tracks. Expenditure on the construction of the railway network alone, stated according to the value of the franc in 1940, was an estimated 11,600,000,000,[10] plus 1,500,000 for the German railway construction in Kamerun and Togo, completed before 1914.

The directly productive sectors enjoyed very low investment, and were, in the main, left to the native population and their pre-capitalist methods of production. Agriculture, stock-breeding and forest exploitation altogether received no more than 30 per cent of the capital. For French West Africa and Togo alone, the proportion dropped below one-fifth, to 18·3 per cent. The weakness of the mining industry will have been noted with 7·5 per cent in French Equatorial Africa, and only 3 per cent in French West Africa. This is one of the few industrial sectors that usually enjoys a considerable development in colonial countries; here it absorbed less capital than industry proper. But one should have no illusions about the latter, which received 9·6 per cent of private investment; it was limited to the basic activities essential for the life of towns and ports and the provision of means of transport.

In French West Africa of the 1,800,000,000 1940 francs invested (10·3 per cent of the total private investment) 35 per cent represents construction and public works (1 per cent for firms producing construction materials: lime, bricks, etc.); 20 per cent the production and distribution of town electricity, 18 per cent port handling, and the rest – some 19 per cent – engineering repair shops and processing industries. In other words, industry and transport, in their very structure, served merely as auxiliaries to commerce. The preponderance of commerce is even more striking if one examines the capitalisation on the stock exchange of the companies under assessment.[11] The statistics of this stock exchange capitalisation for 4 June, 1945, for the total of French Black Africa, give the following division by sectors:[12]

Trade	Plantations and Forests	Industry	Mines
63%	16%	4%	7%

This division is easily explained by the relative profitability of the various sectors under consideration. The commercial companies, taking advantage of their *de facto* monopoly, gained vast profits on little capital, while the mining and forestry undertakings, left to individuals or to speculation, showed far more variable returns. The table below shows the percentage of profits declared in relation to capital invested by a number of companies (1939 and 1940). Under these conditions, of course, the pre-eminence of commercial investments continued to grow. In 1916 commerce in French West Africa absorbed only 36 per cent of investment, and held first place, but was closely followed by agricultural and forestry companies with 34 per cent. In 1940, the proportions were 50 per cent and 18 per cent respectively.

Trade			Mines			Plantations		
	1939 (%)	1940 (%)		1939 (%)	1940 (%)		1939 (%)	1940 (%)
Société commerciale de l'Ouest africain	25	30	Minière du Congo	12	—	Agricole du Gabon	1	5
			Equatoriale des Mines	17·5	—	Plantations de l'Ouest africain	7	0
Compagnie française de l'Afrique occidentale	27·7	30				Société des cultures de Diakandapé	0	0
Maurel et Prom	34	23						

3. The preponderance of foreign (that is to say mainly French) finance capital was overwhelming. The capital of limited companies, which can, in fact, be identified with it, represented 21,000,000,000 out of a total of 28,000,000,000 of private capital imported. The private capital of local (African or Lebanese) origin, which is not included here, accounts for very little. In traditional African society there was no accumulated wealth in the hands of feudal lords or traditional merchants, which could be transformed into capital, as was the case in Japan or, to a lesser degree, in India, China and the Arab countries.

Concentration, as is natural, assumed its most complete form in banking: out of 1,500,000,000 invested, 1,450,000,000 represents the capital of three banks, the Banque de l'Afrique occidentale, the Banque commerciale africaine – which, at the end of the period under consideration, passed under the control of the first-named bank – and the Banque française de l'Afrique, which operated primarily in French Equatorial Africa and went bankrupt during the great crisis. At the end of this period, the banking sector had become the more or less absolute monopoly of the Banque de l'Afrique occidentale which, as we saw, had further been granted the privilege of a bank of issue.

Concentration was equally marked in the field of commerce. The figures that follow do not give the full picture of the degree of concentration, for apparently different organisations are often no other than creations of the same financial groups.[13] Out of the total of 10,500,000,000 invested in commerce, of which 8,700,000,000 came from companies, twenty-three companies ran up a total of 7,700,000,000; eleven companies each made investments of over 200,000,000, making a total of 5,800,000,000, and three companies (the Société commerciale de l'Ouest africain, the Compagnie française de l'Afrique occidental and Unilever) totalled 2,800,000,000.

This monopoly character of commerce dated, as we have seen, from the end of the nineteenth century; but it became worse, and the old 'business houses' of former days became henceforth totally integrated with finance capital. The three 'big' companies just mentioned virtually controlled the commercial sector, providing 50 to 90 per cent of imports and exports of certain products.[14] Less than a dozen companies carried out almost the entire import and export business of the colonies. Industry and the mines were equally 'concentrated': in industry thirteen companies represented a total of 1,300,000,000 francs (of which 328,000,000 alone for the Société française d'entreprises de dragages et de travaux publics) out of the 2,170,000,000 invested in this sector; in mining, seven companies accounted for 1,200,000,000 out of 1,860,000,000 invested in the sector. In forestry and agriculture, leaving aside private investment as before, the concentration was the same: eleven plantation holdings made up a total of 1,300,000,000 and thirty-three companies shared the rest (1,100,000,000); nine forestry companies accounted for 1,500,000,000 invested out of a total of 1,930,000,000.

(b) PHYSIOGNOMY OF THE FINANCIAL OLIGARCHY

It is almost impossible to portray completely and accurately the net woven by finance capital in the territories we are studying, which would allow us to see, behind the anonymous names of the companies, who were their real masters and thus the exploiters of the country.

The integration of business firms with finance capital took place before the Second World War, through the interpenetration of the capital of trading companies, navigation companies and the banks. One sign of this integration was the transformation of the old 'family businesses' or groups consisting of a few associated firms into limited companies. For example, in 1907 the firm of Ryff, Roth became the Société commerciale de l'Ouest africain; 1908 saw the transformation into a limited company of the Etablissements Peyrissac of Bordeaux, and 1919 that of Maurel et Prom, founded in 1822. In 1917 the Société commerciale et industrielle de la Côte d'Afrique was founded, replacing the Armandon company, with the participation of ship-owner Fraissinet; in 1921 the company Le Commerce africain was established and transformed into a holding company of the Etablissements Gradis of Bordeaux, founded in 1688.

The Banque de l'Afrique occidentale, as we have said, dominated the others. Its capital was apparently scanty: from 6,000,000 before 1914 it reached 50,000,000 in 1931, and did not rise until after the war – although in fact nominal capital means little. Established in 1901, this bank was granted the privilege of being an issuing house for all the countries of Black Africa under French domination. It became the principal deposit bank, and from 1904 it enjoyed the right, refused to the Banque de France, of participating in the constitution of companies, on condition that the total sum of its participation did not exceed a quarter of its reserves.[15] By contrast to the Banque de France, which was essentially a 'bank of banks', it was both a bank of issue, a commercial bank, and a deposit and broking bank. In 1923 its board of administration, presided over by Paul Boyer of the Comptoir d'Escompte,[16] which, no doubt, represented the interests of French high finance, showed a majority of Bordeaux interests (Maurel, Gradis) and their associated companies (Delmas).

The privilege of being a bank of issue, which had been granted for a period of twenty years, was prorogued in 1929, then renewed for forty years, as from 1921. A convention signed in 1929 apparently slightly reduced the exorbitant nature of this private bank's privileges, by imposing upon it a state tax on fiduciary circulation and by reserving to the state the right of nominating the chairman of the board of administration and four of the directors. The 1938 board of administration showed no changes. As in 1923, there could be found a Maurel, a Gradis; one Jean Pion had joined them, a former councillor of state and son-in-law of a certain Le Cesne, very likely a member of the family of Julien Le Cesne, creator with Frédéric Bohn of the Compagnie française de l'Afrique occidentale[17] and founder of the Union coloniale française. A few high officials of the ministry for the colonies represented the state. At the time of the 1931 crisis, the general management of the bank was entrusted to Edwin Poilay, previously secretary-general of the Banque de l'Indochine.

The Crédit foncier de l'Ouest africain, the most important land bank in French tropical Africa, with over half of its capital invested by real estate companies, appears to have been a specialised 'double' of the Banque de l'Ouest africain; its boards shared several administrators, and represented more or less the same groups of interests. The Banque commerciale africaine, ranking second in importance, was established in 1924, with a capital of 6,000,000, which rose by stages to 40,000,000 in 1929. Later a deposit bank, it seems at the beginning to have been basically a merchant bank. Here we find again the principal interest groups in Equatorial Africa, represented before the war in the chartered companies: the board of directors included E. Alcan (Société anonyme française pour l'Importation du Caoutchouc, and Alcan et Cie); E. Motte of the Motte dynasty (Textiles du Nord; before 1914 of A. Motte, 'a manufacturer in Roubaix', chairman of the Mines de Lens, director of Caoutchouc de l'Indochine, vice-chairman of the Compagnie forestière de Sangha-Oubangui); J. Weber, in 1931 chairman of the same 'Forestière Sangha-Oubangui', director of numerous other companies in French Equatorial Africa, interested in trade and plantations and also in similar matters in French West Africa (Comptoirs réunis de l'Ouest africain and others).[18] Belonging to the same group of the Forestière Sangha-Oubangui we find the ex-governor-general, Angoulvant, and M. Carton de Wiart, representing Belgian participation in the business.[19]

The Banque française de l'Afrique was likewise a merchant bank with an eye on business in equatorial Africa. Set up in 1904 as a financial company, it changed name several times.[20] On its board in 1923 were Adrien Josse, of the bank R. Josse–A. Lippens and Co., A. Fondère and, once again, Jean Weber. In 1931, we do not find these names any longer, but those of the ex-governor-general, Merlin, and the writer and journalist Pierre Mille, who evidently served as cover.

These two last-named banks, almost certainly used as screens for risky speculations, foundered in the financial crisis of 1929–31: the Banque commerciale africaine, obliged to suspend payments, was refloated by the government, which authorised the Banque de l'Afrique occidentale to issue 15,000,000 francs in promissory notes[21] for this purpose, on strict conditions (capital reduced from 40,000,000 to 6,000,000, and the issue of 1,000 founder's shares, given to the ministry for the colonies). From then on it became a deposit bank, and was henceforth under the control of the Banque de l'Afrique occidentale and the big French banks (Banque de l'Union Parisienne and Crédit commercial de France, in particular, which we shall find again after 1931 interested in West African business). The traditional interests of Equatorial Africa seem to have been represented by Adrien Josse, Robert Josse and a Belgian. The Banque commerciale africaine seems to have controlled the Société immobilière et financière africaine, set up in 1932, dealing in real estate, whose board comprised representatives of the same interests (mainly linked to the Banque de l'Union parisienne, whose chairman was none other than the director-general of the Banque commerciale africaine).

The Banque française de l'Afrique which, it appears, had speculated in Rumanian oil,[22] had to file a petition at the same time, with a deficit of nearly 200,000,000 francs (against 50,000,000 of nominal capital). Its creditors were partly reimbursed by the Banque de l'Afrique occidentale who were authorised to issue 75,000,000 in promissory notes for this purpose.[23] But the bank disappeared. The penetration of the big French merchant banks into African companies and activities showed itself immediately after the First World War with the establishment of holding companies. One of the best known of these was the Compagnie générale des colonies, whose field of action lay mainly in North Africa and Indochina, but which had various interests in tropical Africa. It was established in 1920 by a consortium of banks and construction firms,[24] in which the Banque de Paris et des Pays-Bas played a leading role, and was involved in construction (Construction africaine, Hydraulique africaine, Port de Dakar, Silico-calcaire), industry, with small oil-works in Senegal, and commerce (Maurel et Prom). It was given the task of making preliminary studies for irrigation from the Niger and, in 1926, obtained a concession for the works at the port of Dakar.

In that same boom period, in 1920, the Société financière française et coloniale was established under the auspices of the Banque Lazard and the financier Octave Homberg. It was mainly interested in rubber and Far Eastern business, but took an interest also in various companies of equatorial Africa. Its capital, 20,000,000 francs in 1924, reached 96,000,000 and then fell to 15,000,000 in 1933, when it showed a loss of 86,000,000. It was refloated by a consortium including Lazard, the Banque de l'Union parisienne and the Banque d'Indochine, with E. Giscard d'Estaing as managing director, later chairman, and René Bouvier and Paul Bernard as directors. Also involved was Edmond du Vivier de Streel, already mentioned. It was, undoubtedly, through Du Vivier's mediation that this holding company controlled, from the beginning, the group of Gabon forestry companies which had emerged from the chartered companies, and later their commercial outlet, the Compagnie commerciale de l'Afrique équatoriale (formerly the Etablissements

F. Brandon) founded in 1909, with headquarters at Libreville. Taking advantage of the boom, and the final decline of the rubber trade, Du Vivier de Streel encouraged the growth of the cotton companies, grouped in the Comité cotonnier de l'Afrique équatoriale française – the Compagnie cotonnière équatoriale française, the Compagnie cotonnière du Haut-Oubangui, the Société française des cotons africains and the Compagnie commerciale Ouahm et Nana – all with the participation of Belgian interests, as for example of Compagnie cotonnière congolaise. Du Vivier de Streel will be found again with D. Guynet in the Compagnie minière du Congo français; the former sat on the boards of administration of Say and of Sucreries et raffineries de l'Indochine, companies which also belonged within the sphere of the Banque d'Indochine and through it to the Banque de Paris et des Pays-Bas.

There was also a group of interests whose representatives we have already seen in the Banque française de l'Afrique (A. Josse of the R. Josse–A. Lippens bank; A. Motte of the Roubaix textiles: W. and later D. Guynet (Afrique et Congo, with Fondère, the Compagnie minière du Congo français, the Compagnie équatoriale des Mines, the Société africaine d'entreprises, the Société des Sultanats) – Belgian and Dutch interests. Their main agent until the 1930s seems to have been Jean Weber, and their main base the Compagnie forestière Sangha-Oubangui and its twin, the Compagnie commerciale Sangha-Oubangui, established in 1928 to take over the work of the trading posts. It controlled, among others, the Compagnie congolaise du Caoutchouc, the Compagnie nouvelle du Kouango français, the Compagnie commerciale Sangha-Likouala (transport), all in French Equatorial Africa, the Plantations de la Tanoé on the Ivory Coast, and a trading company the Comptoirs réunis de l'Ouest africain in Dahomey. It does not seem to have managed to escape the bankrupty that hit the banks in Equatorial Africa, and the crisis that followed the expiry of the last concessions (December 31, 1935).

The 'Forestière' company, and most of its subsidiaries, with a capital reduced from 36,000,000 to 9,000,000 in 1934, came under the control of a holding company, Union minière et financière coloniale.[25] It has been impossible to find full details of it but it seems to be identical with the Financière française et coloniale, that is to say, the Banque d'Indochine. In any case, after the Second World War, the Forestière and related companies became branches of the Financière française et coloniale. The Compagnie commerciale Sangha-Oubangui, as well as the Plantations de la Tanoé became, in their turn, branches of the Société commerciale de l'Ouest Africain.

At the end of that period the Fondère-Guynet group supported the Société Afrique et Congo (Bénédic-Guynet) which was limited to trade, and transferred their transportation branch (Congo and Ubangi river navigation) to the Compagnie générale des Transports en Afrique. This Group, which soon came under the protection of the Banque d'Indochine, had interests in the Compagnie minière de l'Oubangui-Oriental and the Compagnie minière du Congo français; on their boards were to be found direct or indirect representatives of the Banque de l'Union parisienne.

Another holding company with African interests (in the Cameroons) was the Société financière des caoutchoucs, representing the Rivaud Bank, whose activities were mainly directed towards Indochina. It controlled the Société africaine forestière et agricole[26] (until 1939 Plantations de la Sanaga) and the Compagnie commerciale de l'Equateur (with the armament manufacturer Vieljeux as owner), the Union tropicale de plantations[27] and the Forestière équatoriale. It seems to have been established immediately after the First World War, taking advantage of the eviction of the German companies.

As has just been shown, it was mainly in Equatorial Africa that French high finance finally imposed its direct grip. West Africa remained the domain of interest groups that had grown out of the traditional trading firms, though the penetration of high finance can be observed here too. Their close interpenetration is visible in the structure of the Banque de l'Afrique occidentale. The Bordeaux group was complex. Its banking elements had interests that were shared between the bank itself, Bordeaux business, and colonial affairs. Among the former was Baron Jean Davillier, who, after the Second World War, became chairman of the Crédit commercial de France,[28] which was linked to the Société de Banque suisse.[29] With Baron Léon de Nervo (metallurgy: Denain-Anzin, Saut-du-Tarn; Chemins de fer de l'Est; colonial companies: Mokta El-Hadid, Phosphates de Gafsa; harbour interests), the former's brother-in-law, we enter the sphere of French high finance. The main agent of this group in the Bordeaux and African subsidiaries was Robert Lemaignen, Léon de Nervo's son-in-law, who specialised in commercial and colonial matters. He acted, in the main, through a holding company, the Société commerciale d'affrètements et de commissions, which controlled a series of companies connected with work at ports: provisioning, lighterage, transit and naval dockyards. On the eve of the Second World War the board of the company was composed of, among others, Robert Lemaignen, chairman and director-general, two British directors, Cyril Hay and Charles Ascherson,[30] and Louis Beigbeder, of a Protestant Bordeaux shipowning family, who seems to have been linked to high finance.[31]

Among the companies controlled by the Commerciale d'Affrètements et de commissions, or linked to it, we may mention the
Société commerciale des Ports de l'Afrique occidentale, the Ateliers
et Chantiers maritimes de Dakar, the Sénégalaise d'approvisionnements, the Charbonnages de Dakar, Sénégal-Mazout, Dakar-
Soutes[32] and others. Baron Jean Davillier also sat on the Crédit
foncier de l'Ouest africain[33] and the Eaux et Electricité de l'Ouest
africain.

In the Etablissement Gradis (a French company for trade with
the colonies and other countries), which emerged in 1921 from the
Anciens Etablissements David Gradis et fils of Bordeaux, we find
the same association between Bordeaux family interests and
Protestant high finance (Banque de l'Union parisienne). Established
in Bordeaux in 1688, the Gradis family founded its fortune on the
basis of commerce with the 'Islands', i.e. the sugar and slave trades.
It remained interested in the colonies – with O.P.T.O.R.G., a
finance company originally centred on Indochina, Crédit marocain,
Comptoir français du Maroc, and others – and in the food business
(Distilleries de l'Indochine, Agricole et Sucrière de Nossi-Bé,
Brasseries du Maroc, Brasseries de l'Ouest-africain, and others).[34]
The board of the holding company was made up of members of the
Gradis family and representatives of the Banque de l'Union
parisienne (in particular its joint director-general Charles Letondot).
The old Bordeaux firms, such as Peyrissac, Devès et Chaumet, Buhan
et Teyssère, Chavanel, Vezia and others, all engaged in trade, or
companies principally concerned with shipping, like Delmas, or in
trade and shipping, like Maurel et Prom – all continued to work
directly in West Africa, mainly in Senegal and the Sudan (today
Mali). They evolved in various ways, each according to its structure.
Certain of them became limited companies, turned to stock market
speculation and merged with the holding companies listed above:
Jean Davillier and Robert Lemaignen sat on the boards of Peyrissac,
and Gaston Gradis on that of Maurel et Prom and Maurel frères.
Chavanel and Vézia did not figure in the financial annuals, which,
however, does not justify the assumption that they were not involved
in finance operations.

The evolution of Peyrissac is characteristic. The founder, who
was first an agent, established himself at Saint-Louis in 1872 and
set up branch offices; in 1866 he became associated with a Bordeaux
shipowner and established a merchant fleet. First he specialised
in gum and Sudan rubber, and in 1908, to maintain and enlarge
the business, he sought outside capital and transformed the business
into a joint-stock company. Between 1920 and 1933 his successors
added numerous subsidiaries to the main offices: Salins du Cap

G

Vert, the Compagnie d'électricité du Sénégal, the Compagnie La Bia (forests and plantations on the Ivory Coast), the Société de Bamako (inland water transport on the Niger) and so forth. The 1931 crisis forced Peyrissac to shut down the majority of its subsidiary companies or to integrate them as participants in more powerful business affairs.[35] Peyrissac was associated with the Delmas group in various deals, principally in the holding company Société auxiliaire africaine (in which the Compagnie française de l'Afrique occidentale participated), which controlled the Manutention africaine (naval repair-yards, machinery, building materials), the Grande imprimerie africaine (the only printing house in French West Africa with a rotary machine, which printed the daily *Paris-Dakar* and various other papers), the Salins du Sine Saloum (with a market extending to Senegal, Sudan and as far as the Niger), the Eaux et Électricité de l'Ouest-Africain (with Thompson-Houston and the Omnium sucrier), the Bananeraies de Kin-San (with the Financière française et coloniale), and so on. In the midst of this kaleidoscope of specialised companies and their subsidiaries, we should remember that the core was formed by the old commercial firms associated with shipping and Bordeaux oil refineries. Peyrissac, first established along the Senegal–Niger route and then in Guinea, controlled in 1946: in Senegal and Mauritania four general agencies and twenty-five branch offices scattered along the railway lines Dakar–Saint-Louis and Thiès–Kayes, on the Saloum and the coast, with an advance post at Port-Etienne (Mauritania); in the Sudan (Mali) two general agencies and thirty-one branches; in Guinea one general agency and six branch offices; in the Ivory Coast two general agencies. Peyrissac 'dealt' in gum, groundnuts and rubber; gum lost its importance at the beginning of the century, rubber after 1914. But other products assured continuation: foodstuffs (millet) for the local market and, in the 1930s, gold from Guinea, of which Peyrissac and Chavanel were almost the sole buyers until 1940 – 600 kilograms per year were handled in that period.

As to imports to the colonies, these included rice, sugar, tea, spirits and cotton fabrics (in 1939, 500 to 600 tons of fabrics were sold in Senegal and the Sudan, representing 35 to 40 per cent of the turnover); then more and more hardware, construction and installation equipment, vehicles, etc. Peyrissac was exclusive concessionaire for the Compagnie des compteurs, Remington typewriters, Peugeot cars and bicycles, Hotchkiss, Thompson-Houston, Mazda lamps, and others. Maurel et Prom were engaged in the following activities immediately after the Second World War. They owned land, property and offices in 148 localities, 111 in Senegal, seventeen in Guinea and the Sudan (Mali) and thirty in Gambia, and a network of eighteen butchers' shops (in the principal centres of Senegal and at Bathurst in Gambia). At Dakar they had a factory and cold stores, the most important in the town, and motor fuel stores in association with Vacuum Oil of America. Their fleet consisted of two cargo ships for mixed cargoes, of 6,200 and 4,200 tons respectively, eleven cutters, twenty-six lighters, and other vessels. To conclude this survey of the Bordeaux group, we must keep in mind the association and interpenetration of this group and Protestant high finance (Banque de l'Union parisienne), probably determined by family ties of the Bordeaux owners.

The Marseilles group seems to have been more homogeneous. It comprised banking elements (Marseillaise de crédit, in which Marseilles ship-owners, merchants and industrialists were involved) and ship-owners (Cyprien-Fabre and Fraissinet); it had as its façade the mighty Compagnie française de l'Afrique occidentale. On its board sat the French ambassador Charles Roux, chairman of the Compagnie universelle du Canal de Suez, Paul Cyprien-Fabre, Edouard de Cazalet, P. Zarifi – later replaced by G. Mitaranga – who represented a group of Greek Marseillais extensively interested in Marseilles big business – oil works, sugar mills, breweries, North African business, and banks and railways in Greece.

The Compagnie française de l'Afrique occidentale, as one of the three great French commercial firms, had a very solid financial position which enabled it to weather the 1929–31 crisis without major difficulties. Its network of offices was spread across the whole of French West Africa and extended also to British territories in West Africa. They ran a number of oil works (particularly at Rufisque and in Dahomey), soap works (Lomé), cotton and kapok ginning (Dahomey) and tanneries (Tanneries de Rufisque, Société Manucuir at Koulicoro). It had subsidiaries (Sénégalaise de précontrainte industrielle, Société des fruits coloniaux) and participated in a variety of business in the Société auxiliaire africaine with Bordeaux firms (in Société Palme with Unilever and the Compagnie industrielle et commerciale d'Afrique, and in the Bank of British West Africa). Among the Marseilles interests should be mentioned the Société commerciale et industrielle de la Côte d'Afrique, set up in 1917, which had branch offices on the Ivory Coast and in Dahomey and Togo. Its chairman was Marc Fraissinet and on its board sat several directors of the Marseillaise de Crédit. After the Second World War, we find there Luc Durand-Reville, the main representative of Protestant high finance in all manner of business. Here, it would seem, he represented the interests of a group whose activities will be described below.

During the 1930s, a Daniel-Dreyfus sat on the board of the

Société commerciale et industrielle de la Côte d'Afrique, who will be found again together with Count Pastré and with Paul and Léon Cyprien-Fabre on the board of the Chargeurs Réunis, a Marseilles shipping company which was associated with Banque Worms et Cie., and had the monopoly of administrative and postal shipping services to the French coastal territories in Africa. The Chargeurs Réunis also owned important landed property in Africa. In this respect it should be noted that there are no tight partitions between the Bordeaux and Marseilles groups. In shipping matters, the Fraissinet-Fabre-Paquet-Delmas-Vieljeux group constituted a truly integrated organisation, a Fraissinet sitting on the board of the Delmas-Vieljeux shipping company.[36] Lucien Maurel was to be found with Daniel-Dreyfus, and Paul and Lucien Cyprien-Fabre in the Compagnie de navigation sud-atlantique, a subsidiary of Chargeurs Réunis. Delmas, Fabre and Fraissinet were on the board of the Union sénégalaise d'industries maritimes, and so on. Moreover, the Fabre firm had retained, from the past, their own branch offices in Dahomey.

With the Société commerciale de l'Ouest africain we come to the second of the commercial giants. Founded by Swiss merchants, its board included Swiss members (Hans O. Ryff, then Mlle. Ryff between the wars; H. Sigg and Maurice Golay, both living in Basle and still on the board after the war, and representatives of the Crédit commercial de France (linked to the Société de Banque suisse), the Banque Lambert-Biltz (Alfred Lambert) and the Banque Jacquier et Cie. of Lyon (Paul Isnard Le Francé). Its chairman was for a long time Jules Exbrayat of the Banque Demachy (linked to de Wendel), director of the Banque de l'Union parisienne. The banking elements seem to have been introduced after the 1929–31 crisis, when the company was in difficulties as the result of imprudent management. Its capital, which had been 157,500,000 in 1931, was reduced by stages to 65,000,000 between 1932 and 1934. Having become owners of the business by refloating it, they annexed the Société commerciale Sangha-Oubangui – which was no more than the trade name assumed by the Société commerciale de l'Ouest africain in French Equatorial Africa – and the Plantations de la Tanoë, the old business of the Sangha-Ubangi group. It participated in the Messageries africaines and the Messageries du Sénégal (with its Africain subsidiary and interests represented by Luc Durand-Reville). This reorganisation quickly improved the situation: its turnover was 800,000,000 in 1938–9, and 25,600,000,000 in 1948–9.[37]

On the eve of the Second World War it comprised the following establishments: in Senegal two branch offices and twenty-five trading posts; in Guinea one branch office and twenty-six trading posts; in Sudan (Mali) one branch office and ten trading posts; in Ivory Coast and Upper Volta six branch offices and thirty-seven trading posts; in Dahomey one branch office and twenty trading posts; in Niger two branch offices and three trading posts and in Togo one branch office and thirteen trading posts – making fourteen branch offices and 134 trading posts in French West Africa and Togo. In Cameroon there were one branch office and eight trading posts, and in Chad there was one branch office. For imports they had an agency in Manchester and an office in New York.

The third 'big' group, Unilever, never appeared under its own name, but in the form of various representative companies. It was not a specialised or localised commercial group, but a world-wide monopoly of exceptional range. Before considering its activities in tropical Africa, we shall review briefly its history and main characteristics. Unilever is a world-wide trust of oils of vegetable origin (60 per cent of its activities), also interested in various connected business undertakings. In 1946 more than one-third of the world trade in these materials was in its hands. It provided 12 per cent of world consumption of soap and two-thirds of soap consumption in the British Empire, and 75 per cent of margarine consumption in Europe and 40 per cent of world consumption. The group took on a definite form in 1937, as a result of the fusion of a British soap trust and a Dutch margarine trust. Thus, at the top are two parallel holding companies, one British, the other Dutch, but having the same board of directors: Lever Brothers and Unilever Ltd., and Lever Brothers and Unilever N.V.; the chairman of the British holding company is the vice-chairman of the Dutch holding company, and vice versa.[38] Effective management is provided from the City of London by a special committee of four, with headquarters at Unilever House. The prime element making up the group is the British soap trust, Lever Brothers. The founder of the firm, William Hesketh Lever (1851–1925), built his fortune on the manufacture of cakes of toilet soap, which, in the retail trade, replaced bars of soap – his Sunlight works was established in 1888. He set up subsidiaries in the whole of Western Europe and the British Empire, and, with the help of the British government, developed the margarine industry during the First World War and established a business of fisheries and fish shops. In 1920 he controlled three-quarters of British soap works. Before 1914 the Lever group was interested in the colonies with a view to obtaining direct supplies of raw materials: coconut palm plantations in the Solomon Islands and oil palms in the Belgian Congo. In 1921 he spent £8,500,000 sterling on the purchase of the Royal Niger Company, a former chartered company which held the monopoly of river transportation on the Lower Niger and Benué, and dominated commerce in Nigeria. In 1929, taking advantage of the crisis, he took over, in association with representatives of the Shell group, the main rival British commercial company (African and Eastern Co.), which had run into difficulties through unfortunate speculations on cocoa. This was merged with the Royal Niger Co. to make the United Africa Company, which from then on was the major incarnation of the Unilever trust in Africa. At the same time, in 1928, the Dutch-German margarine monopoly Jurgens-Van den Bergh-Schicht was merged with Lever Brothers to make up Unilever, which opened up the African resources of the group to European margarine factories. The group added other activities to soap and margarine (in Great Britain fisheries, tinned food, ice cream, Lipton tea, etc.); paper and textile manufacture; and on a world-wide scale the manufacture of toilet articles and cosmetics, as subsidiaries to the soap-manufacturing. In tropical Africa the group is interested in trade (60 per cent of purchases and 50 per cent of sales in Nigeria, and 45 and 30 per cent for all West Africa and almost as much in the former Belgian Congo) and plantations[39] (in the Belgian Congo it employed 40,000 persons producing annually 37,000 tons of palm oil and 16,000 tons of palm kernels). In West Africa, its varied enterprises employ 30,000 persons. In short, Unilever extends over more than forty countries through 516 subsidiary companies, employing 200,000 persons, and fifty-five other companies, in which the group holds a majority.

While in British Africa and in Togo Unilever assumed the trade name of United Africa Company, in French West Africa it was represented by specialised companies, each with its own sphere of action: Nouvelle Société commerciale africaine in Senegal and Portuguese Guinea; Compagnie du Niger français in Guinea, the Sudan (Mali) and Niger, with headquarters at Dakar; and the Compagnie française de la Côte d'Ivoire on the Ivory Coast and in Upper Volta. In Dahomey an old British firm, John Walkden and Co., played this role after the Second World War.

Generally it appears that the United Africa Company steadily extended its influence over the majority of the old British commercial firms, which were important mainly in the Cameroons and in French Equatorial Africa, but which also had branch offices in West Africa, south of Senegal: R. and W. King of Bristol (Cameroons, Ivory Coast); John Holt (Gabon, Cameroons, Dahomey, Togo), Hatton and Cookson (Congo, Gabon) of Liverpool; Paterson and Zochonis of Manchester (Guinea, Sudan, Cameroons); G. B. Ollivant (Ivory Coast, Dahomey, Congo), and Crombie, Steadman and Co. (Togo). Some of these probably agreed to Unilever participation, while others at least concluded agreements with the United

Africa Company, which reduced them virtually to the role of satellites.[40] The Unilever interests extended to French Equatorial Africa where, from 1921 on, Lever Brothers, anxious to lay hold of sources of oil, began to take an interest in plantations, and gained control over the Compagnie propriétaire du Kouilou-Niari –owner, even after the expiry of its concessions, of territory almost the size of Belgium. The Compagnie commerciale du Kouilou-Niari, a twin of the former, traded in Middle Congo, Ubangi-Shari and Chad, and the Société forestière du Niari ran a timber industry in the same region. All of them were entirely under the United Africa Company's control. The 'French' subsidiaries in French West Africa were closely linked to the French subsidiaries in France: Astra margarine, Palmolive soap, Gibbs perfumes, etc., all with headquarters at 33 rue de Miromesnil, Paris. But little is known in detail about their financial structure, and all the shares were held by the Unilever holding company and were not quoted on the stock market. The principal French 'main agents' of the group, in the period 1930–46 seem to have been Amédée Thubé and Arnaud Faure.

In 1938 the three main subsidiary companies (the Nouvelle Société commerciale africaine, Niger français, the Compagnie française de la Côte d'Ivoire) achieved the following volume of exports for French West Africa, Togo, the Cameroons and French Equatorial Africa:

Products	Total production (tons)	Group production (tons)	%
Groundnuts in shells	368,791	91,662	25
Groundnuts shelled	179,153	28,836	16
Groundnut oil	5,681	—	—
Palm oil	29,126	6,965	23·7
Palm kernel	118,905	38,235	32
Karité nut-butter	6,951	3,973	57
Karité nuts	11,657	4,147	35
Cocoa	83,636	19,945	23·8
Coffee	20,966	3,272	15

The group, moreover, maintained its interest in various undertakings (Société des fruits coloniaux with the Compagnie française de l'Afrique occidentale, the Société d'exploitation des acajous de Bassam, and the Société minière du Niger français); it could be found together with the Société commerciale et industrielle de la Côte d'Afrique and the Compagnie Française de l'Afrique occidentale on the board of the Société Palme (Dahomey); and together with the Société commerciale de l'Ouest africain, the Société auxiliaire africaine and the Société du Haut-Ogooué in the Messageries africaines (river transport on the Niger from Koulikoro to Gao) and the Messageries sénégalaises (river transport on the Senegal and coastal traffic). Unilever had concluded agreements with the Compagnie française de l'Afrique occidentale and it seems to have had close links with the Société commerciale d'affrètements et de commissions (where British directors are listed); it seems also to have acquired interests in Bordeaux affairs and links with what we have termed French Protestant high finance (Delmas, Devès et Chaumet and the Société du Haut-Ogooué).

Outside the net woven by the three giants and the Bordeaux group, there remained little room for anything else in West Africa. Beside the small firms which had to resign themselves to the role of satellites, there were a few direct subsidiaries of high finance and of other groups of the financial oligarchy. These were often small businesses refloated and taken over.

We have already indicated the role played by Luc Durand-Réville from before the Second World War, as the main agent of a group of interests controlled by Protestant high finance (Banque de l'Union parisienne). First employed by Maurel et Prom, he later served the Société commerciale, industrielle et agricole du Haut-Ogooué, successor to one of the oldest chartered companies in French Equatorial Africa (Daumas, 1895). Their activity was trade and forest exploitation in Gabon and the Cameroons. Luc Durand-Réville was director-general before taking over from the chairman, Jean Boissonnas, a relative of the Puerari, Mirabaud and d'Eichtal dynasties, and a member of some dozen boards of directors in the group;[41] he presided likewise over the Société des Mines de Falémé-Gambie. It appears that in 1939 the Mirabaud and Rueff banks were the biggest shareholders in the company. It controlled the Société forestière d'Azingo and the Gonfreville textile mill at Bouaké on the Ivory Coast, also directed by Luc Durand-Réville. It had shares in the Messageries du Sénégal, the Société Palme, the Compagnie des recherches aurifères in Gabon, the Société des fibres coloniales and the Syndicat pétrolier colonial. Luc Durand-Réville was on the board of the Société commerciale et industrielle de la Côte d'Afrique with Jean Fraissinet.

Also interested in trade and plantations and forest exploitation was the Mizraki–Lemaître group, which seems to have reached its zenith in 1929. The core of the group's enterprises was the legacy of the firm of Verdier on the Ivory Coast, consisting of the Nouvelle Compagnie française de Kong, the Société des plantations réunies de l'Ouest africain,[42] the Forestière de l'Indénié and the Plantations d'Elima. Included in the group were true commercial companies (the Compagnie générale des comptoirs africains, set up in 1921) and forestry companies (the Société d'importation des bois exotiques,[43] 1919, and the Société des bois de Sassandra, 1925). The multiplication of companies in this group (the Société française des cafés de Côte d'Ivoire, the Société coloniale africaine, the Compagnie pastorale et commerciale africaine, the Plantations et huileries de Bingerville, etc.) leads one to wonder whether the proper object of the company was not largely designed to hide speculation. The group seems, in any case, to have been heavily affected by the 1929–31 crisis, after which it was reduced to a relatively humble position. It controlled, moreover, a whole series of companies in French Equatorial Africa (the Société agricole du Gabon, the Société de la Haute Bokoué, the Union forestière et des palmeraies de l'Ogooué, the Union forestière du Fernan-Vaz) and in the Cameroons (Compagnie pastorale africaine). With the Weber group it participated in the Compagnie générale des plantations et des palmeraies de l'Ogooué and the Compagnie d'exploitations forestières (1920) in French Equatorial Africa. The names of the same directors can be found on all the companies: Mizraki, Lemaître, G. Lévi, Calcat and Merle.

A last group to be mentioned is the Société financière française et coloniale, linked with an impressive consortium of banks (Rothschild, Union parisienne and Catholic high finance), with the chairman of the chamber of commerce at Le Havre (Herrmann du Pasquier) and the Société coloniale de représentation (Hirsch), the last-named interested mainly in cotton and sisal. This whole set-up figured on the board of the Compagnie de culture cotonnière du Niger, on which great hopes were placed and which held a monopoly of the commercial use of cotton in the Sudan (Mali) by conventions granted in 1919–28 and 1936. It began to reap the expected profits from enormous state investment transacted by the Niger office. The composition of the group is a reflection of hopes, which, as will be seen, were not fulfilled.

The Hirsch interest is found in association with a Bordeaux group (the Société coloniale de gérance et d'études, incorporating Devès et Chaumet, Gradis, the Demachy bank) in the Société des cultures de Diakandapé (sisal), the Société des plantations de Casamance and the Compagnie agricole et industrielle du Soudan.

As well as these complex groups, it is worth mentioning finally a few commercial firms of secondary rank, whose financial affiliations are more or less known. Commerce africain (with branch offices and trading posts in Senegal, Gambia and the Ivory Coast and real estate in the Cameroons) emerged in 1920 from the old

G*

firm of Barthes et Lesieur and was absorbed in 1930 by the Comptoirs sénégalaises of the Octave Homberg group. It was a subsidiary of the Lesieur oil group. L'Africaine française, which became the successor of the Bordeaux firm of Dutheil de la Rochère et Cie. in 1910, had a network of trading stations on the Ivory Coast and in Upper Volta. It seems to have been controlled by the Lehideux Bank[44] and by representatives of Protestant high finance.

The Société des anciens établissements Rouchard, successor of the L. Rouchard company which was founded in 1907, had branch offices in Guinea and was interested in public works and, through its subsidiary the Société commerciale et agricole de Ditinn, in orange juice and perfumes. It seems to have been controlled by an association of two groups – the Union française d'Outre-mer, a holding company set up in 1936 (P. Strohl, Rodolphe d'Adler) and partly controlled by the Banque nationale pour le Commerce et l'Industrie and the Société anonyme française pour l'importation du caoutchouc Alcan et Cie. (E. Crémieu-Alcan, director-general, and Maurice Alcan), which was probably linked to the Banque Lazard. The Compagnie coloniale industrielle et commerciale, the former Société africaine des Etablissements Mory, was the subsidiary of an Algerian group, which seems in turn to have been controlled by the Société anonyme de gérance et d'armament, belonging to the Rothschild empire. The Société générale du Golfe de Guinée was established in 1926 by the fusion of the Etablissements J. B. Carbou, the Compagnie cotonnière ouest-africaine, known as 'La Cotoa', the Comptoirs et huileries du Dahomey and the Société française d'entreprises au Cameroun. It was engaged in trade and had industrial workshops in Dahomey, Togo (cotton and kapok ginning) and the Cameroons, and was controlled by the Banque Borgeaud (Raffineries François, Omnium Sucrier). The Compagnie foncière de l'Afrique, established in 1927, seems to have belonged to the same group. The Compagnie soudanaise, also dating from 1927, at first ran agencies in the Sudan; but later turned more and more towards the Cameroons, where it worked almost exclusively after 1944 with ten trading posts. The Entreprises africaines, set up in 1921, ran branch offices in the Sudan (4), the Cameroons (3) and Gabon (3). Both these companies were dependent on a group belonging to Protestant high finance, among them the Hottinguer and Vernes banks, associated with the Loste Bank of Bordeaux,[45] which was interested in colonial business. The Compagnie française du Haut-et Bas-Congo was established in 1929 with the take-over of the Compagnie française du Haut-Congo (Tréchot Brothers, a chartered company whose concession had expired) by the Compagnie française du Bas-Congo, of Brazzaville. It was engaged in trading and had a river fleet which serviced its trading posts and oil palm plantations. The Tréchot brothers remained on its board until 1931. The company became a subsidiary of a holding company, the Société française du Congo français[46] which likewise was controlled by the Crédit foncier du Congo.

These lengthy catalogues should not distort the perspective. Essentially there were three giant companies – or four if the Bordeaux group is taken as a unit. It was on the boards of these big companies that high finance made its influence felt, an influence helped by the 1929–31 crisis, even more than that of 1921. The companies directly controlled by high finance were generally of secondary rank as regards the volume of their business, and less important than the old houses which were not registered at the stock exchange, and so more difficult to identify, such as Vézia, Chavanel or Soucail. Some of them give the impression of being essentially stock exchange enterprises, used as a source of profit and as a cover for all kinds of speculation.

(c) TRADE AND ECONOMIC STRUCTURE

Essentially the methods of the big trading companies did not change. Their *de facto* monopoly and their purely mercantile activities formed an obstacle to all economic progress. In 1958 (that is, well after the end of the period under study) an economist wrote:

> The big commercial companies know the country very well. They have relatively large funds, but tend to limit their investments to certain sectors, viz. purchase of raw materials, sale of imported products, the refinement of local products [this only after 1940] and investments in real estate, for they know the difficulties they would meet in other fields where there is a lack of technicians and equipment. They also know that their services are already sufficiently extended, and that such activities are more or less contrary to the agreements, tacit or otherwise, made with European suppliers or purchasers. But in selling only imported goods and not buying except for export, they implicitly interfere, through their position on the market, with the functioning of any undertaking by enterprising Africans.[47]

In fact monopoly, aided by administrative intervention where needed, enabled the commercial companies to purchase raw materials at such low prices that productive work in agriculture was not profitable in capitalist terms, especially in the less fertile agricultural zones (the savannah). The commercial companies' lack of interest in production was not a matter of routine, but must simply be ascribed to the unprofitability to them of this sector. The exportable produce furnished by the African peasants was certainly mediocre and, considering the peasant's technical equipment, unlikely to expand rapidly. But the companies were not interested in buying in quantity, only in buying cheaply. The size of the profit margin made up for the smallness of the transactions.

In 1945–6 the retail trader and the exporter – often they were one and the same – each made a net profit of 150 francs on one ton of groundnuts, for which they paid the Senegalese producer 3,500 francs, that is an 8·5 per cent profit. Particularly scandalous are the profits made on the sale of coffee:[48] it was sold green at 20 francs C.F.A. a kilo, i.e. 42.50 French francs for 1,250 kg. of green coffee, the quantity necessary for the production of one kilo of roasted coffee. The sales price to the consumer on the official market was 174 francs per kilo, i.e. 24·4 per cent went to the producer: it could hardly be claimed that the costs of transport and roasting were three times those of production. At the same time, bananas[49] sold at 18 francs by the producer were resold to the consumer at 72 francs – 25 per cent of the sales price thus going to the producer. Here, too, it is difficult to justify such profit margins on the basis of transport, handling and conservation costs, even if a percentage of losses are taken into account.

Profit margins of about 300 per cent on these two products are especially significant, for the merchant who did the exporting was not the consumer, while in the case of the groundnuts it was often one and the same, or a single regular customer (oil-producer), which made it possible to hide the true profit margins. These high margins included percentages gained by the monopoly of river transport and port transit (which flowed into the same coffers when all these activities were handled by a single firm). To return to the profit margins of the groundnut merchants, the 8·5 per cent gain on 'pure' trade, excluding transport, represented in 1945–6 the very substantial sum of over 100,000,000 francs C.F.A. for Senegal alone (approximately 354,000 tons sold). One ton of groundnuts represented the average production of a family of Senegalese peasants, the sales price (3,500 francs) therefore representing his annual income. It is easily understandable that with minimum wages at Dakar and Saint-Louis at 20 francs per day (roughly 6,000 francs per year), the exploitation of groundnuts with paid wage labour was definitely not profitable, since all exploitation necessarily involved some investment. Thus the cost price would be certain to surpass the sales price granted to the peasant.[50]

Monopoly and the profit margins expected presented an obstacle to the introduction of free capitalist enterprise and to technical progress at the level of production.[51] In the introduction to his book

Paysans d'Afrique occidentale Henry Labouret cites passages from the opening speech of the British governor-general, Sir Hugh Clifford, to the 1920 session of the legislative council of Nigeria, which was also applicable to the French colonies in West Africa:

> The 'indigenous peasantry' is preferable, in his view, because the European enterprises are less favoured [sic], having to bear the heavy burden of equipment and bush-cutting, to invest important capital which remains unproductive for several years, and finally to recruit the labour force essential to their work from a scattered population.[52]

Clearly, the African peasant was 'favoured' in his competition with capitalist enterprise because his production was the fruit of his immediate labour, with no investment of capital, and because his work was not paid for at its value; the prices imposed upon him in the purchase of his produce were lower than the lowest production prices of a capitalist enterprise involving a minimum of investment and recourse to paid labour. This was the secret of the generosity by which the coloniser left to the African peasant the essential part of agricultural production.

The profit margins were no less advantageous for imports. The only concrete proof we possess on this point also dates from after the Second World War, when prices and margins were fixed by the administration. The 'price rates' were ingeniously calculated on the retail sales price to make the exorbitant nature of the percentages less apparent. These authorised profit margins were net, with the cost of transport, transit, customs dues, and general expenses incorporated in the cost price. Here are a few sample margins, showing percentages on the cost price (or allegedly so) for the period 1945–6:

	per cent
Percale and Guinea cotton	35
Shirts, cloth, napkins	42
Cement	25
Iron and steel	30
Household ware	40
Rice and semolina	20

Since the proportions of the cost price were furnished by the merchant, he was entitled to increase his bills and arrive at improbable cost prices. Thus, in 1946, a ton of cement quoted at Marseilles at 798.35 francs C.F.A. was, on the average, sold at Dakar for 3,035 francs C.F.A. The philosophy of the import trade was to sell little but at a high price, just as that of the export trade was to buy little, but cheaply. The interest of the trading companies was identical to that of the industrial suppliers. Tacit or explicit contacts linked them, assuring the latter of limited but regular outlets at high prices. The absence of all industrial activity on the part of the trading companies except in very limited fields arose not only from their normal practice but from agreements of this kind with suppliers and customers, who were strongly opposed to the establishment of 'competing' industries, which would have in their favour access to cheap labour. When the traders and manufacturers were one and the same firm, like Maurel, exporter of groundnuts from Senegal and owner of oil works at Bordeaux, the problem did not even arise. But if, by chance, isolated individuals tried to go against this policy of the 'colonial pact', the administration, in the service of 'colonial interests', soon managed to put everything in good order. The only tolerated 'industries' were those that were indispensible for the treatment of export products (i.e. the sifting of coffee, pressing of palm oil and shelling of groundnuts) which, until 1940, applied to only a minimal fraction of groundnuts exported – or where the products could not easily be imported like ice, soda water, etc.

The spirit of solidarity which united the commercial firms with their suppliers and customers – all of them more or less merged within the financial oligarchy – must put us on our guard against any over-simple explanation of the profit margins achieved by colonial enterprises. The notion of colonial surplus profits, formulated by Marx and taken up by Lenin,[53] existed before the advent of imperialism. These surplus profits are partly responsible for the underdevelopment of the colonial countries:

> . . . Capital invested in colonies, etc., may yield a higher rate of profit simply on account of backward development, and for the added reason that slaves, coolies, etc. [at that time, thanks to various forms of forced labour and low wages] permit a better exploitation of labour.[54]

To forced labour and low wages must be added pillage and spoilation, achieved through the practice of monopoly prices in export and import, of which a few examples were given and which were not a specific phenomenon of that period. Under imperialism, the trade economy only reproduced and maintained the features of the merchant capital which existed before modern industrial capitalism.

> So long as merchants' capital promotes the exchange of products between underdeveloped societies, commercial profit is not only

a form of swindling and cheating, but also arises largely from these methods.[55]

Where the trader's capital is supreme, it stands everywhere for a system of robbery, and its development, among trading nations old and new, is always connected with plundering, piracy, snatching of slaves and conquest of colonies.[56]

But the surplus profits, which can be seen through all the economic data, did not remain completely in the hands of the colonial enterprises.

We see no reason why these higher rates of profit realised by capital invested in certain lines and then repatriated should not enter as elements into the average rate of profit and tend to keep it up to that extent. This is especially so if such favoured lines of investment are subject to the laws of free competition.[57]

The contemporary monopolies (in contrast to the commercial monopolies of the sixteenth, seventeenth and eighteenth centuries) did not suppress the laws of competition, but only modified the conditions under which they worked. In particular, under conditions of monopoly capitalism as under free market capitalism, capital circulated from one sector to another; the control of all these sectors of economic activity by a small number of large trading banks even facilitated this circulation. The flight of capital from a less profitable sector caused a recession in demand, and hence a rise in prices and profits in all economic sectors. The existence of monopolies did not raise obstacles to the normal working of this law, except in the sense of a growing disparity in the rate of profit between, on the one hand, the non-monopoly sectors (small and medium enterprises) where, as a general rule, the rate of profit was below the average, and on the other hand, monopoly sectors controlled by the financial oligarchy, where the rate of profit was above average, or where a monopoly surplus profit existed.

In brief, the specific surplus profits derived from colonial exploitation came to rest mainly in the joint treasuries of the financial oligarchy, and contributed to the creation of monopoly surplus profit in general. There is reason to think that the profit margins of the colonial trusts were not, except under specific circumstances, much above those achieved in other monopoly sectors of the economy. They were, however, sufficient to provide an above-average net index in the values of colonial stock-exchange transactions throughout that period.

The purchase of exportable raw materials continued to be carried on simultaneously through a network of company trading posts and by agents—Lebanese subtraders, Africans and even on rare occasions Europeans. In the Sahel and Sudan regions, the administration made it illegal to trade except at certain fixed points, under the pretext of control – here we shall see the role of the native provident societies. In fact, the regulation worked in favour of the companies, which could thus easily impose their monopoly price, helped by the administration, whose role was essential where the cultivation and sale of exportable products were made compulsory. This system laid heavy additional burdens upon the peasants: commodities were carried on men's heads, often over dozens of kilometres; in Senegal and the Sudan, recourse was had to muleteers and Moorish camel-drivers who charged up to 20 per cent of the price of the merchandise. This enabled the companies to eliminate the 'irregular' sub-traders; while only those who had agreements with the companies, and who thus became their intermediaries, retained their places, receiving advances on trade and being remunerated by commissions but having, in return, to supply the companies exclusively and taking all the risks on themselves. This system continued to develop, and the companies ceased to open trading posts where the volume of business was not sufficient.

The trading companies' organisation was cumbersome; the disposal of export products and supplies of manufactured goods required the upkeep of branch offices in France and agencies abroad. Between headquarters and the bush trading post there existed a whole bureaucratic apparatus (local management and a regional branch office, to take the simplest structure), but the European agents of trading posts, who lacked any security of employment, were held responsible for their merchandise almost in the same way as the sub-traders, and the toughness of their situation recalls that of managers of commercial firms with multiple stores. The trust thus protected itself against risks and preferred to take on European personnel, more expensive and less adapted to the country, but less likely to disappear with the cash-box.

Trade always requires the advance of capital, but with a turnover limited to four or five months. The Banque de l'Afrique occidentale provided the necessary credit and had the means of eliminating competitors or anybody who was a hindrance to the profits of the big companies. We shall not revert here to the geographical partition of the commercial firms, nor to the degree of concentration characteristic of the commercial sphere, questions which were dealt with in the study of the financial oligarchy. Only the three 'big companies' carried on trade more or less everywhere, including the neighbouring colonial territories. The others were limited to certain areas, or only to a single one. This was the case with several Bordeaux firms

(Buhan et Teissière, Vézia and Devès et Chaumet), which were
limited more or less to Senegal and the Sudan (Mali), while British
firms such as R. and W. King, Ollivant, John Walkden and Co.
were confined to the south – the Cameroons, Dahomey, Togo and
the Ivory Coast.

In theory each firm bought and sold every commodity, but in
practice some specialisation had begun to take shape. The Bordeaux
firms, often closely connected with oil works, were principally
interested in the groundnut trade – hence their geographical siting.
Unilever traded in everything, but as the above percentages showed,
they were interested in oil – seeds and kernels being the mainstay
of their business – rather than in coffee or cocoa, which were of
minor interest. In the export of raw materials, the three giant
companies remained diversified. Evolution was more noticeable in
imports. Apart from fabrics, rice, sugar and traditional hardware,
there began to be imported building materials (iron, cement) and
mechanical devices, together with their necessary fuels and lubri-
cants – first cars, then various kinds of small machinery (pumps,
generators, mechanical saws and articles like gramophones and
radio-sets, where there was lively competition, as in France, between
the different brands. It seems that in the 1920s and 1930s the custom
of 'exclusive representation' was introduced, for which there had
been no cause with the shoddy goods, the import of which hitherto
had become a tradition. In France these articles were sold by
specialised traders. In the colonies the volume of sales was first
limited – the consumers being largely European – so that it seemed
more expedient to the suppliers to turn to firms which already had
at their disposal a sales network and which knew the market
better; for the commercial firms it was advantageous to procure the
'exclusive representation' of a particular brand, if it was a product
for which the market was likely to expand and which could be
backed by publicity.

The commercial firms now became even more diversified: to their
general agencies and trading posts they added, for example, networks of garages and petrol-filling stations. Some form of specialisation was, none the less, established in certain regions and with
certain products. In Senegal, Maurel et Prom were mainly concerned with food products and set up a network of bakers' shops;
Peyrissac and Vézia tended to specialise in hardware and metal
products. One can hardly call this true specialisation; it was rather
a matter of variations in the proportions of merchandise sold. The
economic role of the commercial activities should be appreciated.
As we have seen, commerce was superimposed on the traditional
patriarchal economy based on tribal consumption and, without

destroying it, altered its character. This traditional economy allowed for certain forms of trade, but these applied, for the local markets, only to the excess of production over family consumption, or, in the larger inter-regional trade, to certain products of general use of which the area of production was limited. These traditional forms were not developed to the point of being conducted through the regular use of money.

The spread of market production, and the introduction of money brought about by commerce, had various effects on the traditional forms of trade. Certain major forms of traditional trade were almost eliminated. The Sahara salt trade, which at the beginning of the century still represented one-sixth of the imports from Upper-Senegal-and-Niger (in other words, all the interior zone of Sahel and the Sudan), fell after 1919 to an insignificant level; except for a few regions in the Sahel, all the salt was henceforth supplied through the ocean ports. On the other hand, the inter-regional trade in cola from the forests of the Sudan and Sahel – with its counterpart, the trade in dried fish and cattle from the banks of the Niger or the savannah zones on the edge of the forest – persisted and even developed. But, the number of *dioula* (Guinea and Ivory Coast) or Hausa (Cameroons, Chad, Ubangi) engaged in this, and the volume of their business, were likely to have been reduced. From the beginning of the twentieth century, internal transactions constituted only one aspect of their trade; for the rest, they served as commercial agents. The days of the 'trade caravans' were over. The network of trading posts spread; the coming of the motor-car enabled them to increase in number, not only at traditional 'ports of call' in Senegal, Niger and along the railway lines, but in each main town of a district or sub-division, and often in localities without administrative posts, situated at cross-roads or serving a region highly productive in export commodities. The *dioula* (in Senegal, the Wolofs and Moors) had to find their place, as trading intermediaries in the 'micro-trade', either at a fixed post or within limited districts servicing villages without roads and trading posts. Apart from the trading posts of the big firms or their trade networks, there were numerous retail intermediaries – Lebanese in Senegal and Guinea, Greeks in the Ivory Coast and the Cameroons, Portuguese in Equatorial Africa, and sometimes Frenchmen, to whom the big companies gave preference when choosing their sub-traders. The French, even at this level, could barely stand competition, for their general expenses were too high; retail traders of other nationalities assumed importance during the First World War when their French competitors were called up, and they took root through being more efficient, living more cheaply, rapidly learning the local languages, having more direct contacts with the population, and drawing on family labour.

The practice of 'advances' remained firmly established. Formerly the travelling *dioula* had often had difficulty in recovering his debts. The shopkeeper who gave advances to the peasants in the neighbourhood knew with whom he was dealing, and the local traders could even agree between themselves to refuse to take the crop of someone who paid badly. Advances were given in kind (rice, sugar, fabrics or other import commodities) and were recovered at a usurous rate from the subsequent harvest. There were few African traders who kept a shop and had sufficient credit to take part in the game. Most often they were reduced to itinerant peddling of goods or to conducting their miserable trade on *tabliers*[58] – miniature pavement market stands – which, in the towns, became an open expression of the people's poverty. The subsidiary peasant trade, often practised by women, mainly in the forest zone of the Ivory Coast, was likewise a result of the penetration of money and of the disequilibrium suffered by the traditional economy of tribal consumption. In certain regions of Gabon and the Congo it could even be said that trade was introduced by colonisation.[59]

The penetration of the market economy – or, to be more exact, of the trade economy – differed greatly region by region. The gamut of former French territories in West Africa, the Cameroons and Equatorial Africa is essentially continental, comprising regions of great extent situated far from the coast from which they were often separated by the territorial possessions of other powers, which were subject to different monetary and customs systems. In spite of the railway and the motor-car, prices rose considerably as goods were carried hundreds of kilometres from the coast. The result was that 80 to 90 per cent of the volume of trade was carried on over less than one-twentieth of the area of the country, and involving only a slightly larger percentage of the population. Groundnuts were, in the main, supplied by certain regions of Senegal; they made up 40 to 60 per cent, according to conditions at any given time, of the value of exports from French West Africa. The regions concerned were those served by the railway line: the Dakar–Saint-Louis line to a dwindling extent (roughly one-tenth), the region of Thiès and Le Baol (three-tenths), Sine-Saloum (almost half), and the Tambacounda region (one-twentieth), and finally Casamance (little more than one-tenth) served by coastal traffic.[60] Important regions like the 'River' region (Fouta Toro), through which commerce was introduced into French West Africa, barely participated and were henceforth almost outside the circuit.

Groundnuts produced along the Koulikoro-Kayes line and

exported via Senegal, and those produced in the Sahel Niger and exported mainly via Kano, accounted for very little. Elsewhere, for a long time trade concerned itself with products exploited directly by Europeans (between the two wars, timber from the Ivory Coast accounted for 1 to 6 per cent of the value of French West African exports; and timber from Gabon for the major part of exports from French Equatorial Africa) or furnished by forced labour (rubber and later cotton in French Equatorial Africa), whose income in money did not greatly exceed what was exacted in poll taxes and, hence, could barely contribute to the extension of the market economy.[61] Only Lower Dahomey, a small, densely populated region, owes to palm oil and palm kernels the early introduction of the money economy; but the export of these products did not make any progress, and their relative share in the exports of French West Africa decreased, from 20 per cent in the period 1913–25 to 8·5 per cent in 1937–8 – more than half of this, however, coming from Dahomey. One could add here the coastal areas of the Ivory Coast and the land bordering the railway line from Abidjan to Bouaké, and in Guinea the triangle Boffa–Mamou–Benty with its base in lower coastal Guinea and its apex at the railway line. The trend of these two regions wavered for a long time. On the Ivory Coast, cocoa was still insignificant in 1925, when it represented 1·8 per cent of the value of production in French West Africa; in 1930 it had reached 9 per cent and stayed at that level. Coffee, still negligible in 1930 at 0·30 per cent of the value of exports, began to soar only on the eve of the Second World War (to 3·4 per cent in 1937, and 5·5 per cent in 1938; more or less the same applies to bananas in Guinea, and to a lesser extent in the Ivory Coast, where the percentages were 1 per cent in 1925, 8 per cent in 1930, 4·2 per cent in 1934 and 5·1 per cent in 1938, of the total value of French West African exports.

The trade economy placed the colonial countries in a state of total dependence on the home country. The economic circuit was based on it; the traders made purchases only with an eye to export and sold only imported products. Dependence was even more complete where the market economy was deeply implanted. In the interior territories, where tribal consumption was the rule, the exchange of exportable agricultural commodities for imported finished products remained limited to surplus articles. In the countries truly integrated into the trade system, mainly Senegal, where natural facilities for agriculture were not exceptional, dependence verged on actual need. The peasant produced millet and other crops indispensable for crop rotation based on groundnuts – here one cannot speak of 'monoculture'; it should rather be termed 'mono-speculation'. But there was considerable shortage of food-stuffs. About one-third of the peasant income in the groundnut zone of Senegal was spent on the purchase of food, mainly imported rice.[62]

The circuits of local or regional circulation, apart from tribal consumption, played no more than a secondary role, as we have seen, and did not represent a unit or integrated units but a series of currents moving to and fro in isolation along predetermined routes. This segmentation was still more accentuated in the sphere of trade proper. In this sense, there was not one economy in French West Africa but several, according to the formula which an economist came to apply to a more recent period, viz. 1945–57.[63] Each economic region corresponds to a 'one-line economy', an axis based externally on a port where import and export were conducted and comprising a series of adjacent branches which subdivide in turn until they peter out in the bush. The axis and branches were followed by an ascending current, that of produce imported, and by a descending current, that of exportable products. Each region resembled a kind of lung with its system of veins and arteries running parallel, receiving its oxygen at the level of agricultural production. But the heart was placed outside, far beyond the seas; the impulses that regulated the nature and the intensity of the flow were external ones. Also outside was the body which they kept alive, where the opposing currents rejoined.

The following are the main economic regions:

1. The region having as its axis the railway line from Dakar to Niger, which included Senegal and present-day Mali (formerly known as Sudan). The original axis (Dakar–Saint-Louis and the Senegal river) was reduced to the role of an adjacent branch. Its port was Dakar, more and more exclusively. The secondary ports, Rufisque and Kaolack, became strictly limited to the export of groundnuts.

2. Guinea, with the axis running from Conakry to Kankan, i.e. along the Conakry–Niger railway.

3. The Ivory Coast and Upper Volta, with the axis from Port-Bouët to Abdijan–Bobo Dioulasso, extending its influence to Sudanese regions.

4. Dahomey and Niger, only to the extent that the Niger was not 'split' at Kano, the railway terminus in Northern Nigeria, which was far more accessible, but for the customs frontier.

5. Togo – a north-south axis, parallel to that of Dahomey but having bad communications with it.

6. The Cameroons.

7. Gabon.

8. The axis comprising Congo, Ubangi–Shari and Chad, protected by administrative regulations which made its use compulsory, but hardly traversed except by administrative trade, including the products of forced labour – served, until 1934, by the Belgian port of Matadi, far more than by Loango or Pointe-Noire.[64] The completion, by that date, of the Congo–Ocean railway line gave it autonomous access to the sea, and accentuated the artificial nature of this artery.

In conclusion, this structure, seen either in the context of big administrative units (French West Africa, French Equatorial Africa) or merely as the isolated regions enumerated above, left no place for anything like an integrated market, which could pave the way for the formation of a national market.

(d) TRANSPORT AND INDUSTRY

Taken together, transport and industry provide the means of ensuring the smooth running of trade.

Ports, railways and roads or tracks were installed, as we have seen, partly through loans (for which the colonial budgets – or in the last analysis, the mass of the population – had to reimburse capital), partly directly from the same budgets by means of levies on reserve funds, or through the unpaid labour of the same ultimate contributors – the people. In their mediocrity, these facilities corresponded to trade itself, which, thanks to its high profit margins, remained content with a limited volume.

Ports

The only well-equipped port was at Dakar. Thanks to its subsidiary functions, it developed rapidly after it had taken over from Saint-Louis and Gorée the function of port of access for Senegal and the Sudan. As the first port of call for ships coming from Europe, and the administrative capital of the most important group of colonies, Dakar was naturally destined to play the role of *entrepôt* between Europe and subsequent ports of call. The majority of the trading companies had their principal African offices there, from which they controlled the main branch offices in the other colonial capitals. In addition, Dakar was to play a role as port of call for ships plying from Europe to South America; they refuelled and renewed their supplies of water there. But in this Dakar had rivals in the island ports of call – St. Vincent in the Azores and Las Palmas in the Canaries. Dakar was also an imperial naval base with a dry dock constructed by the Navy between 1903 and 1912. This remained the only one of its kind between Gibraltar and the Cape until the

Second World War. The first port was constructed in 1863, to a depth of only five metres. This barely gave Dakar an advantage over Gorée, Rufisque or even Saint-Louis. Its pre-eminence was established only after 1898, with the building of the first two jetties that permitted the rational use of the water-level of the roadsteads, and which coincided more or less with the promotion of Dakar to the rank of a capital city. Large-scale construction carried out in 1902 to 1912 established the southern zone of the port. From 1910 on, Dakar managed to compete with Saint-Louis as a supply port. But its capacity remained insufficient:[65]

. . . The wharf can take only one ship at a time, and if several cargo boats arrive, as often happened for the Chargeurs Réunis during the construction of the railway line,[66] taking eight to ten days to unload, the other ships were forced to wait or to carry out their transactions on the roadsteads.[67]

Such was the situation on the eve of the First World War. When the southern zone was completed, towards 1925, there were 100 metres of deep-water quays along the southern jetty and two moles 300 metres in length, plus three quays by the waterside, respectively 124, 274 and 325 metres in length. A second series of construction works, entrusted to the Compagnie générale des Colonies (1926–32), was concerned with equipping the northern zone. By 1936 Dakar had two supplementary moles and a half-mole based on the big northern jetty. The total area was 15 hectares and there were 5 km. of quays.[68]

Its monopoly as import terminal for Senegal–Sudan was firmly established, but for exports its role remained secondary. From then on Dakar surpassed Rufisque, where operations were carried out at the roadstead, in the export of groundnuts, but it was outpaced by Kaolack, which was situated on the estuary 120 km. from the ocean proper, accessible only to cargo boats with a 3·50-metre draught, but was also in the heart of the productive Sine-Saloum zone.[69] The other ports on the Senegal coast, including Casamance, were used only by coastal steamers.

Conakry, situated at the end of the Kaloum peninsula, presented a natural landing-stage in the middle of the silted estuaries of the Rivières du Sud, and also benefited from its relatively sheltered position due to the Los archipelago. There was no harbour bar: the inlet Boulbinet, formerly used by the German firm of Colin, was abandoned to the lesser role of a fishing port with the advantage of a landing stage for the Compagnie française de l'Afrique occidentale. A new wooden wharf was constructed where ships with a draught of up to six metres could land. But the depth of access was insufficient; ships could draw alongside the quay only at high tide, hence those not intending to make a prolonged call remained at the roadstead. Between the two wars the installations were enlarged, and in 1940 Conakry had 300 metres of quayside, up to 8 metres in depth. As no export product ever completely replaced rubber, exporting remained limited. The railway construction gave Conakry the import monopoly for Guinea, and the old ports of call on the Rivières du Sud declined in importance. Victoria, at the mouth of the Rio Nunez, Boké, Boffa, Taboria and Benty, were no longer used except for coastal traffic.

Beyond Liberia and up to the mouth of the Niger, the lack of depth made it necessary for transactions to be carried on in the roadsteads. The presence of a bar prevented boats from coming close inshore without serious risks. A wharf built of metal and timber helped to surmount that difficulty.[70] The export merchandise was placed on the end of the wharf where a crane transferred it from the delivery waggons into a lighter which took them to the ship at the roadstead, or to where the ship's crane could reach. Embarking passengers were placed in *paniers* for this purpose – little wooden dinghies with a bench; they too were hoisted aboard the ship, with the risk of an involuntary bath if the crane-operator failed to land them in the lighter or if the swell was too strong. Clearly such a system limited the scope of transactions.

On the Ivory Coast, the wharf at Grand-Bassam, built in 1901 and reconstructed in 1922, was primarily the railway terminus. To avoid Grand-Bassam, which was infested with yellow fever, a new wharf was put into service at Port-Bouët in 1932, linked by 11 km. of railway to the new capital of Abidjan, which in 1933 replaced Bingerville as the colony's administrative headquarters. It was better equipped, so that Port-Bouët became the principal port of the Ivory Coast and Grand-Bassam was gradually given over to local traffic. The deep-water Ebrié lagoon, made it possible to turn Abidjan into a port directly accessible to ocean-going ships; all that had to be done was to cut through the coastal strip of sand which separated it from the ocean. Works to this effect were undertaken in 1904–7, but failed; as the colony's economic activity did not seem to justify the investments necessary to complete the work successfully, it was put off until a later period. The secondary ports that lacked a hinterland (Grand-Bassam, Assinie, Grand Lahou, Fresco, Sassandra, San Pedro) were hardly used except for timber-loading. Tabou, near the Liberian frontier, served for the embarkation of Kroo labourers,[71] who would supplement the ship's company for the manoeuvres of embarkation and disembarkation until the ship sailed for home.

Lomé had a wharf, built by the Germans. Cotonu had one after 1893, and its construction involved quite a story.[72] The French wharves formed a bleak picture alongside the deep-water ports built by the British on the same coast, e.g. Takoradi. In the Cameroons the Wouri estuary (which gave the territory its name)[73] was from 1914 the terminus of the northern railway line; it was essential for foreign trade, which passed through Bonabéri and most of all through Douala, where two wharves had been constructed, which provided access for ships drawing 4 and 6 metres. Kribi, which had enjoyed a certain use with the export of rubber, was soon abandoned. The difficulty of access to the port of Douala meant that mail-boats and cargo ships of any importance had to call at a port 30 km. away, and transit was provided by two small steamers that had been scuttled by the Germans but refloated in 1918; they served in this capacity until 1935. Between 1926 and 1931 the equipment of the port of Douala (dredging, the setting of buoys, and the construction of 564 metres of deep-water quays) was carried out by the Compagnie générale des Colonies with local budget funds, without subsidies or loans. A landing stage was constructed at Bonabéri for banana loading (1933–5) from funds provided by means of a loan.

Equatorial Africa was even worse equipped. Libreville, at the entrance to the Gabon estuary, was a well-sheltered natural port, but access was difficult and there was no deep water, so that it was badly suited to modern shipping. With the absence of a waterway or a railway providing access to the hinterland, its possibilities were limited, in spite of its role as the main town of the colony. It was a sleepy sub-prefecture equipped in the tropical manner. A single commercial wharf enabled only one ship to be loaded or unloaded at a time. Port-Gentil, on Cape Lopez, well sheltered at the mouth of the Ogooué, benefited from a better position and contact with its hinterland. But its island site was not advantageous. Between the two wars timber loading constituted the chief activity of the Gabon ports. The Congo proper had used only open roadsteads for a long time, mainly at Loango, the departure point of the porterage route leading to Pool. With the opening of the Belgian railways, all the traffic passed through the port of Matadi. The construction of a railway line on French territory, decided upon after the First World War, involved the construction of a port. The Lafargue hydrographic mission had chosen the site of Banda-Pointe. Governor-General Auganeur granted full powers for the commencement of work at Pointe-Noire, where a 'friendly' company owned the territory.[74] The technical difficulties resulting from the choice of the site delayed the start until 1932; with the help of a 300,000,000-franc loan it became possible to conclude a deal with the Société des

Batignolles. The foundation stone was laid by Governor-General Antonetti in 1934 – but a long time was to pass before the work was completed. Construction costs were estimated in 1932 at 190,000,000 francs. The technical difficulties proved far greater than had been foreseen; for example, large supplies of stone, which did not exist in the vicinity had to be brought in from outside, since the port was entirely artificial, being built out into the sea. As time passed the loans were 'transferred' to miscellaneous accounts, and only 177,000,000 francs were devoted to work on the port. By the time that the last instalments of the loan were used, the purchasing power of the franc had greatly diminished. The construction of the port gave a semblance of activity to the railway line which brought the stone over a distance of 100 to 150 km. 1,500,000 tons of stone were required. Before the completion of the port from 1925 to 1928, shipments were handled from a wooden pier, and later from one in concrete finished in 1939. The 'reduced' programme was completed only in 1942, in the middle of the war, and the total infrastructure not until 1945.

Shipping

Apart from freighters and tramp steamers, regular services plied along the coast. In 1907 the Chargeurs Réunis obtained the right to conduct mail services, and in 1912, with the approval of the ministry for the colonies, they secured the transport monopoly for all administrative personnel and material. Subsidised and assured of administrative traffic, the French company showed a lack of interest typical of all monopolies. Constant complaints were made about the mail service: letters and parcels were misdelivered, often not reaching their destination in Guinea or the Ivory Coast except on the return trip to Loango. In general, one avoided entrusting perishable goods to the Chargeurs Réunis. Before the war, it was noted that

> almost all the non-requisitioned passengers preferred to use foreign boats since the fares for first- and second-class passages were lower than on French ships, with concessions for return tickets.[75]

In 1929 the main traffic under the French flag was carried out by the Chargeurs Réunis (twenty-four passenger steamers, thirty-six freighters) and by Fabre et Fraissinet of Marseilles (eighteen passenger steamers, twenty-three freighters). Regular cargo services were provided by the Société navale de l'Ouest, Paquet, Delmas-Vieljeux, Maurel et Prom, and Devès et Chaumet – the two last-named mainly ran services for their own enterprises.[76] Regular services under foreign flags were provided by Elder Dempster (British), Woermann (German), and Holland West Afrika Lijn (Dutch). A system of agreements between the shipping companies established a *de facto* monopoly for maritime freight: these companies, as well as those of transit and lighterage, were closely associated with the trading companies. They charged heavily for maritime transport, and helped to consolidate the *de facto* monopoly of the import and export trade in the hands of a very small number of financial groups. Coastal shipping connected Casamance with Dakar, and the Rivières du Sud with Conakry. In Guinea the unprofitable passenger and mail services were handed over to the administration, while in Senegal they were entrusted to a privileged monopoly company, the Messageries du Sénégal.

Railways

The railway network, as we have seen, barely evolved after 1914. It was, in fact, not a network at all, but a series of routes of basic penetration, using a metric gauge. At the start they were strategic routes, constructed at little cost, often with difficult sections that were unsuitable for denser traffic. It had been envisaged that the ports on the navigable stretches of the Niger would be joined. The Roume Plan of 1904 had foreseen a great strategic East–West artery. The Sarraut Plan in 1920 followed up its basic ideas of completing the Thiès–Kayes route and building an interior section, which the railway from Togo would join at Ouagadougou, and the line from the Ivory Coast at Sikasso; then prolonging the southern railway line in the Cameroons from Douala to Yaoundé and Chad, and building the 'Congo–Ocean line' from Brazzaville to the coast. But the necessary credits were not obtained, and with the development of the motor-car the concept behind these plans lost its strategic significance and economic interest in the absence of any integrated market in the interior. Some time later, the minister for the colonies, Albert Sarraut, proclaimed:

> Railways should lead to the sea-ports and pick up all their traffic there.[77]

Between 1920 and 1936 a few missing sections were lengthened or completed – without haste, because railway development was subordinated to that of port capacity. In Dahomey and on the Ivory Coast before the wharf at Port-Bouët was opened, the very limited wharf facilities did not encourage the lengthening of railway lines; it was even said that in Guinea, where the rubber traffic had not been replaced and where Conakry 'was not a port but a simple open roadstead', the railway, running at a deficit, had been constructed too soon.[78] Most of the rolling-stock remained unchanged after 1914. In the Cameroons, German rolling-stock was still in use after the Second World War.

In the Senegalese zone, work continued in 1920 on the Thiès–Kayes line, which had been interrupted during the war. Completed in 1923, this 667 km.-long line provided a direct outlet to Dakar from the Sudan, crossing the most productive groundnut region and serving as an artery for the regional economy – at the expense of the Senegal river route, which involved a double trans-shipment and was impassable from July to October. The Dakar–Niger line was linked in 1923 to the Dakar–Saint-Louis line, purchased by the government. The 46-km. Diourbel–Touba branch line served the sacred town of the Mourides and transported its groundnut production. On the other hand, the 129-km. Louga–Linguère branch line, finished at a time when the centre of groundnut production was moving southward, and running through a semi-desert region, was more or less useless, and had one train weekly.[79]

In Guinea, the railway was not extended beyond the terminus of Kankan which it reached in 1914. Plans for an extension towards Beyla or N'Zérékoré remained on the drawing-board, like the local line of Fouta-Djalon, with a branch line from Tabili to Youkounkoun. On the Ivory Coast, the railway went no farther than Bouaké, reached in 1912 (315 km.). The extension towards Ouagadougou, the principal town of Upper Volta, was begun in 1922, and after extremely slow progress, was never completed: Ferkessédougou was reached in 1926 (558 km.) and Bobo Dioulasso in 1934 (796 km.). The old parts of the line, designed with purely strategic aims, had to be re-made after 1929, and were linked to the stretch Abidjan–Port-Bouët, with a pontoon bridge across the Ebrié lagoon. In Dahomey, three main lines were in existence: the Eastern Dahomey line (Pobé–Porto-Novo), built between 1905 and 1913, was extended to Cotonou in 1928–30, making a total length of 108 km. It belonged to the colony, which purchased it in 1932. The other sections belonged to the Dahomey Railway Company: the main one, the Dahomey central line, reached Savé in 1910 and was prolonged as far as Parakou in 1929–36; the West Dahomey line (Pahou–Segboroué), built at the beginning of the century, formed a branch-line to the central line. The 60-cm. gauge Segboroué–Grand Popo–Athiémé–Lokosa and Abomey–Zagnanado lines provided a sufficiently dense network for Lower Dahomey, but it did not serve the Nigerian hinterland. The Benin–Niger line had 577 km. of line with a one-metre gauge.

Togo had three one-metre gauge lines built by the Germans: Lomé—Anecho, Lomé–Palimé and, in the centre, Lomé–Atakpamé, the main line, which was extended to Blita in 1934. The work undertaken in 1929 laid rail as far as Sokodé – only half way. In the Cameroons, the northern railway line (Bonabéri–N'Kongsamba), finished in 1911, remained as the Germans had left it. The southern line, which they had built from Douala as far as Eseka, was extended in 1922–7 to Yaoundé, the capital of the territory, situated on a plateau, with a better climate. It was completed with a 60-cm.-gauge branch line from Otélé to Mbalmayo, intended to serve the cocoa-producing region. The construction was carried out with 50,000,000 francs from local budget funds and by means of massive requisitioning of labour, which contributed to the spread of sleeping sickness.

In French Equatorial Africa, there was no absence of projects. The railway programme, adopted on the occasion of the 1914 loan, planned for a line from Brazzaville over a stretch of 310 km. to the Atlantic in Gabon; it was to join the navigable section of the Ogooué, which began at N'Djolé and the Ivindo, and a 60-cm. gauge line between Bangui and Fort-Crampel, and to link up the navigable networks of the Chad to the Congo rivers, so eliminating porterage over that route which took a murderous toll. The war prevented the implementation of these projects. By 1921, seven surveying missions had since 1886 undertaken the study of the Congo–Ocean route, at a cost of 4,000,000 gold francs. The Sarraut plan of 1921 dropped the Gabon project, modified the track suggested for the Ubangi–Upper Shari line, and added a project for a line from Logone to Garoua, giving Chad an outlet on to the valley of the Benue. Work was undertaken only on the Congo–Ocean line in 1921 and it was completed in July 1934. A 1.067-metre gauge was chosen, identical to that used by the British and Belgian colonial railways, with a view to a future linking-up of the network with South Africa. The immediate aim was to link up with the projected Belgian railway between the Lower Congo and Katanga, which was to connect Elisabethville and Pool, so giving Katanga an outlet on Belgian territory. This project was soon abandoned in favour of a line from Lobito, which provided a shorter connection through Angola for the Katanga ores. For the sake of the shorter line a difficult terrain was unhesitatingly chosen, involving twelve tunnels, one of them 1,600 metres long, with reinforced ramps and steep curves, all of which prevented trains from moving at a higher average speed than 30 km.p.h. The price per kilometre reached a record level of 445,000 gold francs, as against the average of 119,000 for the French West African network.

The price in human lives was even heavier. The drama of the Congo–Ocean line was such that it stirred public opinion. André

Gide and Albert Londres exposed the essential facts, but the powerful orthodox press did not take the case up, and the mass of Frenchmen remained in ignorance. The scandal, once revealed, remained unanswered, as no commission of inquiry was set up as in 1905; instead, a wall of silence arose, and such means as the censorship of private correspondence coming from French Equatorial Africa prevented the truth from filtering through. The *Revue indigène*, which before 1914 had denounced Angoulvant's repressions in the Ivory Coast, wrote quite seriously that the workers requisitioned for the Congo–Ocean line were so satisfied that they returned as volunteers.[80]

As usual, the funds obtained by loans were destined to provide easy profits for the company that had been granted the works concession, which was none other than the Société des Batignolles.[81] Mechanised work was practically non-existent. The company did not trouble to go to extra expense, and the terms of the loan stipulated that no material was to be purchased outside France, although French industrialists were apparently not able to furnish suitable material. But this would have been unnecessary, for here, as in all preceding constructions, the administration was able to furnish 'requisitioned' labour free of charge.

> The administration had to furnish to the company that constructed the Congo–Ocean line a certain number of labourers per day, or pay an indemnity per man lacking. For a long time there was no claim for labourers and, without touching a single pick-axe, the company received indemnity.[82]

Work clearly made no progress by this means, and Governor-General Antonetti, appointed in 1924, decided to make the Congo–Ocean line the achievement of his period of rule; and for this he resorted to customary procedure. Let us simply cite what was written by General Hilaire, at one time supreme military commander in French Equatorial Africa, a man who can hardly be suspected of systematic anti-colonialism:

> For some five or six years, the cruel problem of native labour has led to a disastrous solution, that of the intensive depletion – yet again! – of a population already sadly decimated by drastic cuts enforced blindly on its weakest elements, over the 500 kilometres of these homicidal construction sites! . . . After the Bakango, the Loango, the Krèche, the Gabonese, the Souma, the Dagba, Baya, Yacoma, and others; even the Sara, the ethnic elite of French Equatorial Africa, magnificent and supreme reserves of farmers and soldiers, have been successively decimated, some of them even exterminated by the prison of the 'machine' – as, in their language of fear, they call the deadly labour on the railway line.[83]

It will be easily understood that the tens of thousands of labourers could not be recruited on the spot in a country that was already under-populated. At first they were made to come from the Middle Congo, in convoys piled onto barges, from the Ubangi and tributaries of the Congo as far as Brazzaville; then on foot, over a distance of 600 km. across the wild Mayombé region to Pointe-Noire. No food was provided. Of the 8,000 men recruited for the first convoys, 1,700 arrived at their destination. After the first 'requisitioning', terror spread through the villages which were deserted on the arrival of recruitment detachments. Man-hunts by the police, the 'punishment' – in other words, the destruction of villages – became customary procedure.

Albert Londres cites figures. The Likouala–Mossaka contingent of 1,250 men was soon reduced to 429. That from Ouesso in Upper Sangha comprised 174 and on its arrival at Brazzaville eighty survived; on arrival at the building site there were sixty-nine, three months later thirty-six. 'Local' resources[84] did not suffice. Appeals went out not only to the Middle Congo and Gabon. New labour was requisitioned from 300 km. away and even farther, from Upper Ubangi and Chad. Apart from the consequences of the journey, epidemics broke out from the overcrowding on barges, for many weeks almost without food and under unimaginable hygienic conditions. The Sara and the Banda of the savannahs showed least physical resistance, being accustomed to a dry climate and cereal food, and now being transferred naked to a damp equatorial climate and forced to eat unaccustomed food. Albert Londres described these Sara, who were known for their athletic appearance, as being now reduced to skeletons, having to burrow tunnels into the rock using their bare hands, with a hammer and mining rod as their only tools. Antonetti, this compound of Himmler and Joseph Prudhomme, proclaimed: 'Either accept the sacrifice of six to eight thousand men, or renounce the railways.'[85] Then, with still greater frankness: 'Monsieur, I need 10,000 dead for my railway.'[86] Albert Londres concluded: 'The sacrifice was far greater. Up to the present, however, it has not exceeded 17,000. And no more than 300 kilometres of line remain to be constructed.'[87] According to official statistics there was an 'improvement' because the 45·20 per cent mortality rate of the total force in 1927 fell to 39·18 per cent in 1928 and to 17·34 per cent in 1929.[88]

But the consequences were only to be expected. In 1928 a general insurrection broke out from the Sanga to the Ubangi, which took several years to quell: we shall return to this later. Meanwhile the railway line had to be finished. Chinese coolies were 'imported' (the word is that of an official writer) from Kuan Chou-wan, then leased by France. The results were not much better. Moreover, however miserable the conditions that had made the Chinese leave their country – although many of them had, undoubtedly, been 'voluntarily taken' by an unscrupulous administration – they had to be fed (with rice) and paid a little. This was considered too expensive and, in the end, labour was recruited from among French or Italian workmen and penniless adventurers wishing to 'get rich quick'. Once more, the African population paid the cost of the operations when 'recruitment' was renewed. The railway line was finally finished in July 1934. But no port was constructed and there was nothing to transport, apart from travelling officials; the latter felt little confidence because of the frequency of accidents, the result of the conditions under which the line had been built.

Roads and Rivers

Until after the First World War there were hardly any proper roads, particularly in the forest zone, where they were difficult to build. 'In 1905 there were only 20 km. of roads in French Equatorial Africa.'[89] There were only tracks for travellers on foot (including porters), which were strictly impassable for any kind of vehicle. Streams were crossed by tree trunks thrown from bank to bank; in the case of larger watercourses there would be fords. Winding tracks made short-cuts up and down steep slopes and rocks. The colonisers had themselves transported on litters carried by porters, called *tipoyes* in the Congo and 'hammocks' in West Africa. In West Africa, military needs and the use of horses or 'Lefèvre carts' (little two-wheeler carts that could be drawn by a donkey or, if one was not available, by a man) had led to the establishment of military routes – the Kayes–Bamako road or the 'Leprince road' from Conakry to Kankan. Strategic roads several metres wide were built even in the forests of the Ivory Coast, not so much for non-existent vehicles as to ease troop movements and limit the risk of ambushes. In 1920 the total length of roads of all kinds in French West Africa was estimated at 20,000 km., mostly no more than dirt roads that were barely levelled, especially in Senegal. Nevertheless, the motor-car was introduced in Africa after the war. The first trans-Saharan car crossing took place in 1923. By 1928 there was a total of 6,000 cars in French West Africa, two-thirds of them imported after 1925. They were in general use from 1929–30 onwards.

The coming of the automobile led to the construction of a network of roads in the years 1920–30. Contrary to the optimistic claims of the panegyrists of colonisation, the self-propelled vehicle brought only limited relief to the harsh forced labour of porterage. The use of porters for long-distance treks was reduced on the major routes, but 'administrative' porterage continued in the regions with few or no roads, and between villages and centres away from any road. The lightening of the burden of forced porterage was countered by the development of forced labour on the roads themselves: the tracks were made and maintained exclusively by requisitioned or statute labour. No consideration was given to the means employed: the chiefs were requisitioned to carry out the construction and upkeep of roads according to instructions received, and it was up to them to arrange matters. The men either escaped or they had already been requisitioned for other labour, so that the women and children were continually employed on this work. No tools were provided; picks and shovels were a luxury which the rigours of the budget did not permit. The only instruments used were bare hands and baskets of woven leaves made by the requisitioned people themselves. André Gide showed how in the Congo the women carried their children on their backs while working with bare hands at road repairs. That was in 1926.[90] In 1943 Father Lelong[91] described in detail the construction of the Boola–Gouecké mountain road in the forests of Guinea by a half-starved crowd of women, children and old men, under the whip of the circle police. As in the Mayombé country of the Congo when the Congo–Ocean railway was being built, the rock was broken with crowbars to save the cost of explosives. Under a photograph showing children at work, Father Lelong observed:

One has to beware of cameras which, under some mysterious effect of the tropical sun, register scenes that never took place, as official reports attest. It is completely untrue, for example, that groups of children have ever been recruited for road construction.[92]

The tracks clearly were of mediocre quality; they were often full of mudholes, which quickly solidified in the dry season, facing vehicles with 'corrugated iron' surfaces. In the rainy season, they became impassable, their low-lying sections were flooded and the bridges carried away. River crossings were (and still are) generally provided by ferry boats, submerged roadways and culverts of logs and planks erected by statute labour under the supervision of public works agents. A few planks just allowed room for vehicles to cross, and quite often an unskilful or unlucky driver had his vehicle sink to the bed of the watercourse, even if the bridge did not completely capsize under its weight. It is unnecessary to give more details of such 'routes'; the wear and tear on the vehicles was infinitely more rapid and their average life-span far shorter than on tarred European roads, besides which drivers and mechanics were inexperienced.

H

But it was an unbalanced picture. In West Africa, where the beginnings of a road network existed before 1914, 64,000 km. of roads had been built by 1930, and 101,000 km. by 1940, of which 27,000 km. could be used throughout the year. In Gabon, however, no more than 100 km. of roads had been built by 1936. In French Equatorial Africa, only Ubangi-Shari, the territory most ravaged by long-distance porterage and with a suitable climate and terrain, was equipped with a network of passable tracks, and a major road linked Bangui with Fort-Crampel; the latter, situated at Batangafo on the Bahr Sara, was the new shipping terminus in Shari, put into service in 1929. On the other hand, between Brazzaville and Bangui there was not, and still is not, any direct road contact, so that the river route alone could be used. The Bangui–Douala road was completed in 1928, but its use, as we shall see, went against the interests of the transport monopolies in French Equatorial Africa and against the administrative frontiers separating French Equatorial Africa from the Cameroons. The Cameroons, which in 1914 had only 40 km. of roads and some 300 km. of tracks leading from Kribi to Yaoundé, had by 1936 4,000 km. of tracks, of which 2,400 were passable during the rainy season, chiefly the two main roads from Douala to Yaoundé and to Fort-Lamy respectively.

In West Africa the river routes, used extensively in the years after the conquest, had only a limited traffic. On the Senegal, navigation was possible between Saint-Louis and Kayes only when the waters were high from July to October. Having lost its transit role with the building of the Thiès–Kayes railway, the river served only to connect its own banks, the economy of which became torpidly self-contained. The same applies to the 'southern reaches' of the Niger (from Kouroussa on the Niger, or Kankan on the Milo, to Bamako), which carried on the traffic of the Conakry–Niger railway in the direction of the Sudan; but it gradually lost the fairly dense traffic it enjoyed between 1911 and 1923. Navigation on the Niger retained its importance only between Koulikoro and Ansongo, where the river flowed through regions of difficult or impossible road access. Steam-boats plied during high water, from July–August to December–February (dates changing as one moved downstream) and flat-bottomed barges during the low water season. Between Koulikoro and Ségou, navigation was totally interrupted during a period that varied from year to year between three weeks and two months, and remained difficult and unprofitable for a far longer period. The volume of traffic increased from 4,000,000 metric tons in 1926 to 13,000,000 in 1930, but from the latter date the competition of the road, with faster traffic avoiding the river crossing, began to be felt.[93]

The lagoons of the Ivory Coast, protected and separated from the sea by the coastal belt, served as timber routes. But, in the absence of roads, navigation kept its former importance in Gabon and the Congo. Particularly in Gabon, the watercourses with access to the forest paths facilitated timber transport. But the main Congo–Ubangi route remained busy in the absence of any other. Downstream from Stanley-Pool, the rapids interrupted navigation, but from Brazzaville to Bangui[94] the Congo and the Ubangi provided a good navigable route; even if it had been poor, there was no other. The swampy zone at the confluence of the Sangha and the two Likoualas presented an obstacle to the construction of a road alongside the river. Several of its tributaries (the Sangha with over 650 km. of shallow water, the Likouala-aux-herbes, the Alima for more than 300 km. of its length, and others) were also navigable. The network of the Shari was navigable only in the wet season, but that was also when the roads were flooded. The volume of traffic, however, remained mediocre in keeping with the development of the country.

Another variant governing the use of roads and river communications was a country's economic system. West Africa, on the whole, maintained 'freedom', under the control of the monopolies; at least this was the case with the roads. After being an appendage of the big companies and the administration, road traffic disintegrated in the 1930s. The Lebanese sub-traders added road transport to their semi-wholesale or retail trade. The big companies, who were the exclusive importers of various makes of cars and lorries, granted liberal credit to their agents. The latter (or their drivers) toiled day and night to repay this debt, and so could not refuse the creditor company the sole rights in sale and purchase. They guaranteed the risks – of bad debts or accidental loss – and these were anything but negligible. All this was to the advantage of the companies.

On the great rivers, the traffic of the Senegal and the Middle Niger,[95] a heritage of the past, remained the monopoly of the old Messageries companies, which received compensation for their inadequate trade by means of budgetary subventions. As we have seen, these were combined offshoots of trading companies long established in the country. On the Middle Niger, a monopoly was established by the take-over in 1934 of the Société de Bamako, and in 1935 of the administrative fleet, by the Messageries africaines. A convention concluded in December 1935 granted them 'navigation service and exploitation of means of transport on the Niger', for a period of twenty-five years. Only the Niger Office and, to a lesser extent, the Compagnie française de l'Afrique occidentale retained a fleet of vessels for their own purposes. The lower reaches of the

Niger (Niamey–Malanville) were exploited by the owners of the railway line, who also provided links between Malanville and Parakou, terminus of the Central Dahomey railway.

In Equatorial Africa, transport as well as the export trade remained under the monopoly system. On the Congo–Ubangi river network, a virtual monopoly of public transport was in the hands of the 'Société Afrique et Congo', set up in 1907, which united the Fondère et Guynet interests and had taken over from the Messageries fluviales du Congo, which was established in 1900 by a group of chartered companies. In 1927 it transferred its river network services to a subsidiary, the Compagnie générale des transports en Afrique. This company had a river fleet of 2,000 tons serving the lines Brazzaville–Bangui (and Mongoumba during the low water season) on the Congo–Ubangi route, and Brazzaville–Nola (and Ouesso during low water) on the Congo–Sangha route. Certain chartered companies or their subsidiaries had their own ships to supply their trading posts. Such, for instance, were the Compagnie Sangha-Likouala, a subsidiary of the company Forestière Sangha-Oubangui, and the Compagnie française du Haut-et Bas-Congo, which owned fourteen steamships and thirty barges to supply its trading posts on the Alima and Likouala. The Shari monopoly belonged to the Compagnie française de l'Ouahm et Nana, a subsidiary of a Dutch chartered company established at Brazzaville (Nieuwe Afrikaansche Handels Gennootschap); its director-general served as Dutch consul at Brazzaville. Its administrative board had as its chairman a former governor of Ubangi-Shari, under whose rule the company had been constituted. It had the monopoly over all public, civil and military transport in the Shari basin. A decree by the governor-general, published in 1932, even gave it a business monopoly; no transport agent or trader who tendered for a contract from the Chad administration could do so except through its agency.

The contract for leasing administrative and postal transport, approved by the governor-general for a period of ten years in October 1931, included the following stipulations, despite protests from the local administration of Chad. Between Fort-Archambault and Fort-Lamy the contract stipulated a freight charge of 6.50 francs per ton, although the normal rate was 3.50 francs. From Bongor to Fort-Lamy, it granted the company a 'forfeit' of 458 francs per ton, although the administration carried it on its own boats at a rate of 100 francs per ton. (Henceforth it was prohibited from doing so.) Finally, the contract granted the company a minimum volume of 750,000 kilos per year on the route Bangui–Fort-Archambault.[96] The company fleet comprised two steam-boats and six whale-boats, the property of the colony of Chad, rented at a tariff that had remained fixed at 50 francs per year per steamer and 10 francs per year per whale-boat ever since the beginning of the century. Towards the 1930s, four of the six rented whale-boats were abandoned and were neither replaced nor paid for. (The company possessed forty-four whale-boats of its own.) Its paddlers were paid at a legal rate, 1.50 francs per day plus food, with unpaid waiting at ports of call, and 0.50 francs per day for the 'empty return' – even if the boats were full. Paying no taxes and with very limited expenses, its position guaranteed by the profits of its trading posts, and refusing all responsibility for the losses that frequently occurred through damage or accident, the company, with practically no capital, made a net profit of 500,000 francs per year. Its prices were almost twice the normal maximum for transport; other carrying firms could use its intermediaries and still make a satisfactory profit since the surplus between the agreed prices and the official tariff received by the company constituted a monopoly income transferred to the budget of the administration.[97]

Under these conditions one can understand the hostility of the 'interests' in French Equatorial Africa to a railway line connecting the Ubangi and Chad through the Cameroons. From Chad, at least, the direct route to Douala was far less expensive; it could be used during every season, or as far as the port of Garoua on the Benue, with trans-shipment to the United Africa Company fleet and the rest of the journey through Nigeria. One could go from Fort-Lamy to Douala in a week via Yaoundé, instead of taking a month to get to Pointe-Noire via Brazzaville – the imposed itinerary. But this change in orientation would have prejudiced a number of interests, especially the Compagnies de l'Ouahm at Nana or Afrique et Congo. And the Congo–Ocean line needed traffic to justify its construction! Thus passengers and 'administrative' products were forced to take the most costly and complicated route. Such products included anything that profited from administrative protection – from the 1930s it was cotton. The route involved two trans-shipments between Chad and the ocean, apart from the initial loading and the discharge at the port; and it was the longest route, thirteen days to travel a thousand kilometres from Bangui to Brazzaville; the distance between Bordeaux and Lomé was covered by passenger ships in the same length of time. 'National' reasons were invoked; it was not certain that the Cameroons, a mandated territory, would remain French, and a 'national' line of communications had to be maintained. The loan of 10,000,000 francs authorised in 1930 to give the Cameroons the benefit of a railway line from Douala to Chad was never launched.

For a long time air transport was only of military interest. The first air crossing from South Algeria to Gao (Mali) was made by Major Vuillemin in February 1920.[98] Several years were to pass before an airmail link was established via Dakar to South America; this still remained something of a feat. The first flight between Morocco and French West Africa was made in 1925, while Mermoz made the first commercial transatlantic flight (from Saint-Louis in Senegal to Natal in Brazil) by seaplane in 1930. The first French Trans-Africa route (Algiers–Niamey–Brazzaville) was established in 1934, followed the same year by a route along the coast from Dakar to Pointe-Noire, established by Aéromaritime, a subsidiary company of Chargeurs Réunis; it was enlarged in 1936 by an air-link from Niamey to Cotonou. In 1938 Air France opened a line from Dakar to Bamako via Kaolack, Tambacounda and Kayes. These lines were used mainly for mail, and only carried a small number of passengers. Air transport remained the privilege of the army and, when needed, it was put at the disposal of the governors and governors-general, but not without risk. In 1935 Edouard Renard, governor-general of French Equatorial Africa, was killed in this way.

Industry

The structure of industrial investment in 1940 clearly indicates the latter's economic role. Thirty-five per cent of investment in French West Africa was in public works enterprises, the Société française d'entreprises de dragages et de travaux publiques (owning the port of Dakar and various railways), linked to the Banque d'Indochine and the Worms and Lazard banks. Several construction and public works trusts were active in French West and French Equatorial Africa, though their activities do not appear in published figures. In the period under review, these companies did not have subsidiaries permanently installed in Africa, but intervened in specific operations as the occasion arose, (mainly in port works and railway construction). Such were the Société de construction des Batignolles (mentioned above, linked to Protestant high finance and Hottinguer in particular), Hersent (associated with Schneider), and others. If we consider only French West Africa, 1 per cent out of the 35 per cent of capital investment was in manufacturing: e.g. Silico-calcaire africaine (1922: bricks and pipes, on the outskirts of Dakar), Chaux et ciments du Sénégal (1926: quarries[99]) and Briqueteries de Bamako (1926: brickworks and public works). These firms met only an infinitesimal proportion of the demand. In spite of rising transport costs – above all to places far from the main lines of communication and in countries of the interior like Upper Volta and Niger – the trading companies considered it more advantageous to limit their activities to imports and the sale of cement, metal building frames and sheet-metal at high prices. Immediately after the Second World War numerous district administrative offices and residences were still made of boards, wooden-walled and with thatched roofs.

The second sector of industrial investment, making up 28 per cent, was that of electricity generation and distribution. Although hydro-electric resources existed in certain regions, particularly in Guinea, the companies concerned – generally groups of specialised French trusts and local commerce – were content to establish small electric power-stations, run on imported fuel, to provide light in the urban centres. They sometimes also managed water supply. This was the case of the Compagnie des Eaux et Electricité de l'Ouest africain, set up in 1929,[100] with power-stations at Dakar, Saint-Louis, Kaolack, Rufisque, Thiès and Louga. On its board of directors were to be found representatives of the French Thompson-Houston company and the Société auxiliaire africaine, and Baron Jean Davillier. Its 1947 accounts showed a gross profit of 73,000,000 francs,[101] which was two and a half times the nominal capital. The Arsenal de Dakar produced electric current at a cost price of 3 francs C.F.A. per Kw/h., while the Compagnie des Eaux et Electricité de l'Ouest africain sold it to the consumer in Dakar for 17 francs C.F.A., the highest rate in the world. The power-stations at Diourbel and Ziguinchor were run by smaller companies,[102] set up in 1920 and 1930, which were concerned with other activities (specifically oil works) and controlled by the Compagnie générale des Colonies. The Union Electrique coloniale, established in 1929 (Sud-Lumière and the Banque de l'Afrique occidentale), ran power-stations at Lomé, Brazzaville, Pointe-Noire and Bangui.

Of the industrial capital in French West Africa, 18 per cent consisted of port management, and 19 per cent various repair shops and processing industries. The engineering sector, apart from garages, was represented by private companies: in Dakar the Manutention africaine (Delmas), the Ateliers et chantiers maritimes set up in 1938, and the Société commerciale d'affrètements et de commissions; others belonged to the state (Dakar arsenal, and repair shops run by the French West African railways at Thiès). The processing industries included palm oil works on the Ivory Coast and in Dahomey, handicrafts in the Congo and groundnut oil works producing mainly for the local market. Groundnut oil was not a significant export before 1936, while from 1937 to 1939 exports ran to 5,000 tons of oil per year, which is 3 per cent of the volume of groundnuts exported.[103] The few existing soap works were, like the oil works, only partly mechanised, and worked only for the local market, providing a fraction of its consumption. During the First World War a factory for tinned meat was established at Lyndiane (near Kaolack in Senegal) making corned beef from local livestock; immediately after the war it closed. Groundnut shelling in Senegal (one-tenth of the groundnuts were exported shelled in 1935, nearly half in 1939), treatment of coffee beans on the Ivory Coast, rice shelling in Guinea and the Sudan, cotton and kapok ginning in Dahomey, Togo, Upper Volta and the Sudan, and the saw-mills on the Ivory Coast were processing industries of the most elementary kind, crafts rather than industries. The only textile mill, the Gonfreville works, was set up during the First World War at Bouaké, on the Ivory Coast, by a former commissioner for native affairs. It supplied only the local market and had difficulty in getting raw materials, despite administrative pressure.

In French Equatorial Africa there were only saw-mills and wood-bark peeling works, chiefly in Gabon, with cotton ginning and pressing in Ubangi.

REFERENCES

1. Huguette Durand, *Essai sur la conjoncture de l'Afrique noire*. Paris, Dalloz, 1957, p. 27.

2. Lenin, *Imperialism, the Highest Stage of Capitalism*.

3. Not published, but made available to the author. It served as a basis for the study by J. Dresch, 'Les trusts en Afrique noire', *Servir la France*, 1946, pp. 30 ff., which was the first scientific analysis of the 'trade economy' (the expression seems to have appeared for the first time in that article).

4. At 20 gold francs to the pound sterling in 1936 and in adopting the co-efficient of conversion of the French inquiry, the figures given by Frankel make 12,264,000,000 1940 francs for public investments (as against 7,033,000,000) and 7,775,000,000 for private investments as against 26,965,000,000. The periods under consideration are not the same, it is true; but private investment was not very important in the periods 1870–1900 and 1936–40.

5. As to the approximate character of these calculations the author himself observed: 'It is very difficult to arrive at an estimate of foreign investment in the French dependencies, . . . on account of the paucity of data, particularly in regard to the non-listed capital.' (Frankel, *Capital Investment in Africa, its course and effects*. London, Oxford University Press, 1938, p. 168.)

6. Including German capital (£15,827,000,000) this figure concerns both territories; what was added after the war concerned only the French Mandate Territories.

7. 624,500,000 1940 francs.

8. 254,670,000 1940 francs.

9. 3,500,000 if one estimates 50 per cent of the total of the loans which were spent on railways, an evaluation that appreciably surpasses reality.

10. In calculating the construction work of the Dakar–Saint-Louis railway-line carried out before 1900 ('Les chemins de fer en Afrique Occidentale Française', *Marchés coloniaux*, Special Number, 14 May, 1949).

11. The capital of the companies is calculated here by taking for each of them the total issued, not at nominal value but according to the stock exchange quotation.

12. Cf. P. Valdant, *Marchés coloniaux*, 23 March, 1946, p. 269.

13. With one exception. We have considered as a single unit the three branches of Unilever: Nouvelle Société Commerciale Africaine, Niger Français and Compagnie Française de la Côte d'Ivoire.

14. As an example, the quotas of food crops imported to Senegal in 1949 by the three 'big companies' are given below (the date chosen is a little after the period under consideration for lack of data, but remains valid in the context):

	Rice	Flour	Sugar
	%	%	%
Nouvelle Société Commerciale africaine	21	20	23
Société Commerciale de l'Ouest Africain	18	9	29
Compagnie française de l'Afrique occidentale	27	16	21
TOTAL	66	45	73

We may add that a 20 per cent quota of each of these products imported officially by the Syndicat des petits commerçants was, in fact, handled by the three big companies.

15. Cf. Marcel Capte, *Traité d'économie tropicale*. Paris, Pichon et Durand-Auzias, 1958, p. 174.

16. Bank which was assured of the financial services of the Banque de l'Afrique Occidentale.

17. F. Bohn was director of the Compagnie Française de l'Afrique Occidentale at Marseilles, Le Cesne in Paris.

18. J. Weber was, within the Union coloniale, chairman of a Union des planteurs de cacaoyers, caféiers, hévéas et palmiers à huile de l'Ouest africain (*Dépêche coloniale*, 25 July, 1931).

19. In 1911 the Forestière Sangha-Oubangui company had on its board M. Jean de Hemptinne, chairman of the Compagnie du Kasaï.

20. 1904: Société d'études et de participations industrielles.
   1905: Société française industrielle et coloniale.
   1909: Banque française industrielle et coloniale.
   1910: Banque française de l'Afrique équatoriale.
   1924: Banque française de l'Afrique.

21. Convention of 26 June, 1931, with the Banque de l'Afrique occidentale (C. Fidel, *L'Afrique occidentale française et la crise*. Paris, 1932).

22. According to R. Monmarson, *L'Afrique noire et son destin*. Paris, Ed. Francex, 1950, pp. 36–7.

23. Cf. note 22.

24. The Banque de Paris et des Pays-Bas represented notably by A. Laurent-Atthalin, the Crédit Lyonnais (E. Enders), the Crédit foncier d'Algérie et de Tunisie, the Société génerale (J.-C. Charpentier), the Marseillaise de crédit (Edouard de Cazalet), Adrien Josse (already quoted) and G. Schwob d'Héricourt. On the 1923 board one finds the names of P. Fougerolles (public works), P. Delmas, the former Minister for the Colonies Messimy and Governor-General Angoulvant. The chair was held by the former minister for the colonies, André Lebon, then replaced by Emile Moreau, chairman of the Banque de Paris et des Pays-Bas. At the onset another person to figure on the board of directors was Fondère, one of the big men in the chartered companies of French Equatorial Africa (Messageries fluviales du Congo, which became Afrique et Congo in 1907, etc.).

H*

25. Participation in the Compagnie Equatoriale des Mines, Compagnie minière coloniale, etc.

26. The Cameroons and Ivory Coast.

27. Huileries africaines from 1920 to 1928. Palm oil plantations and oil works at Dabou (Ivory Coast). In 1939 more than four-fifths of its assets were set up as company securities (plantations of hevea in Indonesia, etc.).

28. Who notably controlled the cement trusts (Lafarge, Chaux et Ciments de Marseille, and their West African branch) and the breweries (which were linked to the Société des Brasseries de l'Ouest Africain – and its group).

29. Who notably exercised control over Nestlé.

30. In 1949, Alexander Hay, a relative – probably the son – of the former, held the position.

31. Before the war, the group Mirabaud-Puerari-De Nervo, later of the Banque de l'Union Parisienne. All met again on the board of directors of the Mokta-El-Hadid, another business of the Nervo group.

32. The work of these companies was often many-faceted: immediately after the Second World War the Ateliers et Chantiers maritimes de Dakar extended their work to all branches of metallurgy; Dakar-Soutes sold chemical products, including insecticides, and ran a firm that disinfected houses.

33. Where the Banque de l'Indochine and the Crédit Commerciale de France seem to be supreme.

34. Represented either by Gradis or Schwob d'Héricourt, German cousins of the Gradis.

35. J. and R. Charbonneau, *Marchés et marchands d'Afrique noire*. Paris, La Colombe, 1961, pp. 73–8.

36. In 1948 one could find on the boards of these companies – Compagnie de Navigation Cyprien-Fabre: directors Paul Cyprien-Fabre and Jean Fraissinet; Compagnie de navigation Fraissinet: chairman Jean Fraissinet, directors P. Vieljeux, etc.; Compagnie de navigation Paquet: chairman Jean Fraissinet; Compagnie Delmas-Vieljeux (La Rochelle): chairman P. Vieljeux, directors Jean Fraissinet, Mme. Frank Delmas, etc.

37. Current fiscal year from 1 April to 31 March of the following year.

38. The data given here concerning the state and structure of Unilever refer, unless stated otherwise, to the year 1946 (source: *Fortune*, December 1947, January, February 1948).

39. These, however, furnished no more than a twentieth of the purchase of African products operated by the group.

40. After the Second World War in any case. R. and W. King were representatives of the trust in the Cameroons, and Hatton and Cookson in Gabon.

41. Mostly replaced on the board by Rémi Boissonas after the Second World War.

42. Established 1926. Plantations on the Ivory Coast and in the Cameroons.

43. Towards the end of this period (on the eve of the Second World War) passed under the control of the banks (mainly Hottinguer-Vernes group).

44. Relative and associate of the automobile manufacturer Louis Renault.

45. It was the Loste Bank which, with the Société des Batignolles, was to grant a loan for facilities for French Equatorial Africa approved in 1914 and only prevented by the war from being put into practice.

46. It held over half the shares and the majority with its other branch, the Crédit foncier du Congo, which equally participated in the Haut et Bas-Congo company.

47. M. Capet, *Traité d'économie tropicale*. Paris, Pichon et Durand-Auzias, 1958, p. 15.

48. Price in October 1947 (sale); purchase price in the 1946–7 season.

49. Price in October 1947 (sale); purchase price in the 1946–7 season.

50. Let us note that the salary of 20 francs applies to 1945, raised in December to 40 francs and in February 1946 to 44 francs.

51. We have assumed that the peasant was paid a 'just' price. In fact, he often received much less; the declassification of the products on the pretext of 'making up' took place with the complicity of the administration (which let them export a mixture as higher quality that they had purchased as average or inferior quality). Fraud generally applied to weights, usurous reimbursement levied by merchants and the Provident Societies, etc.

52. H. Labouret, *Paysans d'Afrique occidentale*. Paris, Gallimard, 1941.

53. Lenin, *Imperialism* . . ., op. cit.

54. Karl Marx, *Capital*, vol. III. Ed. C. H. Kerr and Co., Chicago, 1909. Chapter XIV, p. 279.

55. Ibid., p. 389.

56. Ibid., p. 389.

57. Ibid., p. 280.

58. Little tables or boxes set up on the pavement where vendors sold cola, cigarettes, biscuits, pieces of lump sugar, etc.

59. For a profound analysis of this phenomenon see the penetrating studies of Georges Balandier in regard to Fang Society.

60. Average production 1930–40 (*Les exportations agricoles des cercles de l'Afrique occidentale et du Togo français*. Paris, Secrétariat d'État aux Colonies, 1944, pp. 233 ff.).

61. Except perhaps in Guinea, where the rubber crisis, for lack of a substitute product, led to a recession in the market economy and of trade in comparison with the years 1904–10.

62. Data for 1946.

63. M. Capet, *Traité d'économie tropicale*. 'Les économies d'A.O.F.', op. cit.

64. Even after 1934 the incomplete state of the port kept up a flow of traffic on the Belgian railway.

65. Wharf 385 m. long, of laterite, with a wooden landing-stage 248 m. long, of which 120 m. could be used for the berthing of big ships. Access channel 7 m. in depth.

66. Refers to the Thiès–Kayes line.

67. J. Goulven, 'Les ports maritimes de l'Afrique occidentale', *Bull. Société de Géographie commerciale de Paris*, 1913, p. 523. The foreign navigation companies with regular lines (Woermann and Elder Dempster) protested.

68. Albert Boucher, 'Le port de Dakar', *B.C.E.H.S.*, 1925, pp. 651–75.

69. 1933: 62 per cent of groundnut exports via Kaolack, 28 per cent via Dakar, 10 per cent via Rufisque (Cf. Morazé, 'Dakar', *Annales de Géographie*, 1936, pp. 607–31).

70. Only the British Gold Coast colony (now Ghana) had an artificial deep-water port at Takoradi, opened in 1928.

71. The Kroo are a coastal people in Liberia (right bank of the Cavally); with a high reputation for seafaring; they traditionally provided the crews of ships along the coast of Africa from Cape Palmes.

72. See A. H. Canu, *La Pétaudière coloniale*. Paris, Chamuel, 1894. Viard, a former manager of the sub-office at Cotonou of the firm 'Flers-Exportation' claimed to be an 'explorer' and gained the 'concession' for constructing the wharf from obliging friends. He associated with bankers who furnished the necessary capital of one million francs and gave him for his 'support' 300 ordinary shares (out of 2,000) and 300 'profit shares' out of the 2,000 issued. A loan was raised for the construction. After rising on the stock exchange, the values slumped after a year without anything having been built.

73. From its Portuguese name of the Rio dos Camerões, hence Cameroons.

74. The firm of the Sargos Brothers, later Société forestière et agricole du Kouilou.

75. *Les Colonies et la défénse nationale*. Paris, Challamel, 1916, p. 195.

76. Bordeaux chamber of commerce, *Les ports de la côte occidentale d'Afrique*, Bordeaux, 1929.

77. Albert Sarraut, *La Mise en valeur des colonies françaises*. Paris, Payot, 1923, p. 373.

78. C. Guy, 'L'avenir de l'Afrique Occidentale Française', *L'Afrique française*, 1927, No. 1, pp. 15–17.

79. The convention signed in 1932 provided for the repurchase of the concession of the railway from Dakar to Saint-Louis and the 'leasing' of the railway from Djoloff (Louga-Linguère) against an annual payment of 1,550,000 francs until 1942, 1,375,000 francs until 1956, and 1,165,000 francs up to 1983! The Dakar-St. Louis Railway Company also continues to administer important landed estate. The administration of the railway, carried on largely at a loss, was charged to the budget, as rent paid by the company.

80. *Revue indigène*, May–June 1925, No. 197–8, pp. 106–11.

81. Where other entrepreneurs carried out transport of slag at 9.80 francs per cubic metre, the chartered company received 18.70 francs under its contract (R. Susset, *La Vérité sur le Cameroun et l'Afrique Equatoriale Française*. Paris, Ed. de la Nouvelle Revue Critique, 1934).

82. Denise Moran, *Tchad*. Paris, Gallimard, 1934, p. 295.

83. General Hilaire, *Du Congo au Nil*. Marseille, Edition de l'A.S.C.G., 1930, p. 333.

84. Ouesso was 1,000 km. from Brazzaville.

85. Albert Londres, *Terre d'Ebène*. Paris, Albin Michel, 1929, p. 236.

86. Denise Moran, op. cit., p. 292.

87. Albert Londres, op. cit., p. 236.

88. R. Susset, op. cit., pp. 131 ff.

89. Henri Ziegle, *Afrique Equatoriale française*. Paris, Berger-Levrault, 1952, p. 129.

90. André Gide, *Voyage au Congo*. Paris, Gallimard, 1927, p. 89.

91. M. H. Lelong, *Ces Hommes qu'on appelle anthropophages*. Paris, Ed. Alsatia, 1946.

92. This Father, a Dominican, was not specially anti-colonialist. In the Belgian Congo, in Upper Ouellé, the Dominican region, everything was done to get his works read. But at N'Zérékoré, the administrator was a freemason and anti-clerical, even having a mosque built to annoy the fathers. There was much to settle with the colonial administration. In the first French edition of this book, I believed Father Lelong to be Belgian and had attributed to this circumstance, among others, his indulgence towards the Belgian colonial system. I was mistaken: Father Lelong is French, and in one of his works that have since appeared (*Il est dangereux de se pencher dehors*. Paris, Robert Laffont, 1965) he reprimanded me sharply. In subsequent correspondence Father Lelong, while noting the similarity of the evils inherent in diverse forms of colonial domination and Belgian paternalism, declared to me that 'taken all in all, and without being deceived by the myth of good colonisation' he preferred the methods of adjustment (*la méthode adaptrice*) employed in the Belgian Congo to the assimilation carried out by France (*in litteris*, 23 August, 1966).

93. J. Champaud, 'La navigation fluviale sur le Moyen-Niger', *Cahiers d'Outre-Mer*, July–September 1961, pp. 255–92.

94. As far as Bangui from 15 July to 31 December, and during the other six months – that is to say from January to July – as far as 100 to 200 km. downstream from Bangui.

95. On the southern reaches (Kouroussa-Bamako) the Société de Bamako abandoned exploitation after the completion of the Thiès–Kayes railway, where rates were more advantageous (1923).

96. R. Susset, op. cit., pp. 120–1.

97. Cf. Denise Moran, op. cit., p. 296, and Marcel Homet, *Congo, terre de souffrances*. Paris, Ed. Montaigne, 1934, pp. 155–6. It was superseded after the last war by the Compagnie des Transports Congo-Oubangui-Tchad, a branch of the Compagnie Générale des Transports en Afrique.

98. A second aircraft carrying General Laperrine, the commander of the Territories of Southern Algeria, was lost in the desert near its destination.

99. There was no local cement production in tropical Africa before 1948.

100. By the renewal and fusion of the Compagnie d'Electricité du Sénégal and the Compagnie africaine d'Electricité.

101. 60,000,000 fr. of these profits were set aside as 'reserves'.

102. Société éléctrique et industrielle du Baol, Société électrique et industrielle de Casamance.

103. *Rapport de l'Inspection des Colonies* – February 1942. The first oil works were set up at Diourbel, Kaolack, in 1920 and 1922 by branches of the Compagnie générale des Colonies; others (Ziguinchor, Louga, Dakar) were set up in the years 1929–33.

2. Production

In the trading economy, agriculture remained almost the exclusive source of production. The techniques were still, with few exceptions, those of pre-colonial times: tillage with the hoe on patches of burnt land, and extensive cultivation, involving long periods of letting the land lie fallow. The use of draught animals in ploughing and of mechanical power, even in elementary forms of irrigation with water-wheels, was generally unknown. Intensive cultivation, using manure, was not unknown but was generally limited to kitchen gardens around the huts. It did not become important except where there was a shortage of space, i.e. in mountain or sheltered coastal regions with a great density of population, and it was not a sign of progress even if it did create more civilised landscapes; it required more labour for an equivalent product, and its technical base was identical to that of extensive cultivation, to which the people naturally returned as soon as the opportunity arose.

The products and the selection of crops varied according to the climate. In the forest or humid zones there were 'plantations' of fruit or root crops; in the savannah or the steppe areas there was the field, the *lougan* of the Senegalese, with a predominance of annual cereal crops. We shall not return to this in detail.[1]

The social group also remained essentially unchanged. There was the traditional patriarchal community, tending at times to split into limited family communities – a trend which had already appeared in certain regions before colonisation. There was development only in the nature of production. Export products were added to the traditional food crops, or replaced them: groundnuts and cotton, in the zones with a marked dry season; and coffee, cacao beans and bananas in the humid zones. Harvested crops, which before 1914 represented more than half the exports (gum, wax, oil palm products and, most of all, rubber), dropped to second place – with the exception of timber in which exports continued to develop. Alongside the 'African peasantry', which furnished the essential part of production, European settlers gradually took over a limited but increasingly important place. They monopolised forest exploitation and controlled a large part of plantation crops. But this scarcely ever happened in countries with annual crops, since production on the capitalist pattern was not profitable in cotton or groundnuts. The presence of the settlers brought no important changes either in techniques or in the organisation of African society. The tillage on the settlers' plantations, as elsewhere, remained

almost exclusively manual, limited to irons for slashing and the hoe.
Manpower was provided by requisitioned labour, or it was recruited
for a limited time from among men who had left their families in the
villages and intended to return as soon as possible; there was no real
agriculture proletariat.

(a) THE DEVELOPMENT OF EXPORT CROPS

In 1920 the export production of groundnuts rose to 220,000 tons.
This was grown largely in Senegal, where in 1924–8 the average
annual production was estimated at 600,000 tons in shells, of which
410,000 tons were for export.[2] The other territories of French West
Africa produced another 30,000 to 40,000 tons.

The completion of the Dakar–Niger line and the opening of the
Kano railway in Nigeria extended the potentialities for export production from the Sudan and Niger. The world economic crisis
affected production temporarily; in 1930 520,000 tons were exported
in 1932 less than 200,000, but production returned to its old level
again before 1933. In 1934 the districts of Kayes, Ségou, Bamako
and San, in the Sudan, exported 20,000 tons shelled, the equivalent
of some 27,000 tons in shells; Niger, in 1935, produced 50,000 tons
in shells, of which 30,000 shelled tons were exported via Kano. On
the eve of the Second World War export production rose to 600,000
tons in shells, of which the main portion was supplied by Senegal
and the Sudan (Niger 40,000 tons; Upper Volta and the Korhogo
region on the Ivory Coast 25,000 tons; Dahomey 7,000 tons;
Guinea 4,000 tons).

Groundnuts grow best on light sandy soil, which prevents the
shells from rotting in the soil; this was common in Senegal and
generally widespread in the Sahel zone. Groundnuts were never a
monoculture. They grew as part of a more or less complex rotation
system, alternating with a small millet (mainly of the *souna* variety,
with a rapid vegetative cycle and well adapted to light soil), which
made up the basis of the crop rotation sysem and remained the
staple food crop. To this were added a kind of haricot bean (*niébé*)
and the *voandzou* or ground-pea, an African plant for which American groundnuts had been substituted since the sixteenth century.
Cassava also formed part of the cycle.[3]

On the virgin or fallow land agricultural work began with the
cutting down of the undergrowth at the end of April or beginning
of May, before the start of the rainy season; tools were limited to the
axe, the felling knife and the *rhock*, which served for chopping and
gathering the undergrowth.[4] With only a few exceptions, trees and
bushes were cut to ground level – the stumps were left. The undergrowth was burnt and the cinders scattered over the field, which

was not dug; they simply pierced holes in which they planted the seeds. The rest of the agricultural work (weeding, second dressing and uprooting) was carried out from the middle of June to the end of October, either with the bare hand or with the help of rudimentary utensils (the *daba* and *iler*[5] – various sorts of light rakes). Agricultural techniques did not evolve. Auguste Chevalier observed:

> Everything in tropical Africa has evolved; there are railways and roads that can be used by cars for most of the year, trade is very active, and the inhabitants have reached a higher standard of living, enjoying a certain well-being, and becoming open to ideas of co-operation. But Sengalese agriculture has not evolved – the methods of cultivation are still as primitive, the insects and parasites take a high tithe from the harvest, for the want of measures that are relatively easy to take.[6]

Attempts to that effect were made, sometimes technically useful; as the European plough and harness tools were not suitable, French firms tried to design tools adapted to Senegalese conditions: the 'lark hoe', drawn by a donkey, for ploughing and second dressing, and the 'Bajac *iler*', both used for sowing. All of them involved the inconvenience of clearing the land completely, and eliminating all stumps and roots which traditional agriculture left in the soil and whose shoots played an important part during the fallow period and in soil protection. Their use ran into all kinds of difficulties: the chief obstacle was the shortage of livestock and its incapacity for agricultural work. The horse, where it did exist, was a luxury; cattle and donkeys that lived off the brush plants – that is to say, very badly and only during the dry season – were weak, and riddled with disease and parasites. A donkey or cow could barely be made to work for six hours a day, and even this called for long and difficult breaking in. Any increase in settled stock-breeding was limited by the shortage of drinking water. The use of harness tools presupposed the presence of craftsmen, blacksmiths, wheelwrights and harness-makers, who did not exist or who were driven out by the competition of imported articles. But above all – and this was the essential point – the low income of the Senegalese farmer producing ground-nuts precluded any possibility of even moderate investment on his part. Harness tools spread only very gradually: in 1946, for example, they were used on 3,000 out of 70,000 hectares given over to ground-nuts in the Louga district; they remained essentially the prerogative of a few notables and canton chiefs. In 1921 mechanised cultivation was tried at Laté Mingué, in the Kaolack region, by an agent of the Compagnie française de l'Afrique occidentale;[7] technically, the results were satisfactory, but results proved that such cultivation was not profitable under the economic conditions then existing. Paid labour of mediocre standard 'cost more' than the 'independent workers', besides involving depreciation of the tools.

As to fertilisers, only the Sérères, who practised stock-breeding and agriculture, used manure on their fields.[8] Auguste Chevalier drew attention in 1930 to the useful effects of lime phosphates, but experiments were still needed to show under what conditions and in what form they should be employed. In any case, where the peasant had no capital available for buying fertilisers, this remained in the realm of theory, even assuming that the technical preliminaries had been fulfilled. In consequence, the yields remained mediocre, from 600 to 800 kilos per hectare in a favourable year, although mechanised cultivation would have yielded an average of 1,000 kilos per hectare. (In Egypt and India, with intensive cultivation, manuring and irrigation yields were as high as 2,000 and 2,500 kilos.) Progress of any kind was limited to seed selection carried out at the experimental agricultural scientific station at M'Bambey set up in 1922;[9] and even that was of debatable value.

Apart from groundnuts, the Sudan–Sahel zone produced nothing for export, beyond samples. The 'Fleuve' gum, produced by Senegal and Mauritania, always suffered from the fluctuations of the market: exports (4–5,000 tons) covered just over half the French requirements. Harvested produce included the *karité* (oil-bearing seeds) and textile plants like kapok (Central Togo and Central Dahomey)[10] and raffia. Sisal (4,479 tons in French West Africa in 1938) was supplied mainly by five big plantations in the Kayes and Tambacounda regions. Even at production stage, it was managed by certain companies controlled by large financial interests. Economically, such production was unimportant, and the yields obtained were two or three times lower than those of the other principal producer countries: exports were subject to enormous fluctuations according to economic cycles.

Among the textile plants, cotton seemed to flourish best in the West African climate. In the Sudan, Dahomey and Ivory Coast, the Association cotonnière coloniale, a consortium of French cotton and industrial textile importers set up in 1903, opened several ginning workshops, but without great success. We shall see later what grandiose plans were dreamed up in this field after the First World War. The harnessing of the interior delta of the Niger was to turn the French Sudan into a new Egypt, fully catering for the French cotton industry's demand for raw materials.

The success of the Niger Office did not measure up to the hopes placed in it. Instead of the 300,000 tons of cotton forecast for 1919–21 by the Bélime mission, production had painfully climbed to a few thousand tons in 1939 after twenty years; the cotton was of mediocre quality and sold with the help of substantial subsidies. Private initiative did not succeed any better. The Hirsch group (Compagnie de culture cotonnière du Niger), which in 1919 had been granted the monopoly of cotton purchase in the Sudan, had tried to plant on its own account, besides reaping the profits expected from state production on the irrigated lands. For this purpose it had been granted a concession of 100,000 hectares at Diré near Timbuctu in 1919. Within twenty years 50,000 hectares were put under cultivation, four-fifths of these under cotton. In 1935 cultivation was limited to 1,500 hectares, of which 600 were under cotton – all under the *métayage* system which allowed the company merely to transfer the burden to the peasant.[11] Out of 1,876 tons produced in the Sudan in 1942 the Niger Office furnished 606 tons, Diré 270 tons, and the circles, that is to say compulsory cultivation on the 'commander's fields', 1,000 tons. The same applied to Dahomey, Upper Volta and the Ivory Coast, where compulsory cultivation on the 'commander's fields' produced a few hundred tons. Dahomey furnished approximately 1,000 tons[12] for export, divided between the ginning centres of the Association cotonnière, the Société du Haut-Ogooué, the Walkden company and a few others. The Ivory Coast and Upper Volta produced some 2,000 tons for export, sold in ginning stations of the Association cotonnière, the surplus being supplied to the Gonfreville spinning and weaving works at Bouaké. Cotton exports from French West Africa, which reached their peak of 4,234 tons in 1930, fell to 1,376 tons in 1932, during the crisis, and in 1939 rose to 3,916 tons (Sudan 585 tons; Ivory Coast 2,219 tons; Dahomey 1,071 tons; Niger 41 tons). This was the result of compulsory crops, which were introduced in Ubangi-Shari after 1924, on the initiative of Eboué, to substitute a more saleable product for rubber, the significance of which had dwindled. Compulsory cultivation and the monopoly purchase by chartered companies were instituted in 1927 on the pattern of the Belgian Congo. The methods will be studied below.

The yields were miserable and did not even reach 300 kilos per hectare; the price paid to the producers, 1 franc per kilo of cotton grain in 1925–6, fell to 0·60 francs in 1933–4. Calculating 10 kilos of cotton-grain for 3 of cotton-fibre, the producer earned 2 francs per kilo of cotton fibre at the latter rate. Yet the companies profiting from the purchasing monopoly resold it at 5.50 francs per kilo, and even received a 3.50 francs per kilo premium from the state. In 1936 the rates went up and the premium was abolished, but the purchasing price to the producer was only raised to 0.75 francs per kilo of cotton-grain.[13] It went back to 1 franc in 1939. The renewal of the cotton convention in August 1939 fixed a scale of payment per kilogram of cotton-grain for the producer, linked to the price of cotton fibre on the Le Harve market, but in such a manner that in case of price increases, the profits of the companies rose by twice as much as those of the producers. The purchase price given to the producer was fixed at 1 franc if a ton of cotton was sold at 7,000 to 8,500 francs, and it had to be raised by 0.05 franc for every 500 francs a ton at Le Harve. Thus the production of one ton of fibre, sold for an extra 500 francs, which had called for 3 tons of cotton grain bought for a further 150 francs, kept the companies' profit at 350 francs.

> The colonial administration made a magnificent gift to the cotton companies who could thus gain important profits; for the European war favoured rises in raw material costs.[14]

In spite of the ridiculously low level of prices paid to the producers, production continued to rise, and compulsion by the administration did not lessen: in French West Africa, on the contrary, where cotton was merely an accessory resource, the authorities abandoned it during the crisis. Production was 242 tons in 1928, 810 tons in 1929, more than 2,000 tons in 1932, 5,000 tons in 1933, 9,800 tons in 1937, and nearly 9,000 tons in 1938 and 1939, two-thirds supplied by Ubangi-Shari and one third by Chad. In the whole of French West Africa, French Equatorial Africa and mandated territories, cotton production exports rose from 300 tons in 1913 to 7,400 tons in 1929, and 16,500 tons in 1938, of which Ubangi supplied the major portion. But that was still very little.

Plantation crops (cocoa, bananas, coffee) constituted merely a sample before 1914. While the Gold Coast had already risen to the rank of major world producer in cacao beans, and results had been obtained in the neighbouring coastal sectors of German Kamerun, French tropical Africa remained insignificant in this field.[15] In fact, among the territories suited to cocoa production, Guinea was taken up with 'rubber fever' and neglected everything else; while the Ivory Coast and Equatorial Africa had only just been effectively occupied. Cocoa was introduced to the Ivory Coast by the Angoulvant colonial government in 1908, using the strong-arm method so dear to this administrator.[16] Compulsory cultivation of cacao beans became widespread mainly after 1913, when the rubber crisis had raised an acute problem of substituting other exports. The example of the Gold Coast, where 'indigenous' cultivation was a success, was tempting; but in the absence of any economic incentive, authoritarian methods brought only relative efficiency. Made recalcitrant by the methods used, the people showed anything but enthusiasm; in certain regions they went out at night to water the cacao plants with warm water to ensure the failure of compulsory planting. Production in 1913 amounted to 44 tons. However, in the regions bordering on Ashanti (the big producing area of Ghana), and specially in Indénié, cultivation flourished. In these areas few settlers were involved; from the beginning it was the concern of the African peasants. In 1939 only 8,000 out of the 180,000 hectares under cacao trees belonged to European settlers. Production rose from 2,500 tons in 1922 to 16,000 in 1929, 25,700 in 1932, 48,000 in 1937 and 55,000 in 1939. In 1936, in the Indénié circle, income rose to 25,000,000 francs for a population of 40,000, nine-tenths of the revenue coming from cocoa. Such figures were exceptional in French tropical Africa. Already certain African planters were resorting to paid labour.[17]

In the Cameroons, cacao-bean cultivation had, following the example of Fernando Po, been in the hands of the big plantations until 1905. But it then spread among the African peasants, notably in the Mungo and Ebolowa regions.[18] After the 1914–18 war, it continued to develop among them and became increasingly important, especially when the 1929 crisis forced numerous European planters to abandon cultivation.[19] In 1935 'indigenous production' attained 21,400 tons, 4,200 from the Mungo region, 4,500 from the Nyong and Sanaga regions, and 8,500 from the region of N'Tem. In 1938 exports rose to 31,000 tons. The production zone ran through the Fang country, near the Gabon frontier, where the Woleu-N'Tem region supplied most of the cocoa exported from French Equatorial Africa (1,000 to 1,500 tons). For the whole of French tropical Africa annual production amounted to 86,000 tons; this was the average of the five years 1935–9,[20] although in 1938 the figure rose to 92,300 tons. But already the swollen shoot (a virus disease) was making serious inroads; the dispersion of cultivation made it difficult to apply protective measures.

Coffee, production of which was insignificant before the First World War, with only 10 tons exported in 1913, began to develop later than cocoa; the usual administrative measures were applied to enforce the spread of cultivation on the Ivory Coast, in Guinea and in Equatorial Africa; also Ubangi, where Governor Lamblin had coffee trees planted from 1922. The results were mediocre because of the care required in coffee cultivation; this applied mainly to *arabica*, the most prized variety but also the most delicate. In Guinea, where Auguste Chevalier had considered the semi-mountainous region of Fouta-Djalon suitable for *arabica*, plantations came into full production just at the time of the crisis, which lowered prices, and they were abandoned. Production (average for the five-year period 1925–9) exported from the whole of French Black Africa did not exceed 277 tons on the eve of the crisis.[21] In the period that followed the crisis (generally from the years 1934–5 on) coffee made a real start. But coffee production was still largely in the hands of the settlers, and the very delicate *arabica* was abandoned for a more rustic but less highly valued variety (mainly *robusta*). On the Ivory Coast, too, export production rose from 1,327 tons in 1932 to 10,079 tons in 1937, 17,800 tons in 1939 and 28,360 tons in 1941. In Equatorial Africa (Ubangi, Kouilou, Woleu-N'Tem, etc.) production reached 6,000 tons, but the coffee was greatly inferior to that of the Ivory Coast, which itself was considered 'foxy', and '*dur à la tasse*' by the processors of Le Havre.[22] The Cameroons alone, where production reached 4,250 tons in 1938, continued to supply one-sixth of its production in *arabica*, from the Bamiléké and Bamoum regions.[23] In fact, coffee production in the French-dominated tropical countries could not have stood up in quality or price to South American coffees without the measures of imperial protection devised at the same period. 'Indigenous' production developed, however, and on the Ivory Coast in 1939–40 it supplied two-thirds of total production – with 55,000 hectares as against the 19,000 hectares which belonged to 218 European planters. In short, a real start did not take place until the eve of the Second World War, and the soaring development began only after the war.[24]

At that same time, banana production also had a very rapid take-off; it began, paradoxically, in the middle of the crisis. After providing 0·8 per cent of the value of exports from French West Africa in 1930, bananas accounted for 4–5 per cent from 1934 onwards. A decisive element, apart from imperial preferences and other supporting measures such as premiums, fertilisers supplied on credit, etc., was the organisation of transport and warehousing. From 1935 on, a special banana fleet was in existence.[25] Production in Guinea showed an unbroken ascending curve

1920	114 tons	1933	21,758 tons
1925	1,187 tons	1934	26,000 tons
1928	3,993 tons	1935	30,900 tons
1929	6,112 tons	1936	45,000 tons
1930	8,769 tons	1938	52,800 tons

The total of banana exports from French West Africa reached 65,000 tons in 1938. Most were supplied by Guinea, with plantations spread out along the railway line from Conakry to Mamou. The rest came from the Ivory Coast (regions of Abidjan, Agboville-Tiassalé, a little from Agnéby and around Sassandra), which developed at a later stage (1930, 2 tons; 1933, 196 tons; 1934,

1,378 tons; 1935, 4,378 tons; 1939, 14,000 tons). The variety cultivated was called *sinensis*, more highly valued but more fragile than
the *gros-michel* cultivated in the West Indies and the Cameroons.
Because of the conditions of cultivation (the necessity of mulching,
manuring and either irrigation or sprinkling, and the risks resulting
from the frailty of the fruit) the banana was scarcely cultivated at
all until the war except by European settlers, who from the beginning had sufficient capital, could take advantage of agricultural
credits, and employed 50–100 labourers, without, of course, any
mechanisation. In 1934, 'indigenous production' supplied approximately one-fifteenth of Guinea's total production. The drop in
production during the war was made up only slowly, and after a
very rapid start production came to rest at a steady level or rose
only slightly. The production figures for 1938 were not surpassed in
Guinea until 1951 (1948 in the Ivory Coast) and at that time
Africans made a notable contribution. Production in the Cameroons
followed more or less the same pattern (28,000 tons in 1938).

With the oil palm we return, at least for the major part of production, to the category of products that have to be gathered. Oil palm
products continued to constitute the major portion of Dahomey
exports. But the palm groves were old and the poor living conditions – in over-populated Lower Dahomey – made any replanting
out of the question; the practice of producing intercalated crops
(maize and cassava) contributed to the lowering of yields.[26] On the
Ivory Coast and in Guinea the palm groves were under-productive,
and the produce went for export only in minor quantities. The dispersion of production was an obstacle to the use of modern equipment for oil extraction: presses and crushers (not mechanical ones)
were imported and applied in the Sudan along with the plough or
the seeder and in the same manner. Most of them rusted in the
depots of the indigenous provident societies or were put to use only
during official visits. Only a few canton chiefs found them profitable.
However, the essential cause of stagnation was the unfavourable
level of world prices, which constantly decreased as compared to
those, for example, of cocoa or coffee. Making up 20 per cent of
exports from French West Africa in 1925 as in 1913, oil palm products furnished no more than 13 per cent in 1930, and had dropped
to 5·6 per cent in 1934. The five-year average of exports of palm
kernels did not vary between 1921–5 and 1950–4 (119,000 tons).
Dahomey supplied 50,000 to 60,000 tons, Equatorial Africa attained
a maximum of 15,000 tons, the Cameroons 20,000 tons, Guinea and
the Ivory Coast approximately 10,000 tons each. As to palm oil, in
the same period exports decreased by about one-third (from 32,000
down to 19,000 tons).

Between 1928 and 1933 the price of palm kernels dropped by four-fifths in Marseilles, as compared to a fall of three-quarters in the price of cocoa and two-thirds for groundnuts; the price of palm oil decreased by more than three-quarters. From September 1937 to July 1938, during the minor cyclical crisis preceding the war, the price of palm kernels dropped by 27 per cent, that of palm oil by 67 per cent. In 1938, when the price of groundnuts had settled again close to its pre-crisis level, and cocoa stabilised at approximately 50 per cent, the rate of palm kernels remained at a half of its level in 1928.

Being far more sensitive to economic cycles, timber exports made a spectacular rise immediately after the First World War, more than doubling over the years 1913–29. There had already been an export trade in Gabon before 1914, but the use of *okoumé* as material for cigar-boxes was no more than a limited outlet. It was not until after the war that its suitability for veneers and plywood was discovered. The methods of work remained the most economical one, in other words forced labour; the labourers were compelled to work without mechanical aids, even in transporting logs to the rivers. The narrow-gauge railway did not come into general use for this purpose until 1930.

Speculation lent a peculiar recklessness to the production rhythm. After producing 150,000 tons in 1913, Gabon, where sales were depressed during and after the war since Germany was one of its principal customers, did not reach that level again until 1924 (198,000 tons as against 104,900 tons in 1923). The years 1924–7 witnessed a 'rush', which caused production to rise from 219,727 to 335,454 tons. The peak was reached in 1928 with 469,512 tons. This figure exceeded demand by 60,000, and in 1929 production was back at 310,000 tons. In spite of measures taken by the administration to check production, it rose again to 381,000 tons in 1930. This boom affected the Ivory Coast and the Cameroons rather less. The average five-year level of timber production exported in the years 1925–9, in the whole of tropical Africa under French domination, attained 483,000 tons a year. In Gabon timber represented almost four-fifths of all exports. In French West Africa timber had represented no more than 4·3 per cent of the value of exports in 1913, but it made 6·3 per cent in 1930. After 1930, however, this rate dropped by half. Production in Gabon reached 224,227 tons in 1931. It rose again to 434,800 tons in 1937 but never reached the 1928 record. This level was not surpassed before the 1950s when the average over the years 1950–4 was 500,000 tons for all the countries under consideration.

Rubber lost the importance it had held in statistics before 1911, but continued to play a role in many regions for lack of other exportable goods. In French Equatorial Africa forced extraction for the profit of the chartered companies continued, and exports, taking advantage of the favourable rate, rose from 1,000 tons in 1924 to 1,900 in 1926. In French West Africa, and particularly in Guinea, where no other resources took the place of rubber, the same progress can be observed (1,282 tons in 1924 and 1,913 in 1926). But the results attained before the war were never reached again. After 1929 production dropped again in French West and Equatorial Africa to below 1,000 tons, and the crisis caused it to drop to a sample rate. In 1937, however, production rose to 1,106 tons in French Equatorial Africa.

Ivory, in 1925, held fourth place in value after timber, palm kernels and rubber among exports from French West Africa, at 9,600,000 francs.

(b) COMPULSORY CROPS

The extremely low level of productivity, corresponding to the inadequate technical means employed and the very low production prices imposed by the trading companies and sanctioned in the administrative 'market prices', presented obstacles to the development of economic production incentives. Home consumption within the patriarchal family and a few marginal exchanges on the local market provided the population with their miserable subsistence. The attraction of imported merchandise, often of doubtful utility, was not sufficient to make the peasant plant new crops for the market; furthermore, these new crops generally could not develop without a limitation or cutting back in food crops, which were themselves barely sufficient to assure the survival of populations periodically suffering from famine. For lack of economic incentive, the poll-tax was an excellent means of exerting pressure. To procure sufficient money for its payment (by all adults, male and female), the head of a patriarchal family was forced to devote part of the family fields to market produce, which generally meant export products.

On the Ivory Coast and elsewhere the disarmament of the population led to a reduction in hunting and to their 'direction' into agriculture. However, as a general rule, these indirect means were not sufficient, and the traditional means of compulsory crop cultivation and taxed quotas continued to be used. The system of rubber quotas used before 1914, which became widespread as part of the 'war effort', was susceptible to several variations. The simplest was 'taxing' the circle, or district, which was thus obliged to furnish a specified quantity of products based on assumed production capacity and mainly through the demands of the trading companies involved. It was understood that an administrator would be noticed and judged on the basis of the 'returns' in trading products and taxes from his circle (the two were interlinked). Once the programme was fixed, the circle commander circulated instructions to the canton chiefs – who were taxed in their turn and held responsible, under threat of prison or cancellation of their appointments, for the execution of the production targets. After the harvest, the produce was taken to the markets – often carried on men's heads over dozens if not hundreds of kilometres, and there weighed in a more or less honest manner and paid for by the traders at prices fixed by the administration – generally several times lower than the free market prices.[27] Recalcitrants – those who did not want or could not provide the quantity and quality demanded – were given the necessary 'lesson' in the form of a fine, prison or strokes of the *manigolo*.[28]

As a precaution the crops themselves were measured and controlled. In the Sudan, the practices of the pre-colonial feudal states were simply brought back into being. In the absence of a money economy, the main portion of the fiscal resources came from contributions in kind furnished by the villages; in each agricultural area, a communal field was set aside of which the produce – the fruit of common labour – was destined to keep the chief and his men. Henceforth, over and above the 'traditional' fields of the chief, maintained or established by the administration, the peasants had to cultivate the 'commander's fields' – marked out by the police and periodically checked by them at different stages of cultivation and harvesting. This forced labour was added to the tax in kind instituted by the colonial administration. This system was considered convenient and came into general use; it was introduced even in regions where there was no traditional precedent. The same applied to compulsory cultivation of maize and to cacao-palm plantations introduced by Governor Angoulvant on the Lower Ivory Coast on the eve of the First World War. Angoulvant at the time justified this quite openly:

> As long as the representatives of the trading firms and the European colonial enterprises have to rely on their personal authority to make the inhabitants do work that is remunerative in itself and to their firms, they will fail almost completely, and at great cost.[29]

The same applied to cotton cultivation introduced by Eboué in Ubangi, where no state had existed in pre-colonial times and the chiefs held no feudal political powers. Family solidarity was widespread; effective as this was, it made only the barest impact in the sphere of production where individualism was strongly rooted. The methods of constraint used for the rubber harvest were simply taken over and adapted to Sudanese conditions. Governor Lamblin inaugurated the system immediately after the war – collective cultivation of cassava plantations instead of 'herbal rubber' was instituted under the control of the militia, and rapidly adopted by the administrative chiefs. Then there were a series of compulsory crops:[30] castor oil, rice for the Congo–Ocean railway builders, oil-bearing plants, coffee and so on – each rapidly abandoned. This continued after 1925–6, when Eboué, stimulated by new economic interests, had cotton grown on the rubber plantations, against the wishes of Lamblin and of the chartered companies interested in rubber, like the Compagnie des Sultanats.[31]

Cotton-growing in Ubangi deserves a more detailed description. Cotton was introduced, as we have said, in conjunction with certain interest groups in France dealing with imports of textile raw materials, and with companies of which the controlling interests were Belgian and Dutch. An agreement concluded in 1927, and inspired by the system in force in the Belgian Congo, gave these companies a monopoly of purchase on a given territory. They were bent on setting up ginning mills, or rather workshops, and the administration undertook to supply the cotton for these, and guaranteed the companies an outlet for at least 80 per cent of the cotton produced. The agreement concerned, to begin with, the Société cotonnière équatoriale française, set up in 1926 with a capital of 15,000,000 francs[32] reduced to 11,000,000 in 1935, and the Société textile africaine (later the Société française des cotons africains, with Belgian participation) with a capital of 7,500,000 francs. The privilege was extended in 1930 to the Compagnie commerciale Ouahm at Nana with a capital of 5,000,000, an offshoot of the old chartered company of the same name, with Dutch capital, and the Société de la Kotto (later the Société cotonnière du Haut-Oubangui) with a capital of 4,500,000 francs. These conventions were renewed in 1939 and 1949.

The expenses for the 'recruitment' of producers, which in the Belgian Congo fell on the companies concerned, were here entirely borne by the administration. This recruitment involved a large administrative staff: an agricultural engineer, agricultural foremen and crop agents (European or Senegalese), and agricultural advisers nick-named 'cotton boys' (boys-coton). The production of the commander's cotton' was in the hands of the agricultural foremen, who kept a check on the population: exempt from plantation work were licensed dealers, people in full-time jobs, old men, mothers with five or more children, as well as wives of labourers working on European plantations; all other adults between the ages of fifteen and fifty were liable. The land to be cultivated was chosen by the 'cotton boys' with the assistance of the canton or village chief. The number of taxable persons determined how many plots were to be cleared of undergrowth, the millet patches of the peasants being sometimes taken into account, sometimes not. The area of these plots corresponded to the number of 'cords' allocated to the village; the length of a 'cord' (one dimension of a plot to be cultivated by each taxable person) was fixed beforehand by the administration, generally at some 70 metres. In each village, a special field was set aside to be cultivated by forced labour for the benefit of the chief. Naturally, in the course of their work, the 'cotton boys' and other agents of state power had to be royally entertained by the people, and given everything that they considered necessary for the comfort of their stay; there were armed police to bring any recalcitrants to their senses.

Seeds were furnished to the communities through the agency of the 'cotton boys'. Later, it was also thought advisable to supply tools – in practice this meant a few hoes. The same 'cotton boys' supervised the tilling and the harvest. The work was hard and exhausting: clearing the undergrowth (cotton had to come first in crop rotation on new or fallow ground, which prevented the peasant from planting other crops), sowing, thinning out, weeding – supervised carefully by the 'cotton boys' – then three pickings from November to March. With the onset of the rainy season, the plants had to be pulled out and burnt, an operation also carefully supervised to avoid the spread of disease and parasites.[33] The cotton was then carried on men's heads to the ginning centres, in baskets holding from 30 to 40 kilos. There supplies were checked in order to catch any defaulter, or anyone who had not produced a sufficient quantity. The company agents then proceeded to weigh the supply, generally with slightly 'reinforced' weights, and the producer was paid. Since we have no description of the 'payment' for cotton, we can cite the case of rubber, which continued to be supplied in the regions around the Middle Congo under identical conditions.

At a signal from the 'farmer' [the trading company agent] the militiaman grabs hold of a poor devil who seems to have brought an insufficient quantity of latex. The balls of rubber are thrown on the ground while their owner is given some rough handling. After which, with a rope round his neck, he is sent to swell the ranks of the column of 'bad characters' who will spend that night in prison ready to be transferred to the Congo–Ocean railway line as 'volunteers'.

It goes without saying that no register of committals to gaol bears any record of these arrests. The work proceeds quickly. The liana threads are hooked up in 'the Roman way': one glance and payment is made with a reduction of one-third.

'Not satisfied?' Whack – a big slap in the face for the seller. 'Into the cage', says the militiaman who deals out brutal slaps. In the evening there remains a pile of 'bad' rubber on the ground which has not been paid for. By the morning it has disappeared . . . [34]

As with rubber, payment for the newly introduced cotton was a communal one of tax vouchers; this followed an old-established tradition. It will be clear that the producer, rewarded thus for some six months of labour, showed as little enthusiasm for growing cotton as rubber. A kilo of cotton grain was paid for at the rate of 1 franc in 1925–6, and 1.25 francs in 1927. At the same time a kilo of cotton fibre was sold at Le Havre for 12 francs. Reckoning 10 kilos of cotton grain for 3 kilos of cotton fibre, the cotton companies sold at 36 francs what they had bought for 12 francs. These companies were for ever bewailing their lot and demanding, for reasons of 'national interest', that production prices be lowered; this was particularly ironic as most of the companies were foreign-owned. Prices were lowered during the crisis; the price per kilo dropped to 0.60 francs in 1933–4,[35] and had not risen beyond one considerably devalued franc by 1939. However, the profits of the cotton companies remained untouched: a complicated but highly advantageous system of price 'subsidy' assured them a fixed commission, with all costs paid. The expenses of ginning and transport were largely made good through the transport companies, which were controlled by the same group, receiving highly remunerative 'contracts'. The companies, as we have said, undertook to set up ginning mills, but this promise was implemented slowly and because of a lack of mills at first, forced labour was used for the 'threshing' of cotton.[36] Pressing was carried out with hand presses. One administrator wrote soon after the end of the Second World War:

Real galley work was demanded of the seven labourers in the team. They began by rhythmically pressing the cotton in the container, each with one foot; when the dance was finished the container was taken to the press and the same labourers turned the screw. With sheet-metal roofs above their heads, the men were dripping wet, moving without respite from the container to the screw and back.[37]

Nearly all operations remained manual until 1949. Conventions renewed at that time insisted upon modernisation and the establish-

ment of additional purchasing centres to curtail forced labour and
porterage. But the loading and unloading of lorries, the covering
and tying of bales with canvas, and warehousing remained wholly
manual.

In theory, the employees were free and were paid for their work.
But 'very often when the people resisted signing on, they were made
to work by the canton chief who was given a material interest in the
operations by the company'.[38] The system was in general use in
Ubangi where, towards the end of the 1950s there were 330,000
'planters' out of 473,000 men and women fit for service, and it was
applied to the neighbouring country of Chad and, later, to the
Northern Cameroons.

Its establishment (which coincided with 'recruitment' for the
Congo–Ocean railway) was not unconnected with the outbreak of
the big Baya rebellion in 1928–9; and with a few variations in
products cultivated and methods of execution, the same system can
be found almost everywhere.

Albert Londres described the 'cotton market' of the Bouaké on
the Ivory Coast. The entire village arrived in the district carrying
their loads on their heads, and watched over by a guard armed
with a *manigolo*; anyone who brought cotton that was considered
poor or of insufficient quantity was sent to prison.[39] Purchase was
effected at notoriously lower prices than those current on the free
market. A mill set up by M. Gonfreville obtained its materials in
this way. Before 1914 Gonfreville had been deputy officer for native
affairs at Dabakala, and had quitted the administration to go into
business; after his death his widow continued his business which
was turned into a limited company and taken over by Protestant
high finance (Société du Haut-Ogooué).

In Upper Volta, Delavignette attributed the departure of 100,000
Mossi to the Gold Coast to compulsory cotton cultivation.[40] In his
Les Paysans noirs he complacently describes, in the manner of an
epic poem, the introduction of groundnut cultivation in the Bobo
country of Upper Volta.[41] A Unilever subsidiary set up groundnut
oil works, and it was up to the administrator to provide the 6,000
tons of groundnuts necessary for its economic functioning.

> Already the railway 'machine' of the Ivory Coast, in particular
> the extension of the line beyond Tafiré, used up bearers. And now
> see how a groundnut 'machine' came to gnaw away at the very
> heart of the country. . . . And the country was tired, stupified by
> forced labour on the routes and compulsory crop cultivation.[42]

The 'commander' used trials, promises of wealth from groundnuts
and every kind of scheming to hasten the ruin of the feudal *dioula* in

order to win over the peasants subjected to their rule. When failure occurred, the strong arm came into play; this the commander wisely refrained from mentioning in his reports.

In the groundnut zone of Senegal, which had long since been drawn into the money economy, economic incentives – or rather, necessity – played a major role. The peasant was obliged to use imported products – fabrics, hardware and agricultural tools – which the traditional craftsmen, ruined by competition, could not provide. He had become accustomed to the consumption of imported rice, which did not need to be crushed like millet, and so his own food crop was insufficient. Groundnut cultivation for trade became a habit. But when the rate slumped and the year's produce barely sufficed to pay taxes and the credits given by the traders, the peasant cultivator became discouraged.

The administration, spurred on by the chamber of commerce – which claimed that the colony was ruined – used various means to arouse the producers' zeal. Apart from the canton chiefs, the *grands marabouts*, particularly Mourides, were mobilised to encourage the setting of production targets. They benefited from administrative favours given in proportion to their efforts, and became personally interested in the progress of production, since their faithful, their *talibés*, would reach heaven with all the more certainty when they had ceded their entire gains to the interceding *marabout*. This can be illustrated from the administrative reports addressed to the *marabouts* in a letter to the circle commanders from Wiltord, the governor of Senegal, at the beginning of the agricultural season of 1947–8:

> The Economic Conference at Saint-Louis defined the aims of the 1947–8 agricultural campaign in these terms: develop cultivation and intensify the production of groundnuts to the maximum. . . .
>
> I am fully aware how important, in this respect, your authority, your personal influence, your connections can be to make our action effective. In consequence, I should be obliged if you would lead an active campaign at the start of this new agricultural season and appeal *directly* to the cultivators, telling them how it is in their interest and that of the country in general for them to *produce*; encouraging them to produce *more*[43]; also pointing out to your circle commander the most deserving and serious cultivators who will thus receive the greatest advantages, notably foodstuffs on credit; and informing him likewise about those with bad debts, etc. . . .
>
> Groundnuts are a source of wealth for the country. . . . They will certainly soon bring you prosperity and abundance, and you

know as well as I do that the earth has never deceived anyone.[44] I therefore count upon your close support. . . .

You will be working for the general good, and I leave it to your personal initiative to elaborate, in agreement with your circle commander, the method of propaganda which you think suitable to reinforce the means already applied. Moreover, among your *talibé* there are numerous persons who have left the land, lured by the urban centres. Among them are many who do not have a permanent occupation. This, you will realise, is a bad example and a very grave problem, and you will know how desirable it is to bring them substantial gains.[45] I know that you will take action on this, and that in many cases your voice will be heard and your advice followed.

(*c*) THE INDIGENOUS PROVIDENT SOCIETIES

To complement its functions in the sphere of production, the colonial administration had by degrees to forge an institutional tool: this consisted of the indigenous provident societies.[46] One of their principal official aims was to provide against the 'lack of foresight' of the indigenous population who, with no care for the future, consumed all their harvest without even saving the seeds necessary for sowing the following year. This assumed lack of foresight only reflected the chronic dearth caused in times of hardship by colonial exploitation. Forced to devote part of his work to cultivation of other than food crops, deprived of part of his family labour by requisitioning and conscription, crushed under taxes and various supplementary dues, authorised or otherwise, which were collected by the chiefs, the peasants could not *make ends meet*. The latter expression is highly significant here. Peasants who lack foresight do not exist. The patriarchs of the pre-colonial era were not content simply to keep the essential seeds for the next harvest: they kept vital reserves in the family granaries to ward off a possible bad year – a harvest spoilt by drought or locusts. These reserves amounted, in the Mossi country, to two years' harvests. Colonial exploitation made the maintenance of these reserves impossible, and in case of deficit the peasant was reduced to consuming even the reserves needed for the coming sowing. Delavignette wrote:

What is serious at present is that the family is often reduced to living from year to year. There are few reserves, nor does one find the three years' supply of millet which the former heads of families stored away in time of plenty.[47]

From the beginning of the century, without making it into a general and systematic institution, the administration decided on the creation of 'reserve granaries', collective granaries where, under threat of punishment, each peasant had to deposit a part of his harvest. He was not allowed to touch it until the following year. In certain regions, particularly Niger, this obligation survived until the Second World War. Elsewhere various other schemes were attempted. In Guinea, for example, a circular issued by Governor Roume, dated 28 May, 1907, ordered the establishment of reserve granaries as an experiment. Experimental centres existed at Labé, Kouroussa and Mellacorée – circles chosen in each of the three natural regions of Guinea. To judge from official reports, the 1908 experiment was a complete success, and in 1909 it was decided to extend it to the whole colony.[48] But this general application was never put into practice. The idea met with strong resistance from the peasants. Left to an uninterested administration – preoccupied merely with preventing the peasant from going near the granaries – the 'reserves' were often destroyed by rats or insects. The district officers and agents of the administration regarded this as an additional means of fleecing the peasant and, through advance deductions, the peasant rarely recovered even the approximate amount of his deposit.

Likewise, at the instigation of commerce, still alarmed at the prospect of insufficient harvests, the administration of Senegal provided facilities after 1905 for loans of groundnut seeds to cultivators through the trading firms to which administrative guarantees were given – a profitable operation because these firms demanded reimbursement in kind at harvest time – i.e. after three to four months – with 100 per cent interest. This encouragement to usury met with protests. The idea had arisen from the Algerian precedent which once again provided French colonisation in tropical Africa with an institutional model. It meant uniting two activities within the one set-up of the indigenous provident societies. These became administrative bodies to provide the peasants with seeds, only to recover them with interest at harvest time. A first experiment was carried out in 1865. It became widespread in 1871, and the system assumed institutional form in Algeria through the law of 14 April, 1894, which stipulated peasant participation and compulsory quotas. It was later extended to Tunisia.

The circle commander of Sine-Saloum did a trial test in 1907. Private traders who loaned seeds demanded interest in kind at a rate of 200 to 300 per cent; the provident society supplied seeds at 5 per cent interest, payable in full in equivalent weight at harvest time. It proved a success; but in 1908 a compulsory quota of 5 francs per cultivator was added to the 5 per cent (on the Algerian precedent) and in 1909 the rate of interest was raised to 25 per cent, certainly less than that demanded by private creditors but, none-theless, clearly extortionate. Following on the first two societies, set up in the groundnut regions of Senegal (the circles of Sine-Saloum and Baol), a decree of 29 June, 1910, laid down the institu-tion of indigenous provident societies in French West Africa, bodies which 'have proved their worth in Algeria and Tunisia.'[49] In 1912 there were ten in Senegal spread over nearly all the circles and four in Guinea. The institution, conceived essentially for groundnut pro-ducing regions[50], was favourably received by commerce. Its 'provi-dence' worked to the benefit of trade, rather than that of the peasant. It diverted the latter from the temptation of neglecting export crops in favour of traditional foodcrops; moreover, it per-mitted profitable speculations – in the sale by the indigenous provi-dent societies of the grain recovered and its purchase of (supposedly) selected seeds. The organisation of the societies, at first copied from Algerian legislation, was modified on several occasions (decrees of 8 January, 1915, and 4 July, 1919, modified in 1923 and 1930). The 'advantages' of the societies were so little apparent by the outbreak of the war in 1914 that a decree passed in 1915 imposed compulsory membership (and hence quotas) for all indigenous cultivators. Soon they proved a pretext for supplementary taxes without any appreciable profit to the peasant; and that remained their essential function. In 1920 an observer wrote:

> Lacking clearly determined aims on which to base their activities, these societies, even the richest ones, have achieved nothing at all. The cultivators have concluded that they were simply a pretext for levying supplementary taxation.[51]

On the other hand, the name of these 'societies' evoked the idea of a mutualist or co-operative institution – which would have been incompatible with the bureaucratic and autocratic régime typical of colonial administration. The 'membership' aspect was never other than formal; in theory there was a 'general assembly' of mem-bers (consisting of one delegate from each village or group of villages) who elected an 'administrative council' for a three-year period. This council, according to an order issued on 23 January, 1925, was elected 'according to local customs' (sic) which meant according to the whim of the circle commander, who could, more-over, dismiss council members at will. The 1910 text (imitating Algeria) laid down that the chairman was to be chosen by the governor, from a short list of three candidates submitted by the administrative council on the advice of the circle commander. The chairman was in practice nominated by the circle commander, and was all-powerful. He represented the society in every case and

I

had the right of taking all decisions in its name. During the war (1915) the chairmanship was simply entrusted to the circle commander himself. There was a return to the former system in 1919, but very soon it proved inconvenient if not impracticable. It was, in practice, the circle commander who took decisions; but he needed the signature of the supposed chairman, a dignitary who was often illiterate and who was not always at hand. In 1923 the chairmanship was finally entrusted formally to the circle commander, whose management of the indigenous provident societies (one to each circle or subdivision) became henceforth one of his additional attributes. From that date there could be no mistake on that score: 'The society is, in the most absolute meaning of the word, the administrator's tool.'[52] He was aided by a treasurer, who was at first a special agent (the commissioner for native affairs in charge of circle finance), and a secretary (also a circle official fulfilling these functions apart from his normal duties). The 1930 decree fused these two functions into one, creating a 'secretary-treasurer', a full-time official or European agent, nominated by the governor on the recommendation of the circle commander.

Compelled to file an annual report with the governor, which was then submitted for approval to the inspectors of administrative affairs and colonial inspectors on tour from France, the indigenous provident society appeared from the beginning to be part of the administrative machinery. The economic crisis of 1930–3 led to a growth of state intervention and an extension of the rights of indigenous provident societies, and spread the institution to the whole of tropical Africa under French domination.

This new development of the indigenous provident societies was not determined by the needs or convenience of the peasants but by manoeuvres of private commerce and the convenience of the administration. The latter had got into the habit of using the resources of the societies and often their large staffs (even when this was not essential) to lessen the shortages of normal resources and administrative personnel in the circles. It was tempting to continue in this way since quotas and sale of seeds provided appreciable regular resources. Trade, which found a profitable outlet in sales to the indigenous provident societies, encouraged them along the same road. Each year, there was a campaign by the chamber of commerce 'requesting the purchase of seeds from the traders to avoid the ruin and early disappearance of the colony'.[53]

The slump in prices in 1931 and 1932 reduced the Senegalese peasant to penury; the income from groundnuts did not enable him to buy the quantities of rice he needed for home consumption, and he was reduced to living on his seeds. To 'save the colony' the big commercial firms sold to the provident societies at a high price (almost three times the purchase price) part of the groundnuts which they had bought from the peasants at the nadir of the crisis. These purchases were covered by a loan of many millions on which the provident societies were still paying interest after the Second World War.[54] The commercial companies' zeal to be saviours is thus easily comprehensible. As far as the reserves were concerned, the situation was not as catastrophic as the companies, so devoted to the public interest, claimed. The commander of the Baol circle, quoted above, wrote:

> Contrary to statements by the chambers of commerce, the local people have seeds and are not parting with them as easily as is alleged. . . . In 1931 the reserves covered 70 per cent of needs. In 1932, when the harvest was bad, indigenous reserves still represented 50 per cent of what was really needed.
>
> It should also be said that certain cultivators. . . have formed the habit of relying on the aid of the indigenous provident societies, and they are quickly becoming *improvident* through the existence of the provident societies.[55]

There is even a note from the administrator of Sine-Saloum saying that the quantity of groundnuts taken to the indigenous provident societies' warehouse (the existence of which was called into question by the chambers of commerce) is higher than any noted in the records of the society. The excess is explained by repayments with excessive interest rates demanded by the canton chiefs with a view to feathering their own nests.[56] Consulted on the possibilities of buying from the commercial market, for the whole colony, 25,000 tons of seeds instead of the 20,000 tons forecast, the circle commanders disapproved. They noted a trend suggesting a return to family granaries; the collective granaries were not highly thought of owing to the fear of mixing grain of varying qualities and especially of being cheated of part of the deposit. The commander of the Baol circle proposed individual granaries joined in a special common enclosure; the commander of Sine-Saloum warned against the danger of excessive sowing of groundnuts at the cost of food crops. After an inquiry, an inspector of administrative affairs concluded in a report to the governor of Senegal (10 January, 1933) that a movement was afoot designed to return to family seed stocks and reduce the role of the indigenous provident societies. This trend, though socially beneficial, endangered the financial situation of the societies; it was agreed to put a stop to it. A circular issued by the governor to the circle commanders laid down 'that reserve groundnut granaries should be formed according to the need of getting back interest on seed borrowed from the indigenous provident societies to cover the loans made by the latter'.[57]

But, like the sorcerer's apprentice, commerce had set in motion a process which was to turn against it. In 1933 the drop in the price of groundnuts (from 81 francs per hundredweight in 1930 to 50 francs in 1933 raised doubts about the whole future of a crop gradually being abandoned by the peasants, who were turning away from it to a subsistence economy. The budgetary resources of the federation were reduced to half of what had been forecast. To keep up rates and make up for the shortage of trade, which was waiting for prices to fall still further, governor-general Brévié decided to extend the work of the indigenous provident societies to the sale of members' produce and to authorise the establishment by the colony of a common fund endowed as a legal body, which would allow the resources of the richest indigenous provident societies to be used for advances to less favourably placed societies. A law, passed on 6 August, 1933, and a decree of 9 November, 1933, legalised these new rights, and at the same time gave the aims of the indigenous societies such a broad definition that everything was left to the discretion of the circle commanders and was thus open to abuse of every kind. Article 2 of the decree laid down that the societies aimed at 'taking measures that contribute to the development of agriculture, livestock breeding, fishing and harvesting, as well as the improvement of conditions under which the harvest is carried out, the preparation, circulation, conservation and sale of produce; they shall, notably, be able to organise the sale of their members' produce.' They could sell, buy or hire out agricultural material or agricultural tools and undertake work of collective importance.

The indigenous provident societies were almost confined to Senegal before 1930, but soon became more widespread throughout French West Africa. In 1934, Senegal had fifteen (one to each circle), and the whole of French West Africa 102. In Guinea, where they disappeared in 1920, they were revived in 1932 and there were eighteen of them by 1934, one per circle. On the Ivory Coast, where there had been only one, set up in the Lagunes circle in 1926 for the purchase of palm oil presses, they were widely established from 1930–1 on. In Dahomey, the first made its appearance in 1930, and they came more generally into use after 1932; in the Sudan, where only one existed in 1920, their number increased after 1930; in Niger, they came into existence only after 1933. Indigenous provident societies were introduced and organised in other parts of French Africa by various decrees: Togo (decrees of 1934 and 1937), Cameroons (1937 and 1939) and French Equatorial Africa (decree of 1940). Big business and its representatives (the chambers of com-

merce and the Colonial Union) raised vehement protests against
this interference and 'disloyal competition' in the commercial sector
by para-administrative bodies. The administration replied that

> . . . the intervention of the provident societies will fortunately
> bring to an end the constant scandal of periodic speculation,
> which leads to a rise in the cost of grain as soon as it ceases to
> belong to those who produce it.[58]

But their indignation was more verbal than active. In his report
in 1939 to the government-general, the director-general of economic
services in French West Africa observed:

> The attitude of commerce to the deposit operations has not
> changed. The big export firms, though in principle opposed to
> this activity, do not fail to appreciate the advantages of the
> important shares for which the friendly societies periodically
> invite tenders and the guarantees which they are offered by
> transactions with such bodies. On the other hand, the small
> traders see the societies as serious competitors whose price policy
> is to maintain the rate of transactions at the maximum level.[59]

The quantity of groundnuts put on the market by the societies
still remained modest. The Sine-Saloum circle, which furnished
almost half of the Senegalese harvest, provided 2 to 16 per cent of
the quantity sold, the maximum being reached in the 1940–1 harvest. However, these activities led to the development of fixed
installations such as sheds and drying patches, and to the setting-up
of shelling works at Lyndiane (1937), financed out of a joint fund
of the provident societies.

Outside the groundnut region – that is more or less to say outside
Senegal – the work of the provident societies is more difficult to
describe. Thanks to compulsory quotas, their financial situation
improved: in 1934 the surplus from societies in French West Africa
amounted to over 19,500,000 francs,[60] with an appreciable rise
during the time of crisis; but 'a good financial situation is not always
a sign of great activity'[61]; sometimes it is even the reverse.

On the Ivory Coast and in Dahomey, the societies' funds were
largely devoted to the purchase of presses and crushers for oil palm
products. But the dispersion of production and fear of deductions by
agents of the administration meant that these machines were little
used – except during official visits. On the Ivory Coast in 1935
equipment valued at 1,700,000 francs remained in the warehouses.
In the Sudan, where mainly ploughs had been purchased, tools to
the value of 2,000,000 remained in the stores.[62] At Faranah, Guinea,

it was shown that barely one-third of the ploughs available were used.[63]

In cases where there was no activity connected with agriculture, the administrator – under the pretext of keeping the provident societies running or of coping with public needs – turned the societies' funds into a reserve to be at his own disposal. Cars were thus purchased, in theory the property of the provident society but in practice used for administrative tours by various branches of the administration, or for the transport of visiting Europeans, etc.

It has become known that the cars of the indigenous provident societies are used frequently on credit, for the benefit of the administration. There would be no use in issuing a prohibition, for it will be understood that no district officer would consent to wasting many days making a tour on foot, or would fail to make use of a vehicle when one is at hand.

Nevertheless, the general spread of this custom has placed a heavy cost burden on the societies, as their vehicles soon get worn out. Not only does this involve heavy expenditure on repairs, but the vehicles are not on hand when required for the collection and transport of produce.[64]

The funds were also used to build accommodation for European officials, and dispensaries; even wells were dug and roads constructed, for which the normal budget did not make provision.

The account books showed baths and lavatories, etc., clearly bought with no other purpose than the convenience of the administration. Results were achieved in the sector of public assistance and hygiene, which the hitherto existing services were unable to provide. These establishments were everywhere considered, especially by the beneficiaries, simply as additions to the health services.

With the war the role of the provident societies in providing agricultural loans increased, and they came to centralise the distribution of consumer products – requisitioning and advance supply of foodstuffs, distribution of clothing ration cards, etc. Although under a different name, the indigenous provident societies continued to exist until the very end of the colonial system. However, after the end of the Second World War, they were morally outlawed; their continuation only perpetuated and aggravated the vices that Henry Cosnier had denounced in 1920. More than ever they remained a cog in the administrative wheel. The secretary-general of this group of territories wrote in 1950:

The district officers of French Equatorial Africa have to be convinced that the work of the indigenous provident societies is *one of their principal tasks* [italicised in the text] and that they should devote to it the same care and attention, and the same devotion as to all other tasks of administration: local politics, special agencies, levying of taxes, etc. District officers should not hesitate to comment on the running of the provident societies when making reports on the district chiefs. For my part, I shall pay the greatest attention to this.[65]

The same circular went on to say:

Certain [societies] have clearly limited themselves to the imposition of quotas. . . . One can appreciate the peasants' belief that they are being landed with a supplementary tax. Equally, all activities not properly belonging to the indigenous provident societies should be denounced. It is true that they have at times carried out their function free of charge, if not at a loss, for the profit of the Europeans in the post – on kitchen gardens, small-scale livestock breeding, milk and butter production, etc. – or of the local budget: providing the use of lorries, buildings, tools (carpentry, garages, brickworks, forges, etc.). Such practices are to be prohibited.

And the author added to these benefits *a fortiori* the construction of schools, dispensaries, maternity hospitals and roads.[66]

In 1947 a circular issued by the minister Moutet criticised the indigenous provident societies and recommended their transformation into true co-operative societies, without, however, abolishing them or abandoning them to private forms of co-operation. This was apparently done to satisfy public opinion without opening the way to any real change: the basic vice of these societies was the fact that they were supervised by the administration.

The provident societies were conceived as para-administrative bodies. The administrators often confused the budget of the provident societies with that of their administrative unit and sought to supplement the shortfall of one out of the surplus of the other, robbing Peter to pay Paul.

In the agricultural sector, personnel and labour recruited with the consent of the administration were often used for administrative jobs. Equipment, particularly lorries and cars, did not serve the provident societies exclusively. The societies' agricultural tools were usually the least important part of their equipment and the worst used.

. . . From 1940 to 1945 in particular, [the societies] were no more than auxiliaries to the commander in the intensification of production and the collection of produce. This false step proved their undoing.[67]

But was this particular 'false step' the only one? And had the indigenous provident societies ever had any other real purpose? The colonial administration of the years 1946–58, conscious of how the institution had failed, confessed itself incapable of reforming or replacing it.

(d) MIGRATION AND FORCED LABOUR

We have seen that because of the shortage of means of transport, almost all exportable goods came from zones situated less than 300 km. from the coast. In the interior, where the subsistence economy persisted, the low-quality and barely economic production of compulsory crops hardly sufficed to cover payment of taxes. Since the produce could not be moved by any other means, it had to be carried by forced labour – the 'pipe heads' (*têtes de pipe*), as the forest exploiters of the Ivory Coast called them. This gave rise to streams of migration. Some were spontaneous: young people left to earn tax money or the bride-price of their future wives, sometimes simply to escape raging famine. Others were forced to do so, by 'recruitment' for public works, railways, etc., to which was added recruitment for private enterprise, mining, plantations or timber felling. The spontaneous migrations were of a seasonal character. The oldest and most important one was that of the *navétanes* to Senegal – these were seasonal workers, from the Wolof word *navète*, rainy season.

The centre of groundnut production moved, as we have seen, from Cayor to Baol before 1914, then towards Sine-Saloum, following the railway line. In the newly-developed regions local labour was in short supply. A movement was set afoot to bring labour primarily from regions with exhausted land or those out of the way of commercial trends: the 'Fleuve' region (Fouta-Toro); Oualo, which had become semi-desert, and Cayor.

In 1936 – a boom year, when the adoption of special railway tariffs favoured the influx of labour – over 12,000 out of a total of 76,000 *navétanes* came from those regions,[68] and of these approximately 9,000 from the circle of Sine-Saloum (7,000) and Baol and Thiès. But most of the labour force came from outside Senegal. Most numerous were the Bambara and the Maliné from the Western Sudan and Upper Gambia (some 35,000). They were highly rated as excellent cropgrowers. The second contingent in order of importance was provided by the Fulani of Fouta-Djalon, or rather the overpopulated Labé region (circles of Labé, Pita, Mali): some 20,000 for 1936. They were less sought after, being considered shirkers, little suited to agricultural work, and with a reputation for dishonesty.

The *navétane* was, as a general rule, an annual or seasonal farmer, the month of cultivation coinciding with the rainy season. This seasonal worker brought his labour and a few tools; the *diatigui*, who rented out the land, provided him with accommodation, food, seed and supplementary tools, and rented him a piece of land for the season, which the worker cultivated for his own profit.[69] The seasonal worker worked the fields of the *diatigui* on four 'mornings' per week – i.e. from 6 a.m. to 3 p.m. on Tuesday, Wednesday, Saturday and Sunday. The afternoons and the whole of Monday, Thursday and Fridays were left to him (the day of rest was Monday afternoon for those holding animistic beliefs, Friday afternoon for the Muslims). Such at least was the usual practice in Sine-Saloum. In Casamance, conditions were normally less favourable: the time of work reserved to the employer could be raised to three full days a week, or the seasonal labourer would have to hand over 10 to 20 per cent of the produce of his own field as rent; or he was forced to produce an intercalary crop of millet which went entirely to his employer. The seasonal labourer generally worked on his own. Some examples are cited of 'jobbing' (a contract concluded with one 'overseer' who employed five or six day-labourers on the job); this occurred in the pioneering sectors of the Tambacounda circle.[70] Rent proper (without obligatory labour for the owner) was paid by young workers of Cayor and the 'Fleuve' region.[71] Finally, the seasonal farmers proper were joined for the harvest in October, by supplementary day labourers, generally young men who came in groups, known as *baraguini*.[72] The *navétanes* were generally well fed. Between work and harvest there was nothing to do, and the landlord, whose reserves were also rapidly reaching a point of exhaustion, became less open-handed. Often the *navétane* sought to earn extra as a labourer during this dead season.

It sometimes happened that the seasonal farmer settled in the country he visited, but this was exceptional, and usually occurred amongst young workers from regions where family solidarity was strong and respect was felt for the authority of the head of the family; the latter was generally opposed to the departure of active manpower. Seasonal farmers were hardly conducive to rationalisation in agriculture; they did not look after their fields, from which they had nothing to gain after the harvest. Their sole preoccupation was to derive the maximum from it in one season, without any thought for the future. This 'westward' migration was, as a general rule, spontaneous, though in periods of crisis it was 'encouraged' by

I*

various administrative measures, from free transport to preferential rates for requisitioned labour. The incomes of these seasonal farmers were modest: between 1920 and 1930 they varied from a few hundred to a maximum of 2,000 francs.

> In 1927, the majority of the Sudanese seasonal farmers made no profit, a few of them even had to remain in Senegal for lack of the wherewithal to return to their villages.[73]

The second big stream of migration, which could be called the 'eastward' one, presents quite different and far more complex aspects: the spontaneous migration of people from Niger to Nigeria or Dahomey, and especially of the Mossi, Gourounsi and Dogon, to the Ashanti country of the Gold Coast, which also attracted young men from Northern Dahomey and Northern Togo. Some of them went to settle there for a certain period as traders. Around 1930, more than 12,000 French subjects (including people from Togo) were counted in the Gold Coast colony. The majority of them went on a seasonal basis, to work on the cocoa plantations or in the mines. In 1929 the British administration registered 79,399 Mossi entering the Gold Coast at the Volta crossings, a number certainly far lower than the actual figure. H. Labouret estimated the annual migration to the Gold Coast and Nigeria at about 180,000. Migration to the British colonies represented a means – sometimes important – of escaping compulsory crop cultivation which did not bring in anything, as well as conscription and labour recruitment of all kinds; in short it was a means of preserving liberty. The men were better paid there than on French territory, especially by the Niger Office or the settlers on the Ivory Coast, who were accustomed to using labour more or less without payment. There were periods when this migration swelled considerably, for example shortly before the Second World War. Delavignette estimated that forced cotton cultivation in Upper Volta caused 100,000 Mossi to flee to the Gold Coast.[74]

Alongside this spontaneous migration there existed forced internal migration within the French territories. First there was recruitment for private enterprise on the Ivory Coast – for the forest owners and planters. On the Ivory Coast, in the years of flourishing forest exploitation (1920–30), administrative recruitment for private enterprise was not official but 'tolerated'. Administrators might or might not recruit men as wood cutters. When the forestry concession-holders were important and well-connected people, the administrators never failed to receive instructions requiring them to take measures in aid of the 'economic development' of this work, so beneficial to their district. As to minor concession-holders, things were left to their discretion . . . some used the necessary means to obtain the administrator's consent; others addressed themselves directly to the canton officer, who was highly susceptible to high-flown words or to the gift of a few cases of gin, whisky or aperitif. At Bouaké middlemen took manpower recruited in Upper Volta by lorry and 'supplied the slaves at 200 francs per head to embarrassed entrepreneurs'.[75] To ensure manpower 'stability', the administration made the men 'sign' a contract for one or even two years, which was truly slavery because the settler could request police aid against any who escaped.

Under the pretext of instilling in the workers the idea of 'thrift', they were given no payment but the sums due to them were inscribed in a savings book. That was also a means, not always very efficient, of preventing the workers from escaping; as an absconder a man 'broke the contract' and got nothing, even if he had worked for several months. In any case, his earnings were meagre. With such a system of savings he could buy neither articles for personal use nor merchandise which he might be able to re-sell at a profit in his village. He was obliged to draw his money in full view of the canton chief, village chief, and his family, who did not leave him much of the accumulated savings, after a preliminary sum had been deducted in the form of taxes. Albert Londres wrote ironically:

> Zié earned 77 francs in his month [this example is taken from the forest roads of the Ivory Coast]. The boss paid 88 francs in taxes: 40 for the poll-tax, 48 for buying himself off statute labour. After one month of work in the forest Zié owned 11 francs.[76]

Moreover, in certain circles, the worker had to pay a special 'floating population' tax, and it was a common practice to make him pay the poll-tax twice, one in his own canton, and a second time in the canton where he worked. On the Ivory Coast official wages, not always respected, amounted to 160 francs per month, excluding the deduction of savings but with a daily 'ration' in kind, of which the average monthly value was estimated at 57 francs. On the Gold Coast the wages varied from £2 10s. to £4 10s. (300 to 540 francs) without rations; since a room at Kumasi cost 15s. a month and food in African restaurants sixpence a day, the worker earned more, he was not forced to keep a savings book, nor did he sign a long-term contract of service; the employer engaged him verbally, renewing the term by the week or the month.[77] It will be easily understood that only constraint, open or disguised, could 'direct' labour towards the Lower Ivory Coast (30,000 in 1928, 38,000 in 1929).

The campaigns of Albert Londres, Andre Gidé, the Anti-Imperialist League, and the League for Human Rights and Popular Aid were not entirely without effect. Under the Popular Front government, a circular issued by the governor-general, de Coppet, forbade the administrators of French West Africa to recruit for private enterprise. By 1936 the economy was in full swing again; the lengthening of the railway line to Bobo-Dioulasso absorbed part of the manpower formerly recruited for the lower coast. The forests needed at least 8,000 labourers, the cocoa plantations as many. A spokesman for the colonial settlers deplored that.

> . . . the old system of virtual conscription, which would have been so helpful at the time, was abolished. The entire European colonisation of the Ivory Coast and the exploitation of forests were thus in immediate danger.[78]

In fact, it was not so much the survival of the *colon* that was in danger, as a return to the profits which had enabled timber cutters in the 1920s and 1930s to make fortunes in three years, at least as long as they did not prefer to squander their 'savings', while on leave, on costly fantasies – like the man who, on the opening night of a Bordeaux theatre, hired all the taxis in town. Accustomed to the 'blessings' of Governor Reste, the settlers threatened to rise and throw the Popular Front governor, Mondon, into the sea on his arrival at Port-Bouët. The above-quoted author recalls:

> When the administration wants to construct or open up a track, maintain a road or carry out any kind of public works, it always finds men – to excess. First there is statute labour. . . . Then there are prisoners for all the day-to-day maintenance jobs. Finally there is large-scale recruitment of labourers.[79]

He claimed the same advantages for the settlers, in the name of equality of rights. The settlers were not the only ones to protest; the administrators in Dahomey rose in a body against the restraint on forced labour. In Niger, they found a solution by resorting to the 'second group' of the military contingent, which, instead of being called up for military service, was handed over to private operators for work 'in the public interest'. In 1938 the traditional system was reintroduced, and with the war and the Vichy régime it assumed a statutory character that it had never had in the past. To recruitment for the private sector was added recruitment for administrative works, which never came to an end. A spokesman for the settlers, already quoted, noted with envy:

> For the workshops of the Niger Office, with their military defences, approximately 2,000 labourers were recruited by the administration and placed at the disposal of the consortium.[80]

But the Niger Office was concerned not so much with public works as with agricultural colonisation by the African people on the Office lands, which required an abundance of settled manpower. Here, too, recourse was had to the simple procedure of 'recruiting' from the reserves of manpower in the Mossi country, especially in Yatenga, the nearest at hand. No doubt the records of individuals kept by the settlement and the Office distinguished between 'total volunteers' and 'partial volunteers' (*sic*).

In 1937 the 'settlers' were promised the full tenure of their land after a probationary period of ten years; this promise was not kept and the share-cropping system was established after the Second World War. How could such a promise be believed if given by a military régime imposed on the settlers? An official report noted:

The settlers are not forced to go out together to work the land: but no one is allowed to be in the village between sunrise and sunset, to move about without a permit or *a fortiori*, to leave the Office lands. Punishment is inflicted on those who do not work hard enough.[81]

The work period was between 6 a.m. and noon and from 2 p.m. until sunset, under the direction of instructors. As in the case of conscription during the First World War, the Mossi chiefs sent to this virtual prison convicts or individuals who were unemployable or generally undesirable (including the sick and those suffering from sleeping sickness). This feeble labour force was, moreover, hardly prepared to work on irrigated crops which differed completely from the dry crops normally used in the Mossi country. Under these conditions, not only were the results lamentable, but desertions were continuous, restrained solely by the threat of punishment by the administration. The Bélime mission of 1919–21 envisaged the transplantation of no less than 1,500,000 Mossi. In 1937 there was talk of settling 800,000; on the eve of the Second World War, even after repeated recruitment, only 8,000 had been settled. In 1936 Governor-General de Coppet refused to authorise new recruitment, but decreed that those who had been settled were to remain, regardless of their own wishes. 'One sign from me', he wrote, 'and entire villages are emptied of their inhabitants.'[82]

In view of the failure of local recruitment, appeals for foreign labour were often considered: for example Algerians, brought by the Trans-Saharan route for the Niger irrigation schemes, and Poles; but these projects, aired in the press, did not materialise. As well as those recruited by the Niger Office, there were others intended for employment on the railway lines already mentioned. Most of these came from the Mossi country. In 1922 Upper Volta had to provide contingents of workers, 6,000 for spells of six months, to complete the Thiès–Kayes railway line; these joined the Bambara who were recruited in the Sudan. Another 2,200 had to be provided for the building of the Ivory Coast railway, a 'provision' which continued with fluctuations until 1929.

In Equatorial Africa and the Cameroons, less sensitive to fluctuations in French politics, there was constant administrative recruitment for public and private needs. We shall make no further mention of the labour forced for administrative or para-administrative purposes, already mentioned in connection with the Congo–Ocean line and the roads of Ubangi-Shari. At the beginning of the work on the Congo–Ocean line, 10,000 to 15,000 men were press-ganged, according to an official report by Governor-General Antonetti.[83] Apart from public works, 'recruitment' in Ubangi-Shari provided the labour force for the European coffee plantations and the gold and diamond mines. Requisitioned persons were exempt from compulsory quotas of cotton; this was a source of conflict between the cotton companies, who for this reason were hostile to recruitment, and the administrators, settlers and mining companies, who needed the labour.[84] Cotton had the advantage over rubber of not forcing the entire population to desert the villages. It was different in the forests, partly in the Middle Congo but mainly in Gabon, where the forest workings, mainly during the rush of the years 1920 to 1930, absorbed a labour force disproportionately large in relation to the manpower actually available in these regions.

Because of demands by the companies and the settlers, the governor 'taxed' the administrative divisions of his colony each year, forcing them to provide a fixed number of labourers for the private sector. For example, an order issued by the governor-general, under whom was the administration of the Middle Congo, fixed 'the maximum recruitment for specific needs' for each division of the Middle Congo in 1927 at a level ranging from 400, the minimum, for the Pool *circonscription* (which included the capital Brazzaville), up to 2,000 for the district surrounding Upper Sangha and Likouala-Mossaka.[85] Forest workings and mining absorbed 20,000 to 30,000 'contract labourers' out of a population of 420,000: in other words 40 per cent of the male population between twenty and forty years of age.[86]

The forest workings were situated near transport routes, principally water courses and ocean lagoons, and the 'contract workers' were brought from a distance of 1,000 km. or more under the usual conditions (on foot and with no food provided), crowded in sordid camps for the one or two years' duration of the 'contract', and badly fed; only the women, children and old people were left behind in the deserted villages, to provide 'statute labour' as well as administrative works. They also had to supply, again in the form of requisitioning, 'quotas' of foodstuffs to feed the labour force of private enterprise and the Congo–Ocean line. In 1941, Governor-General Eboué wrote:

Nowadays – and this fact is particularly noticeable in Gabon – the young males from the villages in the interior are taken away from their normal lives and their wives and children, to be transported into camps where all the tribes are mixed, where a man feels at a loss and, to his great spiritual detriment, loses his individuality; there are a few sterile prostitutes who, without giving him the possibility of reproduction, infect him often for life, and in exchange for his pay and the better development of his muscles [sic]; he loses the true sense of his existence, together with the means of perpetuating it. While this male proletariat is formed, the villages, deprived of their best elements, vegetate. The women have no more children, the race vanishes.[87]

In these camps the mortality rate was high, and nothing was done to help repatriate the men at the expiry of their 'contract'. Even the officially-minded Georges Bruel gives the example of a subdivision in Gabon where, in three years, only 423 out of 1,000 'hired men' returned to their villages: 182 died, 395 did not return.[88] The Cameroons, with a less specialised economy, knew the scourge of recruitment to an intermediate degree, between French West and French Equatorial Africa. The administrator of Bafoussam wrote:

. . . Each year, in October and April, the planters of the Foumban region need labour, and for this purpose they transmit their 'order' to the regional labour office at Foumban, which sends me a letter in which I am ordered to send so many men to Mr. X and so many to Mr. Y.

In turn, I summon the chiefs at Bafoussam and apportion evenly among them the number of men they are to provide. As 50 per cent of the men are physically incapable of doing any regular work and 90 per cent of the youth of the country has escaped and is moving about the territory, I demand forty men when I need twenty, for the health service will send at least 50 per cent back as physically incapacitated. The chiefs return home and the man-hunt begins. Nobody wants to go and work voluntarily on certain of the European plantations; but the chiefs' tchindas[89] sooner or later bring in those who had the misfortune not to excape quickly enough.

They are examined by a medical auxiliary, measured and weighed, and sent to the plantations manu praetorii.[90]

As to the conditions under which the requisitioned labourers worked, a witness who can hardly be suspected of extreme views, Father Aupiais who, after the Second World War, became deputy head of the European college of Dahomey and Togo, did not hesitate to write:

It happens (a) that requisitioned labourers are paid less than free manpower; (b) that they are not paid at all; (c) that they are not compensated for the many days they often have to travel to reach their place of work; (d) that unjust deductions are taken from the natives to make them continue work, under the pretext of taxes and of providing them with subsistence and tools.[91]

The 'recruitment' mentioned here does not include 'statute labour' (basically 10 to 12 days a year), which all taxpayers had to render unless they could buy themselves out. The official tax was rarely adhered to; as in poll-tax, the days of statute labour were 'taxed' in each canton according to the population given in the official census: days owed by those absent or deceased were divided among all those present. And to this might be added the completion – under the pretext of urgent necessity – of a given task. Any refusal in this case would be liable to punishment of the population. The administrator Gilbert Vieillard noted in this respect:

For forty years statute labour has taken the form of arbitrary forced labour: it has become a bogy for the people of Fouta-Djalon.[92]

The various forms of forced labour used in the French colonies became the subject of bitter criticism abroad and before various international assemblies. These critics were not always innocent or disinterested themselves; but the fact remains that under the hypocritical veil of the republican slogan of Liberty, Equality and Fraternity, the labour system in the French colonies – especially in French Equatorial Africa – set an example of oppression and arbitrary power such as was rarely attained even in the Portuguese and Belgian colonies.[93] The absence of any genuine labour legislation left the hands of the governors free.[94] The 1903 decree insisted upon recruitment by the administration, and limited the duration of contracts to a maximum of two years. The decree of 7 April, 1911, applicable to French Equatorial Africa, laid down (in its articles 15 and 16) that wages could be paid at the end of the contract. In such cases, the entrepreneurs were obliged to make a public deposit of the sum every six months. In French West Africa the decree of 22 October, 1925, was confined in its application to fixing the limits of labour contracts (minimum two months, maximum two years) and to setting up a council of arbitration presided over and appointed by the circle commander and including one European assessor and one indigenous assessor but no elected member.[95] The institution of 'savings' was left to the discretion of governors. A circular issued by the governor-general stipulated these details:

It goes without saying that in the regions where you have decided to establish the system, savings may be introduced *without provision for the parties concerned to escape this obligation.*

In Dahomey, a local order of 17 August, 1927, fixed the amount of the wages to be thus retained in the form of 'savings' at 50 per cent. This portion was to be paid by the employer to the treasury, which in return issued 'savings stamps' that were fixed to the wage-earner's work book; the amount was to be refunded by the administration at the end of the contract.[96] This system allowed the administration to gain treasury facilities at the expense of the workers without paying the smallest percentage of interest in return.

While statute labour in lieu of taxes was legal, the requisitioning of manpower had no explicit basis in legislation. The existence of requisitioning to satisfy the needs of the administration, under the pretence of public works, is only established by the mention of sanctions to be levied on those who refused such service, in the form of punishment of the local people. In Togo and the Cameroons (analogous texts exist in French West and French Equatorial Africa) decrees of 1923 and 1924 punished 'refusal to submit to requisitioning by the administration for essential public works' (sic). In Madagascar a decree of 3 June, 1926, allowed the 'second group' of the contingent to be used for 'works in the public interest' (which could be carried out by private enterprise). These were conscripts recognised as suitable for service, but not called up, and kept for three years as a reserve at the disposal of the military authorities. During this period they could be requisitioned by decree of the governor-general. This was under the 'Service de la main-d'oeuvre des travaux d'intérêt général'. A similar decree was passed on 31 October, 1926, for French West Africa: but the implementation order for it did not appear until 4 December, 1928, and it was applied only rarely in French West Africa. There was nothing in the text about requisitioning for private enterprises.

The French practice was in blatant contravention of the Convention of the League of Nations of 25 December, 1926, regarding slavery, which prohibited forced labour in the service of private interest. The forced labour scandals in the Congo stirred international opinion, and in 1929 a report was published, accompanied by replies from the governments to a questionnaire on forced labour. It was to be submitted to the 12th Conference of the International Labour Organisation. It proposed the establishment of an international convention prohibiting forced labour.[97] This project brought violent reactions from colonial interest groups and their front organisations (the Union coloniale, the Ligue maritime et coloniale, and the Académie des sciences coloniales) especially during the debates in Geneva when the working delegations tried to introduce international control. The 12th Conference of the I.L.O. finally adopted a convention expressing moral condemnation of the French system by 93 votes, with 50 abstentions (those of the representatives of the French government). The signatories of the Convention undertook to suppress compulsory labour in all its forms 'within the shortest period possible'; only forced labour for public purposes was temporarily authorised. The use of military contingents for civil labour as envisaged by the Service de la main-d'œuvre . . . was expressly condemned. The French government delegates, after opposing the project to the very end, did not dare to take an open stand in favour of forced labour. Their spokesman, M. A. Fontaine, with splendid cynicism, stated before the final vote that France was 'resolutely in favour of the abolition of forced labour' and that it 'would adhere to the general principles set out in the proposed convention', even if it had 'reservations' as to the text.

> Whatever happens to the draft convention, France, which is already putting these principles into practice, will unhesitatingly continue its campaign, supervising the implementation, as quickly as seems practicable, of specific measures the immediate or over-hasty application of which has not seemed possible or in the best interests of the peoples. . . .[98]

In other words, after 'adhering to the principles', they refused to apply them. The French government took no notice of the resolutions of the I.L.O.; on the contrary, under pressure from the Union coloniale, it passed a decree dated 11 April, 1930, renewing that of 1921 on 'repression of vagrancy', whereby heavy punishment could be inflicted on anyone who had escaped from requisitioned labour. Another decree, of 21 August, 1930, under the pretext of 'regulating' labour and preventing the abuse of requisitioning, took care to exclude labour requisitioned in 'circumstances beyond control' or 'customary' labour, exceptions permitting a very loose interpretation. It is hardly necessary to add that no guarantee of 'social security' was ever provided. If a worker were sick he was authorised to return home on his own, which usually meant that he died on the way. If he stayed on the spot his wages and rations were 'cut', which forced him to rely on the goodwill of his friends.

There was no provision for accidents at work. The grant or refusal of indemnity was left to the goodwill of the employer. The 'contracts' of the Congo–Ocean line laid down for cases of complete disablement a total indemnity of 600 francs! Two Sara, who each had a leg amputated, were given 400 francs each, and permitted to return to their country, as best they could – the distance to be covered was 2,000 kilometres.[99] The decree of 2 April, 1932, relating to work accidents in French West Africa, deserves to be included among the finest monuments of human hypocrisy. The derisory 'pensions' envisaged applied only to accidents caused by machines that were powered by sources other than humans or animals, in other words mechanical engines, which were hardly in use at all. The most frequent accidents – falls or injuries on building sites and mine explosions – were not covered.

It was not until the Popular Front came to power, bringing an easing of forced labour (at least in French West Africa, and in relation to requisitioning for private enterprise) that a beginning was made in social legislation: for French West Africa, the decree of 11 March, 1937 authorised trade unions; that of 20 March, 1937, introduced collective agreements and staff representatives; that of 18 September, 1936, regulated female and child labour, as did that of 17 November, 1937, in the Cameroons. These texts, with their limited scope, had little effect as long as such means of execution as on-the-spot control and sanctions were lacking.

(e) THE SPOLIATION OF THE LAND: AGRICULTURAL, FORESTRY
    AND URBAN CONCESSIONS

We have seen that the decree of 23 October, 1904, for French West Africa, and that of 28 March, 1899, for French Equatorial Africa proclaimed the French state's ownership of 'vacant and ownerless lands'. (This last decree was intended to permit the granting of big concessions.) This application of the Roman property concept did not arise, as is sometimes alleged, from a lack of knowledge of the African situation. All colonial authors recognised that in tropical Africa 'not an inch of land is without an owner'. This was clearly stated in 1920.[100] In a report adopted unanimously by the general council of the Ivory Coast, a councillor, J. B. Mockey, recalled:

Not a single square metre of land can be considered as ownerless. Vacant, no doubt, but most often momentarily, periodically, through the crop rotation system, by the intermittent use of pastures, etc. But ownerless? Definitely not. No land in Africa can be so considered. The tribes agreed upon borders among themselves, borders which generally followed natural features such as water courses and mountain ranges; or borders were fictitious ones, their position determined with the aid of landmarks usually placed along routes or taking the form of rocky outcrops. If tribes had borders, *a fortiori* sub-tribes or cantons and smaller territorial units also had precisely defined borders. This applies even on the scale of the village and the family.

In this same report the writer insists on the notion of common land – valid at the village level, in Europe as in Africa – and on the fact of a unilateral breach by the colonisers of the protectorate treaties concluded in the second half of the nineteenth century, which granted them the rights of limited occupation, but on no account the right of possession or ownership of African soil. The legislators of the early twentieth century, inspired by an experienced colonial administration, knew what to do. The disregard for the traditional rights of the African community over the land was deliberate, aimed at demonstrating the absolute power and consequent 'superior rights' of colonisation, untrammelled by any legal restraint. The land system of the French civil code had been largely introduced in Senegal in 1830, but it applied in practice only to a few estates in Gorée and Saint-Louis.

The lands acquired by the settlers – later we shall see under what conditions they were acquired – and lands where the native people wished to have their ownership acknowledged, were subject to a system known as *immatriculation* (registration) inspired by the 'Torrens system' used in Australia. Introduced first in North Africa, this system was applied to Senegal, the Ivory Coast and Dahomey from 1900, in Guinea from 1901, and it spread to French West Africa by a decree passed on 24 July, 1906; it was scarcely practised at all, however, except by the concessionaire settlers, once their obligations for land development had been fulfilled and acknowledged. The Africans, with very few exceptions, did not and could not use it; most of them were unable to understand the necessary preliminaries or to pay the fees; but those who wished to do so met with difficulties owing to the non-existence of absolute individual property rights in the Roman or bourgeois manner. Thus after the Second World War, there were only 1,742 'immatriculated' African owners in French West Africa out of a total of 16,000,000 inhabitants, and together they owned 29,000 hectares of mainly urban property. In French Equatorial Africa, by a decree of 1920, immatriculation was open only to 'non-citizens', and even then with restrictions.

Immatriculation of communal land was not dealt with and was incompatible with the hierarchy of rights normally exercised over

African land.[101] Any request for immatriculation was almost bound to lead to protests and opposition from persons – members of the family, the patriarchal, village or tribal community, etc. – whose land rights co-existed with those of the petitioner. Only chiefs and administration agents, with support in higher places, could overcome these difficulties, with the result that immatriculations for the native population, far from enforcing traditional rights, often led to the sanction of spoliation or usurpation. Faced with such a situation and the troubles to which it often led, a decree issued on 8 October, 1925, without affecting the immatriculation system as such, laid down a procedure of verification and establishment of customary land rights,[102] which proved to be highly involved, and so was hardly used. It only gave the beneficiaries an illusory guarantee – the issue of a title-deed, but no registration: rights were lost if the land was 'abandoned', which could always be invoked during fallow periods.

A decree issued on 15 November, 1935, abrogated and replaced the 1904 text in regard to French West Africa. In theory, it was aimed at respecting customary land rights which had been ignored in the abrogated text, but in fact it gave the administration a free hand by providing a basis in law for the rejection of claims. The 1935 decree had the effect of giving a more precise definition to 'vacant and ownerless lands' preventing, in a good number of cases, the claim of customary ownership. Article I grouped in this category all 'lands not subject to a regular and legal title deed of ownership or use and remaining untitled or unoccupied for more than ten years'. Thus land that was neither cultivated nor in common use (for example, pastures, forests and hunting districts) could legally and without process of law be confiscated and allotted by the state to other persons. The same applied to lands lying fallow for a longer period (fallow periods of ten years or more were frequent and even normal in many of the areas under cultivation).

The governor-general of French West Africa did not hesitate to emphasise:

As a consequence of these new dispositions you will henceforth be able to oppose the claims of certain speculators who are trying, without any right to do so, to immatriculate lands that have been vacant or ownerless for a long time, or to lay claim to them by declaring that their ancestors had once cultivated them.[103]

The 'speculators' here are clearly Africans claiming their rights over lands that had gained in value through town building, or road or railway construction, and which the colonial companies or the settlers had arranged to have 'conceded' to themselves, so that they could 'speculate', in a perfectly legal manner, by parcelling the land out with enormously enhanced values. In effect, the difficulty which the Africans encountered in having their land rights acknowledged was only equalled by the ease with which the companies or individual Europeans arranged to obtain 'concessions' often of immense portions of land claimed by the state. The 'concession' consisted essentially of tenure accorded, under given conditions, to private persons over portions of state land. As a general rule, it gave the beneficiary the possibility of acquiring full tenure of all or certain parts of the concession after a certain period and upon the fulfilment of certain obligations.

We shall not deal here with the origin of the big concessions in French Equatorial Africa and the Cameroons. Before the First World War it was understood that no new ones would be granted. By the conventions passed in 1910, the exorbitant rights of a number of chartered companies in French West Africa had been slightly reduced, but mainly in territories where they had never exercised them and were incapable of doing so. Conventions issued in 1920 renewed contracts dating from 1910 for a period of fifteen years, but reduced their scope. The monopoly of rubber exploitation, which had been conceded over 17,000,000 hectares, was reduced to 5,000,000 hectares; the areas that could be granted on condition of limited development were reduced from 110,000 to 50,000 hectares. By way of 'compensation' the chartered companies received, free of charge and in full tenure, various lands in the proximity of future railway lines.

The process of concentration had left only a small number out of the forty companies, due to legal or *de facto* amalgamation. In Gabon, the powerful Société du Haut-Ogooué and a certain number of others (mostly belonging to the Du Vivier de Streel group) turned, apart from foreign trade, to forest exploitation. In the Middle Congo, the strongest company north of the Lefini was the Compagnie forestière Sangha-Oubangui and its satellites ('Sangha-Likouala'); these monopolised the rubber trade over an immense territory. Farther south, in the region of Likouala-Mossaka and near Brazzaville, was the realm of the Tréchot Brothers: this was the Compagnie du Haut-Congo, which in 1919 took over the concession of the N'Goko-Sangha company, after contracting the part that remained in French hands in 1913 – altogether 5,600,000 hectares – and was coupled to the Compagnie du Bas-Congo, which ran trading posts in the Brazzaville region. The south-west was the domain of proprietary companies which in 1910 were granted land in full tenure in return for abandoning part of their concessions: such were the Société propriétaire de l'Ongomo, the

Société forestière et agricole du Kouilou (Sargos frères); or of companies that benefited from earlier concessions dating back to 1899 – e.g. the Compagnie propriétaire du Kouilou-Niari, which extended over 2,735,000 hectares – an area larger than the whole of Belgium – and was controlled after 1921 by Lever Brothers. In Ubangi, the most important companies were those of the Sultanats, with a system analogous to that of the Forestière Sangha-Oubangui (rubber trade monopoly) and of the Compagnie de l'Ouahm et Nana, mentioned elsewhere.

The year 1930 marked the expiry of the concessions and should have meant the liquidation of the companies[104] – who, in fact, lost nothing. It was quite the contrary. They ceased to pay their dues into the budget and their actual situation was scarcely modified at all. The rubber trade monopoly, which the companies 'reformed' in 1910 were to retain until 1935, had largely ceased to be of economic importance. Those unable to adapt themselves (like the Société des Sultanats or the Forestière Sangha-Oubangui) were finished by the crisis or taken over by other interest groups. On the other hand, some (the Compagnie de l'Ouahm et Nana, for example) turned to new and even more profitable activities such as transport and cotton. But, in any case, the network of trading posts they owned and the connections they had built up within the administration enabled them to survive within their old spheres – a *de facto* quasi-monopoly, in the absence of any legal monopoly. Moreover, the complaisance of the government and the administration assured them, under cover of a voluntary liquidation of rights, immense free grants of land in full tenure. The Société du Haut-Ogooué received 30,000 hectares, of which 15,000 were contiguous with their former concessions, plus one hectare of urban land at Pointe-Noire, which promised a steep increase in value, and 350,000 francs as an indemnity. The Compagnie de l'Ouahm et Nana obtained 10,500 hectares plus 4,000 square metres at Pointe-Noire. The Compagnie forestière Sangha-Oubangui obtained several lots, one of 15,000 hectares in Lobaye and Upper-Sangha, etc.

The benefiting companies did not fully cultivate these lands, any more than they had done under the concessionary system, where they were required to 'develop' the land, and they never had any intention of so doing. They limited themselves in most cases to cultivating infinitesimal fractions, and keeping the rest for speculative purposes. Improvements in the road network, and the construction of the Congo–Ocean railway and the port at Pointe-Noire, permitted them to re-sell, at an advantageous moment and at a high price, the best-appointed lands, which they had been granted free of charge. While areas of the order of a million hectares were no longer conceded after 1899, reduced concessions, still often comprising more than 10,000 hectares, were accorded in growing numbers to companies and individuals, especially in the most fertile and easily accessible regions. Among the provisions of a decree of 1904, which remained in force in French West Africa, were that concessions of less than 200 hectares and urban plots could be made by the lieutenant-governor, in consultation with the colonial administration; for concessions of from 200 to 2,000 hectares he could only present a proposal, the decision resting with the governor-general. A concession of more than 2,000 hectares had to be accorded by decree of the minister for the colonies. In French Equatorial Africa the same provisions applied below 200 hectares. From 200 to 10,000 hectares required a decision of the governor-general taken in council, and more than 10,000 hectares required an order from the minister.

Concessions continued, as before 1914, to be accorded easily and without any thought being given to the rights of the local population. To begin with, they were accorded on a temporary basis, but they were transformed into definite concessions, with full tenure, simply on application from the concessionaire, provided that their 'development' was confirmed by the administration – who often did not take the trouble to verify the facts, one vague installation being sufficient for a state of 'development' to be confirmed. The withdrawal of a concession occurred only very rarely, in a case of total failure, and only if the failed land was claimed by a competitor. Could anyone fight the companies or powerful persons with official connections?

As to the more modest concessions, they were accorded without difficulty, particularly if the beneficiary was well known to the administration, like a colonial official or an army officer who had resigned or retired, or one with suitable recommendations. The Abbé Boganda wrote in 1951:

In Ubangi-Shari, when a newly-arrived settler wishes to establish himself, he chooses a piece of land, regardless of whether or not it is inhabited or whether it is family property, or belongs to a clan or a tribe, and everything is settled over an apéritif.

As for the owner, he is the last to be informed; no one asks his opinion, When there is a dwelling on the earmarked property they sometimes condescend to give him a derisory sum (2,000 to 3,000 francs C.F.A. for an area of 500 to 1,000 hectares). This sum is called 'abandonment indemnity', and it is very often accompanied by threats and beating, or the militia demolish the dwellings in a few hours.[105]

This procedure was applied with variations everywhere; the 'abandonment indemnity' fixed by the governor took into account, under the conditions here described, the type of dwelling and sometimes the value of the harvest on the land under cultivation at the moment of transfer without taking any account of land lying fallow in the cultivation cycle. In general, the buildings were not subject to indemnity, especially in countries of group dwellings: to avoid payment of costs, villages were left outside the concessions, although the best land was taken from them. The inhabitants were left with two alternatives – to take up service under the concessionaire or to move elsewhere. In a circular dated 1937 the governor-general of French West Africa himself recognised that

. . . by the thoughtless grant of definite concessions, particularly in fertile regions, the administrative authority risks finding itself at some future date faced with the impossibility of being able to give satisfaction to the land requirements of a growing indigenous population. . . . It is my view that if the alienation of lands is henceforth not hedged about with absolute guarantees, we shall, sooner or later, find outselves faced with abuse and difficulties, for which the administrative authority alone will be responsible for its lack of foresight.[106]

In spite of these statements, the regular granting of concessions did not slacken off. Only on the eve of the colonial system's collapse were the 'vacant and ownerless lands' explicitly excluded from state property, but the system of concessions was not otherwise modified (decrees of 20 May, 1955, and 10 July, 1956, promulgated in French West Africa by a decree of 7 December, 1956). Henceforth the only lands open to the state or public collectives were those regularly immatriculated in their name: vacant land or land presumed to be vacant had to be immatriculated after an inquiry had given proof that they were not subject to customary rights, or that the owners of such rights had renounced them before they could be brought into the public sector.[107] In fact, from this point on, it was the autonomous governments of the *loi-cadre*, and then the independent states, that were to take charge of the land.

Though only provisional, the forestry concessions (Gabon and Middle Congo, the Cameroons and the Ivory Coast) were no less oppressive and discriminatory for the people.

They are always conceded on a temporary basis, or for a short period: permits for temporary exploitation or for industrial felling (for a basic period of three years, renewable) or in the form of long-term concessions (valid for twenty-five or seventy-five years). The forestry concessions involve considerable areas which, however, are far from corresponding to the effective and rational exploitation of the forest.

Certainly, the grant does not involve the removal of the indigenous people living on the conceded territories. On the contrary, the need for local labour – supplied mainly, and sometimes solely, by the local population – leads to the retention of the villages on the conceded territories. But it is clearly a source of much injustice.

First, every form of pressure is used to make the local people work on the sites, including the more or less flagrant use of forced labour. [The cited text is from the year 1951. It should be understood that, before 1945, forced labour was resorted to officially.] The living conditions of the local people are also affected by the damage, if not the destruction of crops and tree plantations. At the regular session of the grand council of French Equatorial Africa in 1949, Councillor Tchitchelle vigorously denounced the numerous demands made upon the people in the Mayombe forest in the Middle Congo: the destruction of food plantations, palm groves, coconut-palm and banana plantations, various fruit trees, etc.[108]

The difficulties caused by the concessions were increased by the 'classification' of immense forest and savannah areas by the Water and Forest Administration. Under the pretext of combating deforestation, they did not attack the true causes – the ill-considered extension of export crops – but rather the effects, prohibiting the Africans from using the lands they needed for subsistence, and which had often been under cultivation for long periods.

In French West Africa the forestry decree of 4 July, 1935, established a series of categories of land taken from the cultivators (classified forests, protected forests – the term 'forest' being defined very loosely – to which were added 'perimeters of reforestation' that were similarly prohibited. Justified from the point of view of conservation of the natural environment and the soil, the measures taken in putting this decree into practice often took no account of the human situation stemming from the colonial system.

Both in the forest zones and the vast savannah regions, vehement protests were raised against these practices which, under the threat of heavy punishment, fines or prison sentences, forced entire villages to go ten, twenty or even up to forty kilometres in search of free land for their crops.[109]

The discriminatory character of these measures was the more resented since, in practice, the forestry concessions were reserved

for Europeans, who were granted the right to draw on African forest
reserves, the precariousness of which were invoked elsewhere to increase 'classification'.

Circle	Total surface	Conceded forest area	Classified forests	Percentage of conceded or classified forests in relation to total surface area
Agboville	1,052,000	680,000	214,000	85
Grand-Bassam	925,000	530,000	162,000	75
Grand-Lahou	1,320,000	430,000	173,000	45·6
Abidjan	855,000	215,000	184,000	46·6
Sassandra	1,299,000	295,000	250,000	42

In the southern part of the Ivory Coast in 1945, forestry concessions covered more than 2,500,000 hectares, divided among sixty
exploiters with 1,019 timber-yards. Among the principal concessionaires were the Société coloniale de l'Afrique française (400,000
hectares); the Forestière de l'Indénié (245,000 hectares); the
Forestière équatoriale (235,000 hectares), the Société d'Importation des bois exotiques (222,500 hectares), the Société forestière et
agricole de la Côte d'Ivoire (150,000 hectares) and the Société des
Acajous des Bassam (137,500 hectares). In the Agboville and
Grand-Bassam circles (crossed by the railway line) the conceded
forests covered more than half the surface area of the administrative division. In the five circles of Basse-Côte the total conceded
forest area plus the classified forests – in other words territory closed
to exploitation by Africans – made up 3,100,000 hectares out of a
total area of 8,451,000 hectares.

At the end of 1947, out of a total of sixty-nine exploiters on the
Ivory Coast only two were Africans, and one of these was Senegalese.
In 1938 exploitation permits in the Cameroons covered 252,235
hectares, while in November 1947 they covered 2,046,057 hectares,
with four big companies holding 1,050,000 hectares – the Société
des forêts tropicales (300,000 hectares); the Compagnie française
du Cameroun (250,000 hectares); the Compagnie industrielle
française d'Afrique (250,000 hectares) and the Société 'Les Bois du
Cameroun' (250,000 hectares). Felling permits granted to Africans
represented no more than 63,395 hectares of the total area.

In a petition to the United Nations, a representative of the Boulou
people in the Kribi region wrote:

Three-quarters of the forests in our region are already taken over
by the settlers. . . . This unhappy people sees its forests ravaged
and disappearing without any profit to the settlers' companies.
. . . It is as if no one were living in this region.[110]

In Gabon, where lack of communications had saved the interior from being penetrated, the 1,168,000 hectares granted in concessions and almost all the 662,000 hectares of classified forests were situated in the 'first zone', i.e. near the coast.[111] In this zone, conceded or classified forests made up more than half the total. Among the principal concessions were those granted, by the decree of 19 July, 1920, to the consortium of the 'big French railway networks', extending over 197,000 hectares and valid for thirty years. In the Middle Congo, exploitation did not really develop until after the Second World War: 50,000 hectares were granted in concessions in 1945, and 186,500 in 1950. Agricultural and forestry concessions occupied nearly all the land along the railway lines.

In Mayombe, all the land along the railway line is occupied, and the region between Loémé and Cabinda (from the railway to the southern frontier) will soon be completely apportioned in concessions.[112]

A word should be said on urban concessions. From the beginning the colonisers, invoking 'hygiene' as a pretext, appropriated the necessary land to build 'European quarters' in the best positions; they forced the Africans to move to the periphery. The organ of the Rassemblement démocratique africain on the Ivory Coast wrote on this subject in 1950:

The conquered African was forced into the swampy zones if his village stood on the heights. This is what happened at Abidjan: Anoumabo and Cocody, situated on the plateau, were evacuated. Special zones were set aside [for the Africans]: Adjamé with its numerous deep furrows; and the island of Petit-Bassam, marshy and unhealthy, also witnessed the building of the first hutments of the Treichville quarter.[113]

But the moment came when the town grew and the big companies became interested in the 'native quarters'; the administration needed room for its stores, offices and lodgings; so the local people were evicted again. Before the First World War the Germans had acted in this way in relation to Douala, themselves provoking 'trouble', which was put down by 'strong arm' methods with the hanging of King Rudolf Manga Bell in August 1914. The pattern of action was the same almost everywhere, and often with many repetitions. The Abbé Boganda noted:

Even at Bangui, the local population were evicted and their dwellings were demolished more than five times in twenty years.[114]

To carry out these evictions the administration had armed itself with the decree of 15 November, 1935, permitting the governor or the governor-general to decide on the occupation of land necessary to 'establishments or constructions in the public interest', even stipulating the compensation to be paid to the occupiers. Not even the owners of immatriculated property were protected from such arbitrary action; the expropriation procedure could be employed against them for reasons of public utility. Under the terms of Article 5 of the decree of 25 November, 1930 (referring to French West Africa), the governor could order expropriation when it was deemed necessary in the interests of hygiene, on aesthetic grounds, or for the easier realisation of a project of public utility, or even when its execution gave this property a rise of over 20 per cent in value. This very fluid definition set almost no limit to the arbitrary action that could be taken by the administration. The tribunal that followed, pronouncing expropriation and fixing the indemnity, could do no other than ratify the declaration of public utility made by the governor. Whether occupied or expropriated, the land acquired by the administration was divided into lots and 'conceded' at derisory prices to the big trading companies and the settlers, who sold the greater part a few years later at considerably higher prices – thanks to the increases in value that derived from urban development – roads, etc. financed out of public funds.

Such was the concept of 'public interest' which became identified in a special way with the private interests of trading companies and settlers. The 'development' clauses of the urban concessions (concerned with maintaining the buildings up to a certain standard) were frequently invoked against the Africans who lived on the land but who were financially incapable of making the improvements demanded, but never against the big trading companies (unless the latter had agreed to abandon useless concessions).

At Conakry, it was not until independence that concessions situated in the very centre of the old town, that had been granted to the big companies at the end of the nineteenth century and remained open land, were annulled and taken over by the state. We can take as an example the 'parcelling out' of the island of Petit-Bassam. It had been left to the Africans until the Second World War, but the speculators' attention had been drawn to it with the growth of Abidjan and the prospective construction of the Vridi canal. In September 1943, in the middle of the war, applications for its concession were submitted by a group of big companies and settlers, who had 'divided up the cake' in advance. An 'African zone' had been planned, for which the petitioners were Africans, well known as puppets of the big companies. André Latrille, whom

France had sent as governor to the Ivory Coast to replace the Vichy governor, categorically rejected these applications; instead he offered precarious sites, on short terms, without any right of preference, the portions to be adjudicated before the opening of the port, with the aim of letting the Treasury benefit from increases in value. He stood by this decision despite strong pressure exerted on him from above. While he was on leave, however, his successor De Maud'huit hurriedly assigned the land to the speculators (13 March, 1946). Governor Latrille, on his return, tried in vain to annul these concessions.[115] They were upheld and, without having so much as to move a finger, the 'beneficiaries' made profits of hundreds of millions when the port opened a few years later.

Expropriations were not as easy to bring about at Dakar, where the inhabitants had the vote. The resistance of the African community of Leboue on the Cap Vert peninsula gave rise to a notorious and interminable judicial imbroglio, the affair of the 'Tound lands' (*terrains de Tound*). French forces had occupied Dakar in 1853. The colonial administration, invoking treaties concluded in the eighteenth century with the Damels of Cayor, who had 'ceded' the peninsula to France in a highly doubtful treaty,[116] aspired to the possession of the 'vacant and ownerless lands' on the peninsula. The community of Leboue, which had become independent of Cayor at the end of the eighteenth century, invoked its right of communal possession over the whole peninsula, where numerous sales of land to individual Europeans had further complicated the situation. With Dakar's definite accession to the rank of federal capital, Governor-General Roume concluded an agreement with the representatives of the community on 23 June, 1905, through which the urban territory of Dakar (the original territory now greatly extended) was immatriculated in the name of the French state.

A first sector, the 'Bougnoul' lands comprising the 'plateau' and the coast from Cape Manuel to the Madeleines, was ceded on condition that various dues were paid. A second sector, that of the 'Tound land' (dunes), was to be reserved for 'a special village dedicated to the needs of the local population'. This agreement, from the very beginning, aroused numerous protests from the Lebou people who claimed, not unreasonably, that the notables who had appended their signatures had been duped by the governor-general and the interpreter. Tound was never divided up: the relevant decree, issued by Governor W. Ponty in 1915, was never applied, and with the extension of the town the Africans were simply driven out of the centre towards the Medina outskirts where there were no roads or sanitary arrangements, the latter deficiency being invoked as an excuse to have surviving huts in the town pulled down and burnt by the sanitary services. After innumerable vicissitudes a decree passed on 14 March, 1926, enabled the administration to eliminate rightful African claims while recognising the principle of their demands.

The Lebou claims to the Tound lands were upheld; claims to the lots could be made by Lebous who – themselves or their ancestors – had incontestably occupied the land. But the title-deed to the land was only granted (at the cost of the claimants) on the condition, first, that the plots had truly been occupied over the preceding five years, and secondly, that dwellings had been constructed 'solidly' according to prescribed norms; the deeds then remained inalienable for six years. The first condition already opened the way to many acts of dishonesty: for example, how were the true holders of the rights to be determined? On the other hand, the attributions were made individually to heads of families who, according to African custom, acted as managers of the collective rights of the extended family. A number of these, basing themselves on the legislation, later claimed the right to appropriate these lands for their personal profit. One can imagine the innumerable disputes and court cases that resulted. Furthermore, the Lebous of Tound were among the most needy of the community, often incapable of fulfilling the required condition of 'development' with their own means – which is what the colonial administration counted on.

The 'owners' thus had no way out other than to lease their allotments at derisory conditions for long periods of twenty to forty years, to Europeans or Lebanese-Syrians, on condition that the lessees undertook to erect 'solid' buildings according to the required norms so that the title-deed could be delivered; the construction was to return to the owner at the expiry of the lease. There is no need to give statistics to show that the tenants, being obliged to erect buildings that would not remain their own, stuck to the very minimum required for 'development' conditions, and the appearance of the town thereby suffered. In the long run most of the former African occupants were evicted in favour of the Europeans or the Lebanese,[117] and received little compensation.

In conclusion: however vexatious and oppressive the spoliation of the land in the form of agricultural, forestry or urban concession, it was not – for the countries here under consideration – an essential process of colonial exploitation as in such countries as Algeria or South Africa. As we have seen, the system of trade mostly left agricultural production to the African peasant. In the savannah countries the concessions remained few and limited in scope. In the plantations and forest regions they played a more important role, but without depriving the African peasant of all means of subsistence, except in a few isolated cases. In Senegal and Guinea, private concessions occupied in 1912 about 6,000 hectares, in each colony. By 1945, the remaining concessions covered a greatly reduced area. In the Sudan, where they were of insignificant proportions, their total area increased, only through the activity of the Niger Office.

On the Ivory Coast, the area conceded to Europeans rose from 3,290 hectares in 1912 to almost 40,000, of which 27,045 hectares were under coffee bushes, 7,718 hectares under cacao-trees and 1,077 hectares under bananas. The role of the settlers in agricultural production was certainly important there but it was not decisive. In the Cameroons, by 1912–13, during the German régime, 115,147 hectares had been granted in concessions, of which 22,225 hectares were newly planted and 11,393 in full production (fifty-eight plantations). In 1935 the conceded area covered 68,745 hectares, of which 26,739 hectares were cultivated, and 21,969 hectares made up seventy-seven concessions with definite tenure.[118] In 1939 there were 551 European concessions covering about 100,000 hectares of which 35,000[119] were effectively developed. Without being totally negligible, this was little in relation to the total surface of the land and the country's resources.

As for the forest concessions, while they occupied almost a quarter of the forest land on the Ivory Coast, this proportion in the Cameroons was only one-eighth. Only in French Equatorial Africa did the system of concessions play a major role but, in the long run, this was less on account of its legal privileges than the practice of 'recruitment' for forced labour, which was carried out there on an exceptionally large scale. Finally, while in numerous regions of tropical Africa, because of irrational exploitation, usury in land is a tragic reality, and while in some regions the shortage of land caused acute problems, the agrarian problem here, in contrast with what happened in most other colonial countries, does not appear to have been fundamental.

(f) THE MINES

We have already seen the insignificance of the mines in relation to capital invested. In West Africa surface iron and gold mines continued to be exploited by the Africans using pre-colonial methods.

With the competition of imported products, primitive iron smelting slowly declined, reopening in periods of difficulties such as the 1929–33 crisis and the war. The African blacksmiths progressively abandoned the smelting of local minerals and used imported ores almost exclusively; since the wear and tear of ferrous metals was rapid (often through lack of manpower and maintenance and repair services), these became more plentiful. But no overall study of this trade exists, neither do statistical facts.[120]

Traditional gold-washing, in its social setting and employing an age-old technique, was pursued in certain regions of the Sudan, with diggings at Siguiri and Bambouk, and, to a lesser extent, on the Ivory Coast. Production, for which no accurate figures exist, was sensitive to economic cycles; the average revenue of the gold-washer was, in effect, of the same order as that of the wage-worker, and it was the hope of an exceptional stroke of fortune – rare indeed, but always possible – that continued to attract great numbers of men to the gold-fields. Around 1936 it was estimated that between 30,000 and 60,000 men were engaged in gold-washing in the most active region, that of Siguiri. As for capitalist exploitation, its characteristic features did not evolve, but remained more or less the same as before 1914: stock exchange speculations, technical incompetence and failure. The only company to survive from one war to the next was the Compagnie des Mines de Falémé-Gambie, set up in 1911; it was always on the verge of collapse, and was often refloated (in 1927 by the Belgian Mining Company of Kilo-Moto). It used archaic material, lost its mining rights through negligence, and was interested less in production than in the sale of the gold-washers' gold; it survived thanks to beneficial stock-exchange operations at Bordeaux.[121]

The production of gold in French West Africa remained very small, and varied according to economic cycles (from 66 to 460 kg. between 1920 and 1930).

	kg.
1921	460
1928	256
1929	66
1930	286

The essential part was furnished by African gold-washers: 200 kg. in 1928, as against 56 kg. of European production (Falémé-Gambie, 46 kg.; Kokumbo on the Ivory Coast, 10 kg). Attempts made by various companies on the Ivory Coast, under the impact of success achieved on the Gold Coast, were ephemeral or failed for the same reasons as before 1914 (Poura in the Lobi country, Kokumbo, etc.). Nor did the Niger Office succeed any better, as is seen in the failure of the Compagnie minière de Haute-Volta.

In Dahomey, on the other hand, just before the war, the administration launched the Perma workings with some success; for this purpose they sold the rights of the Société minière du Dahomey (1940). Thus the relative boom production after the crisis was attributable to traditional gold-washing. H. Labouret noted:

K

Indigenous gold-washing represents, in contrast to over-capitalised European mining, a very economical mode of development of the local wealth, for it does not involve any immobilisation of capital or outlay of general expenditure.[122]

Two business firms, Peyrissac and Chavanel, specialised in trade with gold, which in 1936 had the highest value among Guinea's exports. The production in French West Africa was: 1934, 3,039 kg. (of which 130 kg. was from European mines); 1937, 3,993·9 kg. (89 kg. from European mines); 1939, 4,530·7 kg. J. Richard-Molard wrote:

Before the war, Upper Guinea could extract officially three to four tons each year, but a good portion escaped official control; more than 100,000 labourers were employed on it and were fed partly on imported rice. When this import disappeared in 1940, the diggings were closed down, and work was not resumed. The official price of gold fixed by an international convention was too low.[123]

Apart from gold, titaniferous sands were mined after the First World War on the Petite Côte (the Joal region in Senegal), and exported in crude form as titanium mineral and zirconium (Société Gaziello and Société 'L'Ilménite'). The results (in tons) varied with the economic cycles:

1921	1922	1923	1924	1927	1930
435	6	492	300	7,260	1,200

1932	1934	1936	1937	1939
0	523	3,228	2,016	4,200

Diamonds, which were abundant in Upper Guinea and the Ivory Coast, in regions that for a long time remained inaccessible, did not attract attention until after the world crisis.[124] Their presence in Liberia had been shown in 1913, and after the war deposits were traced and exploited on the Gold Coast and in Sierra Leone. The results gained in British territories encouraged prospectors in Upper Guinea and the Ivory Coast. The first important concessions were accorded to the Soguinex Company[125] in the region between Beyla and Macenta. A mechanical washing device was assembled at Banankoro in 1936 from pieces transported on men's heads, and at the time of writing it is still in use. Conducted in rough and ready fashion, the exploitation of the Soguinex Company was only a cover: the company was a branch of the Sierra Leone Consolidated Selection Trust and through it of the powerful De Beers Company, the world diamond monopoly; its object seems to have been less to exploit than to block diamond deposits in Guinea, in order to prevent their development by competitors. This was seen clearly when in 1956 individual African diamond miners, armed only with scoops and nets, managed to find diamonds on the perimeters kept under the company's control for twenty years.

As to other minerals, some had been known for a long time, such as bauxite on the Los Islands and iron at Kaloum,[126] but they remained in reserve. For a long time, the officials deplored the backwardness of mining in French West Africa and enviously compared results obtained in the Gold Coast and Nigeria with the meagre achievements in the French territories.[127] At the 1926–7 session of the supreme council of the colonies, the minister, Léon Perrier, declared himself

> struck by the overall backwardness of our West African territories in the field of mining where, by contrast, each year new and remarkable progress is being achieved by neighbouring colonies belonging to other countries.[128]

The situation had hardly changed by the eve of the Second World War. But at least the awareness of these shortcomings led to the establishment of an embryo geological service: young geologists turned to this field that had so long been neglected. But over the greater part of the territory prospecting and even geological surveys had hardly begun by 1940.

In the Cameroons, likewise, mining was limited to sampling: a little gold in the East (with exports of 14 kg. in 1933 and 384 kg. in 1936), tin ore (314 tons of 75 per cent tin-bearing ores in 1935) and titanium oxide mined near Yaoundé (45 tons in 1935). In Equatorial Africa the mining companies did not undertake work until late, (after 1928–30), with the end of concessions and the opening of routes of communication. The Compagnie minière du Congo français, set up in 1905, continued to send 400 to 800 tons of copper ore per year from Mindouli by a narrow-gauge railway, and by the Belgian railways from Kinshasa to Matadi involving three transshipments. Around 1929, the prospective inauguration of the Congo–Ocean railway line, for which copper ore transport was to provide the main local traffic, revived interest in deposits at Niari. A number of companies interested in copper were set up at that time (Congo-Mines, 1929; the Congo-Niari mining consortium, 1929; Compagnie des mines au Niari, 1931). But in 1935, at the very moment when the Congo–Ocean line was able to provide transport facilities, mining was stopped. Some attribute this to the action of Belgian interests controlling Katanga copper, which had refloated the Compagnie minière du Congo français, and had taken over control to prevent this production from competing on the market; others allege the scantiness of deposits and the drop in rates. In fact, the best part of the deposits had been removed by mining the richest ores, the chalcosine: once these were exhausted, mining required on-the-spot treatment of compound and poorer ores from the 'black soil', treatment which met with serious technical difficulties.[129] The very small total of 14,000 tons of mineral ores had been extracted. The place of copper was taken by lead and zinc ores from M'Fouati, near to Mindouli, mined by the same company, where annual output varied considerably according to economic cycles: in 1938, 5,000 tons of lead ore, and for the first time 1,512 tons of zinc ore.

Gold and, later, diamonds were prospected and then mined by the Compagnie Equatoriale des Mines (1927) and the Compagnie minière de l'Oubangui oriental (1927). Gold first appeared in the export statistics of French Equatorial Africa in 1930. Those concerned were content to mine alluvial gold of high gold content, using rudimentary methods, with 'recruited' labour taking the place of mechanisation. Before and during the Second World War, gold mining was done largely by small quasi-family workings directed by the settlers. The main portion was supplied first by Ubangi-Shari and then increasingly by Gabon, where there was a gold-rush in 1938, in the regions of N'Djolé and Etéké, in which Belgian capital participated, and by the Middle Congo (Mayombe). Gold production rose from 500 kg. in 1936 to 3 tons in 1941, but was never to rise as high again. Diamonds, mined mainly in Ubangi-Shari from 1931, furnished 15,000 carats in 1938, having risen from 1,509 carats in 1931.

As in French West Africa, the companies were involved mainly in stock-exchange speculations, but they managed to survive and sometimes to make profits, thanks to their financial backing, mostly stemming from high finance,[130] and to massive recruitment of labourers.

(g) THE CRISIS AND DEVELOPMENT EFFORTS

The Post-War Period

After the 1914–18 war French imperialism had lost between two-thirds and three-quarters of its foreign investments, in spite of its victory and military dominance in Europe. In Russia alone it lost more than 10,000,000,000 gold francs. In the narrowing world of capitalism, with Germany temporarily brought to its knees, and the rising imperialist powers – the United States and Japan – making for sharper competition with the war-weakened older powers, French industrial and political circles dreamed of getting the best out of their colonial empire. Albert Sarraut, minister for the colonies, wrote:

> To repair the ruin and ravages [of the war] the country could draw from there almost unlimited means of industrial and commercial strength. . . . We must make the colonies provide all they can of their considerable resources to *restore the home-country*.[131]

> In growing numbers, financiers, industrialists and merchants have turned with interest to new fields after the armistice, those that they had ignored for a long time, which lay open to their activity, at the precise moment when others were turning their attention inwards upon the partial ruins of our economy.[132]

In the summer of 1920 Sarraut indicated that in the previous year forty new companies had been established in French West Africa and eight in French Equatorial Africa, out of 125 in all the colonies. A few of the more notorious were cited above. The minister for the colonies also referred to the international political situation.

At the moment when France, to justify the firm grip of Britain and France over Germany's former colonial possessions, claimed that Germany had shown herself unfit to be a coloniser, it was hinted in some quarters that France had also shown incapacity. In the United States there was talk of a settlement of the debts of the Franco-British war by the abandonment of part of the colonial empire. At the League of Nations, the Italians protested at the slender share they had been given of the conquerors' spoils – the Greek Dodecanese islands, taken from Turkey.

> Nobody contests the possessors' right to their colonial possessions, nor their legitimate right to the exploitation and fruits of the lands acquired through their sacrifices. But can their right stretch to leaving the soil eternally fallow, where fertility would promise such precious and essential food supplies for human beings?[133]

The time had come to 'develop' the colonies that had been neglected for so long. However, this development ran up against a shortage of equipment, for which the colonial budgets were inadequate, although they were able to support loan issues. At no point was any thought ever given to direct assistance from the French national budget. This was, in any case, sufficiently burdened with the reconstruction of war-devastated areas, and German reparations were required even for national needs. Instead of dispersing the effort in special loans for each colony, as before 1914, the idea of a 'colonial credit' was launched, which would collect the necessary funds by means of savings bonds guaranteed by the state. The wealth resulting from the work undertaken with these funds would lead to a budget surplus, from which the colonies could refund the loans mentioned above.[134]

Albert Sarraut submitted a draft law on the 'development of the French colonies' on 12 April, 1921. The 'Sarraut Plan' envisaged a series of works on major installations: railways, ports, irrigation of the Niger Valley. For French West Africa alone, is allocated 497,000,000 francs for railways, 63,000,000 for ports (40,000,000 for the port of Dakar alone), 62,000,000 for the river control systems, 38,000,000 for urban administration and so on. There was even a plan for the electrification of the Kayes–Niger railway line. Two hundred and eighty million francs were allocated to irrigation works on the Niger (to which we return later);[135] the colonial exhibition at Marseilles, held that same year, stressed this point. However, these illusions were to be rapidly dispelled. The economic crisis of 1921 resulted in a sharp drop in the prices of colonial produce and stopped the movement of private capital. For the same reasons, the 'colonial credit' project was compromised. 'Great caution is called for in public works', the *Bulletin du Comité de l'Afrique française* noted, and it went on to ask the question: 'Was the Sarraut plan well timed?'[136] Germany did not pay the reparations that had been imposed, and French budgetary difficulties became more serious. Albert Sarraut had to take cognisance of this. He remarked:

> We are in 1922. The illusions of 1920 have not lasted. Germany won't pay. The French exchequer has to pay for charges which should have been settled by the contributions of the defeated. . . . On the financial market there is no place for the operation envisaged in 1920. We have to look elsewhere.[137]

The Sarraut Plan was abandoned without even being discussed by parliament. In view of the lack of capital, minor facilities, for what they were worth, could be provided only through forced labour – we have already seen at what price in suffering and in human lives lost.

The local budgets were drained mostly by running costs, and especially by the costly entertainment of French officials, transport costs and paid home leaves in France; any surplus was accumulated in the 'reserve funds', the size of which was an index to the governor's good management. In France there were some who claimed that this 'colonial surplus' should be used to make up the country's deficit. It served in fact partly to finance public works, but mainly for the purchase of imported materials; or else it disappeared into the abyss of fruitful 'deals' made by public works consortia. For the rest, an appeal was made for free forced labour. Albert Londres exclaimed:

Three hundred million in the reserve fund, but not a single tip-lorry or steam-roller. Nothing but blacks and their women, bearing stones on their heads and a harlequin's rod in their hand. In the Sudan, in Upper Volta, on the Ivory Coast, throughout the *pleiade*,[138] there are more than 50,000 kilometres of roads. All the materials used to build them were carried on the heads of the blacks.[139]

French Equatorial Africa alone contracted a loan of 300,000,000 in 1924 to undertake the building of the Congo–Ocean railway, for which the federation budget repaid the loans with interest. Private investment remained minimal. Having been almost non-existent until 1925, it grew to its maximum in 1929.[140] It should be stressed that share issues, by which investments are estimated, were then largely of a speculative character, and did not as such correspond to real investments.

Irrigation Work on the Niger

The only big undertaking that survived from the Sarraut plan of 1920 was the irrigation project on the Niger. This deserves to be considered in greater detail.

Before the war, as we have seen, groundnuts were practically the only cultivated product of any importance exported from French West Africa. Another product, cotton, could be furnished by the Sudanese zone: this was of prime interest to the French economy, and became an essential raw material for the textile trade. From the middle of the nineteenth century, the French textile industry was almost entirely dependent for its supplies on foreign countries. In 1923, out of 261,520 tons of cotton imported into France, French West Africa furnished barely 2,000 tons, and French Equatorial Africa 100: a drop in the ocean. Why could not French West Africa become a national supply source for France, as India and Egypt were for Britain, providing a saving in foreign currency, and supplying capital which could be reinvested in production as a new source of profits? While the tropical climate of the Sudan is, in theory, suited to cotton, the results were disappointing. The soil lacked the richness of the Regur region in India, and with dry cultivation yields were risky. Hence the plan to develop irrigation crops by using the waters of the River Niger, where the middle valley (the 'interior delta') could be turned into a new Egypt.

A Niger irrigation works study mission was sent to the area in 1919–20 with the engineer Bélime as leader, and the draft project produced by that mission was incorporated into the Sarraut Plan: 750,000 hectares of land were to be irrigated, 1,500,000 people were to be transplanted from the Mossi country to remedy the lack of manpower and inhabitants on the spot, and 300,000 tons of cotton were to be grown annually, to cover the needs of the French cotton industry. A loan of 280,000,000 francs was to be devoted to the scheme, which was to be completed within twenty years.

Finance capital at once organised itself to reap the hoped-for profits. A 'Compagnie de culture cotonnière du Niger' was set up, grouping the Société financière française et coloniale, a consortium of high finance (Rothschild, Banque de l'Union parisienne and Catholic·banks), the chamber of commerce of Le Havre (the main French cotton port) and the Hirsch group (Société coloniale de représentation), which specialised in the import of colonial textiles. The absence of textile *manufacturers* in this group is apparent, for these showed little interest, preferring to buy foreign to 'national' cotton, the quality and price of which had not been settled; the financiers involved were also associated with cotton importers. In spite of its name, the company made little effort to promote cultivation,[141] but merely arranged to be granted the monopoly of cotton purchases from the Sudan, by conventions passed in 1919, 1928 and 1936.

The main group involved was the Compagnie générale des Colonies, comprising banks[142] and firms concerned with public works. A contract dated 10 January, 1922, entrusted the company with studying the technical and agricultural possibilities of the interior delta of the Niger (with, as confirmed by the same contract, a preferential right of work at a later stage). While the eventual cotton harvests were far off and problematical, the work to be done with the loan gave rise to hopes of immediate and substantial profits. Bélime, the promoter of the scheme, had professional links with public works firms; Governor-General Merlin could not refuse anything to this powerful company, and his predecessor, Angoulvant, who became a director of the company, represented it at the heart of the Niger committe, set up in 1921 to organise patriotic publicity around the enterprise.[143] Later, another group of interests, linked essentially to the Comité des Forges, tried to link the Niger scheme to that of the Trans-Sahara railway; the latter would have given the irrigated lands of the Niger a direct outlet to North Africa, providing strategic unity for the imperial possessions of France and facilitating a possible southward transfer of North African manpower. The Comité de l'Afrique française set up a special publicity committee for this purpose in July 1927, 'to which the big colonial groups, notably the Union coloniale, gave every support.'[144]

On 23 February, 1928, the committee organised a 'Trans-Sahara luncheon' at the Hotel Continental; the deputy for Lorraine,

Edouard de Warren, of the Comité de l'Afrique française and the Comité des Forges, took the chair in the presence of three Marshals of France: Joffre, Lyautey and Franchet d'Espérey. On 13 March, 1928, the chamber approved a draft law setting up a 'body for the study of the Trans-Sahara route'. A lively campaign was afoot: from 1931 on, the *Bulletin du Comité de l'Afrique française* added to its 'Renseignements coloniaux' a second supplement under the title 'Études et Documents du Comité Algérie-Tunisie-Maroc et du Comité du Trans-saharien'. Violent polemics were launched against opponents of the scheme, among them the geographer Camille Vallaux, who showed that the Trans-Sahara route, which was of little strategic use, would swallow up billions of francs without the hope of any traffic. During 1928–30 the study unit drew up a scheme. Apart from the aims as represented by propaganda, the promoters were evidently interested in obtaining good markets for the French steel industry. Because it was too ambitious, the project was not followed up.

In spite of the Sarraut Plan's abandonment and the disappearance of the anticipated 280,000,000 francs, the Compagnie générale des Colonies and its associates did not abandon the idea. This could be seen with the arrival of Governor-General Carde, who was at first very reserved, if not hostile towards the scheme. National cotton supplies had been given as the *raison d'être* of the project. The boom in the international cotton market, greatly changed by 1923 as compared with 1919, robbed the scheme of much of its interest. Yielding to pressure, Carde nominated Bélime as 'head of the general service of textiles and agricultural water-power' but required him to modify the initial aims. In 1922 Bélime wrote with much assurance:

Foodstuffs are not involved, and from this point of view the irrigation works are, to some extent, superfluous. . . . With but a few exceptions any irrigation system aimed at guaranteeing foodstuff production would be doomed to total failure.[145]

The Carde programme of 1924 demanded, without eliminating cotton, that rice be added, and publicity for the Niger irrigation works was thenceforward limited to improvements in the standard of living of the population and achievement of a 'policy of full stomachs', and an 'island of prosperity' – themes that would easily rouse public feeling.[146] To the council of government of French West Africa, Governor-General Carde declared:

. . . I should like to state that if cotton production is to benefit from this work, this is not, to my mind, the ultimate aim desired.
K*

They [the irrigation works] have as their prime aim that of protecting the natives from starvation, and I say as I said in France: even if we should never harvest a single kilogram of cotton in West Africa, I shall nonetheless pursue the work.[147]

According to Carde, Niger rice ought to suffice to make up for the shortage of food in Senegal and for the shortage likely to affect the Upper Volta and Middle Niger regions when they were reached by rail and the demand for export crops. The years 1924–9 were given up to more detailed studies and the completion of the first very modest piece of work – construction of the irrigation channel of Sotuba – carried out with resources obtained from the government-general's budget of 26,000,000. The inauguration by Maginot, the minister, took place in February 1929. During 1929 the project as a whole was restated clearly: it involved (in the spirit of the Carde directives) the irrigation of 990,000 hectares, of which 510,000 were to be under cotton and 480,000 under rice. Its execution was included in the major works programme of French West Africa, opened by the law of 22 February, 1931, forcing a loan of 314,000,000 out of a total of 1,690,000,000. It involved the construction of a dam at Sansanding, a navigational canal 8 km. long by-passing it on the right side and a supply canal on the left bank leading to two main irrigation channels – the Macina canal 12 km. long and the Sahel canal 24 km. long.

With the arrival of Governor-General Brévié at Dakar, and in the midst of a crisis which made the search for outlets for companies interested in public works more urgent than ever, a new publicity offensive was launched.

In 1931 the sum of 113,000 francs – the annual tax payable by 8,692 blacks in the Sudan – was handed over to the many journals, which kept alive an atmosphere of enthusiasm surrounding the Niger irrigation works.[148]

Finally, in 1932 a decree[149] crowned the victory of the scheme's supporters with the creation of the Niger Office, an autonomous public body in charge of the irrigated lands, representing a true state within the state. Its headquarters were set up at Ségou, Bélime being appointed director-general. Let us examine the balance sheet. Seven hundred and fifty thousand and later nearly a million hectares were to be irrigated. In 1939, on the eve of the war, it was hoped to irrigate no more than 20,000 hectares by 1951; in 1953 there were barely 25,000 hectares of irrigated lands. Instead of the anticipated number of 1,500,000 African settlers, there existed by 1940 only three centres of colonisation – inhabited respectively

by 1,500, 5,500 and 5,268 persons.[150] Gross cotton production in
1937 was 80 tons. In 1944–55 it ranged from 2,000 to 4,000 tons per
year, with 10,000 to 20,000 tons of rice.

A recent study estimated public investment over the twelve years
1928–39 at 14,500,000,000 francs (1959 value), of which 12,000,000,000
were spent by the Niger Office proper and 2,400,000 on roads and
administrative buildings.[151] Under these circumstances it is no
exaggeration to speak of failure, and the causes should be examined.
The first, it seems, lay in the fact that the investment was made by
a consortium of banks and public works firms which profited from
the deal: the 450,000,000 francs spent were certainly not totally lost.
All the resources were devoted to the civil engineering side of the
enterprise, and little or nothing to agronomic and social studies, the
results of which would have determined exactly what work should
be undertaken. An American specialist was given the task of choosing suitable kinds of cotton; the American and Egyptian varieties
were mediocre in quality and yield. Beginning his work in 1922, he
had 'almost' finished by 1940. No study of soils, their reaction to
irrigation and methods for their cultivation had been seriously
undertaken. Only practical experience revealed that irrigation,
after producing less than average yields, eventually sterilised the
soil by washing it out.

The work of preparation and cultivation was carried out largely
with the aid of requisitioned labour, with all its shortcomings. The
colonisation villages, mentioned above, were like concentration
camps, with obligatory labour from 6 a.m. until sunset, restriction
of movement and semi-military discipline. Although this arrangement caused an increase in stagnant water and the curse of malaria,
no health measures were taken by the Niger Office before the war.[152]
When such efforts were made, the costs were charged to the territory:
in 1951, the region administered by the Niger Office absorbed 10
per cent expenditure on social amenities and education in the
Sudan.[153] Finally, the running costs were absorbed in large part by
the enormous administrative staff conceived on a scale of a million
hectares as envisaged in the project, crowded with retired soldiers,
recruited from the lower ranks – less for their knowledge of tropical
agronomy than their 'ability to command', or, in the higher ranks,
for connections that provided them with sinecures.

The Crisis

The world economic crisis, beginning in the United States in 1929,
reached Africa in the middle of 1930. In fact, the first symptoms
were felt in 1927 with the depression following stabilisation of the
franc, and in 1929 with over-production of timber. On the whole,

French tropical Africa 'resisted' the crisis in 1929 and during the first few months of 1930.[154] But the drop in share prices accelerated in the second half of 1930.

> In 1929 the intensification of production still led to an increase in the total value of exports in spite of the quite noticeable drop in the prices of local products. In 1930 this trend was reversed: production was still growing, and greatly so, but the drop in prices led to a cut in the total value of exports. For the first time since the end of the war the statistics for the current year [1930] show a halt even in the growth of exports.[155]

Bankruptcies multiplied, and on 26 July, 1931, the Banque franaçise de l'Afrique suspended payments, followed soon by the Banque commerciale africaine. While world prices fell in general by 50–60 per cent the prices of the principal African export products dropped by as much as 60–70 per cent.[156] The African peoples bore the full weight of the crisis. Prices of imported commodities dropped by far less than did those of export goods, and African purchasing power, already reduced to a minimum, was curtailed even further. The consequences of this will be seen below.

The drop in business and dealing [157] severely affected budget revenue – especially that deriving from customs dues. From 1930 to 1931, customs receipts in French West Africa dropped by 47 per cent. Most affected was the general budget of the Federation; the budgets of the individual colonies remained more stable, as poll-tax, untouched by economic fluctuations, provided the essential revenue. The crisis, with its fiscal consequences and the withdrawal of colonial capital, required state aid to maintain the level of profits; this led to state intervention in economic affairs.

> . . . It is a policy of support: customs dues, a quota system, premiums, compensation funds. Between 1931 and 1941 more than fifty bills and regulations were adopted, measures mostly of an empirical nature, answering the needs of the moment, for a given territory or a given product. Compensation funds for rubber, coffee and bananas, fed by a special tax levied on the products as they entered France, made it possible for subsidies to be given to exporters through the difference between the average rate of the products and their cost price.[158]

Two laws dated 21 March, 1931, organised the 'protection' of rubber, coffee, sisal and cassava;[159] a law of 7 January, 1932, applied to bananas, and one of 28 April, 1932, to pineapples. The refundable subsidies to the exporter colonies given from various compensation funds were payable only if the goods were transported on French vessels.

A law passed on 6 August, 1933, modified the customs tariff applicable to foreign oil-bearing plants, thus assuring a privileged outlet for the produce of Black Africa, a measure reinforced by a decree of 12 January, 1934, setting quotas for grains and oil-bearing fruit, as well as for palm oil and palm kernel.[160]

The 1933 law imposed a special import tariff for foreign oil-bearing plants, of 80 francs per ton of groundnuts in shells and 110 francs per ton shelled; these figures were raised in 1935 to 163 and 234 francs respectively. The revenue from this import was partly returned to the colonial budgets – up to a maximum level of three-quarters – for production development, or, in other words, to maintain prices: abolition of export charges, tax abatement, reduction of transport costs, subventions to the indigenous provident societies, etc. These measures alone raised the price of groundnuts by 45 per cent. The 1934 decree gave mandatory preference to the purchase of oil-bearing products from the empire. Other overlapping decrees[161] made similar provision for colonial products on the French market.

Cotton from French Equatorial Africa benefited from subsidies: the export companies received a premium of 3.50 francs for each kilo exported.[162] Their payment was assured by special loans contracted by French Equatorial Africa (20,000,000 francs in 1931 and 11,000,000 in 1933), and they also benefited from long-term state loans. State intervention extended to the establishment and development of processing services[163] for products, where control and management were left largely to the chambers of commerce, or in other words, to the exporters. There had been controls over exports in the past. But this was just what the trading firms did not want. Control of the quality of produce or the time of sale by the producer enabled the firms to buy less expensively by claiming that the produce should have a lower classification. The staff in charge of processing services often lacked any special competence, having been recruited for the buying season only; they fleeced the peasants, basing their 'classification' on bribes. At the same time, the big firms were skilful at 'diluting' allegedly better quality with inferior quality, and still exporting at a high price. Intervention increased with the development of the indigenous provident societies and their role, which we have discussed above.

Parallel with these defensive measures, efforts were made (as for example immediately after the First World War) to give a new direction to imperial economic activity, which had become seriously run down, towards the protected colonial markets. The international colonial exhibition, held in the Bois de Vincennes, Paris, in 1931, was to contribute towards this by way of publicity.[164] The minister for the colonies, André Maginot, taking measures to combat the crisis, revived the Sarraut Plan and caused the passing of the laws of 22 February and 10 July, 1931. They covered a programme of major works in each territory, and authorised their execution by state guaranteed loans. French Equatorial Africa, with its limited resources and population, was the main beneficiary from these loans which consisted of 1,120,000,000 francs in 1931 and 60,000,000 in 1939. French West Africa received 1,670,000,000 in 1931 and 60,000,000 in 1932; the Cameroons 49,300,000 in 1931–4 and Togo 79,000,000.

The concrete results of these provisions were small, due partly to the fall in the value of money at the end of the pre-war period, and partly to the use to which the borrowed funds were put, as we have seen in the case of the Niger office.[165]

ECONOMIC RECOVERY AND THE SITUATION ON THE EVE OF THE SECOND WORLD WAR

An improvement in production and exports began to be felt from 1934 onwards. The slackening of production, most marked in 1931 and 1932, as a consequence of the drop in prices, never had such deep repercussions as the recession in prices. The latter, however, was only relative in the case of products like timber, which was the main export of French Equatorial Africa and was furnished exclusively by European forestry concerns. Sold at 35 to 50 francs per ton in 1913, timber had jumped to 800 francs in 1929, and in 1933 it was still sold at 500 to 550 francs per ton, which in real terms was twice the pre-war price, and this despite the crisis.[166] The volume of exports (employing constant prices) had only dropped by one-third when it reached its lowest point in 1932 as against the maximum figure attained in 1930;[167] this represented 14 per cent of the 1925 level for all the territories of French Black Africa, excluding Madagascar. The record level of 1930 was equalled in 1934, and in 1937 it was surpassed by more than 70 per cent.[168]

Thus not only did the drop remain limited to one or two years, but the crisis finally ended in a remarkable growth of exports.[169]

We shall not return here to the way that production of each commodity evolved, as details of this were given above. But it is worth recalling that the 1930 record level of more than 500,000 tons for groundnuts, an essential product, was equalled in 1934, rising to 722,600 tons in 1937.

The results of new production were also remarkable, particularly in bananas and coffee; banana exports rose from 6,000 tons in 1929 to 42,900 tons in 1935 and 91,000 tons in 1938; those of coffee from 470 tons in 1929 to 7,600 tons in 1935 and 21,000 tons by 1938.[170]

Those who benefited most from this 'upswing' were the French industrialists, with their protected market in which their products continued to command high prices; the trading concerns, which benefited from subsidies, tax and customs exemptions and preferential freight tariffs;[171] and finally the settlers, particularly those on the Ivory Coast, which attracted large numbers of forest exploiters and coffee planters in 1903–4, encouraged by Governor Reste. Despite the growth in production, the peasant masses, with their limited purchasing power, did not benefit from the recovery until later, in 1936 and 1937. The increased production resulted not from fresh capital investment but essentially from a stepping-up in the degree of exploitation of the native population.

The share issues of French companies with headquarters in French West and French Equatorial Africa did not rise, but steadily dropped to 2,300,000 gold francs in 1936 (as against 9,900,000 in 1931, 8,130,000 in 1929 and 6,100,000 in 1925) and after a brief rise in 1937 to 27,300,000, they fell to almost nothing in 1938 and 1939.[172] French West and French Equatorial Africa accounted for 22·8 per cent of the issues of colonial companies in the period 1927–31; this percentage (of a considerably reduced total) had fallen to 7·8 per cent by 1936. It cannot even be said that state investment took the place of private investment; the total of state loans was out of proportion to the actual results in capital equipment installed. The 'imperial withdrawal' after the crisis was manifested by increased exploitation and redoubled emphasis on the colonial features of the economy in the countries of Black Africa. The Imperial Economic Conference of 1935 confirmed the end of freedom of external trade, and virtually prohibited the colonies from processing their raw materials, which would have been a first step in industrialisation. The customs system introduced before 1914, the complexity of which we have already noted, was modified only in certain details. The Convention of Saint-Germain-en-Laye (10 September, 1919) had renewed the Acts of Berlin (1885) and of Brussels (1890), dealing with freedom of commerce in the Conventional Congo Basin (*le bassin conventionnel du Congo*); it was endorsed by the United States, Japan and Italy, as well as the signatory powers of the preceding Acts, with the exception of Germany. The revision of these Acts was concerned mainly with spirits.

Local manufacture of alcoholic drinks, as well as the import of drinks containing 'harmful substances' (absinthe and commercial alcohol), was forbidden in tropical Africa. This directly affected Germany, the main exporter of alcohol before the war. Spirits were taxed at a minimum rate of 800 francs per 100 litres of pure alcohol. In French West Africa the tax was fixed at an even higher rate; in French Equatorial Africa there was a total ban on alcohol imports. In spite of these measures, the import of alcohol, reduced as it was compared with pre-war times, doubled between 1923 and 1928, mainly in wines and apéritifs.

The Customs law of 13 April, 1928, did not bring any great changes. It brought help chiefly to Gabon, until then 'assimilated' to France, which meant the application of French tariffs to imports, a system against which the European merchants had constantly protested. It concerned merely territories not covered by international agreements (the 'free' zone of French West Africa and Gabon). A 5 per cent *ad valorem* entry charge was made, to which a 7 per cent surtax was added for merchandise of foreign origin, or specific dues for certain products (fabrics, tobacco and, of course, spirits). By virtue of international agreements, the Congo basin, the Cameroons and Togo remained subject to an 'open-door' system, with equal treatment for all imported merchandise; but subsidies, quotas, and exchange control gradually made the system meaningless. In October 1936 the French government denounced Article 9 of the Franco-British Convention of the Niger (1898), which compelled equality of treatment for British and French merchandise on the Ivory Coast and in Dahomey. Tariffs were levelled in the whole of French West Africa (the previous *ad valorem* fiscal dues of 5 per cent in the ex-'free-zone' and 10 per cent in the ex-'conventional zone' were stipulated at a uniform level of 7 per cent).

Foreign Trade of the Countries of Black Africa with the Franc Zone[174]

(in percentage of total exports and imports of the countries under consideration)

	1932		1938	
	Export	Import	Export	Import
French West Africa	66	44·5	82	69
French Equatorial Africa	59	52·5	72	37*
Cameroons	39·6	34·4	56·4	30
Togo	54·2	18·4	67·5	20

* The exceptional percentage of imports in 1938 was due to the completion of work on the Congo–Ocean railway line.

The dependence of the colonial territories on France was reinforced by 'imperial preference'. An artificial price system was created which was alleged to 'favour' the colonies, by providing outlets for export goods at prices above world rates; but it was mainly the parasitic trading firms that profited from this. The mutual trade of France and the colonies grew appreciably in terms both of percentage and absolute value.[173]

It can reasonably be concluded that

all these measures of imperial preference confined the territories to a secondary role as economic satellites of France; this in turn led to the brutal and harmful effects of the suppression of these ties during the Second World War.[175]

In other words, the dependent, colonial character of the economy in the countries of Black Africa was further accentuated – the economy being more than ever oriented towards satisfying France's needs, and more than ever deprived of any possibility of functioning independently. Even before the war broke out, the 'minor crisis' of 1937–8 was enough to put an end to the fleeting prosperity enjoyed in 1936 and 1937. The big companies and settler communities did not fail to blame this on the Popular Front, which had introduced trade unions and social legislation into French West Africa in 1937.

They demanded new measures of 'support' and, when they were refused privileged conditions for their commodities on the French market,[176] followed the example of the Algerian colons by threatening a 'southern' secession.

REFERENCES

1. See vol. I, pp. 70–1 (1st ed.) and pp. 78–9 (2nd ed.).
2. Seeds: 35,000 tons; local consumption: 50,000 tons; losses: 100,000 tons (Auguste Chevalier, 'La culture de l'arachide au Senegal', *Bulletin des matières grasses*, 1931, No. 7, pp. 199–210).
3. On the rotation see R. Portères, 'L'assolement dans les terres arachides du Sénégal', *Revue intern. de Botanique appliquée et d'Agricole tropicale*, January–February 1950, No. 327–8, pp. 44–50.
4. On tools, see J. Suret-Canale, 'Quelques aspects de la géographie agraire au Sénégal', *C.O.M.*, Oct.–Dec. 1948, pp. 348–67 and mainly Auguste Chevalier, 'Monographie de l'arachide au Sénégal', *Revue internationale de Botanique appliquée et d'Agriculture coloniale*, 1936, chapter III, pp. 674–872.
5. Sometimes written '*hilaire*'.
6. Auguste Chevalier, *Monographie de l'arachide*, op. cit., p. 676.
7. Maunoury, 'La culture mécanique des arachides au Sénégal', *Revue internationale de Botanique appliquée et d'Agriculture coloniale*, 1923, pp. 533–54, and 1925, pp. 879–81.
8. Cf. P. Pélissier, 'Les paysans Sérères, *C.O.M.*, 1953, pp. 106–27.

9. The commercial management imposed on the station restricted the possibilities of studying it. The results obtained – mainly after 1930 – were valid for Baol where the station is situated, but not necessarily for regions with different soils and climates (Auguste Chevalier, op. cit.).

10. Respectively 500 and 200 tons per year, on the average.

11. E. Baillaud, *L'Organisation économique de l'Afrique occidentale française*. Marseille, Institut colonial, 1936.

12. The export figures which follow are to be understood in tons of cotton-fibre.

13. Speech by Governor-General Reste to the council of administration of French Equatorial Africa, *L'Afrique française*, 1937, No. 3, pp. 131–40.

14. J. Cabot, *Le Bassin du Moyen Logone*, Paris, ORSTOM, 1965, p. 200.

15. Export 1913: cacao: 150 tons; bananas: 30 tons; green coffee: 10 tons.

16. In the same way, he had wanted to introduce in 1909 the cultivation of maize. 'A big effort of cultivation of the soil was demanded of the people. The endeavour proved a failure, the seeds lost their germinative ability. The result was discontent which, among certain tribes, went as far as rebellion.' (Gaston Joseph, *La Côte d'Ivoire*. Paris, Arthème Fayard, 1914.)

17. Henri Labouret, *Paysans d'Afrique occidentale*. Paris, Gallimard, 1941.

18. Henri Labouret, *Le Cameroun* Paris, Hartmann, 1937.

19. Exports 1929: 8,000 tons.

20. Average over the five years 1925–9: 23,500 tons.

21. On the Ivory Coast: 166 tons in 1926, 405 tons in 1929.

22. J. Richard-Molard, *Afrique occidentale française*. Paris, Berger-Levrault, 1948, p. 209.

23. Two-thirds were supplied by Europeans.

24. Percentage in value of exports in French West Africa represented by coffee: 1930: 0·3%; 1934: 2·3%; 1937: 3·4%; 1938: 5·5%; 1949: 13·8% (in 1949 it held second place in value, after groundnuts).

25. Cf. V. Champion, *Le Bananier*. Paris, Maisonneuve et Larose, 1963, pp. 213–14. In French imports Guinea and the Antilles gradually replaced the Canary Isles, which ceased to supply any appreciable quotas after 1936.

26. J. Richard-Molard, op. cit., p. 213. 120 to 125 kg. of oil per hectare as against 1,500 to 2,000 in a plantation kept rationally.

27. Gide cites the example of a subdivision in French Equatorial Africa in 1926, where the population was taxed 10 tons of millet. As they did not possess this they had to go and purchase it at three days' march away at the price of 3 and 4 francs per 20 kg. cask, for which 1.50 francs, the market price, should be paid (André Gide, *Voyage au Congo*. Paris, Gallimard, 1927, p. 215).

28. Malinké word for the riding-whip of hippopotamus hide used by the circle guards and other agents of public power.

29. 'Afrique française', *Revue coloniale*, 1910, No. 10, p. 320.

30. Cf. Daigre, *Oubangui-Chari*. Issoudun, Dillen and Co., 1947, pp. 129 ff.

31. Cf. Eric de Dampierre, 'Coton noir, café blanc. Deux cultures du Haut-Oubangui à la veille de la loi-cadre', *Cahiers d'Etudes africaines*, No. 2, May 1960, pp. 128–47. The former Governor Bobichon, interested in the cotton business, gave support to this 'reconversion'.

32. Its property extended into the territory of Chad. Below, by way of comparison, are the capital and the profits of this company for the period 1936 to 1945.

	Capital (Francs)	Profits (Francs)
1936	11,000,000	316,000
1937	,,	4,922,000
1938	,,	6,218,000
1939	,,	4,626,000

1940	18,500,000	3,794,000
1941	,,	2,321,000
1942	,,	8,386,000
1943	,,	10,278,000
1944	,,	8,481,000
1945	,,	5,567,000

Quoted from J. Cabot, op. cit.

33. Cf. Jean Cabot, 'La Culture du coton au Tchad', *Annales de Géographie*, 1957, pp. 499–508.

'If one casts a glance at the agricultural calendar, one notes immediately the character of the abusive intruder who takes the cotton, having come last, in competition with the traditional food crops. The same cruel dilemma is posed every year: abandon for a time the care devoted to food plants or suffer the reproach of the "cotton-boy" and perhaps the agricultural guard, which never fails to attract the rage of the "commander" on to the district. This delicate problem was always posed at a season when the daily glance at the bottom of the granaries confirmed the doubtful certainty of a shortage of grain by the end of the agricultural year.' (J. Cabot, *Le Bassin du Moyen Lagone*, Paris, ORSTOM, 1965, p. 177.)

34. Marcel Homet, *Congo, terre de souffrances*. Paris, Ed. Montaigne, 1934, pp. 65–6.

35. At that same time, the cotton companies arranged to receive a state grant to 'support' cotton in French Equatorial Africa, at 3.50 francs per kilo. (Félicien Challaye, *Souvenirs sur la colonisation*. Paris, Picard, 1035.)

36. Cf. Marcel Homet, *Afrique noire, terre inquiète*. Paris, Péyronnet, 1939, pp. 202 ff.

37. Cited by P. Kalck, *Réalités oubanguiennes*. Paris, Berger-Levrault, 1959, p. 167.

38. Jean Cabot, op. cit.

39. Albert Londres, *Terre d'ébene*. Paris, Albin Michel, 1929, pp. 159 ff.

40. Robert Delavignette, *Les vrais Chefs de l'Empire*. Paris, Gallimard, 1939.

41. Robert Delavignette, *Les Paysans noirs*. Paris, Stock, 1931.

42. Ibid., 2nd ed., 1946, p. 24.

43. Italicisations in the text.

44. This socialist governor in 1947 paraphrased Pétain.

45. The price of groundnuts was fixed at 7 francs CFA per kilo for the 1947–8 season, and with the average yield per family being one ton these 'substantial profits' (supposing they remained in the hands of producer) represented 7,000 francs CFA for one year's agricultural work. This does not take into account what the *grand marabout* pocketed for himself.

46. The most complete work on the juridical aspects of the question remains that by Marcel Boyer, *Les Sociétés indigènes de prévoyance, de secours et de prêts mutuels agricoles en Afrique occidentale française*, Paris, Domat-Montchrestien, 1935.

47. R. Delavignette, *Les vrais Chefs de l'Empire*. Paris, Gallimard, 1939, p. 208.

48. Cf. *Revue Indigène*, No. 35, 30 March, 1909, p. 146.

49. *A.F.*, 1911, No. 2, p. 69.

50. Of the four Indigenous Provident Societies of Guinea, two disappeared in 1915, and not a single one remained by 1920.

51. Henri Cosnier, *L'Ouest africain français*. Paris, Larose, 1921, p. 240.

52. Henri Cosnier, op. cit., p. 241.

53. Report by the commander of the Baol circle, 23 April, 1932. Archives du Sénégal, dossier 'Semences', 1930–8.

54. On this subject see Louis Mérat, *Fictions . . . et réalités coloniales*. Paris, Sirey, 1947.

55. Ibid.

56. Letter of 14 March, 1932. Archives du Sénégal. Dossier 'Semences', 1930–8. The abuses stated by the commander of the Sine-Saloum circle were not much corrected. In 1934, the opposition journal *Le Périscope africain* noted: 'It has been shown, among others, that in the course of the trading season 1933–4, in the Sine-Saloum circle, the canton chiefs and certain employees of the Provident Society of that region have diverted more than a thousand tons of groundnuts to the loss of the said society; and, without taking into account all the exactions to which the cultivators were subjected during the course of recuperation and the distribution of seeds, the native received only 75 kilograms per hundred, at the moment of distribution, although he had to reimburse 150 kg. for 125, at a normal rate of interest fixed at 25 per cent and was, moreover, forced to give to the chief a little present in kind to thank him for his kindness.' (*Le Périscope africain*, 5 December, 1934.)

57. Archives du Sénégal. Dossier 'Semences'. 1930–8. A decree, nevertheless, made the reserve granaries a compulsory matter: it was hardly applied.

58. H. Labouret, *L'Afrique française*, 1925, No. 1, p. 47.

59. No. 434, A.E. of 10 July, 1939, A./s. Action des sociétes de Prévoyance au cours de la traite, 1938–9.

60. Statistical Handbook of French West Africa (1933–4).

61. Marcel Boyer, op. cit., p. 176.

62. Emile Baillaud, *L'Organisation économique de l'Afrique occidentale française*. Marseille, Institut colonial, 1936, pp. 61–3.

63. Archives de Faranah, D.I., Rapport 1935.

64. *Le Fonctionnement des Sociétés indigènes de Prévoyance de l'Afrique équatoriale française*. Brazzaville, Imprimerie officielle, 1950, pp. 19–20.

65. Ibid., p. 11.

66. Ibid.

67. Ministerial despatch, circular of 22 October, 1947.

68. 1936: 75,900 seasonal workers, of whom 64,119 were foreigners to the colony of Senegal as against 59,000 in 1935 and 38,000 in 1934 (crisis year). (Archives du Sénégal. *Rapports du service de l'Agriculture*, 1936.) Sine-Saloum employed the main group of the labourers (53,500 seasonal workers); followed by Casamance (13,500), the pioneering company of Tambacounda (3,312), the companies of Baol (1,686) and Thiès (1,173), the majority of the workers in the last two companies came from Senegal. To these 70,000 seasonal workers from Senegal must be added some 10,000 others coming from (British) Gambia.

69. Ph. David, 'Fraternité d'hivernage (le contrat de navétanat)', *Présence africaine*, XXXI, April–May 1960, pp. 45–57.

70. Ph. David, loc. cit.

71. Archives du Sénégal. Rapports du service de l'Agriculture. 1936.

72. From '*M'bé bara guini*': I am looking for work in Malinke (Henri Labouret, *Paysans d'Afrique occidentale*. Paris, Gallimard, 1941).

73. H. Labouret, 'La main-d'oeuvre dans l'Ouest africain', *L'Afrique française*, 1930, No. 5, pp. 240–50.

74. R. Delavignette, *Les vrais Chefs de l'Empire*. Paris, Gallimard, 1939. The figures of 600,000 emigrants to the Gold Coast and 2,000,000 to Nigeria, given by Albert Londres in 1929 (op. cit., p. 126), were probably exaggerated, but the figures taken from an administration source which we present are probably, in an inverse manner, understated. Inquiries in progress indicate that three to four hundred thousand nationals of Niger, Upper Volta and Mali found employment in Ghana, making up 40 per cent of the labour force on plantations and 16 per cent of the number of traders (years 1953–55). Cf. Jean Rouch, 'Migrations au Ghana', *Journal de la Société des Africanistes*, XXVI, 1956, pp. 33–196.

75. Albert Londres, op. cit., p. 165.

76. Albert Londres, op. cit., p. 186.

77. Figures for 1929.

78. Raoul Monmarson, *L'Afrique noire et son destin*. Paris, Ed. Francex, 1950 (1937: *Soudan, Côte d'Ivoire et Guinée*, p. 91).

79. Ibid., p. 93.

80. R. Monmarson, *L'Afrique noire et son destin*, op. cit., p. 93. It concerns a Consortium of Sociétés de Travaux publics which was commissioned to construct the Sansanding canal.

81. Punishment consisted of stoppage of the reimbursable ration (a ration which, the reporter notes, never included any meat). Quoted by Pierre Herbart, *Le Chancre du Niger*. Paris, Gallimard, 1939, p. 106.

82. Pierre Herbart, op. cit., pp. 80–105.

83. Report of 28 April, 1927, to the Union coloniale française (*Dépêche coloniale* of 30 April, 1937). Taken from Gonidec et Kirsch, *Droit du travail des Territoires d'outre-mer*. Paris, Pichon et Durand-Auzias, 1958.

84. In 1950 an administrator declared: 'There is a shortage of a thousand workers in M'Bomou. If administrative pressure in favour of cotton growing were stopped, it would greatly improve recruitment.' Report of the debates at the Conference on Production and Investment held at Bangui between 11 and 16 December, 1950.

85. Decree of 26 November, 1926. *Journal officiel de l'Afrique équatoriale française*, 1927, p. 58.

86. G. Balandier, 'Les problèmes du travailleur africain au Gabon et au Congo', *Bulletin international des Sciences sociales*, Vol. VI, No. 3, 1954, pp. 504–13.

87. Félix Eboué, *La nouvelle politique indigène en Afrique equatoriale française*. Brazzaville, Imprimerie officielle, 1941.

88. Georges Bruel, *La France équatoriale africaine*. Paris, Larose, 1935.

89. Followers and servants of the Bamiléké chiefs.

90. Report on a tour of 25 October, 1944. Quoted by C. Tardits, *Les Bamiléké de l'Ouest-Cameroun*. Paris, Berger-Levrault, 1960, p. 67.

91. National Committee for Political and Social Studies. 'How to behave towards the Black peoples in African Territories?' (Session on 18 March, 1929, p. 47.)

92. G. Vieillard, 'Notes sur les Peuls du Fouta-Djalon', *Bull. I.F.A.N.*, 1940, No. 1, pp. 142–3.

93. After 1919, Germany, defeated and declared by the Allies to be 'unworthy' of holding colonies, replied by invoking testimony from the French themselves on their colonial methods (Reichskolonialministerium, *Deutsche und französische Eingeborenenbehandlung*. Berlin, Dietrich Reimer, 1919). A severe criticism of the French system can also be found in the work of the American writer Raymond Leslie Buell, *The Native Problem in Africa*. New York, Macmillan, 1928, vol. 2.

94. Apart from a decree of 1903 regulating labour contracts, there was nothing on this matter prior to 1920 except ordinances or circulars by the governors. First publications on this matter: decree of 4 May, 1922 (French Equatorial Africa), 4 August, 1922 (Cameroon), 22 December, 1922 (Togo) and 22 October, 1925 (French West Africa).

95. M. Besson, 'La législation ouvrière en Afrique occidentale française', *La Quinzaine coloniale*, 1929.

96. *Réglementation du travail indigène en l'Afrique occidentale française*. Porto-Novo, Imprimerie du gouvernement, 1929.

97. René Mercier, *Le Travail obligatoire dans les colonies africaines*. Vesoul, Imprimerie nouvelle, 1933 (Thèse de droit).

98. R. Millet, 'Le piège du B.I.T.', *Afrique française*, 1930, pp. 380–2.

99. R. Susset, *La Vérité sur le Cameroun et l'Afrique equatoriale française.* Paris, Ed. de la Nouvelle Revue critique, 1934.

100. J. B. Forgeron, *Le Protectorat en Afrique occidentale française et les chefs indigènes.* Bordeaux, Y. Cadoret, 1920.

101. A judgement pronounced on 3 November, 1934, by the Court of Appeal at Dakar acknowledged to the Collection of Customs the right of immatriculation in their name of lands over which they had held authority. The administration was wary of allowing its application.

102. Procedure introduced later by the Cameroons (1927 and 1932), Togo (1934), and French Equatorial Africa (1938).

103. Circular No. 515 S.E./4 of 7 December, 1935.

104. For the eight reformed companies that survived, the concession granted in 1899 for a thirty-year period expired in 1929. The end of the concessionary system was not officially proclaimed until 24 August, 1930.

105. Barthélémy Boganda, *Proposition de loi à l'Assemblée Nationale,* No. 1130. Session of 1951.

106. Circular No. 263 S.E./4 of 27 April, 1937.

107. Cf. J. Chabas, 'Le régime foncier coutumier en Afrique occidentale française', *Annales africaines,* 1957, pp. 53–78, and 'La réforme foncière et le régime des concessions en A.O.F.', *Annales africaines,* 1958, pp. 37–52.

108. Draft law that was aimed at guaranteeing and codifying the African land ownership . . . submitted by a group of Communists to the National Assembly. No. 356, 1951 session. *Exposé des motifs,* p. 8.

109. Ibid., p. 9.

110. Ibid., p. 10.

111. Zone lying between the coast and a line from Cocobeach, M'Foua, N'Djolé, Sindara, Pointe Ste. Catherine.

112. *Bulletin du gouvernement général de l'Afrique equatoriale française,* 15 October, 1949.

113. *Le Démocrate,* Number of 23 November, 1950.

114. Barthélémy Boganda, op. cit.

115. *Proceedings of the Parliamentary Inquiry Commission on the events on the Ivory Coast.*

116. Cf. Claude Faure, *Histoire de la presqu'île du Cap Vert et des origines de Dakar.* Paris, Larose, 1914. No trace has been found of a treaty which was signed by Boufflers with the Damel in 1787 and which the government consequently invoked. The treaties of 1826 and 1830 with Cap Vert made no reference to this.

117. On this affair, see Petition of the Lebon Community to the governor-general dated 13 September, 1944. E. Rau, 'La question des terrains de Tound', *Annales africaines,* 1956, pp. 141–63, and Sylla Assane, 'Vérités sur Dakar', *Présence africaine,* XXIII, Dec. 1958–Jan. 1959, p. 81–7.

118. H. Labouret, *Le Cameroun.* Paris, Hartmann, 1937.

119. Coffee plantations: 12,000 hectares; hevea: 6,500; banana plantations: 6,000; palm groves: 4,000; various: 5,000.

120. The village of blacksmiths of Dianforodou, at the foot of the Simandou range (Republic of Guinea), made the last tapping from local ore in 1960, reserved solely to the production of guinzées, local iron money used in the Toma country. See facts concerning Northern Togo in R. Cornevin, *Les Bassari du Nord-Togo.* Paris, Berger-Levrault, 1962.

121. It did not go into liquidation until 1955.

122. H. Labouret, 'L'Afrique occidentale française en 1934', *Afrique française,* 1935, No. 1, p. 45.

123. Jacques Richard-Molard, *Afrique occidentale française.* Paris, Berger-Levrault, 1952, p. 200. Richard-Molard's appreciation of the war period is a little

too absolute: there were, during that time, attempts to restart gold-washing under administrative control, notably on the Ivory Coast. Production 1954 was 61 kg.

124. Diamond production in French West Africa: 1936, 5,495 carat ; 1937, 52,934 carats; 1038, 62,905 caarts; 1939, 56,300 carats.

125. Société guinéenne de recherches et d'exploitation minière.

126. The Kaloum iron seems to have interested the Americans and an 'elegant' solution was thought to have been found to make them construct the port of Conakry. . . . In the years preceding the war the Germans seem, in their turn, to have been interested and there were worries on account of the strategic position of the peninsula. None of these projects, however vague, was followed up.

127. L'Afrique française, 1925, No. 1, p. 51.

128. L'Afrique française, 1927, No. 1, p. 34.

129. Cf. 'Le cuivre en Afrique équatoriale française', Marchés coloniaux, No. 257, 14 October, 1950, p. 2458.

130. Equatoriale des Mines by the Union minière et financière coloniale (itself probably an emanation of the Banque de l'Indochine), Compagnie minière du Congo français by the Banque de l'Union parisienne.

131. Albert Sarraut, La Mise en valeur des colonies françaises. Paris, Payot, 1923, p. 27.

132. Albert Sarraut, op. cit., p. 51.

133. Albert Sarraut, op. cit., p. 30.

134. Maurice Besson, 'Le crédit colonial', L'Afrique française, 1920, No. 9–10, pp. 285–6.

135. L'Afrique française, Revue coloniale, 1920, No. 6, and L'Afrique française, 1921, No. 3 (Report of Governor-General Merlin to the council of government of French West Africa, December 1920).

136. L'Afrique française, 1921, No. 3, p. 233.

137. Albert Sarraut, op. cit., foreword, p. 21.

138. They were the colonies that made up French West Africa.

139. Albert Londres, Terre d'ébène. Paris, Albin Michel, 1923, p. 124.

140. Share issues by French companies with offices in French West or French Equatorial Africa 1925: 6,100,000 gold francs; 1929: 81,300,000 gold francs.

141. The pitiful results obtained in his concession at Diré were seen above.

142. Mainly the Banque de Paris et des Pays-Bas.

143. The Niger committee was initially presided over by de Monzie, assisted by Governor-General Angoulvant and General Archinard, as vice-presidents. The secretary-general was General Hélo, and the treasury was headed by William Guynet (Afrique française, 1921, No. 3).

144. Jean Vidailhet, Le Transsaharien. Paris, Larose, 1934, p. 11. See also A. J. Schaller, Le Chemin de fer transsaharien. Paris-Strasbourg, Istra, 1932.

145. Quoted by P. Herbart, Le Chancre du Niger. Paris, Gallimard, 1939, pp. 82–3.

146. In 1940 Bélime, having completely changed opinions, opened his report on 'Les Travaux du Niger' (Publications du gouvernement-générale de l'Afrique occidentale française, 1940), with a sombre picture of the famine in 1913–14 in the Sudan, the spectre of which would definitely be removed by irrigation works.

147. Opening speech to the session of the Council of Government, 2 December, 1926, L'Afrique française, Revue coloniale, 1927, No. 1, p. 23.

148. P. Herbart, op. cit., p. 69.

149. Dated 5 January, 1932.

150. E. Bélime, Les Travaux du Niger. Gouvernement général de l'Afrique occidentale française, 1940. For the post-war period see G. Gayet, Les Villages de colonisation de l'Office du Niger, V° C.I.A.O., Abidjan, 1953, pp. 126–30.

151. Samir Amin, *Trois expériences africaines de développement: le Mali, la Guinée et la Ghana.* Paris, P.U.F., 1965. In 1956 the total balance of investments made was counted at 20,000,000,000 francs CFA.

152. P. Herbart, op. cit., refers in this respect to a report dated 7 August, 1937, by Colonel Sicé (medical officer).

153. M. Capet, *Traité d'économie tropicale.* Paris, Pichon et Durand-Auzias, 1958, p. 95.

154. Michel Carsow, *Quelques aspects du commerce impérial de la France.* Paris, Geuthner, 1935, vol. I.

155. Jules Brévié, Opening Speech to the Council of Government of French West Africa, session of December 1930. *Afrique française, Revue coloniale,* 1931, No. 1, pp. 27–8.

156. From 1929 to 1933 the drop in prices was registered as: 58% for groundnuts, 59% for cotton, 66% for skins, 67% for cattle, 73% for gum. ('Le redressement économique de l'Afrique occidentale française', Supplement to *La Presse coloniale,* of 30 October, 1935.)

157. The minimum of fiduciary circulation in French West Africa fell from 174,000,000 in 1926 to 43,000,000 in 1932.

158. H. Durand, *Essai sur la conjoncture de l'Afrique noire.* Paris, Dalloz, 1957.

159. Premium of 1.50 francs per kilo for rubber, 1.40 francs per kilo for coffee, 800 francs per ton for sisal, 100 francs per ton for cassava.

160. H. Durand, op. cit., p. 53. Note that during the 1933–4 harvest, the decree having been put into practice *after* the sale, only the trading companies gained profit from it, not the producers.

161. The granting of quotas coming from abroad (import licences) was subordinated to the preferential or simultaneous purchase (hence the expression *jumelage,* overlapping) of equivalent or higher quotas coming from the colonies.

162. E. du Vivier du Streel, *L'Afrique équatoriale française et la crise.* Bruxelles, 1933.

163. In French West Africa the principles of their organisation had been posed since 1924.

164. Initially planned for 1927 and prepared for from the end of the exhibition in Marseilles, it was delayed and finally fixed for 1931. All the colonial powers participated, including Denmark (Greenland) and the United States (Puerto Rico and the Philippines), with the exception, however, of Great Britain and the Commonwealth, which had organised, a little time before, a separate exhibition in London.

165. Announcing the non-existence of medical equipment in French Equatorial Africa (a single radiographic apparatus, out of use, at Brazzaville; no medicine or transport for its conveyance), the settler-journalist Homet wrote: 'In 1931 Parliament voted and the Government-General invested progressively until 1938 a sum of 75,000,000 francs, exclusively earmarked for the health services in French Equatorial Africa. One asks out of curiosity what has become of these millions.' (Marcel Homet, *Afrique noire, terre inquiète.* Paris, Peyronnet, 1939, p. 218.) We shall see below how they were used.

166. E. du Vivier de Streel, *L'Afrique équatoriale et la crise.* (Rapport à l'institut colonial international, XXIIth session, Lisbon, 18–20 April, 1933.)

167. It was the minimum calculated for the whole (valid for French West Africa and French Equatorial Africa); in Togo, the minimum was reached in 1933, in the Cameroons in 1934. The general maximum for 1930 expressed the real situation for French Equatorial Africa, the Cameroons and Togo. In French West Africa, the maximum was attained in 1929.

168. H. Durand, op. cit., Indices: 1925, 100; 1930, 129; 1934, 128; 1937, 219.

169. H. Durand, op. cit., p. 32.

170. Ibid., pp. 52–3.

171. Tax reliefs reached up to 33 per cent for certain products of the Ivory Coast (*Le Redressement économique de l'Afrique occidentale française*, op. cit.).

172. According to H. Durand, op. cit.

173. Not always; the sum-total of French foreign trade had considerably decreased.

174. In practice with France, as the inter-colonial trade was negligible before 1939.

175. H. Durand, op. cit., p. 53.

176. '. . . Are they not aware that, if this continues, we, the true French, will take up our guns to defend ourselves . . .? How many times, from Dakar to the Congo, have I heard it said that the British dominions and Portuguese Brazil acted in the same way at the beginning.' (M. Homet, *Afrique noire, terre inquiète*. Paris, Peyronnet, 1939, p. 229.)

3. The Economic Balance Sheet

It is now time to draw up a balance sheet of this economic situation,
but the balance will not be a favourable one. The very limited funds
provided by capitalist investment were applied not to progress in
production or in technical fields, but essentially to the extraction of
high profits with no modification whatever of pre-colonial techniques – in other words, principally by intensifying the work
demanded of the population.

The result was a growing disequilibrium between the techniques –
consisting of the local populations' traditional ways of working,
mainly in agriculture – and the demands of production, which
called for an ever-increasing quantity for export, over and above
what was needed to ensure the people's subsistence.

(a) PAUPERISATION

It is claimed as an element of progress that these exports were
compensated for by corresponding imports, placing new products in
the hands of the Africans, and so raising their standard of living;
but this argument is illusory. Rather it should be said that increasing
imports of manufactured goods led to the decline and eventual ruin
of the traditional crafts of the smith and the weaver. While export
products were, in their entirety, the fruits of indigenous labour (the
'independent peasant' workers on plantations and forestry), the
imported products were destined only in part for the local indigenous
population. Part of the imported items provided facilities destined
not to improve the people's lot, but to perfect the manner of their
exploitation – building materials for shipyards and trading posts,
vehicles, and so on. Moreover, an important part of the consumer
goods were intended for the Europeans – officials and settlers –
whose purchasing power was out of proportion to their limited
number: this applies particularly to luxury articles. To appreciate
the importance of this point: in the absence of data prior to 1940,
we can cite those of 1951, given by Capet and Fabre, who estimated
the percentage of the gross national product applicable to the Europeans in French West Africa, at that time fewer than 50,000 as
against 17,000,000 Africans, at 15 per cent.[1]

As we have seen, the foreign trade of the tropical African countries
did not represent equal exchange: thus it was at the level of foreign
trade, and not that of production or the share-out of the alleged
national income, that the process of exploitation was chiefly concentrated. There was far greater instability in the prices of export
goods as compared to imports. All shortfalls had to be borne by the

producer, while rises in prices were largely absorbed by intermediaries.

After the end of the First World War the following variations
occurred in the general wholesale price index of staple colonial
products in the franc, allowing for an average variation of ±10
per cent:

	per cent
Rubber	35·5
Coffee	24·6
Palm kernels	17·7
Palm oil	17·7
Cacao	14·7

By contrast, the variation for rice was 9·7 per cent, and for
cement 3·9 per cent.[2] On the whole, the terms of trade developed
unfavourably, with marked depressions between the crisis and the
war, followed by upswings, which rarely regained the previous
purchasing power except for very brief periods. This was already the
case in French West Africa after the 1921 crisis. While between
1913 and 1922 the coefficient of price increases in cotton fabrics,
known as "Guinea cotton', was 5·7 and in other fabrics 5·0, those
in export commodities were only 1·6 for groundnuts, 1·8 for palm
kernels, and 2·2 for palm oil.

The natives' purchasing power has thus fallen heavily, to the
direct detriment of the consumption of imported fabrics.[3]

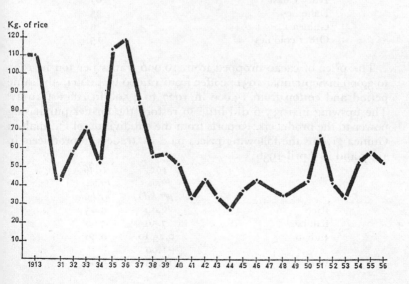

If we follow the evolution of prices in the so-called period of 'prosperity' and up to the crisis, the results will be similar. Between 1913 and 1927 the prices of groundnuts and fabrics moved respectively at coefficients of 7·5 and 9·4 – which is to say that purchasing power expressed in terms of fabrics came close to its 1913 level. But in October 1930, the coefficients dropped respectively to 3·4 and 7·6 and in the first half of 1931 to 2·6 and 7·0.[4] Native groundnuts show the same trend in relation to imported rice. The graph above, which expresses hundreds of kilos of groundnuts as against kilos of rice, reveals that the purchasing power of groundnuts dropped from 110 kilos in 1913 to 42·8 kilos in 1931. It did not exceed 100 except in the two years of recovery, 1935 and 1936, and never again regained that level.

The producers' losses naturally reached their peak in the crisis years. Governor-General Brévié gave the following as their losses for 1930, as compared with a figure of 400,000,000 francs for 1927, divided by products as follows:

	Millions of francs
Groundnut producers	285
Cacao producers	57
Palm-kernel and palm-oil producers	47

and by colonies:

Senegal	274
Ivory Coast	67
Dahomey	35
Guinea	9
Other colonies	15

The price of cacao dropped from 10,000 francs per ton in 1927 to 3,000 in September 1931; coffee from 12,000 to 4,000 in the same period and cotton from 13,000 in 1927 to 4,500 in August 1931.[5] The upswing in 1935–6 did little to restore the former purchasing power to the producers. Reports from the subdivision of Faranah in Guinea give us the following prices paid by traders to producers in 1927 and in April 1936:[6]

	1927 Francs per kilo	1936 Francs per kilo
Rice	2.00	0.65
Rubber	7.50	5.00
Indigo	0.75 to 1.00	0.50
Wax	12.50	5.00

The price of imported merchandise, by contrast, regained and even exceeded its earlier level. The 'minor crisis' of 1937-8 led to a new drop in prices, which was first apparent in October 1937, but affected only tropical produce. In the Cameroons, from October 1937 to July 1938, the drop in prices amounted to 27 per cent for palm kernels, 67 per cent for palm oil, 83 per cent for cacao: at the same time the price of rice rose by 43 per cent, that of salt by 93 per cent and of salted fish by 112 per cent.[7] Production, it is true, rose considerably, but the number of producers for the market grew simultaneously at the expense of the traditional subsistence economy. Progress in export production was also brought about – mainly in Senegal – at the expense of traditional food production, of which the shortfall was not made good by consumption of imported rice. It should be noted that, except in Senegal, the peasant continued as formerly to produce his own food, and imports supplied only manufactured goods.

The pre-colonial crop system, within the traditional social setting, provided a complete and permanent equilibrium between man and nature. Compelled thereafter, with means which were unchanged, to provide for his own subsistence and to furnish a surplus of export products as well, the peasant succeeded only in reducing this subsistence to a minimum, or even below: reserves kept back for traditional feasts or bad years disappeared. Every year there was famine. Malnutrition became a permanent feature. Any natural or economic catastrophe, such as a bad harvest or falling prices naturally resulted in famine, as in the Sudan in 1913–14. This malnutrition was accompanied by intensified exploitation of labour: there were greater areas to be cultivated, an increased demand by the administration for forced labour, and a shortage of manpower resulting from requisitioning and conscription.

On the eve of the Second World War, the peasants of French West Africa had to furnish each year, according to Governor-General Delavignette: 175,000,000 francs in poll-tax and cattle-tax, 21,000,000 days of statute labour and 12,000 soldiers.[8] This catalogue is not complete. To the taxes were added supplementary payments, 'customary' or otherwise, levied by the chiefs; debts paid to the provident societies (in Senegal loans of groundnut seeds were repayable with 25 per cent interest within *three months*; in fact, dishonesty often raised this to nearly 100 per cent, and annual quotas even higher); 'presents' to employees at processing plants; commodities 'requisitioned' for the entertainment of administrators, chiefs on tour and their hangers-on; sales of compulsory crops below cost price; and repayment at extortionate interest rates of seasonal debts – bad times forcing the impoverished peasants to pawn their loin-cloths, jewellery and so on, as pledges for loans at 50 per cent interest, for a minimum of three months. Days of statute labour represented only a fraction of forced labour, excluding extra labour for the chiefs and recruitment for big public works and private enterprise. This perhaps helps us to put in the right perspective claims that the undernourishment of the Africans was due to the vagaries of nature or to their own laziness and lack of foresight. In presenting his report on the state of nutrition among the peoples of French West Africa in 1949, Colonel Pales wrote:

> With the exception of a few small and scattered regions – the coastal lands (Lower Casamance, the Baga country etc.), the banks of the great rivers (fishermen on the Niger at Bozo and Somono) and a few areas in the savannah and the forest, true granaries of millet, rice or tuberiferous roots – it can be said that the people in the whole territory lack balanced nutrition;[9] and this is a *permanent state*.[10]

Naturally, as there were regions where conditions were above the average, in others such as Upper Volta and Fouta-Djalon relative over-population was added to conditions that were basically poor. The same author stated even more clearly:

> The harvest time is one of ease and fullness – in a very relative sense. It is followed by a period of deficiency as regards quality, and later by a period of shortage.
>   This unbalanced diet leads first to a state of mild sub-deficiency (in vitamins C, A, etc.), followed by quantitative and qualitative deficiency combined – this affects roughly 40 per cent of persons.[11]

H. Labouret writes of this period of 'shortage', which 'runs from the moment the old harvest is exhausted until new agricultural products become usable', as follows:[12]

> During this interval, the peasant cheats his hunger by consuming wild plants of little nutritive value, taken chiefly in their natural form or as soups or spinach.[13]

> The daily ration of a rural worker dropped from approximately 3,250 calories after the harvest to 750 and sometimes far below by July.[14]

> The daily ration of an adult might even go down to 208 calories per day, not during famines but simply at times of shortage. So great was the surprise of the personnel in charge of these calculations in France that they suspended their work, believing it an error on our part. There was no error.[15]

The urban workers, apart from the annual famine, suffered from monthly ones, or rather one every fortnight: the daily ration of 2,500 calories in October and November dropped to 1,500 in June and July, but went up, and then down again to 1,250 calories every other fortnight when wages were exhausted.[16] There was a particular shortage of the nitrogenous matter to be found in meat; and this could not always be made up by fish.

Consumption of meat was barely a kilo per inhabitant per year on the Lower Ivory Coast and in Lower Dahomey; it varied from 3 to 5 kilos over a large part of Senegal and the Sudan, from 5 to 8 kilos in Guinea, to over 20 kilos in Mauritania and the north of the Sudan.[17]

In French Equatorial Africa we find the same state of affairs. In Ubangi, Pierre Kalck noted that the average ration everywhere was below the 3,000 calories considered the minimum necessary for a man doing even light work. It was generally less than 2,000 and badly balanced, consisting almost entirely of cassava paste. Meat and fish, formerly eaten on a wide scale, became rare in the two generations following colonial penetration. 'The people of Ubangi were once great hunters, and fresh meat was abundant.'[18] Forced labour had compelled the people of Ubangi to abandon millet, which was rich in fats, for cassava, which required less care in its cultivation; compulsory cotton cultivation worsened this situation by preventing crop rotation. The shortage of salt (sold at 100 francs C.F.A. per kilo, or 5 francs per teaspoonful, though it cost 2 francs a kilo at Cap Vert) was greatly felt. These data, applying to the period after the Second World War, were equally valid for the preceding period.

For the Congo we can mention the following statement quoted in the general report on French Equatorial Africa presented to the Dschang conference, and extracted from a medical report on the Kouilou region:

The prisoners are remarkably healthy since they are the best fed of all the African population.[19]

In view of the 'average' state, one can well imagine what famines were like. In 1924–6 a famine occurred in Gabon which coincided with the forest 'rush' and the vicious recruitment operated on behalf of the forest exploiters. Food crops were abandoned in the coastal regions, all available manpower being used in the forests; in the interior, the requisitioning of food for the forest workings led to the same result. The 1931 famine in Niger and the neighbouring regions, as well as in Upper Volta, was caused by the destruction of the harvest by locusts: but it is clear that the economic crisis aggravated it.[20] One author writes of 'some 15,000 dead of hunger in Niger.'[21] Even at the end of 1933 the governor-general of French West Africa attributed the budget deficit in Upper Volta and Niger to the 'famine', and to 'deaths in the preceding period'.[22] Over a large part of French West Africa, famine and misery, the outcome of the crisis, made their effects felt between 1930 and 1936, in spite of an overall improvement in the economic situation after 1934. Investigations made in Senegal at the end of 1930 showed that in numerous cantons 'the situation appears as critical [in 1931] as in 1930'. To pay taxes, the natives are obliged to sell all their products and part of their cattle.[23] 'In the Diet-Salao canton, even by selling their harvest and their animals, they can only pay part of their dues to the administration. Moreover, they have to reimburse the advances granted by traders and money-lenders. . . .'[24]

In the Baol circle, in January 1931, millet was sold at 4.50 francs a kilo, and the people were in danger of having neither reserves nor resources for a period of three to four months. The Fulani had already sold everything.[25] In the Foss canton, one of the most deprived of the Louga circle, the administrator while on a tour in September 1934 noted that 'the Wolof cultivators have done no sowing, but have eaten the larger part of the groundnut seed crops'; taxes were in abeyance.[26] In the neighbouring Mérinaghen canton the same administrator noted that on 31 May, after officially selling part of the cattle, he did not recover more than one-third of the debts of the canton, where a year's taxes were owed, and in places even a year and a half's or two years'. In Fouta the cattle population decreased by between a quarter and a half, and a strong wave of emigration moved towards the neighbouring colonies, Portuguese Guinea and Sierra Leone. The population did not manage to pay the taxes. The canton chief's henchmen, the *batou-labé*, lived in garrisons, confiscating and selling off cheap all that could be sold, down to kitchen equipment and korans. Even children were pledged to raise ready money.[27] The situation did not improve until 1937.

(b) AFRICA, A DYING LAND

The system of cultivation was not modified, and the imbalance in living conditions spread to the exploitation of the soil. Under pre-colonial conditions a prolonged fallow period generally ensured recovery of the richness of the soil, which received no manure. The obligation to produce more without being able to use any supplementary acreage, and often over an area reduced by concessions to European settlers and classified forests,[28] led to a speeding-up in rotation, a decline in yields, and often the permanent ruin of the soil along with a reduction in pastoral land.

The effect on production did not make itself felt everywhere for, as we have seen, the market economy had not penetrated deeply except in limited zones, and there remained considerable possibilities of extending cultivation; thus, overall, production continued to grow. But certain regions (the first to be affected by groundnut speculation) such as Oualo and Cayor in Senegal were greatly affected.[29] From 1936, the advance of groundnuts in Senegal was due to the penetration of pioneers into the relatively fertile lands of Casamance, and the far less hospitable areas on the eastern and southern fringes of the Baol–Saloum region. The virgin lands were fertile, but the cultivator had to work far from home, the work of clearing the ground was hard and there was a scarcity of water, or rather of the equipment necessary for digging wells. These had to be dug to a depth of 40, 60, and even 80 metres. In a village of 200 people, with 200 oxen and 100 sheep teams working round the clock, could only draw less than one-third of the required water supply could be drawn.[30]

The general misery and the ruin of the soil were taboo subjects until the Second World War. After the war, the inability of the colonial countries to give the impetus necessary to raise essential production so that the local economies would benefit brought to the agenda what later became known as 'underdevelopment'. An answer to this question was given in 1947 in a book by Pierre Gourou, known in its English translation as *The Tropical World*.[31] In his book, which cites numerous examples and provides many new insights, Gourou advanced the view that the tropical countries of Africa are doomed to a retarded civilisation and a low level of life, owing to natural conditions unfavourable to human life and activity.

His thesis can be summarised as follows. The population of the tropical countries is numerically small and in bad physical condition; hence its productive capacity is limited. Its bad state is due to the unhealthiness of the tropical countries, where the climate is hot and damp, for at least part of the year, favouring the rapid multiplication of harmful micro-organisms. The large number of endemic diseases, especially malaria, lead to a high mortality rate, and open the way to other illnesses by lowering physical resistance. Add to this sleeping sickness, yellow fever, and parasitic and bacterial diseases. Natural resources are limited. The tropical soil, contrary to its acquired reputation, has a low fertility, and is quickly affected by erosion or desiccation. It is poor in useful chemical substances. Yields, even in intensive agriculture such as irrigated rice paddies, are greatly inferior to those common in the temperate zone. Traditional agriculture on burnt land devastates the soil, and European methods, like ploughing and continuous cultivation, lead to results

L

worse than the evil they claim to rectify – as, for example, accelerated soil erosion. Intensive stockbreeding, generally apart from agriculture, yields poor returns and leads to equal devastation. Ill-nourished by natural pastures of low quality and weakened by diseases such as sleeping sickness and parasitosis, the animals are inadequate as a source of food and almost useless for work. As to whether these unfavourable conditions can be overcome, the author is sceptical. Industrialisation cannot be considered urgent, as there is insufficient manpower even for agriculture, and the material resources are inferior, the forests are of little use, and there is no coal.

The introduction of modern agriculture, based on continuous cultivation with artificial fertilisers and the association of stock-breeding and agriculture at farm level, envisaged by well-known tropical agronomists like Auguste Chevalier, seem to him utopian.

> . . . To seek to improve [techniques of cultivation] in imitation of European techniques is perhaps a bait.[32]

Only in the ninth chapter does the author touch on the 'problems posed by European intervention', where 'damage involuntarily inflicted on nature and tropical humanity . . . damage directly due to the spirit of profit and violence' on the one hand, and 'the good effects' on the other, seem to cancel each other out. The conclusion is pessimistic:

> The improvement of living standards among the tropical peoples poses very great problems; it may raise many more than it actually solves. Ultimately, at the root of all these difficulties, shall we not find that the poverty of the tropical soils will not permit those who use them to reach the same standard of life as agricultural workers in the temperate zone?[33]

Gourou does not envisage agricultural progress except in plantations and irrigated rice paddies, which preserve the soil. The tropical countries will keep their vocation as providers of 'colonial commodities' to the temperate industrialised countries, which, in return, will provide them with manufactured goods.

Gourou's authority and the wealth of his documentation strongly influenced the geographers of the period.[34] His arguments are scarcely tenable today, and in later works he has considerably altered his position. Even at that period, however, a cursory examination could have shown the weakness of his argument.[35] In studying the characteristic features of tropical countries, Gourou examined only the natural geographical features – climate, the soil, etc. – and left economic and social factors, in other words the hard core of colonial enterprise, in the background. Starting from true facts, copious and often of great interest, the author compromised his position from the start by comparing what cannot be compared. Can one seriously compare the demography and hygiene of the peoples and the yields and results of agriculture in the present tropical countries *today* with the same characteristics of Europe *today*? Yet was the hygiene of European peoples in the Middle Ages, and even at the beginning of the eighteenth century, so different from that of the pre-colonial African peoples? Was their food richer and better balanced?

The results of tilling burnt land with the hoe in tropical countries invite comparison with *analogous* techniques in temperate countries. More than the yields of contemporary temperate agriculture, however, it would be relevant to consider those of medieval agriculture, before the agricultural revolution; but, in spite of the fact that mixed cultivation and the plough existed then, we cannot be certain that the yields of rye or buckwheat on the 'frozen lands' of western France were much higher than those of traditional tropical agriculture.

The tropical soils are fragile, more so than the arid lands in temperate countries. In the United States, the ravages of soil erosion are well known. The content of chemical elements is not of great importance, while bio-chemical processes play a decisive role in matters of fertility; the sandy soils of Senegal, which give good groundnut yields, would be completely sterile in Europe.

Finally, the failure of any attempt at modernisation of tropical agriculture is due, not to its intrinsic nature but to its economic and social setting. The automatic application of methods used in temperate climates, and only valid there, can only have catastrophic results. After the First World War, an attempt was made in West Africa to introduce tillage with the plough, and oxen were requisitioned for this purpose. The chiefs in charge of the operations kept the best for themselves, while the remaining animals did not take to breaking in or stabling, and soon died. The robust imported 'Brabant' ploughs sterilised the soil within a few years. For some years Governor Poiret in Guinea tried energetically to extend the use of the plough, and when he left the colony, the governor-general saluted him as 'father of the plough'. However, what he achieved has almost completely vanished. The use of tractors designed for Beauce or Picardy, produced similar results. Is ploughing by means of either animals or tractors therefore impossible in tropical countries? What is certain is that methods and materials have to be improved before it can be used. But no one – even including the official agricultural services – ever had the means of achieving such improvements, though in the 1950s and 1960s great progress in this respect was recorded. Technical improvements in agriculture are not limited to the methods and the hardware, but apply equally to the species of crops grown. Gourou discusses tropical fodder plants likely to play a role similar to trefoils, lucerne and root-crops in the European agricultural revolution of the eighteenth century. But, even in Europe itself, did the varieties that existed before that epoch play the same role as the tropical plants today? And have the improvements brought about during the last two centuries in crop species cultivated in Europe ever been calculated?

Last and most important of all, techniques cannot make progress unless the social and economic conditions are ready for them. In Europe it was the capitalist farmer and the big landowner, not the small traditional cultivator, who brought about the agricultural revolution. The advance of commerce and the beginning of modern industry provided a stimulus by enlarging the market. In tropical Africa, the native peasant does not have the means of improving his techniques, capitalists show no interest in investing capital in agriculture, and commercial exploitation enlarges yields with fewer risks. Leaving aside the flimsy arguments of opponents of industrialisation in Africa – although Africa is poor in coal it is rich in potential water-power, in uranium-bearing minerals and, no doubt, in oil, and even more in mineral raw materials. In this area it seems privileged by comparison with Europe. But natural resources, while they ease the process of industrialisation, are not indispensable for it. Here again economic and social factors are paramount. Japan and Italy, while short of fuel and power and raw materials, have nevertheless become great industrial powers.

Clearly this does not mean that in Africa either the transformation of agriculture to modern standards, or industrialisation, can easily be brought about. But the backwardness maintained and aggravated by the colonial system is the root cause of all these difficulties; it has nothing to do with nature. The thesis of Gourou ends – involuntarily no doubt – by exonerating, at nature's expense, the colonial system, which he reproaches only for a few abuses and 'blemishes'. This conclusion seems to justify the perpetuation of the system whereby the only vocation open to the colonial countries is to be that of being the supplier of 'colonial' goods.

REFERENCES

1. M. Capet and J. Fabre, 'L'économie de l'Afrique occidentale française depuis la guerre', *Annales africaines*, 1957, pp. 135–94. The *Comptes économiques de l'Afrique occidentale française 1956* (unpublished document) give 17·5% and 27%, if one only considers the money resources, excluding tribal consumption. For French Equatorial Africa (1958) the official data make it possible to evaluate the taxes corresponding to 20% and 35%. In Cameroon (1959) the part of the money revenue attributed to the European population was a quarter to one-third of this revenue (*Marchés tropicaux*, 21 November, 1959).

2. Josué de Castro, *Le Livre noir de la faim*. Paris, Editions Ouvrières, 1961, pp. 80–1.

3. *L'Afrique française*, 1923, p. 435.

	1913	1922
Average price of a metre of Guinea cotton	0,39	2,25
Average price of a kilo of other cloth	4,72	24,34
Average price of 100 kilos of groundnuts	33,00	52,60
Average price of 100 kilos of palm kernels	37,42	66,60
Average price of 100 kilos of palm oil	49,52	111,78

4. Price evolution:

	1927 (francs)	1930 (francs)	1st term 1931 (francs)
Tons of groundnuts	2,500	1,150	875
Kilos of cotton fabric (other than percale)	44,63	36,28	33,59

(Address by J. Brévié to the Council of Government of French West Africa, session December 1931, *L'Afrique française, Revue coloniale*, 1932, No. 1.)

5. Same source.

6. Faranah Archives. D.1. Rapports d'ensemble, 1921–38.

7. George R. Manue, *Cameroun, création française*. Paris, Sorlot, 1938.

8. Robert Delavignette, *Les vrais Chefs de l'Empire*. Paris, Gallimard, 1939.

9. Inter-African Conference on Food and Nutrition (Dschang, Cameroon, 3–9 October, 1949), Paris, *Documentation française*, 1950, p. 152.

10. Underlined in the text.

11. *Documentation française*, p. 152.

12. H. Labouret in 'Le Travail en Afrique noire', *Présence française*, Paris, 1952, pp. 125–6.

13. H. Labouret, ibid.

14. L. Pales, *L'Alimentation en Afrique occidentale française*. Dakar, O.R.A.N.A., 1955, p. 71.

15. L. Pales, *Le Bilan de la mission anthropologique de l'Afrique occidentale française*. Dakar, 1948, p. 22.

16. L. Pales, *L'Alimentation en Afrique occidentale française*. Dakar, O.R.A.N.A., 1955, p. 71.

17. *Encyclopédie coloniale et maritime: Afrique occidentale française*, vol. II, p. 28.

18. P. Kalck, *Réalités oubanguinnes*. Paris, Berger-Levrault, 1959, p. 131.

19. Inter-African Conference at Dschang, op. cit., p. 163.

20. H. Labouret in his pamphlet *Famine et disette aux colonies* (Paris, 1938) mentions it without explanation. The Report of the Cameroons to the Dschang Conference attributes it to locusts. The address of Governor-General Brévié to the December 1931 session of the council of government of French West Africa mentions in its general picture of the economic crisis 'the famine in Upper Volta and in certain areas of Niger'.

21. R. Monmarson, *L'Afrique noire et son destin*. Paris, Ed. Frances, 1950, p. 95.

22. Speech by Governor-General Brévié to the council of government, session of December 1933 (*L'Afrique française*, 1934, No. 1, pp. 19–27).

23. Senegal Archives. Dossier *Semences*.

24. Ibid.

25. Ibid. Discussions at Diourbel (January 1931).

26. Senegal Archives. 1 D 2/28. Report on the circles. 1933–4.

27. G. Vieillard, 'Notes sur les Peuls de Fouta-Djalon', *Bulletin de l'I.F.A.N.* 1, 1940.

28. Which represented, in the savannah country, not 'forests' in the proper sense of the term, but areas where cultivation was prohibited.

29. The impoverishment of the soils in those regions is not as evident as it might seem: in this field one must be sceptical of any simplifying explanations. The study of documents does not reveal in Cayor a lowering of yields, but a far greater irregularity. The abandonment of Cayor was far more an economic phenomenon, due to the lure and higher yields of Baol and Sine-Saloum, regions towards which the cultivators moved as soon as they became accessible by railway. The erosion of Ouala was more evident but it was probably in relation to modifications of the system and the course of the Senegal (cf. for Cayor, J. Suret-Canale, 'Quelques aspects de la géographie agraire au Sénégal', *Cahiers d'Outre-mer*, 1948, No. 4, pp. 348–67). On the other hand, there were the regions where the ruin of the soil is evident through the introduction of colonial crops and too intensive exploitation of means used. For cotton growing in Chad cf. J. Cabot 'Le problème des Koros'' *Annales de Géographie*, 1961, pp. 628–9, and *Les pays du Moyen-Logone*, Paris, ORSTOM, 1965, pp. 173–4.

30. Annual Report of the Agricultural Service in Senegal, 1938.

31. Longmans, Wiley.

32. Op. cit., p. 117.

33. Ibid., p. 181.

34. In particular J. Richard-Molard in his *Afrique occidentale française*.

35. Cf. J. Suret-Canale, 'L'exploitation coloniale est-elle une réalité géographique?' *La Pensée*, January–February 1948, No. 16, pp. 103–4.

CHAPTER II

POLITICAL AND ADMINISTRATIVE OPPRESSION

1. *Colonial Administration*

In the wake of the theories – direct administration, assimilation, or association – empiricism prevailed, and the organisation that came into being on the eve of the war was considered at the time a 'prelude to normal administration'.[1] This organisation, far from disappearing, became further crystallised and gradually took on institutional forms. By the eve of the Second World War it had come to be considered, apart from certain weaknesses in execution, as the best of possible forms, not solely for the colonies. Contributory factors should be seen in the decline of bourgeois democracy and the complacency then shown by leaders of the imperialist states towards fascism and its methods. Governor Delavignette spoke highly in favour of *commandement* as the administrative principle of the future and against the 'impersonal administration' used in Europe.[2] Hitler was to call it the *Führerprinzip*. Since we have already described the formation of the administrative system and its essential features, we do not need to describe it in detail, but to recapitulate briefly the principles and structures and describe their evolution.

(a) GOVERNORS AND ADMINISTRATORS

Sovereignty, as we saw, was entirely suspended in favour of the French state; the sovereign rights that had previously been acknowledged to the ancient African states in the persons of their chiefs and through innumerable treaties, were unilaterally annulled in French Equatorial Africa by the fundamental decrees of 1899, and in French West Africa by the decree of 23 October, 1904. Although the constitutional acts of the Third Republic had instituted a representative, parliamentary system, this sovereignty was not exercised by persons elected by the French people. Parliament only very rarely used its right to pass legislation for the colonies, which remained subject to government by a decree inherited from the Second Empire. In practice, the minister for the colonies, acting in the name of the head of state, held full powers over the territories under his jurisdiction in both the legislative and the executive spheres.

The territorial limits of the countries under study – their external frontiers and internal divisions – were finally fixed, save for a few details, after the end of the war. In question were the boundaries of the French mandated territories of the Cameroons and Togo (19 May, 1919) and the frontiers between Chad and the Anglo-Egyptian Sudan (Paris convention, 8 September, 1919). This area embraces French West Africa, with an area of 4,633,985 square km., and the colonies of Senegal, French Sudan, French Guinea, the Ivory Coast, Dahomey, Upper Volta, Niger and Mauritania;[3] also French Equatorial Africa with an area of 2,510,000 square km., and the colonies of Gabon, Middle Congo, Ubangi-Shari and Chad.[4] To this, finally, were added the mandated territories of the Cameroons and Togo, part of the former German colonies placed under French mandate (432,000 and 57,000 square km. respectively).

The two federations of colonies were administered by a governor-general; and the mandated territories came under a 'commissioner of the republic',[5] who in the Cameroons had the rank of governor-general and in Togo that of governor. In spite of differences in legal status between mandates and colonies, the administrative systems were practically identical in each. Both were ruled from the same offices in the rue Oudinot, seat of the ministry for the colonies. The high commissioner in the Cameroons had practically the same powers as a governor-general. As for Togo, on two occasions, in 1917–21 and then in 1936–46, it was simply attached to French West Africa.[6] Most of the institutions existing in the neighbouring colonies were speedily introduced in the mandates. The only differences from the systems of the neighbouring French colonies arose from international obligations implied in the mandate status: the 'open door' rule in matters of customs tariffs and foreign religious missions; the prohibition of military recruitment, with the exception of a militia whose task was to reinforce the local police force (thus the male population of the Cameroons and Togo avoided conscription); and the entirely formal duty of submitting an annual report on the administration of the territory to the League of Nations. The powers of the republic were vested in the governor-general, who represented, on the spot, the unconditional power of the government which nominated and recalled him. He alone was entitled to engage in correspondence with it. From above, his power was, no doubt, limited by that of the minister for the colonies, his superior in the hierarchy. On the spot, and from below, there was no limitation.

No law or decree emanating from Paris with special reference to the colonies could come into force until it had been promulgated by order of the governor-general, who was subject to no time limit in the exercise of this function. Clearly, discipline did come into play, and the minister had ways of putting pressure on his subordinates; he could recall one who was recalcitrant. But the game would have to be worth the candle, and the governor-general, if he knew how to manoeuvre, and enjoyed support in the right places, did not lack the means himself for counteracting his minister. In fact, the right of promulgation was often employed as a veto. For example, a certain decree on education, passed specially for French Equatorial Africa, was left suspended by successive governors-general over a period of eight years.[7]

The governor-general was assisted by a legal council (serving as an administrative tribunal) and a council of government (an administrative council in the Cameroons, Togo, and French Equatorial Africa after 1934); it comprised the secretary-general (who assisted and in case of need took the place of the governor-general), the military supreme commander, the attorney-general, the directors-general of the principal public services, the governors of the various colonies within the group, some representatives of commerce and the settlers and, in more recent times, a few well-known representatives of the indigenous population, at first nominated by a decree of the governor-general, later elected by limited suffrage. This council, which met no more than once a year over a period of a few days, and most of whose members were, in any case, leading officials directly dependent on the governor-general, merely played a consultative role. It gave opinions on questions where this procedure was required under law; in particular, concessions could be accorded only by decrees which it had passed. There was never any question of its opposing the governor-general. It could, at most, hold up certain schemes.

As supreme head of the administration, the governor-general nominated all employees. He decided on assignments of officials placed at his disposal by the minister for the colonies, and could freely return them without having to state his motives. He was supreme commander of the armed forces; he drew up the general estimates. He was a proconsul, indeed he was assisted by bureaux and by a series of *directions générales* (central offices) which, at the local level, played the part of ministries, but whose heads, the directors-general, were no more than commissioners, appointed and dismissed by him and solely responsible to him. The central office of finance was in charge of the general budget[8] and its supplements (in French West Africa, for example, the port of Dakar); the

L*

treasurer-general directed the treasury service. The central office of political, administrative and social affairs, the most important, played the role of a ministry of the interior. It controlled general administration and the police.[9] The central office of public works directed or controlled the principal technical services – ports, railways, roads, public buildings, mines. Its specialised services (the meteorological service, for example) developed with the passing of time. The central office of economic affairs dealt with general economic questions such as trade and prices, and directed specialised economic services: agriculture, stock-raising, waterways, forests, fisheries, etc. At a later stage central offices of education[10] and public health (developed from the health service for colonial troops) were added. Finally the attorney-general directed the legal services. With the growth of technical services and the growing speed of communications, centralising trends began to appear. Although under the administrative control of the governors, the local technical services were run more and more directly from the centre (in practice by the central offices). This was to cause endless conflict and guerrilla warfare within the bureaucracy.

The scheme we have just traced applied fully only to French West Africa. French Equatorial Africa, as we have seen, vacillated for a long time between a federal and a centralised system. A vast federal bureaucratic machine was imposed upon the services of the four colonies, which were already under-populated and poor in resources, and proved very expensive. Already, for reasons of economy, the governor-general acted in addition as governor of the Middle Congo.[11] During the crisis, in 1934, the local budgets were simply suppressed and the governors made agents of the governor-general, without financial resources and thus without initiative. The decree of 1 July, 1934, which resulted from the resignation of Governor-General Antonetti, made French Equatorial Africa into a separate colony, and the governor-general had under him a deputy-governor resident at Bangui (Ubangi-Shari), a chief administrator in Gabon, and a commander-cum-administrator in Chad. The budgetary saving was expected to be 15,000,000 francs.

Difficulties of communication soon made this system impracticable: a decree of 12 October, 1937, re-established the governors of Gabon and Ubangi-Shari, and after 1940 a 'permanent delegation of power' was granted to the governors by Governor-General Eboué. This re-established decentralisation, however, proved largely ineffective because of the colonies' lack of financial autonomy. This system survived until 1946 – not without its inconveniences, if one considers the size of French Equatorial Africa. 'To understand the need for decentralisation one has to live 1,000 to 2,000 km. from

Brazzaville, to be obliged to deal with all questions in writing through the local administrative offices, with a single letter-box which is not emptied every day, and to have waited weeks or months for the answer to come back. . . .' This was said by the president of the grand council of French Equatorial Africa in 1947.[12] In the Cameroons the problem did not arise, as the administration was unitary with a direct progression to the top.

The colonies themselves constituted the second echelon of colonial administration. At the head, the governor[13] was provided with very wide powers, although the supreme power and the relative proximity of the governor-general set more real limits to these than in the case of his superior in the hierarchy. He could issue ordinances in application of valid laws and regulations; the decree of 18 October, 1904, gave wide scope to his powers of command, and on certain matters he merely had to consult the administrative council, a body composed on the model of the council of government (secretary-general, certain heads of local services, two notables named by a decree of the governor-general).[14] His authority extended over the entire administration and services of the colony. The heads of specialised services and the circle commanders, who were in charge of territorial units of varying size and number per colony, were responsible to him. In French West Africa the territorial units were called 'circles' and there were about 100 of them. They comprised one or more *subdivisions*, each run by its own administrator, and of these there were more than 200. In French Equatorial Africa, until 1934, they were called *circonscriptions*; at that time there were forty-nine of them. For reasons of economy, they were later reduced to twenty and renamed *départements*. Administrative pressures soon forced reconsideration of this reduction, the number was increased once again, this time to thirty, when they became known as *régions*. Each *région* consisted of a number of circles, the equivalent to the *subdivisions* of French West Africa (they had originally been known as such); there were about 150 of them. In the Cameroons the territory was similarly divided into between fifteen and twenty *régions* and between sixty and seventy *subdivisions*. Togo, smaller in size, was split into ten circles of which only two comprised dependent *subdivisions* – making a total of thirteen *circonscriptions*.

Before 1914 the ideal of direct administration had been, as we saw, to establish a network of authority down to the level of villages or groups of villages, and to suppress all indigenous intermediaries. But wartime conditions, with the decreasing number of available officials, entailed the closure of numerous posts and *subdivisions*. The clerks and agents of native affairs (later clerks and agents of the civil service), lower-grade European officials in the general administration, were intended to have exclusively bureaucratic functions (the majority held posts as 'special agent' in charge of circle finances). At the beginning they were non-commissioned officers; a certain number of retired N.C.O.s were taken on after the 1914–18 war, but most were beginners without special qualifications. Shortage of personnel led to their being given administrative responsibilities, no longer as before as 'heads of post' but often as heads of *subdivisions*, attached to circle commanders, and even as commanders of provisional circles. Among the colonial administrators proper, beginners held posts as deputies to circle commanders, then as heads of *subdivisions*; the post of circle commander was reserved in principle to officers of higher rank. Staff were more and more concentrated in major towns. In 1912, there were 341 administrators in service in French West Africa; in 1937 there were 385, half of whom worked in the main towns. In French Equatorial Africa the total number of the general administration (administrators and civil servants) was reduced from 398 in 1913 to 366 (250 of whom were actually in the colony) in 1928. The growing complexity of administration, and the need to control the activities of the growing number of special service agents at circle and *subdivision* level, with more and more office-work demanded of the administrators, led them to improvise, settling on the spot matters for which their juridical and administrative training had not prepared them.

> The officials of technical rank, who no longer operate in the main towns, are given orders by officials whose superior powers they do not always recognise, and who are tempted to add their own, more or less enlightened, views to the transmission of directives from the main town.[15]

According to Governor-General Merlin's doctrine, the governor-general governs, which is to say he fixes the policies to be pursued – which should be done by Paris, but which the distant department cannot do with sufficient mastery of detail; the governor administers, which is even more the function of the circle commander who is at a lower executive level. But this theory, formulated by a governor-general, was not easily accepted in practice by governors or circle commanders. Isolation, slowness of communications, and ignorance on the part of the higher echelon of the real situation on the spot, gave them great latitude. The powers they enjoyed within their sphere would turn their heads, and they would pretend to be carrying out acts of government, while actually they applied their own policies. The functions of colonial 'command' rarely inspired modesty, and the governors and administrators came to write in their reports more and more '. . . my native policy supposes . . .', '. . . my native policy requires . . .', and the like.

Unfortunately this growing self-conceit was accompanied by a growing ignorance of local realities.

. . . The administrator could make no more than short and rapid tours: all his work was devoted to the levying of taxes, numerous questions raised by recruitment of soldiers, native justice (almost as formal as French justice) and current matters.[16]

Before the First World War, each circle in French West Africa possessed an official monograph giving an account of the territory, which was revised and kept up to date every five years. These monographs are of uneven standard, but many of them still provide an indispensable source of information, particularly on local history; they bear witness to their authors' profound knowledge of the country. They ceased to be published in 1914. After the war the administrators, with a few rare exceptions, were incapable of drawing up such reports or even of supplementing them. The generation of administrators who were active at the beginning of the occupation reached retirement age between 1914 and 1920. Many of them, having worked almost continuously in the same area since the conquest, had acquired a sound knowledge, spoke several of the local languages fluently, and spent part of their tours and their leisure in the study of local natural history and indigenous societies.

The new generation lacked this training. Those who graduated from the Ecole coloniale had often made the effort to study one or two African languages and acquired a certificate from the Ecole des langues orientales vivantes, but they rarely had occasion to perfect this superficial knowledge by practical experience. For reasons of economy and administrative convenience, these officials were posted, at the end of their leaves in France, to wherever there was a vacancy to fill, i.e. where an official of equal rank was about to go on leave; any special ability or area of knowledge possessed by an administrator was only subsequently taken into account. A governor in choosing his staff often took greater account of personal links of friendship between himself and his juniors, or recommendations from influential acquaintances, than ever he considered special aptitudes or knowledge of the country. The system of the 'turntable'[17] has been attributed to Governor-General Carde. It meant that officials returning to French West Africa from home leave did not know till the eve of their arrival at Dakar where they were going; their assignment was announced to them on the boat by cable, purely on the basis of vacant posts. A specialist in questions of the Sahara could thus be assigned to the forest regions of the Ivory

Coast, or vice versa. The result was that there were fewer and fewer specialists and more and more interchangeable bureaucrats, applying the same principles or the same methods to Agadès and to Sassandra, based far less on local realities than on their personal whims.

These effects were aggravated by the instability of the official's own position. It was not unusual for him, in the course of his two-year stay in the colony, to hold four or five different posts, always ready to take over his new post in case of another's illness or departure on leave. In Guinea, the average number of circle commanders serving in each of the *circonscriptions* over a sixty-year period was eighty. Such a situation made impossible the direct administration as it was conceived before 1914.

> . . . Under the pressure of circumstances, the circle commanders were obliged to rely more and more on their indigenous chiefs, and to evolve in some ways towards a semi-protectorate.[18]

So, from the theory of assimilation, which was rejected as unworkable, we come to the so-called theory of association, which was, in fact, an admission of failure.

In concluding this general picture of the *commandement*, we must once more make clear that its necessary accompaniment was despotism towards the African peoples. With their own men securely entrenched in the higher ranks of the administration and especially in the rue Oudinot, the big economic interests, on whose behalf colonisation was undertaken, knew how to manipulate the administrative machinery to their own ends. Governors and administrators would resist at times, but, in the long run, they gave in or were crushed. Governor Deschamps wrote:

> There is no native African counterweight to administrative influence. The natives are deprived of representation in France. On the other hand, the influence of the settlers and the businessmen, and especially that of the big companies, is frequently felt in Paris, and 'blows up' governors when they do not show enough 'understanding'.[19]

For Senegal particularly research in the archives reveals how brazenly the chambers of commerce and the 'Committee of Economic Interests of Senegal' presented their demands to the governors, and how prudently and sometimes obsequiously the administration responded. In 1924, before returning to his post as governor-general of French West Africa, Carde felt himself bound, like a council president before parliament, to present and justify the policy that he proposed to follow: but this was done at Bordeaux, in front of the 'Syndicate for the Defence of Senegalese Interests', and before the representatives of the French West Africa section of the Union coloniale.[20] The settlers, although their means of action were in time reduced, knew how to make themselves heard. In 1924 forest exploiters on the Ivory Coast brought about the recall of Governor Brunot, who refused to give in to all their demands in matters of 'recruitment'. In the same territory in 1936, settlers and forest owners threatened to throw the new governor, Mondon, into the sea on his disembarkation at Port-Bouët. Sometimes the economic interests found their allies apparently ready-made. Governor Annet, the 'hero' of the Vichy defence of Madagascar, enunciated this 'main precept' as a former governor without the least embarrassment:

> Always keep pace with commerce. Whether the officials are satisfied with you or not is of little importance: it is the support of commerce which constitutes your strength, as well as your support, in case of need, with the government.[21]

In fact, there were often close links, if not a symbiosis, between the upper administrative echelons and the financial oligarchy. Accommodating high officials knew they could expect handsome 'gifts' and, after their retirement or dismissal from the administration, agreeable bonuses in the form of directorships of companies which they had favoured.[22] We have already seen, in this respect, the venality of a man like Angoulvant, director of numerous companies, a catspaw of the Compagnie générale des Colonies, or like Merlin, director of the Banque française de l'Afrique on the eve of his downfall. Babichon was to become director of the Banque coloniale d'Etudes, and have interests in cotton companies in French Equatorial Africa. Roume was content with the post of director on the board of 'Le Nickel'. These examples can be multiplied and added to from later examples. But to the colonial administration there was nothing special about this. It was a tradition among the high bureaucracy of France (inspection of finance, public works, prefectoral administration) that from the civil service one would move on to trusts, or vice versa.

However, a sweeping generalisation is impossible. There were some high officials of complete integrity who conceived their mission solely in terms of public interest. Even for them public interest remained the interest of the French community, to which that of the African peoples was subordinate; the subtle influence of the colonial atmosphere – and prudence – led them to be tolerant, if not accommodating, towards whatever was going on around them. The best among them upheld the illusion that colonisation would, *ipso facto*, ameliorate the lot of the peoples, or at least that it *could*. One of the most clear-thinking among them, Maurice Delafosse, did not hesitate to write:

> If we condescend to be frank with ourselves, we are forced to admit that it is not altruism that leads us to Africa, at least not as a nation. Granted that pious missionaries, having vowed to devote their lives to save the souls of their fellow-men, have gone there with the sole aim of being useful to their black brothers, in the next life if not in this. But these were not the motives that led us to raise our flags in Senegal or on the shores of Guinea or to fight the natives in order to make them accept our authority.
>
> At times we wished to ensure outlets for our trade, and sources of raw materials for our industry, at others we felt the need to protect the security of our nationals or the need not to be outdone by foreign rivals; sometimes we were moved by the obscure and unconscious desire to procure a little glory or grandeur for our country, at others we simply followed hazardous caprices or the tracks of an explorer, believing that we could do nothing different. In no case do I find as the motive force of our colonial expansion in Africa the real and reasoned wish to contribute to the welfare of our subjugated peoples. That is an excuse that we are all too ready to give after the event, but it was never our intention. . . .
>
> I am far from throwing stones at those who sent France along this path . . . but the generosity of their intentions never went beyond the frontiers of their French homeland, and the national action they set afoot, however admirable it was and remains from the national point of view, is no less egotistical from the human point of view.[23]

In the same article Delafosse protests against the scorn felt for black civilisation, 'for the thousands of creatures in a truly primitive stage of human progress', against the error of ignoring them and wanting to act as if they did not exist.[24] He concluded:

> It is absolutely essential that our intervention should be a cause and element of progress and welfare for [the African communities]; otherwise it would be a condemnation of all colonial endeavour. And it would also be its undoing.[25]

He thus becomes identified with the illusions of the leftist reformers on the possibility of 'good' colonisation, which was quite contrary to the aims, and even the mechanism, of the colonial system.[26] The best men in the colonial set-up could hardly go beyond this pious wish. But for the rest, their very functions obliged them to be agents of exploitation and oppression. The power of the colonial command had one overriding aim: to ensure the maintenance of 'order', so that the monopolies and the settlers could exploit the peoples of the country 'peacefully' and under the best conditions; to extort taxes, human merchandise for forced labour and conscription, compulsory quotas of produce. It was on his performance in this sphere that an administrator was assessed and promoted: every circular reminded him of this.

In the exercise of his function, or outside it, he was given wide scope for arbitrary action – and for caprice and cruelty, provided that he did not cause trouble or public scandal. ('Public' meant likely to spread to France.)

The administrator, so strong in evil, has no power for good.[27]

The administrator's potentialities were limited by his rank and his character, and in practice much obviously depended on each man's behaviour; the people obviously favoured an administrator who was as fair as possible in the application of an unjust policy rather than the blood-thirsty maniacs who sometimes flourished.

To see the situation in perspective, it is useful to provide some data on the recruitment of colonial personnel. The 'men of the bush' of the early period, whose psychology Maurice Delafosse so accurately described, became increasingly rare.[28] On the other hand, the 'colonials of forced vocation' remained numerous. The lower grade posts – especially civil service clerkships – remained largely at the discretion of ministries and parliamentarians. This custom was not confined to colonial administration; in France the custom continued of compensating deputies with good voting records by putting at their disposal, together with crosses of the Legion of Honour and medals of *Mérite agricole*, tobacconist's shops (state monopoly) and jobs as editors or district surveyors. While the metropolitan jobs were given to *protégés* whom it was intended to favour, the colonial jobs were most often granted to *protégés* of a different kind, namely those whom somebody wished to get out of the way.

This was the back door through which people passed who often were not very welcome in France, sons whom families wished to send away, who had had escapades in the capital and who, thanks to the protection of a parliamentarian, were made to enter the colonial administration. There were all kinds of such people.[29]

The French upper and middle classes readily sent undesirables 'to the colonies', as the nobility had once sent theirs to America. The results of such recruitment are easy to imagine. Robert Poulaine gives the example of a *circonscription* in French Equatorial Africa, where the staff was made up as follows: one administrator, a former pupil of the Ecole coloniale, and three clerks: a former dentist, a former non-commissioned officer of the colonial infantry (who amused himself in the evenings, when drunk, by cutting down the flag with rifleshots), and a young man 'of good family', aged twenty-four, who had been guilty of two murders.[30] The liquidation after 1929 of the former rank of 'civil service clerk', and the almost exclusive recruitment of trained administrators from the Ecole coloniale, eliminated by stages this type of recruitment for the general administration. It continued, however, at a lower level in other services, mainly the 'technical' services (public works, railways, etc.), where no one ever hesitated to recruit to the staff adventurers and outcasts of all kinds. Of the former pupils of the Ecole coloniale who came to make up the majority of the administrative corps, a few came from the upper classes, but most were from the *petite bourgeoisie*. In this they were like most other officials at their level. What determined their vocation? The young students who entered the *'Colo'*[31] were generally reared on patriotic and hagiographical colonial literature of the kind that sent others to Saint-Cyr; a taste for adventure and risks was a sizeable element in their choice.

> How did this spirit of escape turn towards the colonies? Are not these the only countries where there is still room for adventure?[32]

The determining element seems to have been something different. Delavignette notes:

> I interviewed the pupils of the lycée when they had succeeded in getting enrolled at the Ecole. 'Why did you want to be enrolled?' A desire for freedom ranked high in all their answers.[33]

That was the key word. But this personal freedom, only limited by the scope of a man's official duties, led to the servitude of others. It was the 'freedom' of the feudal lord, or of the slave owner. The idea of going as a missionary to 'do good' for the peoples did not take root; and if it was sometimes found, it was of lesser importance. On the spot, illusions – if there ever were any – rapidly evaporated. The administrator-cadet or assistant was quickly absorbed into the scene by his 'master' and by the colonial environment in which he soon found his niche. Many of them soldiered on for twenty or thirty years without ever having any real contact with the local people, whom they knew solely through the relations of master to 'boy' or cook, the official to the administered.

Delavignette felt himself obliged to point out to the future commander that the Europeans were only a minority: 'Let him set aside one day a week without colonials, one day entirely devoted to the natives.'[34] Anyone who wished to step outside the colonial environment was barely tolerated. Witness this report in a file on one official: 'Frequented the natives. Even received them at his table. Not suited for colonial life.' He is soon supplied with facile judgments of the native mentality with which every colonial agreed – a big child, 'an incapable minor who has first to be educated'.[35] He is taught, and soon admits, that abuses which are tolerated or covered up by the administration, and about which the literature he read before arrival did not give him an inkling, are inevitable, and necessary on account of the 'native mentality'. He was reassured by constant repetition that 'if we were not here, it would be worse' and that 'every people is bound to pass through this stage'. If he becomes disillusioned it is more likely to be due to red tape and the dreary tasks of every day, after his dreams of excitement and wide open spaces.

Delavignette recalls the disappointment of an administrator who was a weights and measures officer concerned with export produce and a recruiter of manpower for state-controlled offices.[36] He warns against the demands of the merchants and the European colony, who will force him to spend all his time requisitioning food for their own needs and practically turn him into a wholesale grocer. Other, less savoury tasks will be allotted to intermediaries – the chiefs. Administrators were contemptuous of the hypocrisy of official declarations and circulars:

> Which of our colleagues . . . does not sometimes discern a slight dissonance between the official moderation insisted upon in the levying of taxes, and the evaluation of his professional 'yield', when his tax receipts are totalled up? Between paternalistic declarations on the sacred character of food crops, and the order – stemming from unknown sources – which bluntly decrees their abandonment in favour of 'rich' industrial crops? Between the solemnly affirmed principle of freedom of work and the recruitment of 'volunteers' on behalf of enterprises whose vital interests perhaps required less drastic sacrifices?[37]

But these protests could not be made public, nor could they be too readily attached to a man, without compromising his career. So he kept quiet and did his work. The material advantages of his profession and the intoxication of wielding authority contributed to make him accept his fate. It is true that the administrators' 'residences', however impressive in appearance, were only relatively comfortable by European standards. On the eve of the Second World War, the paraffin refrigerator was still considered a luxury and had not been installed everywhere; running water and electricity did not exist. But, as in the *grand siècle*, these deficiencies were made up for by an abundance of domestic servants. The number of servants hired by the commander (and paid for by the administration) was augmented by prisoners, who received no pay, but carried water, kept the vegetable garden and did similar jobs.

Presents were commonly given to win the commander's favour or to accompany a request. People with pleas and requests, and the canton chiefs, did not fail to offer the commander eggs, chickens and sheep; visiting chiefs brought works of local craftsmanship. The majority of administrators readily adapted themselves to this system, which reduced their personal expenses, and enabled them to save from their salaries for going on leave. But it was the exercise of authority which was the best way of keeping the administrator at his post. His office had kept the external trappings of its military origins: a uniform, circle guards, who watched over their master's security and carried out his decisions in the field – suffering imprisonment or rough handling if they committed blunders or caused displeasure; office hours starting and ending to the sound of a bugle, and compulsory salutes to the commander from all and sundry. The young school-leaver, recently terrorised by his masters, found his revenge. It did not take him long to acquire the attitude of a boss, and to feel satisfaction with the system that gave him the means of living it out. He came to tolerate the monotony of his daily work more readily; there were reports to draw up – for which one plagiarised those of preceding months or years, making the necessary alterations; answers to be written for the mail, circulars to comply with or to reject. Some developed hardened arteries and turned into perfect bureaucrats, immune to all human sentiment, thinking only of their careers, advancement, leave, receptions, intrigues to cover up errors, and the habit of speaking and writing like official circulars. These often caused the greatest amount of misery for the people.[38]

There were others, like the S.S. of the concentration camps, who really delighted in the grimness of their work.

> The senior commander whom I saw with a horsewhip placed on his desk, proud of sending for the boy to wipe up the blood which, with his own hand, he had caused to be spilled over the ground, was quite convinced that he was doing a good day's work! He wittily called these crises of brutality 'kindness week'; and all this happened in the year of grace 1943.[39]

This desire for 'liberty', which inspired the colonial vocation, sometimes concealed very murky, even pathological instincts. A colonial doctor openly wrote:

Power-crazy psychopaths are particularly numerous in the colonies – far more so, proportionately, than in France. They belong to the large class of unbalanced individuals who seek out colonial life; their psychic make-up is particularly attracted by the exotic. The life of the tropics attracts them like a lover. It satisfies all their psychic tendencies or passions: for novelty, mystery, authority, liberty, brilliant deeds, tours in the open air, aspirations towards unknown sexual experiences, dreams of opium and hashish intoxication. . . . It gives reality to all the mirages of their spirits.[40]

Delafosse remarked in this respect:

[The unbalanced] are all around us; we rub shoulders with them ceaselessly, in the streets and in the best salons: but their instincts, which are quite at variance with the duties required by their milieu, remain hidden. In Europe these people can live and die with a reputation of unsullied honesty. But send them into the bush, without control, and free of the obligations which, in France, dictate every action and gesture, give them authority which intoxicates them and *above all demand from them results without giving them the normal means of obtaining them* and these same men, who were honest in Europe, become criminals in Africa.[41]

The tragedy was that they were not prevented from doing what they did, or from relating their exploits with amusement to provide entertainment at colonial soirées. Rather, they became well-known among their peers, the terror they inspired among the Africans being considered salutary.

Then there were careerists, more or less successful within the limits of their intelligence, but lacking in scruples. They were most numerous in the higher ranks of the hierarchy. They did not get pushed away into the bush, but made their careers in the main towns, and got themselves transferred as quickly as possible to the private offices of governors or governors-general by supporting official policies or throwing themselves heart and soul into the service of some group of the financial oligarchy. This type of behaviour was not a novelty that only came in after the First World War: it had already been in evidence earlier.[42] As we have said, it was not peculiar to the colonies, but in France, it was less publicly flaunted.

Some made their careers through women, but not in the generally understood sense. Certain governors-general in French Equatorial Africa, in particular, who devised this mania, set up a 'stag park' with the wives of complaisant officials keen on rapid advancement.

In this context, dishonesty could be a pledge of success. A certain administrator who, after the Second World War, left a hole of two million francs in the coffers of the Kaolack provident society, was rapidly promoted to the rank of governor. A high official explained to the writer at the time that, with a history like that behind him, which could cause him to be dismissed at any moment, they were bound to have a governor who would not cause any embarrassment. Some administrators – very much a minority – were not only honest but had a clear understanding of the job they had been called upon to do; however, they kept quiet, except in private, thinking themselves powerless to change the order imposed upon them, and taking refuge in scepticism. Those who identified themselves openly with the anti-colonial struggle were very few; and only in the brief period at the end of the war and immediately after had they any chance to be active. In colonial society they became the targets of an unbelievable intensity of hatred, being denounced as traitors and effectively isolated; some of them were broken. Those with sufficient character to withstand this were sent back to France or were chased out of the administration.

These men deserve special respect, for few could have borne the moral and often the material suffering that was inflicted upon them.

(b) THE SYSTEM OF CHIEFS

The chiefs remained more than ever an indispensable part of the colonial administration, decisive tools of the executive. Being on the bottom rung of the ladder they had to obey every demand made upon them.[43] A sense of ambiguity permeated their whole position. On the one hand, it was extolled as testimony of respect for 'customs' and 'African institutions'; on the other they were always being reminded that they existed only by the good grace of the coloniser and were nothing but tools in his hand. A second contradiction concerned the chief's function: on the one hand, he was the representative, the executive, of administrative authority and, on the other, he was the representative of the African community, who recognised no other. He found himself between the hammer and the anvil. There was no statute or guarantee to protect him. He was simply mentioned in circulars which, in themselves, created no obligations until 1934–6.[44]

The hierarchy of canton and village chiefs, crystallised first in French West Africa, was then extended to French Equatorial Africa where it was given a slightly more flexible character – tribal chief; *chef de terre* – i.e. in charge of a group of several villages; village chief. The same system was applied in the Cameroons and Togo. The administrators naturally realised the need to respect local 'customs' in their selection, in order to guarantee the authority of the chiefs and to put them in a position to exercise their office with dignity (ministerial circular of 9 October, 1929). In the twilight of the colonial era Eboué took up the eternal lament of the need once again to find and restore 'authentic chiefs', and to give them the necessary authority.[45] He cited Lyautey's famous precept:

In every society there is a ruling class, born to direct, without whom nothing is done. We must make it serve our interests. . . .

But in this connection other writings recalled the doctrine, already formulated by Van Vollenhoven, that power belongs only to the coloniser; the chief being a mere instrument, an executive, at the beck and call of his master, who can be dismissed at will.

He is not the successor to the former indigenous king. . . . Even if there is an identity of person, there is nothing in common between things as they were before and as they are now. The canton chief, even if he is descended from a king with whom we signed a treaty, does not hold any power of his own. Nominated by us, after usually careful selection, he is and remains solely our assistant. . . .[46]

And Governor Reste stated more precisely:

The canton consists of a group of villages. It is placed under the authority of an *indigenous administrative agent*, who assumes the name of canton chief. He may be assisted by a secretary who supports him and, in case of need, deputises for him. The canton chief and his secretary are nominated by the lieutenant-governor on the recommendation of the circle commander.[47]

There is no rule, and never will be, governing his nomination. Everything depends on circumstances. The principle, as we have just recalled, is one of careful choice on our part. The chief's status is merely one in the scale of command which we have set up and imposed; it is not a customary institution maintained by us.[48]

The inspector of the colonies who wrote these unequivocal words stated in as many words that the selection of chiefs from among the former ruling families was preferable since their prestige could be put to advantage, but only if no other inconveniences were involved. Governor-General Carde thought along the same lines:

We cannot indefinitely tolerate the hegemony of certain incapable or undesirable families.[49]

In the absence of old families he recommended the use of educated native officials. In other words, all the old abuses were perpetuated. Chiefs without traditional authority, or else strangers to the country, continued to be haphazardly nominated, especially in the regions (e.g. much of French Equatorial Africa, Forest Guinea, Atakora, the Lobi country and elsewhere) where the institution of chiefs as an expression of state power had been unknown before colonisation. In the chiefly echelon there was still room for faithful clients, old soldiers, and even former house servants of important persons. A little before the Second World War difficulties arose in a canton in Guinea over the imposition as chief of a former house servant of the serving governor-general, whom the governor, despite his own reservations, did not dare to turn down. The chief, as indigeneous agent of the administration, was not an official. He had no more than a meagre allowance on taxes to provide for his needs and recompense him for the onerous duties the administration placed upon him. The administration shut its eyes to exactions, 'customary' or otherwise, which he might impose to supplement his income. The difficulties resulting from this caused a tendency for bureaucracy to increase.

Governor Reste, in Dahomey, and later the Ivory Coast, instituted a whole hierarchy and pay-scale for the chiefs; this system became widespread between 1934 and 1936. But again matters remained only half completed. First, the reform instituted by Reste applied only to the upper echelons, i.e. the canton chiefs. The village chiefs had no more than a small rebate on taxes: in the Cameroons 3 per cent if returns were made in the first term, 2 per cent if made in the second, and 1 per cent thereafter. The canton chiefs received 10 per cent of the returns plus wages.[50] The salaries were derisory. On the Ivory Coast, they varied from 2,600 to 18,000 francs per year for canton chiefs and 1,500 to 2,400 francs for secretaries, who were recruited by competition and confirmed in their posts after a year's trial period.[51] In Guinea, in 1934, they ranged from 250 francs per year for the chief of Kassa (Los Islands) to 11,200 francs per year for Almamy Bokar Biro, chief of the Dabola canton.[52] The average was between 2,000 and 4,000 francs.

On the Ivory Coast in 1937 there were 500 canton chiefs who shared out 1,500,000 francs in salaries (average, 3,000 francs per year). Delavignette noted that, by contrast, the European administrators of circles and subdivisions on the Ivory Coast (excluding main towns) earned 7,430,000 francs.[53] In North Dahomey the Paramount Chief of Nikki, the heir of the once great kings of Bariba, 'received a far lower monthly salary than that paid to an orderly of a *subdivision*.'[54] This nominal pay changed nothing in the basic position of the chiefs.

The so-called authority given to the chiefs was put to a harsh test by the demands made upon them.

Taken up with numerous worries [in clearer language, by administrative red tape – *Author*] the circle commander or the *subdivision* chief needed an intermediary to transmit to the natives under his administration his orders and instructions and to supervise their execution.[55]

The circle commander handed over to the chiefs the practical execution of numerous tasks; if any task proved impossible, that was too bad. It was the chief who went to prison or became destitute if the taxes or quotas of the indigenous provident societies were not handed in, if the road was badly maintained, if requisitioned food was not provided in time or in the prescribed volume, and if recruits for forced labour or for the colonial infantry were not enrolled. It was up to him always to find a way out of solving any problem; this had the agreeable effect of freeing the administrator's conscience from considering the means used at any time. It was the chief who had to dirty his hands; the commander remained in ignorance. In return for the few decorations bestowed upon him by the government, the chief was constantly risking his job and his freedom. In theory, the canton chief was removed from contact with the African population and was not liable to administrative imprisonment. But there was never a shortage of motives whereby he could be arrested.

In a letter to his canton chiefs the commander-administrator of the N'Zérékoré circle (Guinea) reminded them:

... You will work the commander's field, the forced labour field and the individual fields. Exempt the rubber teams so that the men in these teams can grow crops.

A canton is worth as much as its chief is worth. If there are very good chiefs in the circle, then it is a very good canton. Unfortunately, there are bad cantons, with mediocre chiefs who have to improve their service if they want to escape the sanctions which I shall not fail to resort to in case of need: dismissal, or simply the suppression of their canton, which will be attached to a good canton.[56]

For the village chiefs, prison sentences (which were legal) and corporal punishment (which was illegal but in common use) were threatened in case of shortcomings or weaknesses. In a report on a tour he had undertaken, the circle commander of Louga, Senegal, wrote:

Thursday the 11th, the circle commander came to introduce a new canton chief. . . . The village chiefs had been summoned individually by circle guards, but four had not complied with the order; they were immediately arrested and brought to Louga, as a first indication of where they stood, and to establish that any disobedience will be punished immediately. . . .[57]

There was no village chief who had not tasted prison at some time. Father Lelong cited the example of a village chief in the N'Zérékoré circle who had never done so as 'quite remarkable'.[58] Eboué, like many others, deplored this situation.

. . . Citizenship is not to be granted to the village chiefs except with extreme prudence. I hold that a subdivisional chief who knows his job does not need to discipline a village chief with prison sentences.[59]

But this advice was incompatible with the demands and convenience of administration, and was little heeded. Being himself under the constant threat of violence, the chief inflicted violence on those he administered. This violence remained, in the final analysis, the only permanent basis of his authority.

Until recently the African chief was a servant in the home of the circle commander. Not being able to communicate with the latter except through the mediation of the circle guard, he based his authority on the pitiless whip. . . . The chief was a man who had requisitioned chickens for the commander, labour for the commander, and so on. In a word, he was the inexorable bailiff of the administration. He was known for satisfying the innumerable demands of the administration as quickly and with as little trouble as possible. Greatly oppressed himself, he oppressed others.[60]

The following are the methods used by a canton chief in levying taxes, described in a Senegalese journal:

To recover overdue taxes in his canton, the canton chief, Salif Fall, had all the natives tied up who, in the course of his inspection tour, were incapable of producing their receipts for the current year. These unfortunates were then whipped in sight of the whole village till they bled, and, as a more effective reminder of the canton chief's authority, their sores were smeared with wet salt through the good offices of the Diaraff.

But Salif Fall was not only a torturer. He was also a chief who loved money, who did not shrink from any means to procure it, and he had instituted a special tax in his canton which was set aside to feed his personal treasury. Each head of an extended family [known as *un carré*, a square] had to pay him an ox. He had already succeeded in forming a herd of seventeen head from the animals with which he was thus supplied. And this without counting the fines inflicted upon unfortunate natives in the canton, which remained in the chief's pocket.[63]

In Fouta-Djalon, where feudal tradition made the chiefs particularly oppressive, the chief's strong arm men (*batoulabé*) and his sons or parents exacted ransom from the country in the course of their tours, made at the time of tax levying or at harvest. The 'customary dues' comprised, in the main, forced labour on the chief's fields and taxes on the harvest and on legacies.

These are *essentially variable* from canton to canton, within the same *circonscription*, for they reflect the personality and the rapacity of the chief and his entourage.[63]

The feudal principle of 'aid' (an exceptional contribution towards exceptional expenses) was more and more frequently applied. For example in 1953 the chiefs of Fouta imposed on their subjects a *per capita* tax for the purchase of a house and an American car, and for financing a pilgrimage to Mecca; they demanded 50 francs per family for each feast-day, 25 per head for July 14 and November 11, and 15 francs per head on the occasions of the census.

Taxes were levied on the death of all persons above the age of seven. For an adult over twenty-five years of age, it was 10,000 francs or two oxen, which were demanded for the 'right of succession', failing which the lands of the deceased were confiscated. If the deceased had no children, his (or her) herd was confiscated, and sometimes the empty granaries, without anything being left for the surviving spouse.

Recalcitrants were given rough handling: their clothing was destroyed, they were left tied up for two days without food, and their cattle were confiscated.[64] They were lucky if they escaped with their lives. Chiefs were quite often dismissed for acts of violence and murder, but more often it was the case that complaints of such deeds were passed over without any reprimand being given.

How many fat dossiers describing exactions have been hidden away in the circle offices. . . . How many suspicious incidents have been far too indulgently treated in the Fouta *circonscriptions*? . . . How much notorious pillaging and worse has been carried out with the full knowledge of the administration and the justiciary, but has remained unpunished?[65]

(c) REPRESENTATIVE INSTITUTIONS

The essentially autocratic system of 'commands' had certain inconvenient aspects. The commander, who had to rely for information solely on his canton chiefs, his circle police and his political agents, could be kept in ignorance of many important happenings in his *circonscription*. Meanwhile public opinion in France and abroad regarded this system with astonishment – maintained as it was by a republic that proclaimed the principles of democracy.

Deputy Diagne had, it is true, obtained citizenship for his electors in the four communes of Senegal, and this concession by Clemenceau had caused reverberations abroad. The Americans, accustomed to racial discrimination of the strictest kind, marvelled at seeing an African, elected by black citizens, take his seat in the chamber of deputies, and were ready to praise French liberalism. But this was not enough. At the moment when Germany was proclaimed unworthy of holding colonies, and the United States, in the name of the right of peoples to self-determination, opposed all the claims of French imperialism, it was important to give some public pledge of France's intention to endow its colonies with representative institutions. This was the background to the decrees of May 1919.

A first decree, promulgated on 15 May, 1919, dealt with the municipalities. Up till then, apart from the communes with full rights, only the territories of 'direct administration' in Senegal had had the right to communal administration. A decree of 13 May, 1891, had authorised the establishment of 'mixed communes', administered by an 'administrator-mayor' assisted by municipal commissioners appointed by the governor, and having no more than a consultative function; it further laid down the institution of 'native communes', which were in fact never organised. Only that part of the decree referring to 'mixed communes' was applied at a few trading posts in Senegal. The 1919 decrees authorised the establishment of such mixed communes all over Senegal.

A second decree, of 21 May, 1919, authorised the establishment, in administrative *circonscriptions*, of 'councils of indigenous notables'. These councils, presided over by the administrator, were to comprise eight to sixteen members nominated by the governor on the recommendation of the circle commander. Their role was a purely consultative one. The actual significance of these measures, as can be seen, was slender enough; their main object had been to make an impression in France and to dampen down the political stirrings which were beginning in Africa itself. In Senegal 'there is talk of setting up communes of full rights in some twenty localities . . . Thiès, Tivaouane, etc.'[66] Those who favoured assimilation hoped for great things. This policy provoked violent protests from the colonials, who demanded the abolition of the privileges of the four communes in Senegal, which in their eyes were intolerable and constituted a dangerous precedent.

After the signing of the peace treaty and the election of the 'blue horizon' parliament in France, colonial reaction grew stronger; it found a ready sympathy among the radicals, who were obviously bound to affirm in public their belief in undying principles, but who had long had associations with colonial big business. The minister for the colonies, Albert Sarraut, proclaimed before the senate:

> While my native policy openly admits the necessity of certain consultative local assemblies, composed of indigenous persons elected by indigenous suffrage, in the indigenous towns, I proclaim quite openly that this does not mean any sort of abdication of our sovereignty.[67]

This confession of faith was translated into practice by the decrees of 4 December, 1920, involving an administrative reorganisation of French West Africa.[68] The government did not dare to renege on its promise to grant citizenship to the people in the four communes, but through suppression of the distinction between 'territories of direct administration' (where the general council of Senegal, elected by the inhabitants of the four communes, approved the budget) and 'protectorate lands', Senegal became unified. The general council became the 'colonial council' comprising two categories of deputies, elected by two distinct electoral colleges. The citizens would elect twenty-four (instead of twenty) councillors; but all the citizens of Senegal now had the vote, and not only those in the four communes. This was a concession to the whites in the interior, who were enraged at not having the vote which the Africans of Dakar and Saint-Louis possessed at that time. To these 'citizen-councillors' were added another sixteen (later eighteen) representing the 'subjects'; these were elected by the province and canton chiefs, i.e. men committed to the administration.

The power of establishing mixed communes was extended throughout French West Africa, at the discretion of the governors-general. Three 'degrees' were involved, reflecting the method of election of the municipal commission.[69] In the first degree, the members of the commissions were nominated by the lieutenant-governor from a list of notables, to serve on a privy council or council of administration. In the second degree, the members were elected by limited suffrage: one half by the citizens, the other half by a college of indigenous notables. Among the citizens, only non-officials were eligible, and the elected were thus inevitably representatives of commerce and the settlers. The college of 'subjects' comprised serving or retired officials, holders of the *Légion d'Honneur* or the *Médaille militaire*, owners of immatriculated land, licensed dealers paying more than 200 francs for a licence, and property owners designated by the administrator-mayor. The third degree, involving the election of members to the municipal commission by universal suffrage, was never applied. The commission, in any case, played a merely consultative role, and the whole administrative power was barely affected by it. In twenty years the system of 'mixed communes' was applied only to the capital cities of the colonies and a few other important towns, where it gave the representatives of business circles and the settlers the right of supervision over municipal affairs. In 1939 there were twenty-three such 'mixed communes', fourteen in Senegal alone. The lieutenant-governors had been given the right to set up 'indigenous communes', but they never made use of this right.[70]

The same was true of French Equatorial Africa, where a decree of 14 March, 1911, remained in force, giving the governor-general the right to establish mixed or indigenous communes and to determine their system of operation. The councils of notables, which Delafosse and some others wanted to make into living bodies, were far too much in opposition to the spirit of *commandement* to have any future. Meeting generally twice a year, they had to be consulted on: (1) the system and modes of indigenous contributions; (2) the fixing of rates at which an African could buy himself out of statute labour; (3) the rendering of statute labour in kind; and (4) the performance of work of direct importance to the *circonscription*. It would be fair to summarise their activity as consisting mainly of drawing up plans for census-taking, the collection of taxes and the recruitment of manpower. In general, experience taught them to be satisfied with telling the commander what he wished to hear. Their influence was nil.

One could not take as 'representative' members who were officials neither of the administrative councils nor of the government (privy council in Senegal). In French West Africa all were nominated by the administration until 1925, except for the delegate of French West Africa to the supreme council of the colonies, who was elected by the citizens of the federation;[71] this was the legal member of the council of government. There were no African members. After 1925 a proportion of the delegates were elected or nominated *ex-officio* (representatives of the chambers of commerce, the colonial council of Senegal, etc.) and finally there were four 'citizens' and four 'natives' (one of each in the administrative council of each colony).[72] Only those representing commerce or the settlers made themselves heard, the others being little more than ciphers. In French Equatorial Africa three indigenous notables, elected by limited suffrage, were added to the three citizens elected by the chamber of commerce, but not until 1936.

Governors and governors-general were obliged only to ask the advice of these councils on certain matters; they were not obliged to follow it. In 1932 a circular by Brévié introduced the formula of village and canton councils. These, however, were not elected, the first being made up of family chiefs and the second of village chiefs, or persons designated 'according to custom'. 'This sort of automatic constitution will avoid the competition that always precedes the designation of individuals.'[74] This system, also introduced in the Cameroons and Togo, had no other practical consequences than the institution of the councils of notables.

(d) THE *Indigénat* – THE JUDICIARY SYSTEM

The disabilities of the non-citizen – or the 'subject', to use official terminology – were not limited to his being without the right to vote. Subjects were bound by the system of the *indigénat* – native status – borrowed, like many other colonial institutions, from Algerian legislation. Even in Algeria its nature had appeared so iniquitous that it had been only introduced obliquely and more or less secretly, as a provisional measure. It consisted of giving the administrative authorities the right to impose penalties on subjects without having to justify their action before any judicial authority. In Algeria, by a decree of 1874, the police court magistrates had the right to punish certain acts that did not properly qualify as contraventions of the penal code – as, for example, a delay in tax payment – by simple police penalties. A law of 1881 'temporarily' transferred this right to the administrators of 'mixed communes', an arrangement renewed from time to time.[75] Local orders, and later a decree of 15 November, 1924,[76] applicable to the whole of tropical Africa under French domination, including mandated territories, gave the various administrations the right to inflict disciplinary punishment on 'subjects'. These penalties were originally limited to a maximum of fifteen days' imprisonment and a 100-franc fine.

At the beginning, almost all the whites in West Africa had the authority to inflict punishment. Later this privilege was limited 'to officials representing the public powers, administrators and their clerks'. For non-administrative chiefs of posts the 'ceiling' was fixed at five days' imprisonment and a 25-franc fine. Offences which justified the imposition of penalties on subject people were limited in a decree of 1924 to twenty-four, but their variety was such and their definition so loose that the effect was arbitrarily to cover anything; moreover, it gave the administrator a list of 'motives', among which he could simply take his pick, and be sure of finding one that would suit a subject he wished to punish. In Guinea a decree of 1 October, 1902, modified by one of 20 September, 1905, included among fifty-six infractions 'complaints or objections, knowingly incorrect, repeated in front of the same authority after a proper solution has been found'. There could thus be no appeal against injustice!

One of the twenty-six infractions defined by the decree of 14 September, 1907, (Senegal) was

(1) Refusal to pay taxes or fines or to reimburse to the full sums due to the colony, or to render statute labour in kind. Negligence [the actual French word] in making such payment and in the execution of statute labour.

It is clear that a wide interpretation could be given to the word 'negligence'.

(5) Refusal or negligence to carry out work or render aid as demanded . . . in all cases referring to interests of order, security and public utility.

It was possible for refusal to do forced labour or lack of zeal in its execution to be punished.

(8) Any disrespectful act or offensive proposal *vis-à-vis* a representative or agent of authority.

Thus through alleged 'failure to salute' a commander, punishment could be inflicted on an unfortunate who had accidentally failed, on passing the administrator, to stand to attention and give him the military salute.

(9) Speech or remarks made in public intended to weaken respect for French authority or its officials.

The same article encompasses 'songs', 'false rumours', and the like.

The slightly more restrictive text of 1924 – it reduced the penalty to five days in prison and a 15-franc fine – still left room for very wide interpretation. It allowed punishment for 'acts of disorder', rumours that were either false or of such a nature as to 'disturb public order', 'the dissemination of seditious writings or remarks, insults to representatives of authority', etc., and the 'damaging of resources belonging to the administration' – such as state forests. In French Equatorial Africa a decree of the government-general added to possible infractions 'refusal or ill-will . . . in the establishment and/or upkeep of crops' (18 December, 1939). This illustrates the restrictions which the *indigénat* imposed on freedom of expression.

In theory, punishment meted out by administrators was invalid until sanctioned by a decree of the governor (beyond which there was no appeal), but this was a mere formality. People were first put in prison, and only afterwards was the decision transmitted to the governor. There is hardly a single instance where the governor disapproved of the proposed punishment. Sometimes neither the decision nor even the prisoner's name was entered on the register of commitals to gaol. This would be rectified in case of an inspection. Administrative imprisonment was in general use when there was a shortage of manpower. According to official statistics for the Cameroons in 1935, there were 32,858 sentences of 'administrative' prisoners as against 3,512 of common law prisoners.[78]

The law forbade corporal punishment. The *Bulletin du Comité de l'Afrique française* praised for humanitarianism the sanctions introduced by the French for the subject-peoples of the Cameroons, replacing the penalties laid down by an ordinance of the imperial German chancellor dated 22 April, 1896, specifying fourteen days in prison, twenty strokes of the cane and twenty-five strokes of the whip as maximum penalties.[79] But while the whip was no longer legal, every circle policeman was provided with a stick and knew how to make use of it. Certain administrators – like the one in N'Zérékoré in 1943, during his 'weeks of kindness' – did not disdain to use it themselves. The strokes were not counted, and it would have been interesting to see if anyone dared to complain.[80]

It was only in very rare circumstances that a subject could reach citizen status. French public opinion was led to think – and some in fact believed – that 'the subject [could] obtain citizenship by abandoning his personal status and submitting to the French Civil Code'.[81] This was not so. We have already seen the numerous conditions for 'naturalisation' made under the decree of 25 May, 1912. By 1926, in all the French colonies together, a total of eighty-four subjects had obtained citizenship.[82] The decree of 23 July, 1937, relating to the admission of natives of French West Africa to French citizenship, laid down *eleven* instead of five compulsory conditions, among them not having manifested any hostility towards France 'in deed, in writing, or by word of mouth'. Article 2 added *seven* optional conditions: when the first eleven had been complied with, one of the subsequent seven sufficed to claim naturalisation. Among these was being the legitimate husband of a French woman and having had a child by her. 'Full' naturalisation could be obtained by retired officers and holders of one of the thirty-five diplomas of higher education – a measure of pure propaganda value since practically no African had the chance to take a higher degree. Graduates and those with polytechnic education were even freed from the requirement to reside in French West Africa.[83] In short, indigenous citizenship remained limited to the 'original members' of the Senegal communes: in 1921 there were 25,000 of these,

M

23,000 of whom resided in Senegal and 1,000 in Kayes; the number of electors in the Senegalese communes did not exceed 10,000 of the twelve to fifteen million inhabitants, and these figures hardly changed. Little by little, however, certain categories were removed from the *indigénat*. On the eve of the Second World War these were the canton chiefs, officials, ex-soldiers, diploma holders and licensed dealers.

Those freed from the *indigénat* did not, however, escape from 'native justice', in which area the commander remained onmipotent. There were two systems of justice in tropical Africa under French domination, the French and the native systems. At the beginning of colonisation, French justice comprised the usual hierarchy of courts: three courts of appeal (French West Africa, French Equatorial Africa, the Cameroons), assize courts (in each colony except French Equatorial Africa) and courts of first instance (in each colony). Unlike the practice of the French courts, this jurisdiction of the first instance was not subject to the rule of collegiality; a single judge could sit without an assessor. He was sometimes assisted by 'justices of the peace with extended competence', where the single judge also had the responsibility of making the preliminary investigation and serving as public prosecutor. These courts, presided over by French magistrates who gave their judgments according to French law, were used in all cases involving a French citizen. According to local custom, they could even sit in cases involving subjects, on a request being made by one or other of the parties. This procedure was even compulsory for members of the four communes who, as citizens, came under French courts but kept their customary legal status. [84]

Indigenous justice applied in all other cases. [85] The judical powers which traditionally belonged to the chiefs were gradually taken from them. In French West Africa the decree of 18 November, 1903, left village chiefs with certain police powers; the penalties they could inflict were limited to 15 francs and five days in prison. The decree of 16 August, 1912, finally deprived them even of this competence in penal matters and limited them to matters of conciliation. The court of first instance (previously called the 'provincial court', then the 'subdivision court') was presided over, until 1924, by a canton chief, assisted by two 'notables' designated by the governor. The decree of 1912 added to these a European 'clerk'. A decree of 22 May, 1924, entrusted the chairmanship of the court to the head of the *subdivision* or some other European official.

The court of second instance (originally called the 'circle court') was presided over by the circle commander, his deputy, or possibly some other European official designated by the governor; the chairman was assisted by two notables designated by the governor. The court dealt with first appeals in civil cases or commercial matters and, exceptionally, with criminal cases, where two European assessors were required. At the level of the *subdivision* and the circle, the administrator held a plurality of powers in his administrative command, with prerogatives in matters of the *indigénat*, and total judicial powers in indigenous matters. The notables recommended by him as assessors – who were, moreover, administered by him – could do nothing against his will. The administrator was a judge with discretionary powers, because he was, at one and the same time, policeman, examining magistrate, public prosecutor, judge, and in charge of the execution of the sentence. This was what gave justice its arbitrary aspect, the more so since the law administered was 'common' law, unwritten and therefore open to every kind of interpretation. In fact, indigenous justice extended the administrator's powers over the African population, while at the same time imposing upon him a more complicated and slower procedure. In theory, nothing could oppose the will of the administrator-judge. But his incompetence and ignorance often gave to his assistants the power to give direction to this will – not always to the advantage of justice or of those to be judged.

For most of the time, the commander remained more or less in ignorance of local custom. The assessors were there, in theory, to put him right. But either they were not fully competent themselves (they were chosen on political grounds) or they were corruptible, especially since they were unpaid, or else received the same pay as a porter. They could easily be tempted to give opinions advantageous to their friends or protégés. Most often, the commander did not understand the language of the accused; in any discussion he could only follow what the interpreter translated for him. If the latter was dishonest and in connivance with the assessors, the judge could be manoeuvred to the advantage of the richer or more open-handed of the litigants. To obviate this drawback Governor Clozel had the common law written down, first on the Ivory Coast and then in the Sudan.[86] This work was undertaken in 1931 on the orders of Governor-General Brévié and finished in 1939 with the publication of *Coutumiers juridiques de l'Afrique occidentale française.*[87]

This publication, however, could not solve the problem. It was, moreover, restricted to French West Africa, and no similar effort was made for French Equatorial Africa and the Cameroons.[88] The collection was not complete and, above all, the initiators of the inquiry, administrators with legal training but insufficient ethnographical and no sociological knowledge, insisted on incorporating into the framework of the civil code notions derived from an absolutely different social order. This error had already been committed in 1903, and it was not rectified now. The compilation was never officially acknowledged; it could simply be consulted 'for information'. To avoid possible errors, there existed for each colony a court of confirmation (from 1931 on, colonial appeal tribunal) which was under obligation to revise cases involving sentences of three or more years' imprisonment and to which were reserved offences carrying a prison sentence of more than ten years.[89] 'Annulment courts' played the role of supreme court of appeal.

As a curiosity, one can mention the Muslim court, left over from the Faidherbe era. It was set up by a decree of 20 May, 1857, and reorganised by decree of 20 November, 1932. It existed only in French West Africa, in the four localities where French domination had first been imposed (Dakar, Rufisque, Saint-Louis and Kayes). They comprised a *kadi*, an assessor and a clerk of the court. In theory, they pronounced judgment according to Koranic law, but in practice they followed custom, in conformity with Muslim law. Their competence was limited exclusively to matters that affected the descendants of the original Muslim members of the communes of full rights in Senegal.

(e) RECRUITMENT

A subject had to comply with innumerable forced labour obligations: statute labour for administrative work, which supplemented the taxes and the duration of which was essentially limited, and recruitment in exceptional cases for major works and for private enterprise. We have stressed this sufficiently and there is no need to recapitulate.

The war added to forced labour the burden of military service, which was conceived first as a temporary expedient but later became a permanent institution. Once it had been successfully tried out in wartime, the massive employment of colonial soldiers became one of the basic institutions of French imperialism.

Black Africa was not the only field of recruitment. Morocco (particularly the Berber regions of the Atlas mountains), Algeria and Indochina had to send contingents. However, Algerian and Annamite soldiers were not considered as valuable from a purely military point of view, and were not considered politically reliable. On the other hand the loyalty, blind obedience and fighting qualities of the Senegalese were highly prized. After using them as auxiliaries against Germany during the First World War, the French imperialists used them, between the two wars, mainly to put down rebellions in the colonial empire. The experience of 1914–18 showed that while the African soldiers did not adapt easily to mechanised warfare, they showed themselves far superior in a war fought largely with archaic weapons – knives or bayonets.[90] The French soldier, on his side, was ill-adapted to colonial wars and punitive expeditions, and there could be no question, for both legal and political reasons, of using troops from Europe for this purpose; and recruited foreign mercenaries (the Foreign Legion) were too few and too costly. In pursuit of these principles, black troops were extensively used in Morocco in the Rif war, in Syria against the Druses, and in Vietnam against peasant insurrections. At the same time the French electorate was able to feel satisfied with a reduction in the length of military service for French citizens, first to eighteen months and later to one year.

Senegalese soldiers thus became the *gendarmerie* of the French empire. They were used wherever need arose on the various frontiers of imperialism (for example, in the Rhineland and the occupied Ruhr), making deliberate use of the terror they inspired and of racism to 'make an impression' on the Germans. It is known that Hitler exploited these sentiments to uphold his racialist doctrines and call for revenge against 'Africanised' France. In applying the principle 'divide and rule' care was taken to set different races and ethnic groups against each other; even in Africa soldiers recruited in French West Africa were used to suppress revolts in Ubangi and Upper Sangha (French Equatorial Africa) and to 'maintain order' in the Cameroons and Madagascar.

The decree of 30 July, 1919, reorganised the 'black army'. Recruitment was carried out partly on a volunteer basis, but mainly by conscription. As in France under the *ancien régime*, lots were drawn. Capacity remained limited; only a part of the conscripts were put into uniform, while the 'second group of the contingent' remained at the disposal of the military authorities, eventually to form battalions of pioneers. Later, as we have seen, this 'second portion' served as forced labour for civilian purposes. The length of military service was fixed at three years for all indigenous subjects of French West and Equatorial Africa. A decree of 1923 stated that citizens of the four communes only needed to do eighteen months of service, stationed in Senegal, while subjects could be sent abroad during their three years. Those going abroad were sent first to France in detachments of 600 men, then, after three months of training, to colonial territories other than French West Africa (e.g. North Africa, Indochina or Syria) and often to theatres of war like the Rif war and the campaign in Syria.[91] This system had the advantage of providing numerous troops at very low cost.

The army objected that quality was on the decline and recalled with regret the era of professional armies when soldiers shared in the profits of a campaign, where the 'black rank and file' permitted the officers 'substantially to encourage their soldiers; there are secret funds belonging to the ministry of the interior . . . why not permit this in military policy?'[92] The officer who could not 'encourage the soldier by gifts' and so 'support' him against the civilian population lost his authority and prestige. The pay was low and voluntary enrolment had fallen off. As the majority were conscripts, those who had voluntarily enlisted or re-enlisted were not looked on with a friendly eye. The professional soldiers (particularly the Bambara), who had formerly been in a majority, were now lost among the recruits, who were less robust and felt no vocation for the army.

The administrators were discontented for still other reasons. First, recruiting operations, to which we shall return later, meant extra forced labour for them. The non-existence of military service in the neighbouring colonies, particularly the British ones, made the young men emigrate, mainly from the border regions. The result was less cultivation, less manpower and thus fewer taxpayers. They were further worried about the state of mind of the ex-servicemen who had brought back new ideas from their visits to France and no longer showed respect for the whites. They were afraid also that military service might become 'a pretext for political rights'.[93] This explains the reduction in the numbers of the West African contingent between 1919, when it stood at 23,000 men, and 1937, when it had fallen to about 12,000. In his speech to the council of government of French West Africa in December 1921, Governor-General Merlin estimated that the contingent of French West Africa would not account for more than, at most, 15,000 men in any year. The colonial army formed of subjects, whose strength had originally been forecast at 300,000 men, was henceforth reduced to 100,000; only 27,000 were garrisoned in France, and their stay there was regarded as a hazard. The lack of manpower and the exhaustion of the country did not allow for any increase.

The total number of soldiers called up in French West and Equatorial Africa amounted in 1920 to 63,000 men (representing three years' intakes), and in 1922 to 52,000, of whom 27,500 served in the colony and 24,500 abroad.[94] The practice of sending half abroad was continued. Each colony of course contributed widely varying numbers.[95] In 1938 the danger of war caused a return to the proportions of 1919. The preamble of a decree of 8 April, 1939, stated that an exceptional call-up in the previous year had almost doubled the number of men in uniform.

Recruiting operations remained the administrators' nightmare. In principle, those called up and subjected to drawing of lots were young men of twenty-one. But how could the young men of the right age be recognised and called up in a country without a civil service?

As the civil service does not yet function in French West Africa, and as it is difficult enough to determine even the approximate age of a black, a sufficiently wide margin has to be left for the designation of men in a given [call-up] class: they are to be over nineteen and under twenty-eight.[96]

In fact, only one man out of ten or twenty of military age was enlisted: but it was a three-year term of service, served thousands of miles away, with increased risk of death from disease or war in other theatres. Under these conditions one could not rely on those concerned being willing to run the risk. Often they did not know their own age! Following the usual methods employed, the chiefs were given the task of supplying the necessary human livestock.

This designation is unfortunately usually made from names given by the canton chief.[97]

Obviously the men sent were of poor background, slaves or undesirable characters, with age a factor of minor consequence. Recruiting was generally carried out between December and the beginning of March. The commission for recruitment (consisting of the circle commander as chairman, an officer, and a civil or military doctor, with an African clerk or interpreter) would summon the recruits to the main town on a fixed day, canton by canton. First, they were medically examined; this often eliminated three-quarters of the recruits, for instead of strong men, the villages sent the ill and the weak, who were certain not to be accepted.

. . . The large proportion rejected or exempted out of the number of young men examined indicates clearly that the natives whose names were put forward are not fit for military service. There are places where this proportion reached 87 per cent. I have often seen chiefs audacious enough to present quite young children. At first glance, this seems to be proof of limitless devotion: had not the commission been sent the very last man out of the fit population? In reality, this keeps up the numbers offered and enables them to hide those who might make excellent soldiers.[98]

Those with the means paid to get a replacement for their own protégé, thus completely hoodwinking the administration, or they bribed a canton chief so as not to appear on the list.

Thus the preliminaries to recruitment are one of the most important sources of revenue for the canton chiefs.[99]

Apart from those who really were unfit, there were often many others who pretended to be so. In the Ivory Coast forest zone, in Dahomey and in French Equatorial Africa the men took drugs to simulate various diseases to perfection, and deceived even the most skilful doctor. After the recruiting visit an appeal was made for volunteers. Each of these received (in 1929) an annual premium of 50 francs supplementary to their pay (50 francs for four years, 100 francs for five years, 150 francs for six years, etc.). They then proceeded to draw lots. Those who remained were enrolled immediately, received their uniform (which consisted of a military cap and a red belt, but no boots or sandals[100]) and were sent on their way. Sometimes the chief's powers could prevail no further and neither those 'fit for service' nor those who attended the commission raised sufficient numbers. Then real operations had to be undertaken with circle police, gendarmes and even troops; the villages had to be surrounded without prior warning and all those who appeared of suitable age were tied together.

The military writer whom we have cited concluded:

Recruiting is like a fisherman's catch, repeated every year.

The 'Senegalese soldiers' – all African recruits were so designated – were not only subject to longer service than French recruits. Commanded almost exclusively by French officers, they were subjected to Prussian discipline, and were forced to speak pidgin French, the debased French which military authority made into a kind of official language, to replace Bambara which was a lingua franca at the time of the conquest. Like commoners before 1789, they could not hold command. 'Officers of indigenous rank' were extremely rare: they could only attain the rank of second-lieutenant after passing out successfully from the training centre for indigenous non-commissioned officers at Fréjus, or after fifteen years of service or experience in war. They could even become lieutenants, but the rank of captain – the summit of their hierarchy – was only given in 'completely exceptional circumstances'.[101] Advancement was exclusively by selection. But even if they did obtain citizenship by naturalisation, they continued to 'serve with indigenous rank'.

There was slightly more advantage attached to service in the police corps, as circle police, gendarmerie, urban police (approximately 15,000 men in French West Africa, among them many retired professional soldiers or veterans of 1914–18), or in the militia and police of the mandated territories (1,500 men in the Cameroons, 400 in Togo). Their pay, nevertheless, was miserable, and their pensions on retirement were calculated

so as to assure retired men just remuneration for their former services, but not enough to allow them to remain idle and thus deprive the territory of precious manpower.[102]

War veterans and soldiers who had completed their three years' service came back from France and the other countries where they had served or fought with their horizons broadened. Contact with the world outside had helped them to become aware of their own situation. In France, outside the barracks, they saw that not all Frenchmen were colonials, and were surprised to be treated as equals, and to learn of Frenchmen who earned their living by working and by fighting against exploitation.

The soldier who came back from abroad, and whose excellent state of mind I pointed out in my speech of 1924, was not always sheltered in France from extremist propaganda, which found him an easy prey with his simple outlook. On his return home he did cause some anxiety.[103]

This is a significant declaration by Governor-General Carde to the November 1928 session of the council of government of French West Africa.

The colonial administration, making a virtue of necessity, tried to turn this superiority complex which the African soldiers had acquired abroad to its own advantage, and against the mass of their fellow-Africans. To prevent them from rising in rebellion they tried to make of them, if not an aristocracy, at least a buffer group. In the absence of adequate pensions they gave them decorations, and special treatment in many ways. They were offered citizenship, and lower officials, such as orderlies and guards, were selected from among their numbers. They were given the option of becoming chiefs. On the eve of the Second World War, with a view to lessening resistance to increased recruiting efforts, two decrees – which never took effect – envisaged ex-servicemen becoming a privileged corps. In Senegal all subjects who had completed military service were to be given the right to elect the colonial council; eighteen additional councillors' seats were created for this purpose, by a decree of 8 April, 1939. The decree of 14 May, 1938, exempted all ex-servicemen in the whole of French West and Equatorial Africa from poll-tax and statute labour, and from the harshness suffered by the native population; these privileges had previously been enjoyed solely by soldiers who had done war service.

(f) THE FISCAL SYSTEM

The principles governing the financial relations between France and her colonies were laid down in Article 33 of the Finance Act of 13 April, 1900. They embodied a system of financial autonomy: the
M*

colonies were to cover the expenditure made by France on their territories. All civil expenditure and the upkeep of the gendarmerie were to be covered by the colonial budgets. The army did not depend on the local budgets but came under the national defence budget; however, its maintenance in the colony was charged to the colonial budgets.

Financial quotas can be required of colonial budgets up to the total amount of military expenditure. . . .[104]

Thus in the 1930s the general budget of French West Africa contributed annually some 7,500,000 francs to defence.[105] However, the Act of 1900 laid down that subsidies could be granted to the colonies out of the state budget, but this exceptional measure was never applied to French West Africa. The mandated territories always provided for their own expenditure. Only French Equatorial Africa, where the scattered, over-exploited and miserable population had to support the costs of a far too heavy superstructure of bureaucracy, was incapable of balancing its budget and had to request subsidies from France of 32,000,000 francs from 1920 to 1924.[106] In 1929 the governor-general stated that French Equatorial Africa had not received any subsidies since 1926,[107] but other sources contradict him;[108] he must have meant exceptional subsidies. The 1929, 1930 and 1931 budgets showed a surplus, but the crisis put an end to this and, as we have seen, even led to the suppression of the budget autonomy of the colonies in French Equatorial Africa in 1934. In 1939, out of a budget of 300,000,000 francs, French Equatorial Africa received 87,000,000 in subsidies, and, even so, registered a 7,000,000 deficit. But it should be emphasised that French Equatorial Africa was the exception; it was the only one before the crisis to obtain loans for building various facilities, such as the 1924 loan for the Congo–Ocean railway. All the other territories were self-sufficient, both for their current needs and the cost of facilities, for which they employed reserve funds. In 1926, the *Revue indigène* stated proudly that between 1904 and 1926, 596,800,000 francs had been spent in French West Africa from the general budget (296,000,000) and from loans (300,000,000), of which in all 308,000,000 francs were allocated for the construction of railway lines and 149,000,000 francs for services.[109] All economic equipment was realised from the resources of the colony, with the exception of the Dakar–Saint-Louis railway and, in part, the line from Kayes to the Niger. In 1931, when income fell to 961,000,000 francs as against the anticipated 1,809,000,000 they even managed to close the account with an 80,000,000 francs surplus!

The Cameroons also covered its expenditure and provided for

the extension of the railway line to Yaoundé without foreign aid or loans. Only the 1931 fiscal year showed a deficit, but reserve funds helped to make it up. In full crisis, the 1932 fiscal year recorded a profit: the railway alone gave surplus revenue of 1,000,000 francs.

Togo, which had balanced its budget ever since 1906 in the German's period and even gained the title of 'model colony',[110] continued to be self-sufficient. It was not enough to have the budgets balanced; the governors made it a point of honour to have a surplus, which was placed in the 'reserve funds'. These reserve funds were used to cover possible deficits and, in case of failure, to subsidise expenditure on facilities. But each governor felt bound to demonstrate his good management by the growth of the reserve funds; since economic expansion caused the budgets to show a regular surplus up to the time of the crisis, the reserve funds were barely touched and continued to grow regularly. The Cameroons with an annual budget that grew from 8,000,000 francs in 1920 to more than 25,000,000 francs in 1925, had by the latter year nearly 12,000,000 francs in its reserve funds. In French West Africa, the joint (federal and local) reserve funds totalled 300,000,000 around 1929 as against 9,800,000 gold francs in 1908.

The price paid for this policy has already been shown: the massive use of forced labour. But let us now examine the origins of the budget revenue. There were basically two: customs dues and poll-tax. Customs revenue consisted of import and export duties, which had a fiscal justification, and of customs dues proper, with their protective character. This revenue naturally rose with the advance of the market economy which, under the trade system, was more or less directly determined by progress in import and export transactions. In the federations of colonies, the import and export dues were fed into the general budget. This budget covered the expenditure of federal bodies, financed certain investments and subsidised the budgets in those colonies showing deficits. Governor-General Bargues, moreover, thought that the federal system – established in French West Africa a little before the Finance Act of 1900 – had financial reasons apart from administrative aims.

The state of mind prevalent in France, of which the Act of 1900 represents but one manifestation, led government and parliamentary circles to think that it is useless for the state budget to subsidise local budgets when territories that are neighbours to those running at a deficit and are linked to them by common interests and development, show a surplus revenue. It seems good financial logic to institute a consolidation of credits and debts between these territories, whose development will thus be assured at less cost and without the intervention of the state budget.[111]

In French West Africa the general budget constantly aided Mauritania, for example, which was short of resources and had a budget deficit.[112] In French Equatorial Africa subsidies from the general budget to the colonies became almost a permanent rule. Already in 1911 over half (1,200,000 francs) of Gabon's budget of 2,200,000 was covered from the general budget; the budget of the Middle Congo (2,570,000) received 880,000. This situation was to continue until very recent times.[113] It partly explains the weakness of the autonomy granted to the colonies of French Equatorial Africa by the government-general. In the years after the First World War a surplus was shown only by Chad, where income from taxes quadrupled between 1913 and 1923, and administrative costs were small. Its reserve funds were regularly plundered by the government-general, and in 1923 were completely cleared of their 3,400,000 francs credit balance. The local administration complained bitterly.[114]

After covering compulsory expenditure, subsidies for facilities and portions set aside for the reserve funds, the surplus of the general budget, if any, could be transferred to local budgets 'in proportion to production and consumption, which in each one [of the territories] motivated the levying of various taxes'.[115] Though easy to collect, customs dues had the drawback of reflecting fluctuations in the economy: in 1931, as we have seen, customs receipts in French West Africa fell by 47 per cent in comparison with the preceding year. The local budgets were far more stable since revenue came essentially from direct contributions, among which the poll-tax, which was unalterable by definition, had chief place. In Guinea the 1931 and 1932 budgets were almost identical; in the Sudan, that of 1932 even recorded an increase on the previous year of almost 4,000,000. Except in Senegal, the poll-tax represented at least half, and often 60 to 70 per cent, of budget revenue.

Percentage of Revenue to Local Budgets Supplied by Poll-Tax

	1925	1928	1930	1932	1933	1936	1940
Senegal	22·3	14·5	13·1	17·9	20·8	24·3	
Sudan	53·4	49·2	49·3	49·4	59·9	51·9	
Guinea	69·5	70·8	61·2	58·4	63·7	54·0	46·0

Indirect taxes formed about a quarter of revenue (in Senegal one-third), the rest being made up of other direct taxes such as patent and licence fees, turnover tax and income tax. Poll-tax formed the almost exclusive revenue of colonies with underdeveloped market economies; as we have seen, it represented a powerful means of compelling the people to produce export crops. It also encouraged emigration: not being able to earn money on the spot to pay the tax, Mossi, Bambara and Fulani seasonal workers went elsewhere to try to obtain it. Its relative weight diminished in proportion as the market economy advanced, the other sources of budget revenue being more or less linked to economic activity. The crisis period, with the accompanying drop in business transactions, caused a rise in the percentage of income derived from the poll-tax. It also increased in absolute terms (from 36,800,000 to 40,500,000 francs between 1930 and 1933 in the Sudan), crushing the people whose real income had considerably diminished.

This fiscal system transferred the burden of the budget on to the mass of the people, particularly the poorest. Poll-tax, raised *per capita*, was fixed at a uniform rate without regard to the resources of those involved. It affected all adults, without distinction of sex, the only exception being mothers of large families. A basis was easily established simply by taking a census of the population. The rate varied from one colony to another and within each colony according to regions; this was theoretically to take into account differences in wealth, but it was also a means of preventing the influx of those without resources towards the towns. In 1926–7 poll-tax, with a rate varying from 2 to 17 francs according to the *circonscription*, was fixed at 25 francs for the main town, Bangui, in Ubangi-Shari; in Gabon, where the rate varied from 2 to 20 francs, 28 francs, representing one month's pay, had to be paid in Libreville.

The level was fixed after the census. However, the census was taken in a haphazard way, seldom on a single day; in any case, the canton chiefs and administrators would be ill-advised to reveal a decrease in the population. The result was that the census figure was often inflated. Cantons and villages were taxed according to their *theoretical* population, and each individual had to pay beyond the legal rate, the surplus representing the tax of those who had emigrated or died, and had not been removed from the census lists. In a report of 12 October, 1933, the administrator of the Zinguinchor circle wrote:

> The instructions given by some of my predecessors to the agents in charge of the census laid down that only increases should be registered. In case of decreases the figures on the previous roll should be maintained.[116]

Moreover, in the same circle, all those passing through were officially inscribed, even if they had already paid taxes or were

registered in another canton. Even those not liable to the tax, such
as children below the age of ten, were inscribed on the lists. Thus in
the Djibélor circle, instead of 20 francs, the real tax paid was from
30 to 32 francs per head. This abuse was widespread almost everywhere. Apart from the tampering with the level of the poll-tax,
other abuses occurred where taxes were raised. The levying of
taxes (poll-tax, cattle tax, quotas and reimbursement of the
indigenous provident societies) was left to the village and canton
chiefs. They had to pay the total sum recovered into the public
counting houses, and only then were the deductions to which they
were entitled paid out to them. If often happened that the canton
chiefs embezzled deductions payable to village chiefs. To prevent
too long a wait the chiefs usually increased the tax to their own profit,
under the permissible pretence of 'customary dues'. If the demands
of the administration exceeded the capacity of the population, the
chiefs bore the consequences. In the miserable Foss canton (Louga
circle, in Senegal) in 1934 the cultivators had only paid 157,000
francs out of the 571,000 francs in taxes due for the years 1932-4.
The administrator sacked the canton chief for 'lack of energy' and
had four village chiefs imprisoned.[117] In the neighbouring Djoloff
circle, the administrator noted that, in the N'Dienguel canton,

> no payment of taxes had been made for 1934. Nine chiefs were
> taken to Linguère for punishment.[118]

To avoid such inconveniences, the chiefs used violence against
the people they admistered and brought official sanctions to bear:
the local population was punished for being 'remiss' in paying taxes,
with great latitude of interpretation. A Dahomey newspaper wrote:

> Every day men and women, even those who owe nothing to the
> fiscal authorities, are arrested, lashed together and beaten under
> the pretext of refusal to pay taxes. . . . Many of them, to comply
> with the payment of their taxes . . . pawn their own children.
> Awéhanson Houcangué, a cultivator in the village of Djégan
> Daho, had already paid his due. Chief Adoto was aware of this.
> None the less, he summoned him, had him thrashed, and made
> him pay two quotas, one for his brother who had died, and the
> other for the latter's wife who does not belong to his district. . . .
> Old Jécha, aged about eighty, was arrested and beaten for not
> having paid his taxes quickly enough. At the time of writing he
> is two kilometres away doing forced labour under the whip.[119]
> On one day, 16 February, 1935, in the village of Djegbi,
> twenty-two natives were sentenced to ten days in prison for having
> only partly paid their taxes. . . .
> About three months ago, one Agassin died on the road to

Savi, the day after he had been set free from Oudiah prison where he had spent ten days for not having found the money for his poll-tax quickly enough at this time of crisis. Rumour has it that he died of blows received in prison.[120]

We read this description of the year 1936 at Fouta-Djalon from an administrator, Gilbert Vieillard:

> ... The young people who left to earn [the tax] did not return; taxpayers who have emigrated are in hiding, in flight or dead, but they are inscribed on the census, and this makes the charges for those remaining even heavier. Too bad, the money had to be found: the people were reduced to selling the goods of those who had paid, but who did not dare to complain too much. First animals were sold – cows, sheep and hens; then grain, cooking-pots, Korans, all that could be sold. Prices were very low. The chief's men and the Syrians fished in troubled waters: the taxpayers rarely received any change between the sale prices and the figure of the tax due. When there was nothing left the coming harvest and the children would be pawned.[121]

In the end, the levying of taxes, as in the first period of colonisation, turned into a raid. The administrator of Louga indicated coldly in his report, already quoted in connection with the Foss canton:

> In the course of his tour of census-taking, the new [canton] chief has been able to recover some of the taxes or sell at Louga the contributed cattle which seemed to him superfluous.

Although it showed no pity for the people, the administration showed infinite indulgence towards the big companies and the settlers. The company taxes, which had to come back to the colonies, were first paid into the treasury of metropolitan France, where these companies frequently had their headquarters. Europeans, not having to pay poll-tax or render statute labour, benefited by way of income tax collections, industrial and commercial grants, etc., which were far more favourable than in France. In Guinea, income tax in 1940 (paid mainly but not solely by Europeans) made up 1·5 per cent of budget revenue, as against 46 per cent derived from the poll-tax. During the crisis the companies and settlers raised a loud outcry and were allowed rebates. In 1930–2 revenue from patents, licences and business turnover decreased by two-thirds in Senegal while that from the poll-tax remained practically unchanged (at 19,100,000 francs as opposed to 20,000,000). In Guinea in the same period, revenue from the former fell from 9,300,000 to

6,100,000 while, at the height of the crisis, the poll-tax rose from 32,400,000 to 33,000,000 francs. Clearly the fiscal system, added to forced labour, made the local people finance the very facilities by which they were exploited, and made them bear the costs of the administrative machinery of oppression which gave assurance that colonial 'order', which was indispensable for this exploitation, would be maintained. At the same time, the exceptionally high cost of this administrative machine concealed one form of colonial exploitation: the abnormal proportion of overpaid sinecures which, to use the term Marx applied to the liberal professions, were a means for the French *grande bourgeoisie* to find employment for part of their superfluous numbers. For the year 1951 (no data exists for previous years) it was established that, in French West Africa, officials (0·3 per cent of the population) consumed 13 per cent of national revenue and 62 per cent of budget returns.[122]

Finally, the fiscal system extended the market and money economy by artificial means, thanks to the importance attributed to the poll-tax: deprived of their reserves and prevented from accumulating resources,[123] the people were obliged to turn to export crops and work as labourers, to the even greater profit of the colonial enterprises.

(g) DIRECT AND INDIRECT RULE

Much has been written about the advantages and otherwise of direct administration as practised in the French colonies and indirect rule as in the neighbouring British ones. In West Africa, the differences were far less deep than was sometimes imagined. The economic system was the same: the economy was controlled by the same trading monopolies (the Compagnie de l'Ouest africain, the United Africa Company, and others) and agriculture was left to the 'local peasants'. The political principles were also the same. Following the example of Van Vollenhoven's famous circular, the Native Authority Ordinance of Nigeria affirmed:

> There are not two kinds of authority, one British, the other native, working separately or collaborating, but one single government in the interior, in which the native chiefs have been given well-defined tasks to do; they enjoy a recognised status like all British officials.[124]

The principles were simply applied in a different style. The British government, not having to find employment for 'poor whites' (or rather, being able to settle them elsewhere) did not send minor officials to its colonies in West Africa; it made wider use of native officials and chiefs whose status and customary privileges received legal sanction. But when colonial interests were at stake, the British colonial administration did not hesitate to interfere with the 'government' of 'protected' kings, to annul or rectify their decisions and, in case of failure, to depose and replace them.

The British obtained better economic results because the territories they occupied were the richest and most densely populated, and because they had created a better infrastructure (mainly railways) at an earlier date. The political system in use had no relevance in this context.

Which system was more advantageous for the African peoples is difficult to decide. The populations of the British territories were, on the whole, exposed to less pressure – more moderate taxes, more restrained requisitioning of manpower, no conscription. Was it the British system, as George Padmore believed, that 'offered the dependent peoples the greatest possibilities of acquiring self-determination by constitutional means?'[125] This may be doubted, even from a formal and constitutional point of view. Moreover, the crystallisation and reinforcement of the feudal system by indirect rule created a serious obstacle to progress in the British territories. Each of the two policies was forged by degrees, empirically, by virtue of the characteristics of French and British colonial imperialism, and it cannot be said that one was 'better' than the other.

REFERENCES

1. H. Cosnier, op. cit.
2. R. Delavignette, *Les vrais Chefs de l'Empire*. Paris, Gallimard, 1939, p. 24.
3. Upper Volta was established in 1919, by the partition of Upper Senegal and Niger, the other part assuming the name of the French Sudan. The territories of Mauritania and Niger were given the status of colony respectively in 1920 and 1921. Upper Volta was suppressed in 1932 for economy reasons, and divided up among the neighbouring colonies, the Ivory Coast receiving the largest part, with the capital Ouagadougou. A supreme administrator was installed in 1937, subordinate to the governor of the Ivory Coast. Upper Volta was finally reconstituted in 1947.
4. The military territory of Chad was detached from Ubangi-Shari and set up as a colony in 1920.
5. Soon called 'high commissioner' in the Cameroons.
6. From 1934 to 1936 further economies had been attempted by merging the functions of the governor and the heads of services in the two territories of Dahomey and Togo: the governor of Dahomey was at the same time commissioner of Togo, where he was represented by a supreme administrator with his seat at Lomé; the head of customs services of Dahomey held the same functions for Togo, etc. This system soon proved impracticable (cf. L. Péchoux, *Le Mandat français sur le Togo*. Paris, A. Pédone, 1939).
7. A. Zieglé, *Afrique equatoriale française*. Paris, Berger-Levrault, 1952, p. 178.
8. The Federation budget, by contrast to the local budgets of the various colonies that made up the Federation.

9. It comprised a 'service of Muslim affairs', set up by Roume in 1906, and first entrusted to Robert Arnaud (author of the novels written under the pseudonym Robert Randau), an Algerian official formerly administrator of a mixed commune, then to Paul Marty, an officer-interpreter whom William Ponty invited to come from North Africa in 1912.

10. Only on the eve of the Second World War in French Equatorial Africa.

11. For quite different reasons, in French West Africa, the peninsula of Cap Vert and Gorée was removed from the authority of the governor of Senegal in 1924, and placed under the direct administration of the governor-general (represented by an administrator) under the name of 'Circumscription of Dakar and dependences'. This was to avoid the difficulties and conflicts of authority resulting when St. Louis, the capital of Senegal, became the federal capital.

12. Quoted by H. Zieglé, op. cit., p. 175.

13. The title of 'governor of the colonies' was a grade in the colonial administration, maintained for a long time, instead of 'lieutenant-governor'. A decree of 14 July, 1937, substituted the term 'governor'.

14. In Senegal, where the elected colonial council had some functions, it bore the title of privy council (*conseil privé*). The council of administration of the Cameroons and Togo and the councils of government of the groups of territories included four notables.

15. H. Zieglé, op. cit., p. 176.

16. *Afrique Française*, 1921, No. 2, p. 560.

17. In fact, Cosnier, in 1920, had already denounced the deplorable effects of administrative instability.

18. *Afrique Française*, 1921, No. 2, p. 56.

19. Hubert Deschamps, *Méthodes et doctrines coloniales de la France*, Paris, Armand Colin, 1953, p. 174.

20. *Afrique Française*, 1924, No. 10, p. 549.

21. Armand Annet, *Je suis gouverneur d'Outre-mer*. Paris, Editions du Conquistador, 1957, p. 101. There is evidently no question of the opinion of the indigenous subjects.

22. The gifts were sometimes poisoned when the companies were of shady character and the responsibilities accepted led to the courts.

23. Maurice Delafosse, 'Sur l'orientation de la politique indigène de l'Afrique noire', *Afrique Française, Revue coloniale*, 1921, No. 6, pp. 146–7.

24. He developed this thesis in the little work *Les Noirs d'Afrique*, Payot, 1921. But he is almost alone in the colonial circles of the time (with General Meynier) to develop this concept which was not allowed to be quoted until after the collapse of the colonial system.

25. Ibid., p. 147.

26. However, in 1922, in commenting on the difficulties that had arisen with mass conscription and recruitment for the construction of the Dakar–Niger railway he wrote: 'Many came to regret the tyranny of an El-Haj Omar or a Samori, more capricious no doubt, but whose caprices had a less general effect and were interspersed with periods of lull.' ('Les points sombres de l'horizon en Afrique occidentale', *Afrique Française*, 1922, No. 6, p. 275).

27. Denise Moran, *Tchad*. Paris, Gallimard, 1934, p. 240.

28. M. Delafosse, 'Broussard ou les états d'âme d'un colonial', *Afrique Française*, 1909, Nos. 2–12.

29. Robert Poulaine, *Exposé au Comite national d'Études politiques et sociales*. March 1929.

30. Ibid.

31. Preparatory class for the entrance examination to the École coloniale.

32. Deschamps, 'La vocation coloniale et le métier d'administrateur', *Afrique Française, Revue coloniale*, 1931, No. 9, p. 498.

33. R. Delavignette, *Les vrais Chefs de l'Empire*. Paris, Gallimard, 1930.

34. Op. cit., p. 62.

35. J. Brévié, *Circulaires sur la politique et l'administration indigènes en Afrique occidentale française*. Gorée, Imprimerie du gouvernement général, 1935, p. 7. This is the official opinion of the governor-general, who later became secretary of state for the colonies under Pétain.

36. Op. cit., p. 10.

37. *Bulletin des administrateurs des colonies*, No. 2, April, 1937 (quoted by Delavignette, op. cit., p. 117).

38. In the book by Denise Moran, *Tchad* (Paris, Gallimard, 1939) can be found a terrible picture of an administrator of this kind and his wife.

39. Father Lelong, *Ces Hommes qu'on appelle anthropophages*. Paris, Ed. Alsatia, 1946, p. 164.

40. Dr. Cazanove, 'Memento de psychiatrie coloniale africaine', *Bulletin du Comité d'Études historiques et scientifiques de l'Afrique Occidentale Française*, 1927, No. 1, p. 140.

41. M. Delafosse, 'États d'âme d'un colonial', *Afrique Française*, 1909, No. 5, p. 164. (Author's italics.)

42. Robert Randau (real name Robert Arnaud, head of the service of Muslim affairs at Dakar 1906–12) described them in his novel *Le Chef des porte-plumes*. Paris, Ed. du Monde nouveau, 1926.

43. The most complete study to date on the chieftainships was written by R. Cornevin 'L'évolution des chefferies dans l'Afrique noire d'expression française', *Recueil Penant* 1961, No. 686, pp. 235–50; No. 687, pp. 379–88, and No. 688, pp. 539–56.

44. Brévié circular of 27 September, 1932, for French West Africa. Decrees passed between 1934 and 1936 in different parts of French West Africa finally settled their status; in French Equatorial Africa, a general decree, issued on 29 December, 1936, fixed their official hierarchy. In the Cameroons on the other hand, the chiefs were given a hierarchy early on, including decorations and even uniforms.

45. Félix Eboué, *La Nouvelle politique indigène en Afrique equatoriale française* Paris, Office française d'édition, 1945.

46. Report by Inspector of the Colonies Maret (5 December, 1930). Quoted by R. Cornevin, 'L'évolution des chefferies dans l'Afrique noire d'expression française', *Recueil Penant*, No. 687, June–August 1961, p. 380.

47. Colony of the Ivory Coast. *Programme d'action économique, politique et sociale*. Abidjan, Imprimerie du gouvernement, 1933, p. 185. Author's italics.

48. Maret Report, op. cit.

49. Circular of 11 October, 1929.

50. Petition to the United Nations, 28 October, 1952, submitted by thirty-five village chiefs of Ndogbessel, Eseka subdivision (Cameroons).

51. The more and more complex functions given to the chiefs, who were generally illiterate, made it necessary to give them a literate secretary as aide (Colony of the Ivory Coast, *Programme d'action . . .*, op. cit.).

52. Decree issued by the governor of French Guinea on 21 December, 1934.

53. R. Delavignette, *Les vrais Chefs de l'Empire*. Paris, Gallimard, 1939.

54. Report by M. Bramoulé, administrator, Quoted by P. Mercier, *Les Taches de la sociologie*. Dakar, I.F.A.N., 1951, p. 78.

55. Colony of the Ivory Coast. *Programme d'action . . .* op. cit., p. 179.

56. Note No. 310 of 23 February, 1944. Quoted by Father Lelong, op. cit., p. 264.

57. Report by Administrator Mercadier, September 1934. Senegal Archives. 1 D. 2/28. Circle reports 1933–4.

58. Father Lelong, op. cit., p. 50.

59. F. Eboué, op. cit.

60. *Le Réveil* (Dakar), No. of 10 October, 1949.

61. Chief of the broader family holding a concession or a 'square'.

62. *Le Périscope africain*, 5 December, 1934.

63. Dalaba Archives (Guinea). Report of 9 January, 1955. Italic original.

64. Dalaba Archives. Complaints (1951–6).

65. Ibid. Report of 9 January, 1955.

66. J. B. Forgeron, *Le Protectorat en Afrique occidentale française et les chefs indigènes*. Bordeaux, Y. Cadoret, 1920.

67. *Afrique Française*, 1920, no. 2, p. 97.

68. Documents which henceforth gave to Niger and Mauritania the status of colony, and returned to Upper Senegal and Niger its former name of French Sudan.

69. Decree of 4 December, 1920, modified by ordinance of 27 November, 1929.

70. Except in one case, Agoué in Dahomey.

71. The citizens of French West Africa and French Equatorial Africa each elected one delegate to the supreme council of the colonies, a phantom body with its seat in Paris.

72. The same principles applied to the Cameroons and to Togo.

73. The composition of the electoral college was analogous to that of the indigenous colleges of the mixed communes: for 3,500,000 inhabitants there were 3,799 electors (*Afrique Française*, 1937, No. 12, p. 599).

74. Circular 421 A.P. of 28 September, 1932.

75. R. Ruyssen, *Le Code de l'indigénat en Algérie*. Algiers, Imprimerie Heintz, 1908.

76. Modified by decrees of 30 November, 1926, and 14 May, 1936.

77. Moreover, a decree of 21 November, 1904, authorised the governors to pass sentences of internment and sequestration for a maximum length of ten years, but subject to confirmation by the minister. They could also impose collective fines. These measures were reserved for 'cases of insurrection against the authority of France or grave political troubles and disorders that threaten public security and do not come under the penal section of the common law' (Article 2). Angoulvant, as was seen, used this widely on the Ivory Coast. Administrative internment continued to be widely used for political reasons.

78. H. Labouret, *Le Cameroun*. Paris, Hartmann, 1937.

79. *Afrique Française*, 1924, No. 10, p. 504.

80. As late as in 1947 the village chief of Akroufla (Ivory Coast), an old man in his seventies was given twenty-five strokes of the whip by a circle guard on order of the commander of Oumé (*Le Réveil*, 3 November, 1947).

81. J. Richard-Molard, *Afrique occidentale française*. Paris, Berger-Levrault, 1952, p. 151.

82. Lamine Gueye, *Etapes et perspectives de l'Union française*. Paris, Ed. de l'Union française, 1955.

83. *Afrique Française*, 1937, No. 9–9, p. 441. This last disposition interested only one single person, today president of the republic of Senegal: Léopold Sédar Senghor, who, at that time, was a grammar school teacher in France. To our knowledge not a single African 'subject' crossed the threshold of the École Polytechnique.

84. One single exception: when 'reserved matters' were involved (questions related to marriages, successions, etc.), and when the interested parties were all citizens of Muslim faith, the cases were referred to the 'Muslim tribunals' which will be discussed below.

85. Cf. H. Labouret, *A la recherche d'une politique indigène dans l'Ouest africain*. Paris, Ed. du Comité de l'Afrique française, 1931, chap. VI, and 'La justice indigène en Afrique Occidentale Française et les coutumes', *Afrique Française*, 1935, No. 7, pp. 411–16. See also J. Chabas, 'La justice indigène en Afrique occidentale française', *Annales africaines*, 1954, pp. 91–152.

86. A circular by Roume ordered the governors to do so: but nothing was done, it seems, in the other territories. For the Sudan, the publication was incorporated in *Haut-Sénégal-et-Niger* by Delafosse. Paris, Larose, 1911.

87. Three volumes. Paris, Larose, 1939.

88. In Togo, a collection of customs was published, but soon proved useless.

89. The 'Homologation Chamber' of the Court of Appeal played the same role in French Equatorial Africa and in the Cameroons.

90. Cf. Abdoulaye Ly, *Mercenaires noirs*. Paris, *Présence africaine*, 1957.

91. George Padmore, *La Vie et les luttes des travailleurs nègres* (Petite bibliothèque de l'Internationale syndicale rouge. XXXVII, Paris, n.d.).

92. Abou Digu'en, *Notre Empire africain noir*. Paris, Charles Lavauzelle, 1928, p. 64.

93. *Afrique Française*, 1922, no. 2, p. 109: letter from an administrator of Guinea, quoted by Camille Guy.

94. Albert Sarraut, *La Mise en valeur des colonies françaises*. Paris, Payot, 1922.

95. Division by colonies:

Upper-Volta	2,500	Ivory Coast	1,500
Sudan	2,000	Dahomey	800
Senegal	1,700	Niger	700
Guinea	1,800	Mauritania	100

96. Capitaine Houdry, 'Le recrutement en Afrique occidentale française', *Afrique Française, Revue coloniale*, 1929, No. 5, pp. 373–8.

97. Ibid., p. 374.

98. Ibid., p. 376.

99. Ibid.

100. At least for the service of the colonies. Certain sadistic officers did not fail to force the young *évolués*, accustomed to wearing shoes, to participate in long marches with bare feet in the name of regulations.,

101. Decree of 29 November, 1926, relating to 'indigenous colonial officers'.

102. V. Chazelas, *Territoires africains sous mandat de la France: Cameroun et Togo*. Paris. S.E.G.M.C., 1931 (International Colonial Exhibition in Paris), p. 131.

103. *Afrique Française, Revue coloniale*, 1928, 11, p. 696.

104. Robert Bargues, *Problèmes financiers en Afrique occidentale française*. Info-Dakar, 1949, p. 5.

105. G. Padmore, op. cit.

106. Opening speech of Governor-General Antonetti to the session of the council of government of French Equatorial Africa in October 1929 (*Afrique Française, Revue coloniale*, 1929, No. 12, pp. 685–98).

107. Ibid.

108. *Afrique Française*, 1926, No. 12, p. 585, mentions a grant of 13,200,000 francs for 1926 and of 10,750,000 francs for 1927 instead of the exceptional grant of 4,000,000 foreseen under the French budget.

109. *Revue Indigène*, No. 205–6, January–February 1926. The article does not state, unfortunately, what francs were involved (gold or paper) nor whether the figures referred solely to expenditure on facilities.

110. Cf. Robert Cornevin, *Histoire du Togo*. Paris, Berger-Levrault, 1959, p. 176.

111. Robert Bargues, op. cit., p. 7.

112. In 1926, e.g. this revenue covered only a little over 50 per cent of expenditure.

113. Even in 1949 50 per cent of the customs dues were paid into the general budget of the colonies of the group (H. Zieglé, *Afrique Equatoriale Française*. Paris, Berger-Levrault, 1952, p. 180).

114. F. Lavit, 'La colonie du Tchad en 1923', *Afrique Française, Revue coloniale*, 1924, No. 4, 6 and 8.

115. Robert Bargues, op. cit., p. 11.

116. Senegal Archives. 1 D.2/28, Circle reports 1933–4.

117. Senegal Archives. 1 D.2/78. Report of a tour by the administrator of Louga, September 1934.

118. Same source. Report of a tour by the circle commander of Linguère, September 1934.

119. *Le Courrier du golfe du Bénin*, 1 September, 1934.

120. *Le Courrier du golfe de Bénin*, 1 March, 1935.

121. Gilbert Vieillard, 'Notes sur les Peuls du Fouta-Djalon', *Bull. I.F.A.N.*, No. 1, 1940, p. 171.

122. Attempt at recapitulation of elements known at Dakar to serve for calculating the national revenue of French West Africa. Dakar, Direction générale des Finances. February 1953. Quoted by J. Lecaillon, 'L'Intégration de l'Union française dans l'Union européenne', *Annales africaines*, 1954, pp. 23–4.

123. For Angoulvant (see above) the excessive 'wealth' of the people in the forests of the Ivory Coast encouraged their 'laziness'.

124. Quoted by H. Labouret, 'Politique indigène et administration indirecte', *Afrique Française*, 1938, No. 5, p. 205.

125. George Padmore, 'Pan-Africanism or Communism?' *Présence Africaine*, 1960, p. 197.

2. *The Missions*

The trinity which, from the beginning, presided over the colonial venture consisted of the military officer, the administrator and the missionary. The last-named, although on the margin of the official establishment, was often more important than the other two. Napoleon, with his usual cynicism, had already observed that the missionary's robe enabled him to 'cover up political and commercial intentions.'[1] On numerous occasions, the persecutions encouraged by the missionaries (most often through their interference in civil or political affairs) had served as a pretext for the first colonial interventions, particularly under the Second Empire. It is this temporal aspect of missionary work mainly that we shall be looking into – without being able wholly to leave aside the religious implications.

We shall consider only the Catholic missions, since the Protestant ones played a relatively minor role in French tropical Africa.[2] Right up until the 1950s missionary work went hand in hand with the colonial venture.[3] This fact is not altered by occasional individual stands on principle or when missionaries took issue with certain aspects of colonial administration.

This solidarity came into being at the very outset of the colonial epoch, with the Portuguese and Spanish ventures in the fifteenth and sixteenth centuries. Imperial conquest was justified and sanctified for the Portuguese and Spanish by their duty to win over souls for the true religion and assure their salvation, if not in this world, at least in the next.

In 1930, on the eve of the international colonial exhibition, Joseph Folliet, later director of the *Semaines sociales*, took up in his thesis on the right of colonisation[4] (sponsored by the Catholic Institute in Paris) concepts put forward four centuries earlier by the Spanish theologian, de Vittoria.[5] According to Joseph Folliet, de Vittoria held that providence, having created the universe for all men, did not place any obstacle to all men having free access to the wealth of this world. Since the Gospel even ordains 'Go and teach the nations', nothing could legitimately place an obstacle in the way of the preaching of religion. If the Barbarian (here the American Indians, but by extension all the colonial peoples) obstruct by force the strangers' desire to take their share of the wealth of the country, the latter have the right to reply with force and to protect their safety by occupying the country and subjugating its peoples. If, spurred on by the devil, the Barbarians attempt to exterminate them, the Spaniards can legitimately exercise against them all the rights of war by plundering them and taking them captive. In modern times, Father Muller has proclaimed:

> Humanity cannot and must not allow the incapability, negligence and laziness of savage peoples to leave for ever unused the wealth which God has granted them with the intention of making it serve the good of all. As long as there are lands that are little cared for by their owners, it is the right of the communities wronged by this defective administration to take the place of these incapable managers and, for the profit of all, to exploit the wealth which they do not know how to use.[6]

Theology here agreed with Albert Sarraut who, in 1931, invoked the right of colonisation to

> distribute resources which the incapable owners held without profit to themselves and to all.[7]

The idea of a particular divine curse hanging over the black race and justifying the slavery of the blacks was frequently expressed, from the sixteenth to the eighteenth centuries, among Catholic writers. As late as the nineteenth century it was expressed by Father Libermann, the founder of the Congregation of the Immaculate Heart of Mary (later amalgamated with the Congregation of the Holy Spirit).

> Blindness and the spirit of Satan are too deeply rooted in these people, and the curse of the Father[8] rests upon them; they need to be redeemed by sorrow bound to that of Jesus Christ, capable of expiating their deadly sins . . . so as to wash themselves of the curse of God.[9]

In brief: the terrible misery of the black people is attributed not to the evil deeds of the traders and colonisation but to a kind of additional original sin lying upon that race. One cannot help seeing only too clearly the relation of such concepts to those of the racialists, who did not hesitate to invoke them. It may be objected that such concepts are in contradiction to the universal teachings of Christianity. But it should be said that this universal teaching was not invoked in favour of the African peoples until after the Second World War, and all positions taken officially by representatives of the Church in the preceding period were in support of colonisation.

Contemporary authors have, however, invoked the theology of de Vittoria – not in favour of the 'right of colonisation', as in 1930, but to justify decolonisation.[10] Thus Father Lelong did not hesitate to present de Vittoria, a Dominican like himself, as a 'progressive'. De Vittoria, in asserting the ownership rights of the Indians, roused the anger of Charles V.[11] But it is also true that elsewhere he had justified, in the name of *jus communicationis et societatis*, the right of the Spaniards to take possession.

That the temporal and spiritual powers differed in their view of certain colonial problems is certain; but there was agreement on all essential points. In the period of colonial conquest, the Church showed complete solidarity with the venture, which at that time was subject to violent criticism from both left and right; it saw the way open for the preaching of the Gospel. Pope Leo XIII gave it his blessing as part of the 'rallying' of Catholics to the bourgeois Third Republic, with its business and colonial interests.

To the extent that [France] progressed in the Christian faith, she could be seen gradually rising to that moral grandeur which she attained as a political and military power. . . . And still today . . . we admire her setting out for distant countries where by her gold, by the labour of her missionaries, even at the cost of their blood, she propagates both the renown of France and the benefits of the catholic religion.[12]

The army and administrators saw in the missionaries' work of conversion a means of rallying the evangelised portions of the population to France and of utilising them against their refractory brethren. A Protestant, Archinard, was prepared to convert Tiéba to Catholicism for political ends. In return for this support, the missionaries proclaimed their solidarity with the work of colonisation. The cathedral at Dakar was conceived as a sort of colonial pantheon on whose walls were to be inscribed the names of all the colonials who had died in Africa. This idea was seen as a means of financing the cathedral's construction; at the ceremony of laying the foundation stone, Mgr. Le Hunsec invited subscriptions from parents and friends 'of those who, up to their last hour, were good servants of colonial France',[13] and whose names would be inscribed on this 'African memorial'.

Quite recently, anxious to dissociate themselves a little from their past stance, the mission representatives claimed that, contrary to what was accepted, the missions had constantly been subjected to persecution by the colonial authorities. Father Bouchaud wrote:

It should be recognised that, as far as the missions were concerned, in French Africa the colonial administration showed itself as a rule far from neutral and undenominational; rather it was often interfering and malevolent, reserving its favour for Islam and in no way easing the tasks of the missionaries. For a long time the ministry of the colonies was a bastion of freemasonry.[14]

To appreciate this opinion, we must examine more closely the situation of the missions in French colonial Africa. A first point to notice is that the missions were never directly dependent on the Church of France, but rather on Rome. They belonged to the Sacred Congregation of Propaganda Fide, set up in 1622 by Pope Gregory XV 'to propagate the faith among the heretics and the infidels'; to use the expression of Bouchaud,[15] it was the 'ministry for the colonies' at the Holy See. Canon 252 fixed its role as appointing and changing missionaries; it had full authority over the religious associations dedicated to missionary work.

Its jurisdiction is limited to regions where the sacred hierarchy is not yet established, and where the missionary status persists. It extends equally to regions which, though already having an established hierarchy, are yet at an early stage of their ecclesiastical organisation.[16]

In short, outside the ecclesiastically independent countries where the episcopal hierarchy was fully established, Catholic geography comprised its colonies (mission lands), run by foreign priests under the direct jurisdiction of Rome, and its protectorates (the newly-established dioceses) where the hierarchy of foreign or indigenous bishops remained to some extent under tutelage. It is a deep question whether the missions should be considered as totally independent of, if not antagonistic to, the colonial power. A colonialist enemy of the Vatican, François Méjean, who vehemently reproached the Church for failing to keep in step with colonisation, did not hesitate to pay homage, at least to its past:

At that period and in the years that followed [the nineteenth and early twentieth centuries] the spiritual and cultural aid which was incontestably given by the Catholic missions to French colonial expansion was not seriously restrained by Rome. Even if the present doctrine of Propagation is in abeyance, as catholic historians claim – without proving it – it has not begun to show openly . . . except in the last few years.[17]

Although, in principle, the civil power had no tutelary rights over the missions, the ministry for the colonies never tolerated the presence of undesirable missionaries. With few exceptions (in the period after the Second World War) only French missionaries were admitted to the colonies. In the Cameroons and Togo, where it was bound by international agreements governing the mandated territories, the French government could not oppose the penetration of foreign Protestant missions – Americans, for example – but it 'nationalised' the German missions, Catholic and Protestant alike, and put them in the hands of French missionaries.[18]

The aim of Rome – not always attained – was to enjoy the constant support of the colonial authorities and to do nothing that might cause them to take umbrage. The principle of their authority was never placed in doubt; yet this authority was rarely applied in favour of the missions. The law on the separation of Church and state (1905) never applied to the African colonies, except in Algeria and Madagascar. The concordat system of earlier times had never applied to the colonies either; as in other spheres, the system open to the missions was left to the discretion of the colonial authorities overseas. Objective examination of these facts leads to the conclusion that this was not to the disadvantage of the missions.

The Napoleonic concordat, by placing the cost of conducting masses and the salaries of the administrative staff on the state budget, gave the Church substantial material advantages. But the church found itself, in return, under the close control of the government, both through express clauses in the concordat itself and through the 'organic' Articles which Napoleon I added unilaterally, and to which the Church submitted without ever accepting the principle. The missions, without ever ceasing to profit from public subsidies – towards staff pay,[19] religious schools and general missionary work – were never subjected to these limitations.

In France the 'Church associations' established after separation, though entitled to receive donations and legacies, could only serve to 'subsidise costs, upkeep or public exercise of divine worship'. In the colonies, local regulations, approved and made general by a decree passed on 15 January, 1939, gave to the 'administrative councils of missions' not only the status of public bodies, but the right to acquire, possess or transfer all personal property and real estate, and all interest, and further to carry on agricultural, industrial and commercial activities. Sometimes even the equipment used in the mass, in schools and for charitable public assistance benefited from tax reliefs granted by local fiscal authorities. Apart from those from the colony, they could receive subsidies from French or foreign institutions. So, from the beginning, the missions were associated with the colonial system.

When it was decided to establish a mission in a certain place, an application was made and a concession granted, as to an ordinary settler. The missionaries (fathers and, under their direction, brothers who devoted themselves not to evangelisation but to material and economic tasks) established themselves and then embarked on the first organisational and building activities: the Church, houses for male religious and nuns, the school, the dispensary, workshops, and so on. The administration gave them support – with varying degrees of enthusiasm – in the form of labour requisitioned by the usual procedure. If reluctance was shown, the fathers protested loudly against 'intolerance'. There were generally gardens and plantations attached to the workshops. The permanent labour force was supplied by the catechumens and later increasingly by paid workers.

On the eve of the Second World War the missions represented an economic force. In the main centres they had joiners' and mechanics' workshops, factories (of carpets at Ségou and Ouagadougou) and printing works which 'usually limited themselves to commercial work destined to supplement the mission budget'.[20] Having obtained vast urban concessions in the first period of colonisation, they possessed valuable real estate which, once developed as building sites for houses or for commercial use, provided them with a considerable income. These economic preoccupations sometimes took priority over spiritual work. The first missions established in the forest regions of Guinea made it their initial task not to spread the Gospel but to produce stabilised coal for export.

In the bush, where Islam did not oppose their influence (e.g. in the Mossi country, the Cameroons and French Equatorial Africa) they did not hesitate to resort to 'administrative' measures involving not only their catechumenate. The chiefs and the population had learnt from experience the cost of opposing the white man. The administration let this happen, but balked when the fathers moved beyond the sacrosanct principles of *commandement* and acted over its head. As late as 1952, the superior of the Brouadou mission, in the Kissi country of Guinea summoned all the canton and village chiefs and taxed them for the reconstruction of the church. The circle commander protested, mainly because he had been neither informed nor consulted. For the population, leaving aside their beards and cassocks, there was often little difference between this particular group of white men and any other. Like everybody else, the fathers issued orders and demanded that work be done for their benefit. Father Bouchaud tried to justify this in the name of his brethren:

> It is perfectly true that the missionaries have forcibly insisted on labour: the reason is that they saw this insistence as a form of apostolate [*sic*], and the work itself as a proof and guarantee of sincere and lasting conversion. In Equatorial Africa, in particular, the dislike for work and the resulting idleness have, for a long time, been one of the main obstacles to the advancement of the population.[21]

We have seen what is to be thought of such a view in the case of the peoples of Equatorial Africa.[22] The same writer also stated that

resentment was felt against the missionaries not only for conse-
crating to material tasks activities that would have been better
employed for spiritual aims, but also for being comfortably
established thanks to the exploitation of the labour of their
faithful.[23]

To exonerate them he recalled that

the missions have no police force, or prisons to impose anything
that might resemble forced labour. As to the moral pressure which
they have supposedly used, whoever wished submitted to it, but
it was easy to elude.[24]

That is easily said. Certain fathers had their 'shock-catechists' and
knew how to use the good offices of the 'friendly' chiefs. Officially,
they had not the means of coercion that were at the administration's
disposal, but they frequently demanded such means. This was the
field where real conflict took place between the administration and
the missions; in this novel antagonism between 'priestcraft and
empire', the 'persecutions' of which the missions complained
generally consisted of refusal or reluctance on the administration's
part to place themselves unconditionally at the former's service. In
certain regions, the missions became openly theocratic. The fathers
demanded of their catechumens the same submission and the same
services as did the canton chiefs or the commander; the collection
after services was taken with as much rigour as the customary poll-
tax. An author cited by Father Bouchaud provided this testimony:

. . . The undisputed ascendancy [of the missionary] and the power
he wielded, however small his material resources, allowed him
to dominate social life with authoritarian methods. . . . In practice,
he had to intervene in disputes between peasants in the fields, as
in conjugal affairs, and sometimes with the holy fury that animated
Christ at His encounter with the money-changers in the Temple.
His main mass on Sundays often resembled a court where the
lukewarm among the faithful received reprimands in a sermon,
such as the most audacious parish priest in Brittany would not
have imagined.[25]

Mongo Beti in his *Pauvre Christ de Bomba* has given a literary
picture of this type of mission and missionary, highly coloured, but
none the less true. At the apogée of the system, under the Vichy
régime, when the theocratic pretensions of some of the fathers were
given official support, a certain Mgr. Thévenoud, vicar apostolic of
Ouagadougou, could be found hiring out his catechumens for money

to the settlers of the lower Ivory Coast, as a labour force for the seasons, just like any canton chief. This excessively temporal tendency, encouraged by the facilities of the colonial system, did far more harm than good to the work of preaching the Gospel. Relations between the missions and the temporal power were none the less not always cordial. However, even at the peak of anti-clericalism during the years 1905 to 1910, there was never any question of applying the law of separation of Church and state, nor of radically lowering the pay and subsidies given to the priests.[26] There were only some evictions of members of religious orders from the public school system and from the three hospitals existing at that time (at the Ballay hospital in Conakry, the chapel was converted into a bath-house). In short, there were a few little wars in the Clochemerle style in which certain aggressive missionaries were not always on the side of the angels. These incidents were always of a local character, and were caused by the anti-clerical fervour of certain administrators, while others at the same time openly supported the missions. The radicals and freemasons in the ministry for the colonies always professed that anti-clericalism – at that time a great subject in France for electoral demagoguery – was not an export article, and that the missionaries, good servants of the colonial venture, were to be maintained and given support.

Conflicts centred mostly round authority, more than any question of doctrine, as in the case of the quarrel in 1932–4 between the Mossi mission, under Mgr. Thévenoud, and the administration of Governor-General Brévié concerning baptism and the freedom of women. The missions took under their protection young girls or women anxious to avoid forced marriages. This led to violent conflict mainly with the chiefs, who considered that their fiancées or wives had thus been 'stolen'; the administration, entirely indifferent to the fate of the women but needing the chiefs, reacted against this interference in their 'indigenous policy', particularly when the Bobo people of Dédougou appealed to the authority of the missions and rebelled against the chiefs imposed on them. It should be noted that the opposition was directed against Brévié (later secretary of state for the colonies under Vichy), whose policy towards the missions was the most favourable on record, while the radical freemason Governor Reste showed himself a strong supporter of the missions.[27] The claim by Father Bouchaud that the administration was constantly favouring Islam to the detriment of the missions must be rejected as an accusation of 'administrative persecution'.

It is a fact that, for a hundred years, its policy has always been pro-Muslim, and that it has always reserved its favours for, and granted its support to, Islam, introducing the marabouts into pagan areas, imposing Muslim chiefs on animist groups, constructing mosques and Koran schools, and organising and subsidising pilgrimages to Mecca.[28]

We have already indicated how, on the contrary, the administration, haunted by the danger of the Senussi brotherhood, pan-Islamism and so on, gave proof of a constant dislike for Islam. From D'Amadu Bamba to Sheikh Hamallah, hundreds of *marabouts* were imprisoned and deported, even when their doctrines had not the slightest anticolonialist character. The fathers were never subject to such treatment. As to the mosques and the Koran schools, it is interesting to draw up a balance sheet of what was constructed by the administration and compare it with the Catholic churches and schools, constructed with subsidies, remembering that Islam claimed 70 per cent of the population, and the Catholic religion 8·5 per cent according to Father Bouchaud's own figure. As regards 'Koran schools' the administration occasionally organised three or four *medersas*, all situated in the Sahel-Sahara region. It is true that the administration made efforts to use Islam and its organisation for its own purposes, closely supervising the *marabouts* and granting them subsidies to the extent that they consented to serve as political agents. The same is true of pilgrimages to Mecca, which were only organised in order to be kept under control. The missions were unable to establish themselves and make progress except through the support of the colonial régime. This was because at the outset they represented a religion alien to the country.

After this account of the material side of their activity, a few words should now be said about the men who represented the missions. Faith being, in principle, the common motive which leads man to enter the ecclesiastical life, we should examine what it was that particularly led to the missionary vocation. We cannot be sure that it was always the desire to win souls – the missions were not the only field in which evangelism could be practised. Without excluding piety as a driving force, one may be forgiven for suspecting that, as in the case of the administrators, the allure of the 'wide-open spaces', the desire to escape, played its part. The taste for 'liberty', in the sense evoked by Delavignette in connection with the administrators, the chance of action, the exercise of authority, together with the conviction of acting for the glory of God and gaining heaven by suffering and sacrifice, were certainly not absent in certain calls. There were the risks to health and life inherent in the job – as elsewhere in colonial employment, civil or military. But what a difference between this ministry, where one could build and work on new souls, and the much less exciting task of priest or curate in a French parish.

The first period of colonisation saw bush missionaries – brothers of the administrators whom Delafosse depicted in his 'spiritual states of a colonial'. They and the administrators shared the same thoughts and the same prejudices. But they also had the same qualities: a perfect knowledge of the country and its languages, which was all the deeper since the missionaries were unaffected by the impermanence of administrative employment. Many of them spent all their lives in the same region, attached to the same mission. Those given to writing have left documents which are often invaluable; in matters of African linguistics, a greatly neglected field, their contribution was vital. Their insufficient scientific training – they were specialists neither in history, ethnography nor linguistics – often detracts from the value of their contribution; but at least the contribution was made.[29] They went on working far longer than the administrators of the same generation – those among them, that is, whose careers were not prematurely ended by sickness. The only retirement age for missionaries was when their physical powers had definitely been spent. After the Second World War there were still men who had been living in the same corner of Africa since the beginning of the century, and who had hardly ever returned to France except during the First World War on military call-up. Among them were those who led saintly lives – who, even without making conversions, dedicated themselves in a totally disinterested way to their works of charity, visiting hamlets and villages without respite, caring for the sick as much as their means would allow, drinking swamp water and sleeping on hard ground.

But there were also those whose worldly taste for authority predominated, who were intolerant and argumentative, soldiers of Christ in the manner of the Crusaders. Such were Mgr. Augouard at Brazzaville and Mgr. Thévenoud at Ouagadougou, whose biography, however favourable, could not hide his difficult character. These were generally the ones who were given executive posts. Their skirmishes with the administration were usually due to their temperament. Bitterness and quarrelling sometimes occurred even within the missions.

We have not yet described the missions' structure. Under the Sacred Congregation of Propaganda Fide's authority, Africa was divided into ecclesiastical areas directed by a prefect or a vicar apostolic.[30] Each region came under an institute, or rather a religious congregation devoting itself wholly or partly to missionary activity. Among such orders involved with Africa were the Capuchins, the Dominicans and the Jesuits; and among specialised congregations, the Fathers of the Holy Spirit, the White Fathers (African missionary society founded in Algeria) and the Lyons Missions. The members of these congregations came under the authority of the 'mother house' in France, where the missionaries were trained, spent their leave and came back on retirement. Each congregation had its 'fiefs'. Senegal, Guinea, French Equatorial Africa and the greater part of the Cameroons were run by the Fathers of the Holy Spirit; at Bamako, Ougadougou, Bobo-Dioulasso, Gao and N'Zérékoro were the White Fathers; in Dahomey, Togo and the Ivory Coast the Lyons Missions;[31] in Adamaoua were the Fathers of the Sacred Heart of Saint-Quentin, and so on. This often led to a narrow *esprit de corps*, and bickering when the time came to adjust frontiers; over this the Holy See had to call them to order on numerous occasions.[32]

As in the administration, so among the missionaries the 'man of the bush' faded away with the generation after 1914. The heroic period was over and the missions were firmly installed. The liking for authority did not disappear, but a taste for comfort made its appearance (to which Father Bouchaud made allusions), and the truly evangelistic temperament became more of a rarity. Throughout successive decades, there remained in the minds of missionaries an unshakeable belief in the oneness of the colonial venture and missionary work.[33] This led the missionaries, with few exceptions, to share the viewpoint of the settler. There was no confidence anywhere in the 'natives', who, as in the administration, could at best occupy subordinate positions in the missions, in particular as catechists. Thought was given to the necessity of training African priests. But the fathers were so convinced of the inferiority and lack of dignity of the 'natives', who were not 'mature', that in practice they discouraged any 'vocation' that might show itself among the Africans. Years passed without a single priest being trained in the seminaries established in Africa; in thirty years, the seminary at Dahomey only trained three priests. In the Sudan and Guinea there was only one indigenous priest in 1944. Even in Senegal, where a seminary had been in existence since 1857, the first three priests to be trained left the country: one died at sea, the second became a parish priest in the diocese of Meaux in France, and the third went to exercise his ministry in Haiti. From 1870 to 1938 there were only three ordinations. This failure must be ascribed to the much more rigorous demands made on the African candidates for the priesthood than occurred in France, and especially to the fathers' desire to keep them at a secondary level. According to a missionary writer, difficulties of recruitment did not stem from any particular lack of aptitude on the part of the blacks over the keeping of their ecclesiastical vows. He even stated that there was

N

> no danger as regards continence . . . the real danger tended to lie in independence of mind and the diverse forms of an easily susceptible pride.[34]

The real trouble was the candidates' refusal to accept racial prejudices.

> The European world adheres to what is called colour prejudice, and this prejudice fights on its own behalf. Without going as far as the Americans, we must admit that one has the right to choose one's acquaintance.[35]

And so,

> if the father [European] is kind and liberal, if the priest [indigenous] remains modest and discreet, they end up not only by loving, but what is often more difficult than loving, understanding one another.[36]

The admission of this state of mind easily explains the delay in setting about training African clergy. Its main causes were the moral 'imperialism' of the missionary congregations and the racialism of many of their members. All this is recognised, with more or less openness, in the Church today, where it is viewed as resulting from a 'historical situation' for which the Church was not responsible. That is one point of view – and it enabled the administrators and the army to wash their hands of the colonial past, and place the whole burden on a situation that was created by history. Father Mosmans admitted:

> The evangelisation of Africa advanced hand in hand with colonial conquest. The Church sometimes supported the colonial regime as being indispensable to peace and prosperity.[37]

Without over-emphasising the 'sometimes', let us simply note the admission that the Church accepted the viewpoint of the apologists of colonisation, which in reality did not bring about peace, except in very relative terms,[38] and which did bring misery.

> The Church often benefited from [the colonial system] to the extent that colonisation favoured dispersion of missionaries across the African continent. If often received subsidies for its schools and its work, sometimes even for its Churches.[39]

And let us add in conclusion that if the colonial power was generous, it was because the work seemed profitable to its own interests.

REFERENCES

1. *Afrique noire occidentale et centrale*, Vol. I, 2nd edition, p. 128, note 1.

2. Except for the Cameroons and Togo, where the French protestant missions replaced the German protestant missions after the war, taking over their possessions and their work, and where certain foreign missions (notably American) installed themselves on these territories on the basis of their international status.

3. On the state of mind of official Catholic circles at the moment of the 'turning-point' in the 1950s, see *Colonisation et conscience chrétienne*, Paris, A. Fayard, 1953. In this collection, with a preface by Mgr. Chappoulie, Joseph Folliet expressed his loyalty to the 'great French tradition of colonisation . . . that of the revolutionaries who set free the Black slaves, those of Schoelcher, Binger, Savorgnan de Brazza, Lyautey, Van Vollenhoven, Félix Eboué. . . .' p. 34). He declared himself 'exasperated by the flightiness . . . of certain left-wing catholics' (p. 13). He contrasted colonisation and colonialism, which he rejected as a 'state of mind'.

4. Joseph Folliet, *Le Droit de colonisation*. Paris, Bloud et Gay, 1930.

5. François de Vittoria, *De Indis recenter inventis; De Indis, sive de jure belli Hispanorum in barbaros*, 1532.

6. Quoted by Joseph Folliet, op. cit., p. 265.

7. Albert Sarraut, *Grandeur et servitude coloniales*. Paris, Editions du Sagittaire, 1931, p. 121.

8. It was a curse upon Ham, the son of Noah and alleged ancestor of the Black race, according to certain interpretations of the Bible.

9. Quoted by Georges Goyau, *La France missionnaire dans les cinq parties du monde*. Paris, Plon, 1948, vol. II, p. 177.

10. For example, Father Ducatillon, 'Théologie de la colonisation', *Revue de l'Action populaire*, July 1955.

11. M. H. Lelong, O.P., *Mes Frères du Congo*. Alger, Baconnier, 1946, vol. I, p. 290.

12. Letter 'Au milieu des sollicitudes' of 16 February, 1892.

13. *Afrique Française*, 1923, No. 12, p. 631 (address of 11 November, 1923).

14. Father Bouchaud, *L'Eglise en Afrique noire*. Paris, La Palatine, 1958, pp. 106–7.

15. Op. cit., p. 14.

16. Based on the translation of the treatise on canon law by Canon R. Naz, Paris, Letouzey, 1948, vol. I, p. 391. Quoted by F. Méjean, *Le Vatican contre la France d'Outre-mer*. Paris, Fischbacher, 1947, pp. 37–8.

17. François Méjean, op. cit., pp. 40–1.

18. Note, however, that the Acts of Berlin and Brussels modified by the St. Germain-en-Laye Convention of 10 September, 1919 (Article 11), obliged the signatories to guarantee the missions of all nations under the convention free movement and the right of residence 'to pursue their work of religion'. But these orders could be twisted by invoking 'security and public order'.

19. Fixed until 1924 according to a salary scale for 'personnel in the service of the Churches', then by the decree of 12 March, 1924, enacted by orders of the governors.

20. Father Bouchaud, op. cit., p. 62. In Togo, until quite recently, the Catholic mission press printed the *Journal officiel*.

21. Bouchaud, op. cit., p. 40.

22. See the texts quoted by Father Daigre above.

23. Bouchaud, op. cit., p. 38.

24. Ibid., p. 40.

25. René Charbonneau Beauchar, 'Missionnaires d'hier', *Cahiers Charles de Foucauld*, vol. XLII, 2nd trim. 1956, quoted by Bouchaud, op. cit., p. 42.

26. Only French West Africa suppressed the school subsidies from 1903 to 1942. French Equatorial Africa continued to pay; in the Cameroons and Togo the provision and amount were stipulated by decree.

27. On this affair cf. Paul Baudu, *Vieil Empire, jeune Eglise. Mgr. V. Thévenoud (1878–1949)*. Paris, Ed. La Savane, 1957.

28. Bouchaud, op. cit., p. 135.

29. The mission journals provide major interest as sources of contemporary local history; they were kept regularly from the beginning of the century, which, with a very few exceptions, was not the case of the administrative *Journaux de poste*.

30. The vicar apostolic held personal episcopal rank in the form of a bishopric *in partibus*.

31. The founder of the Lyons Missions, Mgr. de Marion-Brésillac, had close contacts with the Marseilles merchant Victor Régis, who initiated trade in palm oil and was mainly interested in Dahomey (cf. Georges Goyau, *La France missionaire* . . . Paris, Plon, 1948, vol. II, book VII).

32. Publications of 1919 to 1926 and finally the encyclical *Evangelii Praecones* (2 June, 1951) which stressed: 'The orders and the religious congregations may glory in the mission they have received among the pagans as conquests they have added to the kingdom of Christ; but let them recall that they have not received the territories of the mission in personal and perpetual right; these territories have been confided to them according to the will of the Apostolic See which retains the right and duty to guard over their just and full development.' (Ed. de la Bonne Presse, Paris, n.d., p. 23.)

33. A single knowledgeable criticism of the French colonial system was that of Père Lelong who knew the local conflicts with the anti-clerical administration of N'Zérékoré; it looked different in 1946.

34. Jean-Marie Sédès, *Le Clergé indigène de l'Empire français*. Paris, Bloud et Gay, 1944, 2 vols.

35. Ibid.

36. Ibid., p. 8.

37. Father Mosmans, *L'Eglise à l'heure de l'Afrique*. Tournai, Casterman, 1961, p. 69.

38. His colleague Father Lelong wrote: 'We often exaggerate a little when, among the good deeds that our civilisation has brought to Black Africa, we claim that of peace. The soldiers who lost their lives in Europe in the settlement of accounts among the great white nations could have supplied victims to the internecine wars of the negroes for centuries.' Lelong, *Ces Hommes qu'on appelle anthropophages*. Paris, Alsatia, 1946, p. 56.

39. Mosmans, op. cit.

3. *Culture and Education*[1]

(a) CULTURAL OPPRESSION

In matters of culture the colonial 'achievement' was essentially negative: negation, and if possible, destruction of the cultural values and institutions surviving from the pre-colonial period was its essence. Some colonials, such as Delafosse and General Meynier, recognised this and deplored it as an error; they did not understand that this 'error' was, in fact, a necessity inherent in the colonial system.

Every national culture, using the term in its broadest sense, is conscious. It can turn into a means of resistance. The justification of the colonial system, which its creators presented to the world and even to themselves, was that it was applied to 'infant peoples', incapable and without personality. All their cultural manifestations were regarded as puerile and barbaric. The missionaries, moreover, saw in these manifestations a demonic character. Nobody was interested in culture – folklore, archaeology or 'Negro art' – except as a curiosity and something bizarre. Some administrators became amateur folklorists and archaeologists – and for the uses that might be made of it in 'indigenous policy'. This was the spirit in which Governor-General Clozel set up in 1915 a committee for historic and scientific studies in French West Africa, of which the bulletin included studies by soldiers and administrators interested in ethnography, history or natural science. It was not until 1938 that an Institut français d'Afrique noire (I.F.A.N.) was established at Dakar, conceived, incidentally, as a base for French Africanists and not as a centre for training African research workers. Either African institutions were ignored or attempts were made to use them as political instruments. If they proved rebellious or unsuitable they were destroyed.

It was the same with what Africa had assimilated of Arab culture. This culture was certainly not up to date; all it taught was Arabic calligraphy and the mechanical recitation of the Koran. But this limited endeavour, which at least made possible a written form of communication by applying the Arabic alphabet to African languages,[2] was often surpassed, certainly among the Arabic-speaking peoples of the Sahara (the Moors and the Kounta Arabs, for example). At Timbuctu – however great its decadence compared with past ages – at Djenné and especially in Mauritania, education survived at a higher level in grammar and literature, theology and law. In Fouta-Djalon, at Bondu, there was not a single village without a school. The number of *karamokos* who had a complete knowledge of literary Arabic was very high. In 1907 the inspector of Muslim education, Mariani, summoned by the government-general from Algeria to hold an inquiry, noted with surprise in his report that he had met *marabouts* not only in Fouta-Djalon but even in Lower Guinea capable of conversing in literary Arabic. According to a census of 1906 there were 3,757 *karamokos* in Guinea who taught over 25,000 pupils.

This contribution of Arabic culture was ignored or considered dangerous. The administrative staff as a whole had no knowledge of it. In the course of the conquest, some manuscripts were destroyed, others were scattered among the private collections of officers and administrators as exotic 'curiosities'; while the rest were sent to France where they still collect dust in reserve collections and depositories. When Roume, in 1906, set up a 'Service of Muslim Affairs', several attempts were made to win over and control traditional Muslim educationalists. This quickly came to a stop in the absence of competent staff. As far as Koranic education went, the tour of inspection by the Algerian inspector Mariani was never followed up. It was enough for police control to be exercised over the *marabouts*. At a higher level, the school for the sons of chiefs at Saint-Louis was named *medersa*, and similar *medersas* or, to use a more suitable expression, 'Franco-Arab schools' were set up at Timbuctu, Djenné and Boutilimit.[3] The first inspector of education in French West Africa, Georges Hardy, admitted that these establishments provided nothing resembling higher education. They were 'institutions of a political character, very useful but without scientific pretensions'.[4] Their purpose was to train interpreters, judges and clerks of Muslim courts.[5] Nor did it take long before this was regarded as a suspect concession. The *medersa* of Djenné was soon closed, and that in Saint-Louis changed back in 1922 into a school for sons of chiefs and for interpreters. In short, it was not a question of maintaining or encouraging Arabic learning, but of training a few indigenous officials capable of translating into French the words and writings of notables or Arabic scholars.

Left to its own devices, Arabic culture declined. The Arabic scholars had formerly had the chance of reaching a certain social or poltical rank; they were councillors or secretaries to kings, and some became chiefs themselves. But from now on they functioned only at a lower level, as headmasters of Koranic schools, advisers to canton chiefs (often suspect to the administration), *marabout* miracle-workers living on alms, or at most as heads of mystical brotherhoods, subject to constant persecution. Otherwise they had to accept the role of agents of the administration. In consequence, the level of their knowledge, even within the setting of traditional scholasticism, was reduced.[6] Even in Mauritania, colonial intervention led to the decline of Arabic culture, mainly at the level of higher education.[7]

As to African cultures proper, these were totally ignored and took refuge in secrecy, which was aided by their esoteric character. The sacred forests, which were places of cult and of initiation, provided refuge for 'camps', often of long duration, where young people were given preparation for life and an education, that included physical tests, corresponding to the needs of their environment. This education was in many respects archaic; many of its features had survived from the period when life in the forest and hunting took precedence over agriculture. However, some evolution had taken place: in the nineteenth century the educational system we have mentioned promoted the spread of the syllabic script used particularly by the Vai of Sierra Leone and by the Toma. The training was given in the Toma country, in the sacred forests, and it was used as a form of communication. The colonisers mistrusted the 'witch-doctors' schools', and forced labour made the long probationary period of seven to nine years more and more difficult to maintain.

> Since the economic conditions of life have changed and the young men have been taken away by recruitment, the period of probation has been shortened, so as to allow the villages to regain their workers.[8]

The craze for 'Negro art' after the Second World War, often a sign of intellectual snobbery, proceeded generally from a complete lack of understanding of the dignity and significance of African sculpture (manifested by such phrases as 'spontaneity', 'return to the primitive soul' and so on, in the same category as drawings by children and the insane, or automatic writing). In Africa itself this fashion was expressed in the looting of such objects for the profit of art speculators. During the belated restoration of the royal palaces at Abomey, little was done to ensure the conservation of monuments of the pre-colonial period, which were thrown away or destroyed. In conclusion, colonial action in cultural matters was limited more or less exclusively to education, an education conceived as strictly utilitarian and proceeding from the only culture considered to be of any value – that of the coloniser.

(b) HISTORY OF AFRICAN COLONIAL EDUCATION

Until the beginning of the twentieth century, education was left almost completely to the missionaries, in particular the Fathers of Ploermel, to whom the government had entrusted the two schools at Gorée and Saint-Louis, and the Sisters of Saint-Joseph of Cluny.[9] Lay education was introduced by Faidherbe in Senegal in 1854, with the aim of attracting Muslims, who made up the majority at Saint-Louis and who generally refused to entrust their children to the priests. With the same political aim, he then set up an *école des ôtages* (a significant name), intended to train the sons of vassal chiefs or those who supported France. It was closed down for financial reasons in 1872 after eighteen years. From the Faidherbe period to the end of the century very little progress was made. The number of schools and pupils in attendance was apparently fairly high in 1870, taking into account the extent of effective colonial occupation; but everything was concentrated in a few localities: Saint-Louis, Gorée, Dakar and Libreville. In the Sudan, the army set up numerous schools during the conquest: but these improvised schools run by non-commissioned officers soon disappeared. In 1860, 860 pupils attended the schools of Saint-Louis, including 200 girls. In 1898, even with a growing population, the number of pupils in the nine primary schools had not risen. It should be added that a secondary school was set up in 1884, with a limited number of pupils. The *école des ôtages* was re-established in 1893 with the name of 'school for the sons of chiefs'.

In the Sudan, there were some thirty schools by the end of the century, among them one school for the sons of chiefs at Kayes and one vocational school with some 800 pupils. We hear that from 1886 to 1897 the former was subjected to 'a series of experiments by trial and error. Material provisions were, moreover, very primitive.'[10] By 1902 it had seventy-five pupils in three classes, under the direction of a headmaster and an assistant from Algeria. The vocational school had been a total failure until 1900. For the rest: two urban schools at Kayes and Medina with fifty and sixty pupils respectively, mainly young Wolofs from Saint-Louis families, and twenty-five circle schools. In Guinea, the Holy Ghost Fathers had been put in charge of the school at Boffa in 1878, and later, in co-operation with the Sisters of Saint-Joseph of Cluny, they ran two schools at Conakry, that for boys opening in 1890, and that for girls in 1893. In 1898 two more schools were added, all situated in Lower Guinea and generally run by the Church. Altogether there were 300 pupils in the whole of Guinea. On the Ivory Coast there were seven schools for boys and one for girls, all run by missionaries, and five village schools run by African monitors. In Dahomey, up till 1894, education was provided by Portuguese missionaries teaching in their own language. They were replaced after annexation by French missionaries. There was a total of some twenty schools, centred at Porto-Novo, Ouidah and Cotonou. Finally, in the Congo, the missions had 2,654 children in their schools, with staffs of eighty-five, male and female. In Libreville, where the Sisters of Saint-Joseph of

Cluny were established from 1863, the mission schools, with 300 pupils, took in almost the entire school population.

These figures should be properly understood. Only the schools in the main towns can be considered primary schools in the normal meaning of the term. The village schools, and those run by the rural missions, were largely improvised, and so lacked any stability. Often they closed down suddenly, with the departure of the school-master, who himself only gave lessons as a marginal occupation beside his other jobs. In Senegal, where education had been longest established, a witness noted that there were a large number of schools, but only two teachers with elementary school diplomas. The others were occasional teachers, mainly Fathers of the Order of Ploermel and Sisters of Saint-Joseph of Cluny, whose instruction was mediocre and teaching methods 'frightening'.[11]

In the Sudan, an official report said the following concerning the mission schools:

> These schools, which have benefited to date by fairly high subsidies from the colonial budget, have not brought any appreciable results. . . . The pupils are employed in agricultural work, cultivating the fields of grain and cereals necessary for the needs of the mission throughout the year.[12]

The Act on congregations led the colonial administration in 1913 to withdraw the running of the public schools from the missions. It exempted only those that were attached to the missions proper, and consequently set up private schools to which the administration gave subsidies, at least in French Equatorial Africa.[13] Forced for the first time to concern himself with questions of education, the governor-general of French West Africa issued three ordinances on 24 November, 1903, instituting a school system that was to last, with a few variations, as long as the colonial system itself. The texts were drawn up, on instructions from Roume, by Governor Camille Guy, a university graduate who had entered the colonial administration and who, at that time, held the post of secretary-general.

The system established was as follows: Primary elementary education was given in three types of schools. At the lower level was the village school (*école de village*), where indigenous monitors gave instruction. They taught the 'rudiments of the French language and arithmetic' and set out to 'initiate the children in agricultural work'.[14] At a higher level was the regional school (*école régionale*) situated in the main town of the circle, comprising both preparatory and elementary classes given by assistant teachers, and a middle course taught by a European teacher acting as headmaster. The course as completed by a local 'certificate of primary elementary

N*

studies', of a lower standard than in France. Alongside this, the urban school (*école urbaine*), in the main towns of the colonies and big centres, which educated the children of Europeans and the assimilated population according to the French curriculum leading to the certificate of primary elementary studies.

Vocational education was given at one school only, the École Pinet-Laprade, at Gorée, which existed between 1904 and 1924. It trained overseers, but had to provide its practical training away from school premises 'in public and private workshops'. Higher primary and commercial education was given by the École Faidherbe at Saint-Louis. The higher primary schools, of which only one was established, enrolled pupils who had passed the certificate examination. The course of studies lasted two years, but could be reduced to one year according to the current need for recruiting medium-rank personnel.

Finally a teacher training college (*école normale*) at Saint-Louis trained Africans for the whole of French West Africa in two sections: a section for school-teachers and an administrative section for interpreters and chiefs. It recruited its pupils from among the outstanding leavers from the higher primary schools, and the course of studies lasted three years. This was the old school for the sons of chiefs in a new role. This structure took its inspiration mainly from existing village, regional and urban schools. But any extension it proposed remained for a long time in the realm of theory. Even its author recognised that it was hardly applicable except to Senegal, and an ordinance of 1911 gave the colonies within the group freedom to organise their own schools.[15] The colonial administration showed little interest in education and had not the money to devote to it. Between 1895 and 1908 French West Africa devoted less than 2 per cent of its budget to this purpose.[16] Some schools remained without furniture for over three years.[17] At the start, a few school-teachers were recruited from France; but there were few candidates, and the colonial bureaucracy did not encourage this practice.

The principle was established in 1904 that the post of inspector of education should be created on the staff of the governor of each colony. This inspector was to be no more than an agent under the control of the governor, who meant to retain education under his direct authority. The first inspectors, who took up their posts in 1908, were chosen at random: the governors, by their own arbitrary decision, often hired adventurers who had become temporary school-teachers in the colony without qualifications or proficiency.[18] With the shortage of staff, teachers continued to be recruited from every conceivable source. Bankrupt settlers or merchants, or trading-post agents released by the owners; even army personnel and government officials were pressed to give service in their spare time.

In 1906 there were twelve regional schools in Guinea – that is to say less than one in each circle. Conakry had one urban school and one girls' school, and there existed only three village schools. Altogether 1,345 pupils, among them 234 girls, attended the public schools. The fathers ran a further three schools, with eighty-three pupils. The staff was made up of thirteen male and six female teachers, all European, with eighteen male and two female African monitors. In 1907 the whole of French West Africa had only seventy-six village schools, thirty-three regional schools (two-thirds of the circles had no school facilities) and twelve urban schools. By 1912 the numbers of pupils in the public school system had risen to 11,000; another 2,600 pupils attended private schools.

In French Equatorial Africa the problem of education was almost completely ignored; rather, it was left to the missions. The first budget allocation to be granted, which consisted of 12,000 francs, was allocated in 1906 to the establishment of a secular school at Libreville in Gabon. In 1911, out of a budget total of 2,200,000 francs in Gabon, 25,000 francs were allocated to education in Gabon, and of this only 5,406.84 francs were actually spent; three of the four schools that had existed in 1910 were closed down for lack of teachers. In the school at Libreville, the only one left open, teaching was carried on by civil servants, who thus acquired a supplementary source of income. The same year the Middle Congo spent less than 20,000 francs on education; Ubangi and Chad nothing at all.[19] An order of 4 April, 1911, providing for the training of teaching staff, was not applied; between 1910 and 1919 only five school-teachers were recruited for French Equatorial Africa.

In 1912, French West Africa took the first step toward the implementation of principles suggested in 1903. An education service was established, directed by the governor-general (who thus did not surrender his rights), assisted by an inspector of schools for French West Africa. The first inspector was Georges Hardy, a graduate in history and geography, and a former pupil of the École normale supérieure. The teachers' training college, the Pinet-Laprade school, the Faidherbe school of administration and l'école des pupilles mécaniciens de la Marine, Dakar, were placed under his direct authority, and became federal institutions. The teachers' training college, hitherto merely a training section set up in 1904 at the school for the sons of chiefs, was transferred from Saint-Louis to Gorée. Shortly afterwards it changed its name to William Ponty Training College.

In the colonies the inspectors of education were chosen from among school-teachers holding the higher diploma of the 'certificate of professional aptitude', with five years' experience in French West Africa. Temporary teachers were thus eliminated, but favouritism was not completely rooted out. Although recruitment was 'by competition', the competition was held on the spot, among colleagues, and it was of doubtful value. Moreover, the government-general reserved its right to remove from the competition any candidate considered undesirable. An ordinance of 25 January, 1913, set up a 'higher council of primary education' which was to be consulted on all regular subjects within its competence, and issued a *Bulletin de l'enseignement de l'Afrique occidentale française*. At the end of 1914 the total number of pupils was estimated at 17,000 in French West Africa (Senegal, 4,500; Upper Senegal and Niger, 3,000; Guinea, 2,600; Ivory Coast, 3,400; Dahomey, 3,000; Niger, 400; and Mauritania, 100).[20] But the education brought in French West Africa remained low, being less than 2,000,000 francs in 1914. The war halted the progress that had been made between 1912 and 1914. In 1922 the number of pupils in French West Africa rose to 25,000 in the state system, with at least another 5,000 pupils in private schools. In 1944 the number in the state schools was 57,000, with 19,000 mission school pupils.

Progress, as can be seen, was very slow, and indeed was almost non-existent in certain colonies after the economic crisis. It also nearly ground to a halt during the Second World War, due to shortage of teachers (except in private schools, which benefited after 1942 from a very favourable system of subsidies). The structure of education evolved very little. The ordinances of 1918 and 1923 added only detailed modifications to the 1903 structure. The village school, always a one-class school, was to comprise henceforth basically two stages (a preparatory and an elementary course), and took in children between the ages of six and eleven. From 1920 to 1923 the number of these schools rose from 227 to 275 and the total number of pupils from 16,000 to 22,000. In 1938 there were 310 such schools with 26,195 pupils, of whom 2,625 were girls.

The 'regional schools' comprised three classes, two of preparatory and elementary level, and one at middle level. This last class enrolled the best pupils of the lower course from the local and neighbouring village schools within a radius determined by the region or the school sector. This school sector was in future to be identical with the circle, but in practice it encompassed several circles (in 1922 there were 69 regional schools for 115 circles, in 1938 there were 96). The course was completed by the certificate of primary elementary studies which, in order of merit, gave access to the higher school. The middle course was usually given by a European teacher with a teaching diploma. The number of pupils in the 'regional schools', which varied according to the need for lower-grade administrative staff, rose slowly (4,791 pupils in 1920, 4,831 in 1923). The pupils were given bursaries and were generally boarders, the maximum age being fifteen years.

The 'urban school' likewise comprised three classes: these were divided into indigenous classes, which followed the same curriculum as the 'regional schools', and European classes, reserved for European children and those of assimilated families, which followed the curriculum of French schools. In 1938 there was a total of twenty-six, with 7,944 pupils. In 1927 Senegal succeeded in getting all its 'urban schools' to take up the European curriculum. The latter was clearly unsuitable, but the Senegalese demand is explained by the endeavour to get away from the 'indigenous curriculum', which provided education of a much lower standard.

Finally, each colony had a 'higher primary school', usually in the capital. There were six in 1922 (not in Niger or Mauritania). The average numbers at each school of this type ranged from eighty to a hundred. The 'higher primary school' comprised three sections and one common year. The first section, reserved for sons of chiefs, was intended simply to give some supplementary education; the second took in candidates wishing to become school-teachers and assistant medical personnel, who were then sent to specialised federal schools; and the third led to a second year of a higher course, which 'trained local agents strictly necessary to the needs of the colony',[21] such as postmen, medical orderlies, agents of public works, etc. The secondary course at Saint-Louis, which in 1914 had some fifty pupils and did not go beyond the third form, was provided only for the bourgeoisie of that city. The institution was turned into the Lycée Faidherbe in 1920, but its numbers remained modest – for example, sixty-nine at the end of the school year 1922–3, including primary classes. A decree passed on 28 March, 1924, set up in French West Africa a 'colonial diploma of competence', which was to be the equivalent of the *baccalauréat* offered by the Lycée Faidherbe and the 'Secondary Course of Dakar'; the latter, established in 1925 and turned into the Lycée Van Vollenhoven in 1940, was 'destined mainly for the European population that was growing more numerous at Dakar'.[22]

Now we turn to the federal schools. The Training College at Gorée[23] enrolled trainee teachers and medical students. The course of studies for future teachers lasted three years with a leaving certificate which entitled them to join the ranks of 'secondary education'. The trainee 'assistant doctors', after the common year, took a second year of specialisation preparing for a local qualification: and were then sent to the school of medicine. In 1938 Ponty

College had 220 students. The school of medicine, set up in 1918, trained assistant doctors and pharmacists; the veterinary sections were transferred to Bamako in 1924. It was organised on a military basis and came under the army's colonial health service.

Vocational schools were a local concern, as vocational training was left to the initiative of the colonies. They were gradually set up in the various capital towns, first as manual sections of the 'higher primary schools'; only in 1939 did the growing development of technical services lead to the establishment of 'higher technical school' at Bamako, which took school-leavers from the 'higher primary school' to train as 'lower-rank' officers such as draughtsmen, surveyors or overseers of public works. A second teachers' training college was set up at Katibougou in the Sudan with a predominantly agricultural curriculum, training teachers and also lower-rank officers in agriculture, forestry and water supply services. A school for 'rural education monitors' was opened at Dabou in the Ivory Coast in 1938.

A training college for girls was opened at Rufisque only in 1939, and the numbers it enrolled remained small. It trained school-teachers, and midwives for the medical school. Education for women remained poor: in 1922 in French West Africa, only 1,000 out of 25,000 pupils were girls. In 1938 the proportion was 6,529 out of 56,852, and in 1945, including private education, it was 21,355 out of 110,951.[24] Except in South Dahomey, and to a lesser degree in the big centres of Senegal, parents objected to sending their girls to school, which they considered an introduction to bad morals. The other African territories organised themselves after the pattern of French West Africa at varying rates of progress.

In Togo, German statistics for 1914 recorded 12,000 pupils at mission schools – 7,000 in Catholic missions and 5,000 in Protestant missions. Some government schools trained lower-rank staff for the administration. In 1922, statistics indicated 1,500 pupils in government education, plus 5,000 in private schools, mainly run by French missions. An ordinance of 1928 established one 'higher primary school', but the training course it ran was closed down in 1924 for reasons of economy. An ordinance of 1929 granted a subsidy raising the salaries of the staff at private mission schools by two-thirds on condition that the medium of education should be French, except for one hour a day; the 'catechism' school, where instruction was given mainly in the local languages, did not profit from this measure. In 1930, government education embraced 3,800 pupils, and in 1944, 7,000 – to which must be added 7,000 pupils in Catholic and 1,500 pupils in Protestant missions – making a total of 15,500 pupils, of whom 2,500 were girls.

In the Cameroons, German statistics mention 41,500 pupils in mission schools in 1913. Instruction was given in the local languages and at a low standard. Efforts were made to develop education in German: six German teachers worked in seven public schools in 1914, and there were 1,000 pupils. An ordinance of 21 July, 1921, introduced a system of education based on the pattern of French West Africa. In 1935 there were approximately 8,500 pupils in the public school system: 2,646 pupils were in the eight regional schools, half this number being at Douala and Yaoundé, and 5,904 pupils in the village schools. There were, moreover, a few vocational schools with small numbers of pupils. There was one 'higher primary school' at Yaoundé, opened in 1927; in 1935 it had about eighty pupils. Its third year led to the 'school for hygiene assistants' at Ayos where the course lasted three years.[25] The 'recognised' mission schools, which enjoyed the same advantages as those in Togo, had 6,610 pupils, and the 'non-recognised' schools 81,756. In 1944 the figures were 18,000 in public education (among them 2,000 girls), 16,000 in recognised private education and 100,000 in 'catechism schools'.

The situation in Chad in 1921 resembled that in the Sudan before 1900. One school with fifty to sixty pupils existed at Fort-Lamy, but it closed for six months when the only teacher went on leave. To this were added ten *circonscription* schools, which were left to the care of civil servants, non-commissioned officers, or African monitors whose own education was very slight.[26] In 1928 there were a total of 3,431 pupils in the public schools and 6,000 in mission schools; in 1935 the respective figures were 6,594 and 9,327; in 1939, 9,290 and 12,605, and in 1944 approximately 10,000 and 15,000.

Most lamentable of all was the situation in French Equatorial Africa. An ordinance of 1925 set forth plans for an organisation similar to that in French West Africa, but it was never applied. Fourteen school-teachers were recruited between 1920 and 1924, and twenty-one between 1926 and 1930. It was not until 1935 that a higher primary school was opened at Brazzaville, and an education service run by an inspector only came into being in 1937. Before that, education had been in the hands of the office of political affairs. In 1941, Eboué cited the 'drowsiness' of education as among the factors accounting for the deplorable state of affairs in French Equatorial Africa.

(c) THE SPIRIT AND METHODS OF EDUCATION

Without rejecting Eboué's evaluation, it might be more correct to say that the economic and social backwardness, and the generally miserable conditions which accompany the trade economy, were reflected in the state of education. The greater the economic and technical backwardness, the less the need for educated people. The more oppressive the system, the more precarious did education become.

For the colonial system, the education of the masses presented a dual danger. In raising the qualifications of its sources of manpower, it also made them more costly to employ. Further, it led the masses of the people to become aware of the exploitation and oppression to which they were subjected. On the other hand, the economic apparatus of exploitation, and administrative and political oppression, could not function without a minimum of indigenous lower-grade personnel, to act as executive agents between the European officials and the masses. With the extension of the trade economy; with technical progress, however slow, with the improvement (or growing oppressiveness) of the administrative machine, the colonisers were obliged to train such staff in growing numbers.

Colonial education policy can be explained in terms of this contradiction. For the colonisers, education was a necessary evil. Thus its spread was limited to a strictly controllable minimum both in quantity and quality. And since education could not be dispensed with, the colonies sought to make use of it in the best interests of colonisation. Cultural depersonalisation was one of the means of carrying out this policy. The lesser officials were given a purely French training, which convinced them of the superiority of European culture, of which, as a privilege, they would receive a few crumbs; they were indoctrinated with the idea that this placed them well above their brothers, who remained 'savage' and 'uncultured'. At the same time, efforts were made to give them a sound indoctrination. They were to recognise the superiority of the white and his civilisation, which had saved them from the cruelty of the 'petty barbarian kings', and they were to pledge him respect, gratitude and, above all, obedience. While they were allowed to reveal the distance separating them from the common masses, they were carefully not invited to forget the distance separating them from their European masters. They were told that they could not, within a few years, rise to the level of a 1,000-year-old civilisation. Albert Sarraut, the minister for the colonies, cast no doubt on the role he imparted to colonial education:

> To instruct the indigenous people is certainly our duty . . . but this fundamental duty is performed as an addendum to our obvious economic, administrative, military and political duties.
> In fact the first effect of education is to improve the value of colonial production by raising the level of intelligence among the

mass of indigenous workers, as well as the number of skills; it should, moreover, set free and raise above the masses of labourers the élite of collaborators who, as technical staff, foremen or overseers, employed or commissioned by the management, will make up for the numerical shortage of Europeans and satisfy the growing demands of the agricultural, industrial or commercial enterprises of colonisation.[27]

To those 'afraid of the pernicious effects of education spread among indigenous circles', he replied that

common sense tells us that the effects of the spread of education must be diversely graded and wisely measured according to differences in countries.[28]

And indeed the fear of responsible colonials of the dangers of too wide an extension of education was always in evidence. In the first pages of his book on education in French West Africa, Georges Hardy shows his concern:

We must prevent education among the local people from becoming an instrument of social upheaval.[29]

The strict control of education and the depersonalisation of the pupils meant forbidding the use of local languages. And since the role of the Africans who attended school was to serve as intermediaries in the French chain of command, the study of the French language was a prime object of education. Carde stipulated this study as the exclusive theme of the lower grade (preparatory course) of the 'village school'.

French is to be imposed on the largest number of the local people and to serve as the common language throughout French West Africa. Its study is to be compulsory for future chiefs, and this measure constitutes a standing order.[30] After forty years of occupation it is essential that all the chiefs, without exception, with whom we come into daily working contact should be able to enter into direct conversation with us.[31]

In the absence of positive achievements, French Equatorial Africa prohibited, by orders passed in 1917 and 1922, the use in private schools of teaching materials not of French origin, or of any language other than French. In the Cameroons and Togo, as we have seen, a condition of regular subsidies to the mission schools was the exclusive use of French as the medium of instruction, with no more than one hour per day of instruction in the local language. French colonial policy remained faithful to this approach until the end. In its session of 8 February, 1944, the Brazzaville conference adopted a recommendation, proposed by Félix Eboué, in which Point Three laid down:

> Education must be given in French, the use in teaching of local spoken dialects being absolutely forbidden both in private and public schools.[32]

And a few months later, the 'African educational conference', held at Dakar, brought into focus the decisions of Brazzaville in this field, proclaimed in the words of Inspector-General Delage:

> We must recall that the aim is less to preserve the originality [*sic*] of the colonised races than to raise them towards us.

In this policy – which proceeded from the trend towards 'assimilation' in French colonisation, but above all to ease the task of 'direct' administration – France followed a road diametrically opposed to that used, notably, by Great Britain and Belgium. These colonial powers organised elementary education in the colonies of tropical Africa in the local languages. They were concerned lest the use of English or French might provide access to 'dangerous' ideas or works; in the local languages, apart from the Bible and a few religious books, principally catechisms, issued by the missions – and a few school books, there existed no printed literature which could divert reading and writing from their strictly utilitarian purposes. Under the French system, there was no serious and systematic study of African linguistics, nor was there any printed literature in the local languages nor even any system of transcription. On the other hand, after the Second World War, this system was to favour political awakening of the African peoples, and finally boomerang upon its initiators.

The assimilation aspect of French policy, used in France to claim that the idea was to train 'African Frenchmen', was no more aimed at true assimilation than were any other aspects. The danger which such an assimilation would involve was perfectly understood, and efforts were made to free education of all that was not essential to the practical aims of colonisation. Governor Camille Guy wrote:

> A bit of fresh air! That is what we need. Good curricula are obtained by pruning, not by grafting. Education in French, elementary science, vocational work and technical training appropriate to the milieu; that is all we need. Any other policy produces not French citizens, but vain and eccentric outcasts, who lose their native qualities and acquire only the vices of their teachers. This was the system which created a René Maran and

a novel like *Batouala*, very mediocre from a literary point of view, infantile in conception, unjust and wicked in its tendentiousness.[33]

The curricula thus eliminated all general culture, everything that was capable of developing thought: local history was not taught except in the form of an apologia of colonisation. The insistence was on the need for a 'practical' education, usually reduced to a caricature for lack of means and tools. In this spirit the Carde system of 1924 introduced into the primary school 'agricultural training', and prescribed the provisioning of 'school friendly societies' by the sale of produce from fields and plantations looked after by the pupils. The crisis intensified these trends. When he took up his post in 1931 the governor-general of French West Africa, Jules Brévié, launched the slogan of the 'rural school'. He set out its aims before the academy of colonial sciences in the following terms:

> While this type of school [with curricula similar to those used in France] gives us numerous collaborators of tested loyalty, they also unfortunately created a large contingent of bitter uprooted people, who came to hold us in contempt and become our enemies.
>
> Should these schools be closed as some advise us? A solution as radical as it is impractical would have meant abandoning the education of our subjects to their own inspiration or, even more dangerous, to the initiative of the opponents of colonisation. It is therefore not a question of abandoning but of reforming education.[34]

The spirit of this 'reform' is clearly apparent. Agricultural training became obligatory, and more than half the total of lessons were devoted to it, actual classes being reduced to four and a half hours a day. Fields, plantations and flocks were taken over and attached to the school, and their upkeep became a prime concern. Teachers were judged according to the state and yield of the fields. An official document provides the following evaluation of this system:

> The achievements of the village schools were hardly brilliant. In these schools, the child, sometimes recruited by force, often had to help in running the farm attached to the school, where he did hard work usually of no educational value. That was why some of them preferred to run away.[35]

Being without any modern equipment, these schools could not give any valuable agricultural training; as to traditional agriculture, the young pupils who had worked with their parents from a very early age had nothing to learn and often knew more than their teachers. 'Agricultural training' was thus reduced to manual, forced labour. One headmaster called Capelle cites the case of a school where, every four days, half a day was given over to carrying water-bottles to water the crops.[36] In theory the produce of the farm went to the 'school friendly society' and its sale was to provide the pupils with food, clothing and school supplies. In practice, the produce was frequently handed over to the teacher or to the local European officials; the school farm became a copy of the 'administrative kitchen garden' kept up by prisoners of the subdivision or the circle.

The avowed objective of this education policy, and its result, were to lower the standard of education. Senegal alone, where the presence of the colonial council presented an obstacle to such methods, objected to these 'rural schools'. It will be understood that in numerous regions education, conceived in this manner, became an additional hardship for the population to bear, over and above forced labour and conscription. Chiefs and notables, as was seen, were obliged to send their children to French schools; to have refused to do so would have been taken as a sign of hostility. To avoid this, some bribed the teacher who, if given a suitable present, such as an ox, might consent to inscribe the child in his register. The material provisions of the schools remained at the simplest level. As late as 1949 a teacher at Kédougou in Senegal wrote:

> I have received a visit from the primary school inspector. Together we made a tour of the twenty-one schools of the circle, which are schools only in name, since there is a master and pupils. These schools are lamentable; a few posts fixed in the ground supporting scraps of straw or a few leaves. Public works and the administration do not take any interest in such constructions.[37]

The regional schools were not much better.

> For pupils from far away a rough boarding-house was provided. Food was supplied, as a rule, by the parents. . . . The boarding-house kitchen was extremely rustic, consisting of one hut either with mud walls or built of straw; there was an old woman to prepare the unvarying diet, and one or two grinders to crush the millet; this was the staff of the boarding-house. The dormitory was often in the classroom, or it was a bare room or even a tent (a solution preferred by the Moors or the Touaregs); beds were simple mats stretched out on the ground.[38]

A large part of the time-table was set aside for the construction, or the repair, of the school premises or equipment, by the pupils themselves under the direction of the schoolmaster. The allocation of credits for education was not bound up with the number of pupils. In 1945, when numbers had increased more than sixfold compared with 1908, the percentage of credits allocated to education in French West Africa rose from 2 to 5·75 per cent. Part of the credit remained unused due to lack of materials and manpower, or administrative delays. In other cases, the money was diverted to other purposes: in Chad, a subdivision chief used the credit set aside for the construction of a classroom to build a monumental staircase leading from his residence to the river; another used it to build a stable for his horses. The administrator in charge of accounts controlled the credits, not the teacher.

After visiting French Equatorial Africa, one observer noted:

There is a shortage of money, staff and schools, and I think I saw a lack of willingness on the part of higher authority to spread education among the indigenous masses. . . . I think there is no desire in high places to let the vast majority of black children benefit from education, even at primary level.[39]

The governor of Ubangi-Shari noted in his report of 1932:

It is regrettable that the number of Europeans engaged in teaching has to be reduced owing to financial difficulties at a time when the number of pupils is constantly on the increase. The number of European teachers has, in this way, been reduced to four.[40]

In the Cameroons admission to the 'regional schools' was reduced

so as to make no rash increase in the number of candidates, which is already too high for the employment available.[41]

In Togo, the teachers' training course attached to the 'higher primary school' was closed down in 1934 for reasons of economy. In 1928 the teaching staff for 3,000 pupils in French Equatorial Africa comprised twenty-one European teachers, twenty-six trained African monitors and thirty-three assistant monitors. Credits granted under the 1931 loan permitted the building of a few schools for publicity reasons – the Lycée Van Vollenhoven at Dakar and the 'higher technical school' at Bamako for example, largely used to show off to visiting journalists and to be photographed from all angles as testimony to 'educational achievements'. But most of the other higher institutions worked under far less favourable conditions. In 1947 the William Ponty training college did not possess a single geographical wall map . . . .

(d) THE TEACHING STAFF

The staff itself left much to be desired, both in numbers and quality. In French Equatorial Africa, as we have seen, there was no organised education service until 1937.

Out of several hundred thousand children of school age, only 7,000 attended public schools, and a good half were under incompetent monitors. Curricula, lessons and teaching methods were not clearly defined. There was no inspection; the indigenous teacher was at the same time an interpreter, and the European teacher a post office employee or book-keeper. There were even schools accidentally entrusted to completely uneducated agricultural advisors.[42]

In 1944 the staff in charge of teaching 10,000 pupils in French Equatorial Africa comprised ten European teachers,[43] less than twenty African teachers (with a certificate of elementary primary studies, one preparatory year and four years in a teacher's training college) in a 'materially lamentable' situation with 600 francs monthly pay,[44] and 350 monitors (with the same certificate and one year of vocational training). In the Cameroons the head of the education services from 1922 to 1939 was a former groundnut trader, who entered the administration after going bankrupt and had completed only elementary school education; he rose to the rank of inspector. Among the locally resident European staff were a former bar-tender, a former blacksmith and a non-commissioned colonial officer.

In 1944 the Cameroons had three inspectors, thirty-eight male and female European school-teachers, ten of whom had no diplomas, and 250 African monitors, who had passed through the 'higher primary school' with a teachers' training course of one year. In French West Africa, in that year, the number of European teachers was about 150.[45] Among them were French schoolmasters and schoolmistresses seconded from France. But there were also, as in the Cameroons, European teachers locally recruited, whose qualifications often did not go beyond the lower certificate. The best qualified teachers were employed in the 'higher school' and the 'higher primary schools'. Even the William Ponty teachers' training college was only staffed by elementary school-teachers. Secondary school-teachers were to be found only in the *lycées* at Saint-Louis and Dakar. These elementary school-teachers were often assisted by persons without proper qualifications, by virtue of a decree still in force after the Second World War. There were, for instance, the wives of European officials, who, with a certificate of studies, could be enrolled as assistant teachers, and earn more than African elementary school teachers who had graduated from the Ponty College. Most of the European teachers, it should be said, shared the general colonial attitudes, which were at times intensified by the conditions of life and work; e.g. in French West Africa until 1946 and in French Equatorial Africa until much later the majority of European teachers working in the bush served as 'head of the school sector' and directed the 'regional schools', inspected the village schools and were in consequence exempt from actual teaching. They tended thus to become minor administrative heads, and were more preoccupied with hunting and entertainment than with educational problems.

There were also, however, teachers who were competent and devoted. Within the colonial setting they could not but share the concepts reigning in administrative circles, but they also believed in the 'civilising mission' of France; they believed in their task as educators charged with training 'African Frenchmen', and these views, despite paternalist overtones, often led them to exceed the limits fixed by colonial prudence. Even faced with badly adapted curricula intended to encourage assimilation (the anecdote of young Africans learning about 'our ancestors, the Gauls' is not a caricature, but was often surpassed in reality), they tackled subject-matter designed to make the pupils think. The exaltation of republican principles and the history of the French Revolution, when seen compared with colonial realities, played a major role, however little intended, in arousing political consciousness.

The African staff was composed of elementary school teachers and monitors, the first being generally former pupils of the William Ponty College; the others had passed the certificate of primary elementary studies followed by more or less advanced vocational training. In 1932 there were in French West Africa 436 teachers of 'secondary rank' and only forty-two men and thirteen women monitors – a rank that was dying out. The 'rural school' led to a new massive recruitment of monitors. Around 1945 the number of African monitors in French West Africa was almost equal to the number of teachers.

In French Equatorial Africa and the Cameroons and Togo, the teaching force consisted almost entirely of monitors. The social background of the teachers differed greatly. They came, like all the African officials, from the small élite of children who had gone through school. The administration would have preferred to recruit them from the families of chiefs, the better to attach them to the French administrative machinery. This was the aim of the écoles des ôtages ('hostage schools'). But the chiefs did not like to send their children to a distant boarding school where they were educated

away from home and, at times, in opposition to their home background. Taking advantage of the ignorance of the whites, many
chiefs sent young slaves to the French schools instead of their sons;
and this unexpected social promotion was often regretted by those
who had sent them. These people of humble background formed a
notable percentage among the first drafts of school-teachers.

Their training varied greatly. At the Ponty College, in spite of
a very 'curtailed' curriculum, the training given was solid enough,
at least in French and arithmetic, following the tradition of French
teachers' training colleges. General culture was kept to a minimum;
however, it was difficult to evade the cultural thirst of the young
training college students, and the questions they asked about the
past and the fate of their people. A safety-valve was sought in
folklore – folk tales, traditional games.[46] In 1930 a course on the
theatre was introduced which came to take up a great deal of the
students' free time, with composition of scripts, rehearsals, etc. The
theatre took as its theme tales or historical episodes as told by
travelling musicians and poets. But the contents were carefully
revised and adapted and, when it was thought necessary, given a
frankly colonial bias (African sovereigns described as blood-thirsty
barbarians, etc.). Thus the 'Ponty theatre' became a harmless
diversion.[47]

The Ponty diploma, a purely local qualification, was no equivalent
to French diplomas, and justified keeping the 'indigenous teachers'
in a lower category. No opportunity was offered to young teachers
to study at training colleges, still less to go on to higher education:
the bursaries granted to 'indigenous students' were tied to the 'higher
primary schools'; the *lycées* at Dakar and Saint-Louis were, in
practice, only open to the sons of French or assimilated officials
(sons of 'citizens' of the communes of full rights) whose parents
could afford to pay their fees up to the *baccalauréat* level.

There were many bursaries available for secondary education in
France granted from the colonial budgets, but these were reserved
exclusively for the children of European colonial officials. Orders
passed on 29 October, 1920, and 12 September, 1923, governed the
grant of bursaries to the teacher's training college at Aix-en-
Provence for the benefit of 'selected young schoolmasters' who had
attended Ponty College. These training college students, aged
twenty-five and over, were kept apart from the French students and
subjected to close supervision that went as far as vetting their
reading matter and censoring their correspondence. Two students
were expelled in 1923 by Carde, the governor-general, for having
'bad marks', and a third in October 1924, after being denounced by
the director of the training college as 'bitterly hostile' to the French

administration.[48] In fact, the cause of these expulsions was the students' anti-colonialist spirit, which had been evoked by culture. An inspector-general of education in French West Africa wrote:

The unfortunate example of the teachers' training college at Aix seems to prove that the stay in France exercises on our pupils a troublesome influence.[49]

The experiment was quickly brought to an end. In 1927 the headmaster of the William Ponty training college, a Frenchman named Dupont, obtained a ruling that established examinations for lower and higher certificates in French West Africa on the same basis as in France. French West Africa was attached to the Bordeaux Academy; thus the African school-teachers were able to prepare and obtain the same diplomas as their French colleagues. This decision raised an outcry of indignation in colonial circles and especially from certain European teachers, who considered it intolerable that future African teachers should have the same qualifications as themselves – and in certain cases higher ones – from which would ensue claims to equal position and pay. At the end of his appointment, Dupont left for France and the decree was never applied.

The economic crisis brought a reaction. It was henceforth understood that the colonial peoples were not 'ready' for higher education. Albert Sarraut insisted on the necessity of withholding higher education from the Africans. There was already the danger of an intellectual inflation in France; this danger would be even more serious in the colonies.

Lofty scientific speculations are a heady wine which easily turns heads. Certain temperaments offer no resistance to stimulants. . . . Higher education presupposes hereditary factors, a balance of receptive faculties, a maturity of judgment of which only a small minority of our subjects and protected people are capable.[50] . . . If the administration cannot absorb them they will become social outcasts, bitter, and too often bad spiritual pastors.[51]

At the session of the International Colonial Institute which took place the same year under the chairmanship of Diagne and with the participation of Georges Hardy, one G. Norès, of the French delegation, had the following resolution adopted:

In view of the dangers caused by certain educated indigenous elements, who do not find employment for their real or supposed abilities in society, this house is in favour of limiting the number of higher diplomas issued to them.[52]

It was in this spirit that Governor-General Brévié launched his 'rural schools'; for teaching purposes it was considered that the level of the school-teachers trained at William Ponty College was still too high and too theoretical. For teachers in 'rural schools' the head of the education service of the Sudan, Frédéric Assomption, supported by Governor Eboué, set up a teachers' training college at Katibougou with general education at a lower level than at William Ponty College and a predominantly 'agricultural' curriculum. Since the post of teacher seemed too ambitious, it was proposed to set up training colleges for 'rural teaching monitors' equal in number to the principal agricultural zones. One was opened at Dabou for the forest regions; one at Sévaré for the interior of the Sudan; a third was planned at M'Bambey or Louga, for the groundnut regions, but faced with Senegalese reluctance it never got beyond the planning stage.

After 1945 French West Africa had no native staff who had received higher education. The African doctors who graduated from the school of medicine at Dakar, and the school-teachers who completed the Ponty College course, made up the top rank of the intellectual élite. William Ponty College had 281 students, forty-two of them in the teaching department,[53] and the medical school at Dakar had 106 students. A single African graduate had completed his studies in France and taught at a provincial *lycée*. Kept at a lower rank, the graduate teacher from Ponty College left school, and in the bush came under the thumb of his white superiors and the circle commander. Far from the traditional life, but held at a distance by the settler circles and deprived of any possibility of intellectual life, he often became submerged in routine. Those who put up resistance were broken: stripping of rank as a disciplinary measure was frequent, both among school-teachers and training college graduates. Those who were driven away had hardly any openings except as shopkeepers or small traders.

The conditions of the monitors, the pariahs of the profession, were still worse. Isolated in the bush schools, they were left to their own devices; their standard varied greatly. In French West Africa they had usually taken a certificate after three years of study at a higher primary school and a year of vocational training; elsewhere, as in French Equatorial Africa, their professional training was limited to one year. Their pay was miserable. It was monitors, often more superficially trained, who made up the main body of the teaching staff at the missions. The level of education which they gave was on a level with the targets set.

Why did the missions open schools? To perfect the Christian education of the children, i.e. for the clear aim of preaching the

Gospel, which is their sole *raison d'être*. By reaction and as a matter of fact, it cannot be denied that they have helped the colonies, in raising the number of educated children. . . .[54]

(e) CONCLUSION

The balance sheet is simple. In 1945 it was estimated that in all areas the proportion of illiterates among the population exceeded 95 per cent. In French West Africa the percentage of children of school age who had had some schooling was 3·34 per cent. It varied by territories from 0·82 per cent in Niger to 4·25 per cent in Senegal and 7·8 per cent in Dahomey. To explain this last percentage it has to be remembered that French Equatorial Africa (6·1 per cent), Togo (16·1 per cent) and the Cameroons (17·3 per cent) had a considerable number of private schools – of an extremely low level. Among the negative factors in matters of education must be included the deliberate depreciation and often destruction of the pre-colonial cultural heritage, and the skimpiness and falsely assimilative nature of the instruction itself. Implicitly criticising past methods, Inspector-General Delage was able to state in 1944:

. . . Our colonial education [should not], in any case, be reduced to simple training. It is not a question of giving the black some notions of language, writing, mathematics and hygiene aimed at facilitating the comprehension of orders given by the whites. It is not a question of perfecting an automaton for our service. Our African school should not be conceived as a school for 'boys' [servants].[55]

Among the positive elements were the involuntary consequences of the spread of education – namely, that it opened up the outside world and brought an awareness to some of the educated élite both of their own condition and that of the masses. From this they derived their revolutionary role, dreaded by responsible colonial circles. Tribute should here be paid to the work accomplished, under difficult material and moral conditions, by the great majority of the European and African educators and teachers. Faced with the distrust and often the hostility of the administration, and whatever their illusions about the nature of the colonial system (sometimes even because of these illusions), they did their best to provide more than mere training. The work of shaping human character achieved by many of them played a far from negligible role in the advance of the liberation movement after the Second World War. It was thus that the 'work of education', so often invoked as an excuse if not a justification for the colonial system, acquired its real proportions and its true context.

REFERENCES

1. On this same subject see Abdou Moumouni, *L'Education en Afrique*. Paris, Maspero, 1964. (English-language ed.: *Education in Africa*, London: Deutsch; New York: Praeger, chapters 1 and 2).

2. This procedure did not give rise to written literature except in Fulani and Hausa; but it was, and still is, used for correspondence or announcements in many other African languages.

3. In Mauritania the residence of Sheikh Sidya, the principal ally of France among the Moors of Trarza. In 1939 that of Djenné disappeared, but two others were set up at Atar (Mauritania) and Timbédra (Sudan).

4. Georges Hardy, *Une Conquête morale: L'enseignement en Afrique occidentale française*. Paris, Armand Colin, 1917, p. 40.

5. J. Carde, 'La réorganisation de l'enseignement en Afrique occidentale française', *Revue Indigène*, No. 185–6, May–June 1924, pp. 111–29.

6. On this decline see J. C. Froelich, *Les Musulmans d'Afrique noire*. Paris, Ed. de l'Oronte, 1952, pp. 174 ff.

7. On this point J. Beyries, 'Evolution sociale et culturelle des collectivités nomades de Mauritainie', *B.C.E.H.S.*, 1937, No. 4, pp. 465–81.

8. Capitaine Duffner, 'Croyances et coutumes religieuses chez les Guerzés et les Manons de la Guinée française', *B.C.E.H.S.*, 1934, No. 4, p. 545.

9. Mother Javouhey, the founder of this congregation, sent several young Senegalese to France to become priests. On their return an attempt was made to put them in charge of a secondary school at St. Louis. They were confronted with such obstacles that in the end they had to leave their country.

10. Territories of Upper Senegal–Middle Niger. Report (1900–3), p. 37.

11. Camille Guy, *Afrique Française*, 1924, No. 8, p. 438.

12. Territories of Upper Senegal–Middle Niger. Report (1900–3).

13. In 1928 subsidies to private schools were distributed as follows (for a total of 4,000 pupils):

Apostolic vicariate of Brazzaville	32,000 francs
Apostolic vicariate of Gabon	10,000 francs
Apostolic vicariate of Loango	5,000 francs
Apostolic vicariate of Bangui	7,500 francs

(P. Gamache: 'L'enseignement en Afrique equatoriale française', *Afrique française, Revue coloniale*, 1928, No. 12, pp. 751–9).

14. 'L'enseignement dans les territories d'outre-mer', *Documentation française, Notes et Etudes documentaires*, No. 1896 (19 July, 1954).

15. C. Guy, *Afrique Française*, 1924, No. 8, p. 438.

16. G. François, 'L'enseignement en Afrique occidentale', *Afrique Française, Revue coloniale*, No. 1–2, 1919, pp. 34–9.

17. G. Hardy, op. cit., p. 37.

18. G. Hardy admitted that this recruitment was 'deplorable' and corrupted by 'favouritism'.

19. Government-general of French Equatorial Africa. Final Accounts of Revenue and Expenditure. 1911 Budget. Paris, Larose, 1912.

20. G. Hardy, op. cit.

21. Carde circular, *Revue Indigène*, No. 185–6, May–June 1924, pp. 111–29.

22. A. Prat, Inspector-General of Education in French West Africa, *Afrique Française*, 1926, No. 3, p. 118.

23. Transferred to Sébikotane (between Dakar and Thiès) in 1938.

24. Source: Report by Fily Dabo Sissoko, Deputy for the Sudan, to the Commission de la France d'Outre-mer in the National Assembly: the '*Carnet de documentation No. 5—Afrique occidentale française*' of the French Overseas Ministry gives

88,584 pupils for that year in the whole of public and private education and not 110,951: the figure of 88,584 seems closer to reality. But in the last-mentioned document the number or proportion of girls is not given.

25. It was closed in 1946 and its pupils were sent to the Ecole de Médecine de Dakar. Only four or five pupils were promoted.

26. F. Lavit, 'La colonie du Tchad en 1921', *Afrique française, Revue coloniale*, 1924, No. 4, pp. 117 ff.

27. Albert Sarraut, *La Mise en valeur des colonies françaises*. Paris, Payot, 1923, p. 95.

28. Ibid., p. 96.

29. G. Hardy, op. cit., p. 12.

30. Decree of 1 May, 1924, commented on in the Carde circular.

31. J. Carde, 'La réorganisation de l'enseignement en Afrique occidentale française', *Revue Indigène*, No. 185-6, May–June 1924, p. 155.

32. Cf. J. de la Roche, *Le gouverneur-général Eboué*. Paris, Hachette, 1957, pp. 167-8.

33. C. Guy, *Afrique Française*, 1922, No. 1, p. 43. René Maran, colonial administrator in the Antilles, had denounced the atrocious conditions of the Africans in the Congo in his novel *Batouala*, which won the Goncourt Prize in 1921. He likewise painted the milieu of the administration with great realism. He aroused the fury of the colonials. However, he ended up in complete colonial orthodoxy.

34. Communication by Governor-General Jules Brévié to the Academy of Colonial Sciences, 13 October, 1935 (J. Brévié, *Trois études*. Gorée, Imprimerie du gouvernement, 1936, p. 21).

35. 'L'enseignement dans les territories d'outre-mer', *Documentation française, Notes et Etudes documentaires*, No. 1896, 19 July, 1954, p. 14.

36. *Encyclopédie maritime et coloniale:* 'L'Afrique occidentale française', pp. 272-3.

37. Quoted by J. Suret-Canale, 'L'enseignement en Afrique occidentale française', *La Pensée*, No. 29, March–April 1949, p. 36.

38. *Notes et Etudes documentaires*, op. cit.

39. R. Susset, *La Vérité sur le Cameroun et l'Afrique equatoriale française*. Paris, Ed. de la Nouvelle Revue Critique, 1934, p. 171.

40. Ibid.

41. H. Labouret, *Le Cameroun*. Paris, Hartmann, 1937, pp. 39-40.

42. H. Zieglé, *Afrique equatoriale française*. Paris, Berger-Levrault, 1952, p. 184.

43. Before the Second World War and the consequent mobilisation there had been about thirty.

44. M. Fournier, *Situation actuelle de l'enseignement en Afrique equatoriale française* (African Education Conference, Dakar, 1944). For 1934 R. Susset, op. cit., gives thirty European school-teachers, 116 indigenous monitors with diploma, ten auxiliary monitors.

45. Their number was reduced by the war. Numbers in 1932: 150 European masters and 75 European mistresses.

46. Some of these studies published in the *Bulletin de l'Enseignement* and later in *L'Education africaine* undoubtedly have a documentary interest. The material accumulated was used by Ch. Béart, a former director of the William Ponty training college, in his works on the games and toys of West Africa.

47. Cf. Bakary Traoré, *Le Théâtre négro-africain et ses fonctions sociales*. Paris, Présence africaine, 1958. After 1945 political consciousness led this student theatre to assume an anti-colonialist content; the administration took objection to this. See also R. Delavignette, 'Le théâtre de Gorée et la culture franco-africaine', *Afrique Française*, 1937, No. 10, pp. 471-2 and a special number of *L'Education africaine* (1937). Criticism of Bakary Traoré's theses can be found in Ch. Béart, *Recherche des*

éléments d'une sociologie des peuples africains à partir de leurs jeux. Paris, Présence africaine, 1960, pp. 128 ff. (administrative viewpoint).

48. *L'Afrique occidentale française*, No. of 20 July, 1925. Article by Lamine Gueye: 'Pour notre jeunesse intellectuelle'.

49. A. Prat, *Afrique Française*, 1926, No. 3, p. 118.

50. Albert Sarraut, *Grandeur et servitudes coloniales.* Paris, Ed. du Sagittaire, 1931, p. 152.

51. Ibid., p. 154.

52. Session of 25 July, 1931, *La Quinzaine coloniale*, 1931, p. 357.

53. After one common year the school comprised a medical section (preparatory) lasting one year and a teaching section, providing a two-year course.

54. Father Catlin, *Situation de l'enseignement privé catholique en Afrique occidentale française.* African Education Conference, Dakar, 1944.

55. African Education Conference, Dakar, 1944.

4. *Medical and Health Services*

We now turn to the second element often invoked as a credit to colonisation. Any evaluation of what was achieved in medicine and hygiene calls for a brief preliminary examination of the people's condition of health and its evolution during the colonial period.

(a) HEALTH

Among the long-established diseases endemic to tropical regions, *malaria* appears to be the most widespread and, unquestionably, the most harmful.

Its universality makes statistics difficult to obtain. In adults, malarial infection produced a relative immunity: but there was a frequent incidence of 'pernicious attacks' and haematuria leading to death. In any case, sufferers from malaria had a reduced work capacity as the result of periodic attacks, which weakened the constitution and exposed it to other diseases. Among children chronic malaria, with its direct and indirect effects, produced a high mortality. Although no completely convincing records of the spread of this endemic disease exist for the colonial period, it seems that it was widely distributed geographically and even reached certain oases in the Sahara, where it had been unknown before.

For a long time epidemics of *yellow fever* gave the West coast of Africa a terrible reputation. The regions most affected were Senegal, from Saint-Louis to Dakar, and the Ivory Coast (Grand Bassam). In 1878, of the 1,474 Europeans resident at Gorée, Dakar and Saint-Louis, 749 fell victim to an epidemic, among them twenty-two out of the twenty-six naval doctors and pharmacists sent to combat the epidemic. The 1900–1 epidemic also claimed numerous victims at Dakar and Saint-Louis. The governor-general of French West Africa, Chaudié, 'courageously' and speedily left his post, and Dr. Noël Ballay, governor of Guinea, had to come and take his place. The last major epidemic took place in Dakar in 1927. Later, the use of anti-amaril vaccine limited the effects of the epidemics, which never completely disappeared, since vaccination was not generally enforced. The first year when cases were registered was 1949.

Like malaria, *intestinal diseases* – of microbic or parasitic origin – and indeed all the parasitic diseases are particularly widespread and virulent in tropical countries, due to the heat and humidity. *Amoebic dysentry*, which is transmitted by polluted water, had outbreaks in regions with high rainfall like the coast and forest regions of Guinea, the Ivory Coast, Dahomey, the Cameroons,

Gabon and Congo, as well as among people living on the banks of large rivers, like the Senegal and the Niger. In 1940 there were more than 22,000 registered cases.

Hookworm (ankylostomiasis), the parasitic intestinal worm of numerous varieties, intestinal or vesical bilharzia (transmitted by waters infected with certain molluscs which serve as hosts to the parasites), and so on, were widespread and contributed to general physical weakness. Hookworm infestation, confirmed by various probes, affected 50 per cent of the population of Senegal, 60–90 per cent in Guinea, 74 per cent in the lower Ivory Coast and 45 per cent in Upper Volta. Bilharzia affected half of the children in the forest regions of Guinea, and nearly all the women, due to their regular contact with the marsh water when they were cleaning water bottles, washing clothes, etc.

Embryonic filariosis of the blood affected 18 per cent of the population of Northern Senegal from 15° N., and 66 per cent of those in the South; in the Sudan it affected 18 per cent of the inhabitants of the Sahel zone and near the mouth of the Niger, 31 per cent in the valley of the Upper Senegal, 58 per cent to the East, south of the 14th parallel N., In Guinea, 51 per cent on the coast, 68 per cent along the Upper Niger; on the Ivory Coast 71 per cent and even over 90 per cent at Korogho.

Onchocercosis, which was widespread in the Upper Niger basin, took the form of ocular lesions leading to blindness.

Leprosy, on the other hand, does not seem to have any particular connection with the tropical climate. In 1937, 41,400 lepers had been counted in French West Africa.

Without denying that the special nature of the tropical climate enabled most of these endemic diseases to flourish, some of them such as leprosy were present in Europe in the Middle Ages, and others like cholera existed there until fairly recently. Malaria and various forms of fever also raged in many regions of Europe. Their regression and disappearance does not seem to be related to advances in medical science so much as to the general improvement in living conditions, especially in food and hygiene. It therefore seems to follow that the worsening living conditions that we have described in Africa had the effect of, at the very least, favouring the persistence of traditional endemic diseases, even if it did not aggravate their spread and effects.

Although, with the exception of certain diseases, it is impossible to link increased incidence of disease with the period of colonial rule, it cannot be denied that undernourishment, unbalanced diet and physical exhaustion were direct effects of colonisation while the spread and aggravation of certain endemic diseases and the introduction of new illnesses were indirect effects. Hence it is clear that colonisation had a generally bad influence on the general state of health of the people. Against undernourishment and its consequences, medicine remained powerless.

In his medical report of 1945, the head of the health services of the Cameroons stated:

Diseases, while playing a large role in the decline of the indigenous people, are not solely responsible, and other causes which facilitate such scourges and are of great importance, but escape the notice of the health services, must be blamed: undernourishment and the almost complete absence of nitrogenous food, an inconsiderate economic policy which, in certain regions, had encouraged the growth of money-making crops to the detriment of food crops, and the imbalance between the income of the natives and the price of essential goods.[1]

Numerous diseases in tropical Africa were deficiency diseases, affecting children in particular.

Deficiency diseases have never been counted in Africa. Everyone has spoken of deficiency, but nobody, I believe, deals with this problem, or even its simple clinical expression, perhaps because it is linked to ethnic features, and forms the overall picture. Children are among the worst victims.

The big bellies, swollen gums that are crimson and bleeding, loose teeth, glossitis, conjunctivitis and skin lesions, which for a long time were classified in various ways, are among those which, in the main, make up nutritional diseases.

The examination of 4,000 children in Upper Volta by Major Raoult of the medical service in the course of our last tour showed 20 per cent of cases among this type.[2]

The slowness of demographic progression in French West Africa in the period 1900–40, in spite of a distinctly above-average female fecundity, is explained by the abnormally high rate of infantile mortality. No doubt this mortality rate was caused by a variety of factors: brutality in weaning, which made children pass belatedly but without transition from mother's milk to an adult diet; poor child hygiene, etc. But deficiency factors played an essential role here, too. The majority of women questioned testified that by the time they reached the menopause they had had a high number of pregnancies (generally more than ten, sometimes over fifteen), though frequently the number of living children was no more than two or three. Around 1940, an inquiry held on the Ivory Coast indicated that nearly half the deaths (41·6 per cent) were of children

o

less than fifteen years old. Added to the deplorable food conditions
were other material aspects of life, in particular clothing and housing.
Clothing was not much better than in the pre-colonial period – the
thick and robust fabrics of that time, produced in small quantities
by local craftsmen, were replaced by light imported cotton fabrics.
As to accommodation, living conditions worsened, particularly in
the towns.

Paradoxically, the people of tropical Africa suffered from the
cold. This is true not only of the mountain regions of Atakora and
Fouta-Djalon where, in the dry season, the night temperature could
drop below 10°C. The classic regions of tropical climate were
characterised by violent variations within twenty-four hours: in the
course of one day, when the *harmattan* was blowing, the temperature
could vary from 35° or even 40°C. to 15°C. during the night. Hence,

the natives are badly dressed. A piece of cloth around the body
forms the *boubou*, another covers the lower half of the body
forming the loin-cloth. To protect themselves, when *they had the
means to do so*[3] they put boubous and loin-cloths one on top of the
other. As to the children, when they are not quite naked they
usually wear nothing more than a shirt.[4]

Moreover, in certain regions, such as Senegal, where the huts
often had thin, plaited-mat walls with wide gaps, protection against
the cold was insufficient.

If to this one adds the fact that seven or eight live in one hut
measuring no more than nine square metres, it will be understood
that this was a highly favourable ground for pneumococcal
infection.[5]

The result was that

pneumococcal infections caused each year a large number of
deaths among the native population of French West Africa. The
epidemiological reports on infectious diseases published in the
Annales de médicine et de pharmacie coloniales leave no doubt on
this score.[6]

Sometimes the disease took the classic form of pneumonia, but
sometimes

the pneumococcus passed over the pulmonary condition and
according to the organ affected gave rise to epidemics of meningitis or jaundice, or excessive weight, with a mortality rate that
would reach 80 per cent. These epidemics most often hit native
communities, where large numbers of individuals were gathered,
like work camps and 'military units'.[7]

Epidemics of *cerebro-spinal meningitis*[8] continued to be one of the formidable scourges in the Sudanic regions (Senegal, Upper Guinea, Upper Volta, Chad and Ubangi) where they occurred periodically in the dry season, causing thousands of deaths.[9] The crowding together of requisitioned men for forced labour, or in Ubangi for cotton threshing, in the absence of cotton gins, increased the destructiveness of these epidemics.

It is here that some of the indirect aspects of colonisation made themselves felt. Mobility increased with the development of the market economy; thousands of workers, badly nourished and deplorably housed, were collected together in public works camps, forest workings and plantations; ex-soldiers returned from overseas with fresh infections – all these factors, acting upon a weakened population, helped to spread the existing diseases and to introduce new ones. This has already been mentioned concerning the ravages of *sleeping sickness* in French Equatorial Africa: the disease spread parallel with the establishment of colonisation. The first inquiries made in Guinea by the Martin mission of 1905–6 revealed that sleeping sickness, although not unknown in the pre-colonial period, had steadily increased during the preceding decades. Although it is impossible to be conclusive about these factors, there remains no doubt that the forced migrations of the population and their weakening through undernourishment and excess labour played a role, especially in French Equatorial Africa and the Cameroons, in spreading the disease. Doctor Martin wrote in 1923:

> Physiological weakness is one of the chief elements of the high mortality rate in the Congo resulting from trypanosomiasis.[10]

Among the imported diseases must be included venereal diseases (chiefly syphilis), smallpox, tuberculosis, plague and recurrent lice fever. Syphilis entered the area as long ago as the period of the slave trade. *Yaws*, distributed mainly in the forest zones and very difficult to distinguish from syphilis, is, according to some writers, a primitive form of syphilis which did not evolve in the same manner as in Europe.[11] It is certain, however, that the colonial conquest at the end of the nineteenth century multiplied the sources of dissemination of venereal disease, and greater ease of communication spread it almost everywhere. The only regions little affected were those where traditional patriarchal life remained unchanged and where emigration was not practised. The massive migrations, work sites that kept men for months away from their families, military service and the accompanying spread of prostitution – all considerably aggravated this evil. Although ports were affected most, certain peoples in the interior (Fouta-Toro, Mauritania, Fouta-Djalon) which practised temporary emigration were also greatly involved.[12] *Gonorrhoea* spread in a way similar to syphilis. *Smallpox*, practically eradicated in Europe, continued to cause periodical ravages in the absence of general vaccination. In 1940, more than 1,627 cases were registered in French West Africa, of which seventy-two were fatal.[13] Tuberculosis was certainly introduced by more recent colonisation.

According to the testimony of old naval doctors who worked on the West Coast of Africa, tuberculosis was exceedingly rare on the coast, and was considered as being non-existent among the natives in the centre of Africa. Some people came to think that the blacks had some natural immunity against bacillary infection.[14]

In French West Africa, the first cases were observed in 1880 at Gorée and Saint-Louis. From 1900 to 1910 medical reports attested to its continuous spread. In 1910 an inquiry held by A. Calmette[15] revealed the absence of immunity, and the direct relation between contamination and foreign immigration. The more the subject had previously been protected against infection, the greater was its virulence. Violent and rapidly developing forms, which had become rare in Europe (the galloping consumption of former times), were frequent. The average incidence of tuberculosis in the whole of French West Africa, according to various tests, ranged from 13 per cent in 1912 to 44 per cent in 1930. All those affected were homeless persons, who had been in some contact with Europeans and Syrians. In 1922 the rate among children at Kindia, Guinea, rose to 24·6 per cent, whereas in 1910 it had been 1·8 per cent overall. The repatriation and return to their villages, without medical supervision, of numerous soldiers retired and pensioned off for serious forms of tuberculosis, contributed to the spread of the evil.

Over the years, from seventy to 100 tuberculosis cases are repatriated every season, and they are scattered throughout French West Africa, inevitably creating sources of contagion.[16]

Infection was in inverse proportion to distance from ports. The rate calculated among the soldiers in 1925 was Senegal, 15 per cent; Sudan, 12 per cent; Upper-Volta, 3·6 per cent. At Dakar, in 1925–6, tuberculosis was estimated to account for 23 per cent of the general mortality rate in the local native hospital. The rate of positive skin-tests among the school children at Dakar rose from 38·5 per cent in 1922 to 43·3 per cent in 1927.[17] L. Couvy noted as the main causes of the spread of the disease the appalling hygienic conditions of housing and overcrowding – which even included those living in 'solid' homes.

Faced with these indestructible sordid ruins, true parodies of hygiene, one begins to regret the old straw huts. Inside, one finds rigid division into dark boxes; these house a whole population. One can count up to eight persons in a room measuring 4·60 by 3 metres, provided with one open door.[18]

The plague was also of recent importation. It is not known whence it was imported (perhaps from India, where it is endemic). The first cases occurred in 1899 in Grand-Bassam, then the principal port on the Ivory Coast, then in 1912 in the port of Zinguinchor (Casamance). After 1914, spread by the rat-flea, the disease became endemic on the coast of Senegal, where the sandy soil appears to offer a favourable breeding ground. It did not penetrate to the interior, and the other colonies remained unscathed. From 1920 to 1940, 29,180 cases were registered in Senegal with a mortality rate of 65·6 per cent (100 per cent in its pulmonary forms). Apparently it had disappeared by 1937 thanks to the use of vaccine provided in 1935; it then reappeared in 1940 in the regions of M'Bour and Tivaouane, causing eighty-two deaths.

Recurrent lice fever was introduced into French West Africa in 1921 by soldiers repatriated from Syria and Morocco.

This disease raged in epidemic form and caused frightful ravages among the natives of French West Africa. It started in 1921 and was not exterminated until 1929.[19]

From Kouroussa, where an epidemic broke out among the soldiers being transported by railway from Conakry, it reached Bamako, the Middle Niger, the loop of the river, then Chad and the eastern Sudan. At the same time, it pushed towards Senegal, the Gold Coast and Nigeria. In regions where the epidemic raged, 10 per cent of the population were affected, with a mortality rate varying from 5 to 25 per cent. The number of deaths rose to several thousand each year, reaching a peak in 1923 with 14,000, and 1924 with 20,000. The total number of victims must have amounted to about 100,000.

Among diseases spread by European influence must be counted *alcoholism*. It is true that the African had not waited for the Europeans to make alcoholic drinks: the peoples on the coast and in the forest zones prepared palm wine and *bandyi* (especially in forest Guinea) by fermenting respectively the sap of the palm or *ban* (raffia). The people in the svannah region knew mead and millet beer (*dolo*). Yet the degree of alcohol in these drinks, which were not distilled, remained moderate, and their use, however unconducive to good health, did not have too serious consequences. On the other hand, the advance of Islam in the Sudanic zone undoubtedly reduced the use of mead and *dolo*. As is known, it was trade that introduced alcohol into Africa in its most harmful forms. Industrial alcohol, roughly distilled, often contained toxic substances. From the end of the nineteenth century its consequences were observed in certain coastal peoples – in the Loango region for example – as a form of degeneration. Colonial conquest and the spread of the market economy brought imported alcohols to the interior. The non-Islamic regions – the Ivory Coast forests, Dahomey, the South Cameroons and French Equatorial Africa, with the exception of Chad – were the worst affected.

Alcohol was seen by some as a means of colonisation. In a short booklet on the Ivory Coast, Lieutenant Bonneau wrote, after first deploring the ravages of alcohol:

> While the fatal passion brought by the Europeans is an evil, it must also be admitted that it is a necessary evil. To enable the whites to establish themselves in such countries, to run trade there, it was clearly necessary to create new needs among the natives: alcohol was a sure aid in this.[20]

The application of the Saint-Germain-en-Laye Convention (1919) led to the prohibition of harmful products (absinthe and the so-called commercial alcohols), but without having the intended effect; commercial alcohols were not precisely defined. The high entry duties levied did, however, reduce the importation of spirits (in French West Africa 15,000 hectolitres in 1923, 21,640 hl. in 1924 and 29,664 hl. in 1928, as against 71,900 hl. in 1913). In French West Africa a decree of 30 December, 1924, forbade all importation of commercial alcohol, and in French Equatorial Africa the sale or distribution of spirits to Africans was forbidden by a decree of 18 June, 1927. But this prohibition did not apply to Europeans and so remained in part illusory; it did not include wines less than 14° proof.

Alcoholism as a social evil is caused by general misery and is the constant companion of undernourishment, the effects of which it aggravates. Prohibition or taxation measures were never more than a partial remedy; in fact, these measures led to clandestine distilling, with makeshift stills being used to ferment various products (palm wine, millet or maize beer, bananas, cassava) and resulted often in toxic, if not lethal, spirits. In 1938 the import of brandy and liqueurs fell in French West Africa below 10,000 hl., but the import of wines and apéritifs rose to 11,367 tons, i.e. much more than 100,000 hl.[21] P. Kalck wrote of Ubangi-Shari:

> Alcoholism was very widespread among the chiefs, customary and otherwise, and the 'note-books' kept until now by the local administration nearly always contain some mention of the abuses of alcohol.[22]

In Senegal, the Sudan and Guinea, it seems that widespread alcoholism among the people generally receded with the advance of Islam. It continued, however, to cause ravages among the 'élite', who had the means to procure it and were often led to do so by the example of the Europeans, among whom alcoholism often resulted from frequent, almost obligatory social drinking.

(b) MEDICAL ACTION

The traditional African societies knew how to deal with diseases. A thousand years of experience had accumulated an appreciable body of knowledge. It was indeed largely empirical knowledge, yet European medicine has only recently advanced beyond the stage of empiricism – which still persists in many fields. How much of the treatment and remedies currently prescribed by the 'modern' doctor defy all scientific analysis? And how much of it cannot be justified even as serious experiment, relying, when it succeeds, on the effects of auto-suggestion far more than on medical science?

It is certain that traditional African medical practice contained a strong element of remedies or treatment devoid of justification – on the basis of magic, for example – where any possible effects could only be due to auto-suggestion. But it also contained a valuable part, confirmed by experience, using local products with quite specific effects in the struggle against tropical diseases. 'Numerous empirical remedies of vegetable or animal origin have given proof of their effectiveness', Dr. Aujoulat wrote.[23] And he correctly added: 'They should be more thoroughly known and scientifically used.' He deplored the error of despising traditional African medicine.

The colonial complex had an effect in this as in all other areas of culture. For the colonial doctors, there was no indigenous medicine, only that of 'witch-doctors' and 'quacks' exploiting the credulity of their fellows. It should also be said that the secrecy surrounding the practices of this traditional medicine, like those country healers in an earlier Europe, made any approach difficult. Very little was done in this field, and it can be said that the problem remains unsolved.[24] The first approach of the colonialists to tropical pathology was made by naval doctors, who treated the troops (naval infantry) and the administration of the coastal establishments. Professor

Mahé, of the naval school of medicine at Brest, explained the state of knowledge to young doctors called to service in those regions, as follows:

> Down there, on the infested shores of the Atlantic, you will encounter the redoubtable sphinx of malaria – pernicious Proteus, the delirious phantom of Typhus, the living and icy spectre of Cholera, the yellow mask of *Vomito Negro*. Defy it! The earth and the waters exhale a poisoned breath. . . .[25]

This poetic language simply proved a total admission of ignorance. Beginning with clinical observation, the general practitioners had made efforts to describe and classify the various 'fevers' in hot countries; but, in their ignorance of the causes, they remained perplexed. In the authoritative works of Dr. A. Corre,[26] the arguments of Pasteur, which by then had been fully developed, were contested: Corre turned derisively on the microbes, and did not even suspect the role of insect carriers in the transmission of many diseases. Malaria was attributed to *miasmata* exhaled by the swamp. For lack of a precise definition, Corre said:

> The noxious principle can be considered as a chemical agent. Like the ptomaines, it arises from the decomposition of organic matter; it forms in the soil, under influences that are most favourable to the combustion of this matter, and especially in vegetable substances.[27]

Although the trypanosome was discovered by Forbe in 1901, an inquiry held by the ministry for the colonies in 1903 into sleeping sickness in French West Africa carried out research to see whether food, clothing and customs did not in some way cause this disease. The treatment prescribed ran parallel to this ignorance. To fight against 'malarial anaemia' among its European employees, the Saint-Louis Railway Company, following the prescriptions of the medical corps, gave them 'fortifying wines'. During a yellow fever epidemic at Saint-Louis, people were advised to go up on to the terraces at night to avoid the *miasmata* and breathe pure air, but in doing so, they exposed themselves to the bites of the mosquitoes that spread the disease. In 1888 when the Pasteur Institute was opened, one young naval doctor, Albert Calmette, applied for admission in order to be initiated into new methods of research. In 1896 Dr. Marchoux founded the first African microbiological laboratory at Saint-Louis. In the Congo, the findings of the 1906 study mission on sleeping sickness led to the opening of a bacteriological laboratory under the Pasteur Institute, set up by a convention of 1 January, 1909. It came to be known as the Pasteur Institute of Brazzaville. The laboratory at Saint-Louis, named the Biological Institute of French West Africa after its transfer to Dakar, was established on 1 January, 1924, by an agreement between the government-general of French West Africa and a branch of the Pasteur Institute. At roughly the same time an agreement on 20 November, 1922, granted the Pasteur Institute a concession near Kindia in Guinea to set up a laboratory and a centre for the breeding of anthropoid apes, to give facilities for experiments for the Pasteur establishments. It was built between 1923 and 1927 and became known as Pastoria. Finally a 'leprosy institute' was put into service at Bamako in 1934.

This is not the place to enumerate the work of Pasteur in matters of tropical medicine. It can merely be said that it represents the essence of what was done: the isolation of microbes as the most frequent cause of diseases; the discovery of vaccines and specific serums – among them, in particular, the anti-plague vaccines produced by the Pasteur Institute in Madagascar in 1935 and the anti-amaril vaccine (against yellow-fever) developed in 1927 by the Pasteur Institute at Dakar, and perfected in 1938–40. This scientific work was the more notable since the material and human means with which it was achieved were so pitifully inadequate. The financial bureaucracy demanded weeks and months for formalities such as opening credits, and paralysed the activity of the laboratories which, in the event of an epidemic, would be unable to procure vital materials. Attachment to the Pasteur Institute, a private body, gave its employees financial autonomy: but the colonial administration showed reluctance to grant them the necessary subsidies.

The word 'Institute' should not be misread: the majority of these establishments for a long time had no more than one or two workers with the necessary scientific qualifications, such as doctors or veterinary surgeons. While the Pasteur Institute at Dakar could enlarge its staff, the one at Kindia never had more than one or two staff members. Housed for a long time in delapidated buildings, the Pasteur Institute at Dakar only obtained better accommodation by means of a loan raised in 1931; it moved there in March 1937. The institute of leprosy was opened with the help of the same loan. However limited the contribution of local research workers in aetiology and therapeutics, it has to be said that most of the progress achieved in applied medicine in Black Africa only reflected that being achieved elsewhere, especially in Europe and America.

We should now examine how this scientific knowledge was applied. Starting as the speciality of the naval doctors, overseas medicine devolved upon their heirs, the colonial army doctors[28]

O*

(comprising both pharmacists and veterinary surgeons). Until the First World War they were occupied almost exclusively in treating the personnel of the army and the colonial administration; they also treated settlers. Europeans took first and African auxiliary personnel second place. The colonial health service remained largely a medical service for officials. The number of doctors and the means available to the health service enabled them to do little more: often they were not even sufficient to care for the officials and the settlers. What they were able to do for the masses was only a drop in the ocean, and was done only when Europeans were endangered by epidemics. The missions set up infirmaries and dispensaries, but rarely had qualified personnel, even less doctors. This activity was usually inspired by preoccupations alien to medical aims: 'Often . . . through [the treatment] the first contacts were made with the population, and these led on to the direct work of preaching the Gospel.'[29] The missions provided the hospital staff until 1903.[30]

Only in 1905 did a decree establish a service for general medicine in French West Africa under the name of 'native medical care'. It comprised twenty-one doctors and African assistants. In 1910, native medical care included fifty-three military and thirty-five civilian doctors working under contract, spread over 102 centres, among them three hospitals, respectively at Saint-Louis, Gorée and Conakry. Senegal had twenty-two dispensaries; Upper Senegal and Niger three 'regular health centres' at Kayes, Kati and Timbuctu, and twenty-eight dispensaries; Guinea had thirteen dispensaries; the Ivory Coast had seventeen ambulances and dispensaries, while Dahomey had eleven of the same. Mauritania had five 'medical posts'. In 1920 there were ninety-five civilian and military doctors (including those for troops), twenty of them at Dakar.

The staff, for the most part, did not work exclusively in native medical care, but principally for the troops or as doctors to officials. In 1908, statistics indicate 150,000 sick persons treated, out of roughly 12,000,000 inhabitants. In the Cameroons, even taking into account the difference in population (2,500,000 inhabitants), the Germans seem to have been more advanced: they had forty-two doctors in the health services (including seventeen military doctors) fifteen medical assistants, and ten workers in a special service to combat sleeping sickness, of which the ravages reduced recruitment of manpower and began to cause concern. French Equatorial Africa had a total of forty civilian and military doctors around 1920.

In a book written by a colonial doctor with the purpose of protesting against the novel *Batouala* by René Maran, which had aroused the anger of colonial circles, one can read this clear avowal:

A few figures and a short exposé will suffice to show the almost complete non-existence of this medical aid so freely called 'native'. . . . They [the doctors] are, in effect, doctors for 'the whites' and only very secondarily doctors 'for the niggers'. . . .[31] The 'bush' doctors live in the main town of the circle. In theory, they have to undertake frequent tours, but in practice they hardly move around at all, and when they decide to do so, it is with the sole aim of helping a European, an official or a merchant who is seriously ill. . . .[32]

He adds that the person involved usually turns out to be either dead or already cured.

Medicine for the masses began to appear in a different form: the *Services d'hygiène*. To start with, these were for the towns, aimed at protecting the health of the European population. This was to be done by eliminating places infested with mosquitoes (performed by the mission of Dr. Le Moal at Conakry), improving urban sanitation, and often by introducing segregation – the houses of Africans situated next to European quarters were pulled down, and their occupants moved to the outskirts. Mass medicine was not fully introduced until 1920. It was not due to humanitarian considerations but to a strictly utilitarian point of view. The first effects of the colonial system began to be felt in general undernourishment. Conscription, through the operation of review boards, revealed the physical decline of a large part of the population in the enormous number of rejects for military service. In the Cameroons and French Equatorial Africa, sleeping sickness assumed catastrophic proportions: in 1922 in the Nyong Valley of the Cameroons, 80–97 per cent of the population were infected, with a mortality rate of 22 per cent of cases. Entire villages vanished. Albert Sarraut wrote at that time:

Medical aid . . . is our duty. . . . But it is also, one might say, our most immediate and matter-of-fact interest. For the entire work of colonisation, all the need to create wealth, is dominated in the colonies by the question of 'labour'.[33]

He included the 'necessity, in a word, of conserving and increasing human capital to make financial capital work and bear fruit'.[34] Governor-General Carde coined the phrase *faire du nègre*.

For the more than fifteen years that native medical care has been functioning in French West Africa, I have had the impression that it is marking time and that its impact on the development of the indigenous races remains practically nil.[35]

The failure of curative medicine under native medical care led to the concept of mass preventive medical care. Speaking in favour of the work of the 'African cradle', the director of the Compagnie française de l'Ouest africaine, Julien Le Cesne, first explained:

> You know how, at the present hour, France is trying to overcome her grave financial difficulties. . . . You also know how much she needs to reduce her purchases of raw materials abroad and find at home, in her own colonies, what she needs. . . . But in spite of efforts, the export of major crops has not risen enough.
>
> The reason for this is the lack of manpower. With 12,000,000 inhabitants, French West Africa is under-populated; French Equatorial Africa even more so. More seriously, the question arises whether this already weak population is not going to grow weaker. . . . It is our duty to act: first, in the name of humanity, but equally in the name of our own interests. Growth in production, which is only possible through the growth of population, will enrich France as it will enrich the colony. And each of us, by the extension of commercial transactions, by the resultant growth in raw materials, will reap big profits.
>
> Thus at the present time we must – and you will allow me to stress this point – use a word already coined by others – by M. Carde, I believe, – we must *faire du Noir*.[36]

But between words of this order, marked both by utilitarianism and cynicism, and their translation into reality, there always remained a gulf. French colonialism, particularly in tropical Africa, continued to be remarkable for its narrow-minded spirit, which was pre-eminent in the trade economy. People lived from day to day, concerned only with running profitable businesses upon the backs of the people or at the expense of the colonial budget, and totally disregarded the future. This was true in economic circles, but it was equally true of the administration embedded in its bureaucratic routine, alien not only to human sentiment but to all imagination.

The history of the struggle against sleeping-sickness was an example of this. Its main hero was Dr. Jamot. He began his career at Brazzaville in 1914, and became interested in studying the trypanosomes. He was chief medical officer of the Sangha-Cameroons expedition in the Cameroons campaign, and in 1916 was named director of the Pasteur Institute at Brazzaville. At that time he undertook his first experiments in preventive medicine in Ubangi-Shari. On his initiative a decree of the governor-general of French Equatorial Africa, dated 22 January, 1921, set up a specialised 'sector of preventive medicine' in the group of colonies.

In 1921 he went to the Cameroons to direct the fight against sleeping sickness. The situation was already serious before the war, and as we have seen, the Germans had set up a special service to

combat the disease. The war years and the occupation had aggravated the situation. In certain regions, the population was even in
danger of extinction within a short time; one-third of the inhabitants
were threatened. Jamot got his views accepted and applied the
following methods. He established specialised mobile teams, the
systematic protection and registration of sufferers, and, after
limiting the focal points, mass treatment with atoxyl injections. One
hundred and thirty thousand cases of sleeping sickness were thus
identified in the Cameroons. While the mortality rate among those
who did not receive treatment reached 25–50 per cent a year, it
dropped to 5–15 per cent among those who received treatment.
Jamot did not succeed in having his views accepted without considerable difficulty. Because the centres of infection had to be
isolated and exempted from recruitment, he faced the hostility of
the administration when, in 1923, he wanted to isolate the infection
in the Yaoundé region, where intensive recruitment was required
to complete the railway line. He conducted several preventive
campaigns in the northern Cameroons in 1924–5. Dissatisfied with
his resources he managed to bring about the establishment of a
permanent sleeping-sickness mission in 1926. His demands were
more easily satisfied because at this time Germany, in pressing its
rights to its lost colonies, was leading a campaign against the poor
administration of the mandate powers, especially France. The
Germans showed that, compared to the time of their administration,
the number of doctors had dropped by half in Togo and by 57 per
cent in the Cameroons.[37] From ten doctors, twenty European
assistants and 150 male nurses, the mission had increased by 1931
to eighteen doctors, thirty-six European agents and 400 medical
orderlies. Credits appropriated amounted to 10,700,000 francs in
1929 (more than one-sixth of the revenue of the Cameroons),
14,590,000 in 1930 (with a 3,000,000-franc subsidy from France),
and 15,900,000 in 1931. The south, the worst affected, was systematically treated between 1926 and 1931.

Finally accepted by the administration, Jamot had his moment
of 'glory'.[38] His methods remained, in spite of everything, typically
colonial. In the name of efficiency, he favoured the 'strong arm' in
medical matters. To summon the people, register them and then
proceed to isolate the disease, the mobile teams employed methods
that strongly resembled those used for civil or military recruitment;
in other words, they were like man-hunts. Hence, the lack of
enthusiasm on the part of the people will be easily understood. The
mobile teams and their helpers lived off the country in good colonial
tradition, shamelessly demanding food and women. Lumbar
punctures were indispensable to the bacteriological examinations,

and these were carried out by medical orderlies who were not always skilled and in haphazard hygienic conditions; often serious accidents, and even paralysis and death, were the result. Some of the 'trypano' agents would threaten people with a 'bad injection' if they showed themselves too exacting over the conduct of their wives or daughters. Finally, the treatment used was not without dangers. After 1928 the atoxyl, less efficient than at first supposed, was replaced by tryparsamide, which needed far more delicate handling. Injections had to be carefully graded according to the stage of the disease; any error could have grave consequences for the nervous system – nephritis, blindness, etc. The shortage of doctors, and the need to act quickly among the masses, sometimes made it impossible to observe these conditions. General Sicé of the medical corps defended Jamot in these words:

> This is not the time to discuss the scientific conduct of the struggle he waged without respite; the danger was considerable, urgency was all. The prophylactic method he applied, without the necessary clinical conditions, enabled him to do this well. That is sufficient.[39]

It will be understood how far colonial methods of immunisation differed from those normally in use, if one recalls that the use of widely tested drugs was sometimes suspended in Europe because of a few doubtful individual cases. In the colonies a few dozen or a few hundred 'accidents' were no obstacle to the use of therapeutic methods of recognised mass effect. Given these conditions, one can understand the terror inspired among the people by the trypano teams, a terror which did not arise from congenital obscurantism but from very concrete experiences.

The 'glory' of Dr. Jamot was abruptly terminated by an 'accident' which cost him his post. One of his protégés, Dr. M., had his assistants do his tours, and prescribed injections of tryparsamide at a high dosage (twice or three times as high as that normally prescribed). A number of persons who received this treatment went blind, and Dr. M., when informed, took no notice. Then the scandal broke: the chief of the *subdivision* revealed that in his sector 500 persons treated for sleeping sickness had become blind. Jamot went to the region for an inquiry and made the figure 700. Out of *esprit de corps*, and perhaps because he failed to see anything very serious in this, Jamot covered up for his subordinate. He refused to testify before the board of inquiry set up to look into the work of Dr. M., and the board simply imposed a reprimand on the culprit. Unfortunately for Jamot, the affair leaked out. Diagne, then undersecretary of state for the colonies, read the dossier; and Jamot's protégé threw all the responsibility on his protector.[40] At Dakar, Jamot was taken off the boat which was carrying him to France, placed under arrest, and then relieved of his post in 1931, on a ministerial decision, with the agreement of his superiors. The service which he had set up in the Cameroons was now attached to the management of health services.

In 1932 Jamot was sent to French West Africa where a decree established a service for the prevention of disease.[41] Soon after, and without his being consulted, his service was integrated into the native medical care, which deprived him of any initiative. He settled at Ouagadougou in Upper Volta, where the disease was at its worst; entire villages were being wiped out, with the rate of infection at times reaching 93 per cent. In two years, and by visiting only two-thirds of the population, he discovered 37,000 patients. In North Dahomey, one out of every eight persons examined showed a positive reaction; out of 230 villages in one circle, only eight had remained untouched. In Guinea, according to the official account, the illness disappeared spontaneously: but Jamot found 53 per cent of the villages in the forest region contaminated. In a few months 2,500 sick people were registered in the Kissidougou circle. In the Sudan, where the illness was officially unknown, 2,580 cases were discovered within a few months, some of them on the banks of the Niger, in the immediate vicinity of Bamako. In Senegal, in the region of Niayes, Jamot revealed the persistence of focal points which had been known before the war.

In 1935 Jamot proposed that an autonomous service be created to combat sleeping-sickness, analogous to the service that he had established and run in the Cameroons. He met with scepticism on the part of the administration, for whom sleeping sickness in French West Africa was a chimera; they regarded his demands as a sign of personal ambition and megalomania. Moreover, it was a time of economies, and his demands for credit were turned down. On 9 October, 1935, *Le Temps* announced, moreover, that in the other territories

the few special services that existed to combat this terrible disease have been suppressed to make budgetary economies.

Discouraged, he retired, and died in France a few months later on 24 April, 1937. This story clearly displays Jamot's complex personality; he was undoubtedly devoted to his work and knew no respite, he was churlish and authoritarian, and capable of standing up and speaking bluntly to any governor who did not admit the existence of sleeping sickness,[42] but he shared the reflexes and the *esprit de corps* of the colonial officials.

By 31 December, 1934, he had detected nearly 70,000 cases of trypanosomiasis in French West Africa and Togo out of about two-thirds of the population. As a consequence of 'economies' imposed by the administration, there were 151,000 known cases in August 1938. In 1939, very belatedly, the service he had requested was established on the model of that existing in the Cameroons, with its good and bad points. In French Equatorial Africa the struggle was undertaken on the same principles, and a decree of 18 January, 1928, set up a special service of preventive medicine on the Cameroons model, but numerous focal points of the disease persisted, notably in Ubangi (Upper Sangha) where it had always been widespread. On the eve of the Second World War the structure of the health services was diversified. Alongside native medical care, which treated the sick at fixed posts, there existed hygiene and prophylactic services, sometimes specialised ones, as in the case of sleeping sickness. The autonomy of the services had advantages, like the avoidance of bureaucratic paralysis; its more inconvenient aspects included absence of co-ordination and rivalries going as far as hostility, the effects of which were worst felt in French Equatorial Africa.

Apart from the major work carried out in the field of sleeping sickness – with the specific limits that we have mentioned, the results varied according to the means employed. Means were on the increase, no doubt, but remained totally inadequate to the problems to be solved. In the main centres, there were a few hospitals: in 1920 the Ballay hospital at Conakry, 'the finest in the whole of West Africa', as a publicist noted who accompanied Albert Sarraut on his ministerial trip through Africa, had 100 beds, two doctors and two medical orderlies. Except under special circumstances, it was open only to Europeans. Dakar had a 'native' as well as a European hospital. The Ivory Coast constructed a 'native hospital' in the suburb of Treichville in the 1930s, next to the European hospital in Abidjan. While the European hospitals were passable, the native hospitals were squalid. The patients and the African orderlies were of course held responsible for this situation; but those in charge of the health services did almost nothing to remedy it. In 1948, in the native hospital at Dakar, people in the terminal stages of tuberculosis were lying in wards with open doors, and with neither windows nor wire mesh, covered with flies; their only facility was an empty tin to spit into.

At the same time, credits were often wasted on useless buildings (useless for all but the architects and entrepreneurs). The 'hospital' of Fort-Archambault, built with funds obtained from a special loan of 75,000,000 earmarked for the health services of French Equatorial

Africa, had not a single doctor in 1934, no staff, no operating theatre, no dispensary, no kitchen, no wells. There was no water, except from the river Shari, which had to be brought over a distance of 3 km. At Bangui, the hospital was built in separate small buildings which involved transporting the patients to the operating theatres and carrying them through the open air; the surgical equipment was obsolete and far below the proper minimum requirement. There was electricity in the governor's palace, but not at the hospital, where operations at night were carried out by the light of a kerosene lamp. There was no water: 800 litres per day (instead of the 8,000 needed) were brought by prisoners doing forced labour. One part of the loan had been used to construct the maternity hospitals of Brazzaville and Bangui, which comprised individual rooms with bathrooms (no water!). This was the situation in 1934, and the explanation for the small returns derived from the 75,000,000 francs invested.[43]

Scarecely any of the sixty-nine doctors who worked in French Equatorial Africa (including the sleeping-sickness team) had vehicles for their work, and all were short of drugs. The hospitals had 2,200 beds (for 3,500,000 inhabitants). There were also 115 dispensaries or medical posts where doctors and medical orderlies examined interminable rows of the sick and gave them what care they could. In the Cameroons in 1935 the hospitals had fifty 'European' beds and 3,000 'African' beds. According to statistics, there were 9,300, but 6,200 must be deducted from this for the leper colonies, organised as 'agricultural colonies', and sleeping-sickness hospitals formed of huts or shanties where the piece of matting granted to a pensioner could hardly pass as a 'hospital bed'.

Native medical care employed forty-seven military doctors, two civilians under contract, two pharmacists and one dentist – hardly representing much progress since 1914. It is true that 'care' was free of charge, while that provided by the German administration had to be paid for. But under what condition was free care provided? The African who did not live in the locality had to come to the dispensary on foot, often travelling for weeks over hundreds of kilometres. On arrival, he had to take his place in the interminable queue which formed at consulting hours, often waiting for hours, if not days, to appear before the doctor – unless a willing orderly, with the help of a gift, would agree to do him a favour. Consultation, however, did not settle everything. Drugs were often in short supply. Even if they could be found, they still had to be paid for.[44] Many of the sick became discouraged and attended only when their disease had reached an extremely serious state, or when, as often happened, it was too late. Native medical care represented a drop in the ocean relative to the need, and the marked increase in staff up to 1930 (followed by a slight reduction as a result of the economic crisis) did not change the general situation.[45]

A few isolated initiatives did not add up to much. The hospital at Lambaréné, in Gabon, was for Albert Schweitzer far more a pretext for personal exaltation, in the name of sacrifice and charity, than a truly humane undertaking. However respectable the philosophical concepts of its initiator, the great doctor remained sunk in narrow colonial prejudices as they existed forty years before, faithful to the colonial caste in his refusal to train African collaborators who were *a priori* judged incapable. The sordid hutments at Lambaréné hospital, said by witnesses to have remained unchanged for twenty years,[46] were not great advertisements for this kind of philanthropy.

The record of the fifty years up to 1946 can be summed up by a few figures:[47]

	Number of Beds	Number of Hospitals	Medical Centres	Dispensaries	European Doctors	African Doctors	Health Assistants
French West Africa	23,067	8	152	253	170	335	—
Togo	633	2	7	31	11	16	—
Cameroons	12,897	7	20	81	35	—	42
French Equatorial Africa	13,768	6	44	177	94	19	—

In conclusion, the balance sheet of health care seems to show a medical policy strictly subordinated to the interests of colonisation, the objectives of which were neither humanitarian nor disinterested. The policy worked in two directions. The first was to protect the health of the European administrative personnel, the armed forces and, where possible, the lower-rank African workers on the colonial staff. This was its essential objective before 1914. The second was to prevent a shortage of labour that might hamper the colonial venture; to do this one undertook preventive treatment of certain major epidemics. This was the major objective after the war, but very incompletely achieved due to lack of funds.

So it appears that neither medical nor educational work can be claimed as 'redeeming' the evil deeds perpetrated by colonisation in other fields.

REFERENCES

1. Médicin-colonel Farinaud, *Medical Report*, 1945.
2. Lieutenant-colonel Pales, *Le Bilan de la mission anthropologique de l'Afrique occidentale française*. Dakar, 1948.
3. Author's italics.
4. Médicin-général Mathis, *L'Oeuvre des pastoriens en Afrique noire*. Paris, P.U.F., 1946, p. 307.
5. Ibid.
6. Op. cit., p. 303.
7. Op. cit., p. 306.
8. Due to the pneumoccocus or the meningococcus.
9. In 1848 in Upper Volta there were 2,931 deaths among the 13,876 cases found; in the Natitingou circle (North Dahomey), with a population of 140,000, the epidemic caused 3,000 deaths that year.
10. Provisional report on tuberculosis and sleeping sickness in Equatorial Africa. Geneva, League of Nations, 1923, p. 41. For the spread of sleeping sickness in French Equatorial Africa see the chart and notes by L. Maillot in the *Bulletin de l'Institut de Recherches Scientifiques au Congo*, 1962, 1, pp. 45–54.
11. On this subject A. Basset, H. Boiron and Mme M. Basset, 'A propos d'une enquête sur le pian en Haute-Volta', *Bulletin Société de Médicine d'Afrique noire*, V, 2, 2nd trim. 1960, pp. 186–90.
12. The significance of serological reactions (sometimes with startling results) is under discussion. H. Boiron and A. Basset point out 30 per cent positive reactions among the (adult) Moors in eastern Mauritania, 85 per cent among the Fulani. *Bulletin Société de Médicine d'Afrique noire*, V, 3, 3rd trim. 1960, pp. 328–33.
13. Le Gall and Giordani, *La Situation sanitaire de l'Empire française en 1940*. Paris, Charles-Lavauzelle, 1943.
14. C. Mathis, op. cit., p. 333.
15. A. Calmette, 'Enquête sur l'épidémiologie de la tuberculose dans les colonies françaises', *Annales de l'Institut Pasteur*, 1912, vol. XXVI, pp. 497–514.
16. C. Mathis, op. cit., p. 337.
17. L. Couvy, 'La tuberculose à Dakar', *Bulletin Société de Pathologie exotique*, 1927, vol. XX, pp. 228–32.
18. L. Couvy, op. cit.
19. C. Mathis, op. cit., p. 313.
20. Lieutenant Bonneau, *La Côte d'Ivoire*. Paris, Charles-Lavauzelle, 1899, p. 87.
21. Importation of alcoholic drinks in 1938 (in tons):

	French West Africa	Cameroons	French Equatorial Africa
Wines and various aperitifs	11,367	1,367	2,292
Spirits and liqueurs	840	61	103

(*Annuaire statistique de la France d'Outre-mer*, Volume J (1939–46). Paris, Imprimerie Nationale, 1949).
22. P. Kalck, *Réalités oubanguiennes*. Paris, Berger-Levrault, 1959, pp. 138–9.
23. Doctor L. Aujoulat, *Aujourd'hui l'Afrique*. Paris and Tournai, Casterman, 1958.
24. Some indications of the attempts made on the eve of the war (at least in the sphere of vegetable pharmacopœia) are to be found in E. Perrot, *Où en est l'Afrique occidentale française?* Paris, Larose, 1939, chap. VI: 'Drogues médicinales ou toxiques de l'Afrique occidentale française', pp. 223–52. The importance of the efforts made in China to incorporate the positive contribution of traditional medicine into science are, on the other hand, well known.

25. Quoted by C. Mathis, op. cit., p. 7.

26. *Traité des fièvres bilieuses et typhiques des pays chauds* (1883) and *Traité clinique des maladies des pays chauds* (1887).

27. Quoted by C. Mathis, op. cit., p. 9.

28. Trained at the Ecole de Santé maritime et coloniale at Bordeaux.

29. Father Bouchaud, *L'Eglise en Afrique noire*. Paris, La Palatine, 1958, p. 36.

30. Important hospitals were greatly reduced at the time, and were almost exclusively reserved for Europeans.

31. René Trautman, *Au pays de Batouala*. Paris, Payot, 1922, p. 214.

32. Ibid., p. 215.

33. Albert Sarraut, *La Mise en valeur des colonies françaises*. Paris, Payot, 1923, p. 94.

34. Ibid., p. 95.

35. J. Carde, Speech to the Council of Government of French West Africa, 2 December, 1926, *Afrique française, Revue coloniale*, 1927, No. 1, p. 19.

36. *Afrique française, Revue coloniale*, 1926, No. 2, pp. 65–6.

37. Professor L. Tanon, in an article on this subject, did not deny the facts, but blamed the miserable pay of the French colonial doctors which discouraged the vocation. (*Afrique Française*, 1926, No. 4, pp. 160–3).

38. Professor H. Galliard, 'Eugène Jamot', *France Outre-mer*, 2nd trim. 1959, pp. 12–14.

39. Médecin-général Sicé, *L'Afrique équatoriale française et le Cameroun au service de la France*. Paris, P.U.F., 1946, p. 36.

40. For this affair see Dr. Marcel Bebey-Eyidi, *Le Vainqueur de la maladie du sommeil: Eugène Jamot (1879–1937)*. Paris, n.d.

41. A special service had already been set up in 1928 on the borders of Upper Volta, Togo and Dahomey comprising guards to 'back up the police and the gathering of the people for examination', but only one doctor and seven male orderlies.

42. A picturesque anecdote on this subject will be found in Dr. Bebey-Eyidi's thesis.

43. R. Susset, *La Vérité sur le Cameroun et l'Afrique equatoriale française*. Paris, Ed. de la Nouvelle Revue Critique, 1934.

44. At Grand-Popo (Dahomey), 'the sick complained of a lack of medicines in the circle hospital. They were received very politely for consultation, were examined, were told what they were ailing from, but they were not given anything for treatment. How long will this tragi-comedy last?' (*Le Courrier du Golfe du Bénin*, No. 35, 15 June, 1933.)

45. Comparative numbers (French West Africa):

	European doctors	Indigenous doctors	Midwives
1924	87	26	53
1929	189	88	133

46. Dr. Aujoulat, op. cit., p. 157.

47. *Annuaire statistique de la France d'Outre-mer (1939–46)*, volume C, Paris, Imprimerie Nationale, 1949.

CHAPTER III

SOCIAL AND POLITICAL EVOLUTION

1. *Social Evolution*

We shall deal with this subject only briefly, partly because material
for a study in depth is lacking; also because everything indicates
that broad conclusions are impossible. Economic stagnation is
naturally balanced by social stagnation. What has been said of
social development for the period prior to 1914 remains valid for
the post-war period with only a few exceptions. The old structures
were slow to disappear; and the internal contradictions, generally
ante-dating the colonial era, became more acute. However, no
qualitative changes are discernible in the social structure as a whole.
These did not come until the period following the Second World
War.

(a) THE TOWNS[1]

The towns remained what they had been before: administrative and
trading centres. Industry was more or less confined to the building
trade, public works and port handling operations. Cities with a
pronounced urban character were rare; and, in these, solid buildings were to be found only in the business quarters and the European residential areas. Forced out into the suburbs, the Africans
tried to reproduce the old village set-up with mud or straw and, as
in the village, domestic livestock (sheep, goats, chickens and guinea-
fowl) and, if the size of the plot allowed, a few crops. Streets in the
African quarters (Médina at Dakar, Treichville or Adjamé at
Abidjan, and Poto-poto or Bacongo at Brazzaville) were nothing
but sand or mud alleyways. There was no public highway system;
instead of drainage there were only a few sewers, usually open or
crudely covered with flag-stones; there was little or no water, with
a few public pumps where queues waited from early in the morning. Public lighting was reserved for the European quarters. Overcrowding created a great hazard to health.[2]

The small ports-of-call and the trading posts of the interior consisted of nothing more than the circle commander's 'residence',

offices and a few warehouses, around which crowded groups of African dwellings, forming large villages. Apart from European settlers and Lebanese, there was no bourgeoisie. At Dakar there were a few African traders, but these were individuals rather than a social group. At Saint-Louis and to a lesser degree Dakar (whither they had emigrated from Gorée), there were a few remnants of the families of nineteenth-century traders. These were African or mulatto (the latter by origin only, as they were usually completely Africanised), and constituted a closed circle, despising the 'uncivilised black' and aspiring, usually without success, to gain entry into colonial society, the views and prejudices of which they pretended to share. They lived humbly on what remained of their past fortunes (income from landed estates) or by accepting modest employment in administration or commerce. The same state of mind, though less pronounced, could be found in the descendants of former American Negroes[3] in the Rivières du Sud, of Portuguese in Casamance, of Brazilians in Dahomey and of freed slaves in Libreville. But while the families of Saint-Louis and Gorée had the advantage of citizenship, the latter were as much 'indigenous' natives as anyone else, eventually being admitted to canton chiefdoms. Such were the De Souzas at Ouidah, whose house was hung with family portraits dating back to the nineteenth century, the oldest being very light-skinned, the skin colour growing darker with each generation. The évolués – minor officials or commercial employees who had received an education – did not make up a class, because they played no definite role in the production process but were simply a social stratum or milieu. Though not numerous, they were subdivided into a multitude of categories, according to their level of education and administrative rank, and the colonial administration made efforts to maintain the useful barriers existing amongst them. At the summit, there was the very small élite of former students of Ponty College, of whom many would never consent to rub shoulders with officials of local rank, with their diplomas from the higher primary school, still less with a simple clerk or medical orderly with no certificate of studies. Likewise the latter would not lower himself to be on social terms with policemen or illiterate orderlies, whose 'advancement' took the form of wearing a blue or khaki uniform with metal buttons and, above all, a tropical helmet, and who had, in addition, some knowledge of French.

From the doctor who graduated from the medical school at Dakar to the orderly, a former soldier with the advantage of a reserved job, all suffered from the same alienation between their native milieu and the functions that were given to them. Their education at a French school or in the army to some extent uprooted them and led them to look with disdain, or at least with condescension, upon their fellows who had remained within the traditional society. Considered by the latter as lackeys to the whites, some adapted themselves to their functions with zeal, and sought personal profit by taking part in oppression and the pillage of colonialism. Others, by contrast, indignantly resented the situation created for them. The white constantly reminded them that for him they were 'natives' like the rest; but their revolt did not take the form of effective action, since they were cut off from the masses – from their traditional society – which regarded them with suspicion and irony. They were powerless, reduced to nursing their grievances in private. And the settler constantly pointed out the danger of education in a colonial country, which only produced in those who received it bitterness and a sense of failure.

The working class was only in the process of being born; it was not yet stable or clearly differentiated. The urban masses were still of little importance, being made up either of the uprooted or of a semi-proletariat, peasants who had not broken their links with the villages. The latter were the most numerous and provided almost all the unskilled labourers at ports and railways, and worked as 'boys', cooks and other domestic servants. Some came to Dakar for the season, like the Toucouleurs from Fleuve and the Sérènes from Sine-Saloum, returning to the villages during the three or four months when there was agricultural work to be done. Others left for several years, with the often disappointed hope of accumulating, by skimping, a dowry that would enable them to marry and return to establish themselves in the village. The workers proper were few. By origin they were mainly Senegalese and were scattered over private or administrative work-sites, as masons, joiners, etc. It was only in the ports and on the railways that sufficient numbers were gathered for a class spirit to begin to develop.

(b) THE COUNTRY REGIONS

The patriarchal community survived almost everywhere, under-minded in most cases by the development of the money economy and by a growing conflict of interest between the old, who tend to divert to their own profit the family property and income, and the young, who want to emancipate themselves and assert their exclusive right to the income they have earned by their work. In the regions not much affected by the trade economy or by temporary emigration, evolution remained insignificant. In regions little affected by the trade economy, but where emigration was important, there was no modification of the traditional social order, but internal tensions grew stronger. It is difficult here to estimate exactly to what extent

pre-colonial social relations (slavery, serfdom or patronage) persisted. Official reports generally ignored this. In Mauritania and
the Sahara regions generally, where the French presence was
limited to military establishments and policing (which were only
established late in the day and, in the northern confines, to a superficial extent, traditional relations were barely affected by the new
situation. The warrior aristocracy, partly balked of their traditional
raids against the frontier lands and of the direct or indirect revenue
they had derived from caravan trading, were in decline: enrolment
in *goums* (Arab contingents) and raids against the rebels with the
sanction of the authorities, did not compensate for their losses in
revenue and prestige. The *marabout* tribes, on the other hand, whose
way of life had been precarious before, now enjoyed a rise in their
social importance. Some of them went to seek their fortunes in the
south – in trade or, in a few cases, preaching and begging among the
Muslims of Negro race, who were impressed by their knowledge and
their prestige. Slavery, including the purchase and sale of captives,
continued practically unchanged.[4]

In Niger and Chad the situation was not much different. In the
Mossi country, in Fouta-Djalon, the aristocracy maintained and
even consolidated their privileges – essentially by means of the
colonial authority delegated to them through their chiefs. In the
countries where the system of chiefs was unknown (Atakora, the
Lobi country and Ubangi, for example), the government were to
introduce, with the system, forms of exploitation which had previously been unknown or scarcely developed. Trade took advantage
of poverty, which forced parents to sell their young children, notably
in Ubangi, where the Hausa or Bornu traders exported their merchandise to the feudal courts of Chad and Northern Nigeria.

> It is not rare, for example, in well-to-do families to see children
> of eight to twelve years, boys and girls, in charge of younger
> children. They passed off as relatives in the care of the family,
> although they are, in fact, slaves purchased for money.
>
> By careful observation one can see that they are always poorly
> clad. They are never sent to school, even if they are of school age,
> and even if the true children of the family go there.[5]

The same can be observed in most parts of West Africa. All that
the administration was content to do was to prohibit the use of the
term slave or captive in official documents. Thus the first civil
governor of Chad recommended in 1922 that it should be replaced
by 'not free'. Elsewhere, the euphemism of 'servant' was given pref-
ence. The captive condition persisted even in the oldest centres,
even – the greatest irony of all – in Libreville. Only the word was

proscribed, and the real relationship was camouflaged by the terms 'father' and 'son'.[6] Periods of famine, and especially the general misery which followed the crisis, gave *de facto* slavery a new impetus: children were pawned, as is revealed by concrete evidence everywhere: in Fouta-Djalon,[7] in the Sudan[8] and even in economically developed regions such as Lower Dahomey.[9] Where need arose, even adult members of the family or house slaves would be pawned.

Meanwhile, the institution of slavery continued to change. In French West Africa, many captives set themselves up in the towns and grew relatively rich in trade or manual labour. Their former masters had hardly any control over them, and sometimes the recognised relationship was reversed. The captive, while having no links with his master any more, would not hesitate to invoke traditional ties to extort aid or a present from him in circumstances where custom enabled him to do so, and this the fallen master's pride did not allow him to refuse. For a long time the aristocrats, or masters, did not wish to give their sons as hostages to the French, and sent young captives to school in their place; these became interpreters, clerks or teachers, and were able to escape from their former condition and even to take precedence over their former masters, though traditional prejudices towards them did not disappear. During the war, three-quarters of military conscripts were of slave origin, as the greater number of regular army recruits continued to be. On returning to their villages, spiritually emancipated by their sojourn overseas, possessors of premiums, savings from their pay or pensions, and possibly decorated, or at least having the prestige of ex-servicemen, they found it hard to re-integrate themselves into primitive conditions.

Like the institution of slavery, the patriarchal community itself went through a process of evolution. In the regions most affected by the trade economy, the traditional patriarchal community disintegrated, and although in general customary law did not acknowledge private landed property in the bourgeois sense, certain practices appeared which were to have that result. In Fouta-Toro, it seems that common patriarchal family ownership of the floodlands was replaced in the nineteenth century by family property belonging to the head of the household. This development was probably influenced by the arrival of trade; in any case, this sort of ownership was consolidated and sanctified with the aid of Muslim legal norms prevailing under the theocratic regime of the Almamys. The transfer of inheritance to sons, with equal division among all male heirs, led to the parcelling up of property and the abolition of collective tenure. Slackness in trade, following upon the concentration by business concerns on sites close to railways, led – together with this parcelling up of property – to a decrease in production and to endemic poverty, which in turn encouraged emigration.[10]

In Lower Dahomey, patriarchal collective tenure seems to have disappeared entirely between 1920 and 1940. When the head of an extended family died, his lands were split up among the hereditary heads of households; sometimes they were sold. The density of population in relation to the area of land cultivated (in the Porto-Novo region the average was one person to every six hectares in a family group of ten to fifteen persons) led to individual ownership, but also to the splitting up of the land which obstructed upkeep and renewal of palm groves.

Sometimes there was concentration – estates were to be found covering hundreds of hectares – but this did not happen often.[11] Large properties belonging to Africans were nearly always in the hands of chiefs, as the position of chief alone was possessed of the power to procure the (unpaid) labour necessary to work it. However, there were few canton chiefs, and this remained exceptional. In regions with annual crops, the 'chiefs' fields' could be sited in different places depending on custom. The consolidation of private property appeared only in plantation regions such as coastal Guinea, the forest zones of the Ivory Coast and Lower Dahomey.

In general, the agrarian system inhibited the growth of private property, which was soon to be found almost entirely in towns or suburbs, where it could be sold, or in densely populated regions like Lower Dahomey. In the absence of an entrenched law of private property, mortgages were not possible, except for rights of use. This did not apply to fields with long fallow periods, where such deals would bring little benefit, but to fertile and manured lands of intensive or semi-intensive cultivation on the edges of villages. The mortgagor accepted a field for his use until the settlement of the debt: if need be, the income from the field would amortise the debt and pay the interest. Examples can be found mainly in Senegal. On the other hand, attempts made by the administration to transform traditional slavery and serfdom in Macina, Fouta-Djalon and elsewhere into share-farming on big landed estates do not seem to have met with success, except in so far as they replaced terminology that was judged 'embarrasing' by another acceptable to bourgeois views. For the chiefs, 'rights' always continued to be exercised over men and the fruits of their labour, rather than over the abstract 'landed estate', the very notion of which was often the opposite of local reality.

(c) THE MARRIAGE PROBLEM: MARRIAGE SETTLEMENT AND
POLYGAMY

The problem of marriage remains a central African preoccupation.
It was not a new problem; we have already discussed its traditional
bases, and will not return to them here. With a few rare exceptions,
marriage involved the payment to the wife's parents of what is
wrongly called a 'dowry'; this consisted of gifts in kind and in
money, and promises to provide labour, furnished generally in
instalments before or after marriage. To this were added gifts to
intermediaries and close members of the wife's family, the cost of
the marriage feasts, and so on. Did the colonial system or, to be
more exact, the development of money relations, have the effect of
raising the total given as 'dowry'? Mgr. Le Roy, superior-general
of the Congregation of the Holy Spirit, had no hesitation in replying
in the affirmative:

> Before the European occupation, indigenous customs were a
> framework, rudimentary no doubt, but sufficient. . . . Parents
> were preoccupied with marrying off the young people, who could
> thus set up new homes. The 'dowry' which the husband had to
> furnish to the wife's family was moderate. Adultery was severely
> punished; conjugal union provided a certain stability, and chil-
> dren were born in large numbers.
>
> The European invasion has changed all this. On the one hand,
> as Mgr. Tardy says, the cupidity of parents has grown consider-
> ably, as the result of European commerce. The wife, the young
> girl, the quite small child, have assumed an ever-growing value.
> On the other hand since wealth in the indigenous society belongs
> only to the old, a few old men acquire all the wives. . . .[12]

The result was the enforced celibacy of numerous young men and
adults, with the disorder one would expect to result from this, while
young girls were given to old, infirm, sick or senile old men doomed
to sterility. While this much is certain, did the amount of the dowry
continue to rise throughout the first half of the twentieth century?
It is difficult to give a clear answer to this. An inquiry carried out in
1910 in Guinea gives the amount at 180 gold francs for Upper
Guinea and the forest regions, which at times was raised to as much
as 2,000 francs. At Faranah, this price of 180 francs was given as the
equivalent of two slaves.[13] It is clear that most peasants in that
region (who married nonetheless) did not possess such a sum.

One questions whether the social categories quoted in this inquiry
are valid. In any case, conversion into present-day francs does not
seem to show that the contemporary dowries are higher than

formerly, but rather the contrary. Conversely, it is certain that the rapid rise to wealth of certain individuals, especially in the period 1945–7 which was highly favourable to speculation, could lead in the towns to cross-bidding in dowries. Dowries of 100,000 francs C.F.A. have been mentioned as being paid at Douala during that period, more than the cost of an American lorry.[14] At Dakar there were dowries of 1,000,000 francs C.F.A., arrived at after what amounted to auctions. These examples, however, cannot be applied generally. What appears certain is that the difficulties encountered by the young in getting together sufficient funds for a dowry and getting married grew along with the general poverty. In the old days, payment of the dowry had been incumbent upon the head of the patriarchal family; the accumulation of wealth within the family circle had this aim among others. The disappearance of these reserves and the weakening of family solidarity left the young men to their own devices. They were forced to emigrate to the towns, to groundnut areas or plantations, or to neighbouring foreign territories, to try to accumulate the necessary sum. On the other hand, the aged head of the family would sometimes himself use the possessions with the management of which he had been entrusted, including what the young men under his authority had earned, to acquire additional wives. Tension grew between young men forced to remain celibate and the polygamous old men.

Most of the internal conflicts in African society reflect this tension and its consequences – woman's inferior position and her lack of freedom in the choice of a husband. Adultery, divorce and contests in matters of dowry probably made up three-quarters of the cases coming before lower law courts (native tribunals of the first instance). The colonial authorities showed themselves completely incapable of remedying this situation: no law or decree could have any durable result while the social causes of the situation it strove to modify remained in existence. In the Cameroons no fewer than eleven decrees and ordinances were promulgated between 1922 and 1945 to regulate dowries. In practice they were ineffective, like the 'Mandel decree' of 1939, which laid down the principle of free consent in marriage. Some action was undertaken by local groups, such as the 'Muslim Brotherhood' set up at Saint-Louis in 1938 which, in the name of Islam and pagan custom, spoke out against the high rate of *warougards* (payments in addition to the dowry paid to relations of the bride, etc.)[15] and tried to prohibit them. In certain regions, the missions – because of the authority they wielded – were to be more effective in imposing monogamy; but they would have little impact except on believers, many of whom doubtless lacked the means to indulge in polygamy. The result of their work was much less apparent in the case of the chiefs and other wealthy individuals.

REFERENCES

1. We shall refrain from a full consideration of the urban problem: the question will be taken up in greater detail in a later volume dealing with the present period.

2. Cf. J. Dresch, 'Villes d'Afrique occidentale', *C.O.M.*, 1950, No. 11, pp. 200–30.

3. They bear their names: Wilkinson, Curtis, Lightburne, etc. Slander insinuated that they were descendants of the ancient slaves who took their masters' names.

4. Cf. for the Central Sahara: J. Clauzel, 'Evolution de la vie économique et des structures sociales du pays nomade du Mali, de la conquête à l'autonomie interne', *Tiers-Monde*, III, 9–10, January–June 1962, pp. 283–312.

5. R. P. Tisserant, *Ce que j'ai connu de l'esclavage en Oubangui-Chari*. Paris, Plon, 1955, p. 56.

6. Barthel-Noirot, 'Au Gabon', *Afrique française, Revue coloniale*, 1930, No. 3, p. 152.

7. Cf. G. Vieillard, op. cit.

8. Henri Ortoli, 'Le gage des personnes au Soudan français', *Bull. I.F.A.N.*, No. 1, 1939, pp. 313–24: 'Pawning of human beings exists in all the Sudanese zone and the region between the savannah and the forest'.

9. *Le Courrier du Bénin*, 1 September 1934.

10. Youssouf Gueye, 'Essai sur les causes et les conséquences de la micropropriété au Fouta-Toro', *Bull. I.F.A.N.*, XIX, Serie B, No. 1–2, 1957, pp. 28–42.

11. G. Brasseur, 'La palmeraie de Porto-Novo', *Mémoires de l'I.F.A.N.*, No. 32, Dakar, I.F.A.N., 1953, pp. 49 ff.

12. M. Delafosse and Poutrin, *Enquête coloniale* . . . Paris, S.E.G.M.C., 1930. Preface by Mgr. Le Roy, Archbishop of Carie, pp. V and VI.

13. Delafosse and Poutrin, *Enquête coloniale* . . . Paris, S.E.G.M.C., 1930.

14. J. R. Owono Nkoudou, 'Le problème du mariage dotal au Cameroun français', *Études camerounaises*, No. 39–40. March–July 1953, pp. 41–83.

15. '*Warougards*': money paid in addition to the dowry to the bride's parents, etc.

2. *Political Life*

We shall leave aside here colonial political life proper, which belongs to French rather than to African history. The colonial system restricted the possibilities of true political expression for Africans, and contemporary colonial sources are very discreet, when they are not silent, about this political life. Its presence can, however, be found in three distinct areas. First, there was armed resistance, which continued the resistance that occurred during the period of occupation; though always ultimately doomed to failure, it arose only in regions where this occupation had been delayed or was insufficient. Secondly, there were religious movements which, partly in a secular guise and also partly as mysticism, tried to supply an outlet or at least a consolation for the people who were the victims of this social upheaval. Finally, there was modern political action, of which the first signs appeared, albeit muzzled by the colonial power, in the first working-class centres and among the *évolués*, or colonial élite.

(a) THE LAST ARMED UPRISINGS

In French West Africa, Togo and the Cameroons, these were no more than the last echoes of 'pacification', repressive operations against the people who, until then, had remained more or less on the fringes of the colonial activity. They were undertaken against the 'stateless' populations, which had no natural chiefs, and on which the administration had most difficulty, for this reason, in imposing administrative chiefs and demands for taxes, forced labour and conscripts. Of this kind were the police operations undertaken in 1928 and 1929 in the Lobi country to the north of Bouna, consisting of the southern part of the Gaoua circle, where the last independent Lobi had taken refuge, and the occupation and destruction of the rebel village of Domatéon. Similar were the operations undertaken by Lieutenant Labadie in February–March 1923 against the rebel Konkomba, who refused to pay taxes in Northern Togo, and in 1935–6 by Lieutenant Massu,[1] who destroyed the plantations of strophantus (used for anointing poisoned arrows) and confiscated three tons of the arrows themselves.

Of a different order were operations in Mauritania, where submission was not achieved. Port-Etienne was attacked on 26 March, 1924. In 1925 a raiding party from Seguiet El-Hamra unexpectedly attacked the French troops in the battle of Treyfia (2–5 April), in which Captain de Girval was killed. The panic-sticken authorities could already imagine the redoubtable El Hiba at the gates of Saint-Louis. He was the son of Ma El-Ainin, who in 1912 had seized Marrakesh and proclaimed himself Sultan of Morocco.

The garrisons were scoured for men. . . . The result was disastrous: surprised in a sand-storm, in the desert outside Atar, the detachment lost a considerable portion of its men.[2]

On 13 June, 1927, a new raiding party attacked the trading posts at Port-Etienne and then pillaged a camp 130 km. to the north of Saint-Louis, sowing fresh panic in the capital of Senegal. The years 1931–3 were marked by the last big attacks of the Regueibat based in Rio de Oro: an attack on a camp by a nomad force from Adrar in August 1931, followed in March 1932 by operations against the Regueibat and deserters from the French army who had joined them. The Emir of Adrar, Ahmed Ould Aida, whose attitude had seemed suspect to the French, was killed on that occasion. On 18 August, 1932, French troops suffered a heavy defeat at Moutounsi, where the Trarza nomad contingent was annihilated. Widespread operations were then undertaken: a counter-attack in January 1933 subdued the Regueibat, and the Aubinière counter-attack of 1934 on the Rio de Oro caused Spanish and French protests as some loyal subjects were molested and pillaged in error. In 1934 the motorised troops of General Giraud, coming from North Africa, occupied Tindouf, and on 7 April, 1935, the overland link between French Africa and Morocco was achieved. This was fully established in 1936 under the authority of a military command from the Sahara border.

The great revolt of the Congo and Ubangi in the years 1928–31 had similarities to these other insurrections, but in scope, and above all in its international repercussions, it surpassed them in importance. Ever since Brazza's time, the region of Upper Sangha, the focal point of the revolt, had been the object of repressive operations, which were constantly renewed. The administration had lacked the resources ever to station sufficient occupation forces there: the little-known border areas of the Cameroons had never been completely penetrated, and their peoples had taken advantage of the First World War to achieve emancipation. The local topography, with its mountains and caves, aided resistance. In 1919 and 1920 intensive military operations were undertaken in the area against the Baya, the Pana and the Karé.

The system imposed on the inhabitants of this part of French Equatorial Africa has often been mentioned. It was brought to public notice by André Gide in his book *Voyage au Congo*, published in 1927, which included observations made up to 1926. The description by Father Daigre, quoted on pages 31–3, fully applies here. The villages were deserted. The men were away working on rubber plantations, and the women, including those pregnant and nursing, were on road works; all were housed in huts that let in the rain. The children were likewise pressed into service. Gide met a group tied by their necks, shivering at night by a grass fire, having travelled six days without food to do forced labour clearing the fields for sowing. Gide relates the sinister exploits of Lobaye, the administrator of Boda. In 1924, the Baya of that region refused to do rubber work for the Compagnie forestière Sangha-Oubangui, which paid 1 franc per kilo (as against the normal price of 10 to 12 francs) and demanded its deliveries of cassava at 1 franc per kilo although the market price of cassava was 2.50 francs. Gide quoted the following from an official report:

> M. Pacha announces that he has concluded his punitive activities among the Baya in the neighbourhood of Boda. He estimates (in his own words) the number of dead at 1,000 of all ages and both sexes. Police and irregular troops used in these operations were required to confirm their military exploits by bringing to the commandant the ears and genitalia of their victims. The villages were burnt, and the plantations uprooted.[3]

In a raid against a village that refused to move or abandon its crops, there were thirty-two victims: twelve men were shot, fifteen women slaughtered with the machete and five children burnt in a hut.[4] When recruitment for the 'machine' (the construction site of the Congo–Ocean railway) began, a revolt broke out, bred of complete desperation. The first incidents occurred at Lai (Chad) at the end of 1927, then revolt broke out in the Baboua region in July 1928. The instigator of the latter, according to official documents, was a 'witch-doctor' in the village of Nahing (or Nahim) called Karinou.[5] It seems that the revolt had been caused by recruitment operations for the Congo–Ocean railway in a region with no administrative infrastructure: the subdivisions of Baibokoum, Bouar and Baboua, at the frontier of the Cameroon and Ubangi, had been abandoned between 1924 and 1927. In 1928 an inexperienced agricultural agent was given charge of the Bouar-Baboua *subdivision*, and he proved incapable of coping with events. The revolt was organised within the traditional setting, with the resurrection of the old confederacies of families, and the reappearance of the war chiefs – simple village men unknown to the administration in times of peace.[6] However, *évolué* elements moved among the people and helped to give direction to the uprising – men such as a machine-gun sergeant of the Senegalese infantry, who deserted with his machine-gun and two boxes of cartridges, and the personal interpreter of the chief of the Berberati *circonscription*.[7]

The revolt spread to the regions of Ouham-Pendé (Bouar), a

dependency of Ubangi, and to Upper Sangha, belonging to the Middle Congo. The officer in charge of the post at Carnot was attacked at Balemba on 8 September: Bouar was evacuated and then burnt by Karinou; at the end of October, the chief of the Baibokoum *subdivision* suffered a defeat; and the administrator of Berberati was wounded and had to flee to the post at Boda. At the end of November, a contingent under the command of General Thiry, accompanied by Lamblin, the Governor of Ubangi, moved towards Bouar; as the contingent passed, the village of Yakolé rose up in revolt, and delayed its advance.

On 11 November, 1928, Karinou was killed in a battle preparatory to the seizure of his village.

Unfortunately, the accidental death of the chief of the Berberati *circonscription* a few days later deprived us of any moral victory out of this event.[8]

In his opening speech to the council of government, Governor-General Antonetti mentioned modestly an 'incident' that had remained 'unsettled' at Baboua in Upper Sangha, on the frontier between Ubangi and the Middle Congo.[9] The truth was that the revolt had continued after the contingent had moved on, and had spread, with guerrilla tactics being spontaneously adopted. But the governor-general passed it over in silence. Letters sent by officials and settlers to France were opened, and all allusions to the Baya revolt censored. The year 1929 saw an unprecedented extension of the revolt: in the early part of the year it spread to the whole region between Bangui and Carnot. A counter-offensive undertaken in that area by two contingents brought no appreciable results, and the country was not subjugated again until the end of January 1930. In the Cameroons two contingents, reinforced by irregular troops supplied by the Sultan of N'Gaoundéré, Rei Bouba, proceeded at the same time to launch punitive operations on the border territory inhabited by the Baya; numerous summary executions took place.[10] In March 1929 the revolt spread south to the country inhabited by the Ibenga and Motaba tribes; Bera-N'Djoko, which had been a focal point of revolt in the past, went over to the insurgents and did not submit until 24 June. In June the region of Likouala-aux-Herbes, farther south, joined the rebellion, and Bouboua, the rebel centre, did not capitulate until November. In the north the revolt spread to the Koumra and Moissala regions of Chad, punitive operations following in February–March 1929. In October 1929 the governor-general stated:

For five years the situation has not been such as to cause anxiety in any of the four colonies of the group. The Baya affair has been

P

exaggerated, and would not have spread but for lack of the means of putting it down. The dissident movement, which could, with limited resources, have been stifled completely at the start, has become ever more difficult to stop as it has spread; it is like a dam where one small repair is sufficient to stem a trickle of water, but whose major repairs are called for the moment this trickle is given time to grow.[11]

In 1930 the struggle continued in the Bocaranga region on the borders of Ubangi, Chad and the Cameroons. In Gabon, also, the Bawandji of the Lastoursville region rose up following exactions for statute labour made by regional police in 1928–9. 'The police searched everywhere for hidden weapons, and burnt the people's feet to make them confess.'[12] Chief Wango, who led the revolt, finally surrendered himself and died in the course of transfer to Libreville. We have not been able to determine whether this 'Bawandji war' was in some ways related to the Upper Sangha revolt, nor whether, in Gabon itself, it was strictly localised or spread outside the Bawandji country.

Always laconic, Governor-General Antonetti, in his opening speech to the session of the council of government in November 1930, mentioned 'incidents' in Gabon in the region of Franceville,[13] and declared that the 'disorders' in Upper Sangha were practically over, with only a few trouble-spots remaining at the frontier with the Cameroons. Although there was a shortage of details – even today the picture is hard to reconstruct because of an embargo imposed by Antonetti – information did filter through on the size of the revolt. Public opinion – already sensitive on account of the revelations by André Gide and Albert Londres on methods of colonisation in the Congo and on the work-sites of the Congo–Ocean railway – reacted strongly. The existence of an uprising was made known by *L'Humanité* of 19 January, 1929. Two days later the government was forced to admit the fact.

In the press, parliament, at public meetings, the French communist party expressed its solidarity with the insurgents, and denounced 'bloodstained colonisation'; it gave reasons why the French proletariat should support the Africans in revolt in French Equatorial Africa.[14] This was the time when the French communist party was undergoing savage suppression: in June–July 1929, Maurice Thorez and most of the central committee members were arrested, and the party was reduced to a semi-clandestine condition.

The communist international, at its sixth congress in 1928, had taken a stern line against the communist parties in the colonising countries because of the insufficiency of their action in support of the colonial peoples, particularly those of Central Africa; however, it praised the French communist party for its attitude to the war in Morocco and 'during the insurrections in Syria and the French Congo'.[15] The international and its organs gave much publicity to the events in the Congo, and called for international solidarity with the insurgents. Summing up what he knew of these events, George Padmore wrote:

> The uprising engulfed several important districts of French Equatorial Africa and lasted for more than four months,[16] during which time the indigenous people, in spite of lack of arms, inflicted several defeats on the French troops by taking prisoner a large part of their infantry. Mines were plundered, bridges destroyed, a large number of buildings of French concessionaires were ransacked. The indigenous people showed a degree of courage, even of military valour, which the French bourgeois press, despite attempts to suppress all news, was obliged to admit.[17]

To make its repressive measures effective, the authorities had to send reinforcements from French West Africa and, in particular, three infantry companies from the base at Zinder. Moreover, so-called 'guerillas' and 'auxiliaries' were once more called in, and used the methods already described:

> It was generally understood that the 'auxiliaries' had the right to pillage. . . . But it has not been said that they violated young women and took away girls to sell to Sudanese traders, who were constantly on the look-out for just such prizes.
> It was agreed that every soldier who killed an enemy was entitled to a premium. But he had to provide proof of his achievement. What had not been expected was that these 'proofs', threaded, blood and all, on to a string hung round the warrior's loins, should consist of the victim's male organ. . . .[18]

> Mowed down with machine-guns, raided, eaten, massacred by the thousands, the Baya were subjugated for a long time. . . . The good times of forced labour started all over again.[19]

Thus the pacification of French Equatorial Africa was completed.

(b) RELIGIOUS MOVEMENTS

The development of market relations and communications generally led to the decline and disappearance of traditional animist cults, which were essentially of local significance. Islam in particular benefited from this, being the universal religion best adapted to the social conditions peculiar to tropical Africa at that time. It can thus be said that the colonial system indirectly and involuntarily favoured the spread of Islam. Regions like the Sérère country in Senegal, coastal Guinea and the Bambara country, which at the end of the nineteenth century were still largely animist, had been almost entirely converted to Islam by the end of the colonial era, at least superficially. Islam penetrated deep elsewhere: in Wolof and Manding country and in Senegal, the animist cults still survived at the beginning of the colonial period, but vanished rapidly, as the rigid adherents of Islam waged violent warfare against them.

Christianity profited to a smaller extent from the decline of animisim at points where it did not enter into direct competition with Islam. Christianity's relative failure (despite its greater material means and the missionaries' semi-official position within the colonial system) obviously cannot be ascribed to the character of the religion itself. It has been objected that Christianity is too complicated compared with the simplicity of Islam, and that certain of its demands (strict monogamy, for example) made its adaptation to African conditions difficult. This argument is open to discussion. It can be claimed, on the other side, that the complexity of Christian dogma has far more in common with pagan practices than has Islam, so that animists would find this an element of comprehension and rapprochement. Islam made equally rigorous demands such as daily prayers, in contrast to a mass held on Sundays only, and the prohibition of alcohol.

However, it is indisputable that, as the religion of the coloniser, Christianity laboured under a great disadvantage. This is proved by the large-scale successes obtained in 1914–16 by the Liberian Episcopalian prophet William Wade Harris in the coastal settlements of the Ivory Coast. In 1910 the Ivory Coast had 400 Catholics and a few Protestants, the latter mostly foreigners. In little more than a year Harris made between 100,000 and 120,000 converts, mainly lasting ones.[20] The Protestant missions made great efforts after his expulsion, but with very limited success, to 'assure the spiritual heritage'[21] of his preaching. In 1926–7 another black Christian prophet, Bidjo Aké, again caused commotion among the authorities by his success on the Ivory Coast.[22]

Alongside these general facts, it is interesting to examine the birth and evolution of sectarian or revival movements and to consider their social significance. They reflect the 'spontaneous' evolution of African society within the setting of the colonial system, an evolution which broke up the traditional structures without replacing them, thus aggravating the conditions in which the people – mainly the most oppressed strata – lived, without leaving them any hope of improvement. This is one way of explaining the persistence and renewal of religious movements, which attempt to give to the social and moral crisis a mystical aspect in place of an unattainable temporal solution. This mystical aspect does not exclude – as in Omarian Tidjanism, which preceded it – attempts at a temporal adaptation, nor even revolutionary aspirations.[23]

Among the Muslim movements Mouridism and Hamallism deserve especial attention. In Mouridism, the older of the two, the temporal aspect was the most striking, although the mystical aspect, being the binding force of the temporal organisation, cannot be neglected. Like all new Muslim movements, it at first suffered persecution from the administration, which had been alerted by the traditionalist *marabouts* in their pay. Ahmadu Bamba, its founder, was deported several times.[24] It needed some twenty years, and the establishment of a department of Muslim affairs, for the administration to understand the advantage to be derived from this sect, which did not stand in the way of the régime and which, in the groundnut country, preached the sanctified nature of agricultural work. Before the First World War peace was made and an alliance signed.[25]

Wolof country remained the base of Mouridism. In the south (on the way to the pioneering country) Touba was built as a holy city; in support the administration even consented to build a special branch of the Dakar–Niger railway line to Touba. Colonisation, imposed on Senegal at an early date, enforced the system of direct administration to the utmost and liquidated the big chiefdoms. The extended family was broken down by the advent of groundnuts and the money economy. In this social crisis, Mouridism offered a last resource, a compromise between the groundnut and the social structures it had destroyed but could not replace. It made few demands in matters of ritual or morals. It mattered little if the exact number of prayers was not observed. In conformity with the mystical Islam of the brotherhoods, its founder, and through him his heirs and *marabout* disciples, derived a share of divine power from the prophet, who granted salvation to believers. Discipline and absolute obedience to the chief and his subordinates within the brotherhood were essential conditions. Thus faith (in the full sense of the term) founded a rigorous hierarchy, a true social organisation; within it, moreover, the simple peasant found patriarchal protection for disappearing or dying structures. And because it was the century of the groundnut, and as he had to live, the peasant was called to work the land and to produce groundnuts in large quantities. He gave his groundnuts, or the money they fetched, to the *marabout*, the chief of his zone of cultivation; in exchange he received food for his subsistence. Patriarchal collectivism was revived, sanctified by a religious bond. Hard work was demanded, and in exchange an assurance of eternal salvation and of present survival in a difficult world was given.

Mouridism, like the Tidjanism of Omar, and under new forms adapted to the modern era (working the land instead of holy war), appeared as an escape to all those who suffered from the social crisis and particularly to the most depressed – captives, young men, and women. It was clearly best organised on the *tabula rasa* of the new lands: the Mourides were, above all else, cultivators of the pioneering lands in the south and the east of groundnut Senegal. Each 'square' – the equivalent of a traditional patriarchal family – grouped ten to twenty men with their families around the huts of the *marabout* and his family; these *talibé* (disciples) worked in the hope of one day being named in their turn as persons responsible for a zone of cultivation and of being initiated into the *dikr*, the mystical Mouride lore. Around the *marabout* were gathered young children, who had either been entrusted to his care or who had gone to him of their own accord. He gave them some disciplinary training and, two days a week, instruction in the Koran; the rest of the time they worked in the fields and earned their keep, for the *marabout* provided them with food. The established families worked one field for the *marabout*, to whom they devoted each Wednesday's work.

The villages colonised by the Mourides could be recognised by their geometrical layout; their lands were carefully cultivated in a way that provided better yields but destroyed the soil. The Mourides were enemies of the tree, which caused progressive soil erosion. One example of Mouride colonisation was at Darou Mousti (village of peace), on the borders of Cayor, Baol and the desert zone of Ferlo. The brother of Ahmadu Bamba, Ibra Fati M'Backé, left his village of M'Backé in Cayor in 1912 to settle on virgin land, some twenty kilometres away. With thirty *talibé* he dug wells and was lucky to find a spring which gave a sufficient supply of water. In the years that followed, about 10,000 immigrants came to settle in the region and set up numerous villages. M'Backé had the support of the administration and of the chief of the Louga province, Macodou Sall, who had been placed there by the French at the time of the conquest, and who had 'colonised' the canton chiefships of his 'province' to the advantage of his brothers and his sons.

Ibra Fati was a 'dissident' Mouride who, after Bamba's death, broke with Ahmadu Bamba's son and successor, who had his residence at Baol. The son tried to get the administration to 'reattach' Darou Mousti to the Baol circle, and Macodou Sall opposed this vigorously. In the last years of his life (Ibra Fati died in 1942) the founder witnessed the movement's decline. The well, dug to a depth of 185 metres, dried up; the black water extracted from it was sold at 15–20 francs per 25 litres. Various expedients were tried, such as mechanical pumping (but the motors soon ceased working), and bringing supplies by the indigenous provident society's lorries. The people began to emigrate towards new pioneering sectors.[26]

This colonisation was not always accomplished without trouble. The colonised lands were occupied, though not very densely, by Fulani shepherds. In consequence of skirmishes between Fulani and the Mouride settlers at Baol in 1936, an application was made to the Diourbel court, which handed down a verdict favouring the Fulani the legitimate owners of the land. But in spite of the court's decree, the Mourides went over to the offensive in July 1937 in the contested canton, burnt down the Fulani villages and commited sacrilege – even to the extent of digging up graves.

The exodus of the Fulani was not impeded. Justice of a kind was held in check by policy. *The Grand Serigne* was, no doubt, too powerful for the local administration to speak to him with the necessary firmness.[27]

In 1945, according to official estimates, there were between 100,000 and 150,000 Mourides. From the First World War up to that time, their numbers had continued to grow.[28] They produced one-third of Senegal's groundnuts. The annual pilgrimage to the holy city of Touba united tens of thousands of adherents who came to offer their gifts directly the *Grand Serigne*, the head of the brotherhood.[29] The annual trading turnover of the latter for 1945 was estimated between 15,000,000 and 20,000,000 francs. For the military feudalism of the *Tiedos*, the colonial system and the groundnut had substituted of their own accord, a religious feudalism. Alongside the Mourides, but without attaining the efficiency and the rigours of their organisation, other brotherhoods claiming traditional obedience (the Tidjaniya or Quadriya) played similar roles: El-Hadj Malik Sy at Tivaouane, El-Hadj Ibrahima Nyasse at Kaolack and other leaders of less importance were rivals to the *Grand Serigne* of the Mourides. This Islam of brotherhoods remained a peculiarly Senegalese phenomenon.

Immediately after the First World War, a new trend arose with 'Hamallism'. This came into existence at Nioro in the Sahel region, where historic struggles had caused the miscegenation of peoples of different ethnic origins, and where economic decline had accentuated misery and social tensions. Primarily a mystic, Sheikh Hamallah was little concerned with mundane matters, and the whole setting, including economic conditions, did not favour the birth of an organised brotherhood as in Senegal. The success of Sheikh Hamallah deprived the traditional *marabouts* of their clientele and their income, and as agents of the administration they persecuted him without respite and denounced him to the authorities as a dangerous agitator.

Even more serious [than the progress realised at the expense of other brotherhoods] was the fact that Hamallism set men free – whether within groups created by colonialism or in tribes; whether in huts or under tents; or – in the very heart of the family – women and adolescents.[30]

Incidents provoked by Hamallah's enemies at Nioro (in July 1923) and Kiffa (in July 1924) caused him to be interned by the administration at Méderdra for ten years. Following a new incident at Kaédi in February 1930, Governor-General Brévié had him deported to the Ivory Coast, to remove him completely from his zone of influence. He was set free in 1935, and in 1937, in the more liberal atmosphere created by the Popular Front, the administration supported his reconciliation with his rivals. Though Sheikh Hamallah and his supporters never fomulated a programme of political opposition (they were only opposed to the persecution inflicted upon them), the colonial administration decided to bring about his downfall: the coming of the Pétain dictatorship provided the means. As a pretext they used a bloody brawl over pasture-rights in which his sons were implicated, although he was not involved. This incident took place at Assaba on 23 August, 1940, and caused 400 deaths. In the repressive measures that followed, thirty men were condemned to death and executed immediately, and 500 were interned at Ansongo, of whom one-third died of malaria.

Though 'no positive accusation could be made'[31] against Hamallah, Governor-General Boisson, with the agreement of General Maxime Weygand, then proconsul of North Africa, decided administratively to intern him for ten years in North Africa, and he was sent to Casseigne in Algeria. Then, his stay in that locality being considered dangerous, he was sent to an 'internment centre' (concentration camp) at Vals-les-Bains, where the medical officer warned on 28 August, 1942, that 'his state of health [was] incompatible with a prolonged stay at Vals, especially with the approach of the bad season'.[32] Before the bureaucracy of Vichy had found time to reach a decision on his case, Sheikh Hamallah had to be transferred to the hospital at Montluçon, where he died on 6 January, 1943, from 'pulmonary congestion and a cardiac crisis'.

Hamallism was a religious movement rather than a brotherhood. Its political outlook is difficult to analyse. It should be noted, however, that its most eminent representatives in the Western Sudan

supported the Rassemblement Démocratique Africain in the difficult period when the latter was being repressed by the colonial
government (1946–51).

It is impossible to devote much space to religious movements of
Christian inspiration. The 'Kimbanguism' that came into existence
in the Belgian Congo only affected French Equatorial Africa for a
short time, and only in those parts inhabited by the Bakongo, to
which ethnic group its founder, Simon Kimbangu, belonged. It was
when he was a catechist in an English Protestant mission in the
Thysville region that the revelation of his divine mission came to
him on 18 March, 1921.

The new religion, in its context of the First World War (the war
effort and service in the Cameroons contingent) and the 1921 crisis,
gained a remarkable success on both banks of the Congo – French
and Belgian. Jules Chomé has described the martyrdom of Simon
Kimbangu, brought about by the extraordinary bitterness of the
Catholic missions.[33] Repression took place also on French territory.
Trouble broke out 'when the colonial administration undertook to
put an end to the movement and to prohibit its manifestations; in
May 1921 the administrator of Boko was besieged in his residence
and had to call for troops to come from Brazzaville to re-establish
order and to calm people's minds [sic]'.[34] Kimbanguism survived
in the Belgian Congo, but it seems to have died out on French
territory after 1924.[35] Matswaism, which had a similar political and
religious character, belongs not to the period we are considering,
but essentially after the Second World War.[36]

This development of politico-religious currents in Christian
inspiration took place in that part of Africa where education was
least advanced and, when it existed at all, was left almost completely
to the missions. It was natural that in an intellectual setting such
as this the Bible and Christian ritual should serve to express the
people's political aspirations. But at the same time – and this was
the destiny of Matswaism – their movements were destined to turn
into religious sects, to lose their sense of political realism and take
refuge in messianic hopes, waiting passively for the intervention of
the Saviour.

Social evolution was also expressed through traditional animism
or in forms essentially derived from it. An example can be seen in
the cult or association of the Bwiti among the Fang of Gabon. The
Bwiti was, originally, a secret male society of the classic type, connected with the Mitsago people of Central Gabon. The Bwiti was
introduced during the slave-trade on the coast by the slaves from
Central Gabon. It was taken up and belatedly adapted by the
Fang in 1920–7. The religion that appeared in this association was a

P*

syncretism showing alien influences borrowed from freemasonry and the ritual of the Christian eucharist,[37] but with a dominant African background of spirit possession, sacred musical instruments, songs, and liturgy in the Tsago language.

Georges Balandier has pointed out that the Bwiti developed in a period of crisis when the consequences of the war were beginning to be felt in, among other things, the general spread of the use of money and the weakening of clan links, already of little validity in the traditional structure.[38] Administrative 'regrouping', which organised settlement in artificial villages to facilitate their control, and massive recruitment for forestry work caused a deepening of the social and moral crisis. The Bwiti appeared as an instrument of cohesion outside the traditional limits of the tribe, in which the young clashed with the authority of the old men, an authority to which the colonial system tended to give an oppressive character. Its 'public' cult, open to all regardless of tribal application, was opposed to the 'private' family ancestor cult. The economic up-swing of 1925, which put an end to a political movement among the évolués that had come into existence in Libreville at about that time, gave it a new impetus; massive labour recruitment increased the numbers of the detribalised who had no roots, and so furnished new devotees for the Bwiti. Essentially the Bwiti appeared as a defensive reaction in the traditional and rural setting – expressing human and mystical solidarity, but having no political objective.

Very different were certain practices or associations involving human sacrifices or cannibalism, mainly found in forest Guinea.[39] The cannibalistic associations of 'panther-men' or 'serpent-men' or '*caiman*-men', etc., carried out secret assassinations, and ritually consumed the blood and flesh of their victims; they existed almost everywhere in Africa, and in many other places. Cannibalism, in this as in nearly all other cases, had nothing to do with food pro-curement, as the first explorers naïvely believed, but was ritualistic and mystical in content; its object was communion with divine powers by the absorption of the living strength of the victim. It has existed at related social stages among numerous peoples: witness the re-enactment of the Last Supper – the Christian's holy com-munion – in which the members of the sect consume the body and blood of the Man-God. This is nothing but a sublimation of the ancient ritual cannibalistic meal.

In the early years of the twentieth century these associations underwent a new and formidable development in Sierra Leone and in Liberia, penetrating even as far as the anglicised or Afro-American 'creole' society in these two countries. Their practices took on a new character: the ritual feast became an accessory, or disappeared altogether. The essential object of the human sacrifice became the maintenance, or renewal, of an object or a group of fetishes conserved in a sacred cooking pot, externally of quite normal appearance. This fetish, or rather the blood or the human fat in which it had been steeped, ensured for its guardians strength, authority and youth. A periodical contribution of blood, human fat and certain fragments of flesh was indispensable if its efficacy were to last. Under the name of *kokosalei*, it was introduced from Liberia or Sierra Leone in the Toma country and the south of the Kissi country between 1920 and 1940. Members were recruited exclusively from among the chiefly circles, who saw in this a means of strengthening their power, and who had enough influence to ensure that their practices went unpunished, unless an accident occurred. This was a resurgence of traditional practices in response to European or colonial influences.[40] In contrast to the Bwiti, it did not reflect popular sentiments but it was exclusive to African circles endowed with wealth and authority.

In the Cameroons, among the Mungo, the ravages of groups of 'crocodile-men' appeared, on the other hand, as a reaction against the too rapid enrichment of certain cacao planters, who were suspected of witchcraft and aroused jealousy: they were captured, executed and thrown into the river.[41] Close to these were the traditional secret societies which served the interests of the chiefs or the gerontocracy.

(c) THE FIRST SIGNS OF MODERN POLITICAL LIFE

Various circumstances favoured the evolution of modern political life in French tropical Africa immediately after the First World War. Among these were the first promotions of African officials, mainly teachers, trained in the French school, who became the spokesmen of their people. Up to that time this élite had not existed, or its numbers had been too small outside the communes of full rights in Senegal. Another factor was the return of ex-servicemen who brought new ideas, and who felt little inclination to accept the kind of treatment normally accorded to the African population. The concentration of paid labourers in the ports and along the railways provided the basis for the early signs of a workers' movement. Finally, the suffering of the war – both in the civilian war effort, and at the fighting front – created the need for a *détente* and the anticipation of change. The echoes of the Russian October Revolution did not fail to reach Africa; there had been Senegalese troops among the units stationed in Rumania who had refused to march against the Soviets, and African sailors among the naval units that mutinied in the Mediterranean. Some took part in the mutinies of 1917, and others had witnessed or actively supported the revolutionary movement in France in the final war years and immediately afterwards.

Unfortunately, actual economic and social conditions in tropical Africa under French domination were not yet favourable for modern political life on any scale. There was no industry, nor were there large and vital economic centres where men and ideas could range freely. Dakar was no more than an economic and political command post. *Evolués* and qualified workers were, for the most part, scattered at various posts in the bush, and thus effectively isolated. They had no contacts with the peasant masses, who were totally illiterate and did not understand French. They had not even any contact with ex-soldiers who had acquired some practical knowledge, including – for better or worse – the use of French, but who were illiterate and remained faithful to the ancestral way of life. It was relatively easy for the colonial administration, with its *de facto* power and native laws to nip in the bud any attempts at expression of an emancipation movement. It took care to foment feelings of mistrust and dislike among various strata of society – *évolués*, ex-servicemen, the masses – and had no difficulty in setting one against the other. Haunted by the 'Bolshevik peril', it tried to prevent all contact between African 'subjects' and the outside world. Hence, the few movements which did try to find expression were left to their own devices and deprived of all possibility of outside support.

It was essentially the so-called *évolué* class which, despite the role it was given within the colonial system, provided the framework for the first signs of a desire for emancipation. This class was acutely aware of the contradictions between the French republican principles of liberty, equality and democracy and the situation which they actually enjoyed under the native system (the *indigénat*) of the colonies. Some were not unwilling that the *non évolué* masses should remain in subjection: but were they not the 'African Frenchmen,' entitled to the advantages of citizenship? On this, it can be said that the *évolués* were unanimous, even if not all of them were aware that they had to raise their voices not only for themselves but for all their people. In the name of the policy of assimilation, the growing movement came to claim the abolition of the *indigénat* (native system), and the granting of citizenship on a more or less general basis. Whatever the limitations of its outlook, this movement had, none the less, a general national content, in that it spoke up against imperialism, for which the *indigénat* was one of the essential means of oppression of the colonised people. The movement denounced, sometimes more and sometimes less vigorously, the exactions of the chiefs, the colonial administration and the private companies.

The administration reacted violently against this movement. It used all the means provided by the *indigénat* to quell it; there was neither freedom of association nor real freedom of the press. In French Equatorial Africa a law on press liberty had unexpectedly been promulgated, but the regulations relating to the *indigénat* permitted it to be twisted. Above all, there were so few printing presses that it was easy to prevent groups which lacked financial resources from using them. Anyone who tried to raise funds risked prosecution; since there was no freedom of association, and the collection of all subscriptions and quotas was soon qualified by the administration as 'fraud' and prosecuted as such.

The colonial establishment, from the missionaries to the radicals and freemasons, were unanimous in their opposition to even the most modest claims of the *évolués*. Those who advanced such claims were denounced as 'agents of Moscow' and 'enemies of France'. In France they received support only from the French communist party and from some elements of leftist assimilationists, especially the Ligue des Droits de l'Homme.[42] Normal political life in the colonies was only possible within the four communes in Senegal. But this privilege was limited to an infinitesimal fraction of the population.

As in the 'old' French colonies of the West Indies and the Indian Ocean, the colonial administration tried to reduce the power of electoral rights by tolerating or organising corruption and fraud. Instead of elections being a normal part of the political process, politics were subordinated to elections. Principles and policies were a façade; the essential feature was the struggle among political gangs for jobs – those of deputy (member of parliament) and of mayors of the four communes (reduced to three in 1927 by the incorporation of Gorée, which was almost totally without inhabitants, into Dakar). Until 1914 the whites and people of mixed blood had dominated the political life of Senegal, and had used the African electoral masses for their own ends.

The 1914 elections gave the masses their revenge when they won a deputy's seat for Blaise Diagne, a Catholic from Gorée and a pure African. His predecessor, François Carpot, a half-caste advocate from Saint-Louis, was beaten and a song was sung in Wolof which said: 'If Bilasse [Blaise] gives us the order, we shall kill all the whites.' Intelligent and active, Blaise Diagne ruled over the Senegal electorate until his death in 1934. He knew how to defend himself and his position in face of the narrow-minded colonials who were furious to see an African in the chamber of deputies, and wished rather to bring the 'native' citizens – this constitutional monstrosity – under colonial rule and the general system of the *indigénat*. However, for his own defence he entrenched himself within the system.

He agreed to play the role of a puppet which French imperialism imposed upon him, and even to defend the colonial order; he did the latter more efficiently than the narrow-minded colonials themselves. During the First World War he agreed to become an army recruiting agent for Clemenceau. In 1923, on the eve of elections to the legislature, he concluded the 'Bordeaux Agreement' with the wholesale trade of that city in exchange for the electoral support of the big business companies, and he agreed to become the defender of their interests in parliament. His predecessor François Carpot stated:

> Deputy Blaise Diagne, loving what until recently he heaped with abuse, has become an ally of the Bordeaux treasuries, the collaborator of those whom his friends not long ago called sharks.[43]

At the 14th session of the International Labour Office in Geneva, he became the advocate of forced labour, defending the French government which he had agreed to represent as a delegate, and 'called his less ardent colleagues to order'.[44] In 1931 he accepted the post of under-secretary of state for the colonies in the Laval government and inaugurated the Colonial Exhibition side by side with Marshal Lyautey.

A part of the Senegalese electorate found nothing in this to complain of. Did not three centuries of attachment to France, of good and loyal service to the French colonial venture, deserve the privilege of citizenship? – and was it opportune to extend this privilege to others so soon? The 'Young Senegal' movement, which came into existence immediately after the war, had a slightly nationalistic aspect, and supported the proposal to extend the system of communes of full rights to all the big centres in Senegal (which, incidentally, had been Diagne's electoral programme in 1914); but the movement did not survive the economic upswing of 1924–5 and, particularly, the 1924 elections. Tiécouta Diop, the chairman of the Parti de l'Union Républicaine des Jeunes Sénégalais, opposed Diagne at the beginning of the 1924 election campaign,[45] but it was a European lawyer, Paul Defferre, who campaigned against Diagne, and despite his platform of 'independent republican socialist', he was defeated.

> The indigenous masses joined together to give victory to the representative of their race. They gave their votes not to the man but to his skin.[46]

Diagne, nevertheless, won by a majority reduced by 3,000 votes compared with the 1919 elections. Opposition to Diagne – even if it was from the Left and denounced the injustices of the colonial régime which the deputy supported – was not motivated by principle; it simply strove to take his place and enlisted all his opponents. It placed little emphasis on the extension of citizenship, but a great deal on the claims of the electorate in the four communes (the right to landed property for the Lebou of Dakar, the reconstitution of the general council in its previous form, and the granting of colonial advantages to officials who were Senegalese citizens). Behind the scenes it used less exalted arguments against Diagne: as a Christian married to a white, he was not representative of the Senegalese with citizenship rights, most of whom were Muslims.

Among the leaders of the opposition was a lawyer, Lamine Gueye, who was mayor of Saint-Louis in 1925–7, and succeeded François Carpot in the management of the anti-Diagne weekly *L'Afrique Occidentale Française*. But from 1928, the opposition was headed by Galandou Diouf, a former aide of Diagne, who in turn brought about his election as mayor of Rufisque. Diouf dropped his protector hastily to campaign against him in the elections, and polled 4,396 votes on 3 May, 1928, as against 5,175 for Diagne, who was re-elected.[47] Galandou Diouf was supported by the staff of the *Périscope africain*, a weekly published at Dakar from 1929, which vigorously denounced colonialism. Thanks to *Périscope's* campaigns, Diouf crystallised around himself all opposition to Diagne, and was elected deputy in 1934 on the latter's death. But no sooner was Diouf elected than he broke with his party and his journal to support the list of candidates headed by the European reactionary Alfred Goux in the Dakar municipal elections of 1935. His old friends and *Le Périscope* supported the opposition list which was only beaten by 182 votes, thanks to an electoral fraud.

Galandou Diouf did not have the stature of Diagne and attracted little attention. His political line was the same as Diagne's; supported by the administration, he was re-elected in 1936 against Lamine Gueye (who had the support of the *Le Périscope*) and the former 'Diagnistes', who were united in the Senegalese Socialist Party.

In Dahomey and Togo, at least on the coast, the existence of a fairly numerous educated élite whose members, like the Senegalese, went to other colonies to find employment, favoured the development of a movement with closer links to the masses.[48] After 1914 a reformist movement had been established at Porto-Novo with the support of the rather heterogeneous forces recruited mainly among traditional notables (supporters of one of the two alternately reigning branches of the royal house of Porto-Novo, and Muslims in conflict with the leadership imposed on them by the administration). But its spokesmen were from the 'modern' élite, the most active politician being Louis Hunkanrin, one of the first African teachers to graduate from the teachers' training college at Saint-Louis. Hunkanrin had a powerful sense of justice, as well as inexhaustible energy. These qualities helped him when he had to face his worst ordeals, never allowing him to accept any compromise such as might have enabled him to pursue an easy or an honourable career. Disinterested and with the highest motives, he was sometimes too ready to believe in the good faith of others – which helped the colonial administration to attain its aims in the years before the Second World War. In 1910 at the age of twenty-three, he was dismissed from his job, and sentenced to a term of imprisonment. In 1912–14 he collaborated with the *Démocratie du Sénégal*, a Diagne paper published at Dakar. On his return to Dahomey, he became the object of persecution by Noufflard, the governor, a typical colonial careerist, so that he had to go underground. In 1918 his friend Diagne managed to stop the persecution against him; Hunkanrin then enrolled as a volunteer and was sent to the European theatre of war. On his return to Paris, he quarrelled with Diagne, who never ceased affirming his colonialist leanings and who wanted to use him as a political agent. While he was in the army his correspondence was seized and his revolutionary publications were discovered. He was court-martialled and imprisoned for a year (1919–20). In Paris in 1921 he began, with the co-operation of a lawyer from Guadeloupe, Max Clainville-Bloncourt, to publish a journal entitled *Le Messager dahoméen*. It defended the interests of Dahomey, and attacked the system of the *indigénat* and the basic principles on which the colonial system stood.[49] He took part in the second Pan-African congress of August–September 1921. When he returned to Dakar in that year, he was arrested again and sent to Dahomey to serve the sentence passed on him by the Noufflard administration, which Diagne had shortly before suspended. His friends in Paris succeeded only in fixing its reduction to two years in prison and five years' restriction of movement.

The 1921 crisis, inflation and the unpopularity of recruitment[50] had created a tense situation in Dahomey. Early in 1923 the people were pushed to extremes by a sudden increase in the poll-tax from 2·25 francs to 15 francs for a man, 10 francs for a woman and 5 francs for a child, half of which was demanded in coin, as the paper franc was considerably devalued. In February 1923, demonstrations took place at Porto-Novo against the poll-tax, market dues and statute labour. The movement spread to the regions of Adjohon and Ouémé.

Hunkanrin's imprisonment did not change his views. With the complicity of some of his gaolers, he remained in contact with his friends outside. They had organised themselves by setting up local sections of the Ligue des Droits de l'Homme and the Franco-Muslim committee organisations, which were recognised in France and thus did not need special local authorisation. They corresponded with the Ligue des Droits de l'Homme, with the journal *Le Paria* – published on the initiative of the communist party and directed by Nguyen Ai Quoc, the future Ho Chi Minh – of which they published fifty issues with the help of communist deputies in Paris.

The leaders of the reform movement inevitably found themselves at the head of various militant activities all springing up between 11 and 20 February – street demonstrations, a general strike of workers in the private sector, a boycott of markets, and the extension of the strike to Ouidah and Cotonou, where soldiers were called in to replace the wharfingers. Governor-General Carde declared before the council of government of French West Africa:

> Our intervention was both prompt and firm, and a few days sufficed to re-establish order without bloodshed. The sanctions proclaimed against the leaders had a salutary effect on their compatriots, and have shown our unshakeable resolve not to allow certain factions to imperil the sovereignty of the state.[51]

Repression began on 18 February with a 'raid' on a district of Porto-Novo, involving forty-five arrests. At Adjarra, administrator Chassériaud ordered shots to be fired into the crowds who refused to pay the market dues. A state of siege was proclaimed, and the two main leaders of the Ligue des Droits de l'Homme, Oni Bello and Etienne Tété, were arrested at Cotonou. The arrival at Cotonou of the gunboat *Cassiopée* and the despatch of a company from Togo and a batallion from Dakar as reinforcements made extensive operations possible. At Cotonou, the district chiefs were summoned and ordered to pay the tax within eight days: the levy was accomplished 'with the aid of troops'.[52] The operations were then extended to the whole region, and continued for seven weeks. The tax was levied *manu militari*, firearms were seized, 'recalcitrants' were sent to perform statute labour, and arrested persons were forced into military service. A number of villages were completely destroyed. The legal outcome consisted of dozens of sentences, including those on Prince Sognigbé and Hunkanrin, who were sentenced to ten years' exile in Mauritania.[53] However, the population of Dahomey remained 'critical of the authorities'. The fairly high percentage of literates and the existence of several small printing presses made possible the publication of several broadsheets which were often short-lived because of lack of funds, but which represented a means of denunciation and agitation that had no equal elsewhere.[54] In 1933 and 1934, at the height of the economic crisis, the use of the usual methods of constraint for levying taxes provoked resistance and demonstrations.[55]

The most serious incidents seem to have occurred at Lomé, where on 20 January, 1933, the district and canton chiefs of Lomé canton and its surrounding areas addressed a petition to the chief of police protesting against the market taxes (for stand rights) and the rise in taxes[56] at the same time as incomes had decreased because of the crisis. The petition emphasised the disastrous effects of these measures – especially the increase in the number of children pawned. In this the administration saw a plot, and two notables, Gartey and Johnson, were arrested as instigators of this enterprise. As agents of foreign trading houses (Deutsche Togo Gesellschaft and John Holt) they were alleged to be chairman and secretary of a so-called association of family chiefs, the Duawo, dating back to the British occupation, which the French considered illegal. The same afternoon, the population gave its answer with a general strike: 3,000 demonstrators appeared before the circle offices to demand that those detained be freed – which was granted at 6 p.m. The crowd went to meet them at the prison and chaired them away in triumph. But they thought it more prudent to take refuge in the British zone. The demonstrations continued the following day, and the house of the secretary to the council of notables, Savi de Tové, was wrecked because, as a local journal claimed, 'he was considered, and rightly so, to be a detective in the pay of the local administration'.[57]

The Europeans rallied to the government and were given arms. The administration soon sent for troops from the Ivory Coast, and these were 'let loose' on Lomé. Arrests, pillage and rape multiplied. The village of Kodjoviakopé was sacked by soldiers.[58] On the morning of 4 February, the village of Ahanoukopé was sacked by the soldiers who fired on the people: there were a dozen dead, and innumerable arrests were made.[59] The paper L'Etoile du Dahomey published photos of the 'victims of Lomé', and was seized.[60] Judicial repression was unrestrained: fourteen Togolese were sentenced to death as the result of the demonstrations, thirty-seven were condemned to fines of 600 francs and prison sentences of from six months to five years for having travelled without permits, and numerous fines of 100 francs were imposed for 'failure to salute' Europeans in the administration.[61] Feeling itself in danger, the Dahomey press, which had unanimously denounced the repression, published a signed declaration on 1 May 1933, by six newspapers replying to their accusers:

For these miserable creatures the Dahomey journalists are pretentious and despicable people. They call them 'negro journalists' and find that they do not know how to write. . . . If they do not know how to write, they do not know how to tell the truth.[62]

Even in Dahomey, tax exactions multiplied. At the end of 1933, the new governor, de Coppet, appealed for troops.[63] In March 1934, demonstrations took place at Porto-Novo against excessive taxes and the extortion practised in levying them.[64]

At Libreville, in Gabon, where there was also an important core of 'progressives', the first political party came into being in 1920 under the name of Jeune Gabon. It published a paper and received support from the local section of the Ligue des Droits de l'Homme. It demanded citizenship, and raised its banner against the 'gerontocracy'. Its leader was Laurent Antchouey who, like Hunkanrin, first worked as a journalist at Dakar and edited in France the *Echo gabonais* and the *Voix coloniale* (1923–4). However, the party had no roots among the masses; opposed by the administration and the traditional notables, it disappeared around 1925.[65] Its moving force was André Matswa, a catechist, and later a commissioner for customs. Born near Brazzaville in 1889, Matswa enlisted in the army and fought in Morocco in 1924–5. After being demobilised he was employed in 1926 as an accountant in Paris at the Assistance publique de la Seine. That same year, he set up in Paris a friendly society, which was at first a simple organisation for mutual aid for Africans from French Equatorial Africa, especially the Balali, his own ethnic group. The Amicale des Originaires de l'Afrique equatoriale française was an apolitical body which, under Article 15 of its statutes, enjoyed the exalted patronage of the minister for the colonies and the governor-general, the administration hoping to turn it into an instrument for its own advantage. Governor-General Antonetti received its delegates and granted them an annual subsidy of 1,000 francs. Soon, however, the Amicale turned to political action and demanded citizenship rights. Sections were established in the Congo, run by the *évolués*. Letters were addressed to the president of the council, protesting against the chartered companies, racial discrimination and the system of the *indigénat*, and demanding citizenship. Faced with an extension of the movement, especially in the Bakongo, Basoundi and Balali regions, the administration took action: the delegates were arrested, and subscriptions of 110,154·80 francs were confiscated. In Paris Matswa was searched, and then arrested and transported to Brazzaville in December 1929. All were charged with the classic offence of 'fraud'. On 3 April, 1930, Matswa was sentenced to three years in prison and five years' restricted movement.

When the verdict became known, several thousand African

workers went on strike and marched to the judicial building to demand the liberation of their comrades. The police tried to disperse the demonstration, but were pelted with stones.[66]

This version, first given by George Padmore and then taken up by the press, corresponds very closely to the administration's version given by J. M. Wagret.[67] According to a European eyewitness, it had not, in fact, been an aggressive demonstration. The assembled Balali had been waiting for the verdict; the administration were frightened and ordered them to be attacked, the Africans then defended themselves with stones, and repression was given full rein. The secretary-general, who was governor of the Middle Congo, was wounded. According to Georges Balandier, the demonstrators from the Bakongo quarter of the town shouted 'Death to the Whites!' and '*Bulletin de vote!*' (voting papers).[68] It is not improbable that the first of these cries was invented in the administrative reports. Governor-General Antonetti called out troops who, without warning, fired into the midst of the demonstrators besieging the courtroom. 500 arrests were made. According to the governor-general it had been 'a slight agitation, provoked by a court sentence passed upon common criminals posing as agitators'.[69] In reply to a news item in the Belgian press, *L'Afrique française*, under the title 'False News', spoke of a few unimportant scuffles among the natives and of 'a bit of shouting by a dozen hired and organised natives'.

Those who received sentences and even those arrested following the demonstrations were deported to Chad. However, the *Amicale* went underground and survived, playing the role of passive resistance. For example, the chiefs refused to recover money forcibly collected, and resisted requisitioning for the building of the Congo–Ocean railway. In 1934, after the recall of Antonetti, Governor-General Edouard Renard reauthorised the *Amicale*.[71] Repression continued under the Reste régime, which undertook 'resettlement' in the Bakongo country for the purpose of compulsory groundnut cultivation. The cycle began all over again with resistance, followed by coercive measures, and the imprisonment of 'members of the *Amicale*'. Tension reached its peak in 1938 when Governor-General Reste decided to postpone the establishment of an indigenous provident society, on the pretext that the granting to Brazzaville of a statute similar to that of the Senegalese communes was under consideration. These proposals were rejected by the minister for the colonies Mandel, who demanded the immediate establishment of a provident society and an increase in repression. Meanwhile, Matswa had succeeded in escaping, and reached the Belgian Congo. He returned to Paris, where he joined the armed forces in 1939; in

May 1940 he was transferred to Brazzaville having been accused of 'spying for the enemy'. A 'Free French' court condemned him to life imprisonment on 8 January, 1941. On 12 January, 1942, he died at Mayéma in Chad. Officially the cause of death was given as 'bacillary dysentery', but according to public rumour, he died from blows received while in detention.

Matswa had made his attack at the point of contact between a socially undifferentiated, traditional world (this enabled him to involve all his people as one, including the chiefs) and the plural modern world. This was a deliberate innovation. Although he received the greatest response among his own people, the Balali, Matswa was not a tribalist and always insisted on his desire to organise and represent all the indigenous inhabitants of French Equatorial Africa. But the contradictions within the social milieu, Matswa's premature death and the execution by the Free French colonial authorities of the main leaders of the movement, explain the paradoxical fate of Matswaism, which became transformed into a messianic religious movement after the Second World War.

The trade union movement was another field of 'modern' action. Workers' strikes in tropical Africa were nothing new, as they had existed already at the time of the attack on Ahmadu by Archinard. The year 1919 saw the first strike by workers at the port of Conakry.[72] At the beginning of 1925 the railwaymen on the Dakar–Saint-Louis line went on strike, and later the same year there was agitation among the Bambara requisitioned for the completion of the Thiès–Kayes line. The administration had the three ring-leaders arrested and beaten; a general strike was the result. The troops, among whom were many Bambara, refused to march against the strikers, so that, to put an end to the strike, the administration was forced to set the agitators free, and to open an inquiry into their demands. Other movements, which cannot be dated, took place among the railwaymen on the Dakar–Niger line, the first relatively important working-class centre in Black Africa under French domination.

The effects of the crisis and the coming of the Popular Front gave the trade union movement its first impetus. A decree of 11 March, 1937, made the provisions of the labour code applicable for the first time to the trade unions. These provisions were, however, singularly restrictive, as they required that any person wishing to be a member of a trade union should be able to speak, read and write French fluently, while for French West Africa and the mandated territories they made the possession of a *certificat d'études primaires*, or an 'equivalent attestation' by the governor, a further condition! This is to say that the working class, properly defined, remained deprived of union rights. Only the Europeans could benefit from them fully – in itself a novelty. So the first trade unions came into existence, and organised Europeans and Africans separately. The European unions were often little less racialist than the colonial administration. The 'poor whites', who were in direct competition with the Africans of equivalent qualifications, showed the most determination, in defending their racial privileges.

A decree of 20 March, 1937, introduced collective agreements and the election of staff delegates in firms with more than ten employees. Because of this decree, or perhaps in spite of it, the union organisation acquired new categories for which it had not been prepared, to the great fury of the settlers. Marcel Homet indignantly denounced the 'scandal of fetishistic [sic] cooks and chauffeurs' at Zinguinchor (Casamance), who set up a union of house servants and demanded a collective agreement.[73] At the November 1937 session of the council of government, de Coppet, the governor-general, announced that 119 associations had come into existence since May 1936, among them forty-two trade unions.[74] Demonstrations of solidarity between the French working class and African workers took place. Marcel Homet cited the 'deplorable' example of the sailors on a French ship who, while calling at the port of Assinie on the Ivory Coast, had incited the Kroo sailors there to put in claims. When the latter were dispersed by troops, the French sailors went on strike and the Kroo obtained satisfaction.[75] On the other hand, the local European employees with their racialism gave no sign of solidarity. This lack of goodwill caused the failure in 1937 of an attempt to found a federation of trade unions at Dakar. Only in 1938 was such a federation established in the Dakar *circonscription*, with only African unions participating; the European unions did not ask to be represented.[76]

The most important unions were those of the railway workers on the Dakar–Niger line and of enlisted men in the merchant marine. It does not appear that any notable strikes took place before the railway strike on the Dakar–Niger line from 27 September to 1 October, 1938. This strike broke out spontaneously outside the union. On 27 September the auxiliary railwaymen (irregulars) struck at Thiès and Dakar in protest against the arbitrary dismissal of one of their comrades. The following day, at the Thiès depot, the strikers organised a barricade to keep out 'blacklegs'. The special railway police tried to intervene, but were quickly thrown out. The railway management appealed to the administration: troops were sent in, the strikers defended themselves with stones, the army opened fire and the result was six dead and thirty wounded. The strike now spread to the whole network. On 30 September, an agreement was signed between workers' representatives and the government-general, that there would be no sanctions, no obstacle to the right of association, indemnities for the needy families of the victims, and an inquiry into the demands. On 1 October, the union ordered work to be resumed. *Le Périscope africain*, the *de facto* organ of the Popular Front, dissociated itself from the strike, but held the circle commander and the army responsible for the incidents.[77] The report was relegated to page two. The colonials protested against the 'scandalous weakness' of the governor-general, de Coppet, who was for a long time the target of a hostile campaign from the right. The new minister for the colonies, Georges Mandel, a sworn enemy of the trade unions, sent his director of political affairs, Gaston Joseph,[78] on a mission of inquiry. A decree of 18 April, 1939, transferred de Coppet to Madagascar.

In spite of its isolation, black Africa was not wholly cut off from contact with the movement which was defending its cause abroad. The Pan-African Congress, which had been in existence since 1900,[79] had been a group consisting almost entirely of coloured Americans, British West Indians and the African élite of British West Africa. However, the second congress, held in Paris on the initiative of Dr. W. E. B. DuBois, had wider repercussions. DuBois had gone to Paris after the signing of the armistice in 1918, with the intention of presenting a petition on behalf of the rights of the coloured people to the peace conference. This initiative cast a bad light on American imperialism which, while proclaiming the right of peoples to self-determination, left the field open to its own ambitions, trying to bridle the appetites of its British and particularly its French allies. In his magazine *The Crisis* DuBois denounced not only segregation among American troops, but the instructions given to the French military authorities demanding the same discrimination, so as not to 'spoil' coloured American troops with too egalitarian an attitude on the part of the authorities and the French people. Wilson's staff, wanting to teach the French a lesson, did everything in its power to prevent a congress or demonstration taking place that would put lynching[80] and racial discrimination in the United States on trial. Clemenceau, however, was pleased to have this opportunity to put the Americans in their place, and not only allowed it to take place but encouraged Diagne to take part and sing the praises of French policy. 'Don't just proclaim it to the world in general', he said to Diagne, 'but go to the congress itself.'[81] The congress, held at the Grand Hotel in Paris on 19–21 February, 1919, was attended by fifty delegates, nearly all West Indians, Americans and Africans resident in Paris, since the American government had refused to grant visas to participants travelling from the U.S.A., and all public preparation ran the risks of a request by the U.S. government to prohibit the congress. A few coloured officers in the American army participated.

A petition was presented to the League of Nations demanding that the administration of the former German colonies should be entrusted to an international authority, that the Africans' right to land should be respected, and that improper concessions should not be allowed. It also demanded the prohibition of slavery and forced labour, and the Africans' right to free education and to participation, by stages, in the government of their own country. The *Bulletin du Comité de l'Afrique française* was satisfied with this moderation and the fact that deliberations were kept within a general framework without touching those 'burning questions of local interest'.[82] It noted furthermore a great preoccupation with the condition of American Negroes, but that nothing was said about the French colonies. With Diagne to represent them, this was to be expected.

In French-dominated Africa the echo of these events was certainly faint.[83] However, the possible repercussions of Garveyism aroused greater concern. Marcus Garvey, a Jamaican settled in the United States, had proclaimed himself in 1920 the emperor and provisional first president of Africa. He was highly successful among the Negro proletariat in the cities of America who were disappointed in the post-war period, and he coined the slogan of 'Return to Africa'. His publication *Negro World* appeared in three languages, and soon coined another famous slogan, 'Africa for the Africans', and called for the expulsion of the whites from Africa – which caused it to be banned in the French colonies. Garveyism would appear to have won some of its support through its anti-colonialism, but the megalomania of its founder and the 'Liberian' manner in which he conceived the decolonisation of Africa denied him the success in Africa that he enjoyed in the United States. In 1925, ruined by the failure of financial ventures he had launched to organise American-Negro colonies in Liberia, he was arrested and sentenced, and his movement collapsed. His influence was in any case a purely moral one and did not turn into any concrete action, as it did not even propose any for the Africans who had remained on their own continent. In 1923, Governor-General Carde, in his address to the council of government, estimated that 'it might almost be said that Garveyism disappeared at birth', but showed himself far more preoccupied with 'extremist doctrines'. In 1925 he denounced the danger of propaganda by 'organs of disorder':

The danger exists: the speedier, more frequent relations between

West Africa and Europe, badly affected by the commotion of the war, periodically bring in seeds of *tares*.[84]

In 1927 he turned on the anti-colonialist groups in France: 'Their tracts and their journals multiply as they reach West Africa'.[85] A decree of 27 March, 1928, prohibited the sale of sketches, pictures, reproductions and printed sheets, periodical or otherwise, likely to lessen the respect due to the authorities in French West Africa. Jules Carde proclaimed:

It would be vain to pretend that the number of individuals affected by pernicious ideas from abroad does not continue to grow under the repeated assault of subversive propaganda. It has seemed to me indispensable to adopt a set of legal precautions against the latter. Not only are journals or suspect tracts infinitely more disastrous for the colony than they would be in France, but certain publications, even when sincerely inspired by respectable philosophical doctrines and the principles underlying our methods of colonisation and our system of education, are often distorted or badly assimilated by their readers and cause unexpected claims.[86]

In brief, everything seemed dangerous, not only communist propaganda, the prime danger, but even the proclamation of the principles of the Republic and the motto 'Liberty, Equality, Fraternity', which was indeed difficult for people living under the system of the *indigénat* to comprehend. More dangerous still was propaganda issued by Africans in Paris speaking to Africans in their own continent. Among the small group of African activists settled in Paris, was a Dahomey lawyer, Kodjo Tovalou Houénou, who in 1924 founded the Ligue universelle de défense de la race noire in Paris. He established contact with Garvey and the communist party, and published a journal *Les Continents*. From France he contributed to the local press in Dahomey. When Tovalou tried to return to Africa he was arrested at Lomé on a warrant issued by the public prosecutor of Cotonou, sentenced and placed under house arrest. In 1927 his movement turned into the Comité de defense de la race noire, with Lamine Senghor as its moving force. Senghor was a former serviceman, disabled in the war, who had settled in Paris where he pursued his studies at the Sorbonne. As secretary of the committee he was present at the foundation in Brussels in February 1927 of the Anti-imperialist League. Albert Einstein was made honorary chairman of the inaugural congress, which was also attended by Mme. Sun Yat-Sen, Jawaharlal Nehru and Barbusse. Senghor, in his address, threw out this warning:

The Africans have been asleep for a long time. But be on your guard, Europe! Those who have been asleep for so long will not go back to sleep once they wake up. Today the Africans are awakening!

He was elected a member of the League's executive committee. But in 1929 he was arrested in the course of repressions, and died in prison.[87] His companion at the 1927 congress, the Sudanese Kouyaté, represented the committee at the second congress of the League held at Frankfurt in July 1929. He collaborated with the Comité international des ouvriers noirs set up by the Internationale Syndicale Rouge and encouraged by George Padmore. This body had its headquarters in Hamburg, and worked mainly among the African workers in European ports. Kouyaté was arrested by the Nazis during the occupation of France and shot. The Committee published a magazine, which changed its name to escape the various bans – it was successively *La Voix des nègres*, *Le Cri nègre*, *La Race nègre*. Government decrees prevented it from being given regular distribution in the colonies. It took part in the Anti-imperialist Assizes held in Paris under the aegis of the League on 31 March, 1935.

It was at that time that reaction, after succeeding in getting Laval into power following the fascist disturbances on 6 February, 1934, finally gave satisfaction to the colonials who had long clamoured that the few rights for Africans existing in the colonies should be liquidated. The instrument of this repression was to be the Régnier-Rollin decrees. The Régnier decrees applied to Algeria, while the Rollin decree of 10 April, 1935, referred to all the colonies apart from Martinique, Guadeloupe and Réunion. Article 1 of the Rollin decree prescribed from three months to two years' imprisonment, and fines ranging from 500 to 5,000 francs, on 'anyone who, by publications of any kind whatever, incites resistance to the application of laws, decrees, regulations or orders of public authority'. Article 2 imposed from three months to one year's imprisonment and from 100 to 3,000 francs fine on 'those who by any means whatever publicly impugn the respect due to the French authority'. In the case of officials being culpable, the punishments were to be doubled and accompanied by a ban on their holding public office for from five to six years. All criticism of French authority and all forms of political expression were thereby stifled. The local press was more firmly gagged than ever.

The coming to power of the Popular Front a year later brought some relaxation. At the same time, over and above the local problems of the struggle against imperialism, the threat of Hitler's fascism came to weigh more and more heavily. A contradictory situation arose. On the one hand, it was true that a fascist or racialist hegemony, which the territorial ambitions of Germany and Italy made a possibility, represented a major danger for the peoples of the world, including those of Africa. On the other hand, French colonialism, which envisaged the making of concessions to the Nazis even in the colonial sphere, used the fascist danger to try and discourage all popular resistance to the colonial system. Africa was aware of the fascist threat. Italian aggression against Ethiopia, and with it the barbaric crushing of one of the two remaining independent African states, aroused strong emotions; Hitler's racialist dogmas, and his aggressive plans with regard to the black race, were known. The colonial press congratulated itself openly on the 'success' of the Italians in Ethiopia; and Laval, under the Rome Agreements of 7 January, 1935, ceded to the Italians a frontier strip of 110,000 square km. in the north of Chad (the northern half of the Tibesti massif). This region was admittedly almost deserted, and the agreement was never executed, but the whole proceeding was full of foreboding.

Germany, in search of indispensable *Lebensraum,* noisily claimed the restitution of its former colonies, particularly the Cameroons and Togo. German companies established themselves in Portuguese Guinea (notably in the Bissagos islands, where they were suspected of setting up a submarine base), in Liberia, in Spanish Guinea and at Fernando Po. In the Cameroons and Togo from 1920 on, the German-educated former élite (recruited mainly among the coastal peoples – the Douala of the Cameroons and the Ewe of Togo) were suddenly deprived of employment and persecuted as suspect; the mere fact of speaking German and not French, and thus being able to correspond with their former German masters, was held to be dangerous to the security of the state. As a reaction, the opposition movement readily assumed a pro-German orientation. The German colonial administration had indeed been strict, but it had not been hypocritical; at least it had made its policy plain to all. This was the setting in which the first attempts at political expression developed (e.g. the Douala paper *M'Balé-Vérité,* launched by subscription by Richard Manga Bell and Gaston Kingué-Jong in Protestant parishes). Political suspects were seized and sent for years of confinement to the prison at Mokolo, in the Northern Cameroons. Men who had been sentenced were taken there on foot, and dozens of them died on the way. Repression reached its peak in 1930.[88]

However, while these movements sometimes supported Germany (e.g. the Bund der deutschen Togoländer, which used the pre-1918 imperial flag) they basically reflected a desire to fight the existing régime. This was the case with the Pan-Douala movement which, in 1918, presented claims for a Douala republic in the Cameroons; the same applied later to the Pan-Ewe movement in Togo. After Hitler's advent to power, when certain circles in France envisaged colonial concessions to Germany, those directly involved in the affairs of the Cameroons and Togo became worried, and in the name of anti-racialism tried to gain support among the population. In 1939, for instance, Brunot, the governor-general, authorised – or perhaps even supported – the establishment in the Cameroons of an African organisation under the name of *Jeunesse camerounaise française* (Jeucafra), which set out to oppose the German colonial demands.

> But no half-measures are possible. No one who speaks his mind on the German claims can keep quiet on the subject of his own claims.[89]

Jeucafra soon raised other questions, such as exemption from the *indigénat* for the *évolués*, and the pay of Cameroon Africans in government service.

The coming of the Popular Front was to leave a mark on the political movement in Senegal. Up till then, even if the existing parties used the terminology or labels of the Left, they had remained strictly local. The opposition – Galandou Diouf in 1928, Lamine Gueye in 1936 – were treated as 'communists' by the party in power, and defended themselves vigorously against this. In the 1928 campaign, when Diagne denounced the support given to his adversaries by Tovalou, and had himself saluted by the troops with shouts of 'Vive Diagne!' and 'Down with communism!',[90] Diouf defended himself with vigour, and seized upon an article in *L'Humanité* which treated him and his friends as 'agents of imperialism'.[91] But in 1935 Diagne turned against Lamine Gueye. The congress of the Senegalese Socialist Party, which at the end of the year rallied all Diouf's opponents, 'stigmatised tendentious rumours, which ascribe extremist tendencies to the Parti socialiste sénégalais'.[92] It was possible to feel reassured by the presence in this 'socialist' party of Turbé, president of the Dakar chamber of commerce. In the 1936 elections, Diouf, elected after a fight, did not regard it as his duty to rally to the Popular Front. His opponents afterwards linked up with the winning party in France against him, and supported the popular anti-colonialist movement.

In July 1936, Popular Front committees were set up at Dakar and Saint-Louis, with the basic aim of organising the Bastille Day demonstrations on July 14. At Dakar, the committee grouped the

Senegalese Socialist Party, the League of Human Rights, the French Section of the Workers' International (which, incidentally, was not organised but only represented by isolated individuals) and the Confederation of Labour. The president of the chamber of commerce took part as a 'social republican'. The committee appealed for a demonstration which, as soon as the official ceremonies were over, drew thousands of African demonstrators across the town, following tricolour flags, the red flag of the Popular Front and a green and red flag with a white arrow, the emblem of the Senegalese Socialist Party. Posters with demands were carried. *L'Afrique française* denounced with horror the presence in the demonstration of some Europeans;[93] Galandou Diouf wrote violently against the demonstration in the Parisian daily *L'Ordre*.

In September 1936 the Popular Front committee, with great ceremony, received the minister for the colonies, Moutet (a member of the French section of the Workers' International [S.F.I.O.]), and the new governor-general, de Coppet; toasts were drunk in their honour. The S.F.I.O. became organised, mainly with the support of European officials; on the 5 and 6 June, 1938, the Senegalese Socialist Party voted to fuse with the S.F.I.O. whose constituent congress was held at Thiès on 11 and 12 June. The S.F.I.O. clearly wished to absorb the local opposition (against the sitting deputy who was discredited) and to provide a base for local politicians. But for all its liberal affirmations, and in spite of its break with the president of the chamber of commerce over the price of bread and rice,[94] the 'Senegal Federation' of the Socialist Party – S.F.I.O. never departed from a position of colonial orthodoxy, and was satisfied with the timid measures on social questions enumerated above. It also proclaimed its loyalty to the governor-general. Such was the fate of a doctrine founded not on the condemnation of the principle of colonialism but on claims for its 'improvement'.

In 1931, *L'Afrique française* commented as follows on the speech of the S.F.I.O. spokesman, Sixte-Quentin, in the debate on the budget of the ministry for the colonies.

After his criticism, what we have to recall is the speaker's affirmation that there could be no question of abandoning our overseas territories. . . . Little by little, the socialist party will end by becoming colonialist.[95]

REFERENCES

1. The future general, who gained his first experiences in colonial repression here.

2. Abou Digu'en, *Notre Empire african noir*. Paris, Charles-Lavauzelle, 1928, p. 68.

3. André Gide, *Voyage au Congo*. Paris, Gallimard, 1927, p. 93.

4. Ibid., pp. 85–8.

5. The word means 'chief of the land'.

6. P. Kalck, *Réalités oubanguiennes*. Paris, Berger-Levrault, 1959, p. 48.

7. M. Homet, *Congo, terre de souffrances*. Paris, Ed. Montaigne, 1934.

8. 'Les évènements de la Haute-Sangha', *Afrique française*, 1929, No. 2, pp. 171–3. *Le Journal officiel de l'Afrique équatoriale française* mentions the death of Leroux (Louis-Charles), Administrator-in-Chief of the colonies at Berberati, on 25 December, 1928, without comment.

9. *Journal officiel de l'Afrique équatoriale française*, 1 December 1928, pp. 1127–8.

10. *La Dépêche africaine*, No. 13, April 1929.

11. Speech to the session of the Council of Government of French Equatorial Africa, October 1929, *Afrique française, Revue coloniale*, 1929, 12, pp. 695–6.

12. Hubert Deschamps, *Traditions orales et archives au Gabon*. Paris, Berger-Levrault, 1962, p. 57.

13. *Le Journal officiel de l'Afrique équatoriale française* announced the deaths on 24 August, 1930, near Booué (Gabon), of Captain Carrot and Lieutenant Hutinel without stating the circumstances and without mentioning whether their deaths were connected with these events.

14. *L'Humanité*, numbers of January and February 1929.

15. 'The work of the French Party in the colonies' (adopted by the Secretariat of the Executive Committee of the Communist International, 16 December, 1929) *Cahiers du Bolchévisme*, 1930, No. 4, pp. 439–46.

16. The movement reached its peak between November 1928 and March 1929.

17. George Padmore, *La Vie et les luttes des travailleurs nègres*. Paris, Petite bibliothèque de l'Internationale syndicale rouge, XXXVII, s.d.

18. M. Homet, *Congo, terre de souffrances*. Paris, Ed. Montaigne, 1934, p. 38.

19. Ibid., p. 41.

20. On Harrisism see testimony by a Protestant missionary in J. Bianquis, 'Le prophète Harris . . . (1914–24)', *Foi et Vie*, Paris, 16 November and 1 December, 1924. Excellent study in J. Rouch, 'Introduction à l'étude de la Communauté de Bregbo', *Journal de la Société des Africanistes*, 1963, XXXIII, I, pp. 129–200. See also B. Holas, *Le Séparatisme réligieux en Afrique Noire*. Paris, P.U.F., 1965.

21. Richard-Molard, *Afrique occidentale française*. Paris, Berger-Levrault, 1952, p. 165.

22. Cf. Carde, Speech to the session of the council of government of French West Africa, December 1927, *Afrique française, Revue coloniale*, 1928, No. 1, pp. 19–41. See also B. Holas and J. Rouch, op. cit., as well as De Billy, *En Côte d'Ivoire*, Paris, n.d. and W. Platt, *An African Prophet*, London, 1934.

23. See among others *Afrique noire occidentale et centrale*. Paris, Ed. Sociales, pp. 119–21 (1st edition, 1959), or pp. 127–9 (2nd edition, 1961).

24. In Gabon (1895–1902), then in Mauritania (1902–7).

25. After the death of Amadou Bamba (1929), dissension among the members of his family led to administrative prosecution of some of them: his brother Sheikh Anta, condemned first to eight months in prison, was administratively interned for ten years at Ségou in 1930.

26. Darou-Mousti benefited in 1949 from a first deep drilling, which had to dig to more than 284 m. before finding water.

27. *Afrique française, Revue coloniale*, 1938, No. 8–9, p. 203.

28. In 1959 Abel Bourlon put their number at 400,000. (A. Bourlon, 'Actualité des Mourides et du Mouridisme', *L'Afrique et l'Asie*, 46, 1959, pp. 10–30.)

29. Mainly because, as we saw, there was disagreement among the parents and heirs of Amadou Bamba following their rivalry.

30. A. Gouilly, *L'Islam dans l'Afrique occidentale française*. Paris, Larose, 1952. This work gives the religious details of Hamallism which are not dealt with here.

31. Circular of the governor of Guinea of 19 June, 1945, with extracts of a report by the national security board relating to the death of Sheikh Hamalla.

32. Ibid.

33. Jules Chomé, *La Passion de Simon Kimbangu*. Bruxelles, Amis de Présence africaine, 1959.

34. J. M. Magret, *Histoire et Sociologie politiques de la République du Congo (Brazzaville)*. Paris, Pichon et Durand, Auzias, 1963, p. 41.

35. Cf. Georges Balandier, *Naissance d'un mouvement politico-religieux chez les 'Ba-Kongo' du Moyen-Congo* (III C.I.A.O., Ibadan, 1949). Lagos, Nigerian Museum, 1956, pp. 324–36.

36. Matswa's role, purely political, will be discussed below. The religious movement was born after and despite him.

37. See P. Alexandre and J. Binet, *Le Groupe dit Pahouin*. Paris, P.U.P., 1958.

38. Georges Balandier, 'Aspects de l'évolution sociale chez les Fang du Gabon', *Cahiers internationaux de Sociologie*, IX, 1950, pp. 76–106. See also A. Raponda-Walker and R. Sillans, *Rites et croyances des peuples du Gabon*. Paris, Présence africaine, 1962.

39. Cf. E. Rau, 'Le juge et le sorcier', *Annales africaines*, 1957, pp. 305–20, and 1958, pp. 179–206.

40. The work of the Afro-Americans in Liberia did not differ, in this respect, from that of other colonisers.

41. Iwiye Kala-Lobe, 'Mun'a-Moto, cultivateur camerounais', *Présence africaine*, No. 37, 2nd trim. 1961, pp. 90–118.

42. At least at the beginning; later retired high colonial officials came back on to the central committee of the league and caused obstacles. As a result of their activity, several of the militant representatives of the anti-colonialist movement (F. Challaye, Elie Reynier) handed in their resignations (Louis Hunkanrin, *in litteris*, 8 June, 1963).

43. *L'Afrique occidentale française*, No. of 1 May, 1924.

44. *Revue Indigène*, No. 256–7, May–June 1930, p. 105.

45. *L'Afrique occidentale française*, 21 February, 1924.

46. *L'Afrique occidentale française*, 8 May, 1924.

47. He got 9,000 votes in 1919 and 6,000 in 1924.

48. To a lesser degree, there was on the Lower Ivory Coast an ancient body of Europeanised African traders (notably at Assinie, Grand Bassam, Jacqueville, etc.) and planters, also offering scope for the development of a modern political life. N. Gavrilov (*Le Mouvement de libération en Afrique occidentale*, Moscow, Progress Editions, 1965, p. 29) indicated the role played by the *Eclaireur de Côte d'Ivoire*, an African journal founded in 1935, as the spokesman of that milieu. We have not been able to verify this information nor, *a fortiori*, can we add complementary data.

49. The editorial writer of No. 4 (15 July, 1921) wrote: '. . . Everything happens in its given time. Voltaire made Mohammed say: "The time of Arabia has come at last." That of the Congo, of Dahomey will also come . . .' And he concluded by citing Marcus Garvey: 'We shall not ask England, or France, or Italy, or Belgium: "Why are you here?" We shall simply order them to go away. What is good for the White man is good also for the Black man, that is to say: democracy and liberty.'

50. Recruits were obtained only by force, and desertions were very numerous. (Captain Cluzel Martinot, 'Une tournée de police au Dahomey en 1923', *Revue militaire de l'Afrique Occidentale Française*, No. 28, 15 January, 1936, p. 57.

51. J. Carde, opening speech to the 1923 session of the Council of Government of French West Africa, *Afrique française, Revue coloniale*, 1923, No. 12, p. 431.

52. Captain Cluzel Martinot, op. cit.

53. Cf. Captain Cluzel-Martinot, op. cit.; J. Suret-Canale, 'Un pionnier méconnu du mouvement démocratique et nationale en Afrique: Louis Hunkanrin (1887–1964)'. *Etudes dahoméennes* (Nouvelle série) No. 3, December 1964, pp. 5–30. J. A. Ballard: 'Les incidents de 1923 à Porto-Novo', *E.D.*, Nouvelle série, No. 5, October 1965, pp. 69–87.

54. They never included less than half a dozen weeklies, bi-monthlies and monthlies. After the accession of the Popular Front there were a dozen (December 1936).

55. Cf. Speech by J. Brévié to the council of government of French West Africa, session December 1933, *Afrique française*, 1934, No. 41, pp. 19–27.

56. According to *Le Phare du Dahomey*, No. 85–86, 16 January–1 February, 1933, twelve new taxes had been imposed on Togo in one year.

57. *Le Courrier du golfe du Bénin*. No. 33, 1 May 1933. *Le Phare du Dahomey*, No. 171, 10 November 1938, accuses him of being an 'agent of the Deuxième Bureau'.

58. *Le Courrier du golfe du Bénin*, No. 27, 1 February, 1933.

59. Ibid., No. 30, 15 March, 1933.

60. Ibid., No. 31, 1 April, 1933.

61. Ibid.

62. Ibid., No. 33, 1 May, 1933.

63. Ibid., No. 44–47 (October–December 1933).

64. *La presse porto-novienne*, No. 43, March 1934. *Le Courrier du golfe du Bénin* protested (No. 55, 15 April, 1934) against sending the Porto-Novo convicts to Kandi (North Dahomey): 'It is a public scandal that none of the convicts of Lower Dahomey sent to Upper Dahomey to serve their sentences return home alive.'

65. Cf. G. Balandier: 'Aspects de l'évolution sociale chez les Fang du Gabon', *Cahiers internationaux de Sociologie*, IX, 1950, pp. 76–106.

66. G. Padmore, op. cit., p. 128.

67. J. M. Wagret, *Histoire et sociologie politiques de la République du Congo (Brazzaville)*. Paris, Pichon et Durand, Auzias, 1963, chap. II.

68. G. Balandier, op. cit.

69. Opening speech to the session of the council of government of French Equatorial Africa (November 1930), *Journal officiel de l'Afrique équatoriale française*, 15 November, 1930.

70. *Afrique française*, 1930, No. 4, p. 228.

71. According to J. M. Wagret, op. cit., public rumour attributed responsibility for the plane crash that caused the death of Edouard Renard to the 'Antonettiste' clan (headed by the secretary-general of the governor-general).

72. *Afrique française*, No. 2, p. 57.

73. Marcel Homet, *Afrique noire, terre inquiète*. Paris, Peyronnet, n.d.

74. *Afrique française*, 1938, No. 1, pp. 19–25. Note the date, which shows that the unions were formed after the electoral victory of the Popular Front, and without waiting for a decree that legalised such action.

75. Marcel Homet, op. cit.

76. *Le Périscope africain*, 9 July, 1938.

77. Ibid., No. of 1 and 29 October, 1938.

78. *Afrique française*, 1938, No. 10, p. 368.

79. Ibid., 1900, No. 8, p. 283 gives an account of the first Congress held in London on 25 May, 1900, and of the establishment of a 'Pan-African association',

which elected as honorary chairmen Emperor Menelik and the presidents of the republics of Haiti and Liberia. It protested against slavery in South Africa both on the part of the British and the Boers (then at war).

80. In the single year 1919 seventy-six negroes were lynched in the U.S.A., among them one woman and eleven soldiers; fourteen of these were burnt in public, eleven burnt alive (W. E. B. DuBois, *Dusk of Dawn*, p. 264).

81. W. E. B. DuBois, *The World and Africa*. New York, Viking Press, 1941, p. 236.

82. *Afrique française, Revue coloniale*, 1919, No. 3–4, p. 53.

83. The following Pan-African congresses, in which few, if any, of the countries under French domination participated, caused even fewer reactions.

84. *Afrique française, Revue coloniale*, 1926, No. 1, p. 10.

85. Ibid., 1928, No. 1, p. 20.

86. Ibid., 1928, No. 11, p. 696.

87. According to the official communiqué, lung tuberculosis.

88. Cf. Iwiye Kala-Lobé, 'Mun'a-Moto, cultivateur camerounais', *Présence africaine*, No. 37, 2nd trim. 1961, pp. 90–118.

89. Marc Ducat, 'Du Mandat à l'Indépendance', *Marchés tropicaux*, No. 737, 21 November 1959, pp. 2547–54.

90. *La France coloniale*, Nos. of 22 and 29 March, 1928.

91. *Le Périscope africain*, 30 November, 1935.

92. Ibid.

93. *Afrique française*, 1936, No. 8–9, p. 474.

94. *Le Périscope africain*, No. of 27 November, 1937.

95. *Afrique française*, 1931, No. 3, p. 233.

Q

3. *The Second World War, 1939–1945*

The First World War and the Russian Revolution of October 1917 breached the façade of world imperialism, and so began a continuing crisis for the colonial system. In 1921 the colonial powers were still deluded by the intoxication of their victory in 1918; they counted on the rapid collapse of Soviet power under the blows it was receiving from within and without. But in 1931, when Albert Sarraut wrote *Grandeur et servitude coloniales*, these illusions had been dissipated.

> Such is the situation, and there is no point in disguising the truth. Everywhere, colonialism is in open crisis.[1]

In Asia the crisis was visible for all to see. In India the British had decided to hang on for as long as possible: but the political and administrative circles directly involved, with few exceptions, did not believe that the colonial regime would last for ever. In Indo-china the French colonial circles, less clear-sightedly, were unwilling even to contemplate withdrawal, but everywhere tension was becoming manifest; fear and racially-inspired hatred frequently broke into the open, to be answered by fierce repression and the most retrograde legislation which the colonial system ever enforced.

The calm that reigned in black Africa, on the other hand, produced an illusion. Paternalism went hand in hand with avowed colonialism. The colonial masters kept repeating – and ended up by believing – that, as a whole, the Africans were satisfied with a system of government suited to their situation, and felt for France a filial recognition of the benefits she had bestowed. In Africa it was the Second World War and its consequences that led to the crisis in the colonial system which, until then, had been mainly an Asian problem but which now became general. The war marked the beginning of a great turning-point in African history.

(a) AFRICA IN THE WAR

The French colonies in tropical Africa were catapulted into the world conflict in the wake of France. As in 1914–18 they made their contribution to the number of combatants: 80,000 men sailed to Europe in 1939–40; to be followed in 1943–5 by some 100,000. Again they were called upon to make a 'war effort', to provide food and raw materials for the European war machine. At the same time, in the eyes of a population whose judgement and critical capacity had matured, the intolerable nature of the colonial system became more obvious, as the incapacity and weakness of the representatives of colonialism stood exposed for all to see.

In 1939, in Africa as in France, the semi-dictatorship of the Daladier government had swept away the hesitations and irresolution of the years of the Popular Front. The early, timid demonstrations of the working class were becoming a thing of the past, and the administrators who favoured the 'strong arm' had a free hand. The declaration of war gave the pretext of a 'breach of state security' to smash any movement that was an embarrassment to the administration. But 1940 was to show the weakness of colonial power. In June of that year, France was invaded. The possibility of seeing France occupied by the enemy had become a reality. In colonial circles nobody at first saw any other course than to pursue the struggle on the side of the Allies – who were, furthermore, the two big colonial powers in Africa: Great Britain and Belgium.

On 9 June, 1940, during the Anglo-French–Belgian mobilisation at Leopoldville, Boisson, governor-general of French Equatorial Africa, vowed solemnly to 'do his duty beyond the bounds of possibility'. King Leopold III of the Belgians had just capitulated to the Germans and, breaking with him, the colonial authorities of the Belgian Congo decided to pursue the war by the side of Great Britain. On 18 June, 1940, the day the Franco-German armistice was signed, Boisson summoned his service chiefs and announced his decision to pursue the struggle. Similarly General Husson, commander-in-chief of troops in French Equatorial Africa, gave as his objective the continuance of the struggle, even if this meant withdrawal to British territory. In the Cameroons Governor-General Brunot declared himself in more or less the same terms.

The official announcement on 22 June of the signing of the armistice, and, at the same time, the liquidation at Vichy of the Third Republic and the formation of a fascist-type state under the authority of Marshal Pétain, precipitated trouble, dividing the colonial staff into two opposing camps. With only a few exceptions, the administrators and, especially, the officer corps in the army were men of the Right, who since the 1930s had been in sympathy with or actual supporters of the fascists or pro-fascist groups. They had execrated the Popular Front which had sown a great deal of trouble for them and made inroads into their 'command'. For many of them the first shock of defeat appeared, as it did to Charles Maurras, a 'god-given surprise', and they were ready to reap its 'golden fruits'. Furthermore, the armistice government was headed by the 'victor of Verdun'. Weygand and many other prominent army officers who, like Pétain, were idols of the Right, rallied to it. Who could doubt the Marshal's patriotism?

Thus, as a general rule, the colonials were in favour of the Vichy régime, which they identified with what had always been their

dream. A conclusive point was that Vichy had legitimacy on its side.
The colonial administration and the military staff were completely
permeated by bureaucratic pusillanimity, and many of them lacked
not only patriotic and human sentiments but even, seemingly, all
imagination. All they cared about was their personal position,
advancement and pension rights. All this was threatened if they
broke with 'legitimacy'. And wasn't German victory inevitable?
The circumstances were unprecedentedly dramatic, but the highest
authorities were visibly incapable of adapting themselves, remaining
obsessed with their minor preoccupations to the point of losing all
sense of honour and patriotism. What could one oppose to Vichy?
A few almost unknown men like de Gaulle, who addressed his message particularly to the colonials, asking them to join Great Britain
or the British territories, and continue the struggle there. What a
risk! To answer this appeal meant endangering relatives in France,
jeopardising careers, perhaps inviting a court-martial.

Thus the colonials split into two groups: Vichyites and Gaullists.
Among the Vichyites two groups can be distinguished: on the one
hand, those whose choice had been primarily a political one, whose
pro-fascist sentiments took precedence over patriotism, and on the
other, those whose choice was dictated by faint-heartedness and
conformism. In this second category were General Husson, who has
been described by the medical general Sicé as paralysed by conformism and preoccupations with his career, and the governor of the
Ivory Coast, who declared to a witness:

> Can you understand my dreadful situation? I am a Corsican, my
> family is in Corsica; everything leads me to fear that our island
> will become Italian and our defeat final and total. If I want to
> protect my position, without which I cannot keep my family, I
> have to make a choice. So I cannot place myself in opposition to
> Vichy policy.[2]

Still in the second category but in a different style was the in-
credible Governor Armand Annet, 'hero' of the Vichy resistance in
Madagascar, a perfect bureaucrat, to whom conformism was a
matter of heart and soul, and who ten years after the event did not
understand what had been wrong in obeying Vichy.[3]

The Gaullists were in the minority in colonial circles, and were
mainly to be found in the higher echelons of the hierarchy. They
scarcely differed from the Vichyites in their political concepts, and
with very few exceptions they shared the right-wing views of the
others, their admiration for Pétain and Weygand, and their dislike
of democracy and the Popular Front. But the national reflex prevailed. Those who knew de Gaulle knew that he was a conservative

who had been close to the Pétainist clique. The idea of a 'double game' by Pétain (which the Marshal's supporters used for a long time to come to terms with his betrayal) made some of them think that in carrying on the struggle they, who were not under the direct threat of the enemy, were obeying his secret will. The future Governor Louveau, who was in the Sudan after the war and one of the fiercest agents of the repression conducted against the Rassemblement Démocratique Africaine, admitted in his Resistance memoirs: 'At one moment in 1940 I was, I admit, a Pétainist as well as a Gaullist',[4] and he confessed to having sent a telegram of loyalty to Vichy.

The British attack on the French fleet at Mers-el-Kébir strongly reinforced anti-British sentiment and contributed to a crystallisation of attitudes. Some days later on 7 July, a British destroyer that appeared at Dakar was forced back by Governor-General Cayla. The next day the battleship *Richelieu* was attacked and immobilised in the port of Dakar: but the crews of five auxiliary cruisers in the port refused to obey when the command was given to clear the decks for combat. On 23 July Boisson, nominated high commissioner in Black Africa by the Vichy government, came to Dakar to replace Cayla, who was posted to Madagascar. He entrusted his functions in French Equatorial Africa on a temporary basis to General Husson.

Parallel to anti-British sentiments was a growing defiance of the increasingly suspect position of Vichy towards Germany. On 24 July Boisson cabled to Vichy:

> The crisis has become acute, sometimes extremely so. To overcome it, we must use far more psychology and proceed by successive stages.[5]

Boisson exaggerated, but did so to establish his position. At the same time he revealed his duplicity with a certain cynicism, but once again to gain Vichy's confidence. This man does not fit into either of the two categories of Vichyites referred to above. For some, he was a great administrator: Richard-Molard remarked on his relative moderation.[6] But Governor Louveau did not spare him:

> Traitor to his past [as a wounded veteran of the 1914–18 war], traitor to himself, traitor to the republic, traitor to the country, traitor by a monstrous pride which finally deprived him of all lucidity by letting him believe in his own infallibility.[7]

There is an element of truth in these astonishing denunciations by a man who had himself sent a telegram of loyalty to Vichy.

Boisson's intelligence and ability cannot be disputed. He did not reach the upper levels of the colonial administration by the easy way; a former teacher, he rose by hard work to the difficult rank of inspector of the colonies. But this devotion also expressed frantic ambition and an unbounded pride, tainted with scepticism and cynicism. Boisson did not believe in Vichy; he believed only in himself. Vichy gambled heavily in appointing him high commissioner; and from then on, Boisson played the cards of Vichy. His 'moderation' merely reflected his cynicism, and at the same time an ability to 'calm' certain excited spirits in colonial circles. Vichy's position, the isolation of French West Africa, and the reliance on authoritarianism in the 'New State', gave him a fullness of power which no proconsul preceding him had enjoyed. This plenipotentiary status intoxicated him and led him to do his utmost to retain the confidence of Vichy.[8]

Now that French West Africa had been taken in hand by Boisson, the locus of the struggle was to shift to French Equatorial Africa. At Brazzaville, the close proximity of the Allies in Leopoldville facilitated preparations for a surprise attack. However, the Gaullists were not in one mind. At the last moment, the plot was foiled by the arrival, in the Belgian Congo, of one of the officers of the group, Colonna d'Ornano, who believed there was nothing to be done but move over to the ranks of the British. There was only a handful of plotters, all belonging to the colonial establishment: some army officers, some officers of the health service, and two directors of companies. On 19 August, 1940, one of General de Gaulle's earliest companions, Edgar de Larminat, a colonial infantry officer, arrived at Leopoldville. The pamphlets and proclamations which he directed at Brazzaville were typical of the state of mind of colonial circles. The great concern of the Gaullists was to clear themselves of being accused of anti-Pétainism; their views on the causes of defeat remained faithful to those of the pro-fascist and anti-republican right wing; they were in fact a copy of Vichy. In his pamphlets, de Larminat excused Pétain and Weygand on account of their age, and threw the responsibilities on the 'sceptical and cynical intellectuals'; they were outflanked by their entourage of 'professional politicians'. Of de Gaulle he wrote:

> A former immediate subordinate of Pétain and Weygand, he has not revolted against the chiefs he loved and respected, but against the disastrous policy for the country for which irresponsible subordinates made them accept responsibility.[9]

In his proclamation of 26 August, he excused Weygand and Huntziger, offering to 'stand guarantee for their patriotism', having formerly served under them. Their excuse was that they were not free.[10] As is known, the initiative did not come from Brazzaville, but from Chad. Isolated from the other French colonies, Chad had a common frontier with the Anglo-Egyptian Sudan to the east and Nigeria to the west; from this position it derived a certain freedom to manoeuvre. But it was also the only French colony sharing a common frontier with enemy-controlled territory: Italian Lybia to the north. Disarmed during the armistice, Chad lay at the victor's mercy. But the decisive element was the personality of its governor, Félix Eboué. Born at Cayenne, in French Guiana, in 1884, he was a Negro, one of the few serving in the colonial administration who had been born in the Americas. A former student of the École coloniale, his career had mainly been in French Equatorial Africa, especially in Ubangi, where he took up his first post in 1908. He took part in the 'pacification' of that region, and later, with the support of certain interest groups and in opposition to others, he initiated cotton-growing there – we have discussed its characteristic features above. His colonial doctrine could not have ben more ortho-dox: one could even say that he contributed a touch of conservatism. This French citizen of the black race was resolutely opposed to assimilation, citing Lyautey: 'There is a class in every society born to rule, without which nothing can be done. It should be made to serve our interests.' At least verbally, he went beyond the contradic-tion implicit in traditional politics, which rejected assimilation, proposed respect for customary institutions and at the same time recalled that the chief was nothing by custom and everything by the will of the coloniser. Eboué condemned the principle of direct administration and extolled what, before 1914, had been called the 'protectorate policy'.

> No constituted council shall be omitted, no guardian turned out, no religious prohibition neglected, under any pretext, be it absurd, embarrassing or immoral. . . . Who should be chief? I shall not answer, as the Athenians did, 'the best'. There is no best chief, there is a chief, and we have no choice. . . . There is a chief designated by custom, and we must recognise him. . . . The chief pre-exists.[11]

This is completely different from Van Vollenhoven's doctrine, followed by Carde and reaffirmed by the inspector of the colonies, Maret. Eboué showed preference for the Belgian and British methods as opposed to those of direct administration. For him it was neces-sary not to destroy customs, but to let them evolve – with the help of the religious missions. As far as colonial doctrine went, there was nothing to distinguish him from the men who opted for Vichy, and

Governor Deschamps could point out the similarity between the native policies of Boisson and Eboué.[12]

It was probably because he was a coloured man that Eboué chose Gaullism. For the mass of racialist administrators, whose prejudices Vichyism encouraged, a black administrator, even more a governor, was intolerable. Like his colleagues in the Caribbean, Eboué had suffered innumerable affronts on account of colour prejudice. To succeed in his career he had, on the one hand, to give proof at the rue Oudinot of perfect colonial orthodoxy and, at the same time, to try to gain the political support of the Left. He was a freemason, and even enrolled in the socialist party – S.F.I.O. In these circumstances he knew that he could save his position only by turning to 'dissidence', which the colonial staff of Chad, civil and military, generally favoured. He took the step after a period of uncertainty, during which he concluded a secret agreement with the British governor in Nigeria, and rallied firm supporters around him. On 26 August, Eboué and Colonel Marchand, his military commander in Chad, officially announced their support of de Gaulle. On 27 August, General Leclerc, of the Free French forces, carried out a surprise attack on Douala, and rallied the administration of the Cameroons.

During that time Larminat and the conspirators at Brazzaville made good use of the situation. Vichy had committed an error in calling Boisson to Dakar and not replacing him immediately by a safer man.[13] General Husson, overtaken by events, tried to take security measures on 25 and 26 August, but on the 27th the conspirators carried out a surprise attack on the general staff. Husson was arrested and sent to Leopoldville, and Larminat made his entry into the capital of French Equatorial Africa. Then, on 30 August, Ubangi rallied (in spite of the opposition of the military commander, and most of the officer corps, who were finally arrested and expelled). Gabon followed. The French committee in London nominated Larminat high commissioner.[14]

The African people had no part in all this, but were content to watch how the colonials settled their accounts with each other. London's support was due to a handful of determined men, in the face of inertia on the part of the majority, mainly in the army, where most of the senior officers were in favour of Vichy, or lacked the courage to move over to 'dissidence', alleging family problems, careers, and other excuses. Those who opted for Vichy were repatriated.

The instability of the situation was manifested in September 1940 by the sudden change of mind of Masson, the governor of Gabon, who had first announced his support for the new authorities at

Brazzaville. The cause of this move was the arrival at Libreville of Armand Annet, appointed governor-general of the Cameroons by Vichy, but who had not been able to take up his post; then came the air force General Têtu, whom Vichy appointed governor-general of French Equatorial Africa. Two naval vessels, the gunboat *Bougainville* and the submarine *Poncelet*, arrived to reinforce their positions. At the same time Governor Masson was under pressure from pro-Vichy colonial circles, with the vicar apostolic, Mgr. Tardy, at their head – the latter, leading a delegation of settlers, presented him with a petition protesting against his joining the 'dissidents'.[15] Masson yielded, and declared that his support was an error resulting from inaccurate information; he opted for Vichy, and resistance to the Anglo-Gaullists. Two Gaullist contingents, from the Cameroons and Congo, converged on Libreville.

During this time, Governor-General Annet chafed at his inactivity, and his colleague Têtu was irked at the unimportance of the post he had been given – he was now governor-general of a fraction of Gabon – and at his air force colleagues who had sent him there to prevent his appointment to the secretaryship of state for air in the Vichy government, to which he had aspired.[16] Major Parant, who had laid siege to Lambaréné, captured it on 5 November, and joined up with the contingent coming from the Cameroons. On 9 November Libreville surrendered to Colonel Leclerc, Port-Gentil following on the 11th. Five days later Governor Masson committed suicide. Governor-General Annet, untroubled in conscience, escaped from Libreville at the last moment to replace Léon Geismar, the secretary-general at Dakar, the latter having been dismissed because he was a Jew.

Thus French Equatorial Africa and the Cameroons entered, or rather remained, in the war. Because of the defection of the Vichyites the Europeans, except for a small number of volunteers, were not mobilised. The African population, however, provided men for the small detachments which were to represent France on the side of the Allies in the African theatre of war. One of these detachments, commanded by General Garbay, took part in the campaign against the Italians in Eritrea, and a motorised detachment from Chad, with great daring, raided the Italian positions in the Sahara. The raid caused panic in Fezzan (its leader, Major Colonna d'Ornano, was killed on 11 January, in an attack on the airfield at Mourzouk) and then, under the command of Leclerc, it seized the Koufra oasis on 1 March, 1941. It continued throughout 1941 and 1942 to harrass Italian positions at Fezzan, which was finally occupied; they then joined up, in January 1943, with British forces in operations on the Libyan coast against the German Afrika-Korps.

Q*

Throughout that period, French West Africa and Togo remained under Vichy control. The surprise attack on Dakar, planned by the Gaullists with the support of a few Free French naval units and the British fleet, failed. The captain of the corvette *Thierry d'Argenlieu*, who took a small launch to deliver a message to Boisson to propose his joining them, was machine-gunned as he left the harbour, and a battle broke out between the French and British naval units. The latter shelled the town, causing some 200 casualties. The British fleet withdrew, and Boisson celebrated the 'Dakar victory' (23, 24, 25 September, 1940). Numerous *croix de guerre* were distributed, even to officers who had prudently taken cover in cellars during the bombardment. Early on in the incident numerous 'suspects' were arrested, and three of them (including the mayor and the president of the Dakar chamber of commerce) were interned in North Africa. The Italian and German armistice commissions visited the areas under Vichy rule to check that the agreed terms were being fulfilled. Seventy-five thousand African soldiers ordered to be repatriated, were sent home between April 1940 and June 1941, and 90,000, who had been mobilised on the spot, were likewise returned home with neither pay nor equipment; there were some incidents in the course of these operations in the army camps at Kindia in Guinea and Kati in the Sudan at the end of 1940. A German diplomat Mülhausen came, under the name of Martin, to gather military intelligence – which was supplied to him by Colonel Salan (later, as a general, to achieve notoriety in Algeria) under the pretext of preparing German 'aid' for the defence of French West Africa. Polish and Belgian gold held for safe-keeping at Bamako was handed over to the Germans.[17]

The reign of Vichy in French West Africa was the Indian summer of the 'true' colonials. The ambiguities of the policy of 'assimilation' including the citizenship of the Sengalese in the three communes, the criticising of politicians, and the possibility of being denounced in the French press – all vanished. Republican hypocrisy was complete. For the administration the policy of *commandement*, reserved formerly for the colonies only, was now the policy of metropolitan France. In this respect the Vichy régime was nothing new for the colony: it was merely a continuation – and a culmination.

> To establish [the dictatorship] in France, a *coup d'état*, as at the time of Bonaparte, and the official erasure of the words Liberty, Equality and Fraternity, had been necessary. In French West Africa, on the other hand, it was enough to have the old Faidherbian régime fully restored . . . and the law, or rather decrees, applied.[18]

In other words, the illegal practices current under the Republic –
illegal requisitioning, corporal punishment, etc. – met with no
obstacles. Racial discrimination without a basis in law (Vichy was
interested only in the Jews) was now openly practised. Resistance,
on a feeble scale, was found only in the defection of a few officials or
members of the armed services to the British territories or in the
activities of a few underground centres. When repression was carried
out, racialism came into the open. The authorities showed no sign
of tenderness towards the European Gaullists; they were condemned to heavy prison sentences or forced labour. But it was
arranged that no death sentences should be passed except *in absentia*,
mainly on those who had fled to British territories. Africans, on the
other hand, were shot, often simply for making contact with, or
working for a Gaullist. One such, Adolphe Gaëtan, was shot at
Dakar on 19 November, 1942, eleven days after the Allied landing
in North Africa.

If the administration, with few exceptions, accepted the Vichy
régime as the answer to its progress, the same was true of the settlers.
The more prominent businessmen were usually circumspect, but
the settlers of small and medium means were enthusiastic, and consequently set up a *Légion des Combattants*. Fanatics established a
secret society, a sort of Vichyist freemasonry, called *La France de
Pétain*, which spied upon and denounced those suspected of Gaullism
or who simply lacked their own enthusiasm.

Racial discrimination permeated every aspect of life, even in
Dakar and the principal towns where before 1940 attempts had been
made to camouflage its most blatant symptoms. In the Senegalese
communes, at least, the protests of the 'local' citizens would have
proved an effective obstacle. For example, when rationing was
introduced, normal food ration cards were given only to Europeans
and, at the discretion of the circle commander, to a few African
officials classed as 'living in the European manner'. Other Africans
living in the towns were put on a short allowance. Clothing and
sugar coupons were, in practice, entrusted to the canton chiefs, who
kept them for their own cronies or used them to supply the black
market. In public places, in queues and on the railways, discrimination was introduced. Even if he had paid for a first-class ticket, an
African was forced to travel in 'carriages for natives', dirty and
without any comforts, while the best carriages were reserved for
Europeans. Discrimination spread even to the economic sphere. In
the harvest season of 1942–3 on the Ivory Coast, cocoa was bought
from the Africans, who supplied nine-tenths of production, at a
price of 2.60 francs per kilo, while the European planters received
4.50 francs. At Kouroussa, a good cow sold 'at the administrative

price' (*sic*) fetched 2,000 francs. The same cow sold among Africans could go as high as 3,000–3,500 francs.[19] These practices were not new, but their incidence became much greater.

The various forms of forced labour reached their peak, and requisitioning of manpower for the settlers' enterprises became the rule. On the Ivory Coast, on the eve of the suppression of forced labour early in 1946, there were up to 36,000 administrative 'recruits' for labour. All African 'subjects' were forced to submit, and it was not a rare sight to see an African planter forced to abandon his plantation to work, with his wife and children, on the plantations of a neighbouring European settler. In Guinea men were recruited throughout the forest regions for the coastal banana plantations. . . . 'A Guerzé sent to work in the region of Conakry', Father Lelong noted, 'is like a Dutch peasant exiled to the Ukraine.'[20] The administrator of Kouroussa, a circle that officially had 67,450 inhabitants, noted in his 1942 report:

> The circle at present supplies: 490 labourers for the Conakry–Niger railway line (tree-felling at Nono and Tamba); 80 labourers for the Baro plantation (Kankan circle); 80 labourers for the Delsol plantation; 15 labourers for the African Banana plantations; 40 labourers for the Linkeny banana plantations; 200 labourers for public works at Kankan; 100 labourers for charcoal burning at Conakry; 100 labourers for road-repair work – making a total of 1,105.
>
> This is a heavy burden on the circle; there are many desertions, for the natives of the circle object to working for others, even when paid and fed [*sic*], hence there are frequent complaints by the corporate employers and the planters. All deserters caught are sent to the court of the first instance (Article 28 of the native penal code).

Ration cards for clothing, oil and other commodities, which were intended for workers, were frequently diverted by the owners of the firms from their true purpose. On the Ivory Coast a planter neither fed nor paid his labourers; administrative recruitment for this planter was only suppressed when Governor Latrille came to the Ivory Coast at the end of 1943, after two warnings had failed to have effect. Another planter on the Ivory Coast, in the Toumodi region, systematically applied the following 'treatment' to his labourers when they were sick: no food, rubbing the body with pigmented oil, and exposure to the sun. In this case also it was not until the arrival of Governor Latrille that the man was brought to justice, and even then he was only given a small fine. The head of the *Légion des Combattants* on the Ivory Coast, classifiable as a 'poor white' in

1940, had amassed a fortune three years later amounting to 15–20,000,000 francs through a wine and petrol distributing agency, with profitable outlets on the black market. In June 1943 the Vichy governor still in residence on the Ivory Coast fixed a rule for inspectors of labour that they should 'state the facts' and not 'make judgments', and

> never tell the labourers that they have the right to such and such a privilege or that they should not do such and such work; an observation of this nature should only be made to the employer himself.[22]

For Catholic missionaries the Vichy period was, likewise, a halcyon age. The 'French state' had abolished the laws governing the relationship between Church and state in France and given the Catholic Church an official position. The effects were felt in Africa. Instead of subsidies, which had formerly depended on the arbitrary will of the local authorities, whose generosity varied, the missions in French West Africa and Togo received from 1942 onwards official subsidies for their schools by decree. These subsidies included a clause which at first worried the fathers.

> But when a letter from the governor-general [Boisson] stated that a 'moderate' contribution could be received for religious instruction, quite apart from the question of schools which did not go in for religion [sic], grants were applied for. If some contributions are too large, that is a matter to be settled later.[23]

Boisson's support made it possible to create an office of private education under the direct control of the governor-general, a private training college at Ouagadougou, and four private écoles des moniteurs in the other colonies. Catholic action organisations were authorised and started to develop, while freedom of association, even in the limited forms that had existed in 1937–9, was entirely suppressed. They obeyed the rules of racial discrimination: the Jeunesse ouvrière chrétienne had separate sections for whites and for Africans.[24] Over and above the material advantages which the missions derived from 'establishment', there were moral ones. With the official support of the state, they were secure against the chicanery of French politics or of administrators who were anti-clericals or freemasons (the most notorious of whom had already been eliminated). The missionaries now assumed a special niche in public life. The administrator who did not completely approve of this situation had much to fear from a denunciation in high places; thus an enforced 'harmony' was at last achieved between the admini-

stration and the missions. The latter were also the most fervent
defenders and propagators of the 'national revolution'. They did
not accept the break of 1943; and even in 1944 the Marshal's por-
trait hung prominently in the mission centres. In the refectory of the
mission at Abidjan it faced a picture representing the 'Dakar Victory'.

On General de Gaulle's first visit to Abidjan in January 1944, the
bishop left for a tour on the morning of his arrival in order not to
have to receive him. When the Allies landed in Normandy in June
1944, the Catholic missions at Abidjan refused to put out flags; the
same was true of the liberation of Paris in August, when the missions and religious buildings on the Ivory Coast did not fly flags and
refused to have the bells rung. It was not until 1945 that the missions gave in and admitted the final defeat of Vichy.

The African inhabitants suffered under all this and formed their
own judgment. At the same time, as Richard-Molard stressed, the
people of Europe were also suffering under dictatorship:

> But they knew that it was illegal and that legal liberties would be
> restored. The Africans, on the contrary, know that their subjec-
> tion is legal, and this is the cause of their concern.[25]

For this reason, while some far-sighted Africans sympathised
from the beginning with the Allied cause against the Axis that
officially professed racialist doctrines, the majority of the population remained indifferent to the quarrels between the colonisers.
They understood only too well that the administrators and settlers
who went over to the Anglo-Gaullists did not behave very differently
from their Vichyite colleagues, and they failed to see what more
they could expect from one than from the other. With the exception
of a small group led by Abd El-Kader Diagne, linked to the Free
French mission at Bathurst in the Gambia, which recruited its
supporters almost exclusively among the citizens of the Senegalese
communes, the Africans who took part in the Resistance played
only a minor role – as liaison officers, for example – but they earned,
in return, the privilege of getting shot.[26]

Here and there incidents broke out, some directly related to the
Resistance, others with different causes. The most spectacular concerned the Abron in Bondoukou, Ivory Coast. In January 1942 the
Abron king, his son, his canton chiefs and his principle notables, with
quite a large entourage,[27] moved across the frontier of the Gold
Coast, and offered their services to the Free French mission at
Accra. It was difficult to know what had been the determining
factor in their decision – whether local politics or wider considerations. A punitive detachment was sent out by the French colonial

power to take possession of the houses and goods of the defectors, which were then burnt.[28] Another king, of a rival branch, was put in his place by Vichy in June 1942. To the surprise of the Boisson régime he fled to Abidjan in September 1943, taking a part of the family treasure with him. He was arrested and sentenced, while the old king and his supporters returned from Accra to the Ivory Coast.

At Bobo-Dioulasso also, bloody incidents took place in 1942. At Porto-Novo King Gbehinto, arrested for aiding the Gaullists, committed suicide in prison (1940). Hunkanrin was arrested and deported to the Sudan. Other incidents were without direct political causes, but fitted into the traditional pattern of resistance to colonial exactions. Such were those among the Lobi of the Gaoua circle, and the Diola and the Floup of Casamance. In 1942 the administrator of Dakar learnt from his opposite number at Ziguinchor that the Diola had large stores of rice, and so he demanded their immediate release. The delivery quotas were fixed at a far higher level than the actual stores, and a ridiculously early deadline was fixed for delivery, taking into account the time needed for shelling. Led by a woman, the Queen of Kabrousse, who had acquired great prestige by making rain in a period of drought, the Diola refused to obey. Troops were sent. One soldier was killed, whereupon the usual repressions came into effect: the village of Effoc was 'broken up', its shrines were ransacked, and the queen herself was punished. The frightened people moved to Portuguese Guinea and did not return until ten years later.[29] They had to wait for the independence of Senegal before their war-drum, seized by the military authorities, was returned to the village inhabitants.

The 1942 landing in North Africa made French West Africa change camps. Boisson at first reaffirmed his steadfast loyalty to Marshal Pétain and his decision to fight to the last against the Anglo-Saxon aggressors. But when Admiral Darlan went over to the Americans, Boisson realised that the game was up, and General Bergeret, who was sent by Darlan, had little difficulty in getting him to change his position. But he had, first of all, to win over his immediate subordinates and, in particular, the military chiefs. The latter did not consider it a matter of patriotism; they merely demanded that a commision be sent to Algiers to verify if Admiral Auphan's telegrams conveying to Darlan the marshal's commendation for his action were really authentic! In the meantime, Boisson, to cover himself, tried (in vain) to obtain Pétain's approval for his change of position by emphasising that 'the longer the wait becomes, the more deeply rooted in people's minds becomes the disinclination to fight against the Americans'. In a cable on 21 November, Pétain enjoined him not to negotiate and to prepare for resistance.

Boisson's letter of reply to the marshal contained the following:

> At this point in the situation in French West Africa it is impossible to take the people and the army in hand, as you ask, and to lead them into resistance against aggression.[30]

It was only on 22 November, when reassured of the 'legitimacy' of Darlan, that army personnel declared themselves in favour of 'token support'. During this time, they continued to shoot Africans accused of Gaullism. On 7 December, 1942, Boisson signed an agreement with Eisenhower in the Darlan's presence, declaring the entry of French West Africa into the war against Germany. Boisson took his place on the *Comité de l'Empire français* which, under the direction of General Noguès, continued the work of Darlan, who was assassinated at Algiers on 24 December. French West Africa was still governed in the name of the marshal, and in pursuance of his 'true will'. Vichy continued its existence with the support of the Americans, whose sympathy towards the Pétain regime was not feigned, and who saw General de Gaulle as the tool of Britain. Only through the official telegram 10119/P/S of 14 December, 1942, did the administrators of Guinea receive orders to liquidate their network of anti-British and anti-Gaullist intelligence. The administrator of Gueckédou was proud of the network he had set up, which 'closely shadowed' the activities of Gaullists who had taken refuge in Sierra Leone. In November, 1942, he drew up a plan to defend his position against the 'enemy', and did not resign until 12 February, 1943.[31]

Vichyism was officially condemned only in June 1943 with the elimination of the former Pétainists and the final triumph of the committee at Algiers. But this committee did no more than replace Boisson, his governors and some high officials who were too deeply compromised; all the others – administrators, armed service chiefs, secretaries-general – remained in their jobs. The same policy continued in support of the increasingly burdensome 'war effort'; the contradiction between the methods employed in its implementation and the aims that were invoked to justify the sacrifices demanded appeared more and more unbearable to the Africans. In French Equatorial Africa under Free France, the position of the African masses was no better, the more so since the 'war effort' had been imposed sooner and upon a population in an even greater state of wretchedness. French Equatorial Africa, for ever in debt, had all of a sudden to become self-sufficient and, in part at least, to finance the activities of Free France. The 1939 and 1940 budgets showed deficits of 7,000,000 and 15,000,000 francs respectively, including subsidies from France amounting to 100,000,000. With growing expenses and without subsidies the subsequent budgets attained deficits of 22,600,000 in 1941, 34,300,000 in 1942 and 40,000,000 in 1943.

Opponents in the European conflict, Boisson the Vichyite and Eboué the Gaullist, shared the same views on matters of 'native policy'. When the old Balali chief Goma Tsé-tsé wrote to de Larminat to declare his loyalty and demand authorisation for the *Amicale* (friendly society), he was refused. Imprisonment and execution, carried on under Eboué, took their toll of members of the *Amicale*: Malanda, shot at Boko on 5 December, 1940; M'Biémo and Milongo, shot at Majama on 11 December, 1940.[32] It was under the Free French régime that André Matswa was sentenced to life imprisonment and, in all likelihood, murdered in his prison cell. The decrees of July 1942, in which Eboué's 'native policy' found expression, were aimed only at modifying the traditional system so as to avert disastrous consequences; but, apart from a declaration of principles, they had no practical effect. To attenuate the ravages of large-scale recruitment and offset the effects of detribalisation, he proposed the 'integration' of races on work-sites and, when men were displaced, to let them take their families with them. On the pattern of the Belgian Congo, he established the status of *notables évolués* (*sic*), allowing in the villages for a class freed from the *indigénat*, but without benefit of citizenship. The practical effects went no further than the naturalisations on an individual basis which were planned for after the First World War. The status was of interest to no one apart from a few officials. By 1 April, 1943, only eleven persons had been established as *notables évolués*; by 23 August, 1943, ninety-three; by 30 December, 103. Throughout 1944 there were 218 promotions to this status. A third decree authorised the formation of African communes; like previous documents dealing with 'native communes', this decree remained a dead letter.

(*b*) THE WAR EFFORT

For the African population, the war period, as in 1914–18, took the form of an intensification of all their burdens. The colonies, with their economy entirely oriented towards the needs of France – supplying it with raw materials and absorbing its manufactured products – had to live on their own resources. Imports fell almost to zero. In Vichy-controlled French West Africa this was because the Allies controlled the seas, and France, bled by Germany, had nothing to export. From November 1942 the other territories and French Equatorial Africa were shut off from France, and the Allies were waging total war. Very little got in. No petrol or coal reached

Africa; fire-wood was used to stoke locomotive engines. The small quantities of fabrics and sugar that entered the territory were rationed.

The black market flourished at all levels, but most of all at the level of big business. Firms worked out their import quotas in the same proportions as in 1938-9. When retail traders approached them with vouchers signed by the administration they were not refused goods but forced to buy, at exorbitant prices, untaxed or unsaleable commodities: rubbish of all kinds, and, after 1943, Algerian wines and spirits which were difficult to resell. The importer always made a 100 per cent profit. To recoup his outlays the retailer was obliged to sell essential products (fabrics, sugar, etc.) at excessive prices, demanding illicit supplements, or to pass his merchandise entirely on to the black market. Some more than managed to cover their expenses in this way. The remainder of the merchandise sold on the free market was divided each month among African sub-traders under the same sordid conditions to feed the black market in the bush. As to ration cards and coupons, those to which the peasants were entitled (mainly for sugar and textiles) were distributed by the canton chiefs. This led to the obvious abuses. The weaving trade started up once more, and blacksmiths tried to compensate for the lack of imported hardware by working from scrap-iron. Traditional crafts revived to some extent, but in an atmosphere of general penury. The peasant received little in the way of imported goods; but this did not prevent everything from being taken from him, particularly what could contribute to the strategic needs of the countries at war. First he was taxed in the form of food products, in which commerce had never shown any interest, and which the cultivator produced only for his own sustenance or for small local markets.

Then imported rice vanished: Senegal suffered a shortage and the towns had to be fed. Shortage of transport and administrative inefficiency caused enormous stocks to accumulate and become spoiled, while the population was dying of hunger. The methods employed were the time-honoured ones; we quote, as an example, the service order addressed by the administrator of Kissidougou to his canton chiefs at the very moment when the war was ending:

Service order for the canton chiefs of [complete list follows]:
I give you until 31 May at the latest to deliver your quota of millet for the current trading season to the Société commerciale de l'Ouest africain.
On 15 May . . . kilos still remained to be delivered.
Unless you fulfil this order within the term stipulated, you will

be brought physically to Kissidougou and subjected to the necessary sanctions until the quota of your canton is fulfilled.

Kissidougou, 20 May, 1945
THE CIRCLE COMMANDER[33]

In the Guerzé country, situated in the forest area of Guinea . . .

the rice harvest has defied every means of transportation. American trucks arrived in time to prevent considerable stocks of badly stored rice from rotting on the spot while the people starved....[34]

The sacks needed for transporting the rice did not exist. To make good this lack, the villages were forced to make mats. The Guerzé of the south did not do so. They bought them elsewhere, at 50 francs apiece, and at the place of requisitioning were paid only 10 francs for them. Where no trucks were available, porterage was reintroduced.

To transport one ton of rice to the nearest station, 300 km. away, 600 men were requisitioned, who each carried 15 kilos on their heads for ten days, their return journey on foot taking another ten days; so for a total of more than three weeks they ate only what they found along the road. . . .[35]

Obviously, 'strategic' materials or those needed to feed the armies were the first to be demanded. Under Boisson, until 1942, this was to satisfy the demands of Vichy and Germany; but lack of transport created considerable obstacles.[36] Next, materials were needed for the Allied war effort; the *Comité française de Libération nationale* no less than the *Comité de l'Empire français* declared that the honour of France was bound up with the size of its material effort in the war.

The colonies have to help remedy the shortage in France with an unprecedented war effort. The war effort demanded of the federation, of each colony, circle, canton or village, was worked out by pre-war statistics, often greatly augmented. These ideal statistics of the past took little note of present-day material conditions, which prevented realistic calculation. Impossible requests were made, under draconian threats, to be carried out, if need be, immediately.[37]

Richard-Molard (author of the passage quoted above) mentioned the anecdote of the administrator who was sanctioned, when his circle had been taxed in honey, although it did not produce any, for telegraphing the governor: 'O.K. for honey. Stop. Send bees.' But in general the administrator and the canton chiefs were not found wanting. It was up to the people to find a way out, and the goods they did not produce they had to buy elsewhere, at higher prices, to deliver at derisory prices to the trading firms that benefited from 'quotas', as we saw in the case of the sacks and the mats.

Rubber gathering, which for a long time had been more or less abandoned, was now revived; in the absence of precise data, the circles were taxed haphazardly. In French West Africa, a 'rubber service' was established, in which all kinds of 'ne'er do weel' Europeans who happened to be available exercised their sorry talents. In 1944 the official of this service arrived at the village of Layadi in Dabola circle to find the place deserted, the population having fled into the bush at his approach. Under the pretext of conducting a search, he had the huts sacked, glass and furniture smashed, and the roofs torn down. While one case of this kind gave rise to an inquiry (which brought no result), there were many more which never appeared in administrative reports.

At Kissidougou a report by a circle commander gives the following data. The rubber trade ended in 1920, but in 1941 the circle produced nine tons, 'the major part of which was bought outside the circle'. In the Dialakoro canton, 476 out of 566 kilos were bought in the neighbouring circles of Kankan and Kouroussa at 40 to 50 francs per kilo; in the Tinki circle, 345 out of 360 kilos were bought outside, at prices rising to 80 francs per kilo. Because of the labour needed to obtain a few tons of rubber, the rice harvest was endangered by a delay in sowing.[38]

On the Ivory Coast, the governor wrote:

> From an economic point of view, given the dispersion of settlements and their distance from the villages, a day's labour brings in one to three francs according to the region.
>
> From a medical point of view, it is a monstrosity against which the sleeping-sickness service has protested. The natives have to go deep into the forest, several days' journey from their villages, with no protection against the tse-tse fly, which abounds in the very regions where the latex plant grows.[39]

In French Equatorial Africa, where the plantations were exhausted, gathering was resumed on a large scale using the same methods. Eboué wrote in a circular:

> We shall not lose sight of the fact that in becoming suppliers of rubber – and it is well understood that supplies must reach a minimum of 4,000 tons in 1943 – we also have to preserve the cotton fields of the Sara peasant, the palm-groves of Sangha, the timber yards and even the gold.[40]

But the governor-general forgot to say how all this could be achieved, while still avoiding the consequences he deplored. In 1943 only 2,505 tons of the target of 4,000 tons were produced. The latter figure was approached in 1944 but production dropped again to 2,725 tons in 1945. The sale of rubber for military purposes to the British Rubber Control was certainly beneficial to the finances of French Equatorial Africa and to the firms acting as intermediaries, but P. Kalck noted that the collection of this rubber 'gave rise to new abuses which discredit Free France in the eyes of the village masses'.[41] The final economic balance-sheet was deplorable, quite apart from human considerations.

In Senegal progress in groundnut production had caused a deficit in foodstuffs. In the course of 1935–9, that colony imported an average of 64,000 tons of rice from Indochina annually .In compensation, groundnut exports over the same period amounted on average to 580,000 tons. The freezing of C.F.A. prices (at the point of sale in France) established at the end of 1939 caused traders to pay lower prices to their producers – so leading to discouragement among the cultivators from 1940 onwards. The depression grew during the 1940–1 harvest, with transport difficulties and the absence of imported goods to attract the peasants. The administration fixed a minimum price for the producers, varying according to the transport costs involved, and this system lasted until 1945. Due to lack of demand, the indigenous provident societies sold only 16 per cent of production. There were no longer any seasonal workers, and so the administration resorted to forced recruitment, which produced labour of mediocre quality (Fulani shepherds were sent who had never reaped a harvest) and in insufficient numbers; about 25,000 seasonal workers were employed in 1941 and 20,000 in 1942, as against 50,000 before the war. In 1941, production dropped to 220,000 tons and exports to 174,500 tons. Food crops increased correspondingly: the area under cultivation in millet was estimated to have increased by one-third. Even so the deficit, estimated at no less than the equivalent of 80,000 tons of rice (100,000 tons of millet), was not made good. In 1942, groundnut production was 231,000 tons; the indigenous provident societies increased their distribution of seed, but this was partly eaten by the famished peasants. Land under millet increased by an estimated third, but yields decreased; the deficit in cereals for human consumption was estimated at 184,500 tons of millet. Germany had demanded supplies of castor-oil, and 20,000 hectares were accordingly put under cultivation to produce it, by requisition. From 1943 groundnuts expanded, and in that year the harvest was estimated at 460,000 tons, in 1945 it was 429,400.[42] But progress was not due to economic stimulus, or only marginally so; it was due to the 'war effort' that production rose, with massive forced recruitment of seasonal labour (45,000 in 1943).

The war brought one positive result for Senegal: it made possible the beginning of industrialisation, with the development of oil works. For a century, every attempt to develop a groundnut processing industry on the spot had been impeded by the veto of the French exporters and oil-producers, who in many cases were one and the same. Until 1933 there were only a few small oil works in Senegal, producing for the local market. The law of 6 August, 1933, made the oil-bearing plants grown in the colonies preferential imports to the whole French customs zone, which encouraged the Senegalese oil producers to develop production – for example, 2,100 tons were exported to Algeria in 1936 and 5,300 tons in 1937. In 1936 the French oil works reacted by obtaining a rise in export dues for oil from French West Africa successively to 9.75, 14 and then 18.70 francs per 100 kilos. These measures failed to bring the expected results, and the French oil-producers forced the local ones to sign an agreement, sanctioned by a decree dated 8 April, 1938, freezing the duty-free oil quota from French West Africa at 5,800 tons. In 1938, oil production rose to 9,000 tons (from six oil works), of which 3,500 tons were intended for the local market, the rest for North Africa.

The war put an end to this policy. In 1939 it became necessary, in order to economise in the use of shipping space, to give preference to supplying North Africa with groundnut oil directly from Senegal, and to avoid the double transport of groundnuts from Senegal to France and French oil to North Africa. The quota was raised to 12,000 tons. In 1941, even greater shipping difficulties led to a rise in the quota, admitted duty-free, to 45,000 tons. A French company, Lesieur, obtained permission to set up a works at Dakar in place of its premises at Dunkirk, which were out of use. Oil production was 11,000 tons in 1939, 20,800 tons in 1940 and 40,000 tons in 1941.

In spite of the clearest possible economic necessity for this development, the government-general received an order to impose restraint – French industrialists were not losing sight of the future. By 1942, production had dropped to 27,000 tons and requests for permission to build new oil works were refused. A decree of 29 June, 1942, ratified by a law of 30 October, 1946, subjected all building or extension of oil works in French West Africa and Togo to approval by the governor, authorisation only being granted after consultation among, in effect, trade competitors. But they were allowed to establish themselves in North Africa. The Lesieur oil works produced only crude oil, which had to be refined in their works at Casablanca. But the trend thus begun was irreversible: oil exports took on a rising trend and little by little replaced exports of groundnuts.[43]

> In spite of opposition by French industrialists, oil works developed in Senegal as a result of the shortage of raw materials inherent in the state of war and because of lack of transport.[44]

In Guinea, the Ivory Coast, the Cameroons and French Equatorial Africa traditional production involving transport difficulties or of perishable goods (timber, bananas[45] and, to a smaller degree, cocoa) suffered considerable falls. On the other hand, coffee and cotton continued to make progress. To supply local needs, tobacco growing was started in the forest regions of Guinea. French Equatorial Africa in 1940 and French West Africa in 1943 had to give up the old 'protected prices' and conform to the prices imposed by the Allies, lower for exports and even higher for imports.

The result was a 'drop in the purchasing power of the natives', which the governor-general, Bayardelle, illustrated by the following figures: between 1939 and 1944, the price per kilo of rice at Brazzaville rose from 2.60 francs to 3.85 francs; of sugar from 4.75 to 6.40 francs; of milk from 3.50 to 10 francs; of soap from 2.50 to 4.50 francs; of meat from 6 to 12 francs; of a bicycle from 700 to 2,700 francs; of a cotton blanket from 10 to 68 francs. All these prices were the official rate and did not apply to the black market, which was often the only place where these goods could be obtained. During this period the price paid to the cotton producer rose from 1 to 1.50 francs per kilo.[46]

Finally we should note a further form of exploitation which accompanied the 'war effort', namely the abuse of 'voluntary subscriptions'. The chiefs were encouraged to outdo one another in this matter to show their 'loyalty': the Lebanese merchants were likewise made to contribute. In turn the chiefs obtained contributions from the people under their administration. This procedure had already been used in 1914–18 and occasionally at other periods.[47] It occurred again in 1939. In November 1939 a correspondent from Guinea wrote:

> Subscriptions for national defence never cease to flow in, both at Conakry and in the circles of the colony. They have already reached 500,000 francs, and are accompanied by gifts in kind. Among them should be noted the gift of a herd of 100 head of cattle offered by Tierno Oumarou, the chief of the Dalaba canton.[48]

Under the Vichyite régime in French West Africa subscriptions were raised for the 'national emergency' for 'the marshal's winter aid', and so forth. In French Equatorial Africa, and in French West Africa after June 1943, new subscriptions were raised for national defence, to aid the French Resistance. The Resistance never benefited from the sums collected, as they mysteriously vanished in transit.[49]

(c) THE CONFERENCE OF FRENCH AFRICA AT BRAZZAVILLE
(30 January–8 February, 1944)

All the sacrifices demanded for the war effort were in the cause of France, with more and more insistence on the cause of democratic and republican France in the struggle against fascist and racialist Germany. This trend, which was not apparent in 1942, nor at the beginning of 1943, least of all in French West Africa under Boisson, was established with the triumphant establishment in Algiers of the Comité français de Liberation nationale.

While the men of the Left joined Gaullism in 1940, the Gaullist clan itself, mainly derived from the extreme Right and from the Cagoule, did not conceal its political opinions, which were very close to those of its Vichy adversaries; its representatives readily blamed intellectuals and politicians in general, and the Popular Front in particular, for the defeat. They did not reproach Vichy for its home policy; often they even approved of it, deploring only that it was being put into practice under the German aegis.[50] The position changed after 1942, largely on account of the rivalry that grew up within the Allied camp between the British and the Americans, and to considerations of internal policy. The Americans were hostile to de Gaulle because they considered him an instrument of British policy. Against him they used the Vichy régime which was now on the side of the Allies, and in North Africa and French West Africa they allowed the rule of the Pétainist proconsuls to survive. To eliminate his enemies, who personified the most extreme conservatism, de Gaulle had to win the support of the French Resistance at home, which was taking up a position more and more to the Left. Gaullism in its early years had spoken only of France; now it referred more and more to the Republic. This trend in Gaullism, based by its leader on opportunism rather than principle, corresponded to changes in the character of the war. At the beginning, the imperialist conflict had not differed greatly from that of 1914 – the defence of the rights of oppressed peoples appeared to the Allies rather as a pretext than as a dominant cause. But later the war took on a more popular character. The attack on the Soviet Union and the growth of the Resistance among the people of Europe subdued by Nazism gave it the character of a people's struggle for national independence and democracy against Nazi imperialism and dictatorship.

The imperialist Allied powers – the United States and Britain – were forced by necessity and tactical interests to follow the current of the times. The solemnly proclaimed Allied 'war aims' (cf. the Atlantic Charter) assumed as their central theme the right of mankind to self-determination. Naturally the French and the British, in adhering to these principles, had Europe in mind not the colonies. Roosevelt, however, following the example of Woodrow Wilson in 1917–19, deliberately insisted on the universal application of these declarations. Internal agitation in the British and French colonial empires, which grew as the metropolitan powers lost their grip, gave an entrée to American imperialism, which had previously been denied opportunities there. Washington was not displeased. The French empire, cut off from its enemy-occupied capital, appeared a particularly tempting prey. So, in order to defuse American intrigues, and to have the increasingly crushing war effort accepted more readily (the years 1944–5 were the hardest in this respect), changes had to be promised. This was the task of the Brazzaville conference, which was held a few months after the elimination of the Vichyites from French West Africa. De Gaulle, as president of the Comité français de Libération nationale, set the context in his opening speech.

As always, war itself speeds up evolution. First, from the very fact that, up to the present, it has been largely an African war, and because on the same score, the absolute and relative importance of African resources, communications and contigents has become apparent in the harsh light of the theatres of operations. But finally, and above all, because this war has put at stake the whole condition of man, and because under the impact of the psychic forces it has unleashed, every nation, like every individual, is raising its head and looking to the future, questioning its own fate.[51]

He stated explicitly further on:

But in French Africa, as in all the other territories where men are living under our flag, there will be no real progress unless the inhabitants benefit from it, morally and materially, in their native land; unless they rise, stage by stage, to the level where they will be capable *of participating, within their own country, in the management of their own affairs.* It is France's duty to make sure that this comes to pass.

Such is the goal towards which we are set. We do not close our eyes to the length of the successive stages.[52]

However vague this declaration of principle, and despite the escape clause accompanying it (the length of the stages), it undoubedly constitutes an irreversible step in French colonial policy, going far beyond the tactical motives that dictated it. Such men as Jules Harmand and Régismanset ridiculed 'humanitarian' colonisation and stated – strictly in accordance with the facts – that the aim of colonisation was exploitation and that its effective basis was force. In 1931, during the crisis, Albert Sarraut proclaimed it a 'duty' to improve the conditions of the natives, as the only justification for colonial enterprise. But responsible colonials never envisaged the participation of their subjects in the management of their own affairs, not even in the distant future. De Gaulle, concentrating on the tactical considerations of the moment, evidently did not appreciate the impact of his declarations. Their prime aim of stopping American manoeuvres was fulfilled. They had the secondary aim of opening the road to 'colonial representation' which – de Gaulle and his advisers did not doubt – would be exactly what the government intended. It could affect the balance of parliamentary representation in France, which had resulted from universal suffrage, the possible direction and independence of which they feared.

The very composition of the Brazzaville conference left no doubts about the immediate, concrete significance of these principles. It was not of a democratic or even a representative character, but it was rather a conference of governors and governors-general of Black Africa and Madagascar, presided over by M. Pléven, commissioner for the colonies in the French National Liberation Committee. Also associated with its work were heads of transport, commerce and industry, and the missions – the chief figures of the colonial establishment. A delegation of the provisional consultative assembly was present; it included three members representing respectively the Confédération française des Travailleurs chrétiens, the Confederation Générale du Travail (the socialist Albert Gazier) and the Section française de l'Internationale ouvrière (Jules Moch). Care was taken to exclude the Communists. Above all, no African was invited to take part.[53]

There was nothing revolutionary about the recommendations which were adopted. To avoid ambiguity the conference stated specifically at the outset that the principle of the colonial system remained beyond dispute. At the very beginning of the recommendations, it declared:

The Conference of French Africa at Brazzaville, before proceeding to that part of the general problem which it proposes to examine [i.e. political organisation], thought it necessary to affirm the following principle:

The aims of the work of colonisation achieved by France in the colonies *make it impossible to entertain any ideas of autonomy, any possibility of evolution outside the French empire: an ultimate self-governing constitution for the colonies, even at a distant date, is to be rejected.*[54]

The conference considered mere improvements in parliamentary representation for the colonies to be insufficient, and it proposed a federal assembly. This was not to be native representation; the idea was rather to give the 'colony' – that is to say its administration, its commerce and its industry – the chance of being represented in Paris, and of bringing some pressure to bear on French policy. As for internal matters, the conference asked for an extension of gubernatorial powers.

In matters of 'native policy' the conference adhered to Eboué's concepts: a status of *notables évolués* and respect for custom – modified by the establishment of matrimonial freedom (already advocated before the war by the Mandel decree). The use of local languages in education continued to be strictly forbidden, and there was no question of citizenship for African subjects. All that was promised was a 'progressive suppression' of the hardships of the *indigénat,* after the end of hostilities.[55] Freedom of labour was to be established within a period of five years (France had already reluctantly agreed to this step in 1930); a body of labour inspectors was to be set up at places of work. However, one year's labour service was made obligatory for all young men not enlisted in the army (this was an extension of the system of the 'second group', condemned by the International Labour Office).

In short, these recommendations are all one needs to form a judgment on the alleged 'breadth of vision' supposed to have been expressed at the Brazzaville conference. They testify rather to the inability of the colonials and the Comité français de Liberation nationale to understand the wide scope of the movement that was was taking place among the mass of the people.

Accusations of not respecting the peoples' right to self-determination were met by the simple promise of African *participation* in the management of their own affairs, in a form and at a future time which were both left vague – only when the people had been 'raised, stage by stage, to the level where they would be capable [of this]'. The conference, in other words, believed that a way out could be found by making vague promises, qualified by reticence and delays, intended less for the African masses (convinced as they were that these were 'under control' and would so remain) than for world opinion. The pretext of the African peoples' incapacity, of their being below the age of discretion, continued to be invoked to oppose any substantial change in the foreseeable future.

Above all, the principle of colonial sovereignty remained sacrosanct. It might even be said that it was the main object which the conference wished to affirm. Already one could discern future drama inherent in this way of thinking, which was unaware of the profound movements stirring within the African masses and which, above all, remained determined in its refusal to give up more of the privileges of colonial domination.

REFERENCES

1. Albert Sarraut, *Grandeur et servitude coloniales*. Paris, Ed. du Sagittaire, 1931, p. 219.

2. It was Governor Croccichia (quoted by E. Louveau, *Au bagne: Entre les griffes de Vichy et de la milice*. Bamako, Soudan-Imprimerie, 1946).

3. See Armand Annet, *Aux Heures troublées de l'Afrique française (1939–43)*. Paris, Editions de Conquistador, 1952.

4. E. Louveau, op. cit., p. 22.

5. Quoted by medical General Sicé, *L'Afrique équatoriale française et le Cameroun au service de la France*, Paris, P.U.F., 1946, chap. VII.

6. Richard-Molard, *Afrique Occidentale Française*, Paris, Berger-Levrault, 1952, p. 167.

7. E. Louveau, op. cit., p. 21.

8. Boisson had great ambitions; his adherence to the Vichy cause was very sudden.

9. Tract of 22 August, 1940. Quoted by Sicé, op. cit., p. 143.

10. Ibid.

11. Circular of 8 November, 1941. Quoted by H. Zieglé, *Afrique équatoriale française*, Paris, Berger-Levrault, 1952, p. 167.

12. H. Deschamps, *Méthodes et doctrines coloniales de la France*. Paris, Armand Colin, 1953, pp. 177–8.

13. A very young inspector of the colonies, M. Tézénas du Montcel, had been sent from France to assist General Husson, arriving at Brazzaville by plane on 27 June. He was too young and inexperienced to assume the necessary authority. 'Inspector Tézénas was no fool. As soon as he arrived in Leopoldville [after the Gaullist surprise attack on 27 August] he undertook to demoralise our supporters at Brazzaville by announcing that he had all the requisite lists, and promising repression against families.' (E. de Larminat, op. cit., p. 159.)
Interned for three years at Fort Rousset, Inspector Tézénas du Montcel was 'rehabilitated' by volunteering for the Italian campaign in 1943. After the war he became a director of the Institut d'émission monétaire de l'Afrique occidentale française (today Banque centrale des Etats de l'Afrique de l'Ouest).

14. Eboué was appointed governor-general of French Equatorial Africa in November.

15. '. . . Governor Masson was a protégé of Boisson, who kept an eye on his career and sharply called him to order at Dakar.' (E. de Larminat, op. cit., p. 183.)

General de Larminat gave this opinion of the Apostolic Vicar: 'Mgr. Tardy, holding Maurrasian opinions, had been the firmest support of the ephemeral and dissident [Vichyist] government of Gabon, and a virulent member of the Vigilance Committee, whose activity consisted of denouncing bad citizens and having them interned in the hold of the banana-boat *Cap des Palmes* before sending them to the Vichy prisons; a curious occupation for an ecclesiastic.'

16. Cf. Armand Annet, *Aux Heures troublées de l'Afrique française*. Paris, Edition du Conquistador, 1952.

17. Pro-Vichy sources: *L'Agression de Dakar* (Dakar, Information Service of the High Commissioner of French Africa, 1940); P. Chenet, *Qui a sauvé l'Afrique*, Paris, L'Elan, 1949 (Apologia of Boisson); J. Mordal, *La Battaile de Dakar*. Paris, Ozanne, 1956.

18. J. Richard-Molard, *Afrique occidentale française*, Paris, Berger-Levrault, 1952, p. 167.

19. Kouroussa Archives, Political Reports. 1945.

20. Lelong, op. cit., p. 188.

21. Kouroussa Archives, Political Reports. 25 August, 1942.

22. Ivory Coast Archives. Note by the governor, dated 5 June, 1943.

23. Catlin, *Situation de l'enseignement privé catholique en Afrique occidentale française*. (African Conference on Education. Dakar, 1944.)

24. Paul Baudu, *Vieil Empire, jeune Eglise*. Paris, Ed. de la Savane, 1957, p. 220.

25. J. Richard-Molard, *Afrique occidentale française*. Paris, Berger-Levrault, 1952, p. 167.

26. The complete list of those shot at Fann is not known. E. Louveau (op. cit.) gives a few names.

27. Amon d'Aby, *La Côte d'Ivoire dans la cité africaine* (Paris, Larose, 1951) gives the figure of 10,000 persons which is perhaps an exaggeration.

28. This, at least, is the version of the administrative reports of 1944, adopted by M. Georges Chaffard (*Les Carnets secrets de la décolonisation*, Paris, Calmann-Lévy, 1965, p. 32); he attributes the responsibility for the repression to the administrator of Bondoukou. M. Jubert Deschamps (*in litteris*, 5 May, 1964) points out, however, that when he arrived on the spot after the flight of the King he saw or learnt nothing of the kind. The cause of the conflict came from the refusal of the administration to give the king's succession to his son, which would have been contrary to local practice. It was, as one might suspect, a local incident rather than a matter of general policy.

29. Cf. L. V. Thomas, *Les Diola*. Dakar, I.F.A.N., 1958, vol. I, p. 22.

30. Texts quoted in the deposition of Procurator-General Mornet during the Pétain trial. (*Le Procès du maréchal Pétain*. Shorthand records. Paris, Albin Michel, vol. II, p. 949.)

31. Gueckédou Archives (Guinea). Confidential records. 1941-7.

32. J. M. Wagret, *Histoire et Sociologies politiques de la Rèpublique du Congo (Brazzaville)*. Paris, Pichon et Durand. Auzia, 1963.

33. Kissidougou Archives.

34. Lelong, *Ces Hommes qu'on appelle anthropophages*. Paris, Alsatia, 1946, p. 261.

35. J. Richard-Molard, op. cit., p. 168.

36. With old re-cast rails, the first stage of the Trans-Sahara line was extended from Colomb-Bechar, though the undertaking did not get very far for lack of funds.

37. Richard-Molard, op. cit., p. 168.

38. Kissidougou Archives. Report of 8 February, 1943.

39. Ivory Coast Archives. October 1945.

40. Circular of 19 April, 1943. Quoted by Zieglé, op. cit., p. 112.

41. P. Kalck, *Réalités oubanguiennes*. Paris, Berger-Levrault, 1959, p. 159.

42. Senegal Archives. Agricultural Reports: 1940–5.

43. Oil exports from French West Africa (in tons): 1938, 5,681; 1939, 5,231; 1940, 13,193; 1941, 23,383; 1942, 11,020; 1943, 19,439; 1944, 27,842; 1945, 30,859; 1946, 35,121.

44. J. Fouquet, 'La traite des arachides dans le pays de Kaolack', *Études sénégalaises*, No. 8, 1958, p. 125.

45. There was a rise in the production of dried bananas which could be preserved and transported at reduced weight.

46. A. Bayardelle, speech to the council of administration of French Equatorial Africa (2 December, 1944).

47. In 1927 appeal was made for voluntary contributions 'for the financial rehabilitation of the metropolis'. Each number of the *Journal officiel de l'Afrique équatoriale française* gives a list of subscribers and the amount of their contribution. They were mostly chiefs: the Sultan of Chad gave 15,000 francs.

48. *Afrique française*, 1939, No. 10–11, p. 245.

49. Here is the 'effort' demanded of the subdivision of Dalaba (Guinea) with 60,000 inhabitants—according to official reports (where the subscriptions are mentioned on the same level as taxes, statute labour, the obligatory provision of foodstuffs):

1942. 'Voluntary subscriptions' for National Emergency: 81,761 francs; for victims of bombing in the Paris area: 24,900 francs.

1943. National Emergency: 102,000 francs; African Loans: 658,000 francs; National Subscription for the Resistance: 390,000 francs. (In the course of the year the Resistance took over Pétain's National Emergency funds.)

1944. Subscription: 350,000 francs.

50. In his *Mémoires de Guerre* de Gaulle pays homage to its 'incontestable achievement in economic and social organisation'.

51. *La Conférence africaine française*. Brazzaville, Ed. du Baobab, S.d. (1944), p. 38.

52. Ibid.

53. The sending of six memoranda (edited, among others, by Fily Dabo Sissoko and by the Cercle des évolués de Brazzaville) cannot be considered participation, and the conference does not seem to have taken them into serious consideration.

54. Ibid., p. 45.

55. Ibid., p. 54.

BIBLIOGRAPHY

ABBREVIATIONS

A.E.F.   *L'Afrique equatoriale française* (French Equatorial Africa).
A.F.   *L'Afrique française* (Bulletin du Comité de l'Afrique française).
A.F., R.C. *L'Afrique française, Renseignements coloniaux* (suppléments).
A.O.F.   *L'Afrique occidentale française* (French West Africa).
B.C.E.H.S. *Bulletin du Comité d'Etudes historiques et scientifiques de l'A.O.F.*
C.I.A.O.   *Conférence internationale des Africanistes de l'Ouest.*
C.O.M.   *Cahiers d'Outre-Mer*, Bordeaux.
E.D.   *Etudes Dahoméennes.*
I.F.A.N.   *Institut français d'Afrique noire.*
R.I.   *Revue indigène.*

PART I (1900–1919)

Abadie (General), *La Défense des colonies.* Paris, Charles-Lavauzelle, 1937.
Abou Digu'en, *Notre Empire african noir.* Paris, Charles-Lavauzelle, 1928.
Adloff (R.), *West Africa: the French-speaking Nations Yesterday and Today.* New York, Holt, Rinehart and Winston, 1964.
Afrique Equatoriale Française, Gouvernement général de l', *Comptes définitifs des recettes et dépenses, 1911.* Paris, Larose, 1912–3; Brazzaville, Imprimerie du gouvernement général, 1914.
— [Gouvernement général de l'], *l'evolution économique des possessions françaises de l'Afrique équatoriale.* Paris, Alcan, 1913.
— [*Emprunt de l'*]. Paris, Larose, 1913
— [*Une étape de la conquête de l'*]. Paris, Fournier, 1912.
— [*Victor Augagneur et l'*], by S., Colonial settler in the Congo. Bordeaux, Imprimerie coopérative, 1923.
Afrique Occidentale Française (Gouvernement général de l'), *Situation générale de l'année 1908.* Gorée, Imprimerie du gouvernement général, 1909.
— [Gouvernement général de l'], *L'Afrique occidentale française en 1910.* Rapport d'ensemble annuel. Laval, Imprimerie Barnéoud.
— [Gouvernement général de l'], *Rapport d'ensemble annuel 1912.* Paris, Larose, 1916.
[Allemagne] *Les Crimes allemands en Afrique.* Paris, Comité de l'Afrique française, 1917.
Anfreville de la Salle (Dr. d'), *Notre vieux Sénégal.* Paris, Challamel, 1909.
Angoulvant (Gabriel), *La Pacification de la Côte d'Ivoire.* Paris, Larose, 1916.
Annet (Armand), *En colonne dans le Cameroun.* Paris, Debresse, 1949.
Arcin (André), *La Guinée française.* Paris, Challamel, 1907.

[Armée] *L'Artillerie aux colonies*. Paris, Imprimerie Villain et Bar, 1931.
— *Le Train des équipages aux colonies*. Paris, Imprimerie Villain et Bar, 1931.
Aspe-Fleurimont, *La Guinée française*. Paris, Challamel, 1900.
Augagneur (Victor), *Erreurs et brutalités coloniales*. Paris, Ed. Montaigne, 1927.
— 'Le mouvement de la population en Afrique Equatoriale Française', *Revue d'hygiène*, vol. 46, no. 6, pp. 509–40.
— Voir: Afrique Equatoriale Française.
Augier (Ch.) et Renard (Ch.), *Le Régime douanier colonial*. Paris, Ed. des Lois nouvelles, 1914.
Aymerich (General), *La Conquête du Cameroun*. Paris, Payot, 1933.
Barot (Dr.), *Guide pratique de l'Européen dans l'Afrique occidentale*. Paris Flammarion, 1902.
Basset et X . . . : 'Ce qui se passe au Congo', *La Revue*, XXXVIII, 1901, pp. 337–50 and 459–73.
Beslier (G. G.), *Le Sénégal*. Paris, Payot, 1935.
Betts (R. F.), *Assimilation and Association in French Colonial Theory (1840–1914)*. New York University Press, 1961.
Bohn (Frédéric), *Le Développement économique de nos colonies d'Afrique occidentale*. Marseille, 1898.
— *C.F.A.O.: Rapport adressé à M. Cotelle, conseiller d'Etat, président de la Commission des concessions coloniales*. Marseille, Imprimerie marseillaise, 1900.
Boisboissel (Y. de), 'Origine et historique sommaire des unités de tirailleurs et spahis sénégalais et soudanais', *Revue internationale d'histoire militaire*. Dakar, 1956.
Boni (Nazi), *Crépuscule des temps anciens*. Paris, Présence africaine, 1962.
Bouche (Denise), 'Les villages de liberté en A.O.F.', *Bull. I.F.A.N.*, 1949, nos. 3–4, pp. 491–540, and 1950, no. 1, pp. 135–215.
— *Les villages de liberté en Afrique noire française, 1887–1910*. Paris-The Hague, Mouton, 1968.
Bourdarie (Paul), 'La colonisation du Congo français', *Questions diplomatiques et coloniales*, 4e année, IX, 1 Jan., 1900, pp. 1–13.
Boutillier (J. L.), 'Les captifs en A.O.F. (1903–1905)', *Bull. I.F.A.N.*, XXX-B, 2 April, 1968, pp. 513–35.
Britsch (A.), *Pour le Congo français: La dernière mission de Brazza*. Paris, L. de Soye et fils, 1906.
Bruhat (J.), 'Jaurès devant le problème colonial', *Cahiers internationaux*, March, 1958, pp. 43–62.
Brunschwig (Henri), *Mythes et réalités de l'impérialisme colonial français*. Paris, A. Colin, 1960. As *Myths and Realities of French Imperialism*, London, Pall Mall Press, New York, Praeger, 1965.
— 'Politique et économie dans l'Empire français d'Afrique noire', *Journal of African History*, XI, 3, pp. 401–17.
Caillaux (Joseph), *Agadir. Ma politique extérieure*. Paris, Albin Michel, 1919.
[Cameroun] *La Conquête du Cameroun et du Togo*. Paris, Imprimerie nationale, 1931.
Cario (Louis) et Régismanset (Charles), *La Concurrence des colonies à la métropole*. Paris, Challamel, 1906.

Chailley (Commandant Marcel), *Histoire de l'Afrique occidentale*. Paris, Berger-Levrault, 1968.

Chailley-Bert (J.), *Dix années de politique coloniale*. Paris, Armand Colin, 1902.

Challaye (Félicien), *Le Congo français. La question internationale du Congo*. Paris, Alcan, 1909.

— *Un aspirant dictateur: André Tardieu*. Paris, Editions de la Révolution prolétarienne, 1930.

— *Souvenirs sur la colonisation*. Paris, Picard, 1935.

Chudeau (R.), 'Le grand commerce indigène de l'Afrique occidentale', *Bull. Soc. de Géographie commerciale de Paris*, 1910, pp. 398–412.

Collery (M.), 'Origine historique des cantons de la subdivision d'Athiémé', *Etudes dahoméennes*, VIII, 1952, pp. 89–108.

[Colonies] *Les Colonies et la défense nationale*. Paris, Challamel, 1916.

Cookey (S. J. S.), 'The Concession Policy in the French Congo and the British Reaction, 1898–1906', *Journal of African History*, 1966, VII, 2, pp. 263–78.

Coquery-Vidrovitch (C.), 'Les idées économiques de Brazza et les premières tentatives de compagnies de colonisation au Congo français (1885–1898)', *Cahiers d'Etudes africaines*, 1965, V, 1, No. 17, pp. 57–82.

— 'Quelques problèmes posés par les choix économiques des grandes compagnies concessionaires du Congo français', *Bulletin de la Sté. d'histoire moderne*, 1968, 15e série, No. 5, pp. 2–18.

— 'L'échec d'une tentative économique: l'impôt de capitation au service des compagnies concessionaires du "Congo français" (1900–9)', *Cahiers d'Etudes africaines*, 1968, VIII, 1, No. 29, pp. 96–109.

Cornet (Capitaine), *Au Tchad*. Paris, Plon, 1910.

Cosnier (Henri), *L'Ouest africain français*. Paris, Larose, 1921.

Cousin (Albert), *Concessions congolaises*. Paris, Challamel, 1901.

Coutouly (F. de), 'Le cercle de Kadé-Touba', *A.F., R.C.*, 1916, no. 4, p. 96.

Crespin (M.), 'Alpha Yaya et M. Frézouls', *Revue indigène*, 1906, no. 2, pp. 45–6.

— 'La question du Coniagui', *Revue indigène*, 1906, no. 4, pp. 88–93.

Crowder (Michael), *West Africa under Colonial Rule*. London, Hutchinson, 1968.

Cuvillier-Fleury (Henry), *La Mise en valeur du Congo français*. Paris, Larose, 1904.

Cuvillier-Fleury (Robert), *La Main-d'œuvre dans les colonies françaises de l'Afrique occidentale et du Congo*. Paris, Sirey, 1907.

Daigre (R. P.), *Oubangui-Chari, témoignage sur son évolution (1900–40)*. Issoudun, Dillen et Cie., 1947.

Debrand (Lieutenant), *La Conduite des petits détachements en Afrique équatoriale*. Paris, Fournier, 1911.

Deherme (G.), *L'A.O.F., action politique, économique et sociale*. Paris, Bloud, 1908.

Delaisi (Francis), 'Comment on lance une conquête coloniale', *Le Crapouillot*, special number: *Expéditions coloniales. Leurs dessous, leurs atrocités*, by F. Delaisi, A. Malraux, Galtier-Boissière, Jan., 1936, p. 47.

R

Desbordes (J. G.), *L'Immigration libano-syrienne en A.O.F.* Poitiers, Regnault, 1938.

Désiré-Vuillemin (G.), *Contribution à l'histoire de la Mauritanie.* Dakar, Ed. Clairafrique, 1962.

Duboc (General), *La Mauritanie.* Paris, Fournier, 1935.

Dumas (Charles), *Libérez les indigènes, ou renoncez aux colonies.* Paris, Eugène Figuière et Cie., 1914.

Etienne (Eugène), *Les Compagnies de colonisation.* Paris, Challamel, 1897 (Collection of articles published in *Le Temps*).

— *Son œuvre coloniale, algérienne et politique (1888–1906).* Paris, Librairie de *La Dépêche coloniale*, 1907 (vol. I), and Paris, Flammarion, n.d. (vol. II).

Ferrandi (Lieutenant-Colonel Jean), *La Conquête du Cameroun-Nord.* Paris, Charles-Lavauzelle, 1928.

— *Le Centre-africain français: Tchad, Borkou, Ennedi. Leur conquête.* Paris, Charles-Lavauzelle, 1930.

Fillot (Henri), 'Alpha Yaya et M. Frézouls', *Revue indigène*, 1906, no. 4, pp. 85–8.

Forgeron (J. B.), *Le Protectorat en Afrique occidentale française et les chefs indigènes.* Bordeaux, Y. Cadoret, 1920.

Fralon, Capitaine, 'Le siège de Tabi, dernier épisode de la pacification du Soudan, octobre-novembre 1920', *Revue militaire de l'A.O.F.*

François (G.), 'L'Afrique occidentale française en 1908', *Questions diplomatiques et coloniales*, XXVII, 1 April, 1909, pp. 425–37.

Ganiage (Jean) and Deschamps (Hubert), *L'Afrique au XXe siècle (1900–1965).* Paris, Sirey, 1966.

Gann (L. H.) and Duignan (Peter), *Colonialism in Africa (1870–1960).* Cambridge University Press, 2 vols., 1969.

Garcia (Luc), 'Les mouvements de résistance au Dahomey (1914–1917)', *Cahiers d'Etudes africaines*, 1970, X, 1, No. 37, pp. 144–78.

Gnankambary (Blami), 'La révolte bobo de 1916 dans le cercle de Dédougou', *Notes et Documents voltaïques*, 3 (4), July–Sept., 1970, pp. 56–87.

Girault (Arthur), *The colonial Tariff Policy of France.* Oxford, Clarendon Press, 1916

[Guerre] *Historique des troupes coloniales pendant la guerre de 1914–1918.* Paris, Charles-Lavauzelle, 1922.

— *Les Contingents coloniaux.* Paris, Imprimerie nationale, 1931.

— *Les Troupes coloniales pendant la guerre 1914–1918.* Paris, Imprimerie nationale, 1931.

Gueye (Lamine), *De la situation politique des Sénégalais originaires des communes de plein exercice.* Paris, Ed. de la Vie universitaire, 1922.

Guignard (A.), 'Zig-zags en A.O.F.', *A.F.*, 1912, no. 8, pp. 309–16.

Hargreaves (John D.), *West Africa: the Former French States.* Englewood Cliffs (N.J.), Prentice-Hall, 1967.

Harmand (Jules), *Domination et colonisation.* Paris, Flammarion, 1910.

Harris (Joseph E.), 'Protest and Resistance to the French in Fouta-Djallon', *Genève-Afrique*, VIII, 1, 1969, pp. 3–18.

Hauser (Henri), *Colonies allemandes, impériales et spontanées.* Paris, Nony, 1900.

[Haut-Sénégal-et-Niger] *Rapport d'ensemble sur la situation de la colonie du* —, *1906*. Bordeaux, Gounouilhou, 1909.

Hébert (Jean), 'Révoltes en Haute-Volta de 1914 à 1918', *Notes et Documents voltaïques*, 3 (4), July–Sept., 1970, pp. 3–55.

Henry (Yves), *Le Caoutchouc dans l'Afrique occidentale française*. Paris, Challamel, 1907.

Hervet (G.), *Le Commerce extérieur de l'Afrique occidentale française*. Paris, Larose, 1911.

Hilaire-Mamie (G.), *Les Douanes en Afrique occidentale française*. Paris, Jouve 1910.

Histoire et Epopée des troupes coloniales. Paris, Les Presses modernes, 1956.

Hubert (Lucien), *L'Eveil d'un monde. L'œuvre de la France en Afrique occidentale française*. Paris, Alcan, 1909.

Jeaugeon (R.), 'Les sociétés d'exploitation au Congo et l'opinion française de 1890 à 1906', *Revue française d'histoire d'Outre-mer*, 1962, pp. 353–437.

Joseph (Gaston), *Manuel des palabres*. Bingerville, Imprimerie du gouvernement, 1916.

Kersaint-Gilly (F. de), 'Essai sur l'évolution de l'esclavage en A.O.F.', *B.C.E.H.S.*, 1924, no. 3, pp. 469–78.

Lacheroy (colonel), *Les Libano-syriens en A.O.F.* Paris, C.M.I.S.O.M. 1953 (duplicated).

Lagrillière-Beauclerc (Eugène), *Mission au Sénégal et au Soudan*. Paris, Ch. Taillandier, n.d. (1898).

Lefébure (J.), *Le Régime des concessions au Congo*. Paris, 1904 (thesis).

Lefranc (Georges), *Le mouvement socialiste sous la IIIe République*. Paris, Payot, 1964.

Lorin (Henri), 'La crise du Congo français', *Questions diplomatiques et coloniales*, no. 91, 1 Dec., 1900, pp. 674–85.

Louis (Paul), *Le colonialisme*. Paris, Société nouvelle de Librairie et d'Edition, 1905.

Madrolle (Claudius), *En Guinée*. Paris, H. Le Soudier, 1895.

Maguet (Edgar), 'La condition juridique des terres en Guinée française', *A.F.*, *R.C.*, 1926, no. 3, pp. 121–6.

— *Concessions domaniales dans les colonies françaises*. Villefranche. 1930 (thesis).

Maillard (Jean), 'Au Ouadaï, de 1909 à 1912', *Encyclopédie mensuelle d'outre-mer*, Nov., 1953.

Mangin (Ch.), *Troupes noires*. Coulommiers, Brodard, 1909.

— *La Force noire*. Paris, Hachette, 1910.

Martin (G.), Lebeuf (A.) et Roubaud (A.), *Rapport de la mission d'études de la maladie du sommeil au Congo français (1906–1908)*. Paris, Masson, 1909.

Marty (Paul), *La Politique indigène du gouverneur général Ponty*. Paris, E. Leroux, 1915.

Massiou (Jacques), *Les Grandes concessions au Congo français*. Paris, Sagot, 1920 (thesis).

Masson (Paul), *Marseille et la colonisation française*. Marseille, Barlatier, 1906.

Mazenot (Georges), 'L'occupation du bassin de la Likouala-Mossaka, 1909–1914', *Cahiers d'études africaines*, 1966, VI, 2, No. 22, pp. 268–307.

Mbaye (Gueye), 'L'affaire Chautemps (avril 1904) et la suppression de l'esclavage de case au Sénégal', *Bull. I.F.A.N.*, XXVII-B, 1965, 3–4, pp. 543–72.

Meinecke (G.), *Wirtschaftliche Kolonialpolitik*. Berlin, Deutscher Kolonialverlag, 1900, 2 br.

Mermeix, *La Chronique de l'an 1911*. Paris, Grasset, 1912.

Mille (Pierre) and Challaye (Félicien), 'Les deux Congo devant la Belgique et devant la France', *Cahiers de la Quinzaine*, No. 16, Series 7, 1906.

Mondjannagni (A.), 'Quelques aspects historiques, économiques et politiques de la frontière Dahomey-Nigeria', *E.D.*, new series, 3e trimestre, 1963, 1, pp. 17–58.

Morel (E. D.), *The British Case in French Congo*. London, Heinemann, 1903.

— *Red Rubber*. London, Unwin, 1907.

— *The Black-Man's Burden*. Manchester-London, n.d.

Mveng (Englebert), *Histoire du Cameroun*. Paris, Présence Africaine, 1963.

Newbury (C. W.), 'An early Enquiry into Slavery and Captivity in Dahomey', *Zaire*, XIV, 1, 1960, pp. 53–68.

— 'The formation of the Government of French West Africa', *Journal of African History*, I, 1, 1960, pp. 111–28.

'Niger, Les révoltes de 1906 au', *Revue militaire de l'A.O.F.*, No. 41, 15 April, 1939, pp. 1–13.

Olivesi (A.), 'Les socialistes marseillais et le problème colonial', Mouvement social, No. 46, Jan.–March, 1964, pp. 27–66.

Paré (Isaac), 'Les Allemands à Foumban, *Abbia* (Yaoundé), March–June, 1966, No. 12–13, pp. 211–31.

Picrochole, *Le Sénégal drôlatique*. Paris, Imprimerie Paul Dupont, 1896.

Possessions du Congo français et dépendances. *Rapport d'ensemble sur la situation générale en 1906*. Paris, Larose, 1908.

Prévaudeau (Albert), *Joost Van Vollenhoven*. Paris, Larose, 1953.

Rapport confidentiel au G∴ O∴ de France et aux RR∴ LL∴ de la Fédération. Dakar, Imprimerie de la L∴. *L'Etoile occidentale*, 1904.

Rébérioux (Madeleine), 'La gauche socialiste française, la "guerre sociale" et le "mouvement socialiste" face au problème colonial', *Mouvement social*, No. 46, Jan.–March, 1964, pp. 91–104.

— and Haupt (G.), *Le socialisme et la question coloniale avant 1914*. 'L'attitude de l'Internationale', *Mouvement social*, No. 45, Oct.–Dec., 1963, pp. 7–38.

Reclus (O.), *Lâchons l'Asie, prenons l'Afrique*. Paris, Librairie universelle, 1904.

Régismanset (Charles), *Essai sur la colonisation*. Paris, Mercure de France, 1907.

— *Questions coloniales (1900–12)*. Paris, Larose, 1912, 2nd series (1912–19), 2 vols., Paris, Larose, 1923.

Reichskolonialministerium, *Deutsche und französische Eingeborenenbehandlung*. Berlin, Dietrich Reimer, 1919.

Rotté (Charles), *Les Chemins de fer et tramways des colonies*. Paris, Larose, 1910.

Rouard de Card (E.), *Traité de délimitation concernant l'Afrique française*. Paris, Pédone, 1900.
— Supplément 1910–13. Paris, Pédone, 1913.
— Supplément 1914–25. Paris, Pédone, 1926.
Rouget (F.), *La Guinée*. Corbeil, Ed. Crété, 1906.
— *L'Expansion coloniale française et le commerce austro-allemand*. Melun, Imprimerie administrative, 1916 et 1917.
Roux (E.), *Manuel des administrateurs et du personnel des affaires indigènes de la colonie du Sénégal*. Paris, Challamel, 1911.
Saintoyant (Jules), *L'Affaire du Congo (1905)*. Paris, Editions de l'Epi, 1960.
Sangha-Oubangui (*La compagnie forestière*). *Ses origines, ses méthodes, ses résultats, ses aspirations*. Paris, Imprimerie Chaix, 1911.
Séché (Alphonse), *Les Noirs*. Paris, Payot, 1919.
Seidel (A.), *Deutsch-Kamerun*, Berlin, Meidinger, 1906.
Servel (André), *Etude sur l'organisation administrative et financière de l'Afrique équatoriale française*. Paris, Larose, 1912 (thesis).
Simon (Marc), *Souvenirs de brousse*, 2 vols. (1905–10 and 1910–12), 1961.
— *Souvenirs de brousse: Dahomey-Côte d'Ivoire (1905–1918)*. Paris, Nouvelles Editions latines, 1965.
Soubbotine (V. A.), *French Colonial Expansion at the End of the Nineteenth Century (Equatorial Africa and islands in the Indian Ocean)*. Moscow, Ed. orientalistes, 1962 (in Russian).
Stoecker (Helmuth), *Kamerun unter deutscher Kolonialherrschaft*. Berlin, Rütten und Loening, 1960.
Suret-Canale (Jean), 'La Guinée dans le système colonial', *Présence africaine XXIX*, Dec., 1959–Jan., 1960, pp. 9–44.
— 'L'anticolonialisme en France sous la IIIe République: Paul Vigné d'Octon', *Cahiers internationaux*, no. 107, Sept.–Oct., 1959, pp. 57–68.
— 'L'Economie de traite en Afrique noire sous domination française (1900–1914)', *Recherches africaines*, 1960, no. 2, pp. 3–39.
— 'A propos du Ouali de Goumba', *Recherches Africaines*, 1964, Nos. 1–2–3–4, pp. 160–4.
Tardieu (André), *Le Mystère d'Agadir*. Paris, Calman-Lévy, 1912.
Terrier (A.) et Mourey (Ch.), *L'Œuvre de la IIIe République en Afrique occidentale, l'expansion française et la formation territoriale*. Paris, Larose, 1910.
Teullière (G.), 'Alpha Yaya et la politique indigène', *Revue indigène*, 1911, pp. 615–20.
Thomas (R.), 'La politique socialiste et le problème colonial de 1905 à 1920', *Revue française d'histoire d'Outre-mer*, 1960, pp. 213–45.
Tisserant (Father Charles), *Ce que j'ai connu de l'esclavage en Oubangui-Chari*. Paris, Plon, 1955.
Toqué (Georges), *Les Massacres du Congo*. Paris, 1907.
Vallier (Capitaine), *L'Organisation militaire du Congo français*. Paris, Charles-Lavauzelle, 1909.
Venel et Bouchez, *Guide de l'officier méhariste*. Paris, Larose, 1910.
Verdat (Marguerite), 'Le Ouali de Goumba', *Etudes guinéennes*, 1949, no. 3, pp. 3–81.

Vigné d'Octon (Paul), *Les Crimes coloniaux de la IIIe République. La Sueur du burnous.* Paris, Ed. de la Guerre sociale, 1911.

— *La Nouvelle gloire du sabre.* Marseille, Petite Bibliothèque du Mutilé, n.d.

Vignon (Louis), *Un Programme de politique coloniale. Les questions indigènes.* Paris, Plon, 1919.

Vincent (J.F.), 'Traditions historiques chez les Djem de Sonanké (République du Congo-Brazzaville)', *Revue française d'Histoire d'Outre-Mer,* L, 1963, pp. 64–73.

Violette (Maurice), *A la veille d'Agadir. La N'Goko-Sangha.* Paris, Larose, 1914.

Vivier de Streel (E. du), 'Le caoutchouc en Afrique équatoriale', *Bull. Société de Géographie commerciale de Paris,* 1912, pp. 5–31.

Willard (Claude), *Les Guesdistes.* Paris, Editions sociales, 1965.

Wondji (Christophe), 'La Côte d'Ivoire occidentale, période de pénétration pacifique (1890–1908)', *Revue française d'histoire d'Outre-Mer,* L, 180–1, 1963, pp. 346–81.

Zévaès (Alexandre), *Les Guesdistes* (vol. III de l'*Histoire des partis socialistes en France*). Paris, Marcel Rivière, 1911.

PART II

CHAPTER I

ECONOMIC PERIODICALS

Annuaire S.E.F. Cote Desfossés.

Annuaires statistiques de l'A.O.F. 1917–38.

Annuaires statistiques de l'A.E.F., 1936–50.

Annuaire statistique de la F.O.M. Paris, Imprimerie nationale, 1949.

Bulletin économique de l'A.E.F.

Bulletin de l'Agence économique de l'A.O.F. 1924–36.

Bulletin trimestriel de l'Association cotonnière coloniale 1933–9.

Rapports annuels à la S.D.N. (Cameroons and Togo).

Suppléments statistiques au 'J.O.' de l'A.O.F. 1924–36.

A.O.F. [Le redressement économique de l'—]. Supplement to *La Presse coloniale,* 30, 10, 1935,

A.O.F. [Réglementation du travail indigène en —]. Porto Novo, Imprimerie du Gouvernement, 1929.

[Alimentation] *Conférence interafricaine sur l'alimentation et la nutrition.* Dschang, Cameroun, 1949. French documentation, 1950.

Baillaud (Emile), *L'Organisation économique de l'Afrique occidentale française.* Marseille, Institut colonial, 1936.

Barbé (Raymond), 'Caractéristiques du colonialisme français', *Cahiers du Communisme,* Sept., 1960, no. 9, pp. 1376–417.

Bélime (E.), *Les Travaux du Niger,* Gouvernement général de l'A.O.F., 1940.

Bonafos (Capitaine V.), 'Taoudenni hier et aujourd'hui', *Revue militaire de l'A.O.F.,* 15 April, 1934, No. 21, pp. 1–24.

Bosc (Philippe), 'Résultats et évolution de l'aide technique et de la coopération ferroviaires apportées par la France aux pays d'outremer', *C.R.S. Acad. Sc. outre-mer,* XIX, June–July, 1959, V–VI, pp. 294–304.

Boyer (Marcel), *Les Sociétés indigènes de prévoyance, de secours et de prêts mutuels agricoles en A.O.F.* Paris, Domat-Montchrestien, 1935.

Cabot (Jean), 'La culture du coton au Tchad', *Annales de Géographie*, 1957, pp. 499–508.

Cap Vert ['La presqu'île du —']. *Etudes sénégalaises*, no. 1, 1949.

Carbon (J. de), 'La culture du coton en milieu africain' (*West African Cotton Research Conference, held at the Regional Research Station*). Ministry of Agriculture, Samaru, Northern Nigeria, 1957, pp. 50–3.

Carsow (Michel), *Quelques Aspects du commerce impérial de la France.* 2 vols., Paris, Geuthner, 1935.

Castro (J. de), *Le Livre noir de la faim.* Paris, Editions ouvrières, 1961.

Cépède (M.) and Lengellé (M.), *L'Economie alimentaire du globe.* Paris, Librairie de Médicis, 1953.

Chabas (J.), 'Le régime foncier coutumier en A.O.F.', *Annales africaines*, 1957, pp. 53–78.

— 'De la transformation des doits fonciers coutumiers en droit de propriété', *Annales africaines*, 1959, pp. 73–108.

Champaud (Jacques), 'La navigation fluviale sur le Moyen-Niger', *C.O.M.*, 1961, pp. 255–92.

Charbonneau (J. and R.), *Marchés et marchands d'Afrique noire.* Paris, la Colombe, 1961.

Chardy, 'Le chemin de fer Thiès-Niger', *Revue militaire de l'A.O.F.*, 1930–1, Nos. 7–8, pp. 45–58.

Chpirt (A. I.), *African Resources in Raw Materials (1913–58).* Moscow, Editions orientalistes, 1961 (in Russian).

Cousturier (Lucie), 'La forêt du Haut-Niger', *Les Cahiers d'aujourd'hui*, no. 12, Paris, 1925.

Dakar [*Le port de—*], Dakar, Grande Imprimerie africaine, 1929.

Dampierre (E. de), 'Coton noir, café blanc', *Cahiers d'études africaines*, no. 2, May 1960, pp. 128–47.

David (Ph.), 'Fraternité d'hivernage (le contrat de navétanat)', *Présence africaine*, XXXI, April–May, 1960, pp. 45–57.

Dresch (Jean), 'Les trusts en Afrique noire', *Servir la France*, 1946, p. 30.

— 'Questions ouest-africaines', *Boletim cultural da Guiné portuguesa*, no. 17, Jan, 1950, pp. 1–21.

— 'Recherches sur les investissements dans l'Union française outre-mer', *B.A.G.F.*, 1953, no. 231–2, pp. 2–13.

Durand (Huguette), *Essai sur la conjoncture de l'Afrique noire.* Paris, Dalloz, 1957.

Eboué (Félix), *Les Peuples de l'Oubangui-Chari.* Paris, Comité de l'Afrique française, 1933.

Edouard (Father), *Sur les pistes de l'Oubangui. La mission de Berberati en Oubangui-Chari.* Grenoble, Allier, 1954.

Faure (Claude), *Histoire de la presqu'île du Cap Vert et des origines de Dakar.* Paris, Larose, 1914.

Fidel (Camille), 'L'Afrique occidentale française et la crise économique', *La Chronique coloniale*, Feb., 1932.

Fouquet (Joseph), 'La traite des arachides dans le pays de Kaolack', *Etudes sénégalaises*, no. 8, 1958.

Frankel (S. Herbert), *Capital investment in Africa*. London, Oxford University Press, 1938.

Gayet (G.), 'Les villages de colonisation de l'Office du Niger', Ve. *C.I.A.O.* Abidjan, 1953, pp. 127–30.

Gide (André), *Voyage au Congo*. Paris, Gallimard, 1927.

— *Retour du Tchad*. Paris, Gallimard, 1928.

Goulven (J.), 'Les ports maritimes de l'Afrique occidentale', *Bull. Soc. Géogr. commerciale de Paris*, 1913, pp. 505–44.

Guillemin (R.), 'Evolution de l'agriculture autochtone dans les savanes de l'Oubangui', *Agronomie tropicale*, 1956, No. 1, pp. 40–61, No. 2, pp. 143–72, No. 3, pp. 276–309.

Harroy (J. P.), *Afrique, terre qui meurt*. Brussels, Marcel Hayet, 1944.

Herbart (P.), *Le Chancre du Niger*. Paris, Gallimard, 1939.

Hoarau-Desruisseaux (Ch.), *Aux colonies*. Paris, Larose, 1911.

Homet (Marcel), *Congo, terre de souffrances*. Paris, Ed. Montaigne, 1934.

— *Afrique noire, terre inquiète*. Paris, Peyronnet, 1939.

Laurelli, *De l'application des régimes douaniers dans les colonies*. Paris, Domat-Montchrestien, 1939.

Lelong (M.H.),*Ces Hommes qu'on appelle anthropophages*. Paris,Ed.Alsatia,1946.

— *N'Zérékoré. L'évangile en forêt guinéenne*. Paris, La Librairie missionnaire, 1946.

Lenoir (Robert), *Les Concessions foncières en Afrique occidentale française et équatoriale* (sic.) Paris, Librairie technique et économique, 1937.

Londres (Albert), *Terre d'ébène*. Paris, Imprimerie Busson, 1929.

Manot (Michel R. O.), *L'Aventure de l'or et du Congo-Océan*. Paris, Librairie Secrétan, 1950.

Maunier (René), *Eléments d'économie coloniale*. Paris, Sirey, 1943.

Mérat (Louis), *Fictions . . . et réalités coloniales*. Paris, Sirey, 1946.

Mercier (René), *Le Travail obligatoire dans les colonies françaises*. Vesoul, Imprimerie nouvelle, 1933 (thesis).

Mersadier (Yves), 'La crise de l'arachide sénégalaise au début des années trente', *Bull. I.F.A.N.*, XXVIII-B, 3–4, 1966, pp. 826–77.

Monmarson (Raoul), *L'Equateur français*. Paris, Editions Baudinière, 1932.

— *L'Afrique noire et son destin*. Paris, Ed. Francex, 1950.

Morazé (Charles), 'Dakar', *Annales de Géographie*, XIV, 1936, pp. 607–31.

Ninine (Jules), *La main d'oeuvre indigène dans les colonies africaines*, (thesis) Paris, 1932.

Perrot (E.), *Où en est l'Afrique occidentale française?* Paris, Larose, 1939.

Peter (G.), *L'Effort français au Sénégal*. Paris, De Boccard, 1933.

Poquin (J. J.), *Les Relations économiques extérieures des pays d'Afrique noire de l'Union française (1925–55)*. Paris, A. Colin, 1957.

Ports de la côte occidentale d'afrique (Les). Bordeaux, F. Pech, 1929.

Portères (R.) and Pales (L.), *Les Sels alimentaires*. Dakar, Gouvernement général de l'A.O.F., n.d.

Rau (E.), 'La question des terrains de Tound', *Annales africaines*, 1956, pp. 141–63.

Rivière (J.), 'Etude commerciale des riz de la vallée du Niger', *Suppl. au 'J.O.' de l'A.O.F.*, 1911, pp. 151–86.

Rondet-Saint (Maurice), *Un voyage en A.O.F.* Paris, S.E.G.M.C., 1930.

[Rossignol] *Les Exportations agricoles des cercles de l'A.O.F. et du Togo.* Paris, Direction des Affaires économiques du Secrétariat d'Etat aux Colonies, 1944.

Rouch (Jean), 'Problèmes relatifs à l'étude des migrations traditionnelles et des migrations actuelles en Afrique occidentale', *Bull. I.F.A.N.*, XXII-B, 3–4, 1960, pp. 369–78.

Saint-Genest (Jean), *Un Voyage de M. Albert Sarraut, ministre des Colonies, en Afrique.* Paris, Imprimerie de *La Dépêche coloniale*, 1922.

Sarraut (Albert), *La Mise en valeur des colonies françaises.* Paris, Payot, 1923.

— *Grandeur et servitude coloniales.* Paris, Ed. du Sagittaire, 1931.

Sautter (Gilles), *De l'Atlantique au fleuve Congo.* Paris, Mouton, 1966, 2 vols.

— 'Notes sur la construction du Congo-Océan', *Cahiers d'Etudes africaines*, VII, 1967, pp. 219–99.

Schaller (A. M.), *Le Chemin de fer transsaharien.* Paris-Strasbourg, Istra, 1932.

Sociétés indigènes de prévoyance de l'A.E.F. [*Le fonctionnement des—*]. Brazzaville, Imprimerie du gouvernement général, 1950.

Spitz (Georges), *Sansanding, les irrigations du Niger.* Paris, S.E.G.M.C., 1949.

Sylla (Assane), 'Vérités sur Dakar', *Présence africaine*, XXIII, Dec., 1958–Jan., 1959, pp. 81–7.

Vidailhet (Jean), *Le Transsaharien.* Paris, Larose, 1934.

Vivier de Streel (E. du), 'L'Afrique équatoriale française et la crise', *Institut colonial international*, XXIIe session, Bruxelles, 1933, pp. 355–82.

Volle (M.), 'Le Niger', *Marchés coloniaux*, No. 47, 5 Oct., 1946, pp. 1046–7.

CHAPTER II

A.E.F. [*L'enseignement en—*]. Historique et organisation générale. Paris, Agence économique de l'A.E.F., 1931.

Afrique Occidentale Française [*Le redressement économique de l'*—]. Supplément à *La Presse coloniale* (30 Oct., 1935).

Annet (Armand), *Je suis gouverneur d'outre-mer.* Paris, Ed. du Conquistador, 1957.

Arnou (Father), 'Le problème social aux colonies', *XXIIèmes semaines sociales de France*, 1930, pp. 341–61.

Asmis (Dr.), *La Condition juridique des indigènes dans l'Afrique occidentale française.* Paris, Marchal et Godde, 1910.

Basset (A.), Boiron (H.) et Basset (Mme M.), 'A propos d'une enquête sur le pian en Haute-Volta', *Bull. Soc. médicale d'Afrique noire*, V, 2, 2e trimestre, 1960, pp. 186–90.

Baudu (Paul), *Vieil Empire, jeune Eglise: Mgr. J. Thévenoud (1878–1949).* Paris, Ed. de la Savane, 1957.

Bebey-Eyidi (Dr.), *Le Vainqueur de la maladie du sommeil, Eugène Jamot.* Paris, 1951.

Beurdeley (E.), 'La justice indigène en A.O.F.', *A.F., R.C.*, 1916, no. 3, pp. 45–57.

Beyriès (J.), 'Evolution sociale et culturelle des collectivités nomades de Mauritanie', *B.C.E.H.S.*, 1937, no. 4, pp. 465–81.

R*

Boiron (H.) et Basset (A.), 'A la recherche de la syphilis endémique', *Bull. Soc. médicale d'Afrique noire*, V, 3, 3e trimestre 1960, pp. 328–33.

Bouchaud (Father Joseph), *L'Eglise en Afrique noire*. Paris-Genève, La Palatine, 1958.

Bouffard (Dr.), 'Fonctionnement des services de santé ... de Côte d'Ivoire', *B.C.E.H.S.*, 1927, no. 3–4, pp. 368–419.

Brévié (Jules), *Circulaires sur la politique et l'administration indigènes en A.O.F.* Gorée, Imprimerie du gouvernement général, 1935.

— *Trois études*. Gorée, Imprimerie du gouvernement général, 1936.

Carde (Jules), 'La réorganisation de l'enseignement en Afrique occidentale française', *Revue indigène*, May–June 1924, nos. 185–6, pp. 111–29.

Cartier (Henri), *Comment la France 'civilise' ses colonies*. Paris, Bureau d'Editions, 1932.

Cazanove (Dr.), 'Memento de psychiatrie coloniale africaine', *B.C.E.H.S.*, 1927, no. 1, pp. 133–77.

Chabas (J.), 'La justice indigène en A.O.F.', *Annales africaines*, 1954, pp. 91–152.

— 'La justice européenne en A.O.F.', *Annales africaines*, 1955, pp. 79–108.

Chazelas (Victor), *Cameroun et Togo*. Paris, S.E.G.M.C., 1931.

Colonisation et conscience chrétienne. Paris, A. Fayard, 1953.

Cornevin (Robert), 'L'évolution des chefferies dans l'Afrique noire d'expression française', *Recueil Penant*, 1961, no. 686, pp. 235–50, no. 687, pp. 379–88, and no. 688, pp. 539–56.

[Côte d'Ivoire (Colonie de la)] *Programme d'action économique, politique et sociale*. Abidjan, Imprimerie du gouvernement, 1933.

Coulibaly (Ouezzin), 'L'enseignement en Afrique noire', *Europe*, no. 41–2, May–June, 1949, pp. 56–70.

Crowder (Michael), 'Indirect Rule, French and British style', *Africa*, XXXIV, 3, 1964, pp. 197–205.

Delafosse (Maurice), 'Etats d'âme d'un colonial', *A.F.*, 1909, nos. 2–11.

Delavignette (Robert), *Les Vrais chefs de l'Empire*. Paris, Gallimard, 1939. (Republished in 1946 with the title *Service africain*.)

— *Christianisme et colonialisme*. Paris, A. Fayard, 1960.

Deschamps (Hubert), *Méthodes et doctrines coloniales de la France*. Paris, Armand Colin, 1953.

Doublet (P.), Traité de legislation fiscales des T.O.M. 2 vols., Paris, Sirey, 1952.

Ducatillon (R. P.), 'Théologiede la colonisation', *L'Action populaire*, July 1955.

Duchêne (Albert), *Histoire des finances coloniales de la France*. Paris, Payot, 1938.

Duffner (capitaine), 'Croyances et coutumes religieuses chez les Guerzés et les Manons de la Guinée française', *B.C.E.H.S.*, 1934, no. 4, pp. 525–63.

Eboué (Félix), *Politique indigène de l'A.E.F.* Brazzaville, Imprimerie officielle, 1941.

François (G.), 'L'enseignement en Afrique occidentale', *A.F.*, *R.C.*, no. 1–2, 1919, pp. 34–9.

Galliard (Prof. H.), 'Eugène Jamot', *Europe-France Outre-mer*, 2e trim. 1959, pp. 12–14.

Girault (Arthur), *Principes de colonisation et de législation coloniale*. 5 vols., Paris, 1927–31.

Goyau (Georges), *La Congrégation du Saint-Esprit*. Paris, Grasset 1937.

— *La France missionnaire dans les cinq parties du monde*. 2 vols., Paris, Plon, 1948.

Hardy (Georges), *Une Conquête morale. L'Enseignement en A.O.F.* Paris, Armand Colin, 1917.

Ingold (F.), *Lec Troupes noires au combat*. Paris, Berger-Levrault, 1940.

Kerillis (Henri de), *De l'Algérie au Dahomey en automobile*. Paris, Plon, 1925.

Körner (Heiko), *Kolonialpolitik und Wirtschaftsentwicklung: das Beispiel französich-Westafrikas*. Stuttgart, Gustav Fischer Verlag, 1965.

Labouret (Henri), *A la Recherche d'une politique indigène dans l'Ouest africain*. Paris, Ed. du Comité de l'Afrique française, 1931.

— *Famine et disettes aux colonies*. Paris, 1938.

Lampué (P.), 'La promulgation des lois et décrets dans les T.O.M.', *Annales africaines*, 1956, pp. 7–26.

Lapeyssonnie (L.), 'Jamot parmi nous', *Médicine tropicale*, XXIII, 4, July–Aug., 1963, pp. 461–9.

Leclerc (R.), 'Problèmes scolaires en A.E.F.', *Bulletin des missions*, XXIII, 3, 3e trimestre 1949, pp. 156–67.

Le Gall et Giordani, *Etat sanitaire de l'Empire français*. Paris, Charles-Lavauzelle, 1940.

Le Révérend (Arlette et Gaston), *Deux saisons au Dahomey*. 1940, published privately; collection of serials in the *Journal de Caen*, from 17 Feb. to 20 Oct., 1939.

Leslie-Buell (Raymond), *The Native Problem in Africa*. 2 vols., New-York, The Macmillan Co., 1928.

Lesourd (Paul), *L'Œuvre civilisatrice et scientifique des missions catholiques dans les colonies françaises*. Paris, Desclée de Brouwer et Cie, 1931.

— *Histoire des missions catholiques*. Paris, Librairie de l'Arc, 1937.

Maillot (L.), 'Notice pour la carte chronologique des principaux foyers de la maladie du sommeil dans les Etats de l'ancienne fédération d'A.E.F.', *Bulletin de l'Institut de Recherches scientifiques au Congo*, 1962, I, pp. 45–54.

Mathis (médecin-général), *L'Œuvre des pastoriens en Afrique noire (A.O.F.)*. Paris, P.U.F., 1946.

Maunier (René), *Sociologie coloniale*. Paris, Domat-Montchrestien, 3 vols., 1932–49.

— *Répétitions écrites de législation coloniale*. Paris, Les Cours de Droit, 1943 (duplicated).

Mazé, *La Collaboration scolaire des gouvernements coloniaux et des missions*. Maison Carrée, 1934.

Méjean (François), *Le Vatican contre la France d'outre-mer*. Paris, Fischbacher, 1957.

Missionnaires d'Afrique (*La société des Pères blancs*). 1 vol., Maison Carrée, 1935.

Moumouni (Abdou), *L'éducation en Afrique*. Paris, F. Maspéro, 1964.

Muraz (médecin-général), *Rapide enquête médicale en A.O.F.* Paris, Masson, 1951.

Padmore (G.), *Les Ouvriers nègres et l'intervention armée antisoviétique.* Petite Bibliothèque de l'Internationale syndicale rouge, XXXII, Paris, n.d.

— *La Vie et les luttes des travailleurs nègres.* Petite Bibliothèque de l'Internationale syndicale rouge, XXXVII, Paris, n.d.

Paillard (Jean), *La Fin des Français en Afrique noire.* Paris, Les Œuvres françaises, 1936.

[Paludisme]. *Rapport de la conférence sur le paludisme en Afrique équatoriale.* Genève, O.M.S., 1951.

Paternot (M.), *Lumière sur la Volta.* Lyon, 1946.

Péchoux (L.), *Le Mandat français sur le Togo.* Paris, A. Pédone, 1939.

Randau (Robert), *Le Chef des porte-plume.* Paris, Ed. du Monde moderne, 1926.

— *Les Terrasses de Tombouctou.* Alger, P. et F. Soubiron, 1933.

Robert (André P.), *L'évolution des coutumes de l'Ouest africain et la législation française.* Paris, Ed. de l'Encyclopédie d'outre-mer, 1955.

Rolland (L.) et Lampué (P.), *Précis de législation coloniale.* Paris, Dalloz, 1940 (3rd ed.).

Rueff (Capitaine), 'L'organisation militaire de l'A.O.F.', *Revue militaire de l'A.O.F.*, No. 1, 1929, pp. 1–8.

Runner (Jean), *Les Droits politiques des indigènes des colonies.* Paris, Larose, 1927.

Ruyssen (R.), *Le Code de l'indigénat en Algérie.* Alger, Victor Heintz, 1908.

Schnapper (B.), 'Les tribunaux musulmans et la politique coloniale au Sénégal', *Revue historique de droit français et étranger*, 1961, no. 1.

Sédès (Jean-Marie), *Le Clergé indigène de l'Empire français.* 2 vols., Paris, Bloud et Gay, 1944.

Solus (Henry), *Traité de la condition des indigènes en droit privé.* Paris, Sirey, 1927.

Suret-Canale (Jean), 'Problèmes de l'enseignement en A.O.F.', *La Pensée*, no. 29, March-April, 1950, pp. 35–52.

Susset (Raymond), *La Vérité sur le Cameroun et l'A.E.F.* Paris, Ed. de la Nouvelle Revue critique, 1934.

Teil (Baron Joseph du), *L'Antialcoolisme aux colonies.* 1911.

Traoré (Bakary), *Le Théâtre négro-africain et ses fonctions sociales.* Paris, Présence africaine, 1958.

Trautmann (René), *Au pays de Batouala*, Paris, Payot, 1922.

[Tuberculosis], *Rapport provisoire sur la tuberculose et la maladie du sommeil en Afrique équatoriale.* Genève, S.D.N., 1923. Rapport complémentaire, Genève, S.D.N., 1925.

Vernier de Byans (J.), *Condition juridique et politique des indigènes.* Paris, Alfred Leclerc, 1906.

CHAPTER III

Afrique Equatoriale Française, Les réalisations coloniales de la France combattante en, (duplicated) 8 Feb., 1943.

Annet (Armand), *Aux Heures troublées de l'Afrique française*. Paris, Ed. du Conquistador, 1952.

Arnaud (R.), *L'Islam et la politique en A.O.F.* 1911.

Balandier (G.), 'Naissance d'un mouvement politico-religieux chez les *Ba-Kongo* du Moyen-Congo', *IIIe. C.I.A.O.*, Ibadan, 1949. Lagos, Nigerian Museum, 1956. The many works of this author, although they have a bearing upon our period, are more directly concerned with the contemporary period, which will be dealt with in a later volume.

Ballard (J. A.), 'Les incidents de 1923 à Porto Novo: la politique à l'époque coloniale', *E.D.*, new series, No. 5, Oct., 1965, pp. 69–87.

Bianquis (J.), 'Le prophète Harris ou dix ans d'histoire religieuse de la Côte d'Ivoire (1914–24)'. *Foi et Vie*, Paris, 16 Nov. and 1 Dec., 1924.

Bonafos, Capitaine, 'Notes marginales prises en étudiant la pacification de la Mauritanie', *Revue militaire de l'A.O.F.*, No. 13, 1 April, 1932, pp. 51–66.

Boulègue, M., 'La pressure au Sénégal avant 1939. Bibliographie', *Bull. I.F.A.N.*, XXVII-B, July–Oct., 1965, 3–4, pp. 715–54.

Bourlon (Abel), 'Actualité des Mourides et du mouridisme', *L'Afrique et l'Asie*, 46, 1959, pp. 10–30.

[Brazzaville] (*La conférence africaine française de* —). Brazzaville, Ed. du Baobab, n.d. (1944).

Chassin (L. M.), *Histoire militaire de la seconde guerre mondiale*. Paris, Payot, 1947.

Chenet (D.), *Qui a sauvé l'Afrique?* Paris, L'Elan, 1949.

Chomé (Jules), *La Passion de Simon Kibangu*. Bruxelles, Les Amis de Présence africaine, 1959.

Chpirt (A. I.), *L'Afrique dans la seconde guerre mondiale*. Moscow, Ed. orientalistes, 1959 (in Russian).

Cluzel-Martinot (Capitaine), 'Une tournée de police au Dahomey en 1923', *Revue militaire de l'A.O.F.*, No. 28, 15 Jan., 1936, pp. 53–71.

Cros (Charles), *La parole est à M. Blaise Diagne*. Paris, 1961.

[Dakar] (*L'agression de* —). Dakar, Haut-Commissariat de l'Afrique française, n.d.

Dehon (Father Emile), *La nouvelle politique coloniale de la France*. Paris, Flammarion, 1945.

Delafosse (Maurice), 'Le Congrès panafricain', *A.F., R.C.*, no. 3–4, 1919, pp. 53–9.

Delafosse (M.) et Poutrin (Dr.), *Enquête coloniale dans l'Afrique française occidentale et équatoriale*. Paris, S.E.G.M.C., 1930.

Deschamps (Hubert), *Traditions orales et archives au Gabon*. Paris, Berger-Levrault, 1962.

Diagne (Abd El Kader), *La Résistance française au Sénégal et en A.O.F.* (duplicated, n.d.).

Doriot (Jacques), *Les Colonies et le communisme*. Paris, Ed. Montaigne, 1929.

Eboué (Felix), *L'Afrique française libre*, n.d.

— *L'A.E.F. et la guerre*. Brazzaville, Ed. du Baobab, 1943.

Gautherot (Gustave), *Le Bolchévisme aux colonies et l'impérialisme rouge*. Paris, Editions de 'La Vague rouge', 1930.

Gavrilov (N.), *Le mouvement de libération en Afrique occidentale*. Moscow, Editions du Progrès, 1965.

Glélé (M. A.), *Naissance d'un Etat noir: le Dahomey*. Paris, Librairie générale de droit et de jurisprudence, 1969.

Gueye (Lamine), *Itinéraire africain*. Paris, Présences africaines, 1966.

Grall (A.), 'Le scorbut à Dakar', *Médecine tropicale*, 1945, no. 3, pp. 255–7.

Ho Chi-Minh (N'guyen Aï Quoc), *Procès de la colonisation française*, Paris 1925 (republished in *Œuvres choisies*, vol. I, Hanoi, Foreign Language Editions, 1960).

Ingold (F.), *L'Epopée Leclerc au Sahara*. Paris, Berger-Levrault, 1945.

Kala-Lobe (Iwije), 'Muna-Moto, cultivateur camerounais', *Présence africaine* no. 37, 2e. trimestre 1961, pp. 90–118.

Klein (M. A.), *Islam amd Imperialism in Senegal*. Stanford University Press, 1968.

Köbben (A.), 'Prophetic Movements as an expression of Social Protest', *Inernational Archiv für Ethnographie*, 49, I, 1960, pp. 117–164.

Langley (J. C.), 'Panafricanism in Paris, 1924–36', *Journal of Modern African Studies*, 7, 4, April, 1969, pp. 69–74.

Larminat (Edgar de), *Chroniques irrévérencieuses*. Paris, Plon, 1962.

Le Cornec (J. L.), *Histoire politique du Tchad de 1900 à 1962*. Paris, Pichon et Durrand-Auzias, 1963.

Louveau (E.), *Au bagne. Entre les griffes de Vichy et de la milice*. Bamako, Soudan, Imprimerie, 1946.

Madeïra-Keïta (M.), 'Aperçu sommaire sur les raisons de la polygamie chez les Malinkés', *Etudes guinéennes*, 1950, no. 4, pp. 49–56.

Manouilski, 'Rapport sur la question nationale et coloniale au Ve Congrès de l'Internationale communiste', *La Correspondance internationale*, no. 60, 27 Aug., 1924.

Michel (Marc), 'Les débuts du soulèvement de la Haute Sangha en 1928', *Annales du Centre d'Enseignement Supérieur de Brazzaville*, vol. II, 1966, pp. 33–49.

Mordal (Jacques), *La Bataille de Dakar*. Paris, Ozanne, 1956.

Moynet (Capitaine Paul), *Les campagnes du Fezzan*. London, Publications de la France combattante ,1944.

Ortoli (Henri), 'Le gage des personnes au Soudan français', *Bull. I.F.A.N.*, no. 1, 1939, pp. 313–24.

Owono-N'Koudou (J. R.), 'Le problème du mariage dotal au Cameroun français', *Etudes camerounaises*, no. 39–40, 1953, pp. 41–83.

Padmore (George), *Panafricanisme ou communisme?* Paris, Présence africaine, 1960.

[Pétain] *Le Procès du Maréchal Pétain*. C.R. sténographique. 2 vols., Paris, Albin Michel, 1945.

Poulaine (Robert), *Etapes africaines: voyage autour du Congo*. Paris, Editions de la Nouvelle Revue critique, 1930.

Renaud-Molinet (Charles), *Problèmes de politique coloniale*. Saint-Louis-du-Sénégal, Imprimerie Lesgourgues, 1933.

Roche (Jean de la), *Le gouverneur général Eboué*. Paris, Hachette, 1957.

'Sahara: Aperçu d'ensemble sur la campagne saharienne, 1936–7', *Revue militaire de l'A.O.F.*, No. 39, 15 Oct., 1938, pp. 1–30.

Senghor (Lamine), *La Violation d'un pays*. Paris, Bureau d'Editions, n.d.

Sicé (médecin-général), *L'A.E.F. et le Cameroun au service de la France*. Paris, P.U.F., 1946.

Sophie (Ulrich), *Le gouverneur général Félix Eboué*. Paris, Larose, 1950.

Stiéklov (I.), 'Le réveil d'une race', *La Correspondance internationale*, no. 91, 25 Nov., 1922.

Suret-Canale (J.), 'Un pionnier méconnu du mouvement démocratique et nationale en Afrique: Louis Hunkanrin', E. D. (new series), No. 3, Dec., 1964, pp. 5–30.

Vassilieva (V.), 'Ce qu'on montre à Vincennes', *L'Internationale communiste*, no. 16, 15 Aug., 1931, pp. 1137–41.

Wagret (J. M.), *Histoire et sociologie politiques de la République du Congo (Brazza-ville)*. Paris, Pichon et Durand-Auzias, 1963.

Weinstein (Brian), *Gabon: Nation-Building on the Ogooué*. Cambridge (Mass.), M.I.T. Press, 1966.

INDEX

A.B.I.R., 22
Abadie, General, 140
Abbeys revolt, 99, 100, 101
Abéché, 94, 133, 143
Abidjan, 196, 474
Aboisso, 44
Académie des sciences coloniales, 254
Acafou, 96
Act of Annexation (1896), 124
Act of Berlin (1885), 9, 17, 23, 283
Act of Brussels (1890), 9, 17, 283
Adrar, 93, 94
Afrique française, L', 157, 448, 457
Afrique Occidentale française, L', 443
Agadir coup, 122
Agboville, 98
Agni, 142
Ago-li-agbo, 73, 74
agriculture, 218, 302–4, 383–4
Aguibou, king of Macina, 73, 74
Ahmadu, Sultan of Zinder, 107
Ahmed Ould Aida, Emir of Adrar, 93, 94, 427
Ain Galakka, 94
air transport, 209–10
Ajoulat, Dr., 403
Akoué, 101, 102
Alcan et Cie, 169
alcoholic drinks, 283–4
alcoholism, 401–3
Aldan, E., 169
Alfa Alimou, 66, 78
Alfa Yaya, 66, 73, 75, 78–9, 105
Aliou Tierno, 76
Alis, Harry, 18
Almamy Baba-Alimou, 76
Almamy Bokar Biro, 77
Ambidédi, 46
Amicale des Originaires de l'Afrique Equatoriale française, 447–8, 477
amoebic dysentery, 395–6
Anciens établissements David Gradis et fils, 173
Anglo-French convention (1898), 9

Angoulvant, Governor, 95–103, 107, 142, 169, 229, 277, 315
Annet, Governor-General Armand, 315, 469
Antchovey, Laurent, 447
anti-colonialism, 123–9
Anti-Imperialist League, 247–8, 453–4
Anti-Slavery Society of France, 61–2
Antonetti, Governor-General, 198, 310, 429, 430, 448
Arabic culture, 369–71
Archinard, 62, 73, 357
armed uprisings, 426–31
arms tax, 99
Asherson, Charles, 172
Assémat, 8
Assikasso, 96
assimilation, theory of, 83–6, 314, 382, 440
Assinie, 6
association (of races) policy, 84–5, 314
Assomption, Frédéric, 390
Ateliers et Chantiers maritimes de Dakar, 173
Attié, 101
Augagneur, General, 111, 197
Augouard, Mgr., 36, 74, 364
Aymerich, General, 144

Babichon, 66, 315
Bafobakoro, 104
Bafoussam, 251
Bakel, 63
Balandier, Georges, 448
Ballay, Governor, 10, 17, 22
Ballay hospital, 413
Ballieu, Captain, 50
Bamako, 88, 378, 385
Bamba, 104
Bamba Ahmadu, 433
Bambara, 140
Bambouk, 49, 50
bananas, 225–6
Bananeraies de Kin-San, 174

Bandama, 103
Bandiagara, 131
Bangui, 33, 413
Banque (de l') Afrique occidentale, 5, 60, 166, 168, 169, 170, 172, 188
Banque commerciale africain, 103, 166, 169, 170, 280
Banque française de l'Afrique, 166, 169, 170, 171, 280
Banque (d') Indochine, 170, 171, 172, 210
Banque Lazard, 170, 210
Banque nationale pour le Commerce et l'Industrie, 182
Banque (de l') Ouest africain, 169
Banque (de) Paris et des Pays-Bas, 170, 171
Banque (du) Senegal (later, Banque de l'Afrique occidentale, q.v.), 5, 60
Banque (de l') Union parisienne, 169, 170, 172, 173
Baol, 14, 46
Baoulé, 96
Baram-Bakié, 110
Bargues, Governor-General, 343
Barthié, 105
Bassin Conventionnel du Congo, see Conventional Congo Basin
Batanga, 42
Bateke, 7, 74, 111
'Bawandji war', 430
Bayardelle, Governor-General, 483
Beigbeder, Louis, 172
Belgian Congo, see Congo
Belgian interests, 21, 169, 171, 230, 271
Bélime, 275, 278
Bell, Richard Manga, 455
Bell, Rudolf Manga, 113, 264
Benin, 88
Bera N'Djoko, 109, 110
Bergaret, General, 475
Bernard, Paul, 170
Beti, Mongo, 361
Beyla, 104
Bidjo Aké, 432
Bilma, 94
Binger, Governor, 19, 100–1
Bingerville, 99
Bofosso, 104
Boganda, Abbé, 264
Boggio et Cie, 18
Boisson, Governor-General, 436, 463, 465–6, 473, 475–6, 477, 484

Boké, 43
Boloma, 6
Bondoukou, 474
Bordeaux group, 8, 11, 172–4, 181, 189, 442
Borelli, Georges, 22
Borkou, 94
Bornu, 32
Bossou, 105
Bouaké, 233
Bouboua, 429
Bouchaud, Father, 357, 361
Boulou, 112, 263
Bouré, 49, 50
Boussédou, 105
Bouvier, René, 170
Boyer, Paul, 168
Brazza, Pierre, 17, 30, 35–6, 51, 74, 127
Brazzaville, 29, 52, 86, 89, 111, 379, 382, 405, 484
Brazzaville Conference, 484–7
Brévié, Governor-General Jules, 278, 296, 331, 335, 362, 383, 389–90, 436
Broadhurst and Sons, 8
Brouadou, 360
Bruel, Georges, 34, 35, 36, 37, 251
Brunot, Governor-General, 315, 456, 463
Brunschwig, Henri, 125
Brussels Conventions, 4
Buhan et Teyssère, 8, 173
Bulletin du Comité de l'Afrique française, 277, 333, 452
Bulletin de l'enseignement de l'Afrique occidentale française, 376
Bund der deutschen Togoländer, 455–6
Bunua, 24
Bwiti, 437–8

CACAO BEANS, 224
Caillaux, 36, 121, 122, 123
Caillet, Major, 140
Calisti, Captain, 110
Calmette, Albert, 400, 404
Cameroons: administration, 122, 250, 308; budgets, 342–3; education, 385, 386; health services, 397; plantations, 42; provident societies, 240; resistance to conquest, 112–13; subsidies, 282; taxes, 324; trade, 41–2, 268
cannibalism, 438–9
capital investment, 24, 160–7, 211, 272

Carde, Governor-General, 277–8, 313, 314, 323, 341, 383, 388, 407, 445, 452–3
Carde Programme (1924), 277
Carpot, François, 441
Caudrelier, General, 99
Cayor, 14, 46–7
census figures, 36, 38–41, 47–8
centralisation, 86–90
cerebrospinal meningitis, 399
Cesne, Julien Le, 168, 408
Chad, 7, 27, 32, 60, 66, 89, 93, 94, 379, 467
Challaye, Félicien, 34–5, 121, 127, 128
Chalons Congress, 126
Charbonnages de Dakar, 173
Chargeurs Réunis, 176, 198
Chatelier, Le, 18–19
Chavanel company, 8, 11, 173, 270
Chevalier, Professor Auguste, 33–4, 156, 220, 221, 224
chiefdoms, 77, 79–83, 322–7
Christianity, 432, 437–8; see also missions
Christophle, 17
circonscriptions, 311, 328
Clainville-Bloncourt, Max, 444
Clemenceau, Georges, 123, 138, 328, 451
Clifford, Sir Hugh, 185
Clozel, Governor-General, 369
coffee, 224–5
colonial administration, 307–49
colonial exploitation, 24–6, 68, 95, 107, 129
Colonial Union, 241
Colonialisme, Le, 125
colonialisation, 37, 59, 156, 355, 399, 434–5
Comité (de l') Afrique française, 18, 276
Comité cotonnier de l'Afrique française, 171
Comité (de) défense de la race noire, 453
Comité (de l') Empire français, 476
Comité (des) Forges, 277
Comité français de libération nationale, 484
Comité international des ouvriers noirs, 454
Commerce Africain, Le, 168
Committee of French Africa, 18, 276
communist influence, 430–1, 439, 445

Compagnie (du) Bas-Congo, 258
Compagnie coloniale industrielle et commerciale, 182
Compagnie commerciale de l'Afrique équatoriale, 170
Compagnie commerciale de l'Equateur, 172
Compagnie commerciale Ouahm et Nana, 25, 171, 208, 230, 259
Compagnie commerciale Sangha-Likouala, 171
Compagnie commerciale Sangha-Oubangui, 171
Compagnie (du) Congo occidental, 23, 109
Compagnie congolaise du Caoutchouc, 171
Compagnie cotonnière équatoriale française, 171
Compagnie (de) culture cotonnière du Niger, 181, 277
Compagnie (des) Eaux et d'Electricité de l'Ouest africain, 173, 174, 211
Compagnie (d') electricité du Sénégal, 174
Compagnie équatoriale des Mines, 171
Compagnie (d') exploitation forestières africaines, 103
Compagnie forestière de Sangha-Oubangui, 40, 103, 110, 169, 171, 208, 258
Compagnie française (de l') Afrique occidentale, 5, 7, 8, 9, 11, 22, 167, 168, 175, 207
Compagnie française (du) Commerce Africain, 9
Compagnie française (de la) Côte d'Ivoire, 161, 179
Compagnie française (du) Haut et Bas Congo, 182, 208
Compagnie française (de) Kong, 19
Compagnie générale des colonies, 103, 170, 195, 211, 277
Compagnie générale des Transports en Afrique, 172, 208
Compagnie (du) Haut-Congo, 258
Compagnie (de la) Kotto, 25
Compagnie La Bia, 174
Compagnie Manutention africaine, 174
Compagnie (des) Mines (de) Falémé-Gambie, 269
Compagnie (des) Mines (au) Niari, 271
Compagnie (des) Mines (de) Siguiri, 50

Compagnie minière (du) Congo français, 52, 171, 172, 271
Compagnie minière (de) Falémé-Gambie, 50
Compagnie minière (de) Haute-Volta, 269
Compagnie minière (de l') Oubangui-Oriental, 172
Compagnie minière (du) Soudan français, 50
Compagnie (de la) Mobayé, 25
Compagnie (de) navigation et des transports de Congo-Oubangui, 25
Compagnie (du) Niger français, 161, 179
Compagnie nouvelle du Kouango français, 171
Compagnie propriétaire du Kouilou-Niari, 19, 41, 179, 259
Compagnie Sangha-Likoula, 208
Compagnie (des) Sultanats, 25, 142
Comptoir commercial français, 9
Comptoir français colonial, 22
Comptoirs réunis de l'Ouest africain, 169, 171
Conakry, 8, 12, 43, 195–6, 265, 362, 407, 413, 449
concessions, 20–4, 34, 38, 259, 260, 264; see also map, xiv
Confédération française des Travailleurs chrétiens, 486
Confédération Générale du Travail, 486
Congo, Belgian, 28, 230
Congo (French, cap. Brazzaville): administration, 74, 88, 108–11, 122, 143; concessions, 20, 22, 23; education, 372–3; exploitation, 26–34; health standard, 299; trade, 8, 9, 19, 37–40; see also French Equatorial Africa
Congo Free State, 21, 23, 28, 119
Congo-Mines, 271
Congo-Niari mining consortium, 271
Congo revolt, 427–30
Coniagi, 105
Conrart expedition, 104
conscription, 132–3, 135, 165, 203, 244–55, 442, 472
Continents, Les, 453
Convention of Saint-Germain-en-Laye (1919), 283, 402
Conventional Congo Basin, 17, 18, 23, 121, 283

copper, 51, 271–2
Coppolani, 93
Coppet, Governor-General de, 248, 249, 447, 450, 457
Cornet, Captain, 135
Corre, Dr. A., 404
Cotonu, 22, 197
cotton, 222–3, 230–1, 233, 281
country region evolution, 419–22
Courrier européen, 121, 128, 157
Cousturier, Governor, 22, 75
Couvy, L., 400
Crébessac, Lieutenant, 104
Crédit commercial de France, 169, 172
Crédit foncier du Congo, 17, 183
Crédit foncier de l'Ouest africain, 169, 173
Crimes Coloniaux de la IIIe République, Les, 128–9
Cri nègre, Le, 454
Cunliffe, Major-General, 144
Curea, Dr., 33
Customs Act (1892), 9
customs dues, 280–1, 343–8
Customs Law (1928), 284
Cyprien-Fabre, 176

DABOU, 25, 101
Daboula, 77
Dahomey: administration, 88, 324; concessions, 25; education, 372; provident societies, 240–1; railway, 22; revolt, 141–2, 444–7; trade, 4, 9, 10, 269; wage rates, 253
Daigre, Father, 31–3
Dakar: administration, 84, 88, 266, 456; air transport, 210; cathedral, 357; hospital, 412; port, 194–5; railway, 16, 46; trade, 16, 170, 211, 418; 'victory' at, 470
Daniel-Dreyfus, 175
D'Arboussier, 106
Darlan, Admiral, 475–6
Daumas, 18–19
Davillier, Baron Jean, 172, 173, 211
decrees: on administration, 88, 237, 310, 328–34; on African rights, 454; on arms carrying, 101; on army recruitment, 135, 137, 337, 338, 341; on company formation, 20; on construction works programme, 278; on education, 377, 381; on expropriation, 113; on forestry, 262; on

decrees—*cont.*
labour relations, 252–5, 449, 450; on land use, 31, 256, 257, 261, 265; on medical care, 406, 408, 411; on mining, 49; on Muslim Court, 336; on porterage, 30; on prohibition, 402; on provident societies, 237, 240; on railways, 264; on relations with France, 84, 91–2, 142, 255, 307; on repression of vagrancy, 254; on rubber adulteration, 43; on slavery, 62, 65; on subversive literature, 453; on taxation, 10, 29, 62, 101; on transfer of de Coppet, 451
Defferre, Paul, 442
Delafosse, Maurice, 316, 321, 369
Delage, Inspector-General, 382, 391
Delavignette, Governor-General, 297, 307, 318–19, 363
Delcassé, 18, 118
Delmas, 8, 168, 173, 174, 198
Démocratie du Sénégal, 444
départements, 311
depopulation, 36, 37
deportation, 101
Déroulède, Paul, 124
Deschamps, Governor, 314
Destenaves, Lieutenant-Colonel, 27
Devès et Chaumet, 8, 11, 173, 198
Diagne, Deputy Blaise, 84, 138, 328, 389, 410, 441–3, 451, 456
diamonds, 270–1, 272
Dinguiraye, 45
Diop, Tiécouta, 442
Diorodougou, 104
Diouf, Galandou, 443, 456
dioula, 6–7, 43, 65, 190–1
Dioulafoundi, 50
Diourbel, 46
disarmament, 100–1
Djenné, 59
Djerma, 106
Djouah Sembé, 42, 109
Dodds, General, 124
Dogon, 106, 130
Dolisie, Lieutenant-Governor, 27
Dominik, Major Hans, 112
Döring, Major, 144
Doroté, 94
Douala, 7, 42, 112, 113, 197
Doumergue, 29, 137
dowries, 423–4
DuBois, Dr. W. E. B., 451

Dumas, Charles, 127
Dupont, 389
Durand-Réville, Luc, 175, 180
Dutch interests, 171, 230

EBOUÉ, GOVERNOR-GENERAL FELIX, 229–30, 251, 310, 323, 326, 379, 382, 390, 467–8, 477, 480
Economic Conference (Saint Louis), 234
economic crisis, 278–82
economic recovery, 283–5
economic regions, 193–4
economic structure, 183–94, 294–304, 348–9
Edea, 42
education, 371–85, 391
Einstein, Albert, 453
Ekoreti, 110
El-Ainin, Ma, 93
El-Hiba, 94
electricity, 211
Elima, 6, 24
emancipation, 440
embryonic filariosis, 396
Entente Cordiale, 23, 118
Eseka, 42
Estaing, E. Giscard d', 170
Établissements F. Brandon (*later* Compagnie commerciale de l'Afrique équatoriale, *q.v.*), 170
Établissements Gradis, 168, 173
Établissements Peyrissac, 168
Étienne, 17–18, 20
Étoile du Dahomey, L', 446
Exbrayat, Jules, 176
exchange by barter, 11–12
export protection, 280–1
exports, 42–9, 219–28

FABRE ET FRAISSINET, 198
Fabre, Lieutenant, 107
Faidherbe, 3, 62, 71, 72, 87, 134, 371
Faidherbe, Lycée, 377
faire du Noir, 407, 408
Falémé Golden Valley Company, 50
famine, 45, 299–300
Faranah, 155–6
Fashoda affair, 118
Fathers of Ploermel, 371, 373
Fatoya, 50
Fernan Vaz, 18, 19
Fez, 93, 122

Finance Act (1900), 87, 341–3
First World War, 45, 134–43, 211–12
fiscal system, 341–8
Flaissières, 124
Folliet, Joseph, 355
Fondère, 52, 121–2, 169, 171
Fontaine, M. A., 254
Forbe, 404
forced labour, *see* conscription
forestry, 262–3; *see also under* timber
Fort-Archambault, 34, 412
Fort-Crampel, 28, 30, 34
Fort-de-Possel, 25
Fort-Sibut, 30
Fotoba, 76
Fouta-Djalon, 45, 66, 76, 78, 252, 327, 347, 369, 420
Fouta-Toro, 421
France de Pétain, La, 471
Franceville, 110, 111
Franco-German agreement, 122
Franco-Liberian negotiations, 104
Frankel, 161
free trade, 3–4, 29, 59
'free zone', 9; *see also* Guinea; Sénegal; Sudan
'freedom villages', 62–4, 66
Freetown, 10, 17
French citizenship, 84
'French Congo' (name), 89; *see also* Congo and French Equatorial Africa
French Equatorial Africa: administration, 310, 330, 334, 431, 441; concessions, 20, 260; development funds, 130; education, 375, 379, 381, 385, 386, 387; medical work, 413; outside influences, 112, 122, 476; population and labour, 36, 95, 107, 250, 252, 360; railways, 201; ration levels, 299; regional divisions, 89, 146, 243, 308; roads, 204, 206; subsidies, 87, 282, 342, 476; trade, 17, 20, 25, 37–41, 42, 51, 197, 208, 212, 240; uprising, 431; *see also* names of component states
French Guinea, 88
French Sudan, 88
French West Africa: administration, 73, 78, 86–9, 257, 265, 310, 329–30, 334, 335, 341; budget, 342, 344; concessions, 22, 260; education, 374, 375, 381, 387, 389, 390; forestry, 262; investment, 210–12; medical work, 33, 397, 404, 406; mining, 51;

monographs, 313; Muslim Court, 336; nutrition, 298; pacification, 129; population, 66, 333; provident societies, 240; recruitment, 135–9, 338–9; revolts, 141–2; roads, 204, 206, 207; slavery, 421; subsidies, 282; taxes, 29; trade, 6, 9–10, 12, 13, 16, 22, 24, 42–9, 223; *see also* names of component states
French West Africa Company, *see* Compagnie française de l'Afrique Occidentale
French Workers' Party, 124
Freycinet, 18
Frézouls, Governor, 75
Fulani, 66–7, 105, 435
Fulconis, Major, 36

GABON, 9, 37, 40, 41, 87, 88, 108, 110, 111, 130, 143, 206, 258, 264, 437
Galliéni, 62, 72
Garbay, General, 469
Garnier, 109
Garvey, Marcus, 452–3
Gaud, 34–5
Gaud-Toqué trial, 34, 127
Gaulle, General de, 474, 485–6
Gaullism, 464, 468–9, 484–6
Gazengel, 18
Geismar, Léon, 469
Gentil, Commissioner, 29–30, 35–6
German interests, 9, 11, 60, 89–90, 110, 112–13, 118–23, 144–6, 264, 406, 455–6
Gide, André, 205, 247, 427–8
Giraud, General, 427
Gloire du sabre, La, 128
Goibina, 143
gold, 49–51, 269–70, 272
Gold Coast, 51, 87
Gonfreville, 233
gonorrhoea, 400
Gorée, 6, 84, 87, 374, 377
Gouecké, 104
Gourou, Pierre, 301–4
government-general (system), 86–90, 108
Grand-Bassam, 6, 196
Grande imprimerie africaine, 174
Grodet, Governor Albert, 63, 65
groundnuts, 10, 14, 46–7, 191, 219–21, 233, 236, 239, 240, 281, 282, 301, 433
Grüner, Dr., 112

Guerre sociale, 128
Guesde, Jules, 124
Gueye, Lamine, 443, 456
Guignard, Lieutenant, 105, 135
Guilhon, 63
Guillain, 20
Guin guinéo, 46
Guinea: administration, 88, 104, 324; cannibalism, 438; education, 372, 375; provident societies, 240; railways, 200; rubber, 43, 45; slavery, 63; trade, 4, 8, 9–14, 24–5, 50
Guy, Governor Camille, 373, 382–3
Guynet, D., 171
Guynet, William, 18, 29, 52, 171

HAMALLAH, SHEIKH, 435–7
Hamallism, 433, 435–7
Hardy, Georges, 370, 381, 389
Harmand, Jules, 85–6, 486
Harris, William Wade, 432
Hatton and Cookson company, 17, 23–4
Haute-Fleuve, 88
Hay, Cyril, 172
health, 395–403
Héquet, Captain, 105
Hérisse, Le, 135
Hervé, Gustave, 128
Hilaire, General, 94, 133, 202
Hirsch group, 181, 222, 277
Hitler, Adolf, 454–5, 456
Homberg, Octave, 170
Homet, Marcel, 450
hookworm, 396
Houénou, Kidjo Tovalou, 453
Hubert, 36
human sacrifice, 439
Hunkanrin, Louis, 444, 475
Hunsec, Mgr. Le, 357
Husson, General, 463, 464, 468

IBISSA, 106
immatriculation, *see* registration
imperial preference, 285
import restrictions, 4, 294
impôt personnel, *see* poll-tax
Indigénat (native status), 331–6
indigenous provident societies, 235–44
industry, 210–12
Institut français d'Afrique noire (I.F.A.N.), 369
International Colonial Institute, 389

International Labour Organisation, 254, 442
Internationale ouvrière, 486
International Syndicale Rouge, 454
intestinal diseases, 395
irrigation project (River Niger), 170, 275–9
Isasa, 33
Islam, 4, 67, 78, 361, 362, 424, 431–5
Italian-Turkish war, 94
Ityo, 106
ivory, 228
Ivory Coast: administration, 88, 107, 255, 324; concessions, 24–5; education, 372; medical work, 412; pacification, 95–103; ports, 196, 207; provident societies, 240, 241; recruitment, 246–8; revolts, 142; trade, 7, 19, 44, 45, 48, 49, 51, 263, 268

'JACK-JACK', 7
Jamot, Dr., 408–11
Jaurès, 36, 126
Javouhay, Captain, 103
Jeucafra, *see* Jeunesse camerounaise française
Jeune Gabon party, 447
Jeunesse camerounaise française, 456
John Holt company, 17, 23–4
Joseph, Gaston, 451
Josse, Adrien, 169, 170, 172
Josse, Robert, 170, 171
Jurgens-Van den Bergh-Schicht group, 178

KABAKITANDA, 106
Kabré, 112
Kamerun, 87, 89–90, 112, 113, 119, 144–6; *see also* Cameroons
Kankan, 59
Kannenberg, Captain, 90
Kaolack, 46
Kaossan, 140
Kaouar, 94
Karinou, 428–9
Kayes, 44, 46
Kimbangu, Simon, 437
Kindia, 44
Kingué-Jong, Gaston, 455
Kissidougou, 104, 480
Kokosalei, 439
Koko Tolno, 104, 105

Kong, 59
Kouamé Guié, 96
Kougouloutou, Chief, 109
Kouila-Niari, 17
Kouilou, 19, 111
Koulikoro, 46
Kouroussa, 7, 43, 44, 236
Kousseri, 3, 93
Kouyaté, 454
Koyama, 105
Krebedjé, 25
Kribi, 42
Kuonkan, 104, 105

LABADIE, LIEUTENANT, 426
Labé, 75, 236
Labouret, H., 298
Lambaréné hospital, 413
Lamblin, Governor, 230
Lamibé, 113
Lamothe, Commissioner-General de, 26
Land Act (1904), 74, 75
land spoliation, 255–68
Largeau, Colonel, 94, 132
Larminat, Edgar, 466, 468
Larroque, Captain, 103
Lastoursville, 110, 111
Latrille, Governor André, 265–6, 472
Laurent, Captain, 98
Lazard Bank, 170, 210
League for Human Rights and Popular
    Aid, 248, 445
League of Nations, 145–6, 253, 273, 452
Lebon, 21
Lecerf, Lieutenant, 104, 105
Leclerc, General, 468, 469
Légion des Combattants, 471, 472
Leist, Chancellor, 89
Lelong, Father, 205
Lemaignen, Robert, 172–3
Leopold II, King of the Belgians, 21,
    51, 119
Leopoldville, 17, 463
leprosy, 396
Leroy-Beaulieu, Paul, 18, 20
Letondot, Charles, 173
Lever Brothers, see Unilever
Lever, William Hesketh (first Lord
    Leverhulme), 177
Liberia, 42, 104
Libermann, Father, 356
Libreville: administration, 86; political
    party formed, 447; port, 197;

schools, 130, 372–3; slavery, 62,
    420–1; taxes, 29; trade, 23
lice fever, 401
Ligue française pour la défense des
    indigènes du Bassin conventionnel du
    Congo, 121, 128
Ligue maritime et coloniale, 254
Ligue universelle de défense de la race
    noire, 453
Lindequist, Dr., 123
Lisbon Protocol, 9
Liverpool Chamber of Commerce, 23
Loango, 31
Lobaye, 108, 109, 428
Lomé, 197, 446
Londres, Albert, 157, 203, 247, 274–5
Loomax, Colonel, 105
Louga, 47
Louis, Paul, 125–6
Louveau, Governor, 465
Lower Guinea, 24
Lycée van Vollenhoven, 377, 385

MACADOU SALL, 434
Macina, 130
Madagascar, 84, 124, 253
Mademba Seye, 73, 74
Madola, 113
Maginot, André, 278, 282
Mahé, Professor, 404
Malamalasso, 51
malaria, 395
Mandara, 112
Mandated Territories, 308, 342, 358;
    see also Cameroons; Togo
Mandel, 448, 451
Mandel decree, 424
Manding plateau, 43
Mandja, 28, 34
Mangin, General, 27, 30, 34, 108, 109,
    134–5
Mante et Borelli Company, 9, 22
Manzan, 51
Marabout Saidou, 106
Maran, René, 406–7
Marchand, Colonel, 26–7, 34, 468
Marchoux, Dr., 404
Mariani, 370
Mariotte, Dr., 105
Maroua, 112, 113
Marrakesh, 94
marriage problem, 423–5
Marseillaise de Crédit, 5

Marseilles group, 175
Martin, Dr., 33
Masson, Governor, 468–9
Massow, Lieutenant von, 112
Massu, Lieutenant, 426
Matswa, André, 447–9, 477
Matswaism, 437, 449
Maud'huit, de, 266
Maurel, Emile, 5
Maurel, Lucien, 176
Maurel et Prom company, 8, 11, 168, 173, 189, 198
Maurel Frères, 11, 173
Mauretania, 14, 66, 88, 93–4, 426
Mavouroulou, 109
Mayombe, 109
M'Backé, Ibra Fati, 434
M'Balé-Vérité, 455
medical work, 395–414
Méjean, François, 358
Mellacorée, 236
Merlin, Governor-General, 87, 109, 111, 169, 277, 312, 315, 338
Messager dahoméen, Le, 444
Messageries africaines, 176
Messageries fluviale du Congo, 25, 121, 207, 208
Messageries (du) Sénégal, 176
Messimy, 121, 135
Meyer, Colonel, 144
Meynier, General, 369
migration, 244–55
Mille, Pierre, 121, 128, 169
Milliès-Lacroix, 120
Mindouli, 52
Mines de Lens, 169
mining, 49–52, 165, 268–72
missions, 355–66, 372–3, 473
Missoum-Missoum affair, 119
Mizraki-Lemaître group, 180
Moal, Dr. Le, 407
Mocabé, 109
Mohammed-es-Senoussi, Sultan of Dar Kouti, 94
Moll, Colonel, 94, 131
Moncorgé, Lieutenant, 105–6
Mondon, Governor, 248
monetisation, 12–13
money economy, 59–60
Mongumba, 36
monopolies, 18, 23, 24, 183–7, 259–60
Monthaye, 18
Mopi, 143

Mora, 112
Morel, Edmund D., 23, 128
Morocco, 3, 93, 118, 120, 122, 134
Mosmans, Father, 366
Mossaka, 111
Mossi, 73, 74
Motte, A., 171
Motte, E., 169
Mount Cameroon, 42
Mouret, Lieutenant Colonel, 94
Mouridism, 433–5
Mourin, Lieutenant, 109
Moutet, 457
Moutet circular, 243
M'Palé, 105
M'Poko, 109
Muller, Father, 356
Muslim Court, 336
Muslim movements, 433

NANA, 35
Nanafoué-Kpri, 103
Napoleonic concordat, 359
Native Authority Ordinances of Nigeria, 348
Native Reserves, 31
N'Diolé Boni, 103
N'djolé, 18
Negro World, 452
Nervo, Baron Léon de, 172
N'Gaoundéré, 112
N'gban, 102, 103
N'Goko-Sangha, 108, 109
'N'Goko-Sangha' company, 20, 118–21
Ngoso Din, 113
Niadou, 104
Niari, 19
Niger: forced labour, 248; insurrection, 106; occupation, 94; railway, 22; slavery, 66; trade, 7
Niger Office, 155, 181, 207, 221, 222, 248–9, 278–9
Niger River irrigation project, 170, 275–9
Njoya, 113
N'Kiambour, 47
N'Kongsamba Bonabéri, 42
Nogues, General, 476
Noirot, 75
Nome, 143
Nord-West Kamerun company, 21, 22
Norès, G., 389
North Cameroon, 60

Noufflard, Governor, 444
Nouvelle Société commerciale africaine, 161, 179
Nunez, see Rio-Nunez
N'Zapa, 104, 105
N'Zérékoré, 105

Octon, Vigné d', 128–9
Office du Niger, see Niger Office
Ofia, 111
Ogooué, 17, 18, 23
Ogooué-Ngunié Company, 23
oil palm, see palm oil
Okano, 110
Olivier, Aimé, 6
onchocercosis, 396
Ornano, Colonna d', 466
Osrou, 98, 100, 101
Ouagadougou, 411
Ouassou, 103
Oubangi-Shari: administration, 37, 89, 260; child slavery, 420; cotton, 230; education, 385; military operations, 110, 143
Oubangi revolt, 427–30
Oulata, 93
ousourou, 62

Pacification, 95–107, 129, 426–31
Padmore, George, 454
Paix-Séailles, 121, 128
Pakpa, 35
palaeonegritic people, 60, 95, 129
Pales, Colonel, 298
palm-oil products, 10, 44, 47–8, 226–7
Pan-African Congress, 451
Pan-Douala movement, 456
Pan-Ewe movement, 456
Parant, Major, 469
Paris Convention, 308
Passarge expedition, 112
Pasteur Institute, 33, 404–5, 408
Pastré, 6
Paterson-Zochonis, 8
pauperisation, 294–300
Pelizaeus, 8
Périscope africain, 443, 451
Perrier, Léon, 271
Pesséma, 106
Pétain, Marshal Philippe, 475
Petit-Bassam, 265
Peyrissac, 11, 173–4, 189, 270
Pichon, 121

Pion, Jean, 168
plague, 401
plantation crops, 223
Plantations de la Sanaga (later Société africaine forestière et agricole), 172
Plantations de la Tanoé, 171, 176
Plantations réunies de l'Ouest africain, 103
Plomion, Captain, 103
pneumonia, 398
Poilay, Edwin, 168
Poincaré, Raymond, 123
Poiret, Governor, 303
political life, 439–57
poll-tax, 28–9, 96, 129, 192, 228, 247, 343–8, 444
polygamy, 424–5
Ponty, Governor-General William, 78, 82, 99, 135, 266
Ponty circular, 64, 65
Popular Front, 454, 456–7
Port-Bouët, 196
Port-Gentil, 197
ports, 194–8
porterage, 11, 26–8, 30, 33, 96, 132
Porto-Novo, 88, 443, 475
Portuguese Guinea, 6
Poulaine, Robert, 317–18
Proche, 34
profit margins, 184
Prokos, Captain, 109, 110
'protectorates', 74–5
Protectorate of the Cameroons, 21
provident societies, see indigenous provident societies
Puttkammer, von, 42

Rabaud et Cie, 8
Race nègre, La, 454
racial discrimination, 471
railways, 18, 19, 22, 42, 46, 72, 98, 155, 165, 197, 199–204, 209, 450
Railway Company of Dahomey, 22
Rassemblement Démocratique Africaine, 465
recruitment, 135–9, 336–41
'Red Nigger', 43
régions, 311
Regis et Cie. (succeeded by Mante et Borelli Company, q.v.), 18
Régismanset, Charles, 85, 486
registration, 256–7, 266–7
Régnier-Rollin decrees, 454

religious movements, 431–9 *see also* missions

Renard, Governor-General Edouard, 135, 141, 448

repression of reform movement, 445

re-settlement, 102

resistance (war-time), 139–43

Reste, Governor-General, 248, 283, 323–4, 448

Revue indigène, 157, 202

Rio de Oro, 96

Rio Nunez, 43, 63

Rivaud Bank, 172

rivers, use of, 206–10

Rivières du Sud (*later* French Guinea, *q.v.*), 6, 43, 87, 88

roads, 204–10

Rollin decrees, *see* Régnier–Rollin decrees

Roman Catholic Church, *see* missions

Rome Agreements, 455

Romilly Congress (1895), 124

Rouanet, Gustave, 36, 127

Roume, Governor-General, 236, 266, 315, 370

Roume Plan (1904), 199

Royal Niger Company, 177

rubber, 12, 20, 31, 38, 40, 41, 43–5, 48, 130, 227, 231–2

Rufisque, 46, 84, 195, 378

rule, direct and indirect, 348–9

Russian Revolution, 146–7

Ryff, Roth et Cie, 8, 11, 168

S.F.I.O. (WORKERS' INTERNATIONAL: French Section), 457, 468

Sacred Congregation of Propaganda Fide, 358, 364

Sahel, 7

Saint-Louis, 6, 16, 46, 84, 88, 94, 374, 404–5, 418

Saintoyant, Commandant, 25, 30

Salaün, Captain, 135

Saléfoué, 103

Salekrou, 103

Salins du Sine-Saloum, 174

Samba, Captain Martin, 113

Samoe, 105

Samory, 96, 104

Sampouyara, 104

Sangha, 40, 42, 108

Sarraut, Albert, 137, 199, 273–4, 329, 356, 380–1, 389, 407, 413, 462, 486

Sarraut Plan, 199, 201, 274, 275, 282

Satadougou, 51

schools, *see* education

schoolteachers, 386–91

Schweitzer, Albert, 414

Second Empire, 71, 84, 307, 355

Second Republic, 62

Second World War, 462, 488

Semler, 121

senatus-consult, 71

Senegal: administration, 74–5, 79, 84, 86–8, 91, 332, 334; education, 371; investment, 24–5; politics, 442, 456; provident societies, 240; railway, 200; river navigation, 206; slavery, 62–3; trade, 7, 8, 9, 13, 14, 44, 48–9, 112, 481–2

Senegal River, 46, 74

Sénégalaise d'approvisionnements, 173

Senegalese Socialist Party, 456–7

'Senegalese soldiers', 336–7, 340

Senegambia and Niger, 88

Senghor, Lamine, 453–4

Services d'hygiène, 407

Shell group, 178

shipping, 198–9

Sicé, General, 410

Sicre, 109

Siguiri, 7, 50, 65

Sine-Saloum, 14, 46, 236, 241

Sisters of Saint Joseph of Cluny, 372, 373

slavery, 60–7, 421; Act for abolition of, 62

sleeping sickness, 399, 404, 408–12

smallpox, 400

social evolution, 417–25

social organisation, 67–9

Société africaine d'entreprises, 171

Société africaine forestière et agricole, 172

Société Afrique et Congo, 121, 172, 208

Société (des) anciens établissements Rouchard, 182

Société anonyme française pour l'Importation du Caoutchouc, 169, 182

Société auxiliaire africaine, 174, 211

Société (de) Banque suisse, 172

Société coloniale (de la) côte de Guinée, 9, 25

Société coloniale de représentation, 276

Société commerciale d'affrètements et de commissions, 172

Société commerciale et industrielle (du) Congo français, 19
Société commercial et industrielle (de la) côte d'Afrique, 168, 175, 176
Société commerciale et industrielle (du) Haut-Ogooué, 19, 41
Société commerciale et minière de Satadougou, 51
Société commerciale, industrielle et agricole du Haut-Ogooué, 180
Société Commerciale (de l') Ouest Africain (S.C.O.A.), 8, 11, 167, 168, 171, 176
Société commerciale (des) Ports de l'Afrique occidentale, 173
Société commerciale Sangha-Oubangi, 176
Société (de) construction des Batignolles, 202, 210
Société cotonnière équatoriale française, 230
Société (de) dragages aurifères du Tinkisso, 51
Société (des) études et d'exploitation du Congo français, 18, 19
Société (d') exploration coloniale, 119
Société (des) factoreries de N'Djolé, 121
Société financière des caoutchoucs, 172
Société financière française et coloniale, 170, 171, 181, 277
Société forestière et agricole du Kouilou, 259
Société forestière (du) Niari, 179
Société forestière Sangha-Oubangi, 121, 259
Société française (du) Congo francais, 183
Société française (des) cotons africains, 171, 230
Société française (d') entreprises de dragages et de travaux publiques, 167, 210
Société française (des) gisements aurifères du Comoé et affluents, 51
Société générale du Golfe de Guinée, 182
Société (du) Haut-Ogooué, 258, 259
Société immobilière et financière africaine, 170
Société (des) Kémou, 51
Société (de la) Kotto, 230
Société (des) Mines de Falémé-Gambie, 180

Société minière (du) Dahomey, 269
Société minière (de) Kokumbo, 51
Société navale de l'Ouest, 198
Société (de la) N'Kémé-N'Keni, 20
Société (de l') Ogooué-N'Gounié, 121
Société propriétaire de l'Ongomo, 258
Société (des) Sultanats du Haut-Oubangi, 20, 171, 259
Société textile africaine, 230
Soguinex Company, 270
Sous, 94
Spanish Guinea, 122
Streel, Edmond du Vivier de, 21, 41, 52, 170–1
Sucreries et raffineries de l'Indochine, 171
Süd-Kamerun Company, 21, 22, 42, 119, 120, 121
Sudan: administration, 72, 88–9, 95; education, 372, 373; 'freedom villages', 63–5; provident societies, 240; slavery, 65, 66; taxes, 62, 229; trade, 7, 8, 9, 44
Syrians, 12–14, 68

TABOU, 196
Taoudéni, 94
Tardieu, André, 120
taxes, 99–100, 101, 106, 131, 327, 447
teachers, 386–91
Têtu, General, 469
Théassou, 105
Thévenoud, Mgr., 361, 362, 364
Thierno, Ibrahima, 106
Thiès, 46
Third Republic, 71–2, 83, 307, 357, 463
Thiry, General, 429
Thomas, Albert, 121
Thomasset, Captain, 27
Thoreau-Levaré, 76, 78
Thuo, 105
Thys, Colonel, 22
Tiassalé, 44
Tibati, 112
Tichit, 93
Tidika, 93
timber, 10, 48, 227
Timbuctu, 59
Tindouf, 3, 95
Toffa, King, 77
Togo: administration, 89, 308; budget, 87, 343; conquest, 144–6; education, 378, 385; insurrection, 112; provident

Togo—*cont.*
  societies, 240; railway, 200–1; subsidies, 282
Toma, 104–5
Toqué, Georges, 27–8, 34–5
Toucoleurs, 14
tougourou (militiaman), 77
Toulouse Congress (1908), 127
Tound Lands, 266–7
town evolution, 417–19
trade, 167, 183–94
trade union movement, 449–50
trading firms, 4–7
trading procedure, 11–16
trading stations, 5, 6, 14–15
transport, 194–210
Trans-Sahara route, 276–7
Tréchot Brothers, 182, 258
Trentinian, General de, 65
trypanosomiasis, *see* sleeping sickness
tuberculosis, 400
Turkey, 94, 140

UBANGI, *see* Oubangi-Shari
Unilever group, 167, 177–80, 233, 259
Union coloniale française, 168, 254
Union Congolaise, 25
Union Electrique coloniale, 211
Union française d'Outre-Mer, 182
Union minière et financière coloniale, 171
Union tropicale de plantations, 172
United Africa Company, 178–80
United Socialist Party, 123
Upper Falémé, 51
Upper Ibenga, 109
Upper Kotto, 108
Upper N'Gounié, 109
Upper Ogooué, 18, 110
Upper Oubangi, 29, 37, 109, 110
Upper Sangha, 29, 427, 429
Upper Senegal and Niger, 7, 24–5, 88

Upper Shari, 35
Upper Volta, *see* Sudan

VALLAUX, CAMILLE, 277
Verdier, 6, 19
Vézia Company, 8, 173, 189
Vichy régime, 463–9, 470–1, 473, 476
Vieillard, Gilbert, 347
Vieyres, 106
Vilers, Le Myre de, 11
Vittoria, de, 355, 356
Voix des nègres, La, 454
Vollenhoven, Joost Van, 82–3, 129, 136–7, 348, 377, 385
Volz, Dr., 105
Vridi, Baram Bakié, 108

WADAI, 133
Wadi Kadja, 94
Wagret, J. M., 448
Wango, Chief, 430
Warren, Edouard de, 277
Water and forest administration, 262
Weber, Jean, 169, 171
Weber group, 181
Wehlan, Judge, 90
Wiart, Carton de, 169
Wilhelm II, Kaiser, 118
William Ponty Training College, 375, 377–8, 385, 386, 387, 388, 389, 390; *see also* Ponty, William
Wilson, President Woodrow, 145
Wiltord, Governor, 234
Woermann, 17, 22
Woleu-N'Tem, 110
Wolofs, 6, 433

YALOU-TÉNÉ, 105
yaws, 399
yellow fever, 395

ZIMMERMANN, COLONEL, 144